AMERICAN GLOBAL LEADERSHIP

AMERICAN GLOBAL LEADERSHIP

**Ailing US Diplomacy
and Solutions for
the Twenty-First Century**

EDITED BY

G. DOUG DAVIS AND

MICHAEL O. SLOBODCHIKOFF

Legacies of War | G. Kurt Piehler, Series Editor

UNIVERSITY OF TENNESSEE PRESS | KNOXVILLE

Library of Congress Cataloging-in-Publication Data

Names: Davis, G. Doug, editor. | Slobodchikoff, Michael O., editor.
Title: American global leadership : ailing US diplomacy and solutions for the twenty-first century / edited by G. Doug Davis and Michael O. Slobodchikoff,
Description: First edition. | Knoxville : The University of Tennessee Press, 2024. | Series: Legacies of war | Includes bibliographical references. | Summary: "This edited volume consists of contributions from American statesmen who have guided US foreign policy through the Cold War, the Iraq and Afghan wars, the 2008 economic crisis, and the instability that emerged during the Trump administration. The chapters allow diplomats and military professionals such as Gen. Wesley Clark, NATO ambassador Robert Hunter, and others to reflect on their experience. The volume takes its cues from George Kennan's 1950 University of Chicago lectures that were the most widely read account of US diplomacy in the first half of the twentieth century. The insights collected here touch on international crises over the past seventy years and provide a critical assessment of the way forward for diplomats and scholars of American statecraft"— Provided by publisher.
Identifiers: LCCN 2024008519 (print) | LCCN 2024008520 (ebook) | ISBN 9781621908845 (hardcover) | ISBN 9781621909033 (paperback) | ISBN 9781621908852 (pdf) | ISBN 9781621908883 (kindle edition)
Subjects: LCSH: United States—Foreign relations—21st century.
Classification: LCC JZ1480 .A964 2024 (print) | LCC JZ1480 (ebook) | DDC 327.73—dc23/eng/20240316
LC record available at https://lccn.loc.gov/2024008519
LC ebook record available at https://lccn.loc.gov/2024008520

To George Pratt Shultz,
Secretary of State from 1982–1989,
a man dedicated to diplomacy
and a true statesman.

CONTENTS

ix   Foreword
     MARY N. HAMPTON

xiii Foreword
     JAMES A. BAKER III

xv   Acknowledgments

  1   ONE | G. DOUG DAVIS AND MICHAEL O. SLOBODCHIKOFF
     The Challenge to American Diplomacy

 13   TWO | JACK F. MATLOCK JR.
     Diplomacy That Ended the Cold War

 25   THREE | RICHARD "DICK" MILES
     An Amazing Diplomatic Career

 49   FOUR | GENERAL WESLEY CLARK
     Reflections on Diplomacy and the Use of Military Power

 73   FIVE | ROBERT E. HUNTER
     The Challenge to US Foreign Policy

123   SIX | DAVID DUNFORD
     Effective Diplomacy is a Team Sport

159   SEVEN | EARL ANTHONY WAYNE
     Modern American Diplomacy:
     Core Skills, New Demands, and a Changing Global Stage

231   EIGHT | KEN GROSS
     On Diplomacy

255   NINE | MARC GROSSMAN
     What is the Purpose of American Diplomacy?

269 TEN | RONALD E. NEUMANN
     Reflections on Half a Century of Diplomacy

301 ELEVEN | THOMAS PICKERING
     A Prescription to Heal US Diplomacy in the
     Twenty-First Century

343 TWELVE | P. MICHAEL McKINLEY
     From Morning in America to January 6:
     Perspectives on Diplomacy, 1982–2022

375 THIRTEEN | J. STAPLETON ROY
     Superpower Diplomacy

419 FOURTEEN | MICHAEL McFAUL
     Twitter Diplomacy:
     Lessons from an American Experiment in Russia

441 FIFTEEN | MICHAEL O. SLOBODCHIKOFF AND G. DOUG DAVIS
     Morning or Twilight:
     American Diplomacy in the Twenty-First Century

449 Contributors

461 Index

FOREWORD

MARY HAMPTON

Critical to the US role in the world over the last century has been statecraft. Henry Luce, one of the most powerful and influential public figures of the last century, aptly called the twentieth century, "the American century." It began at the end of the First World War, when US President Woodrow Wilson sought to craft an international order reflecting what he defined as American values. The US emerged as a global power for the first time after the war. Yet, Wilson's failure to persuade the victorious European Allies of his vision, and his even greater inability to persuade the US Senate, doomed the blueprint to failure. If the vision were to continue, American statecraft had to change.

The lessons learned from that failure informed the generation of American policymakers who guided US foreign policy after the Allied victory over Nazi Germany in 1945. The US-led postwar order reflected American unrivalled power but was also much more than that: it was a triumph of visionary design, diplomacy, and persuasion—successful statecraft. US leadership in international institutions like the United Nations (UN), World Bank, the International Monetary Fund, and especially through the creation of the North Atlantic Treaty Organization (NATO), helped prevent chaos and dangerous instability in Europe immediately following the incredible destruction left by the war. Important was the farsightedness of US leadership in integrating West Germany as a respected and stable member of the emerging Western democratic order.

The international order held more-or-less steadily for the next half century. That said, it was always a bifurcated order. The US-led Western order was just that—Western. It faced off against the Soviet-led Communist order. Yet, alongside that fierce competition emerged accommodation and even cooperation. Thus, by the last two decades of the century, the sharp edges of the Cold War were smoothed over, followed by the disintegration of the Cold War system, without a great power war. Soviet leaders loosened their grip over Central and Eastern Europe; Germany reunited peacefully, surrounded by allies; there were indications that the Soviet Union, soon to be Russia, was finding its way westward. The Western community of liberal democracies grew, as President George H. W. Bush led the way and called for a Europe whole and free. His Secretary of State, James Baker, delivered a watershed speech in Berlin in 1989, heralding the diminished military identity of NATO in favor of its increasing political and diplomatic roles in securing a free, democratic, and open Europe.

The first decade of the twenty-first century witnessed developments that challenged the initial post–Cold War optimism. Under Vladimir Putin's influence, Russia turned increasingly away from Western aspirations. NATO and the US once again assumed the role of adversary, and the Russian forceful quest for recovering lost great power status ensued. Far away from the Western order, China began asserting itself on the world stage, showing signs of challenging US leadership and Western dominance. Alongside the challenge from Russia and the rise of China came the concomitant ascendancy of India. Further, the regions of the world that had been somewhat managed through Cold War competition now often seethed with domestic unrest and foreign policy challenges. In short, the world was tending toward multipolarity, and the US-led order was increasingly challenged, including in American domestic politics. Not only had the American public grown very skeptical about the benefits of continued US leadership, the tendency of political leaders to regularly seek military solutions for resolving foreign policy crises began to undermine the American image and reputation. The role of the powerful American military, and its employment alongside diplomacy, have been especially difficult to adjust in the post–Cold War era.

Thus, the "American century" gave way to an embattled and uncertain twenty-first century. Ongoing problems within the US policymaking complex have made adaptation to changed circumstances difficult. The multiple challenges presented by the pervasiveness of social media, the complexities of integrating American organizational missions, the problems incurred in trying to make necessary adjustments within those organizations based on changing political and social pressures: these complications have made adaptation to a changed international environment more difficult. Yet, American diplomacy continues to seek ways and means with which to persuade allies, neutrals, and rivals, and to navigate the changing landscape of a multipolar world. US leadership has stepped up at pivotal moments but has been found wanting at other times, both reflected clearly by post–Cold War NATO which has experienced a range of successes and failures.

The contributions in this excellent volume assembled by G. Doug Davis and Michael O. Slobodchikoff are written by authors who each played a role in imagining, constructing, maintaining, or transforming American statecraft, whether during the "American century" or afterward. Leading lights of American foreign policymaking, the contributors helped guide the ship of state through the various phases of US-Soviet (and Russian) relations, who helped solidify and then transform NATO, who led and helped change the State Department, and who have led and advised through ongoing alterations in world politics, including the rise of China, the Russian war on Ukraine, and the slipstreams created by pandemics. There is much insight to be gained by reading their chapters, in understanding their perspectives, and in viewing the opportunities and challenges of statecraft as they saw and currently see them. Their insights and criticisms are drawn from firsthand experiences, reflecting the knowledge and wisdom of insiders. As an academic who has spent decades studying, teaching, and writing about American foreign policy during the Cold War and post–Cold War years, I can honestly say that this volume is invaluable for those who are interested in the formulation and conduct of American foreign policy, and in understanding why the US role in the world is so uncertain today.

How appropriate as well that the volume should be dedicated to George Shultz, a foreign policy leader whose heralded diplomatic skills played such a pivotal role in the maintenance of the US-led order, and during the delicate transition from the Cold War to post–Cold War period. His tenure at the State Department during the culmination of US-Soviet relations and the fall of Berlin wall offered a masterclass in leadership. In short, this book sheds much light on how and why American foreign policy has so often succeeded through the Cold War years and into the post–Cold War era. Just as important, the authors speak honestly and openly about the problems and challenges that marred success, the likes of which current and future makers of statecraft must be aware of and address.

Few people in U.S. history came to their jobs as well prepared for success as George Shultz. I can say that because I served as President Ronald Reagan's White House chief of staff when George became Secretary of State and continued to work with him after I became Secretary of the Treasury. He was—in a word—brilliant. During his six and a half years at State, U.S. dialogue with the Soviets blossomed as he laid the groundwork for the peaceful end to the Cold War. Before then, he had flourished in academia, earning a doctorate in economics from Massachusetts Institute of Technology and later working in the University of Chicago economics department. He was also successful in business at one of the world's largest construction companies. In short, George Shultz was a giant in the annals of 20th Century American diplomacy because he had mastered all the tools for success— and he used them with deft precision.

George understood that one of the biggest obstacles to successful diplomacy is often opposition within the American government. To be effective in guiding U.S. foreign policy, a Secretary of State needs to be intimately familiar with Washington politics. His unparalleled government experience and knowledge gave him the capacity to navigate the complex dynamics that influence presidential decisions regarding national policy. After all, he is one of only two people who has served in four cabinet positions. He knew that success requires one to maneuver through numerous obstacles, institutional gridlock, and substantial political opposition. George Shultz used intelligence, hard work and personal relationships to in some of the most difficult jobs in government.

Direct and forthright, he understood the importance of trust in building the bridges needed to overcome barriers to success. He played the long game with his interlocutors and formed relationships that advanced the interests of our partners as well as our own. George also understood that successful diplomacy requires hard work. Before taking part in serious negotiations with Soviet leaders, for example, George spent days with key personnel to gather as much information as possible and to hear the insights of local staff. While this effort may not have conformed to the pressure for immediate publicity imposed by the contemporary news cycle and social media, it ensured that the agreed upon policies met the national interest.

George Shultz remains an important role model for anyone who wishes to serve the country. He definitely was an important one in my career. In fact, he was my predecessor at Princeton University, the U.S. Marine Corps, Secretary of the Treasury, and Secretary of State. I learned a lot from my friend, and I knew I could always count on him for thoughtful, honest and forthright advice.

George also had an important trait shared by successful diplomats— the ability to learn from the past. The ambassadors, foreign service officers, and other diplomats who contributed to this book have experiences that stretch from the Eisenhower administration to the immediate past. These men and women worked diligently for years to make sure that the Cold War never degenerated into a hot war and their perseverance helped bring about its peaceful end. They opened the doors to our relations with other nations and preserved the Atlantic Alliance when its survival was threatened. All of them dedicated their lives to the conduct of American foreign policy.

Within this book, they share their experiences and wisdom so that future generations might learn from their experiences and considerable accomplishments. They offer insights on how diplomacy has changed from the Cold War to the present, and how technology is changing it today. For example, as social media has increased and interpersonal relations are replaced with soundbites, the human dimension of diplomacy is lost. This is a dangerous trend because the ability to have frank conversations behind closed doors is essential to any successful foreign policy.

Though the world has changed, and new rivals and challenges confront the United States today, I remain optimistic regarding our future. Our national prosperity has been bolstered by multilateral agreements that brought about stability and worked to increase trade and prosperity. The United States must maintain its alliances and partnerships as this helps to advance international peace and solidarity and build new ones. The brand of American diplomacy practiced by George Shultz and the contributors to this book can continue to play a big role in helping us preserve our important place on the world stage.

ACKNOWLEDGMENTS

We would like to acknowledge the many people who contributed to our work to make it a reality. We cannot thank enough the contributors who were willing to engage in the difficult labor of moving their thoughts to text. This work would not exist without their hard work and generosity. Their selfless contributions to the diplomatic efforts of the United States have been amazing and are important stories that need to be told. In addition, their observations about US foreign policy over their careers should be read by all aspiring foreign service officers as well as policy makers.

It is impossible to thank everyone who spoke with us to give us their valuable insights on diplomacy and US foreign policy. Conversations we have had with foreign ministers, ambassadors, diplomats, generals, strategists, academics, and writers have all helped us to understand important context of US foreign policy and to appreciate the difficulty foreign service officers face as they represent the interests of the United States. Each person that we spoke with has shared her or his experiences and thought, which worked to improve the intellectual foundation and structure used to build this work. We are grateful to all who have helped us along the way in our education and work. We wish to acknowledge Troy University, which provided institutional and library sources to help us in this effort. Further, Nick Olguin and Andrew Bowie, two amazing students, really helped with transcribing interviews and providing background information for this project. We would like to thank both Dr. William Dean and Dr. G. Kurt Piehler for reading previous drafts of the manuscript and providing excellent recommendations for improving it. Any mistakes within this book are the fault of the editors and not those of the reviewers.

Lastly, we wish to thank our wives and children for all their sacrifice, love, and support as we engaged in this project. As with any significant project, there are both highs and lows that must be overcome as completion draws near. Our wives and children have listened to our thoughts, concerns, and provided much-needed support. They have been invaluable in helping us finish.

ONE

MICHAEL O. SLOBODCHIKOFF

AND G. DOUG DAVIS

The Challenge to American Diplomacy

The twentieth century was a time when ideological divisions and great conflicts required states to prioritize diplomacy to facilitate dialogue. Through open exchange, rival powers found mutually beneficial areas where agreements could be made to reduce conflict and war. The contributors to this book were those whose work secured a peaceful resolution to the Cold War. The United States and Soviet Union were able to reach a temporary period of peace through dialogue where mutual respect produced hard-won agreements and both sides made compromises.

The Cold War was a challenging time because of the always-impending possibility of a war between the Soviet Union and the West. As the United States lost its monopoly on nuclear weapons after the Soviets tested their first nuclear device in 1949, diplomacy grew in importance since the potential for unprecedented destruction increased apprehension on both sides. Fortunately, direct military engagement between the USSR and the West never occurred. In looking back at this time period, it is imperative to recognize the diplomats whose long, dedicated, stressful labor managed to prevent open conflict. Their contributions to US and global security averted armed confrontations and allowed the Cold War to end peacefully. Their perspectives are invaluable and need to be passed down to future generations so that the importance of dialogue can always be recognized.

The United States and Soviet Union were originally allies and fought on the same side in World War II. Their joint effort worked to defeat Germany and Japan, setting the stage for the international system that would govern the Cold War era. However, cooperation between the two powers was short lived and once the war ended, their relationship quickly deteriorated. The United States and Soviet Union divided Europe into spheres of influence, where the East was controlled by Moscow and the West by

Washington. The USSR sought to consolidate its control over Eastern Europe and erect buffer states that would protect Moscow from future invasions. Moscow required states under its influence to participate in a joint alliance called the Warsaw Pact, which created and maintained political, economic, social, and cultural separation from Washington and Western Europe. The United States, on the other hand, sought establish a world order based on liberal democracy, which was contrary to the Communist authoritarian system established by Moscow. Needless to say, these two ideologies clashed. Not only this; they were pitted against each other as part of Communist ideology was to spread its influence and sow international revolution. To prevent this, and thus to forestall Soviet expansion across the continent, Washington had to maintain a military presence in Europe. As a consequence, geopolitical competition emerged between Washington and Moscow, thus giving rise to the Cold War.

In 1947 Winston Churchill, the Prime Minister of Great Britain, gave a speech in which he described an Iron Curtain descending between the East and the West, where the Soviet Union and its allies were in conflict with the United States and its allies. This was a new era, and instead of a direct conflict, the world entered a period known as the Cold War. During this time there was competition and proxy wars, but there was no direct conflict between the United States and the Soviet Union. The Soviet Union created a defensive alliance, called the Warsaw Pact, which centered around keeping Western values and influence from spreading Eastward. The Soviet Army remained stationed in much of Eastern Europe to maintain Moscow's control over the alliance. In response to the Soviet military presence, the West created its own mutual defense alliance to prevent the spread of Soviet ideology and influence into Western Europe. The United States and its allies established their own treaty—the North Atlantic Treaty Organization (NATO) to protect Europe. NATO had three main purposes: to keep the United States active in Europe, to keep the Soviet Union out of Western Europe, and to make sure Germany did not rise again as a power that would threaten peace and stability in Europe. Ambassador Stapleton Roy, a contributor to this volume, started his career in the foreign service during the Eisenhower administration, when the Atlantic Alliance was in its infancy.

The Cold War presented Washington with a new strategic environment which required the United States to maintain its global diplomatic efforts to combat Communism. Communism was a threat to the peace and stability of the liberal democratic order. The United States was convinced that the seeds of the destruction of Communism lied within Communism itself. To allow Communism to annihilate itself, the United States had to ensure that it would not spread to other countries and become the dominant ideology. The United States employed a policy of fighting the spread of Communism through trade, influence, and even military means when necessary known as strategy of containment. The US and its allies did not confront the Soviet Union with open military force, but actively worked in other regions to prevent its advance.

Nevertheless, indirect conflict emerged through proxies throughout Asia, Latin America, and Africa. The Korean War (1950–1953) and the Vietnam War (1955–1975) were both a result of the policy of containment. While the Soviet Union and United States did have open war, Washington was a direct participant in both conflicts, which the Soviet Union treated as proxy wars by arming and aiding the United States' opposition. The U.S. used the same methods to oppose the USSR when it acted offensively. Similarly, when the Soviet Union invaded Afghanistan in 1979, Washington armed the mujahedeen to oppose the Soviet army and sent weapons and special advisers to help fight against it, thus using the war in Afghanistan as a proxy war against the Soviet Union. The USSR eventually withdrew, thus bringing temporary success to the West—until its return in the early 2000s.

The great power tactics of providing arms to support their clients in other regions almost led to a full-scale nuclear war. In 1962, a new American President was to be severely tested by the Soviet Union. Moscow began arming Cuba, which had just had a revolution and became Communist. Castro's Communist revolution was a particular threat to Washington because of its geographic proximity to Florida and the US sought to destabilize and overthrow the communist regime. Havana sought Soviet help and Moscow began to send weapons to the island. More serious for the United States was the fact that Moscow sent nuclear missiles to Cuba that would be able to directly attack the United States.

A tense standoff began as Washington ordered a blockade of Cuba in the attempt to prevent nuclear missiles from being delivered to Havana. The Soviet and American navies directly faced each other in open water, knowing that both countries were on the brink of nuclear war, which would have led to mutual destruction. Jack Matlock, a contributor to this volume, was a new State Department employee stationed in Moscow during this time and he worked to translate the correspondence between Kennedy and Khrushchev. He returned to Moscow as the last American Ambassador to the Soviet Union under President Ronald Reagan and was deeply involved in the negotiations that brought about the end of the Cold War.

The Cuban Missile Crisis allowed both the US and USSR to perceive the danger in the status quo where unforeseen events could lead to open war—a conflict where neither side would prevail. Washington and Moscow recognized the importance of diplomacy to preserving peace. Constant dialogue and personal relationships needed to be fostered so that future international agreements could be reached and informal networks developed. Diplomacy became important not only at official levels, but also through peer and personal relationships. Agreements were made to notify military personnel ahead of exercises so that war would not accidentally break out, and yet even when bridges were built, the foundation was often weak. The US and USSR realized they needed allies if they were to maintain their superpower status. Neither power was strong enough to manage and preserve the international system alone as each had grown more dependent on allies. Washington knew it would face a much stronger Soviet Union if Moscow continued to be aligned with China. Thus, President Richard Nixon began an effort to drive a wedge between Moscow and Beijing. One of the ways to do this was to have Congressional Delegations with foreign service officers from the Department of State visit China annually to discuss a mutual relationship and begin to build trust. J. Stapleton Roy, a foreign service officer, was tasked with aiding the Congressional Delegations to China several times. Ambassador Roy, a contributor to this volume, would later serve as US Ambassador to China. The architect of the new policy towards China was Secretary of State Henry Kissinger. He recognized the need to isolate the Soviet Union by gaining allies, and more specifically the necessity of ensuring a fissure in the relationship between Moscow and Beijing. During that period of time, Thomas Pickering served as a special assistant to Kissinger. Pickering would later have a long and very important career, serving as one of the first US Ambassadors to Russia following the end of the Cold War as well as eventually becoming Under Secretary of State for Political Affairs and earning the State Department's highest rank, Career Ambassador.

Despite the fact that diplomacy during this period of the Cold War was so important and used as a tool to advance the competition, politically, it was necessary for each side to demonize the other. In the United States, leaders would often talk about the Soviet Union as the "Evil Empire." In 1985, Mikhail Gorbachev came to power in the Soviet Union. Gorbachev saw the Soviet system as having become complacent and truly believed in

Communism. He believed that there didn't need to be conflict between the Soviet Union and the United States, and rather began to try to de-escalate the tension between the two superpowers.

Gorbachev and Reagan began to meet and engage in the difficult task of finding mutually beneficial agreements that were facilitated through compromises. A new era in relations was born where they reached agreements on reducing the number of nuclear weapons maintained by each country as well as allowing for each side to monitor the other to ensure compliance, which had not been possible prior to Gorbachev. Negotiations continued throughout the end of the 1980s, and eventually, both sides came to a consensus that the Cold War needed to end for the benefit of both Washington and Moscow. Both sides mutually negotiated an end to the Cold War.

Soon after the end of the Cold War, the Soviet Union collapsed. This created fifteen new states and many new difficulties for diplomacy. The United States was the only superpower and was always negotiating from a position of power, often leading to the threat of military force as a tool of diplomacy. Several countries have had issue with Washington's super-power status and challenged US supremacy. Countries such as China and Russia have specifically taken measures to test Washington, while other countries like India have remained non-aligned, yet have argued for the creation of a multipolar world as opposed to having one superpower. The challenge to the United States' world order makes diplomacy even more important in the present period than during the Cold War era.

The end of the Cold War saw policymakers in the United States euphoric and develop the attitude that we had prevailed in the long and difficult contest with the Soviet Union. The United States was undisputedly recognized as the most powerful country in the world. The economy and domestic political system were strong and attractive internationally and the American armed forces were dominant. No country could challenge the United States and expect to prevail in a conflict. American weapons were the most advanced globally and our soldiers were deployed at strategic points throughout the world. This gave us the capacity to project military power anywhere in the world.

American diplomats were able to capitalize on this power because the military's global-dominance meant that other states had to consider whether Washington was willing to use force when it made a request. Following the Soviet collapse, the United States failed to adequately incorporate diplomacy into its strategy and came to over-rely on military force.

This led to several mistakes that made us take our allies for granted and we failed to build consensus or international support for military conflicts. We did not maintain long-term relationships and relied on our unparalleled military might to achieve our desired goals. No other country had this capacity and we had many successes, but we came to rely less on our diplomats and failed to develop a comprehensive strategy—one that used all resources—to accomplish our goals. America's Cold War victory led to complacency and efforts to manage conflicts without an overarching plan or comprehensive multi-dimensional foreign policy.

The Department of Defense and military leaders are engaged in diplomacy and are critical to maintaining alliances and managing international crises. The problem was that often the military did not partner effectively with our state department and it was called to intervene in issues without appropriate diplomatic support. In his contribution, General Wesley Clark argues that it is important for diplomats to work in tandem with the military. Over relying on military power and neglecting diplomacy is a recipe for failure, while diplomatic under-utilization works to impair our armed forces. Focusing on one foreign policy tool while letting other elements decline also weakens the element we wish to feature. The US was not able to maintain its diplomatic prowess in the post-Cold War world. The wars in Afghanistan and Iraq and the subsequent failure to build democracy in those countries and maintain peace have challenged US credibility as a moral power in the twenty-first century.

China's economic and military growth is testing the United States and a resurgent Russia is openly opposing American interests in Europe, the Middle East, Asia, and Latin America. Today's international climate is fundamentally different from what occurred at the end of the Cold War and the US is facing great power opposition to its agenda. Our failure to maintain strong relationships with our allies means that the West is no longer unified as it confronts adversaries. The challenge to the liberal order—established and defended by the United States—is real and one implication is that diplomacy will become increasingly important for Washington. The experienced diplomats who have written chapters in this volume have served in every administration from Eisenhower through Trump. They have dedicated their lives to improving and serving the United States of America. In this work, they have outlined and discussed the realities of diplomacy in the United States as well as the difficulties facing diplomats, foreign policymakers, and military leaders today. We should all be very thankful that despite the hardships they have faced throughout their careers, we have such a dedicated and capable people ensuring the future of diplomatic relations in the United States. It is thanks to these hard-working individuals that the United States has been able to achieve such power and moral authority as it has at the end of the last century. The challenges our country faces moving forward are unprecedented and should really worry policymakers in the years to come. Will the United States be able to maintain its moral authority and global power or will it be forced to eventually cede it to countries like China and Russia?

Ultimately, diplomacy is a vital part of statecraft and must be maintained. The United States is at a crossroads. It can either revitalize its efforts in diplomacy or it can wither away its power in the future. Diplomacy and the art of diplomacy are even more important in the twenty-first century than in the past. While the United States still has one of the most powerful militaries in the world, its efficacy to bring about changes in behavior or resolve many crises is limited. The military is very skilled at waging war and defeating enemies, but less so at nation-building and creating permanent change. The wars in Iraq and in Afghanistan have resulted in sectarian violence, and limited gains in governance.

In addition to the difficulty with achieving long-term goals through the use of military force, the economy of the United States, one of its greatest strengths in the past, has slowed. The crisis in 2008 highlighted how interconnected many economies were and how difficult economic pressure can be used to achieve long-term change. While in the past the United States has been able to use economic pressure and sanctions to achieve changes in behavior such as with the apartheid regime in South Africa, these tools have not been as effective in the twenty-first century. Further, the growth in the economy of China and India are threatening the economic situation in the United States. While almost all trade and economic interactions helped the United States at the end of the twentieth century, countries now have more choices and the ability to achieve economic gains without involving the United States.

Another great obstacle to US superiority in the global system is demography as the US population is shrinking. National populations are also quickly declining in much of Western Europe, South Korea, and Japan—our traditional allies—and their armed services will be smaller going forward, while, on the other hand, the population in many African states and India is increasing. The relevance of the United States as a global superpower is slowly deteriorating. What this means is that the US can no longer afford to use its might and strength to force other states to comply with its wishes. Instead, the US must rely on what most countries have long relied upon, which is effective negotiation and compromise with other states. Most other countries have a professional cadre of diplomats who devote their lives to mediation and achieving the goals of the countries they represent. They do not rely upon non-professional diplomats to negotiate outcomes. The United States also has a professional cadre of diplomats who are extremely well trained and very professional at their task. However, increasingly the posts of diplomats and ambassadorial positions are given to political and financial supporters of the incoming president. There is sometimes mistrust between politicians and professional diplomats because politicians' question their loyalty and see professional foreign service workers as blocking their ideological or policy positions.

The importance of diplomacy in the twenty-first century cannot be understated. However, our current system in the United States needs to be revised greatly. It has been argued by some in this volume that more training needs to occur, that there needs to be more reliance upon professional diplomats, and that politics needs to be less present in the State Department. One very interesting recommendation comes from former ambassador Marc Grossman, who suggests developing a cadre of reserve diplomats who are well-trained and can be called upon in moments of crises. They can be sent to countries to help resolve political conflicts and to help in negotiations. This is a very interesting proposal and one that we believe deserves a lot of discussion from policymakers.

While we will not reiterate the points made by all the contributors in this volume, we will state that all of the recommendations made by these professional diplomats and people who have devoted their lives in the service of the United States should be taken very seriously in policy circles. Their decades of experience and focus on American diplomacy mean that the subjects and issues they present merit attention and are central in allowing the United States to regain its diplomatic prowess. Their contributions shed light into America's foreign policy for more than half a century and under twelve different administrations, from Eisenhower to Trump.

We have dedicated this volume to the memory of former Secretary of State George Schultz. In discussions with many ambassadors, it became apparent how important the former secretary was to ending the Cold War. While he was extremely familiar with the political battles occurring in Washington, Secretary Schultz nevertheless truly focused on the professionalism and abilities of those who worked within the Department of State. He relied upon their counsel, took time to listen to their arguments, and in an era where technology was making it difficult to be fully briefed on all events, he would often take several days to become acquainted and thoroughly informed on issues before entering into negotiations. Former ambassador Jack Matlock, the last US ambassador to the Soviet Union, tells how Mr. Schultz would fly into Finland before summit meetings with the Soviet Union, and would bring Mr. Matlock and other officials from the Soviet embassy to Helsinki to work for three days to allow him to meet and discuss the major issues with the personnel who best understood them. This allowed him to better grasp the subjects that would be discussed and to more comprehensively recognize the elements that were in our national interest. This also ensured that everyone was on the same page and clear about their various roles in the negotiation processes. This approach was vital to creating a bilateral settlement to end the Cold War, to negotiating treaties on de-escalating the arms race, and setting the groundwork for a more peaceful world order. Former Secretary of State George Schultz's contributions to US foreign policy and to diplomacy in general are much greater than is commonly understood. It is wholly fitting that this volume is dedicated in his honor.

This volume begins with a touching preface written by former Secretary of State James Baker III. Baker was very involved in the State Department and had an amazing way of navigating the political pitfalls in Washington. He succeeded former Secretary of State George Schultz and had a lot of respect for his predecessor. We are very thankful for his contributions to US foreign policy and for his personal tribute to his friend and mentor.

The work provides an introduction to the life-work of career diplomats. The chapter written by former ambassador Richard "Dick" Miles discusses his career at the end of the twentieth and beginning of the twenty-first century. While his record was truly extraordinary in many ways, he also provides an illustration of a "typical" professional career.

Chapter 3 is written by the former supreme Allied Commander Europe, General Wesley Clark. Typical studies of diplomacy do not examine the military aspect of diplomacy, therefore, General Clark's chapter is unique in that it examines how military policy and military force can be used as a very effective diplomatic tool. He also points out the problems of using force in the wrong way which actually hurts diplomatic efforts. In other words, the use of military force can be an effective tool in promoting diplomacy providing it is used in an effective manner and not only on its own. It must be used in tandem with other diplomatic efforts.

The next section of the book identifies problems and challenges facing

US foreign policy. For example, former ambassador Robert Hunter discusses a myriad of complex issues facing policymakers and diplomats regarding US foreign policy. Former ambassador David Dunford discusses how many different entities are involved in the foreign policy process and often are not coordinated in their efforts to achieve US foreign policy goals.

Several contributors, for example former ambassador Ken Gross, provide overview perspectives on lessons and skills diplomats should possess. Similarly, former ambassador Earl Anthony Wayne discusses not only the core competencies that diplomats must have, but also identifies the specific challenges faced by diplomats in service to the United States.

Former ambassador Marc Grossman writes about US foreign policy not being geared towards the middle class, but rather serves the interests of the policy elites. The middle class has largely been forgotten in the pursuit of US foreign policy goals. Mr. Grossman's proposal of having a reserve cadre of diplomats available in times of crisis is very interesting and one which we believe should be pursued.

Former ambassador Ronald Neumann discusses the global order established by the United States following World War II. He identifies that the global order is currently under attack by China and Russia and further laments that the credibility of the United States is at a low point. He argues that alliances are necessary to maintain the current global order. The US needs to prioritize its alliances and attempt to improve its relations with its current allies. He also argues that US diplomacy must be revitalized if the United States is to fend off challenges from other states globally.

Former ambassador Thomas Pickering deeply analyzes US diplomacy. First, he looks at what motivates countries. Second, he examines current global crises and discusses the relevance of diplomacy in resolving them. Specifically, he shows how diplomacy can mitigate disputes and prevent conflicts when used effectively. Finally, he analyzes the current structure of US diplomacy and makes recommendations on how to improve so that the United States can become more effective at dealing with global challenges.

Former ambassador P. Michael McKinley offers a historical view of US efforts in diplomacy from the Reagan administration through the Biden administration. He has a unique experience within the leadership of the US Department of State and, therefore, can offer a very unique perspective of US diplomacy efforts from an administrative perspective as well as the perspective of a former ambassador. He is able to effectively show how diplomacy has evolved from being driven by ideology during the Cold War era to being in serious jeopardy and unable to meet the challenges of the present era.

Former ambassador Stapleton Roy highlights the fact that superpower diplomacy is different from diplomacy in the rest of the world. While other countries use diplomacy to convince other states to cooperate, the United States has too often relied on its military to threaten other countries and resolve disputes through force as opposed to negotiation. He argues that this approach has to change for diplomacy in the twenty-first century to be successful. It is very interesting to contrast the views of ambassador Roy with those of general Clark. They highlight the same problem from very different perspectives.

To conclude, this volume is extremely unique in that it brings together specialists with many decades of experience in US foreign policy. Their expertise is unmatched and vital for policymakers to consult during this transitional era of US foreign policy. It is very difficult to determine whether or not the United States can overcome the challenges that it is currently facing in its foreign policy. However, if it is to be successful in doing so, it must truly reform its diplomatic institutions, its approaches to foreign policy, and rely more upon the knowledgeable and professional Americans working to further American interests.

The roots of American power have always lied within the wealth of its country citizens. The United States is truly a unique melting pot of world cultures, languages, and diversity. The United States is a natural leader in the world, and should not relinquish this role. The authors in this volume represent just some of the wealth working to advance US foreign policies and interests. In the future, the United States needs to rely on their expertise in order to weather the current storm. In other words, it is as yet unclear if it is morning or twilight to American diplomatic efforts in the twenty-first century. The future remains hazy. However, with people such as these experts working to represent the United States, it is more likely that US diplomacy will adapt and become more and more successful in the twenty-first century and beyond.

TWO

JACK F. MATLOCK JR.

Diplomacy That Ended the Cold War

My thirty-five years in the American Foreign Service (1956–1991) started when the Cold War was at its height. They ended only weeks before the Soviet Union broke up into fifteen independent countries, but at least two years after the Cold War itself had come to an end. Eleven of these years were spent at the American embassy in Moscow, seven of them in Washington dealing with Soviet and European affairs, and most of the rest in Africa and Central Europe when the Cold War was the central preoccupation of US foreign policy.

One of the most damaging misperceptions about international relations in the late 1980s and the beginning of the 1990s is the idea that the Cold War ended with the break-up of the Soviet Union at the end of 1991, and that this constituted a "victory" for the US and "Western" policy. As one who participated in the negotiations that ended the Cold War, I can testify that this interpretation distorts, to the point of misrepresentation, what actually happened. The Cold War ended by negotiation and the results benefited all parties, especially the Soviet Union, by ending the expensive and dangerous arms race and the division of Europe into hostile blocs. Subsequently the Soviet Union shattered into fifteen independent states as the result of internal pressures, not external compulsion. The United States would have preferred to live with a voluntary federation of twelve Soviet republics—that is, one without Estonia, Latvia, and Lithuania—as President George H.W. Bush made clear in his speech to the Ukrainian parliament on August 1, 1991. Events in the Soviet Union itself, particularly the policies of the elected president of the Russian Socialist Federated Soviet Republic (RSFSR), Boris Yeltsin, made this impossible.

I will return to these thoughts later as I discuss international relations following the end of the Cold War, but first let us consider what we mean by diplomacy and then how it was used to end the confrontations of the Cold War.

When I google for a definition of "diplomacy," I get the following reply: (1) "the profession, activity, or skill of managing international relations, typically by a country's representatives abroad" and (2) "the art of dealing with people in a sensitive and effective way." These are not two variant definitions. They are two aspects of what should be a single definition. One cannot be an effective diplomat—that is, one that facilitates a settlement of differences acceptable to both parties—without sensitivity to the position and views of his or her interlocutors, in other words without at least the appearance of personal respect. That means, *inter alia*, avoiding public demonization of people who hold power in other countries.

President Reagan was a sharp critic of the Soviet system; in one of his speeches early in his presidency, he referred to the Soviet Union as an "evil empire." However, he never personally insulted the Soviet leaders. Indeed, when he met them his first words were likely to be something like, "We hold the peace of the world in our hands. We must find a way to co-operate to insure peace." In time—by 1987—he and Soviet leader Mikhail Gorbachev had implicitly agreed on the same negotiating agenda. And then, in December 1988, as he was preparing to leave office, Reagan noted in his diary: "The meeting [with Gorbachev on Governors Island] was a tremendous success. . . . Gorbachev sounded as if he saw us as partners making a better world."[1] Earlier that year when he visited Moscow, Reagan had been asked by a journalist if the country was still an "evil empire." "No," he replied, "that was another time, another era." And then, when he was asked who was responsible, he said, "Mr. Gorbachev, of course. He is the leader of this country."

That was in 1988. Just five years earlier, on September 28, 1983, Soviet leader Yuri Andropov had announced on Radio Moscow "If anyone had any illusions about the possibility of an evolution for the better in the policy of the present American administration, recent events have dispelled them once and for all."[2] Andropov then withdrew Soviet negotiators from all ongoing arms control negotiations. Many observers, especially those in Europe, began to talk about a "Second Cold War" as if the Nixon-Brezhnev détente period had ended the first. (It hadn't.)

My personal involvement in these events began in the spring of 1983 when I was asked to take a position on the National Security Council to work out a negotiating approach to deal with the Soviet Union.[3] Although Reagan had earlier made some gestures intended to begin a useful dialogue with the Soviet leader, such as a handwritten letter to Brezhnev in 1981 when he was still recuperating from an assassin's bullet, and also his decision to end the embargo on grain sales imposed by the Carter administration, his forceful criticism of communism and of Soviet policy overshadowed such gestures. He needed to make clear his desire for a negotiated solution to the issues that had divided the world into competing power blocs and produced a dangerous and costly arms race. He noted in his personal diary just before I took up my duties on the NSC: "Some on the NSC staff are too hard line and don't think any approach should be made to the Soviets. I think I am hard line and will never appease. But I do want to try to let them see there is a better world if they'll show by deed that they want to get along with the free world."[4]

Even though Reagan was eager for a personal meeting with the Soviet leader, that proved to be impossible until Gorbachev was named General Secretary of the Communist Party of the Soviet Union in March 1985. Reagan immediately sent a letter to Gorbachev suggesting a meeting, which was delivered by Vice President Bush when he attended Konstantin Chernenko's funeral in Moscow. Gorbachev accepted in principle, and by summer it was agreed that the two would meet in Geneva in November.

Meanwhile, US policy had been revamped, articulated in greater detail, and—most important—had shifted its focus to concentrate on cooperation to achieve a mutually beneficial outcome and to implement private consultation before proposals were publicized. In other words, US policymakers tried to replace a "zero-sum" game where one party loses all that the other side gains, for one that was potentially "win-win" with both sides coming out better off.

This was done by describing a more accommodating posture in a series of speeches President Reagan delivered in 1984. In the first, delivered on January 16, Reagan set forth a policy that later became a four-part agenda: to cooperate in arms reduction, particularly nuclear weapons; to end fueling conflict in third countries; to better protect human rights, and to build a better working relationship (a euphemism for raising the Iron Curtain).[5] A second speech, delivered in June 1984, described the need for freer contacts across the East-West divide and the fact that both sides would benefit from it.[6] A third, delivered to the United Nations General Assembly on September 24, 1984, proposed regular consultations between senior US and Soviet officials on all topics of the broad agenda he had described in his earlier speeches: "I will suggest to the Soviet Union that we institutionalize regular ministerial or cabinet-level meetings between our two countries on the whole agenda of issues before us, including the problem of needless obstacles to understanding."[7]

As we defined goals and cooperative methods to achieve them, we also defined—for internal US government use—three topics or objectives that were not in our stated agenda: (1) challenging legitimacy of the Soviet system; (2) military superiority; (3) forcing collapse of the Soviet system.[8]

These policies were in place before Reagan's first meeting with Gorbachev. Once we started preparing for the Reagan-Gorbachev meeting in November, 1985, we began to put them into effect. We would propose a list of possible cooperative projects through diplomatic channels and request Soviet comment before describing them in public. We also invited our Soviet interlocutors to suggest projects of particular interest to them. Reagan's staff set aside extensive time to brief him on the main issues and also on relevant history; we put together the equivalent of a college-level course with the help of specialists in the State Department and Central Intelligence Agency.[9] We also turned to many specialists outside the government to write papers on important topics and sometimes come and discuss them personally with the president.

Reagan read the reports avidly, and often commented in the margins. What interested him most, however, was not so much the details of the political and military issues, but the Soviet leader's mode of thinking.

Just before he left Washington to meet Gorbachev, Reagan wrote out his thoughts on a yellow legal pad, had them typed, made a few corrections, and sent them to me with a request to discuss them during the briefings in Geneva. They gave valuable clues to his approach. First, he recognized that Gorbachev was not a dictator but had to justify any concessions to the Politburo at home. Second, Reagan considered protection of human rights to be one of the most important issues but recognized that public condemnation could do more harm than good. (As he put it, "Front page stories that we are banging away at them on their human rights abuses, will get us some cheers from the bleachers but it won't help those who are being abused.") He resolved to deal with those issues privately rather than by shouting demands in public. He made the development of trust one of his most important goals. Finally, he observed, "Whatever we achieve, we must not call it victory."[10] He understood that claiming triumph in a negotiation would undermine the possibility of solving other problems.

I have described in detail how US-Soviet relations developed during the 1980s in my book *Reagan and Gorbachev: How the Cold War Ended*. Despite occasional setbacks, relations moved from what seemed to be a total stalemate in the fall of 1983 when Andropov announced that it was impossible to deal with the Reagan administration, to the sense of partnership

Reagan described in his diary when he and Gorbachev parted in December, 1988. After some hesitation, President George H.W. Bush and his Secretary of State, James A. Baker, III, adopted key elements of the Reagan approach, though without attribution and without the help of important members of Reagan's support team.

In short, from 1983, the US shifted its approach to the USSR from one of challenges and accusations to proposals for cooperation to achieve mutually beneficial aims. Ending the arms race was in the interest of both countries, but it had to be done in a way that neither would feel that the agreement was a defeat. It was also in the interest of both countries to withdraw from proxy conflicts in third-party countries; regular meetings by the US and Soviet officials who dealt with policy in these areas resolved most of the confrontations by the late 1980s. Gorbachev's reform initiatives, *glasnost'* (openness in the media) and *perestroika* (reform or reconstruction of the political and economic system) gained momentum in the late 1980s and facilitated expanding contacts and communication across borders that had been blocked by what Winston Churchill had called an "Iron Curtain" in his 1946 speech in Fulton, Missouri.

Secretary of State Shultz made a special effort to develop a personal relationship with Gorbachev's foreign minister, Eduard Shevardnadze. The first time Shevardnadze visited Washington, Shultz invited him and his wife Nanuli to a private dinner at the Shultz residence in Washington. The Shevardnadzes reciprocated the next time Shultz and his wife came to Moscow. Soon, they were dealing with each other on a first-name basis. Of course, both knew that personal friendship did not automatically solve problems. As a result, however, they were increasingly able to deal with each other with confidence and without rancor. When he replaced Secretary Shultz, Secretary of State Baker and his wife continued to maintain a warm personal relationship with their Soviet counterparts.

Personal relations matter. International relations are in fact not comparable to billiard balls colliding on a pool table, as some theories hold. Nation states are led by people and international diplomacy is heavily influenced by the personal relations of those who exercise power in their respective countries. US policy sought to achieve ends compatible with the long-term interests of both countries; these could be defined in practice only if the political leaders and their diplomats were able to communicate with each other privately in candor, and with confidence that they would not be confronted with embarrassing disclosures to the public. By defining all of US foreign policy goals as cooperation to achieve ends beneficial to both, as President Reagan did in his January 1984 speech, and then pursuing these goals increasingly through private diplomacy when that became possible with Gorbachev's assumption of power, we ended the Cold War to the benefit of all.

Exclusion of certain goals was an essential part of the Reagan approach. As noted above, from 1983 Reagan's policy excluded denying the legitimacy of the Soviet system, seeking military advantage, or trying to replace the communist system in the Soviet Union with something else. The first would have made real negotiation impossible; as for the second, defining a military balance would be difficult, but any overt effort to retain a military edge would undermine the possibility of agreement; as for the third, trying to achieve what later was called "regime change" would actually strengthen the police state system and make any attempt at reform impossible.

Another feature of US policy was a commitment to dialogue and negotiation. In the past, the leaders of both countries had tended to break off negotiations if the other side did something they objected to. The Carter Administration, for example, withdrew from cultural exchanges and cooperative agreements when the Soviet Union invaded Afghanistan. When the US began to deploy missiles in Europe in response to the Soviet SS-20s, Andropov terminated all arms-control negotiations. Reagan's instincts told him that dialog and consultations were particularly important when something happened to increase tensions and distrust. He pledged never to withdraw from negotiations.

The ideological cold war, which underlay the arms race and the geopolitical divide, ended in December 1988, when Gorbachev, in a speech to the United Nations, announced that Soviet policy would be based on "the common interests of mankind," rather than the traditional Soviet aim of supporting the "proletariat" in an international class struggle. Events of 1989 and 1990, when the countries of Eastern Europe asserted their independence and the Berlin Wall came down, proved that he meant it. The Cold War was over. At the same time, resistance to reform was growing in the Soviet Union: many non-Russian nationalities were pressing, first for autonomy and then for independence, and the country was experiencing an erratic supply of food and consumer goods as Gorbachev tried to introduce more elements of a market economy into a state-controlled system.

In August 1991, a cabal of senior officials tried to take power from Gorbachev. They failed, but their attempt so weakened Gorbachev's authority that Boris Yeltsin, who had been elected president of the RSFSR, was able to enlist the cooperation of the leaders of Ukraine and Belarus to abolish the USSR altogether. The Commonwealth of Independent States, which replaced it, was a loose association lacking sovereign authority to govern. A country that had been seen as a superpower, a military match for the United States, simply collapsed. In its stead there were fifteen sovereign states, all struggling to solidify their independence, restructure their economies and develop independent bureaucracies rather than branches of USSR ministries. The Russian Federation, by far the largest, had only half the population of the Soviet Union. By effect, the huge Soviet military establishment was in total disarray.[11]

The United States had an opportunity at the beginning of 1992 to help build a post-Cold-War order based on shared responsibility for security and development. Military deployments and military spending could be sharply reduced and strong encouragement given to building inclusive security arrangements. This did not occur. In fact, thirty years after the Soviet Union collapsed and ceased to be a military threat to the United States, we now find ourselves involved in multiple conflicts and confrontations reminiscent of the Cold War, with two major powers: China, whose economy is now growing faster than America's, and Russia, whose nuclear capability, if ever used, is adequate to demolish the United States (and to invite its own destruction).

How has this come about? Doubtless for many reasons, but it seems to me that a misunderstanding—or in some instances, willful misrepresentation—of the way the Cold War ended has been a major contributing factor, maybe even the principal one. Instead of continuing to practice the sort of diplomacy that ended the Cold War, the United States has too often done the opposite. The prevailing idea that the United States "won" the Cold War in the sense that it defeated the Soviet Union is flat-out wrong. As Professor Beth Fischer observed in her detailed study, *The Myth of Triumphalism: Rethinking President Reagan's Cold War Legacy*: "The Cold War was resolved through diplomacy. President Reagan focused on the superpowers' mutual interest in reducing nuclear arms and engaged in meaningful dialogue so as to ease security concerns and build trust. It was this policy of reassurance and engagement that led to the peaceful conclusion of the Cold War."[12]

Looking at the end of the Cold War as a victory of one country over the other rather than an outcome that served the vital interests of both led to the unfounded conclusion that an American-style political system suited the entire world and that in fact it was the inevitable future of mankind. As Francis Fukuyama put it, "What we may be witnessing is not just the end of the Cold War, or the passing of a particular period of post-war history, but the end of history as such: that is, the end point of mankind's ideological evolution and the universalization of Western liberal democracy as the final form of human government."[13] This statement, the philosophical basis for the attempt to use America's military and economic power to create clones of "Western liberal democracy" in other countries, had not the slightest confirmation in historical experience.[14] Even the definition of what constituted a "liberal world order" was subject to constant change.

The break-up of the Soviet Union also fed another unfounded myth, that of a "unipolar world." The idea was that the world of the Cold War had been run by two superpowers, the United States and the Soviet Union, but now that the Soviet Union had collapsed the United States stood astride the globe with power to change it in its own (largely imagined) image. Few commentators questioned the absurdity of the proposition. They mainly argued over whether this was a permanent characteristic of global politics or a temporary one ("the unipolar moment").

Now, of course, both the United States and the Soviet Union had in their possession weapons that, if used, could destroy the other, and in so doing also render the planet uninhabitable for anybody. Call it superpower if you wish, but it is power to destroy and not create. Even with reduced numbers, both the United States and Russia still have enough nuclear weapons on station to wipe out civilization on earth. So, if possession of nuclear weapons by the thousands is the qualification for superpower status, the United States and Russia still qualify.

Power to destroy is not power to change other societies. The idea that outsiders can "build" a nation or create a government in a different country of, by, and for its people (to use Lincoln's definition of democracy) is a self-contradicting oxymoron. Yet it has been an essential element of the foreign policy of all of our post-Cold War presidents. Even our spectacular and costly failure in Afghanistan has not yet led to a fundamental rethinking of impossible goals.

The idea that "Western liberal democracy" is "the final form of human government" and that it can be achieved by the application of US power reminds me of the Soviet Union's Brezhnev Doctrine. Based on the Marxist-Leninist theory of world revolution—that the proletariat (working class) would take power by revolution and create first a "socialist," and then a "communist" society—it held that once a country was declared "socialist," it was the duty of other "socialist" countries to defend "socialism" and prevent backsliding into the control of "imperialists." That was the official rationale for the Soviet invasion of Hungary in 1956 and of Czechoslovakia in 1968.

One of its assumptions was that socialist countries would always be allies of the Soviet Union. It assumed that the form of government determined a country's geopolitical orientation. But this assumption was contradicted by Marshal Tito's Yugoslavia, which broke from Stalin's Soviet Union, and Mao Zedong's China, which for a time became a virtual enemy. The same form of government did not necessarily guarantee a willing alliance after all. Gorbachev's renunciation of the Brezhnev Doctrine permitted "a Europe whole and free," and was a key factor in bringing the Cold War to an end.

Despite the evidence that the Brezhnev doctrine had been an expensive burden to the Soviet Union and that its motivating tenets were proven falsehoods, in effect the United States adopted a version of it when it set out to create a "liberal world order," founded in the presumption that the United States could build nations and create democratic governments in other countries. This implied a diplomacy *based on* the three approaches President Reagan *excluded* when he negotiated the end of the Cold War.

The fact is that the United States, since the end of the Cold War, has more often than not replaced the techniques of effective diplomacy—settling disputes peacefully by negotiation—with hypocritical moralizing,[15] direct interference in the domestic politics of other countries,[16] censuring others for behavior it has indulged in, itself,[17] and outright bullying less affluent countries with financial and economic sanctions.[18] It has asserted the goal of a monopoly of military power ("full spectrum dominance" in the words of one Pentagon document during the second Bush administration), and assumed it has the right to enforce rules without itself abiding by them.[19]

The ability to conduct effective diplomacy with Russia suffered further damage when the Obama administration, along with the leaders of both parties in Congress, began systematically blaming Russian president Vladimir Putin, alone, for the rising tensions. Prominent US newspapers and television networks joined in what, to suspicious Russian eyes, had all the appearance of a coordinated campaign of personalized vilification.

In fact, Putin was reacting to what he viewed as US efforts to isolate Russia and build a military cordon along its borders, and—he suspected—even encourage "regime change" in Russia, as it had in Ukraine and Georgia. President Obama extended the hostile rhetoric to insult the Russian nation as a whole when he made public statements about Russia not producing anything anybody wanted and ridiculed the idea that Russia was a Great Power. (At that time, the only way the US could take astronauts to the International Space Station was by Russian rockets and the US was trying to prevent Iran and Turkey from purchasing Russian anti-aircraft missiles! Obama's comment that Russia was not a Great Power but only a regional power seemed to imply, first, that might makes right, that Great Powers have rights which are denied to less powerful nations, and second, that Russia had no business protecting its interests even in its own region. After all, the two areas most in contention, Ukraine and Syria, are much closer to Russia than they are to the United States.)

On top of this, the United States, from January 2017, started expelling large numbers of Russian diplomats on one pretext or another. Predictably, Russia, reciprocated tit for tat with the outcome by the summer of 2021 that the staffs of diplomatic and consular missions of both countries had been slashed to the point that basic services such as visa issuance had to be suspended at the American embassy in Moscow. The result was a campaign against the very instruments of international diplomacy. The governments of both countries seem bent on crippling their capacity to cooperate in dealing with common problems.

The US attempt to police and remake the world diverts it from dealing most effectively with the most serious threats it and the world as a whole face. We are still in the midst of a pandemic which will not be ended or controlled in the United States until it is also managed elsewhere. Nuclear weapons are still a potential threat to mankind and we seem to be on the brink of yet another nuclear arms race, having withdrawn from the key agreements that helped us end the Cold War. Global warming and environmental degradation also threaten all countries. Failed nation states and mass migrations will stress even the most affluent.

None of these problems can be alleviated without cooperation among all major powers. None can be solved or even ameliorated by military action. The current rise in geopolitical competition and the replacement of diplomacy with threats, sanctions, and attempts to mind other countries' business can only divert us from dealing effectively with our problems at home and the more serious dangers that now threaten to engulf mankind as a whole.

Notes

This essay was completed some three months before Russia invaded Ukraine. It is included without alteration since the editors believe these subsequent events add forceful evidence to the author's arguments about the nature of and need for diplomacy. The author believes that diplomacy which took into account the security interests of all the parties would have avoided the war in Ukraine that started in February 2022 and the earlier annexation of Ukrainian territory by Russia.

1. Ronald Reagan, *An American Life* (New York: Simon & Schuster, 1990), 715.

2. Reported in *Pravda*, September 29, 1983.

3. Described in Jack F. Matlock, Jr., *Reagan and Gorbachev: How the Cold War Ended* (New York: Random House, 2004), ix–xi.

4. Reagan, *American Life*, 572.

5. *Weekly Compilation of Presidential Documents* 20, no. 3: 40–45. Also available on the internet at: https://www.reaganlibrary.gov/archives/speech/address -nation-and-other-countries-united-states-soviet-relations.

6. Ibid., vol. 26: 945.

7. https://www.reaganlibrary.gov/archives/speech/address-39th-session-united -nations-general-assembly-new-york-new-york.

8. See "US Policy Guidance," In Matlock, *Reagan and Gorbachev*, 76.

9. Documents 60 and 74, *Foreign Relations of the United States (FRUS) 5, Soviet Union, March 1985–October 1986* (Washington: United States Government Printing Office, 2020), 214–220 and 298–305 are examples of papers prepared for the president.

10. Matlock, *Reagan and Gorbachev*, 150–54.

11. William E. Odom, *The Collapse of the Soviet Military* (New Haven: Yale University Press, 1998).

12. Beth A. Fischer, *The Myth of Triumphalism: Rethinking President Reagan's Cold War Legacy* (Lexington: University Press of Kentucky, 2020).

13. Francis Fukuyama, *The End of History and the Last Man* (New York: Free Press, 1992).

14. For a more extensive discussion of the implications of Fukuyama's thesis see John Gray, *Black Mass: Apocalyptic Religion and the Death of Utopia* (New York: Farrar, Straus and Giroux, 2007), *passim*; also the discussion in Jack F. Matlock Jr., *Superpower Illusions: How Myths and False Ideologies Led America Astray—and How to Return to Reality* (New Haven: Yale University Press, 2010), 115–16.

15. For example, the passage of the so-called Magnitsky Act during the Obama administration. Based on allegations—never proved—of a single miscarriage of justice—prominent Russians were "sanctioned" for alleged human rights violations. It would seem that members of Congress should have more properly turned their attention to numerous miscarriages of justice in the United States rather than unproven allegations regarding acts under foreign jurisdiction. At the same time, the Obama administration covered up the tortures committed by the second Bush Administration and actually prosecuted the whistleblowers who revealed these human rights abuses by the United States.

16. For example, overt support for Yeltsin in the 1996 Russian election, the "color revolutions" in Ukraine, Georgia, and Kyrgyzstan, plus direct support for "regime change" in Russia itself.

17. For example, accusing Russia of "aggression" against Ukraine, when the United States had illegally made war against Iraq with far greater casualties, and also had illegally attempted to remove the president of Syria, the head of a government the US recognized.

18. Economic sanctions have become a favored tool of coercion, however, when they involve issues that the other country's government considers vital to its national security, they normally fail. For example, the various sanctions against Russia in response to its actions in Ukraine make resolution of the issues more difficult.

19. For a more expansive discussion of events in the 1990s and the first decade of the twentieth century, see Matlock, *Superpower Illusions*, 131–265.

THREE

RICHARD "DICK" MILES

An Amazing Diplomatic Career

I have had a lot of luck in my life. Of course, "luck" is sometimes self-caused, brought about by taking risks or seizing an opportunity. I think the best illustration of pure luck in my life was when I enlisted in the Marine Corps in December 1954. I was seventeen years old, a high school dropout at sixteen and aware only of the thought that my future prospects in Richmond, Indiana, appeared dull, in the extreme.

To my mind, the Marine Corps offered a chance to see something of the world and perhaps a bit of excitement. The Marine Corps has two centers for basic training: Parris Island, South Carolina, and San Diego, California. Traditionally, recruits enlisting east of the Mississippi River went to Parris Island and those west of the river went to San Diego. The Marine Corps decided to send me to San Diego. I don't know why they did this, but that simple stroke of the pen or clicking of a few typewriter keys changed my life significantly. Thanks to that minor bureaucratic event, I would eventually be assigned to duty as a member of the Marine Detachment on the USS Lexington, where I first heard of the Department of State and the Foreign Service. A young naval officer, who was simply doing his required tour of duty after having gone through college in the naval ROTC program, had volunteered to teach an evening class on the ship. While the topic was American government, he dwelled on the State Department because he planned to join the Foreign Service when his military tour of duty was up. I was sufficiently intrigued by his description of the Foreign Service and the color slides he had made during a tourist visit to East Berlin, for me to decide—at the tender age of 19—that I would do the same thing. I'm glad I did not confide this idea to anyone because I would surely have been counseled to give it up as an impractical dream.

I had encouraged my parents to move from Indiana to California and when when my three-year enlistment was up, I returned home and enrolled in the junior/community college in Bakersfield, California. I have now been married for more than sixty years to the truly wonderful woman, Sharon O'Brien, whom I met at Bakersfield College—another bit of luck in my life that would not have happened without that fateful decision to send me to California instead of South Carolina.

I owe a lot to Bakersfield College. I made up a few required high-school level courses—algebra, geometry—and I did well enough in all my classes to be accepted for further study by the University of California at Berkeley, where Sharon and I got our bachelor's degrees. I then went on to get a master's degree at Indiana University in the school's Russian and East European Institute.

Fast-forward to January 1967. After six and a half years of college and two and a half years in the civil rights movement, I passed all the entrance tests and other requirements, and became a Foreign Service Officer.

The State Department was always good to me regarding assignments abroad and at home in Washington. I was able to serve in both Eastern and Western Europe, receiving truly excellent language training along the way. In Washington, I served on the Soviet and the East European-Yugoslav Desks, and also in the Politico-Military Bureau. You can read more about these early years in the oral history memoir I made in 2008 for the Association for Diplomatic Studies and Training (www.adst.org).

The more interesting assignments in my career began in 1988 when I became the Consul General in what was then Leningrad. This three-year assignment came at a turbulent period in Russia. At that time, Leningrad had a population of four and a half million people. Times for the Soviet citizens were very difficult. Basic food items were rationed and often were not available at all. Change was in the air, although no one, literally no one, foresaw the imminent collapse of the Soviet Union.

Due to a long-standing American policy of non-recognition of the incorporation of the Baltic States—Estonia, Latvia and Lithuania—into the Soviet Union, the American Ambassador in Moscow was not allowed to visit the Baltic States. Since 1972, when the Consulate General in Leningrad was opened, the Consul General had made periodic but perfunctory trips to those areas. In the late 1980s, however, these visits took on a much more important and even dramatic role as the independence movement in the Baltic States grew, despite Moscow's attempts to suppress these developments by pressure, including the use of force.

For the Leningrad Consulate General, the result was the transformation of an interesting but somewhat sleepy post into one of the nerve centers of

American policy toward the Soviet Union. Happily, I had an excellent team of officers and staff in Leningrad who rose to the occasion—I won't to try to name everyone, and although eventually everyone played a valuable role, I would like to mention my office manager Linda Price, who remained with me for the rest of my career. Further, I have to name the deputy principal officers, first Tom Maertens, then Jon Purnell, and also the political officers, Doug Wake and George Krol, plus Bob Patterson—four of these five became ambassadors later in their careers.

Due to the sensitivity of the changing situation in each of the Baltic States, the National Security Council asked the Consulate General to maintain a constant presence in the region. This was not easy due to the relatively small size of the Consulate General staff. We managed by calling on officers who normally would not have participated in active missions of political and security-related reporting.

We did have difficulty communicating with Washington, our Embassy in Moscow, and with other appropriate addresses. Following an earlier discovery of listening devices deeply embedded in the structure of the Consulate General building, we were forbidden to send classified cables from the Consulate General. Any such messages—and there were many—had to be written in longhand and sent to Embassy Helsinki by diplomatic courier, to be typed and sent from there. Our poor, designated secretary in Helsinki not only had to read the handwritten messages of many different officers, but also had to try to provide the correct spelling of names and places transliterated from Estonian, Latvian, Lithuanian and Russian languages.

Not for the last time in my career, I worked hard to ensure that neither I nor the officers in the field provided any false hopes of American intervention, either to the leaders of the democratic opposition in Leningrad or to the Baltic leaders of their national movements. We did provide moral encouragement but I was always mindful of the Hungarian Uprising of 1956, when false hopes were raised by overwrought American propaganda. I did not want that to happen on my watch.

Developments in Leningrad itself were also moving in a progressive manner and those received our moral encouragement, as well. To my own amazement, free and honest elections were held, first for delegates to a new entity which would then select deputies to the Supreme Soviet, i.e., the national parliament in Moscow. Shortly afterward, elections were held in Leningrad for the City Soviet. In both cases, the traditional Communist Party elite were voted out and members of the democratic opposition were voted in. The new Mayor of Leningrad, Anatoly Sobchak, brought a former law student of his, one Vladimir Putin, into his administration, thus starting Putin's rise to later prominence in the new Russia.

Leningrad was followed by my assignment to an unusual post in Berlin. When the Berlin Wall came down in 1989, the now-united German government decreed that all diplomatic missions in both East and West Berlin were to be closed and the foreign countries could then choose whether to open consulates, consulates general, or what were known as embassy offices, in the new, unified city. The embassies, of course, remained in Bonn until the federal government moved from Bonn to Berlin. Most of the big powers opted for an embassy office and I succeeded Harry Gilmore as Head of the Embassy Office in Berlin in 1991. I loved the title: *Leiter der Aussenstelle der Botschaft.*

I was in Berlin for less than a year, and there was no crisis or difficulty in the bilateral relationship that affected the Embassy Office. Sharon and I spent much of our time calling on officials and business and cultural leaders in the former GDR, some of whom had never had the opportunity of speaking to an American official, before.

The collapse of the Soviet Union in late 1991 brought an end to this briefly idyllic diplomatic life. James Baker, then-Secretary of State, wanted US embassies and ambassadors in all the new, independent states of the former Soviet Union, immediately if not sooner—and Russian-speakers with Soviet experience were suddenly in high demand. I was not only asked to fill one of these positions, I was even given a choice. I selected Azerbaijan.

In mid-March 1992, Robert Finn had formally opened the "Embassy"— actually a series of rooms along a corridor in a lugubrious, former Soviet Intourist hotel. He was accompanied by an extremely capable political officer, Philip Remler. I arrived, sans wife, in early May. In a most unusual move, the Congressional leadership allowed the ambassadors-designate to proceed to their posts before being confirmed by the Senate. After a few months, in my case, in August I went back to Washington for several weeks to be confirmed and then returned to Baku, this time with Sharon.

These were very difficult times for the Azerbaijani government. The former Communist leaders had been overthrown in a relatively bloodless coup shortly after my arrival in early May and the new government lacked the experience and means to bring about serious economic and political reform while simultaneously fighting opposition in and around the province of Nagorno Karabakh. The Azeri population had largely fled that province and the ethnic Armenian population which supported separation from Azerbaijan was receiving moral and physical support from the newly independent Armenian government.

Communication with Washington and appropriate US diplomatic and military entities was not easy. We could usually send and receive classified cables on a limited basis, but we had no means to secure unclassified files. And classified telephone conversations were even less successful due both to the relatively low level of the technology at that time and also to the lack of a secure space in our hotel arrangements to carry on such conversations. For several months, we had no vehicles of our own, so we hired cars and drivers. One officer bought a used car only to have it stolen from the hotel parking lot.

Much time was spent on the simple tasks of finding outside housing for our small staff, not to mention finding a permanent location for the Chancery itself. Sharon and I decided we would not move out of the hotel until all other members of the staff had found adequate housing in the city. We stayed in that miserable hotel for sixteen of the eighteen months we were in Azerbaijan.

Just to keep things interesting, the democratic government which had replaced the former Communist government was itself hounded out of office after scarcely a year in power. The nationalist leader Abulfaz Elchibey resigned and was replaced by Heydar Aliyev, the former Communist Party leader, KGB general, and later, Politburo member. Aliyev, who had been removed from his Politburo position in Moscow several years earlier, had returned to his native Nakhchivan, an exclave of Azerbaijan bordering on Iran, Turkey and Armenia. Sensing his potential return to power, embassy officers and I had developed a friendly relationship with him, one that paid off when he did return to power. This second change of government in not much more than one year was also bloodless, although some members of the former, short-lived nationalist government were arrested. We were able to intervene successfully on behalf of some, but not all, of the arrested officials.

I have only scratched the surface of the many difficulties embassy personnel and spouses put up with during those turbulent times, but it seems to be the general rule in the Foreign Service that morale is higher in posts, especially smaller posts, that are under duress. People tend to pull together, and work and play together with less quibbling than in larger, less stressful posts.

In any case, my wife and I, joined occasionally by our adult son and daughter, enjoyed our stay in Azerbaijan and we were not particularly happy to leave after only a year and a half.

It came about in this way:

Tom Pickering was appointed Ambassador to Russia in 1993. One of the superstars of the Foreign Service, he was an excellent choice for the job—experienced, accustomed to crisis situations, and blessed with creative energy and impeccable judgement. The downside was that he did not speak Russian and, indeed, had never served in the former Soviet Union.

He lost his very qualified deputy, Jim Collins, an Indiana University classmate of mine and later, Ambassador to Russia himself, who was needed in Washington for a high-level job dealing with US policy toward the new states of the former Soviet Union. And so the search was on for a deputy in Moscow who had experience serving in the former Soviet Union and who spoke Russian.

Strobe Talbot, then Deputy Secretary of State, asked me if I would fill that vacant slot. I was not eager to leave Azerbaijan, and I even suggested several alternate names to Strobe, but in the end, I agreed to go. The Moscow Embassy had been large enough when I was there in the 1970s, but by 1993 it had grown enormously, surpassed only by a very few other foreign service posts. It was made larger by the inclusion of the three consulates general in Russia: St. Petersburg (the former Leningrad), Vladivostok and Yekaterinburg.

I think Pickering and I made a good team. We have different personalities and I think the resultant balance was good for the overall life and work of the Embassy.

As Deputy Chief of Mission, my job was basically to manage the day-to-day work of the Embassy and the problems of the wider Embassy community, but occasionally I would get involved in operational matters, for example protecting American interests in international property rights. I did have one specific role which drew heavily on my previous experience in the Soviet Union. The Deputy in Moscow was always the chairperson of the American delegation to a bilateral commission, set up in prior years to organize the spending of funds deposited by the Russian Government for humanitarian food supplies which were provided to Russia by the American Government. An accumulated fund amounting to some forty million dollars was to be spent on loans of money for entrepreneurial projects in the agricultural sector. In what I thought was a clever part of the agreement, the loans provided were to be repaid at a favorable rate of interest—not to the commission itself but to the appropriate local governmental entity for infrastructure maintenance and development. All of the agreements were negotiated by Russian staff members of the commission and approved by the Russian and American delegations to the commission. The monthly meetings went well for the first two years of my involvement, but then there was something of a palace coup on the Russian delegation side, and the congenial former members were replaced overnight by people steeped in the corrupt ways of the old Soviet system. The changed situation required an increase of my time and attention, not to mention a great deal of stress on the part of the Russian staff of the commission, who came under constant and insidious pressure to bend procedures in favor of projects of interest to the new members of the Russian delegation to the commission. I once mentioned to Ambassador Pickering that if he ever doubted what I was doing with my time, he should be grateful that I was keeping this bureaucratic mess from landing in his lap. I did at one point ask him to call on the Russian Minister of Agriculture to hear our complaints about the behavior of the Russian commission members, and that did help to some degree. When my tour in Moscow was nearly over, I advised my very capable immediate successor, who later became American Ambassador to Moscow, John Tefft, to try to dispose of the remaining funds available to the commission (down to about eighteen million dollars, as I recall) and to declare the terms of the original bilateral agreement to have been fulfilled and to close the commission down.

Moscow was followed by my appointment in 1996 as Chief of Mission in Belgrade. The fighting in Bosnia-Herzegovina had stopped as a result of the 1995 Dayton Accords, and we were in the process of restarting normal, or at least more normal, diplomatic relations. Despite this, the United States, unlike our Western allies, did not appoint a new ambassador to the Federal Republic of Yugoslavia (FRY) by 1996, so I went to Belgrade as "Chief of Mission", that is, without confirmation by the US Senate, thus bypassing the Senate confirmation required for someone with the title of Ambassador. In practice, this distinction did not particularly affect my status or my work in Belgrade. My wife and I lived in the Ambassador's residence; I was driven about in the Ambassador's car, albeit without the flag on the fender, and I was treated by the FRY Government and by fellow diplomats as though I was a duly appointed and confirmed ambassador.

While the 1995 Dayton Accords had solved many, if not all, problems of the situation in Bosnia-Herzegovina, they had not touched on the long-standing problems of the ethnic Albanian population in Kosovo. This was not pleasing to the leaders of the Albanian separatist movement in

Kosovo, or to younger hotheads who, by the late 90s, had turned increasingly to armed struggle to achieve their goals.

These difficulties between ethnic Albanians and ethnic Serbs had been brewing for decades and I had often dealt with them myself during my previous tours of duty in Belgrade in the early 1970s and late 1980s.

There had never been a shortage of weapons in civilian hands in the former Yugoslavia and by the late 1990s an increasingly large amount of weaponry from the collapsed Communist Albanian state began to appear in the hands of militant ethnic Albanian nationalists operating under the rubric of the Kosovo Liberation Army, known in the region by the Albanian acronym, the UÇK (pronounced oo-che-kah); I say more on this later.

Political differences between the ethnic Albanian population of Kosovo and the Government in Belgrade had brought a collapse of efforts to achieve political reconciliation. A parallel, semi-formal, political, economic and social structure had been established by the leaders of the Albanian community. Ad hoc educational and medical systems were organized and funded by locally imposed taxation and by donations from members of the Albanian diaspora, including those residing in the United States. There was no effective dialogue between the leaders of the Albanian community and the Serb representatives in the formal governmental structure in Kosovo or with the Government in Belgrade. It must also be said that there was considerable lack of unity among the leaders of the Albanian population.

Into this volatile situation came an increase of sporadic but growing violence by armed groups representing the UÇK which were often met with disproportionate punitive acts of violence by the paramilitary force of the Serb Ministry of Internal Affairs. It is interesting to note that General Perisic, Chief of the General Staff of the Yugoslav Armed Forces, refused to allow the deployment of military units to Kosovo until he was replaced by President Milosevic. The Defense Attaché, Colonel Bill Fischer, and I had many interesting conversations with the General before he was removed.

To try and calm things down, Washington decided to appoint a special envoy. There were two individuals comprising it. The first one, Bob Gelbard, did not handle President Milosevic very adroitly, and after Milosevic said that he would no longer speak with him, he was replaced by Richard Holbrooke. Holbrooke had worked closely with Milosevic in the negotiating process leading to the successful Dayton Accords in 1995. He was an excellent choice.

The relationship between an ambassador and a special envoy with similar responsibilities is not always an easy one. Books have been written by and about Ambassador Holbrooke. I will limit my remarks to say that, while he was not always easy to get along with personally, I do not believe anyone could have done more than he did to make Milosevic see reason. Holbrooke asked Chris Hill, the US Ambassador in Macedonia, to assist him. He had known Chris since the Dayton negotiations. This was a bit awkward but Chris and I were determined to make the team effort work, and I believe we were successful at this.

Holbrooke was certainly smart, in fact very smart, and he had an abundance of creative energy. He used this to good effect with Milosevic—and with the civilian leaders of the Albanian community—in lengthy, sometimes very lengthy, conversations and negotiating sessions. Richard was often accompanied in these sessions with Milosevic by General Wes Clark, then the Supreme Allied Commander Europe, along with other military officers.

Holbrooke discouraged note-taking during these sessions. He also forbade written reports back to Washington and interested posts abroad. He would either report back personally, or on a secure phone if one was available and use an open line if one was not necessary. I have often regretted that, at a minimum, I did not write what is known as a Memorandum to the File, after each of his many visits to Belgrade and Kosovo. Sent back to Washington in due course, these would have made valuable historical records.

Milosevic accepted several of Holbrooke's creative ideas. There were many, but two stood out. The first was the formation and deployment to Kosovo of large contingents of foreign diplomats, military officers and what have you, to provide objective information about the increasingly violent clashes between the UÇK and the Serb paramilitary forces. Unarmed and organized into separate national groups, including the US, Russia, the U.K., France, Germany and Italy, the organization was called the Kosovo Diplomatic Observer Mission (KDOM), and reported through the national units to their representative ambassadors in Belgrade. This was, of course, a rather clumsy arrangement. Even so, the courageous members of the various KDOM components provided very useful and objective reporting on the situation, in what was increasingly becoming a battlefield.

As the situation on the ground worsened, KDOM was replaced by a similar and equally large but much more unified organization under the auspices of the Organization for Security and Cooperation in Europe (OSCE). Headquartered in Vienna, this organization, known as the Kosovo Verification Mission (KVM), had a single leader: the former American Ambassador

William Walker, who reported directly to the OSCE in Vienna. The KVM performed extremely valuable work, but as the international diplomatic situation deteriorated, KVM was withdrawn from Kosovo in March 1999.

In early 1999, international negotiations at the Château de Rambouillet in France had reached a consensus of sorts—neither Russia nor the FRY, however, agreeing to its terms. After some delay, these terms were presented to the FRY government in the form of an ultimatum. Not to make light of the situation, but rejecting foreign ultimatums is historically a kind of national sport in Serbia. Belgrade has always taken pride in its rejection of the ultimatum from the Austro-Hungarian Empire in 1914 and also the Nazi ultimatum of 1941, preferring to go down in glorious defeat, rather than acquiesce to external dictation from abroad.

In any event, Holbrooke and I found ourselves in my office on March 23, 1999, watching Serbian President Milutinovic, the FRY negotiator at Rambouillet, speaking to the Parliament and rejecting in acrid language the terms of the Rambouillet Agreement. I translated his remarks for Holbrooke and said, "This means war." Richard delayed his planned departure in hopes of a meeting with Milosevic but, when it was apparent that no meeting was forthcoming, he left.

Under instructions from Washington, I informed the Ministry of Foreign Relations that we would close the Embassy and that my greatly reduced staff of nineteen, including six Marine security guards, would depart for Budapest the next day, March 24, 1999, to join the remaining Embassy staff and families already there. We didn't know whether we would actually be allowed to leave Belgrade, since in the event of war, we could have been interned until agreement on the exchange of all diplomatic personnel could be arranged. We did leave, in a US Navy military plane early on the morning of March 24. Hostilities began later that same day.

We had already drawn down spouses, dependents and all other Embassy American personnel, led by the Deputy Chief of Mission, to safe haven in Budapest. Before that, Gil Sperling, head of the Consular Section, had worked out arrangements with the State Department to allow those locally employed Serb employees and their families wishing to relocate to the United States the opportunity to do so, for fear of reprisal if they stayed in Belgrade. Many took advantage of this opportunity and, while some returned to Belgrade after the fighting stopped, many remained in the United States, eventually becoming American citizens.

There are two interesting footnotes to all this drama. In the early morning hours of March 24, the Marines and I took down the American flag from the front of the Chancery. I carried that flag to Washington and expected to turn it over to the State Department Secretary or another high-ranking official. I never saw Secretary Albright and no one else seemed to want the flag, so I took it overseas with me a few months later, once I was confirmed as Ambassador to Bulgaria.

A year or so afterward, when diplomatic relations were restored with the FRY, I told our new Ambassador, Bill Montgomery, that I had the flag and that I would send it to him to raise once again over the Chancery. Bill very kindly invited Sharon and me to bring it to him in Belgrade and proposed that we raise it together. Some of the former Yugoslav employees of the Embassy joined us—perhaps twenty or so people were assembled—and tears were shed all around.

The second footnote concerns the selection of what is known as a "protecting power." When diplomatic relations are broken for some reason, each country selects another friendly country willing to take on the responsibility of looking after its interests in the about-to-be-abandoned country.

The Swedish government agreed to act in our stead in Belgrade, and I dutifully informed the Ministry of Foreign Affairs. However, we encountered a stubborn head-in-the-sand attitude on the part of the Yugoslav government in which they steadfastly refused to name a protecting power to handle their interests in the United States.

After the beginning of hostilities, however, Washington was informed, I believe through the Yugoslav representation at the United Nations, that the FRY government would like China to assume this role. We refused to accept China. Although it's the prerogative of the host country to agree to a foreign country's choice of a protecting power, in my admittedly limited experience, disagreement is rare to the point of being almost unheard of. We offered suggestions such as Sweden, Switzerland, and others. FRY officials refused all offers—it was China or nothing. We never reached agreement and ultimately the FRY Government in turn informed the Swedish Government that it would not be allowed to perform this function on our behalf. Well, this maneuver had consequences.

We had spent some time in Belgrade showing the Swedish Embassy officials and workmen how to maintain the antiquated electrical, heating and plumbing systems in our Chancery, at the Ambassador's residence and various other properties in Belgrade, and in Pristina in Kosovo. Now, however, the Swedish workmen were not allowed to enter these buildings. The results were predictable: electricity was cut off, winter came, the water pipes froze and burst, and in the spring, the water continued running. There was an enormous mess all around which took months to clean up and repair when diplomatic relations were finally restored.

In this chapter, I won't give Bulgaria the full attention it deserves. Bulgaria was a very pleasant assignment for both Sharon and me; it happily did not contain the drama and the stress of either Serbia/Kosovo or the assignment yet to come, in Georgia. We had the full range of programs in Bulgaria—USAID, Peace Corps, Trade and Development Agency, and such. Now many of the new, independent states of the former Soviet Union had developed arrangements of military cooperation with the National Guard units of various states in the US I did make innovative use of the very successful cooperative relationship between the Tennessee National Guard and the Bulgarian military. Through the Adjutant General (TAG) in Tennessee, we arranged for the Governor of Tennessee and many of the heads of various state organizations—education, commerce, agriculture—to fly to Bulgaria on an Air National Guard plane for a week of intensive travel and talks with their Bulgarian counterparts. A good time was had by all, and in addition to the exchange of many ideas, a scholarship program was established between the chief universities of Tennessee and Bulgaria.

By the way, when accompanied by the very competent and politically savvy TAG of the State of Georgia, the late David Poythress, I tried to sell this same concept to George "Sonny" Perdue, then Governor of the State of Georgia. Unfortunately, he had no interest at all in such a project, even asking sarcastically if I knew how many voters of ethnic Georgian background lived in his state. So much for good ideas.

Sharon and I came to like Bulgaria and the Bulgarians, and we still have friends there; Sharon still travels there occasionally. Much could be written about the day-to-day work of an American Embassy in such a country, still in transition from its Communist past to a modern democracy, including the return of the former boy King of Bulgaria to political prominence. But, continuing the focus of this chapter, I will move on to my three tumultuous years in the Republic of Georgia.

The very assignment was somewhat novel. In Bulgaria I had reached the mandatory retirement age of sixty-five. During my last year in Bulgaria, I had written to the Secretary for European Affairs, Beth Jones, and Deputy Secretary Rich Armitage, saying that I was prepared to retire as required, but that I was also willing to take on another assignment if there was an opportunity to do so. As it turned out, there was. An old friend of mine had been selected to be the Ambassador to the Republic of Georgia and had gone through the lengthy vetting process, but before he was actually nominated, he had decided for personal reasons to withdraw his name from consideration.

Sharon and I were just returning in our car to our hotel after a day of talks with local leaders on Bulgaria's beautiful Black Sea coast, when Beth Jones called me on my mobile phone. I was standing on one side of the car and Sharon was on the other side. I asked Sharon if she would like to go to Georgia; she said, "Yes," and that was that. My friends and colleagues who have had to go through the slow, agonizing process of being nominated and confirmed as ambassadors found this story almost unbelievable, but that is what happened.

I did have to resign from the Foreign Service due to my age and, of course, also had to submit reams of paperwork to the State Department, the White House and the Senate, but everything moved quickly and smoothly, and so, shortly after leaving Bulgaria, we arrived in Tbilisi, Georgia, in the early fall of 2002.

There is one incident I would like to mention if only to show that despite my comment about Governor Perdue, I am not biased politically. In the spring of 2002 before I left Bulgaria, I attended the annual conference of the European chiefs of mission held in Washington. We were all taken to the White House for a one-on-one photo op with President Bush. When my turn came, I said to the President, "Sir, I'm here under slightly false pretenses. I am your Ambassador to Bulgaria, but you have also nominated me to be your Ambassador to Georgia." Without missing a beat, the President said, "Good man. Tell President Shevardnadze that we will help him take care of the situation in the Pankisi Gorge." Now the President may have just finished reading his briefing notes, but I was still impressed not only by his statement, but by the fact that he pronounced "Shevardnadze" and "Pankisi" correctly.

When Sharon and I arrived in Georgia, things were in a rather bad state. Ethnic separatists had taken control of the provinces of South Ossetia and Abkhazia, and in the province of Adjara a tin-pot despot named Aslan Abashidze had virtually stopped cooperation with the government in Tbilisi, including refusing to send collected tax money to the capitol. And there was money to be collected, because the commercial Black Sea port of Batumi is in Adjara.

In general, taxes in Georgia were not being collected on a regular basis and thus the salaries of government workers were not being paid—in Georgia this meant teachers, hospital workers, the police and the military, in addition to civil servants. The small but vital pension payments—something like our Social Security System—were not being paid, either. Electric bills were not being paid to the American company AES which also, with subsidies from the US government, was engaged in modernization of the Georgian electrical grid. A few people had been electrocuted because they had unsuccessfully tried to steal electricity off the grid. Many others had actually been successful in tapping the power lines and stealing energy.

Meanwhile, Georgia faced serious pressure from the Russian Federation to stop the annual movement of ethnic Chechen men, called Kists in the Georgian language, from the Pankisi Gorge into Chechnya to join the Chechen resistance forces in that region. President Bush had responded positively to President Shevardnadze's plea for help in dealing with this problem, and almost simultaneously with my arrival, contingents of the US Army began to arrive to operate a training center for the Georgian military. The program was known as the Georgia Train and Equip Program (GTEP). This very successful program went through several subsequent iterations, culminating in a training program for Georgian soldiers deploying to Afghanistan in support of international military operations there.

Georgian law did not permit the use of regular military forces to engage against the citizens of Georgia. The role of the newly trained GTEP soldiers was to provide a visible force to back up the paramilitary forces of the Ministry of Internal Affairs as they moved into the Pankisi Gorge. Because of this, I was able to get US military approval and a rare State Department waiver (of US legislation which did not normally allow military training for nonmilitary forces) to provide simultaneous GTEP training for paramilitary units of the Ministry of Internal Affairs and a few Georgian border guards. Helpful in its own right, this also facilitated communication between elements of the two ministries involved.

The program was a distinct success. Cross-border traffic of ethnic Chechen fighters into Chechnya virtually ceased and Russian military pressure against Georgia eased considerably. Multinational border observation posts were established including both Russian and American military officers under the auspices of the OSCE.

The defense attachés at the Embassy and I spent a good deal of time helping GTEP succeed. Housed at an abandoned Soviet military base (actually more of a camp than a base), the facility lacked decent barracks, potable water, mess equipment, medical support or even a paved or graveled access road. Solving all these problems required meetings with the Minister of Defense, the State Secretary—something like a Prime Minister—and, on occasion, with President Shevardnadze himself.

Meanwhile the usual Embassy programs—educational and cultural exchange programs, USAID projects and many others—were proceeding as well.

While Georgia had the attributes of a democratic state, the institutions of government and the people who led them often had difficulty escaping the experience of their Communist-era past. As a result, problems which should have been soluble at working levels of both the Embassy and the Georgian government required my intervention with President Shevardnadze. Happily, he was always available to see me and I suppose not a week went by without a meeting between us, and on occasion, several meetings during a week. Less happily, these meetings, while providing understanding and even agreement, did not always produce actual results.

A case in point was the persistent effort by my predecessor, Ambassador Ken Yalowitz, and then by me, to get the Georgian consumers of electrical energy to pay for the electricity they used. In 1995, the American energy company AES had purchased the Georgian energy company Telasi. USAID subsidized AES's efforts to modernize much of the company's electrical grid. For example, USAID provided several million dollars to the company to pay for the acquisition and installation of individual electrical meters at homes and apartments. In the Soviet period, there had never been such a system. Despite these and other efforts, the consumers—individual, corporate and state—were not paying for the energy they consumed and the Georgian project was hemorrhaging money.

At my urging, President Shevardnadze called a domestic summit meeting at which the AES project manager, the appropriate regional governor and Shevardnadze were all present. The American side made its presentation and answered questions. Shevardnadze told the governors to enforce payment of all electric bills and to stop what had become repeated examples of using force on citizens resisting efforts to collect past-due bills. Perhaps I should not have been surprised, but I was nonetheless when, one by one, the governors told their president that they could not and would not enforce his order. "The people will not support such measures," they said. Shevardnadze repeated his order. The governors remained silent and the meeting was over. Shortly after, AES sold its ownership to the Russian energy company RAO UES, owned by Putin confidant and former Russian government official Anatoly Chubais. I had known Chubais when I was Consul General in then-named Leningrad. After he purchased AES's holdings, I saw him when he came to Tbilisi on business. "Well, Anatoly Borisovich," I said, "You now have a real mess—*nastoyashchiy bardak*—on your hands." "What do you mean?" he said. "I'm sure you know," I said, "but, if not, you will soon find out." Shortly after, a full-page article appeared—I don't recall if it was a Russian or Georgian/Russian language newspaper—describing all the difficulties that RAO UES was having with the Georgian energy project. If one were to substitute "AES" for "RAO UES" in the article, no other words would need to be changed.

It was clear from the day I arrived in Georgia that the real test for the country would be the presidential election scheduled for 2005. There was a parliamentary election scheduled for November 2003. We and other countries with ties to Georgia saw the parliamentary election as a forerunner of what we believed would be the pivotal presidential election to come. Accordingly, the US government, with the cooperation and support of many of the other diplomatic missions in Tbilisi, embarked on a major effort to ensure that the parliamentary elections would be open and honest.

Quite a bit of US taxpayers' money went into such projects as transforming the messy handwritten voter rolls into computerized voter lists. Under the umbrella of the National Democratic Institute (NDI) and the International Republican Institute (IRI), experts were brought from America to provide nonpartisan training in campaign management, poll watching, and exit polls.

The efforts of other interested embassies were loosely coordinated by weekly meetings of the ambassadors and key aides under the chairmanship of the Director of the U.N. Development Program (UNDP). While I don't recall the attendance of either the Russian or Chinese Ambassadors, officers from their embassies were often present at these meetings.

An interesting development took place in the summer of 2003. Negotiations between the Georgian government and the opposition representatives, over the composition of the State Election Commission had reached a stalemate. Failure to move forward on this issue would result in postponing the election, something no one wanted to see happen. I would like to claim credit for solving this problem, but, actually, the idea of asking former Secretary of State James Baker to fly to Tbilisi to help negotiate a solution to this issue came from Washington.

It was an inspired idea. Baker had a close and warm relationship with Shevardnadze, from the time when the latter was the Soviet Foreign Minister. Due in part to a common-sense solution Baker had thought up on the flight to Georgia, in part due to his congenial relationship with Shevardnadze, and in part due simply to his prestige and personal charm, Baker surprisingly succeeded in quickly getting all sides to assent to his proposal. I recall an informal meeting Baker had with Shevardnadze after an agreement had been reached. Baker described the importance the United States placed on the necessity that the forthcoming parliamentary elections would be open and honest. "So, James," said Shevardnadze, "you are telling me that the way we conduct these elections will determine our relationship with the United States." "Yes, Eduard," said Baker, "that is correct." "I understand," replied Shevardnadze.

In Peter Baker's fine biography, *The Man Who Ran Washington: The Life and Times of James A. Baker III*, he quotes Secretary Baker, saying that this was the only time Shevardnadze ever stiffed him. Unfortunately, at the time the Secretary apparently heard what he wanted to hear. All Shevardnadze actually said was that he understood what Baker was telling him.

In the end, of course, the November 2003 election was deeply flawed. Mass protests rose almost immediately and continued on an almost daily basis even in the face of wintry weather.

I spent a good deal of time going around to the power brokers on both sides of the barricades, urging continued avoidance of violent acts by the opposition and continued restraint from the government agencies—the police and the army—in dealing with the almost constant and sometimes volatile demonstrations.

At one point, after the leaders of the opposition and Shevardnadze had refused to meet with each other, Russian Foreign Minister Ivanov came to Tbilisi to try to bring the opposing sides together. I had arranged for Secretary Powell to phone Ivanov as soon as he landed in Tbilisi. The Secretary encouraged Ivanov's mission, noting that the Patriarch of the Georgian Orthodox Church had offered a neutral venue for a proposed meeting, and in addition Secretary Powell said that the American Embassy was available for assistance should need arise. In the event, I am not aware that Ivanov did anything more than thank Secretary Powell for the phone call, but it was a nice gesture nonetheless.

Events then moved quickly. Under Ivanov's urging, the opposition leaders, Mikheil Saakashvili, Zurab Zhvania and Nino Burjanadze, did in fact meet with Shevardnadze. The story is, though I can't confirm it, that Ivanov accompanied the opposition leaders to the meeting and was going to attend the meeting with them, when they thanked him for arranging the meeting and said, "This is now between us Georgians," as they shut the door behind them.

Whether this is true or not, Ivanov then flew to Batumi in Adjara Province where he met with the local ruler, Abashidze. He was there when he learned of Shevardnadze's resignation and he flew straight back to Moscow without stopping in Tbilisi.

The "troika", Saakashvili, Zhvania and Burjanadze, then formed an interim government and announced there would be a special election in forty-five days. It was later announced that Saakashvili would be the candidate for the presidency.

Almost immediately after Shevardnadze resigned, I was called on the phone late in the evening by Zhvania. He pleaded for urgent financial assistance from the United States. "The cupboard is bare," he said, "and we must pay the police, the army and essential workers." I informed Washington and every available account of possible relief was searched for spare funds. I don't recall the exact amount of money that was finally provided—twenty million dollars would not be far off the mark. The special election was held on schedule and Mikheil Saakashvili became President of the Republic of Georgia.

Secretary Powell came to Tbilisi for Saakashvili's inauguration. He promised US support for reform efforts in Georgia and said that an extra effort would be made to include Georgia in the Millennium Challenge program—a program newly authorized by Congress to allow developing democracies additional leeway beyond the usual terms of our USAID programs, including longer-term projects, road building and local procurement of supplies. In conversation with the Secretary, Saakashvili also asked for US tanks. The Secretary, a former US Army general, seemed taken aback. I certainly was. The Secretary noted that tanks were basically an offensive rather than defensive weapon, and further said that it did not seem that the mountainous terrain of Georgia was conducive to the use of tanks. "We'll think about it," he said, meaning "No". Much later, we did bring in Marine Corps armor teams to modernize the Soviet-made tanks in the Georgian arsenal.

Saakashvili quickly embarked on an anti-corruption, anti-crime campaign. After efforts to reform the notoriously corrupt traffic police failed, he fired all the members of that department—several thousand strong—

and hired replacements. He acquired a fleet of new police cars from Germany. Billboards were put up along Georgia's highways listing a hotline to call if any traffic policeman attempted to extract a bribe. These measures were extremely popular with the general population.

Dramatic police raids on criminal gangs were shown on television and publicity was provided to Georgians on the arrest of businessmen who were accused of "stealing" money from the people. Some of those arrested were told they would be released from jail if they "returned" their "stolen" money. A son-in-law of Shevardnadze was pressured in this manner. Fortunately for him, his American partner-company came to his aid with high-level legal assistance from the United States and with enough cash to reach a satisfactory solution to the issue. He was freed from jail after a payment of several million dollars by the American business partner.

Saakashvili and some of his associates engaged in rather strong rhetoric against the Russian Federation and also in terms of solving the problem of the breakaway provinces by force. This was troubling enough, but it was accompanied by the acquisition of serious weaponry from Ukraine, Israel and other countries.

On several occasions, I urged Saakashvili to tone down this bellicose rhetoric and weapons acquisition. There had always been a large map of the Caucasus and Southern Russia hanging in the President's office. I had never once had to refer to it in my many meetings with Shevardnadze, but I did so several times with Saakashvili. "Look at the map," I would say, "here is Georgia and here is Russia. You do not want to have a military conflict with Russia. Russian air power can destroy all your newly acquired arms, self-propelled artillery and the like in a few hours. Please think about this." I don't think he ever did think about it and, in fact, he attempted a military push into South Ossetia in August 2004 which quickly turned into something of a debacle as the Georgian forces were forced to withdraw. That exercise ended quickly and the Russians did not intervene.

Not long after that, I was in Washington for consultations and was asked by Ambassador Dan Fried, then serving at a senior level in the National Security Council, what could be done to prevent another such military push by the Georgians. I said the only thing that might work would be a strong message from President Bush, preferably delivered personally by the President. Fried liked the idea and said he would see what he could do. The result was the successful, at least for a few years, visit of President Bush to Tbilisi in May 2005. In my presence, the President twice warned Saakashvili not to try to solve the issue of the breakaway provinces through force of arms. "If you do that," he said, "the Russians will intervene and the US cavalry is not going to come riding to your rescue." This may not be an exact quote, but it's close to the President's actual words, which he used on two occasions: once in a small meeting with Saakashvili and once with Saakashvili and his ministers.

This warning by the President did deter Saakashvili for a few years. I finished my three-year assignment to Georgia in the summer of 2005 and the Georgians did not try using military force against South Ossetia until August 2008. Then the Russians did intervene, exactly as President Bush had predicted—the result being not only the withdrawal of Georgian forces from South Ossetia but the loss of additional Georgian territory, a situation which continues to this day.

I then returned to private life in 2005 until I was recalled to active duty to serve as Chargé d'affaires in Turkmenistan, an authoritarian, energy-rich state which borders on Iran and Afghanistan—in other words, a tough neighborhood. I was in Turkmenistan for about one year and will say only that the experience gave the word "authoritarian" real meaning to me. The one unusual aspect of my stay in Turkmenistan is that many of the cables allegedly sent by the Embassy were published on the internet, in the Wikileaks scandal. This was most unfortunate, and, among other things, caused the recall of the Dean of the Diplomatic Corps in Ashgabat, the very competent Turkish Ambassador. I felt very bad about this.

Unfortunately, for health reasons, Sharon was unable to accompany me to either Turkmenistan or Kyrgyzstan, where I was next assigned, and so, while I enjoyed being in charge of an embassy again, life as a grass widower had considerably less sparkle than I was accustomed to.

Back to private life again but, once more in 2015, I was recalled to serve as Chargé d'affaires in distant Kyrgyzstan, a small but very beautiful country south of Kazakhstan and bordering China, Tajikistan and Uzbekistan. In 2001, the United States had established an air base on a section of the international airport near the capital city of Bishkek. The Manas Air Transit Center, as it was called, saw considerable use as a stopover for troops being ferried in and out of Afghanistan. At Kyrgyz insistence, the base was closed in 2014. The aftereffects of closing the base were still felt when I arrived in 2015 for a six-month stay. The Kyrgyz seemed to feel the pull and tug of Russia. The Russians had a small air base of their own near Bishkek and thousands of Kyrgyz citizens worked at temporary jobs in Russia.

While we tried to have a normal relationship with the Kyrgyz Government and the people of Kyrgyzstan, this was not always easy. For example, the Kyrgyz President, Almazbek Atambayev, refused to see me. I met the man only once, shortly after my arrival, when I shook his hand and offered my condolences at a memorial service for his father. This lack of access to the president was annoying, but did not interfere greatly in my interaction with government ministers or the president's bright, young Chief of Staff Sapar Isakov, or with various local officials all around Kyrgyzstan.

By the way, in the manner of "what goes around comes around", I would note that both former President Atambayev and his Chief of Staff Isakov, who later was Prime Minister, are presently serving prison sentences in Kyrgyzstan.

Diplomatic relations did reach a low point toward the end of my relatively short stay in Kyrgyzstan. Before I arrived in Bishkek, the Embassy had nominated a Kyrgyz citizen (and ethnic Uzbek) named Azimjon Askarov, to receive the State Department's annual Human Rights Defender Award. This was approved in Washington, and I duly informed Isakov that the award would soon be announced. He was not happy to hear this, of course, but only asked if the announcement could be postponed to avoid influencing a local election at about the same time. I passed this on to Washington and the requested postponement was granted. So far, so good.

After the announcement was made, I was called in by the Foreign Minister. I had expected a verbal head scrubbing as a show of governmental displeasure, but the Minister went well beyond that. He predicted widespread violence by Kyrgyzstan's ethnic Uzbek population down near the border with Uzbekistan. He said the blood of those people would be on my hands. I said I resented such rhetoric and I noted to him the overwhelming international interest and support for Mr. Askarov. By the way, there was no such violence on the part of the Uzbek community.

Then the Minister fired the second barrel of this verbal attack. He said they were going to abrogate the 1992 agreement with the United States on the operation of USAID (in essence, the agreement allowed duty-free entry of goods for USAID programs). He added that they were going to isolate the Embassy and that no one from the Embassy would be able to meet with anyone in the government at the minister level or above. I protested strongly, noting that these decisions would harm our ability to carry out programs which were of direct benefit to the citizens of Kyrgyzstan. This did not faze the Minister in the slightest.

Now, in a post-Soviet country like Kyrgyzstan, the inability to speak directly to the appropriate minister of the government meant that many day-to-day problems simply could not be resolved. In addition to the general malaise which these decisions placed about the US assistance program and other mutually beneficial programs, lower ranking officials were just not willing to make decisions, operating under the very probable assumption that positive decisions would not be well received at higher levels.

In actual practice, we were not importing large quantities of equipment and supplies. Many of our programs were self-sustaining and needed only local problem-solving, the advice of consultants, and moral encouragement. But still, these punitive measures were unpleasant and unhelpful.

A related problem arose with the Peace Corps. Our Peace Corps volunteers (PCVs) served two years in two separate groups, one overlapping the other by one year. This hardening of the Kyrgyz attitude unfortunately occurred just as half the volunteers had finished their two-year tour of duty and were soon to return to the US The Kyrgyz authorities informed the Peace Corps director that the group could leave, but the incoming group would not be allowed to replace them. Meanwhile the usually uneventful extension of Kyrgyz documentation for the remaining half of the Peace Corps contingent was put on hold by the Kyrgyz authorities.

I asked the Peace Corps director to assemble all the volunteers in Bishkek. I explained the situation to them, answered their questions and said that, in the event their present Kyrgyz documents expired, we were prepared to move all PCVs to Kazakhstan until we could obtain Kyrgyz government approval to allow them to complete their two-year assignment. For whatever reason, the documents were approved shortly after this meeting and the volunteers returned to their places of assignment all around Kyrgyzstan. I don't know what happened to the second team waiting in the US for approval to enter Kyrgyzstan since I left the country not long after these unfortunate events.

Even before this hullabaloo, I had been subject to an unusual degree of harassment by Russian-inspired trolls. Their state television network had carried footage of me calling on a known Kyrgyz dissident; social media carried dire warnings of my nefarious background and equally nefarious intentions; and small groups of protestors assembled near the Embassy, chanting and carrying signs, in English: "Ambassador Miles, Go Home." When Sharon, still in the United States, saw pictures of the demonstrators, she sent me a message saying, "Yes, come home!" With the arrival of the duly nominated and confirmed ambassador, I did return home after only six or so months in the country.

Well, what did I learn from all this? One of my favorite quotations is from George Eliot's *Middlemarch*: "Among all forms of mistake, prophecy is the most gratuitous." All embassies and the Department of State itself does spend a great deal of time on plans for the future—in other words, on "prophecy". Now, I don't think that one should not try to plan for various contingencies that might arise, and certainly not least in the area of foreign affairs and national security. But in my experience, in many cases the success of predictions in this area can be mixed.

For example, I was involved in contingency planning for Yugoslavia following the death of President Tito in 1980. The lengthy interagency study of all manner of contingencies concluded with estimates of how long the Yugoslav regime would hold together. The State Department's estimate was overly optimistic, the Pentagon's was overly pessimistic, and the CIA's was amazingly accurate.

The question is not whether the foreign affairs and intelligence agencies of the government should engage in "prophecy," but rather to what degree and for how long false prophecies and subsequent faulty decision-making should be allowed to influence later analysis and decision-making. We have seen this play out in Vietnam, Lebanon, Iraq and Afghanistan, to name only a few significant places.

In retirement I have often served as a mentor to groups of military officers at the Army Command and General Staff College, the Army War College, the Joint Forces Staff College and other such institutions. I've been struck by the difference between the general approach of our military and that of our civilian officers. In my experience, the civilians seem much more willing to contemplate the use of force than their military counterparts. State Department officers tend to have a sometimes commendable "Yes, we can do it" approach while the military people who do have a "can do" attitude of their own also want to know precisely what is being asked of them. What resources are available now and what will be available later? What is the desired end result of this requested action? What is the time frame to achieve this end result?

A final comment about training. Again, between our civilian and our military establishments, there are different institutional attitudes about training. I can't speak for the intelligence agencies but, in general, our military people spend considerably more time in training than their State Department counterparts. To a degree, this is understandable due to the enormous disparity in size between the Department of Defense and the Department of State. But the issue of training is deeper than that. I have always enjoyed training; I've spent several years in language training and I had a very productive and educational year on Capitol Hill working as an American Political Association Fellow in the office of Senator Hollings (D-SC). I also had a wonderful year as a Fellow at Harvard University's Weatherhead Center for International Affairs. But an alarmingly large number of my State Department colleagues avoid extensive training as though it were the plague. They fear being effectively removed from the promotion cycle by receiving only a perfunctory training report in lieu of the Department's complex and lengthy annual efficiency report. True, we do have an "up or out" promotion system in the Foreign Service. At any particular rank, there are only so many chances to be promoted, and failure to be promoted can ultimately lead to dismissal from the Service. From time to time, efforts have been made by the State Department to improve this situation, but I don't believe they've been very successful. Secretary Powell was the only Secretary of State in my memory to place an emphasis on training—unfortunately to little avail in changing the attitude of many of my colleagues in the Department.

In relating my story, I've often mentioned the value of teamwork. I would never have been as successful in my career as I was, without the absolutely essential value of the teams with which I worked, starting with my wife Sharon, and ending with the last-hired, locally employed Embassy employee. I owe a tremendous debt to my office manager Linda Price who accompanied me to numerous, sometimes dangerous posts over a twelve-year period. Pat Moller, herself an ambassador, was an excellent resource of advice, support and management both as Administrative Counselor in Belgrade and as Deputy Chief of Mission in Tbilisi. And, to paraphrase Garrison Keillor, "All the officers (ok, with a very few exceptions) were above average." And indeed they were. I am sorry I'm unable to name them all here.

All in all, I had a wonderful career, aided to an enormous degree by Sharon, and by my many colleagues, bosses, and subordinates, and many more from civilian, military, and other agencies. I am very grateful for the "lucky" opportunities I was given.

FOUR

GENERAL WESLEY CLARK

Reflections on Diplomacy and the Use of Military Power

Diplomacy and Military Power

Diplomacy is the art and science of communications between states, as states attempt to persuade others to act in their interests. Among the various tools used in the practice of diplomacy, military power has always been significant, and perhaps, ultimately the most significant. But the exact interrelationships are intricate, and difficult, for both diplomats and military professionals as well as the public, to understand. It's easy to get it wrong, sometimes with disastrous consequences.

For members of the military, there should be little confusion about such matters. As nineteenth-century philosopher of war Count Karl von Clausewitz observed, "war is a continuation of politics by another means." But even among the military, misunderstanding is rampant.

The reasons for persistent American misunderstanding are both historic and cultural. American victory in World War II achieved "unconditional surrender." There was no negotiation with Hitler's Germany or with Japan. The advent of nuclear weapons soon afterward brought the possibility of the "unthinkable," the total destruction of mankind in a nuclear holocaust and subsequent "global winter." At NATO, during the Cold War, once the conflict began, the planning was that the military would do the fighting; the only political discussion required was "nuclear release". Interwar negotiation and deterrence were abstruse subjects discussed occasionally by academics, but never understood by either the public or the military itself.

Part of the problem has been cultural. We see things in simple terms. Much of America still longs for the "justice" of the frontier, the lawman with the six-shooter. There is also a tendency to see the world in moral terms. President George W. Bush's charge that "you're either with us or against us" and his evocation of the "Axis of Evil" perfectly captured American culture and temperament.

But successful diplomacy requires a much more nuanced approach to issues, and hence to the relationships between diplomacy and force. This is the subject of this chapter, and I shall draw upon my personal experiences in uniform as well as a lifetime of study of statecraft, and the uses of military power.

The historical context is critical. The United States for almost two centuries was protected by its oceans, and by the absence of strong neighbors north and south. Our first President, George Washington, warned in his Farewell Address against "entangling alliances." In 1825, our fifth President James Monroe, warned European powers against intervening in the Western Hemisphere. We isolated ourselves from the nuances of nineteenth-century European "balance of power" diplomacy, even as we grew to become the foremost industrial power of the world. Meanwhile the US military racked up victory after victory against opponents, invading Mexico, and crushing the Confederate Army during the US Civil War. Union Commanding General Ulysses S. Grant was nicknamed "Unconditional Surrender" Grant, for this is what he demanded of his vanquished foes.

In 1918, as World War I neared its bloody conclusion, General John Pershing, Commander of the American Expeditionary Force in France, warned his French and British colleagues not to accept German pleas for an armistice, but instead fight to the finish to destroy the German Army. It was the tradition of Grant, and the US military. However, in his memo to political leaders, General Pershing was strongly rebuked for stepping out of line, and very nearly lost his position. The European Field Marshals understood the politics behind the war, and the need to end it. They understood the military is the servant of political leadership, and that military aims must serve diplomatic or political purposes. (Of course, political here does not refer to American political partisanship, but rather to the fact that the military is an institution of the state and is therefore subordinate to elected leaders in democracies.)

In the post WWII era, with the US no longer isolated by its ocean barriers, the US record in its use of military force as an instrument of statecraft has been mixed at best. Certainly, nuclear deterrence has to be judged a success. US strategic nuclear power was, as my former boss, General Alexander M. Haig, Jr, often explained, "the ultimate arbiter in world affairs." There has been no use of nuclear weapons in conflict since World

War II, and neither has there been intense direct conflict between nuclear-armed states.

But below the level of nuclear war, the US has been engaged in multiple military actions, some preventive deployments, others full-blown and difficult conflicts. And in several it is clear in hindsight that neither military nor political leaders understood the use of the military as an instrument of diplomacy. There was a tendency by the diplomats and policymakers to "turn over the problem" to the military, and on the other hand, the military was sometimes unable or unwilling to seek the proper guidance and direction at the right time from the diplomats.

In the Korean War, General Douglas MacArthur smashed the invading North Korean army with his amphibious landing at Inchon in October 1950, only to blunder northwards, apparently with the aim of eliminating North Korea as a state. The Chinese intervened, and MacArthur's forces were thrown back. The US political objective—the purpose of the war—was never made clear enough to rein in his overreach, and when he later sought negotiations with the enemy by hinting at a nuclear threat in an open letter to China, he was removed from command. The accusation was that he had trespassed on civil authority—the same offense that General Pershing had committed three decades earlier. Two years later the war ended with an armistice, as a result of two years of negotiations. The US learned a painful lesson—that it must talk "talk" while it fights "fights," to paraphrase the Communists' approach.

After President Kennedy's assassination in 1963, US military engagement in Vietnam quickly escalated from an advisory and support role to direct combat operations. In order to isolate the South from North Vietnamese direction, support, and direct interference, the Joint Chiefs recommended an invasion across the 17th parallel into Laos to cut off the Ho Chi Minh Trail. It was rejected by the Johnson White House. The political leadership instead sought a graduated response, proportional to the threat and our interests as they saw them and which also minimized the political signature of warfare. So, the war was waged largely inside South Vietnam, at first seeking to eliminate the enemy's main force units and then later to build up South Vietnamese defensive military and civil capabilities, along with various "pin-prick" air strikes on the North, through Operation Rolling Thunder, to further demonstrate US resolve. The US also tried extensive bombing of the Ho Chi Minh Trail through Laos into the South, but without great success. There were inartful attempts at negotiations in 1968, of diplomacy backed by force, but the use of force was not compelling. It was only when President Nixon launched a massive bombing campaign in December 1972, in frustration at North Vietnamese diplomatic intransigence, that "diplomacy backed by force" succeeded. Even then, the diplomacy was flawed by a secret agreement that allowed the North to maintain its Army inside South Vietnamese territory. In addition, The South was cut out of the negotiations, bludgeoned into support with promises of continuing assistance which were then blocked by Congress. South Vietnam collapsed militarily in April 1975.

Sometimes the US got it mostly right. Cases in point are the 1989 invasion of Panama, and the 1991 Gulf War. In both cases end-state political objectives were clear and achievable, and the US military planned and coordinated appropriately. Rules of engagement were clear. There were still quibbles and accusations about imprecise diplomatic communications in advance of the military operations. And, in the case of the Gulf War, commander in chief of US Central Command General Norman Schwarzkopf, made the mistake of directly negotiating with Saddam's representative to end the fighting. Although he was acting with authorities granted by US political leadership, he put himself out front, violating two key rules: never negotiate with someone of inferior rank (in this case, an Iraqi two-star General) and always have a "back-stopping" team that can review draft agreements and look for traps and mistakes. In Schwarzkopf's case he permitted the Iraqis to continue use of helicopters south of their designated no-fly zone, which enabled Saddam to slaughter tens of thousands of Iraqi Shia "marsh Arabs."

To recap, use of the military tool in diplomacy runs a spectrum from discussions of military capabilities, through casual ship visits and overseas deployments, into private diplomatic warnings and direct threats, then actual public warnings, and finally into the use of force itself. And also, in related matters—correctly identifying political objectives of the military operation and the rules of engagement for military use of force. Are the objectives regime change? Restoration of territory? Attitude adjustment? Protection of the population? Are the objectives clear and attainable by military means? Does the military have the right to shoot without warning? Accept collateral damages to what degree? And take other actions as necessary to attain the objectives? And finally, in considering the all-important post-conflict political aims, the restoration of a government: of what form, by whom, and how will the US disengage and exit?

Simplistically, it is the military's job to deliver the forces to the operational area and engage or protect designated forces, groups, or sites—

everything else should fall to the diplomats and policymakers. Or as General Colin Powell is reported to have said to the incoming Clinton Administration, "Tell us what you want us to do, and we will tell you the costs and the risks." In practice, this doesn't work, and Powell knew this. The planning and the execution must be integrated, both military and diplomatic, as well as iterative. Issues must be raised and explored freely by all parties.

Diplomacy and Military Power, 1994
Learning Diplomacy and the Use of the Military

The experiences of the Clinton Administration provided a key laboratory for working these issues. As the Director of Strategic Plans and Policy, J-5, 1994–96, I was the principal staff officer responsible for ensuring that military policies and plans reflected the guidance of elected and appointed civilian authorities; I and my team of some three hundred officers were daily in the White House or at the Department of State working on these matters. Later, as Supreme Allied Commander Europe, 1997–2000, I was responsible for proposing and implementing many of these plans and policies.

In late spring, 1994, a vast ethnic cleansing operation began in the small African country of Rwanda. A 2000-man UN detachment was in the country for peacekeeping but was equipped with only light weapons and given a mandate to use force only in self-defense. As violence mounted, perpetrated by a savage Hutu tribal uprising and supported by a militia movement, the UN force retreated into the soccer stadium in the capitol city of Kigali. Bit by bit the horrors emerged, some captured by US intelligence, others leaked through open media and press. A slaughter of unprecedented scale was occurring.

As J-5, I was dually tasked as the military advisor to the US Ambassador to the United Nations. Ambassador Madeleine Albright asked for a notional US plan to intervene. My staff drafted such a plan within two days, and I then approached my boss, General John Shalikashvili, Chairman of the Joint Chiefs of Staff. "Fly 2,000 troops into the heart of Africa, at a cost of $2 billion," he asked, "six months after the murder of nineteen Americans in the infamous 'Blackhawk Down' incident in Somalia?" He queried as I sketched out the concept. "Wes," he asked, "do you seriously believe Congress will support this?" "Probably not," I said. "I agree," he said, and added, "I will take care of this." He called Anthony Lake, the

National Security Advisor, and explained the plan; it was never presented to the President.

Some 800,000 Rwandans died in the ethnic cleansing. There was no diplomacy in the conceptual plan, just an idea that a small American force could arrive with shock effect, join with the UN, and together restore order in Kigali and beyond. Had there been a decision to proceed with actual planning, we would no doubt have required a much stronger force, more precise aims and rules of engagement. But with those, we might have saved hundreds of thousands of lives—if we could have exited successfully. President Clinton said years later, "where we can make a difference, we should." And there, we didn't.

In early 1994, seeking to restore democracy to Haiti, the US imposed a total economic embargo on the island nation, only to find that the economic measure was not sufficient to dislodge the leaders of the November, 1991 coup. Planning began in early 1994 for a military invasion to displace the coup leaders and restore elected President Bertrand Aristide to the presidency there. My first look at the military plan was in June 1994. It was only a plan for strategic entry, with no planning for what to do with our forces once inside Haiti. As J-5 I was tasked with creating the political-military framework for the military, and so, I asked: who would provide services, assure public order, retrain the Haitian police, recreate the economy, provide medical assistance, and so on. There was also no plan for an exit strategy. I traveled with then-Ambassador Madeleine Albright to New York to negotiate with UN Secretary-General Boutros Boutros Ghali and Assistant Secretary-General for Peacekeeping Kofi Annan for a handover to the United Nations of the occupation at the six-month point. This was agreed and provided the US with an exit strategy.

For several weeks we continued the political military planning, which culminated in a new procedure, the first interagency operations plan, that would deal with police training, support for a new government, economic revitalization, and humanitarian efforts. Soon it became clear that the DoD really shouldn't be ordering around other Executive branch agencies, so I turned the plan over to Richard Clarke and the National Security Council Staff. The process was later formalized in Presidential Decision Directive 55, which created the framework for future interagency political-military planning.

A date was set for the invasion, with a two-division, approximately 30,000-man force under command of the 18th Airborne Corps. The political-military plan was actually rehearsed in a gymnasium at Fort McNair, with various cabinet members in attendance including the Deputy Attorney General. The planning was designed for either forcible or permissive entry: a 3000-man brigade of the 82nd Airborne Division would parachute into Port au Prince and secure all key facilities as necessary; and it would be followed by a sea-landed and heliborne force from the 10th Mountain Division. In the event that the Coup leaders surrendered, there would be no need for the airborne forcible entry.

In a wise move, President Clinton dispatched a negotiating team to Port au Prince in advance of the invasion. The team consisted of former President Jimmy Carter, Senator Sam Nunn, and recently-retired General Colin Powell. Arriving on a Sunday morning, they were promptly detained and placed under custody by Haitian authorities. On Sunday evening, September 18,1994, as multiple aircraft took off from Fort Bragg for the parachute assault, someone with Haiti's intelligence service who was located near Fort Bragg called coup leader General Cedras to report that the airplanes were taking off. Immediately after receiving the call, General Cedras summoned the three-person team and asked for asylum in Panama, to leave immediately. The aircraft all turned around and returned to Fort Bragg. This is a prime example of diplomacy backed by the threat of force.

The 10th Mountain Division came ashore the next day, met no resistance, disarmed the corrupted Haitian militia ("the FAHD"), and secured the return of President Aristide and his team to the Presidency. The next day there were riots in the streets of Port Au Prince, there were fatalities, and there was no police force to maintain order. To avoid Congressional criticism, the US military had been told explicitly they were not to do "police work," according to their rules of engagement. We had to fix this; someone had to maintain public order, and that would have to be our military until a new police force could be constituted. After a quick conference call with the White House, Undersecretary of Defense Walt Slocombe and I rewrote the rules of engagement that evening and sent them forward. Lesson learned: however unpalatable it might be politically, a military force cannot execute an operation among a civilian populace without police support.

President Aristide was returned to the Presidency, and US forces departed and turned the mission over to the UN in February 1965. As part of the agreement, the US authorized LTG Joseph Kinzer to command the UN force.

By April 1994, the Clinton Administration was facing yet another crisis: North Korean nuclear weapons. The North had reneged on an agreement to allow nuclear waste from its Yongbyon plant to be inspected by the International Atomic Energy Agency. As a means of leveraging an inspection, the US was considering calling for an economic embargo of North Korea; the North could not be permitted to reprocess the nuclear waste materials into plutonium which could be used for a nuclear weapon. North Korea was responding by asserting that an economic embargo would constitute an act of war, and the US commander in Korea was insisting that we take the threat seriously. By mid-June, after a series of planning meetings, the US was preparing to call up its reserve air-refueling assets and begin activation of an "air bridge" of tanker planes in order to deploy reinforcing fighter squadrons to South Korea and Japan. This was the first step in the war plan to defend South Korea, and it was highly possible that this action itself might be seen by the North as sufficient provocation, leading to open conflict.

This was the fundamental dilemma of using the military as a "tool" to send signals of resolve: what could be meant as a signal of resolve diplomatically could also be interpreted as the first step to seize an advantage in a budding conflict. A principal's meeting was held one afternoon the third week of June 1994, to make the recommendation to the president to commence the air bridge and reinforcing aircraft flow.

In the midst of the discussion, a call came in from former President Jimmy Carter. He was in Pyongyang, North Korea. It was 2 AM. He had just received a pledge from North Korean dictator Kim ill Sung that he would surrender the nuclear waste materials in return for receiving two nuclear power plants so that they could generate electricity, and 500,000 tons annually of heavy fuel oil in the meantime! It was a shock to the Principals to learn that Carter had been secretly dispatched by the President to head off the crisis, even while the national security team was working on a plan to escalate, and force the North to abide by its pledge to the IAEA. And he had apparently succeeded.

Assistant Secretary of State Robert Gallucci was made responsible for conducting the actual negotiations to bring South Korea and Japan together with the US to provide North Korea the fuel oil and nuclear reactors, in return for permitting the fuel to be inspected. I was part of the Pentagon "backstop team" for the negotiations. There were many equities at stake, and so all US positions were fully explored and agreed to by the interagency, before Gallucci submitted them to North Korea.

As with many negotiations, the devil was in the details. Yes, the North wanted the reactors, but it also wanted to hold onto the nuclear waste as a bargaining chip, and it was never clear whether the spent fuel had in fact been reprocessed, or otherwise tampered with, in violation of the IAEA agreement. A compromise was reached in which, without inspections, the nuclear fuel rods would be sealed but retained inside North Korea, thereby neither confirming nor refuting that the North had acquired or attempted to acquire plutonium from the waste materials. It was an artful ambiguity which met the requirements of both sides.

Unfortunately, after the first deliveries of the heavy fuel oil the Republican-controlled Senate balked at sending more, and during that same period Japan and South Korea both encountered delays in fulfilling their commitments to fund and equip the promised nuclear reactors. North Korea complained loudly. After a few years of frustration, and President Bush naming North Korea as a member of the Axis of Evil, the so-called Agreed Framework collapsed. North Korea forged ahead with its own bomb-making project. No doubt President Clinton's decision to move ahead with reinforcing US forces in Northeast Asia was known to the North Koreans and contributed to their willingness to settle for an agreement, an example of diplomacy enabled by implied military threat. But agreements entered into must be executed, and in this case the US and its allies failed to do so.

Then there was also the problem of warfare and ethnic cleansing in the former Yugoslavia. By 1994, the US and NATO were enforcing both an arms embargo on and a no-fly zone over war-torn Bosnia. UN forces supplied by Britain, France and other countries, were on the ground in attempts to protect the populations. Safe zones had been established for the Bosnian Muslim populations of eastern Bosnia-Herzegovina, which had been ethnically cleansed by Serb forces in 1992. The city of Sarajevo remained a war zone, a small part still occupied by Serb forces, but the bulk of the city, occupied by Bosnian Muslims, was surrounded and under sporadic artillery, mortar and sniper fire. Serb military operations were constrained by the UN force, the NATO-enforced no-fly zone, and a keen awareness by the Serbs that an International Criminal Tribunal on Yugoslavia had been established under UN auspices to investigate and prosecute the very war crimes they had committed in ethnically cleansing large portions of Bosnia. A third ethnic group, the Bosnian Croats, were at times hostile and in conflict with the Muslims, but by 1994, at Western urging, had become somewhat aligned with the Bosnian Muslims.

In the spring of 1994, US diplomat, Ambassador Charles Redmond, was completing negotiations with the warring parties on a peace agreement that envisioned a cease-fire and a 51–49 percent split of territory between the Bosnian Muslims and Croats on the one side, and the Bosnian Serbs on the other. All knew that Serb President Slobodan Milosevic was behind the Serb aggression, but he was artful in concealing his direct control.

In June 1994, on one of my returns to Washington, I met with Ambassador Redmond to examine the draft agreement. As I looked at the proposed lines of separation, it was clear that these would not be militarily enforceable. In some places the lines were not readily identifiable on the ground. In other places, they were placed to the obvious disadvantage of one side or the other. As I discovered, no one on the Joint Staff had been consulted in the process of preparing or negotiating the agreement. I went to my boss, General Shalikashvili, and asked, "Sir, don't we have military equities in this, since we might have to observe or enforce it?" He agreed, and so we became engaged in the negotiating process.

Over the next thirteen months I made several trips to the region, including a visit to Sarajevo to meet with the Bosnians, and to Banja Luka to meet with the infamous General Maldivian, already accused, but not yet indicted for war crimes. I explored with the Bosnians whether covert military assistance, if authorized, would persuade them to accept a peace agreement; I asked General Mladic to sign the agreement, and I gathered enough firsthand impressions to help draft the US policy paper on the Balkans in the summer and fall of 1994. I also ran into trouble: unknown to me, the US Ambassador in Sarajevo, not in town when I visited in August 1994, had forbidden meetings with General Mladic. His Defense Attaché, who accompanied me throughout my visit, apparently didn't know this either. When I returned to Washington, the Ambassador was leaking information that I had violated his guidance and, enlisting help from a friendly Senator, was calling for me to be fired. At the same time, others were critical of my having discussed covert assistance, even though I was careful never to offer or promise such. I weathered the storm with a supportive letter from the President and his warm reception of my findings. My meeting with the Bosnians, and with General Mladic, gave me a much deeper understanding of the nature and intensity of the conflict.

In May 1995, the Bosnian military tried a military breakout of the siege of Sarajevo. It was easily repelled by the Serbs. In the following weeks, new leaders in Britain and France reinforced their UN troops on the ground, as the Serbs retaliated against the UN-protected safe areas of Zepa and Srebrenica. Pushing aside flaccid Dutch resistance and ineffective UN leadership, the Serbs occupied Srebrenica, separated the men and boys from the women and children, and summarily executed some 8,000 Bosnian Muslim men and boys in the nearby forest. It was an outrageous war crime. President Clinton, British Prime Minister John Major, and French President Jacques Chirac met together with their military chiefs; it was agreed that any further Serb transgression would be met by a devastating NATO reprisal. In addition, President Clinton directed National Security Advisor Anthony Lake to draft a new peace proposal to stop the fighting there and create a political settlement. By early August 1995, the seven-point plan that emerged included a 51–49 percentage division of territory, a separate Serb entity in the 49 percent portion, a 25,000-man US contingent as part of a larger NATO peacekeeping force, elections within a year, return of refugees, and provisions for punishing whichever side failed to accede to the agreement.

At a Sunday night meeting with Secretary of Defense William Perry and General Shalikashvili, the peace plan was discussed, and it was noted that Ambassador Richard Holbrooke would be leading the negotiations, a kind of shuttle diplomacy to have the plan adopted. Since Holbrooke was on his honeymoon, Anthony Lake would lead the initial phase, selling the concept plan to allies. I volunteered to lead the Joint Staff element with Holbrooke—I had seen him at close range in many meetings and knew that he had a tendency to seek overly robust military actions, and I felt that I would be able to protect military equites by being part of his delegation.

In actual fact, I had a broader set of responsibilities for the Joint Staff, ranging worldwide, while Holbrooke as Assistant Secretary of State for European Affairs, had a narrower portfolio. But he was older, a civilian, and far more experienced. He had been in Vietnam, had participated in the early stages of the 1968 Paris Peace talks, and had been the youngest-ever Assistant Secretary of State twenty years ago in the Carter Administration. I knew working with him would be an interesting experience.

Shuttle Diplomacy, Ending a War

The Seven Point concept proposal for peace in Bosnia first had to be coordinated with our allies. With Tony Lake in the lead, our small interagency team jetted to London, Paris, Bonn, Russia and Turkey, briefing the concept and winning concurrence. Holbrooke arrived to take over for Lake after the round of capital cities, and we jetted into the region. In his detailed recounting in his best-selling book *To End a War*, Holbrooke describes the negotiations in detail. Here I will focus on what I believe are the major lessons and the military role.

In the initial phase, Holbrooke took us to Zagreb to meet Croatian President Franjo Tudman and then Belgrade to meet with Serb President Slobodan Milosevic. We returned to Croatia after the meeting with Milosevic and on Saturday, August 20, 1995, we helicoptered to Mount Igman for safe passage down a narrow mountain trail to Sarajevo to meet Bosnian President Alijaha Izetbegovic. En route down the mountain, a French armored car broke through the edge of the narrow trail and tumbled some 400 meters down the steep mountainside. Deputy Assistant Secretary of State Robert Frazier, Deputy Assistant Secretary of Defense Joseph Kruzel, and Colonel Nelson Drew of the National Security Staff, along with three French soldiers died in the accident. We returned to Washington with our fallen diplomats and under instructions from President Clinton reconstituted our team.

Holbrooke insisted that affected agencies be represented on the new team. I represented the Joint Staff and US military; Colonel James Pardew represented the Secretary of Defense; Brigadier General Don Kerrick represented the National Security Council staff, and senior Foreign Service Officer Christopher Hill backed up Holbrooke for State.

The shuttle diplomacy was reconstructed visit-by-visit, conversation by conversation, speaking first with one leader then another, while raising and discussing each of the points in the proposed agreement. With the support of a USAF Gulfstream, we jumped from Belgrade to Zagreb, to Sarajevo, to Italy, to Brussels, to Paris, back and forth. Holbrooke described it as a combination of mediating and negotiating. He took the lead in the discussions, sometimes one or the other of us would be brought in. The discussions were intended not only to generate general agreement but also to draw out the salient issues, tradeoffs and specific concerns which would need to be addressed. We also took advice from the European Contact Group—the top diplomats from UK, France, Germany, and the EU—and also allies and neighboring leaders. Holbrooke was tireless in seeking advice, building consensus, and surfacing the sticking points that would obstruct the agreement. Our team contributed by constructive listening to most of the conversations and holding ancillary meetings with key people along the way.

At the outset of the mission, a Serb mortar round killed thirty-two

Bosnians in a market in Sarajevo. NATO began a targeted bombing campaign against Serb military assets in Bosnia. This greatly empowered our diplomacy.

In a visit to Belgrade a few days after the start of the bombing, Milosevic asked Holbrooke and me to end the bombing, saying, "this is not good for peace." Clearly, we were into "diplomacy backed by the use of force." As Milosevic later admitted to me, "We Serbs stood no chance against your NATO."

I met with the military leaders in each country, working in Zagreb to head off a potentially devastating artillery barrage designed to punish the retreating Krajina Serb civilians as they fled from a Croatian military assault east of Zagreb. Together with Jim Pardew, there were extensive meetings with the Croatian Minister of Defense, Gojko Susak, who seemed to be in the lead of advancing Croatian military efforts. I dealt often with Serb Chief of Defense Momcilo Perisic, listening to his propaganda that was trying to undermine German-American relations and other nonsense, but also gaining a sense of his relationship to Milosevic, and his character and intent, and pushing our interpretation of the way ahead for Serbia.

The process of shuttle diplomacy moved forward by fits and starts. Issues would arise and be dealt with, or sometimes put aside for later. Advice would be sought. Holbrooke kept in close touch with Deputy Secretary of State Strobe Talbott as well as the National Security staff, both through Don Kerrick, and directly with Deputy National Security Advisor Sandy Berger. I kept contact with the Chairman of the Joint Chiefs and the NATO commander. The idea was to keep Washington united behind the effort.

There were key moments in the shuttle: the plea by Milosevic to stop the bombing, a meeting with indicted war criminals General Radtko Mladic and Bosnian Serb President Karadzic, and seeking advice from Bulgarian President Gligorov and other regional leaders. My role was not without risk—after the meeting with Milosevic, Karadzic, and Mladic, I was assigned to write a cease-fire agreement that the Serbs could sign to have the bombing halted, while Holbrooke, Milosevic and the others in the delegation met elsewhere to continue discussions. I drafted it out on a clumsy laptop; it called for lifting the siege of Sarajevo and the withdrawal of all Serb heavy weapons, in return for a halt to the bombing. There was no previous document to draw on, in the late-evening hours at Milosevic's hunting lodge outside Belgrade. No experienced lawyer was available. I simply made it up. It was an imperfect effort, in which my definition of "heavy weapons" was different than the Bosnian definition, but nevertheless it was accepted by all sides, and the Serbs did pull their "heavy weapons" out. This was tangible progress in ending the conflict.

In another moment, we arrived in Zagreb early on a Sunday morning in the midst of the rapid Croatian military advance across northern Bosnia. Pardew and I were instructed by Holbrooke to meet with Minister Susak to tell him to call off the offensive. Holbrooke, Hill and Kerrick meanwhile gave the same instructions to President Tudjman. As we met with Susak in the darkened MoD headquarters, he excitedly exclaimed that Croatian forces were about to overrun the key city of Banja Luca. He was obviously caught off-guard when we instructed him to halt.

Later I argued with Holbrooke that the halt was a mistake, but Holbrooke's reasoning was clear: the Serbs' territory had already been whittled down to the planned 49 percent and the most important thing was to "stop the killing." It was a sophisticated view, and Holbrooke had his instructions from the White House. I saw it in practical terms: the more the Serbs lost, the greater their willingness to settle. And also, I saw it more in moral terms—this was aggression that legitimately should be rolled back—and I often asked, would we have cut a deal with Hitler in 1943, if we could have "stopped the killing?" On reflection, though, I have supported the imperative of "stopping the killing."

In addition to accompanying the team to its meetings, I broke off at one point to accompany Strobe Talbott to meet with the generals in Moscow. I had met them on previous occasions, so this was a familiar journey. Talbott got Moscow's support at the political level. I got a different view from the generals, however, "You are going into our countries in Eastern Europe; you say you will be gone in a year, but you won't be." When I protested that the plan was indeed to depart in a year, the generals protested, "Please, we know you Americans; you won't depart. Anyway, if we were in your position, we would do the same thing."

My responsibilities also included preparing the military annex which was crucial guidance for the NATO military enforcement and would have to be agreed upon by the respective warring parties, the actual division of territories, and additionally, preparing the police annex which would give NATO authority over the rough, heavily-armed Serb Ministerial Special Police.

As September moved into October, it became clear that Milosevic was quite willing, even eager, to end the conflict if he could achieve terms acceptable to him, but he was firm on wanting a separate Serb entity inside

Bosnia. Bosnian President Izetbegovic was equally firm in rejecting the division of the country he had been elected to lead. Holbrooke maneuvered Izetbegovic out of Sarajevo in order to press him to give in—and he did, under pressure, agree to what he termed the "most unjust" decision ever taken against his people.

Finally, it became clear that the agreement could not be done without sustained face-to-face contact with the respective parties and our team, and that we might even benefit by their ability to talk to each other occasionally. Wright Patterson Air Force Base in Dayton, Ohio offered an excellent location, could be sealed off from the press if necessary, and took each of the parties away from their more extreme supporters at home. Over a period of three weeks, we hammered out the details of the agreement. Under Holbrooke's leadership, I worked the details of the military annex and the map, wrote the police annex, and fussed with refugee repatriation. Finally, I made sure the military had the authorities necessary to protect the peace and enforce the agreement. Then, it was done. The killing was stopped. It couldn't have been achieved without Holbrooke, and it was a diplomatic triumph for President Bill Clinton.

Enforcing the Peace

As NATO Supreme Allied Commander, Europe, July 1997, I was responsible for the military actions of sixteen member-nations, plus twenty-four members of NATO's Partnership for Peace. I was also responsible, as Commander-in-chief, US European Command, for US military activities associated with eighty-nine nations, ranging from Norway to South Africa and including Israel. But in practice, and out of necessity, most of my attention fell on the Balkans. This is where the Dayton Peace Agreement, which I had helped write and negotiate, was being implemented, and where a new conflict would unfold.

On my first day of command, British forces seized a Bosnian Serb who was indicted for war crimes. The action reflected new responsibilities for the NATO Implementation Force; the Bosnian Serbs responded with a series of riots and demonstrations against NATO, but remained always careful to refrain from using lethal force. Meanwhile, an election among the Bosnian Serbs was underway, as well as the first efforts to resettle refugees in Srpska, the Serbian entity.

During the eight months from July 1997 until February 1998, there were critical incidents that shaped the ongoing implementation of the agreement. In early September, US forces reacted to a threatening Serb riot by advancing on the rioters' strong point, an important Serb communications node. Unexpectedly, NATO forces now had control of the Serbs' backbone for microwave communications. The Serbs demanded NATO surrender the position, staging a noisy and threatening protest; the on-scene commanders agreed without consulting me, and prepared to move away. The move was instantly seen by the local and international press as a feckless, UN-style surrender to Serb pressure and would have seriously compromised the overall credibility and enforcement of the Agreement. I intervened and ordered the force to hold onto the communications site until we extracted commitments from the Serbs to cease threatening behavior. What may have appeared to the on-scene commanders as a military action to deescalate violence actually had strategic-level political and diplomatic implications. This should have been clear to the NATO commanders, but they lacked the background of the UN experience to understand fully that they were falling into the same pattern of performance. These were the kinds of nuances that were hard to convey in standard military orders.

A few weeks later the Serbs in Banja Luka were holding a rally for the Serb candidate for President of Republika Srpska, Ms. Biljana Plavsic, an anti-Milosevic Serb. Intelligence indicated a likely assassination attempt would be perpetrated by Milosevic's agents during the rally. We asked the UN representative, Mr. Jacques Klein, to postpone or cancel the rally; he said he could not do that. The Serbs were calling for "all patriotic young Serbs" from across Bosnia to attend the rally, and several busloads were coming from Pale, the center of Milosevic's influence. To break up the rally we used "forces without using force." We simply stopped the buses every few miles, called on passengers to dismount, then searched the buses and confiscated the clubs and planks that were intended to be used as weapons. This stretched a three-hour bus ride into an eight-hour journey. By the time the buses neared Banja Luka, the small rally was over, and Ms. Plavsic, surrounded by her supporters, were safe. The next morning Milosevic called me to complain that his agents—the suspected assassination team—were under threat in a hotel in Banja Luka and needed NATO to rescue them. We did rescue them, to prevent violence, but confiscated their weapons and subjected them to humiliating searches.

Then it was time to take the long-barreled weapons from the Serbs' Ministerial Special Police. I issued the order in response to sensing that politically this would further reduce Serb prestige, reduce the chance for violence and make return of refugees easier. My commanders on the ground resisted the order, fearing violent Serb resistance. Finally, I simply ordered it done; there was no Serb resistance and the weapons were meekly surrendered.

By this time, I had three years' experience in the Balkan theater, and knew well the culture, temperaments, and leadership of all parties. Our Army commanders, however, did not. They rotated in and out. This is a fundamental flaw in peace enforcement missions—they require extensive cultural intelligence, not just a set of military capabilities. It was a weakness again exposed later on, in Afghanistan and Iraq.

In late-February 1998, Serb forces in southwest Serbia, in the region known as Kosovo, surrounded the farm estate of the Jashari family, firebrand Albanian nationalists, and murdered some sixty of their family members, including the children.

A few days later I flew into Macedonia to inspect Task Force Able Sentry, a small contingent of US forces deployed to help maintain security over the poorly delineated border between Macedonia and Serbia. When I landed in Skopje, US Ambassador Chris Hill asked me to come meet with him and President Gligorov. Gligorov minced no words: "There will be war in Kosovo," he said, "These Albanians will fight back. You must do something; war there will harm my country." "Should the US reissue the 'Christmas Warning'?" I asked. "Yes," he said.

On December 25, 1992, in an earlier round of violence in the portion of Serbia known as Kosovo, which had a ninety percent Albanian majority, President George H. W. Bush had warned the Serbs to cease their violence against the Albanian population or face American action. Specifically, "in the event of conflict in the Kosovo caused by Serbian [military] action, the United States will be prepared to employ military force against the Serbians in the Kosovo and in Serbia proper." It became known as "the Christmas Warning." During the Dayton negotiations Holbrooke had unsuccessfully sought to bring Kosovo into the agreements, but each time Milosevic refused to discuss it. Now Milosevic was once again raising the stakes.

Upon returning to the Pentagon, I messaged the Pentagon of imminent trouble and suggested the warning be reissued. Nothing was done. Fighting in Kosovo, aimed at civilians by Serb special police, escalated that spring. Albanian leaders came to NATO and to my headquarters expressing fear and anger at Milosevic. NATO members became alarmed and asked me for advice. Madeleine Albright, then-Secretary of State, asked my advice. I returned to the discussion of US airpower that had been used to break Milosevic's will in Bosnia in 1995.

In June of 1995, with permission from the Pentagon, I met with National Security Advisor Sandy Berger and sketched out a concept of bringing the fighting to a halt by using the threat of NATO airpower in an escalating manner. "Will it work?" asked Berger. "No guarantees but having met with Milosevic for over a hundred hours, and listened to him, with his fear of NATO, it could work." A few days later, Berger called me to give me the Ok on the concept; subsequently the Pentagon called to warn me it was "unlikely to work," and ask rhetorically, "when it doesn't work, will you invade with ground troops?" "Yes," I replied. I was thinking, No More Vietnams. Once the US engages, it must fight to win—the Weinberger Doctrine, in essence. If necessary, we will take the fight all the way to Belgrade; we cannot let Milosevic get away with this. He would destabilize the entire region, including Bosnia. I saw the concept as a spectrum of diplomacy backed by presentation of force, then the threat of force, then the use of force, and finally force, backed by diplomacy, and if necessary, with each step becoming more coercive.

NATO asked me formally for concept plans, and our headquarters provided them. First an air demonstration of fighters circling outside Serb airspace, then next a limited strike campaign against Serb targets in Kosovo, and then an expanded campaign including targets in Serbia, and after that, a limited ground campaign inserting forces into Kosovo, and finally a major-cover land campaign, from multiple directions, against Serbia. The concepts plans were approved.

NATO began its air demonstration in late June, empowering Holbrooke to travel to Belgrade to meet Milosevic there. "I see your NATO aircraft," Milosevic said to me on the telephone, then lying that "These Albanians are my people; we would not harm them," even as thousands were already being displaced by ethnic cleansing including armed attacks by Serb paramilitaries and heavily armed police in their villages.

Neither Holbrooke, nor later on Ambassador Chris Hill, made any headway in stopping the attacks. European leaders warned me that NATO and American credibility was at risk. NATO Secretary-General Javier Solana described Milosevic's salami tactics as "A village a day keeps NATO away." By September some 400,000 Albanians had been driven from their homes; Milosevic was carefully preventing them from escaping the country, so they were hiding in the rough, forested mountains, anxiously awaiting help.

I brought the situation to Secretary of Defense William Cohen in early September and asked for his intervention in NATO's September Defense

Minister's meeting. Despite his reluctance—he was focused on Iraq—he realized he must act. As a result of his leadership, NATO issued its first ACTWARN a few days later, an alert to nations to begin planning with NATO on committing their aircraft to NATO command for air operations.

Roughly at the same time, the US prevailed upon the UN Security Council to issue UNSCR 1199, ordering a cease-fire and calling on Serbia to withdraw its excessive forces in Kosovo, while also authorizing nations to act in the humanitarian crisis in Kosovo "using all necessary means." This provided a foundation in international law for NATO's actions.

The ACTWARN and UNSCR empowered Holbrooke in a renewed set of meetings with Milosevic in Belgrade. Milosevic was once again charming but unmoved. The Holbrooke mission gained no traction. Holbrooke returned to ask NATO to move one step further, by converting the ACTWARN to an ACTORD, meaning nations would actually assign aircraft to NATO. Under pressure from Holbrooke, Milosevic agreed to a "diplomatic observer mission" on the ground in Kosovo. He promised to remove his forces. Holbrooke returned to the US. No forces were withdrawn, despite Milosevic's promise.

Over the next three weeks I made three separate trips to Belgrade to meet with Milosevic and his generals to force implementation of the UNSCR. In the first trip I brought NATO Secretary General Solana, on the second, I went by myself, and the third time I brought with me NATO Chairman of the Military Committee, German General Klaus Naumann. In the first meeting Milosevic denied he had excess forces in Kosovo; I named them, and then he promised to withdraw them. We departed, but again no forces were withdrawn. A week later I was back, this time with authorization from the White House to actually deliver a direct threat of air attack to Milosevic. I did so. He asked me to speak with his generals, which I also did. It was a remarkable conversation, in which they described the locations and activities of these "Albanian terrorists," and I warned them that their tactics would only worsen the crisis. I left with some hope that they would withdraw, but no forces were withdrawn. A week later I returned with General Naumann, and this time we hammered out a specific agreement in writing committing to the immediate withdrawal, which we pressed Milosevic to sign. (I knew from previous experience that a signed agreement in writing had some greater hope of implementation.) Naumann and I left believing he had achieved something.

By late the next day no forces had been moved; I called the US Ambassador in Belgrade the next morning and warned, *on an open line*, so Milosevic could monitor, that we were preparing to commence the bombing campaign. Within a few hours the heavy Serb forces began to withdraw from Kosovo.

In November, 1998, Ambassador Hill returned to Belgrade for another bout of fruitless diplomacy with Milosevic. But he hosted a Russian military delegation and, always with a keen eye to Washington, understood that Washington saw Saddam Hussein—not Kosovo—as its biggest problem.

By January, the heavy Serb forces had returned to Kosovo. Fifty-three Albanian farmers were found murdered in a ditch. This was the very type of action that called for commencing the limited air strikes against Serb positions in Kosovo. NATO debated. I was sent back to Milosevic to ask him to permit a UN investigation team on the ground, and not to discontinue the diplomatic observer mission. Milosevic resisted; he refused to acknowledge the murders, railed against Ambassador Bill Walker who headed the diplomatic mission, and refused to allow the UN investigators to enter.

French President Jacques Chirac hosted negotiations between the warring parties at the Rambouillet Palace (about fifty km southwest of Paris), in an effort to seek a peaceful resolution prior to commencing military action against Serbia. My headquarters prepared a peace enforcement plan modeled on the military annex of the Dayton Agreement, which was offered to both Albanian and Serb negotiators. I offered to help, based on my experience at Dayton and my knowledge of the Serb team. I felt that I also might have some personal leverage in persuading Milosevic and his team to accept the agreement, but I was not permitted to participate. Ultimately, the Serbs rejected the proposed plan, while the Albanians accepted. This and renewed Serb aggression against the Kosovars triggered the ultimate decision by the US and NATO to commence the bombing campaign.

NATO was now moving from diplomacy backed by the threat of force to diplomacy backed by use of force. The first strikes began the night of March 24, against Serb air-defense radars and ammunition bunkers in Kosovo. All planes returned successfully.

Many in Europe expected that after the first strikes, or certainly within a few days, Milosevic would give in to NATO and accept the Rambouillet Agreement. Instead, on the third day he struck back with an attempted air strike on US forces in Bosnia. It was easily turned back, with two Serb fighters shot down as they attempted to move into Bosnian airspace. A US stealth fighter was downed over Belgrade the next night, as it prepared to release its bomb load and suddenly became visible on Serb radar. The pilot was rescued after two hours on the ground, evading Serb troops.

I couldn't deny publicly that the campaign might be brief, and I hoped it would be, but I had to prepare for a campaign of indefinite duration. Accordingly, I directed the campaign to avoid the loss of aircraft, to avoid collateral damages to Serb civilians, and to maximize strikes against the Serb forces conducting the tonic cleansing, rather than simply striking fixed targets. These were my "measures of merit" for the campaign.

Pre-campaign targeting had been poor, due to the US fixation on targeting Iran and Iraq. My air commanders were frustrated that the initial strikes were so light, but this was a deliberate choice to soothe NATO sensibilities; we lacked the deep targeting to do much more. As we escalated operations, we began to be constrained by limited numbers of targets. Gradually the target sets were extended. We increased the numbers of aircraft, we moved strikes to the daylight hours, and I secured permission from Bulgaria and Romania to overfly their airspace, so as to deliver strikes from all azimuths around Belgrade. It was a campaign of deliberate, measured escalation. In order to break Milosevic's will, we needed to achieve "escalation dominance," convincing him that further resistance was hopeless. It was a concept I had learned early in my career, from study of the mistakes in Vietnam. I concluded each press conference by stating, "we're winning, he's losing, and he knows it." I knew Milosevic would be watching these press conferences, and I wanted to increase the personal pressure on him. And I understood, it wasn't the bombing itself that would win, but the growing Serb sense that they were powerless to stop the escalation that eventually would break their will.

At my urging Secretary Solana also adjusted the political aims of the campaign. We already had the end state set with NATO occupation forces, but now we called for the full departure of all Serb forces in Kosovo. After their intense campaign of clearing villages and killing civilians, they could not remain in the country even when hostilities with NATO were ended.

Two weeks into the escalating campaign I met with Secretary of State Albright in Brussels. "Well," she said, "it's now all up to your air campaign; I can't get the Russians to talk to me." We had earlier arranged the air strikes so that a Russian delegation could fly into Belgrade to meet with Milosevic. Now the Russians were refusing to intercede diplomatically. Still, we agreed, the bombing will only work if we take advantage of the pressure to force fruitful negotiations. The US subsequently enlisted Finnish President Marti Ahtisaari and Russian Vice President Victor Chernomyrdin to bring a peace proposal to Milosevic. The plan was originated at my headquarters in Mons and based on the proposal presented to the Serbs at Rambouillet, except that it required total withdrawal of all Serb police and military forces. This was diplomacy backed by force.

I also asked for permission to begin planning for the next steps, an invasion by ground forces. President Clinton had said early on, that he had "no intention" of committing ground troops. The plan was a masterly, lawyeresque formulation, allowing plenty of wiggle room, while heading off partisan attacks in Washington. Inside the US circles, there was discussion back and forth with no resolution. On the eve of NATO's Fiftieth Anniversary Summit Meeting in Washington, British Prime Minister Tony Blair came to my headquarters for a one-on-one meeting. "I want to know if you will win with this air campaign with air power alone," he inquired. "Possible" I said, "but no guarantees." "Will you get ground troops if you need them?" he asked. Without a moment's hesitation, having in mind British Prime Minister Churchill's close relations with General Eisenhower during World War II, I answered, "For that, Prime Minister, I will depend on you." "I'll get them for you," he said. As a result of PM Blair's private intervention in Washington, NATO announced it was prepared to do "whatever was necessary," and I received permission to begin planning for ground forces.

We continued to intensify the attacks. Serbia's neighbors all wanted to become NATO members—so I was able to isolate Milosevic geographically from overland reinforcement and use their airspace. By May, Milosevic was hearing reports that NATO had begun planning a ground invasion of Kosovo. Albanian resistance inside Kosovo was being augmented by hundreds of Albanian volunteers from the US and Western Europe. Ahtisaari and Chernomyrdin made several visits to Milosevic in efforts to crack his resistance. Finally, on May 25, 1999, based on diligent research and my recommendation, he was indicted by the International Criminal Tribunal on Yugoslavia. The combination of all this broke his will to resist. Following a week of intense negotiations at the military level, Milosevic acceded to NATO demands and on June 10, the UN authorized NATO entry into Kosovo.

Solana congratulated me for winning. "You'll be my friend for life," he said.

The next day, Russia removed its peacekeeping battalion in Bosnia, nominally under my control, and headed it to Kosovo. It was a Russian Special Operation, and it threw NATO into a new crisis, this time directly with Russia. It was apparent that the battalion's purpose was to seize the airfield in Kosovo and hold it to permit Russian reinforcements to be flown in to block NATO's authorized entry, or at least to contest the NATO occupation and perhaps split the territory.

Unknown to me, and despite my backstopping of the previous week's talks, my British commander on the ground, Lieutenant General Mike Jackson, had apparently agreed to a sly Serb request not to take any early action to occupy the airfield. It was another case of a capable general not understanding the full implications of his actions, and he made this agreement without clearance from my own State Department advisor who was present at the negotiations. Nor did he seek permission from me. French intelligence picked up a warning about the airfield, and I was called by the head of the French military, General Jean Paul Kelche. "Something is going to happen concerning the airfield," he warned. Still, even when I pressed Jackson after the warning, on June 9, he failed to acknowledge anything specific about the airfield. Now on the morning of June 11, he was caught flat-footed and went through British channels to beg off taking any actions to preemptively seize the airfield.

The Russian battalion arrived at the airfield in the early hours of June 12. Jackson's forces arrived late that afternoon, some fifteen hours after the Russians; when Jackson entered the airfield, he was harassed by a Russian armored vehicle, and he withdrew.

The Pentagon suggested we land a couple of helicopters on the runway to block any incoming Russian aircraft. I passed the suggestion to Admiral Jim Ellis, the theater commander, and he passed it down to Jackson. Jackson refused, citing poor weather that evening.

I met with Jackson early morning the next day. Obviously exhausted, he was almost hysterical in warning that he would "not start WWIII" by trying to enter the airfield or block Russian landings of reinforcements. Neither Washington nor London was prepared to act. We settled for surrounding the Russian force at the airfield, leaving them in control. Working with Hungarian, Bulgarian, and Romanian officials, we denied Russian requests to transit these countries' airspaces. Sill, our intelligence reported Russian airborne regiments loading into aircraft for departure from Russia. At the request of my Air Force commander, I sought Washington's guidance on whether to shoot down any Russian troop transports that violated Hungarian, Bulgarian, or Romanian airspace.

It was brinkmanship, and the Russians blinked; their reinforcements were called off and NATO was not challenged. One and a half million Albanians flooded back into their homes, despite General Jackson's efforts to restrain their return. They were joyous in being liberated. NATO conducted its occupation, even incorporating the Russian battalion on the periphery. The Russians soon left, but to this day a small NATO contingent still remains, as a guardian in a rough neighborhood. Kosovo today is an independent, democratic, and Western-aligned nation, thanks to NATO and the courageous resistance of two generations of Albanians. This was diplomacy backed by force.

Lessons Not Learned

From the perspective of the Clinton years, US military and foreign policy have been badly handled over the past two decades. The list of mistakes in using the military as one of the tools of US diplomacy, and using it properly, is egregious—ranging from attacking Afghanistan in 2001 without a clear desired end state or plan to eliminate Osama Bin Ladin in the beginning, through a series of serious mistakes and misjudgments, all the way to the end.

I've tried to explain that no action should be undertaken without a clear and attainable military objective, that this objective must support the desired political end state, and that the political end state must also be attainable. By this standard we failed in Afghanistan in 2001, in Iraq in 2003, and in Libya in 2011. Diplomacy backed by force works when escalating the force—it doesn't work well when the decision to negotiate has been preceded by a decision to withdraw. By this standard we failed multiple times in Afghanistan.

In negotiating to end a conflict, all warring parties must be engaged; by this standard we failed in Afghanistan, as we had earlier in Vietnam. In both cases we were seeking an exit from intransigent and fearful allies.

In dealing with Iran, we lost an opportunity to use the leverage of the 2003 invasion to shift the course of Mideast politics. In Syria, in 2011, and into 2015, we wavered when we could have enforced a no-fly zone, invoked NATO to stem the refugee tide into Europe, and used the NATO commitment to keep Russia out and Turkey within bounds.

In the multipolar world of the 2020's the United States faces potential adversaries in China and Russia. But this further depends on geography as well as technology and demography. The Soviet Union under Stalin was the provocateur and ultimate beneficiary of WW II. We must not let Putin drive China nor the US to hostilities.

FIVE

ROBERT E. HUNTER

The Challenge to US Foreign Policy

Introduction: Determining the *What* of the Challenge

For anyone who has been involved in either studying, writing/speaking about, deciding, or implementing US foreign policy over a period of several decades, there have obviously been profound changes. The different nature of the world and the US role in it of course have been critical—certainly since the end of the period of relative statis called the Cold War. Technologies (particularly in communications) have had an important and growing impact, but there have also been matters of process that bear inspection and understanding: both for what has more or less stayed the same, and for what has changed, in some regards significantly.

Notably and probably of greatest impact at least for the next few years, has been the Russian war of aggression against Ukraine which began on February 24, 2022. As important for the long term, if not more so, is the rise of China as a major factor on the world scene and in various ways as a competitor to the United States. Of lesser significance but still of potential major consequence is the congeries of issues in and around the Persian Gulf, including the possibility of a war involving Iran in the not-too-distant future (observing from early 2023). And there are global challenges that did not exist during the Cold War: one is the COVID-19 pandemic which might be transitory, but another is climate change—and that will easily be the most important challenge ever to face the United States and the world in general.

Besides striving to meet the long-term, existential challenge of climate change, *sine qua non* for the planet, the three major areas of challenge to the United States today—Ukraine/Russia (and Russia's long-term role), China, and the Persian Gulf (especially relating to Iran)—are very much in play at the time of writing (March 2023). Hence I will not dwell on the specifics of what is now happening which inevitably and rapidly will become dated.

In sum, however, it is already clear the United States will face major challenges to a degree it has not faced at the least since the end of the Cold War (and indeed well before it settled into predictable patterns). Any thought of America continuing to assert some form of hegemony can no longer be sustained. The meaning of the slogan "rules-based order" will have to be rethought and reconfigured. Redefining it will involve far more countries than before, with the United States playing a diminishing role in the process, though for now still *primus inter pares*. Analysis and planning for the long term have become increasingly important, well beyond immediate challenges. At heart, the requirement is for strategic thinking of a quality and intensity not required in the United States for decades if not even longer, and certainly not now present in sufficient quantity and quality. This chapter will discuss some of the specific requirements that, whether well or badly met, will have a major impact on America's role in the world.

Prior to the Russia-Ukraine war, the most important breakpoint in recent decades was the end of the Cold War, centering in most popular imagination on November 9, 1989, with the historic opening of the Berlin Wall. That heralded not only the opening up of Central and Eastern Europe but also a transformation of power on the Continent (and much of the world) with the December 1991 collapse of one of the two superpowers, the Soviet Union.

These events and all that attended them ushered in a period that many observers called a unipolar moment, though that term itself is an oxymoron, and for a while left the United States with no enemies or, at least, threats to the homeland, of any significance. It regained its traditional security of two broad oceans (three, if one counts the Arctic). US foreign policy also lost two of its three key elements of an overarching Cold War paradigm, in competition for which nothing else in the world mattered as much. The three could be summarized as 1) containing Soviet power; 2) confounding Communism; and 3) leading a growing, global economy. Only the third component survived, though regarding Russia, a need for the first began to reemerge in 2014 and with a vengeance in 2022.

At the beginning of the 1990s, so many things thus seemed possible for the United States, both alone and with its friends and allies abroad. (This included one conclusion that seemed to me to be absurd even as it was being uttered: "The end of history.") At least in the European theater, much opportunity was seized upon, leading to a reconstruction of security throughout most of the Continent, and including changes proposed by

President George H.W. Bush to create a "Europe whole and free,"[1] to which the words "at peace" were added. That led to the most profound transformation in European security and politics since the beginning of the Cold War in the late 1940s and, like that earlier period, the process was a compound of several elements: political (both national commitments and diplomacy); economic (encompassing the Marshall Plan through to the European Union's enlargement into Central Europe); and security-military (from the creation of NATO to the development in 1993 of the Partnership for Peace, then bringing several Central European countries into NATO and finally, reaching out to Ukraine and Russia—the last-named of which failed.)[2]

Despite the important work done from 1989 through the early 1990s to tidy up after the end of the Cold War (especially in Europe)—where President George H.W. Bush, his team, and some European counterparts (especially German Federal Chancellor Kohl) deserve such credit—to a great extent the United States, especially its elites, lapsed into what I later called a "holiday from history," until 9/11 (see below). Foreign policy did not seem to be as important as before the Soviet collapse. That was particularly true in the so-called think-tank world, in what I judged as time went on to have been a period of large-scale intellectual disarmament. While there was almost an explosion of new foreign policy institutions, many of which did good work on individual regions and on the tactics of foreign policy, virtually none did serious work on overall US goals and strategy in the world, other than remaining, to use the over-popular phrase, "Number One."[3] This was perhaps natural; since the US was no longer facing any vital threat to the homeland, the impetus for intensive critical thinking such as had characterized the periods of World War II and the development of the Cold War, was not there. The skills eroded. This, in fact, has been the worst negative consequence that came from the end of the Cold War: downplaying the need for first-class, highly trained people in the profession of foreign affairs, capable of relating "apples to oranges," and to think and act at the high-end of strategic analysis—something that was a staple of the Cold War period (at least until the main lineaments and key elements were well established). Even more absent are people who can legitimately be considered to be grand strategists, a rare talent which few are practicing at the moment, and none of whom have served in any of the last few administrations.

Rarely understood is that foreign policy and diplomacy are crafts requiring much skill, training, and experience. But there is a built-in handicap.

Even though international relations (a generic term) is one of the most complex and difficult branches of the social sciences, especially to get right, the access by just about anyone to the field's basic notions provides a widespread belief in their capacity to make judgments. This is a built-in problem, given that it is necessary, at heart, to be able to relate America's role in the world to American politics and society. When that link is broken—as happened in Vietnam—disaster can occur. Among other things, the need for accessibility in a democracy means that, except in areas that are necessarily highly-technical and abstruse, notably nuclear deterrence, foreign policy has to be available to the layman. Unlike law or medicine or much of science, there is no ersatz priesthood that keeps outsiders out, in part by design, by the sheer opacity of nomenclature.

The halcyon period of American's holiday from history was not to last. A second major breakpoint came on September 9, 2001.[4] The events of that period do not need recapitulating, but the impact on United States foreign policy is very much germane, here. It was as though the instruments of foreign policy and security had come out of a summer slumber to full-awake mode. In addition to rapidly devised responses for the attacks on the United States—the first on the continental US since 1812—there was a shift from the former Cold War emphasis on threats from abroad, in major part aimed against interests abroad (notably in Europe), to a focus on threats at home, even though emanating from abroad and not involving a major competitor (the Soviet Union), but what in effect was an inexpensive "mom-and-pop" operation, the 9/11 terrorist attacks.[5] The shift, reflected in widespread perceptions throughout the United States, in government as well as the thinktank and commentary communities—indeed, in US public opinion virtually across the board—was that of a potential major threat of continuing terrorism mounted from abroad against the United States itself (in addition to a secondary concern of terrorism against friends and allies abroad). This led to what became known as the Global War on Terrorism (GWOT) which was, however, a gross exaggeration of what the United States was facing.

A keynote element of this development was psychological rather than actual. As I wrote at the time, 9/11 was not a matter of WMD (Weapons of Mass Destruction, e.g., notably nuclear weapons), but of what I called a War of Mass Psychological Disruption (WMPD)—that is, the impact on the American body politic from the shock of 9/11. One result was the mobilization of so much of the Washington community and its outliers to focus and build upon capabilities to deal with "terrorism," not only abroad, but also at home. (The response included people for whom democracy was and still is a flawed commodity.) This produced, among other things, the Patriot Act[6] and creation of the Department of Homeland Security. In the process, some limits were imposed on civil liberties in the US which, at least formally, still exist.

Thus in effect the US Constitution's checks and balances in this area were suspended. Perhaps even worse, the new atmosphere, working outward from elite opinion, set the stage for widespread acceptance of the 2003 US-led invasion of Iraq, probably the worst foreign policy and national security mistake by the United States since Vietnam if not even before. There were of course many reasons for supporting the invasion of Iraq, but a sense of vengeance against "someone," was involved, in addition to escalating the US presence in Afghanistan in October 2011 which transmogrified into America's longest war, lasting ten years. (Its duration in major part was because no reasonable, achievable, or even important goals were ever determined.)

Notably, in the wake of the political atmosphere following 9/11, debate in the United States regarding the invasion of Iraq—certainly across mainstream media—was stifled in favor of getting on the bandwagon, and many people who opposed the invasion were blacklisted by these media.[7] With regard to the Middle East, there has still not been a resuscitation of open debate about US policies, which has cost the nation dearly in both blood and treasury, as well as diversion of attention.

Another factor that is still with us is that many people in the United States who occupy major roles in the shaping of public opinion and government policy have difficulty in getting over a "cold war mentality." The GWOT gained strength in part from this. This mentality has also had a major impact on US efforts to deal effectively with post-Cold War Russia, beyond tangible challenges it does pose to us and others. There is also a risk of failing to find ways of avoiding a new cold war with China (in addition to Russia which, as of time of writing in March 2023, is now virtually a certainty, at least in the perceptions of almost all the US foreign policy community), from a failure of foreign policy at the top, as well as in much of the commentariat which, among other things, has limited the capacity of American diplomats to pursue alternatives. This is already becoming a major cost.

To put the issue in broader perspective: since the time when the United States became fully engaged in the outside world (Pearl Harbor) until about the time of the Russian invasion of Ukraine, it did not have to deal with a world in which it is only one player among others, however much *primus inter pares* as we still are, but now it must learn the techniques of pursuing US interests in a world where dealing with the ambitions and actions of other major powers has become unavoidable. In short, from now on it is clear that, in many situations, some of critical importance, many other countries "get a vote," in addition to the United States along with its friends and partners.

In effect, the aberration in US and global statecraft is not from the era in which we now live but the Cold War, when the United States did not have to operate within the classic laws of foreign policy that the rest of the world operated in prior to Cold War rigidities and within which the United States now also has to live. Further, the difficulty of seeing both the valuable roles of diplomacy and a must-needs understanding of other cultures and significant accommodation to others' interests and perspectives, tends to create rigidities in thinking—as happened during the Cold War, with greater reason than now. Thus the military threats that were such a centerpiece of the Cold War were essentially dealt with (and widely understood as such) by 1962–1963, with the onset of the mutual deterrence policy with the Soviet Union (denominated in the amazingly ironic term, MAD, for Mutually Assured Destruction). Even so, it took another twenty-seven years for the politics to come into alignment so the conflict could end. Such rigidities of thought and psychology limit the capacity to debate differences regarding the US role in the world and in competition with other countries (notably, now Russia and China, and at a lower level of power-contention also with Iran). Here again, public discussion of alternatives is also limited, thus constraining the needed flexibility for top policy people as well as American diplomats to operate effectively (if they don't themselves succumb to this disease).

Some of the other impacts that post-9/11 conditions have had on making and conducting US foreign and security policy (including diplomacy) in today's world will be examined below.

Determining the *How* of the Challenge to American Foreign Policy

Most of us writing for this volume were engaged in US foreign policy, in one way and another, through most if not all of the last several decades, and each has his or her story to tell. My own story has included many different elements. Notably, unlike others writing in this volume, I was not a Foreign Service Officer. All my government service has been through one form or another of civil service or political appointment. In summary, my experience has covered a broad spectrum of interconnected elements that have punctuated a long period of learning and have reinforced one another:

- Three summers (1961–1963) in the US Navy's Polaris Project (the third summer in the London Admiralty), which brought practical experience in issues of nuclear deterrence and of cooperation with America's key European ally;
- A year (1964–1965) working in the LBJ White House at the time of the Great Society (primarily education, but also some limited elements of foreign policy, including European security and non-proliferation), which brought a domestic and political perspective to policy across the board;
- Principal author (mostly domestic issues) of the 1972 Democratic Party National Convention Platform;
- Three-plus years (1973–1977) as Senator Edward Kennedy's first Foreign Policy Advisor, which entailed not just work on issues (and foreign travel with him) but also provided understanding of both the role of Congress in US foreign and defense policies and the critical importance of bipartisanship in these areas;
- Four years (1977–1981) on the Carter NSC staff, as leader first in European policy and then in Middle East policy, in which I played important roles during a consequential period for both areas. In addition to issues, this position also provided invaluable experience in what is called the interagency process, as well as some diplomatic activity;
- Four and a half years (1993–1998) as US Ambassador to NATO, covering the most important transformative period of the Alliance since its founding, while building on the work of the George H.W. Bush administration. Under Clinton, I was principal architect of NATO's transformation and negotiator of virtually all elements of European security development. Although based abroad, this again included being engaged in the U.S interagency process and also working with fifteen allied ambassadors under conditions where each of us had wide latitude in shaping policies to which

our respective capitals would adhere. (This work also included NATO's unit veto, thus requiring subtle diplomatic skills to produce consensus, even though the United States was—and more than any other country still is—the Alliance's "800-pound gorilla.") This period further included my negotiating NATO's use of airpower in the Bosnian War, which provided critical leverage to diplomacy (which to that point had not succeeded) and eventually brought the war to an end.

Mixed amongst these formal jobs were additional engagements: I was Lead Consultant (1983–1984) to the National Bipartisan Commission on Central America (the Kissinger Commission); advisor on Lebanon (1983) to the Speaker of the House of Representatives; and representative of the House Majority Leader on a congressional delegation to the Persian Gulf (1990), just prior to the Persian Gulf War.

I also have had broad academic training and experience, including my PhD in International Relations at the London School of Economics (dissertation on the origins of NATO), as well as teaching at several universities including LSE and working at a number of so-called think tanks in the United States and England.[8] I was also president (2003–2008) of the Atlantic Treaty Association, the Brussels-based collective organization for NATO's forty-two national Atlantic Councils, and served as Chairman (2001–2014) of the Council for a Community of Democracies.[9]

I list all this background not to provide a resume or to claim any particular expertise, but rather to illustrate the value of broad engagements in a full spectrum of activities and institutions related to the learning and practice of foreign and security policies. That is, not only about the issues, but also about what is called policy making, which entails active diplomacy related thereto, the role of the US Congress, and the embedding of foreign policy in domestic politics. Through luck, accident, and outstanding mentors, I thus believe I can bring perspective to what Aristotle argued should be the combination of both study and experience in politics (an area clearly related to foreign policy): "Surely, then, while collections of laws, and of constitutions also, may be serviceable to those who can study them and judge what is good or bad and what enactments suit what circumstances, those who go through such collections without a practised faculty will not have right judgement (unless it be as a spontaneous gift of nature), though they may perhaps become more intelligent in such matters."[10]

Domestic Political Influences on Diplomacy.

"Politics," the old saw goes, "should stop at the water's edge." There is wisdom in that saying, but it assumes that there are identifiable national interests to be pursued regardless of how they play in domestic politics. There can and will be disagreement about those interests, which will also affect the nature and conduct of US diplomacy. It probably has always been so. In the period from about 1960 until the late 1980s, perhaps the most notable disagreements were about how to deal with the Soviet Union—in summary the two principal passions were pro-détente versus anti-détente. The overall objective, however, was more-or-less the same: to prevail in the Cold War (though what prevail meant in practice was also subject to debate). The debates were mostly on the merits rather than results of domestic politics (though with exceptions, as discussed below) that depreciated debate on genuine security interests.

But there are also many issues, especially now in the post-Cold War period, where debate cannot be so easily compartmentalized—that is, in terms of different interpretations of national interests or the best way of pursuing them, including through diplomacy. These are issues where domestic politics more often come to front and center. Since the end of the Second World War, the first, and for some time the most prominent, differences of view about foreign policy affected by domestic politics, were in regard to the coming into being of the People's Republic of China. "Who lost China?" was a frequent question, begging the issues of whether China was "ours" to "lose" in the first place, or that US policies had much to do with the 1949 communist triumph on the Chinese mainland. What one might call objective assessment was rapidly lost, as on the one hand Chiang Kai-shek became a potent force in US politics (both on his own and through his wife, Soong Mei-Ling), along with some Americans who had been involved in China during the Second World War, most notably General Claire Chennault (of Flying Tigers fame) and his Chinese-born wife Anna.[11] On the other hand, there were some fervent anti-communists, notably Sen. Joseph McCarthy (R–WI), who took up the cudgel, destroying a lot of careers (especially in the State Department, a purging that some analysts arguably weakened the department's capacity to assess Vietnam adequately a decade later) and placing out of bounds any rational debate about whether the United States should accept the reality of Communist Chinese control of the mainland. Honest debate was further stifled, following General Douglas MacArthur's insubordination in moving US forces in Korea up to the Chinese border along the Yalu River, prompting China to intervene, and Washington and Beijing found themselves at war.

An historic irony, of course, is that Richard Nixon, one of the American politicians who most "made hay" in domestic politics over the supposed fecklessness or even perfidy of the Truman administration on China, in 1971 created the US opening to China and had even signaled that approach in an October 1967 article in *Foreign Affairs* magazine.[12]

Meanwhile, debate about the best approach to the Soviet Union—a genuine threat to the US and allies, about which there was broad consensus—also was affected by US domestic politics, beyond pro- and anti-détente. In particular, US ethnic supporters of the so-called Captive Nations in Central and Eastern Europe played a role, though they were never as influential as the so-called China Lobby had been.

There was also an effort, initiated by an anti-détente staffer in the office of Senator Henry Jackson (D–WA) to link US-Soviet Union relations to permitting Jewish emigration which Moscow was severely limiting. The resulting Jackson-Vanik Amendment prevented trade agreements with non-market economies (but was primarily targeted at the Soviet Union). The objective—securing freedom for Jews to emigrate—was unimpeachable; but as Jackson's staffer made clear to those of us working for other Senators, his real objective was to try killing off détente. Indeed, Jewish emigration from the Soviet Union—which the Kennedy office in the Senate had long been working to promote (led by my colleague Marc Ginsberg), with considerable success[13]—was cut off immediately, with predictable political results in US debate on relations with the Soviet Union, including arms control.[14]

My first direct experience of the impact of domestic politics on foreign policy, at the time of my working on the National Security Council staff in 1977, involved the issue of the Crown of St. Stephen, the historic relic of the Hungarian monarchy and a major symbol of Hungarian nationalism—indeed, probably their most important such symbol. It was unknown to me until Mary Rose Okar, a US Representative from Ohio, responding to some Hungarian-American constituents, wrote to Soviet National Security Advisor Zbigniew Brzezinski seeking assurance that the Crown would not be returned to the communist government in Budapest. My NSC colleague Bill Hyland and I were dispatched to Capitol Hill to calm the waters. He knew what the Crown was; I had never heard of it.

This piqued my curiosity, and I did some research: long story short, the Crown plus the rest of the state regalia had, by means worthy of a spy novel, come into the possession of the United States Army at the end of World War II and in 1977 was locked away in Kentucky at Ft. Knox. Given that we were trying to weaken the hold of the Soviet Union on East European countries through stimulating nationalism and also promoting the objectives of the Helsinki Final Act of 1975, I had the inspiration: why not give back the Crown, even though the government in Budapest was communist? Again, long story short, I put forward the idea as part of a long memo to President Carter (signed by Brzezinski) on various European issues, and he checked "Yes." The State Department managed to drag out the implementing negotiations for nearly a year, but the deed was done and helped to have the effect I had desired for it, as Hungary a decade later in 1989 was at the vanguard of moving Central European states beyond communism. This was the impact of a domestic lobby on diplomacy in reverse gear: but for the remonstrations by some Hungarian émigrés, I might never have heard of the Crown of St. Stephen.

After the end of the Cold War, domestic politics have arguably played an even more important role in influencing US foreign policy. Thus while I was Ambassador to NATO, in 1994 President Clinton supported NATO enlargement beyond Partnership for Peace (of which I was co-author), which helped the newly "liberated" Central European states adapt to independence and develop as democracies, as well as work out non-member relationships with NATO, for some of them to prepare for eventual membership in NATO. There also developed significant strategic reasons for taking a handful of new members into NATO, even beyond the value of helping states to find a modern, democratic place in the West (Partnership for Peace). Thus, the newly unified Germany was surrounded with NATO (and soon after, also with the European Communities) by bringing in Poland, the Czech Republic, and Hungary which was thrown in for good measure as one of the four so-called Visegrad states, with Slovakia being the outlier. This was designed to reassure Russia and Germany's neighbors against risking any repetition of the German past.[15] Clinton has never revealed the extent to which he backed NATO expansion for geostrategic as opposed to domestic political motives (such as gaining the votes of ethnic Americans from this part of Europe). Perhaps it was significant that in the 1996 presidential campaign the only foreign policy speech he gave (which notably promoted NATO enlargement) was in Hamtramck, Michigan, a community surrounded by Detroit and home to people who hailed from Central Europe. Of course, all US politicians were aware of the number of Polish-Americans in Chicago.

Captive Nations were not the only domestic lobbies with some impact on US foreign policy during the Cold War. In 1974, while I was Foreign Policy Advisor to Senator Edward Kennedy, the military dictatorship in Athens was overthrown and, in the ensuing melee, champions of unity (*Enosis*) between Greece and Cyprus got into the act, deposing the Cypriot president Archbishop Makarios III (a fanatic of the first order). In response to the Greek and Cypriot coups and proclamation of a Hellenic Republic of Cyprus, the Turkish government in Ankara decided to intervene militarily on behalf of the Turkish-Cypriot ethnic minority in the northern part of the country.[16] But what happened next was striking. The US Greek lobby rose up and, through Greek-American members of Congress (notably Rep. John Brademas, D–IN), got sanctions imposed, not on Greece but on Turkey! (To this day, the standoff on the island has not been resolved.)

Other lobbying efforts stimulated at least in part by domestic politics had more salubrious results, particularly for the ending of apartheid in South Africa. The extent to which US and international pressures, including sanctions, actually helped bring about the decisive change, if not entirely clear, nonetheless involved strong domestic pressures—in this instance with a strong moral case that was not contradicted by any particular *realpolitik* considerations—though many US (and other nations') corporations with extensive involvement in South Africa were pushing the other way.

Economic and other sanctions have become a major part of US foreign policy, as well as for some other Western countries, such as the limits imposed on trade with the Soviet Union and communist bloc nations (COMECON) during the Cold War.[17] They have been a regular staple of US foreign policy, particularly in the last three decades. But, except for South Africa (though success is not entirely clear) and Iran in regard to getting it to negotiate seriously over its nuclear program (sanctions likely were a significant factor), imposing sanctions has almost never worked. To "work," there have to be virtually airtight sanctions by all countries, which rarely happens.[18] Furthermore, sanctioned countries have to judge that the economic costs of sanctions outweigh their sense of important national interests," which, again, rarely happens. There also have to be limitations on work-arounds for sanctioned countries, that is, their ability to develop indigenous alternatives. And, in countries that are sanctioned, leaders will pass on the costs to their populations as much as is possible, while continuing to enjoy their own luxurious lifestyles.

At this point, it should be clear that I don't think much of this tool. In

US statecraft, sanctions have essentially been used to appease domestic political pressures by appearing to be "doing something." They are, however, usually less risky than moving up the scale of actions to the direct use of force. One major problem, however, is the general belief in US administrations (and much of Congress) that it is possible to impose sanctions on the one hand while simultaneously trying to build relations on the other, which often seems to be an absurdity by leaderships in targeted countries. US sanctions on Russia and China in the last several years are major cases in point, as well as the Trump administration's maximum-pressure campaign against Iran, still continued by the Biden administration. These sanctions have only played into the hands of Iranian hardliners and gained nothing for US interests, though this campaign has been strongly supported by Israel, some of the Persian Gulf Arab states (notably Saudi Arabia), and their political lobbies in the United States.

The United States (and some other countries) will no doubt continue to use sanctions as a major tool of foreign policy, although they are mostly "feel good" tools in domestic politics and can interfere with statecraft rather than strengthen it—risking an emphasis just on "sticks" instead of also offering "carrots." Most often, however, they are still preferable over going to war and do serve domestic political purposes with respect to taking, at least seemingly, a moral stance.

One evergreen (so to speak!) foreign policy issue that is deeply immersed in US domestic politics involves Ireland, in particular relations between the Republic and Northern Ireland (still part of the United Kingdom), plus the inferior economic and political position of Catholics in the North. This became particularly significant in the early 1970s, as Irish-Catholic American supporters of the Provisional IRA were urged to give money to buy arms for the Northern Ireland cause—the so-called "jars in bars" in Boston-area Irish pubs. It was rapidly getting out of hand, potentially embroiling the United States in United Kingdom politics, thereby straining relations. Four Irish-American politicians, Senators Edward Kennedy and Daniel Patrick Moynihan, New York Governor Hugh Carey, and House Speaker Tip O'Neill, backed by the Northern Irish leader John Hume and spearheaded by a member of the Irish Embassy, Michael Lillis,[19] pushed to put the United States on record as opposing violence, supporting a peaceful resolution of the conflict, and promising major economic investments if that were achieved. I wrote much of President Carter's August 30, 1977, statement to that effect, the first such formal intervention by the US government in the "troubles" in Ireland.[20] US engagement—led mostly for domestic political reasons—continued through (and after) former Senate Majority Leader George Mitchell's important contribution to the April 1998 Good Friday Agreement.[21]

All the above examples of impacts by US domestic politics on foreign policy and diplomacy, save for the role of the China Lobby, were small beer during the Cold War era, because of the overarching near-consensus on Soviet Union containment and its central role in US foreign policy. With the end of the Cold War, however, there was no longer a need for domestic interest groups to take a back seat to reasons-of-state (as I predicted at the time). Since then, and possibly even now with countering Russia's invasion of Ukraine and dealing in a different manner with the rise of Chinese power and influence, there has been no central organizing principle for US foreign policy as there was during the Cold War. For many years, the most obvious and heavily pursued effort to have a central organizing principle became in shorthand the Global War on Terrorism (GWOT) that followed 9/11. Given that it was always limited in scope, GWOT was never a substitute for the Cold War, although it did include a commingling of domestic politics with foreign policy, both in the tools developed inside the United States and the choice of targets abroad. Should either Russia or China truly become the central organizing principle(s) in US foreign policy, in addition to whatever courses of action are suggested by circumstances, accepting the rigidities of cold war in both government administration and Congress plus the media and think tanks, carries major risks for the United States along with countries following in our wake, of becoming locked into psychology, structures, actions, and politics that likely will constrain the West (especially the United States) in abilities to craft and pursue flexible policies that promote our interests long-term. A cold war paradigm is thus only accepted, much less actively pursued, with utmost caution and even trepidation.

Judging the three decades following the end of the Cold War, it would be difficult to discern adequately the extent to which some activities of US foreign policy were products of accurate assessments of US interests and threats to them abroad and to the homeland, or were at least a significant result of domestic political support for the tools and methodologies of military force, combined with the popular desire to "do something," as in Afghanistan following 9/11. In retrospect, it is hard to see that the US accomplished much of anything in Afghanistan that directly relates to US (or allies' and partners') interests and security. But until President Trump (moving toward US withdrawal) and President Biden (actually withdrawing

US military forces) it was not possible in US domestic politics to accept the reality, not so much of failure in Afghanistan but of not having at any point a sense that anything that happened there meant very much to the United States, as opposed to quelling some residual sources of exportable terrorism. This can be accorded in large measure to a disconnect between objective US interests and domestic political support to pursue unclear goals which were unattainable for that very reason (and others). US peace diplomacy with the Taliban, but without including the Kabul government, was doomed from the start and was only a way of delaying the inevitable (which suddenly and predictably—by me and others—came to pass in August 2021), while surrounding the developments with a bit of verbal fog.

In the post-Cold War period, one other set of domestic pressures carried over from the previous era. This was the role of the US military and, clearly enmeshed with it, what President Eisenhower called in his farewell television address to the Nation the "military-industrial complex."[22] These domestic political and economic interests continue to play major roles, with their impact on US involvement in the outside world and the tools employed (individually or in combination with other tools) to pursue US interests. The overwhelming budget primacy of the Defense Department has confounded many administrations; but the integration of instruments of power and influence (see below) in the post-Cold War world now needs more than ever before, to deal effectively with the guns-versus-diplomacy tradeoff.

Another area where US domestic politics has clearly determined US foreign policy and diplomacy in the post-Cold War period has been Cuba. It was obvious to many Americans—I included myself in that number—that, as Soviet financial subventions to the communist regime on the island disappeared following the USSR's collapse, Cuba would suffer mightily in economics and thus also would the stability of the government. It was an ideal time for the United States simply to lift all sanctions and permit a flood of investment and money, etc., into the island (while hopefully avoiding at least most of the prior problems that led to Castro's overthrow of Fulgencio Batista in 1959). But the Cuba lobby in the United States, located primarily in presidential-election swing-state Florida, blocked that course. Despite some efforts to change things, made mostly by the Obama administration, Trump reimposed almost all the sanctions and Biden followed suit—even though the Cuba lobby in Florida is arguably less potent in state politics as new generations of expatriates grow up simply as unhyphenated Americans. (Of course, there has remained the important role of Senator Bob Menendez (D-NJ), Chairman of the Senate Foreign relations Committee, who was able to hold hostage some key Biden foreign policy matters.) Cuba is no longer very important to the US, in any strategic sense, but US policy, aided by US sanctions, as well as Cuban government practices, both continue to fail basic human-rights standards—while blaming the government in Havana not just for its own abysmal human-rights record but for all of the failures.

Among various domestic-interest groups that have had influence in the post-Cold War world, with little doubt the area of the world, and of US diplomacy and other engagements that has been most affected has been the Middle East. The part of the region that has been most obviously involved, from the late 1940s until now, is the Levant and, more particularly, issues directly related to Israel. While there may be few if any issues regarding Israel's relations with its neighbors that are not subject to debate and disagreement, there has been and continues to be strong support within the American body politic for Israel's creation and continued existence, thriving as a prosperous democracy, and its security in a difficult, often dangerous region. There is little debate about whether the United States should continue to provide tools for Israel's defense and broad support for its security, including in international institutions, most notably the United Nations. Nor did this support flag even after conclusion of the Egypt-Israel Peace Treaty in March 1979 (just prior to my assuming the lead role in Middle East policy on the National Security Council staff). Though that treaty removed the risk of any serious Arab military attack on Israel (with Egypt out of the military balance) along with any US-Soviet confrontation over a possible Israeli-Arab conflict, thus dramatically reducing the importance of this geopolitical reason for the United States to support Israel diplomatically, the moral and values dimensions of US support did not decrease.

In my judgment, the strength of the US commitment to Israel lies primarily in this moral and values dimension. Not surprisingly, that has not been enough with regard to Israel, which has also needed to remain strategically important for the United States. (This requirement was most likely reinforced when President Eisenhower pulled the rug out from under the 1956 Anglo-French-Israeli invasion of Suez.) I learned this lesson on my first official visit to Egypt and Israel as part of a team led by Secretary of State Cyrus Vance, that was sent to be present for Israel's return of major parts of the Sinai to Egypt, pursuant to the Egypt-Israel Peace Treaty. Afterwards in Jerusalem, Prime Minister Menachem Begin confronted Vance with what Begin said was the cancelling of a strategic dialogue between the two countries. Neither Vance nor anyone else in the American party knew what the Israeli prime minister was talking about, and I took on the task of finding out. As it turned out, there had been a series of low-level (colonel and below) US-Israeli talks being hosted by Andrew Marshall, the Pentagon's Director of Net Assessments. It had proved of little value, so Marshall had cancelled it. It was, in a term of art, a "nothing-burger," but Begin made a big deal of it with Vance. I immediately (and accurately) interpreted that, following the conclusion of peace with Egypt,[23] Israel needed a new, strategic common-interest with the United States to guarantee their relationship, and that the moral basis—the most solid basis possible for a US commitment to another nation—was in Begin's view and that of other Israeli leaders, simply not sufficient. One could not really blame them.

This requirement has been important in US-Israeli relations ever since and has been a major factor in Israel's concerns to gain reassurance that the United States will remain steadfast, and the same has applied to the so-called Israeli Lobby in US domestic politics. This factor has deeply colored virtually all US diplomacy in the Middle East. It was present, for example, in Israel's quiet but firm support of the US-led second invasion of Iraq in 2003—one of the worst US foreign policy decisions ever made, and present in America's overall dealings with Iran, long-term, whatever the objective merits were in terms of US interests. The one exception regarding Iran was President Obama's negotiation of the 2015 Joint Comprehensive Plan of Action (JCPOA), designed to trammel Iran's capacity to gain nuclear-weapons. That exception was marked by an extraordinary and unprecedented speech given by Israeli Prime Minister Netanyahu to a joint session of Congress, in which he exhorted its members to choose his vision of US interests over that of the President of the United States.[24] Israel (and many of its most committed US supporters) thus pressed President Trump to withdraw from the JCPOA in 2018, supported his maximum pressure measures on Iran, and also welcomed President Biden's dilatory and failed diplomacy in rejoining it, despite his verbal commitment to do so.

The foregoing are examples from my direct experience with the role that US domestic politics has had in shaping and in some cases distorting America diplomacy, including some issues of considerable importance to the United States. This factor also reflects the frequent tension between what may be generalized as interests and values. Interest-group efforts to shape US foreign policy is a time-tested practice in US politics and diplomacy. No doubt it will continue; part of both the art and craft of US political leaders (rather than diplomats), charged with protecting the nation's security and other interests, is to prevent parochial domestic pressures from inflicting damage to the nation's role in the world and possibly even its security.

Throughout much American history, there has been a dualism in approach to the outside world. One is interests, defined as supposedly objective requirements for protecting the Nation's security, and to pursue advancement in the outside world as well as shape an international environment congenial to the United States; also, mainly in the post-World War II era, requirements for what is termed a "rules-based international order" and "liberal internationalism." (This territory is too well-trodden to warrant recapitulation here.) At times in US foreign policy toward many other countries, there is little to no conflict between what, in shorthand, I will call interests and values. (That does not include some religion-dominated countries, like some of the Sunni Arab states, notably Saudi Arabia. Nor has there been tension in US policy arising from conflicts between interests and values in relations with communist states, and religion-based states like Iran, where the two can reinforce one another in terms of generating alienation from the United States.) The relative lack of tension between interests and values is especially true with close allies, as in Europe and parts of East Asia, although in recent years that has not always been so. In some other parts of the world, that is more often not true. (US sanctions policy often relates to the issue of values rather than interests.)

When I served for four years on the NSC staff in the Carter administration, I would often see tensions between interests and values—the latter often expressed as human rights. Indeed, human rights was a centerpiece of President Carter's approach to the world, as it continues to be in his unprecedented post-presidency.[25] It is a truism to say that not everyone in his administration, in Congress, or in the commentariat agreed with him. Nor was it always true even among European allies, many of which have high standards for promoting human rights internationally, some higher than the United States. Thus at the time of the Helsinki Final Act (1975), Henry Kissinger was heavily criticized by many Europeans for what they perceived as his ambivalence toward human rights.[26] They therefore should have welcomed Carter's commitment on this score. I was surprised, as the lead for Europe on the NSC staff, to find that this was not so among many of the allies. They worried that President Carter would put too much emphasis on human rights as opposed to a military and security focus, principally regarding the Soviet Union. (This behavior related to an aphorism I coined during my many years in the US government, working in senior positions of helping to manage relations with Europeans: "They will complain when the US does too much, and they will complain when the US does too little—the constant is 'complaining.' I would rather be criticized for doing too much in support of the alliance!")

There is little doubt that undergirding much of US foreign policy with significant respect for values, including human rights, is necessary to gain broad approval from Americans for US engagements in the outside world. World War I was sold in part as "a war to end all wars." World War II was presented as a war for democracy and the US as the Arsenal of Democracy. Since then many of America's military interventions were portrayed in part as a way of advancing democracy and in some formulations, even as "the American way of life." US military failure in both Vietnam and Afghanistan were related to an effort to achieve too much in terms of "values" (or in the case of Vietnam, *realpolitik* dressed up as American values). Thus US commitment to its European allies derives at least in significant part from the promotion of democracy, and efforts like NATO's Partnership for Peace (1993) had a major element of democracy-promotion. As US Ambassador to NATO, I would tell US military and civilian personnel working in PFP countries that in effect they were individual ambassadors for the United States, especially with regard to living democracy, as exemplified by the way they conducted themselves in these countries and practices of a Western way of life that they brought along with them.[27] Earlier, the major US role in the transformation of Japanese and West German societies was not just about geopolitics but also about democracy-promotion in those societies, which worked—indeed, in large part because both societies were ready for democratic governance and, before Nazism and Japanese militarism, had underlying Western political and social systems (albeit moreso in Germany than Japan).

The tension between interests and values in future US foreign policy will no doubt continue, and the people who develop US foreign policy as well as those who implement it, both military and civilian (the latter focusing on diplomats), will need to reconcile both elements on an almost daily basis.

During my time in and observing US government activities in the outside world, I noted that not many politically active Americans or US institutions were committed to human rights as an absolute; many people often made judgments concerning "friends" and "enemies" on an ideological basis before deciding whether to promote human rights as a major element of US foreign policy. That was of course largely true during the Cold War: American foreign policy in general favored human rights in communist countries[28] but there was often less support for human rights in authoritarian countries that happened to be on "our side" in political and security competitions. There will continue to be major areas of competition; regrettably, not enough universalism in human rights was practiced during the period immediately after the Cold War (or, in some cases, there was too much proselytizing), when there were few tensions between power on the one hand and promoting human rights and democracy on the other. Thus it has been one thing to help nurture efforts to build or preserve democracies, as was the case with the Community of Democracies (and in support of which, I chaired for more than a decade the US-based Council for a Community of Democracies), and another, in the often heavy-handed effort to impose democracy without due attention to its requirements for flourishing in different societies: Iraq and Afghanistan have been major cases in point.

In 1982, while I was at the Center For Strategic and International Studies, I worked with a colleague, Allen Weinstein, who saw value in what the West German political parties had been doing, each with an institute (*Stiftung*) with government funding, to help democracy-promotion by individuals and institutions in other countries: fostering, not imposing. Building on some earlier work, he and I played lead roles in developing the concept. Weinstein's idea led to congressional chartering of the National Endowment for Diplomacy, with four quasi-independent subsidiaries, one for each of the two political parties, plus one for Labor, and one for private industry. These have been mostly successful.[29] There are also many similar human-rights organizations in the United States and abroad which could be said, from the US perspective, to be "doing well by doing good."

In all my years in international relations (as student and practitioner) of dealing both with power and with human rights, I have worked out a formula for the US government in its approach to the tension that often arises between the two. It may become necessary, for good and legitimate reasons of state, to give second place to human rights considerations. But that should never happen at the start of policy debate, as too often occurs, especially with people who see non-power matters as of minor value. If need be, giving second place to human rights should only happen at the end of policy deliberations, and even then only after the human consequences—and price—are fully understood. This methodology is obviously not perfect. But it is better than that which often is followed, today.

Instruments of Power and Influence

It is perhaps a truism that the craft of diplomacy, ancient as it is, has not changed all that much, although I will bow to superior historical and analytical knowledge. What I have observed, however, is that "diplomacy" between states never stands alone (except, at the "lowest level," e.g., negotiation of some minor issues between countries X and Y, say, over cultural relations). There are also other factors; what I have seen change, primarily, is the mix of those instruments, in the way they work together (or don't!), and the relative priority each is given by the people who "make" foreign and security policy and then carry it out.[30]

In my experience, the same has been largely true in terms of the relative primacy of different agencies of the US government (counting the NSC staff and the White House as "agencies"). In sum, the essence is the integration of instruments of power and influence—not with any one instrument standing by itself—and with overall strategic purpose as lodestar. Sometimes this is done well, as in wrapping up the Cold War, and sometimes less well, such as in Vietnam, too often in the Middle East and most prominently the failures following the 2003 invasion of Iraq (as well as the assessments leading up to that invasion).

Reflecting on my historical studies in particular as a "World War II buff,", during that period, primacy in the conduct of the nation's "foreign engagements" most definitely lay with the Navy and War Departments, and especially the latter in its direct land contacts with enemies and liberated countries. The State Department (and its then-secretary Cordell Hull) played secondary roles. Notably, however, US president Franklin Roosevelt was the master of grand strategy and reconciliation of many if not most of its key elements.[31] Late in the war and soon afterwards, however, diplomacy as such gained a larger role, especially in creation of the great postwar institutions, the UN, IBRD, IMF and others, and the creation in and for Europe of the Marshall Plan, the Organization for European Economic Cooperation (now named the Organization for Economic Cooperation and Development), and of course the North Atlantic Treaty and NATO. Notably, in the last mentioned, the US strategic and political commitment to the eleven Canadian and European allies came April 4, 1949, nearly two years before creation of the military arm of NATO, initially in the form of Allied Command Europe (April 2, 1951) and then Allied Command Atlantic (January 30, 1952). As noted earlier, the US engagement in Europe was three-legged: political/strategic, economic and military, with additional major roles for both public and private sectors.

In my first government job as an administrative management intern with the Navy's Polaris Project, emphasis was exclusively military until the third summer (1963) when, as a result of the US-UK Nassau Agreement[32] under which the US provided Polaris missiles to Britain, I also got a taste in the British Admiralty of "diplomacy" mixed with "military."[33] Then, to the extent that my role in the LBJ White House (1964–1965), which focused on education, also had a foreign policy dimension, it was political-military, in co-authoring the president's 1965 speech to the International Atomic Energy Agency and in helping to derail the ill-begotten NATO Multilateral Force (MLF). Meanwhile, the Vietnam War was primarily about military instruments, even after the long, drawn-out diplomacy with the North Vietnamese had begun.[34]

However, by the time I was foreign policy advisor for Senator Ted Kennedy (1973–1977), in addition to military matters, which at that point were well-settled into their Cold War patterns, diplomacy was gaining in importance at the major geopolitical level, especially as it related to arms-control efforts with the Soviet Union. Ted Kennedy was deeply engaged in supporting efforts to promote the success of détente (e.g., a diplomatic emphasis).[35] I was helped in my role on his staff (and in my later government service at the NSC and NATO) by the six-plus years I spent at the London School of Economics, plus the then-fledgling (International) Institute for Strategic Studies, and at times by my experience at Chatham House, learning from many of Britain's best academic scholars and government officials in the fields of foreign policy and defense, and being taken seriously by them despite my youth (!). This included my thorough training as a nuclear strategist and my work on European integration (now the European Union).[36] These British academics and officials did not suffer from the ideological constraints of Cold War analysis in the United States. The lesson of endeavoring to see matters in analytical rather than ideological terms has stuck with me ever since, though sometimes that has been a handicap, given the all-too-frequent "need to choose sides" approach to foreign policy analysis in the US government and US think tanks.

With the blessings of Secretary of State Kissinger, Kennedy also dispatched me, with Spanish-speaking staff colleague Mark Schneider who

I took along, to Cuba for a week at the end of 1974, as a sort of "smelling things out" visit which included a four-hour meeting with Fidel Castro. This nibbling at US diplomatic alternatives to isolation of Cuba came to naught when Castro sent troops to Angola.

Also during my years with Kennedy, I handled foreign-aid legislation and budgeting. I benefited from my three years at the Overseas Development Council, just prior to joining Kennedy's staff. US "foreign aid," to use a summary term, has a long history and has had many different primary purposes at different times, ranging from purely humanitarian causes to economic and political development for their own sake and instrumentally (for example, to limit global population growth), to competition with other countries for "hearts and minds," as against the Soviet Union and now to a lesser degree China. As then-president of the Overseas Development Council (James Grant) had told me when I worked there (1970–1973), "It doesn't matter what the reason, just so we get money for the LDCs [Less Developed Countries]." That term, itself, has evolved as part of "political correctness." and is now "the Global South."

But this instrument has never been straightforward, in part because of the sense among many US political leaders and constituencies that foreign aid is a giveaway of precious American financial assets.[37] Thus the Foreign Assistance Act (rarely renewed in its entirety) was and is larded with a large number of conditions or hoops that recipients have to jump through to get help. At one point in the Kennedy office, I counted eighty-seven statutory or procedural hoops, with all sorts of US domestic-interest groups wanting (for good or ill) to get their oar in, often in an effort to project American "values" onto others. This practice continues today. It is no wonder that the use of foreign aid has been so lacking in coherence over the years, along with its administration by the various agencies and its numerous various types, ranging from foreign military assistance (a major Pentagon instrument) to economic and social aid of the "purest" sort. And thus it will no doubt continue to be.[38]

I also by then had become a champion of the United States Information Agency (USIA) and its representation abroad, the US Information Service (USIS), as what I believed was an invaluable means of promoting, as accurately as possible, a view abroad of the nature of American society, warts and all. Most foreign visitors on these US government-sponsored programs, who are allowed to choose what to do, where to go, and whom to see, learn that the "warts" are the exception, not the rule. Early in my career, beginning in London (and elsewhere in the world throughout it, from Germany to Georgia), I started to lecture for USIS and came to understand its value. I coined a maxim that Foreign Service Officers represent the policies of the US government abroad, whereas USIS officers "represent the American people," even though both sets of officers worked out of the same building (the embassy) and under the local authority of the ambassador. The distinction was almost always understood by foreign nationals, and thus through USIS attention and support were gained for the United States (and the American "way of life") that otherwise would not have been possible for regular diplomats.

USIA's merger into State in 1999 was thus a great loss, as information and education officers know that their career paths depend on not rocking the boat with top State officials and US foreign policy positions. USIA should be resuscitated as an independent agency, although today it would be of less value in many parts of the world, in view of the growth of international communications and travel. But it won't happen.[39]

As my career and experience advanced, I increasingly came to understand the difficulties within the US government of integrating the instruments of power and influence. Much of the problem is interagency competition and bargaining, and efforts to get as big a piece of the budget pie as possible. In Vietnam, the United States did try economic projects in parallel with military fighting, but it was never large enough to be very effective[40] and, given the nature of the war—essentially with the heavy appeal of anti-colonialism on the communist side—it probably would never have been effective, as has so proved elsewhere in American experience, from the Philippines (1898–1913) to Afghanistan and Iraq.

Throughout my time in government, competition among agencies (and functions) for money has been a central issue. There is no need to rehearse the many complexities of budgets, especially for the Defense and State Departments, other than to say that the relative size has always (in my time in government, and at least after the Cold War) been grossly imbalanced to serve the nation's overall interests, with the military gaining so much of the overall budget that a good deal of diplomacy (and other instruments, like foreign aid) have been short-changed and at times even crippled.[41] Unfortunately, diplomacy (and foreign aid) have no natural political constituencies on Capitol Hill or in the private sector—resources to buy things in individual members' districts—so the contest is always uneven. There is no easy fix, unless a president is prepared to take on the entrenched interests, which has proved beyond any president's capacity to do.

Sometimes the Defense Department is prepared to help. Thus Secretary of Defense Robert Gates transferred some funds to State from the foreign assistance budget, but these were always a pittance. Also, just before he left the Department, he proposed (2014) that each NATO ally spend at least two percent of its GDP on the military. Even though that was adopted as a goal at the 2014 Wales NATO summit, only a fraction of the allies have met that goal, and all will not have met it by the 2024 target date. Of course, this proposal was popular with Congress, which has difficultly computing inputs and outputs—that is, how much money is spent on the military (and other foreign policy inputs) results in how much security, writ large; and it is easy for members of Congress and even presidents (notably Donald Trump) to claim that allies are getting a "free ride."[42] Ironically, when this test is applied to Central European allies, at least up to the Russian invasion of Ukraine in 2022, it ran counter to an approach we adopted when I was at NATO: to get these countries to spend less on military forces and more on economic and political development, also important elements (if not moreso) of security" in Europe. Instead, I have long supported a goal of three percent of GDP per European ally (at least in the richer West), with much of that going to non-military instruments, especially economic, social, and political development in Central Europe (including Ukraine). There have been no takers in US administrations or on Capitol Hill.

A further limitation on the State Department's capacity to be a competitor in developing and integrating instruments of power and influence stems from its training and promotion processes. In the US military, each serving officer can expect to spend about one-third of his or her career in some form of formal education; the figure is far less at State. Further, while the State Department does superb work in the craft of diplomacy, as a rule there is inadequate training in the area of strategic thinking, the framework for diplomacy. Indeed, the "clearance" process of policy recommendations within State usually just files off the rough edges of prior proposals from the bowels of the Department, yet often these "rough edges" provide useful creativity and strategic analysis. In addition, State's personnel promotion system inordinately relies on the nature of annual performance reviews, which contain much subjectivity.[43] I also discovered over the years that one of the best ways for a young Foreign Service Officer to gain career advancement was to latch on to a senior "high flyer" and rise with him or her, on the basis of propinquity. This may be a problem in all professional career structures, and no doubt also occurs in the military, but a lot of talent in the State Department and Foreign Service is lost thereby, because "go along to get along" is encouraged too much.

When issues and ideas then were passed on to the NSC interagency process, I discovered that the State Department regularly came up short. In fact, sometimes in preparing materials for President Carter, I would be in touch with relatively junior State Department officers (e.g., office director or even desk-officer levels) to find out what ideas would best serve the president. I was often told of good ideas that these officers said they had put into drafts of briefing papers destined for the White House, but which then were cut out at upper levels.[44] I would then take the best of them and put those into briefing papers actually going to the president!

I learned both at the NSC and later at NATO that the crafts of diplomacy and strategic thinking are not the same, and few people are able to do both well; further, in the Foreign Service, the latter too often gets sacrificed to the former, in terms of State's focus on what is considered as its more important task (diplomacy).

At times, State is also let down by its formal training process, centered on the Foreign Service Institute (FSI).[45] One of its most useful devices was called the Senior Seminar, which for a few months brought together FSOs ranked just below ambassador level, to work collaboratively on issues across the board and to bring different national and regional perspectives together. But for budgetary reasons the Senior Seminar was eliminated more than a decade ago. Additionally, a recent FSI director also killed courses in regional affairs, thus depriving trainees of the chance to see how issues needed to be dealt with across a region and not just country-specific applications. Proper leadership could deal with all these problems.

As part of my education and government experience, I also learned about some other gaps in the adequate understanding and analysis of different elements of power and influence. Thus, when I was Lead Consultant to the Kissinger Commission on Central America (1983–1984), one of my duties was to assemble lists of people to testify to the Commission and also to research political and security issues related to the region, I was surprised to learn that, while there was copious literature on economic and political issues, there was none on Central America's strategic significance to the United States. In choosing people to testify before the Commission, I thus sought out some officials and experts—few and far between—who could fill in the gaps: just what did developments in these countries mean to the United States, notably other than competition with Cuban and Soviet influence, and widespread fear of that from communist and other left-wing ideologies? Political attitudes tended to split along ideological lines and there was little conversation across these divisions.

At that time, I also got a fiery baptism in the "take no prisoners" attitude, especially from some right-wing officials, among whom UN ambassador Jeanne Kirkpatrick was as prominent, forceful, and at times vindictive as any of them. She saw her task as making sure the Kissinger Commission would produce nothing that did not conform to her own vision of Latin America and the region's communist inroads. At one point, when I had invited the US ambassador to Pakistan to testify (he also had a lot of Central American experience), I had to rescue his diplomatic career once Kirkpatrick set her gunsights on getting rid of him. Later, Kirk O'Donnell, key aide to House Speaker Tip O'Neill, tried to put together a small bipartisan group, composed of appointees by the four Democratic and Republican leaders of the two congressional chambers, for the purpose of examining Central America. Kirkpatrick killed the project, telling O'Donnell it was in part to keep O'Neill from appointing me.[46]

The issue of the integration of instruments of power and influence became central with the end of the Cold War. Many American analysts and political leaders became convinced that the collapse of the Soviet Union would necessarily give the United States greater influence in international affairs but if it chose, also the ability to be less engaged abroad. I soon became less certain that we could continue to "call most of the shots," for two reasons. First, during the Cold War, America's allies had had to shelter under the wing of US power and purpose because of the patent threat from Soviet power and communism; but with the collapse of the Soviet Union and its Central European satellites, along with its history of perpetuating European communism, America's allies no longer needed to look to the United States for protection against a major threat. They were thus in a position to make decisions more according to other factors and didn't need almost automatically to "cut the US slack" when in disagreement with things Washington did (for instance, as they had done during the Vietnam War). Of course, there were exceptions, and thus, even before relations with Russia went sour and well before Putin's aggression against Ukraine (beginning in 2014 and escalating in 2022), the European allies continued to understand that only the United States could deal with Russian power. They continued to look to Washington for leadership in this area (and still do, even moreso in the wake of Putin's prolonged aggression against

Ukraine) although with some differences of view within the Alliance. This factor largely explains why the allies supported the United States after 9/11,[47] and also sent troops into Afghanistan: it was not for fear of terrorism at home (which did occur, but was never a serious threat), but rather to make sure that the United States would not become so preoccupied with the Global War on Terrorism that it would forget about its leadership in coping with Russia, especially under Vladimir Putin.

Second, with so much of international politics "let loose" and "in play," the United States, still *primus inter pares*, needed to reexamine not just its interests in the world but also the instruments for pursuing these interests. These were not only military but also the full range of non-military instruments. Adjustment to utilizing both these factors was done imperfectly in the United States, in both the public and private sectors. Not only was there overall less interest, but also, habits are hard to overcome, especially with the bureaucratic practice of worst-case analysis having become so central to much American thinking, both in and out of government.[48] Thus, in a personally memorable moment, a group of the nation's leading experts on Europe met one morning in 1989 at one of the Washington think tanks to consider political rumblings in Central and Eastern Europe. Many predictions were made, but none of us suggested that the Berlin Wall might open. And the group's ignoring of that possibility was right—for four whole hours (November 9, 1989)!

This incident and others like it illustrate the inertia of expectations and behavior, such as in the Cold War which had provided a central organizing principle for so much of global politics (certainly for the United States). This inertia was hard to overcome and it was difficult for many people in and out of government to adjust to the need to think more broadly. Indeed, even before Putin began rattling sabers and China began accelerating its military/naval activities and major economic outreach, many members of leading research organizations in the United States, as well as in the US government could not think of competition with Russia and China except in cold-war terms—a major failing. At the time of this writing (2023), the war in Ukraine has virtually set in stone US (and some European) perceptions of lasting confrontation with Russia, with all of its risks and rigidities, however that war turns out. While Putin is most to blame for bringing about this situation of cold-war mentality, virtually no one in the United States has been thinking about the problem of dealing with a Russia that almost inevitably will again be a major factor in trying to fashion any long-run strategic stability in Europe that is not just based on zero-sum attitudes and actions. Among other things, if this proves to be the future, hopes in the United States of being able to lessen major, costly military engagement in Europe in order to focus far more on China will go a-glimmering. Perhaps there will be no other viable alternative. But paucity of strategic thinking, intellectual and psychological inertia and difficulties in breaking analytical habits of extending the present into the indefinite future, will limit US flexibility in critical aspects of its foreign policy.

My own definition of "cold war" is both simple and direct: a situation in which it becomes difficult if not impossible to separate out areas between us (country X) and "hostile" country Y, where there can be accommodation in our interests, from those areas where there cannot be, because of security and at times some other interests. Thus the idea exists that a relationship, for instance with China, can be a mixture of "competitive when it should be, collaborative when it can be, and adversarial when it must be."[49] While analytically valid, this methodology is difficult to apply in practice, especially due to the habits of mind that emerged at the time of Pearl Harbor and that have never been entirely outgrown. Indeed, the United States has historically been one of the few countries with difficulty thinking and acting in such a complex, nuanced fashion but tends to default to "adversarial"— perhaps the penalty of historically having had so much power in the world from the moment of its total engagement and, save for the nuclear balance with the Soviet Union, so few direct threats to its homeland. (9/11, while of immense psychological impact in the United States, was strategically insignificant.) Further, a country like China is unlikely to comprehend America publicly espousing such an almost naïve, three-part proposition as-noted above—good in the classroom, perhaps, but hard if not impossible to apply to a comprehensive set of policies and hence to diplomacy.

Following my time at NATO and while at the RAND Corporation, I put together a project on integration of tools of power and influence, which included many top experts and senior former officials both civilian and military (US and European), and co-chaired it with a former SACEUR, Gen. George Joulwan, and a former US ambassador to several posts (especially in the Middle East), Edward "Skip" Gnehm.[50] It was a root-and-branch survey of the many tools available to the United States—from political, economic, military, cultural, and public, private, and NGO sectors— covering how they do and should relate to one another, the process needed both to blend them into a whole and to make strategic judgments, and the means for introducing this process most effectively into the "interagency process," beyond what existed at that time. Little of this study was ever implemented, but either it or some similar analysis is very much needed now, especially after the "process" shambles of the Trump administration. One casualty of the post-Cold War limitations on strategic analysis and planning in the US government and think tanks is that such systematic efforts as have been made following the end of the Cold War remain inadequate for the need.

The integration of instruments of power and influence of course needs a process. Learning from my four years on the Carter NSC Staff, first as lead for Europe and then for the Middle East, my experience is that the center for so-called policymaking—and certainly for strategic direction and integration—has to be close to the president, at the NSC level.[51] Put simply, none of the individual agencies—notably State and Defense (civilian and military), or others like Treasury (and now Homeland Security)—can be the locus of this effort. The purview of none of them is adequate and, in institutional terms, none of these agencies would sit still for "their" issues to be adjudicated anywhere except in "neutral territory;" that means close to the president in the White House, including the central role of the National Security Advisor and his or her staff. Some administrations have tried different arrangements, sometimes under the guise of so-called cabinet government, but all these efforts have failed and would continue to do so. It is, as I have argued, an "iron law."[52] The Secretary of State can and should be the president's chief diplomat (the NSC Advisor should in almost all situations keep their hands off diplomacy or there will be confusion, including in the outside world), but he or she can't be the chief "policy-maker."[53]

In summary, the work of the National Security Council staff (from the National Security Advisor downward) has four essential parts: 1) to keep the president informed of what he (or someday, she) needs to know, yet not overload him with information—a fine art; 2) tasking the bureaucracy to analyze issues and policies and present them, within the NSC structure, for recommendations to the president along with any dissenting views; 3) coordinating the making of policy, from strategy to tactics, but in day-to-day operations only when interagency cooperation is required; and 4) checking, when the president has made a decision, on whether the bureaucracy has carried it out (not always a sure thing).

This system also implies that there is, in the White House (NSC staff), a capacity for genuine strategic thinking, which has been true in several administrations but unfortunately for many years not to the degree needed. Presidents need to take this point most seriously, and not appoint anyone to lead at the NSC who does not have a keen strategic sense. Each agency will also have a policy-planning staff, but these tend to be skewed in their work toward their own instrument (diplomacy, military, economics, et al.), and for many years the State Department's Policy Planning Staff has not been up to snuff.[54]

A further requirement of a functional system, as I learned on the Carter NSC staff, is to keep that staff small, including a mix of career officers (civilian and military) seconded from agencies, plus outside experts. Under Carter, the NSC staff had fewer than seventy people, all-told; it subsequently ballooned, until by the G.W. Bush, Obama, and Trump administrations it had as many as 600 people (though that number also included staff working on Department of Homeland Security issues). The virtue of a small staff is that each regional or function-based officer has to think broadly, across countries and often also across regions. The more staff members, the narrower their individual purview and the less chance there is for strategically relating and structuring decisions. By contrast, on a small and well-functioning NSC staff, its members learn how to "think presidentially," in other words how to present analysis and choices to the president that are worthy of his job description.[55] Otherwise, a president may find himself or herself "all at sea" on occasion. Again, this is an iron law of management.

A well-run NSC System also has to include the political side of the White House, and there is proven value in informal meetings of the president with the top few of his cabinet-level foreign policy and national security teams (about four or five people), such as regular breakfast or lunch meetings in the Cabinet Room; the president cannot permit himself to become a prisoner of the system, especially on difficult or sensitive matters. This worked well in the Carter administration. Further, depending on the president's style, he should get regular (daily under Carter) brief reports on his top advisors' activities and perspectives. These often can lead to presidential decisions, especially in a crisis. Indeed the better the NSC system functions, operates, and builds trust among all its members, the easier it is to short-circuit the process when need be to deal with a crisis, without confusion for all other issues.

Often neglected is the role of Congress; although this is the White

House's job (from the president on down), each agency will also have its congressional liaison office. Further, staff of key agencies need to be trained in understanding the congressional perspective (or perspectives).[56]

Of course in the execution of policy, different agencies will take the lead, depending on objectives and tools used to achieve them. Diplomacy is the State Department's business although of necessity all actions in the field will involve diplomacy with counterparts in other nations. A useful tool is the secondment of personnel from one agency to others, as well as career training in each agency on the perspectives of others. The more that can be done without reference back to the NSC interagency system, the better. But this delegation needs to be done wisely. Over time, in every administration, "practice makes 'less imperfect'." Naturally, experience and mutual trust within the government are key elements of success.

Communications and Control

In the history of diplomacy that is conducted not just *in situ*, countries have to consider the means whereby their chosen diplomats and other representatives abroad communicate with home capitals. In days when communications were primitive by today's standards, that required giving diplomats sent abroad to take care of the nation's business either through tightly-written instructions or trust in their judgment (e.g., the ambassadors'), within a broad mandate, to convey a good sense both of the nation's interests and objectives, and of their chief executive's thinking—in the US case, the president. The US was well served, for example, by Thomas Jefferson, Benjamin Franklin, John Adams, and James Monroe.[57]

These qualities were particularly important before the transatlantic (and transpacific) cables and other means of rapidly conveying instructions. Thus supposedly, US diplomat Nicholas Trist, sent to Guadalupe to negotiate the end of the war with Mexico (1847–1848), considered himself on a long leash and, going beyond what President Polk had asked him to do, worked out an agreement with the Mexican representatives and brought the result back to Washington.[58] The president had no choice but to accept what already had been done and sent the resulting document to the Senate which ratified it as the Treaty of Guadalupe Hidalgo. A better-known example of the consequences caused by lack of rapid communications was the 1814 Treaty of Ghent which ended the War of 1812.[59] The negotiators (the US team was led by John Quincy Adams) worked out a deal on Christmas Eve and sent the result to their two capitals, the British ratifying it on

December 30th. But the fact that peace had been concluded did not reach Washington (and then New Orleans) in time to avert the major battle on January 10, 1815, thus quite useless in those terms, although the victory did launch Andrew Jackson's political career.[60]

For diplomacy to be effective, it is essential that a government (I reference the United States for this purpose) be able to keep its negotiating strategies and tactics from the opposite number's sight. Of course, there can be "false flags"—e.g., leaks to the public—designed to mislead an opponent, but over the long term these can impose costs: effectiveness of diplomacy also depends on credibility and that means a high level of trust that what is conveyed is indeed authentic.

The control of information (and reporting) in diplomacy has become more difficult with advances in technology. When I worked in the Johnson White House, a transatlantic phone call was a rarity for most Americans. I did discover that in the nuclear age there was a dedicated phone line from the White House to #10 Downing Street,[61] and also the Blue Line to the Elysée Palace. (This was a year after the creation of a hotline between Washington and the Kremlin, which was actually a teleprinter.) Most communications with US missions abroad were by "cable," the name that is still used for formal communications, although the technology has changed radically. Thus, when I worked at the NSC during the Carter administration, it was relatively easy for the State Department and White House to keep communications more or less under control. (I would note that the Defense Department, and the military in general, had their own means of rapid communication.) It was also rare in those days for communications to US missions abroad not to go through a formal process, with clearances, including at the NSC level, even for all but the most routine State Department cables. Then and now, all are always signed with a single word: the name of the Secretary of State (or acting secretary), which authenticates the cables and, when appropriate, can commit the nation to a course of action. (The same is true of cables signed out from a mission abroad going back to the State Department. The ambassador's name goes at the bottom.) No ambassador worth his or her salt will commit the US government to another government without that official confirmation: woe betide an ambassador who goes off on his or her own and something goes wrong!

This is not just about keeping control and coherence over policy and diplomacy but is also a matter of human nature. In foreign policy and diplomacy, and generally, all other aspects of governance (as well as in human life), the craft is conducted by people with the full range of human emotions. Jealousy, beyond competitiveness, is certainly one of those emotions and there is always someone in Washington waiting to pounce on an ambassador who "gets off the reservation," so to speak; or others who believe that "I could have done a better job." These people are not in the majority, but there are enough to make an ambassador's life difficult—especially an ambassador who has been successful! The problem is particularly acute at State where, unlike many other domestic agencies, there is a narrow pyramid leading upward to the secretary, or at least to the small number of people on the seventh floor. Further, the jealousies are especially intense when an ambassador is a political appointee as opposed to being a career officer. It is up to the secretary, and if need be, the president, to try and keep this from getting in the way of US policy and diplomacy.

I noted this in one special way, in the realm of communications. For many Foreign Service Officers as they climb the career tree, knowledge is power in the sense that it is a precious commodity, kept close to the vest and shared only when there is some advantage. Thus, during the time I was at NATO, one key roving ambassador almost never reported his activities in cables, but communicated by phone back to Washington, and that, on a selective basis where it would do him the most good personally. At NATO, this caused us problems on a regular basis and was recognized as such by all of my colleagues. By contrast, I discovered that the military with whom I worked were exactly the opposite: senior US military officers would share virtually everything with their foreign counterparts; knowledge was not a "good" to be hoarded and traded. My insight: that with the military, if you don't share information, there is risk that someone will get killed!

While I was at NATO, even when I would work out something informally with an allied ambassador, I made it clear that I would never make such proceedings official until I had a piece of paper (a cable) either backing me up, or instructing otherwise! This was how the NATO French ambassador and I worked out a major departure in France's relationship to NATO in July 1993: I proposed that the United States would remove its objections to a major role for France in the Western European Union, a French desire, but which was opposed by the "keep control" people in Washington who wanted only NATO to be important, long after that made any practical sense. This was provided that France would move back toward full membership in the military side of the Alliance, from which President De Gaulle had withdrawn in 1967. Both governments subsequently blessed our initiative,[62] In what proved to be a major development at NATO.

As time went on, the telephone became a regular channel of communication, including secure phone calls on the so-called STU (Secure Telephone Unit), so both reporting from the field to Washington and issuing instruction often used that means. But ambassadors have to be careful about who is giving the instructions, not only whether they have authority to do so but, at the same time, whether some negotiations are moving so rapidly that waiting for a cable would be too slow or there is a need for flexibility that can only be judged adequately on site While I was at NATO, however, when a negotiation with fifteen allies was underway (in this instance, on Bosnia), it was almost always with some underlying cable-sanctioned policy in place.[63]

USNATO may be unique among US missions. The US Mission to the United Nations, for example, is in the same time zone as Washington, is only a short flight away, and has an active American press corps nearby. The UN ambassador and his or her mission in New York City thus tend to be kept on a tight leash, even though in some administrations the UN ambassador is also a member of the president's cabinet.[64]

I also learned during my tour of duty on the National Security Council staff that there were different processes of conducting diplomacy with other countries, depending on who they were and importance of the issue. In general, the less important the country is to the United States (!), the greater the latitude the US ambassador had to work with levels of the State Department below the seventh floor, which is where the secretary and his or her immediate team work. There would still be cables sanctioning policy, but without a lot of interference by senior people.

But that was not true, in particular, in our working with the "big three" governments, Britain, France, and Germany. Many of the key negotiations and other interactions (e.g., on major security issues) were done directly between senior officials in the respective capitals, often by phone and without involving the local ambassadors directly. The rule, however, was that the US embassies in London, Paris, and Bonn would be kept informed, in order that there would be no glitches or embarrassments. Of course, at times the US president would talk on the phone directly to his European counterparts, especially in London, Paris, or Bonn, and the same practice was true regarding other regions. Thus if President Clinton were on the phone, say, with the French president, I would be on another line taking notes. I would then write a memo to make sure that the other players in Washington knew what had been discussed and agreed, and also dictated a cable for State to dispatch to the US ambassador in Paris.

There was (and is) a lot of travel back and forth for diplomacy, which has added its own complications. Most notorious, perhaps, was when President Wilson spent months at the Paris Peace Conference in 1919, certainly a factor for the US Senate in later rejecting US membership in the League of Nations. Decisions taken at the head of state and government level on issues of the moment remained a rarity for many years, with the World War II summits being most notable exceptions, all of which left at least some questions in their wake; the Yalta conference of February 1945 is still being debated eight decades later. For regular diplomats, summits are generally seen as a curse, with the chance that a president will go off on his own, or when he meets with his foreign counterparts with only interpreters present (when needed), with doubts arising as to what was actually discussed and, more important, agreed upon.[65] Most notable, perhaps, was the 2018 Helsinki summit meeting between Presidents Trump and Putin. It is still not known, beyond the people who were actually present (the two leaders and two interpreters), what was discussed and agreed, and it can fairly be said that the subsequent joint press confidence was a shambles, haunted US-Russian relations and sidetracked useful ideas that the two leaders had informally agreed to between them. In process terms, the fact of President Trump not having a third party present or not at least debriefing, say, the secretary of state immediately afterward, made him grist for the mill of American media who were only interested in showing Trump in a bad light. There was a lesson here that Trump should have been taught: the media travelling with presidents abroad are not from the State Department, with a background in foreign policy, but from the White House, with their domestic political interests and agendas. Thus at the Madrid NATO summit in July 1997, one of the most consequential ever, all the questions that President Clinton got at his post-summit press conference with the US media were related to domestic issues, especially *l'affaire* Monica Lewinsky—to Clinton's obvious frustration! (This example is another argument for minimizing summit meetings.)

In general, no president is able to master much more than the headlines of the issues under discussion at a summit meeting (some, like Richard Nixon, Jimmy Carter, Bill Clinton, and George H.W. Bush, have done better than others), and regular diplomats often have to "clean up the mess," even going to the length of comparing notes with their opposite numbers.[66] That happened to me with Carter's second foreign visitor to the White House, Canada's Prime Minister Pierre Trudeau. Afterward, his notetaker, a senior diplomat, and I compared our notes. On a couple of points, our notes disagreed significantly. He said that "Trudeau surely didn't mean that, so I will put it in the record the way he would have meant!" This was a lesson for me in diplomacy-craft.

In general there is in fact an effort by seasoned diplomats and policy people to leave open only an item or two in a pre-negotiated final communiqué to be agreed upon at a summit meeting, so that the president can be seen to have made his mark by putting a few finishing touches on diplomacy carried out at lower levels. For professional diplomats, there is no liking for the invention of jet aircraft, and the media tend to inflate the significance of summit meetings.

By contrast, however, many complex negotiations can only be undertaken by getting diplomats (or experts) from different countries together in the same room. Sometimes this is done formally and regularly (e.g., for arms control and other negotiations in Geneva or Vienna), and sometimes spontaneously on an ad hoc basis. This is particularly true at NATO, where the number and breadth of negotiations on subjects below those of major issues means that meetings have to go on all the time. During my time there, these included cooperation on arms standardization, budgets, relations among national military procurement agencies, and a hundred other housekeeping matters, some quite important but where only the experts could do the job, and without any need for interference by me as ambassador, but all within an agreed framework of cooperation. Thus, when I was at NATO, we averaged more than 7,000 official visitors per year from Washington, and in almost all cases there was nothing of sufficient political (as opposed to functional) significance to require formal cables. Without these kinds of arrangements, NATO (for one) could not function.

The exception for many US embassies is with an agency represented abroad that is involved in key political and security matters and wants the ability to communicate directly and independently back to its home base in Washington, including analyses of what was happening in a host country. Most important are intelligence agencies. I did not have any such personnel at NATO, but savvy ambassadors who do have them will usually not try to interfere with independent reporting and rather will only ask to be copied on whatever is transmitted. Once that ambassadorial authority is established, it rarely (I am told by ambassador-level colleagues) has to be invoked. When an intelligence agency is involved in operations on an ambassador's turf, however, that is another matter. The same is also true where there are US military commands and personnel present in the ambassador's country. Working out arrangements there are often more difficult. But an ambassador who is not kept in the loop either by intelligence agencies or the military is likely to see trouble for US foreign policy at some point and compromise of the ambassador's authority as the president's in-country representative. At NATO, my working closely with the military, whether on my staff, the next-door US Military Representative to NATO,[67] or the Supreme Allied Commander Europe (SACEUR), was daily fare; but both formal and practical arrangements would have been worked out successfully long before I went to Brussels, and I made sure that my relations with US military elements were high on my list of priorities.[68]

Over the years, the increasing ease of foreign travel has also led to the growth, in numbers far greater than the State Department's, of personnel from Washington agencies who are stationed at embassies abroad. Embassy London probably has fifty or more such on-the-spot permanent representations which deal with just about every function of government. (At NATO when I was ambassador, we had only State, Defense both civilian and military, and the United States Information Service until it was disbanded, plus from time to time someone from the Federal Emergency Management Agency, since natural disasters are also an important area of allied cooperation. In a mission as small as mine with about 120 personnel, all of whom because of security concerns were US citizens (no foreign nationals worked there other than as drivers), keeping control over communications was relatively easy. Further, with my Washington experience, I had thought about the problem of leaks and end-runs, either back-channel to Washington or to reporters. I thus kept my top staff completely informed of all that was going on, to give them ownership of issues, and also to give everyone and every element at the mission—State and Defense, civilian and military—a fair hearing before I made a decision, and moreover to develop team loyalty; in my four and a half years as NATO ambassador, we never had a leak. Senior staff from, say, the uniformed military, when they got push-back from the Pentagon about a decision I had made (or recommended formally to Washington), which the Washington-based military did not like, could at least say that they had the opportunity to make their case with me.

Related to travel is also the temptation of some national security advisors and even some of his or her staff to get directly involved in diplomacy.[69] Some is unavoidable, given the expectation by many foreign governments of having contacts with the center of power, namely the US president and his immediate entourage in the White House. When this works well, there will be interagency representation (beginning with State Department), except in the most limited interactions between the president and a foreign counterpart. But many national security advisors are also tempted to travel themselves and often without State Department representation (other than to make housekeeping arrangements), even though keeping State (and other agencies) fully informed is important, if only to prevent some form of retaliation. Thus, for example, during the Carter administration, almost all negotiations over Euromissiles (and the neutron bomb) were conducted by travelling parties of a few senior officials, usually consisting of the Assistant Secretary of State for Europe and me as NSC staff lead for Europe—denominated for this purpose (as also our three European counterparts) as US Political Director and Deputy Political Director. At the time, the method worked, because it was "State lead, but NSC included." We had a good personal relationship, and we made sure that everyone in Washington who needed to be engaged was engaged. That is not always true.

In general, however, problems can arise if the national security advisor himself or herself travels abroad, unless with the secretary of state and (always) with the president. There is potential for crossed wires, even with close personal relations between the national security advisor and the secretary of state, given that there is always some institutional tension, no matter the relations, at the top. And foreign governments may come to wonder where the locus of policy and diplomatic influence really is in Washington: at State, or also (or only) in the White House. In my time in the Carter administration, I saw both the good and bad of this, which at the time was not just about the much-discussed tensions between two senior cabinet-level officials.

All these arrangements relating to communications and control have become much more difficult in the age of digital technology and media saturation (including so-called social media). There continues to be a need for embassies/missions abroad, plus their "home bases" in the United States, both organized formally through the State Department, to deal directly with one another. Communications possibilities have proliferated, and many are useful, especially as informal channels for trying out ideas. And whether secure or otherwise, more than just cables and phone calls, but also email and social media like Twitter, Facebook, and others, are all possibilities today.[70]

The video conference, including classified, also has now become a staple means of interacting, creating further temptations for people both in Washington and in US missions abroad to bypass the more cumbersome cable route. But as with informal phone calls this new medium also creates inherent and potentially serious problems in potentially committing the United States to a course of action, even though people who follow this informal practice in lieu of authorized channels will claim that speed is of the essence.[71] In particular, as head of mission, an ambassador may not know all he or she needs to know about what is being said back and forth to Washington; the same is true for communications of the State Department and other agencies in Washington to US representatives abroad.

In recent years especially, staff at the National Security Council have become increasingly involved in reaching out directly to US personnel serving abroad (leaving aside direct communications with foreign governments). Risk of serious confusion is the inevitable result, as well as a loss of control by Washington on what US foreign policy and diplomacy" actually are. There may be no easy way around what is a serious problem, except for rigorous observation of rules within each mission abroad— rules mandated both by ambassadors and the home agencies—as well as controls on Washington-based personnel. As noted elsewhere, with the dramatic rise in the number of NSC staff personnel, the temptations to use these uncontrolled means of communication tend to increase, even leading to informal instructions from NSC staff, a practice that can do nothing but cause trouble. Presidents and agency heads need to lay down the law with subordinates, but it is probably a lost cause.

Finally, this discussion has been designed to show that for the United States, meeting the challenges in today's and tomorrow's world will require a complex set of understandings, ranging from analysis of changes taking place in power configurations, to comprehensive strategic thinking about US interests, values, and their interaction, to creation or adaptation of methodologies for adequately addressing challenges, to integrating different tools of action, to placing the US role in the world and choices related thereto in the context of domestic politics, to organizing the government (including a proper role for Congress and the private sector) for effectiveness, and intelligence, vision, and finally, to competence of the Chief Executive and his or her team. The demands will be greater than at any other time since at least the end of the Cold War and entail, potentially more than at any other time in its history, America's full, ineluctable and permanent engagement in the outside world.

Notes

1. President George H.W. Bush. Address to the citizens of Mainz, May 31, 1989, Rheingoldhalle. Mainz, Federal Republic of Germany. Accessed at: https://usa.usembassy.de/etexts/ga6–890531.htm

2. See Robert E. Hunter, "Toward NATO Enlargement: The Role of USNATO," in Daniel S. Hamilton and Kristina Spohr, eds., *Open Door: NATO and Euro-Atlantic Security After the Cold War*, PDF (Washington: Paul H. Nitze School of Advanced International Studies, Johns Hopkins University, 2019), ch. 14, *passim*. Accessed and downloadable at: https://transatlanticrelations.org/wp-content/uploads/2019/04/14-Hunter.pdf.

3. It has never been clear, then or since, precisely what the phrase "number one" means or what essential elements are involved.

4. The period I call here the US "holiday from history," was between "the two 9/11s." Europeans write dates the opposite way from us. Their "9/11" (November 9) was the day the Berlin Wall opened; ours (September 11) witnessed the terrorist attacks in New York, the Pentagon in Washington, D.C., and the plane crash at Shanksville, Pennsylvania.

5. Given the multitudinous responses to 9/11, which are continuing, it is clear that the most consequential figure in the twenty-first century so far was Osama bin Laden.

6. US Congress, "Uniting and Strengthening America by Providing Appropriate Tools Required to Intercept and Obstruct Terrorism Act of 2001 (USA Patriot Act)," 26 Oct., 2001, Public Law 107–56. PDF. Accessed at: https://www.congress.gov/107/plaws/publ56/PLAW-107publ56.pdf.

7. The analog was the ignoring of those people—I was not among them at the time—who accurately warned that the Vietnam War was less about communism than about anti-colonialism, thus making it a war that was unwinnable. In general, the United States had learned nothing from the French experience in Indochina. It was only later, about 1967, that the anti-war movement took significant shape.

8. These have included the Institute for Strategic Studies (now IISS), the Overseas Development Council, the Center for Strategic and International Studies, the RAND Corporation, the National Defense University, and the Johns Hopkins (SAIS) Center for Transatlantic Relations.

9. I have also traveled to more than ninety countries; made several thousand speeches and lectures; done more than a thousand radio and television appearances; and written about 1,500 publications—all mostly on foreign policy and defense. I have played a senior policy role, mostly foreign policy but also domestic policy, in eight presidential campaigns, and written speeches for more serious candidates campaigning for US president than anyone else in US history, including three presidents and four vice presidents.

10. Aristotle, *Nicomachean Ethics*, translated by W.D. Ross, digital reprint PDF (Kitchener: Batoche Books Ltd., 1999), 181. Accessed at: https://socialsciences.mcmaster.ca/econ/ugcm/3ll3/aristotle/Ethics.pdf.

11. In 1968, Anna Chennault was the go-between linking the Nixon presidential campaign and the South Vietnamese Embassy, urging the Saigon

government to block progress at the Paris peace talks, with the promise that the South Vietnam government would get a better deal under a Nixon presidency. President Johnson learned about it from intercepted communications, but he and democratic presidential candidate Hubert Humphrey decided not to go public with the information, which might have tipped the election. What Chennault did was very likely treason.

12. Richard M. Nixon, "Asia After Vietnam," *Foreign Affairs*, October 1967. Accessed at: https://www.foreignaffairs.com/articles/united-states/1967–10–01/asia-after-viet-nam.

13. The most prominent people for whom Senator Kennedy secured exit visas from the Soviet Union, by direct appeal to Chairman Leonid Brezhnev during our April 1974 visit to Moscow, were cellist Mstislav Rostropovich and his wife.

14. Years later, when I was in charge of Middle East matters on the National Security Council staff, the deputy minister of the Israeli government in charge of *Aliyah* (in effect, meaning "in-migration") visited me and complained about how Jackson-Vanik was stifling the emigration of Jews from the Soviet Union to Israel. I expressed support for his position but said he should take up the matter with Senator Jackson's people!

15. While Russia would have preferred that no state in Central Europe would join NATO, it largely kept quiet about Poland and the Czech Republic for the reason noted here, just as it accepted that a unified Germany would join NATO, where the United States could keep an eye on it! West German Federal Chancellor Helmut Kohl had the same ambition. As I put it at the time, this generation of Germans wanted to make sure that their children and grandchildren could not repeat what their parents and grandparents had done.

16. See "Turkish Invasion of Cyprus," *Wikipedia.org*. Accessed at: https://en.wikipedia.org/wiki/Turkish_invasion_of_Cyprus.

17. A key moment for the League of Nations, which undercut its purposes and ultimately its role, was the failure to impose an embargo on shipments of oil to Italy after its 1935 invasion of Abyssinia (Ethiopia) until some limits were imposed, too late (1936). See "Failure of the League in Abyssinia," History, *Tutor2U.net* (Boston Spa: Tutor2U Ltd., 2002–2023), *passim*. Accessed at: https://www.tutor2u.net/history/reference/failure-of-the-league-in-abyssinia.

18. When, in 1976, I visited internationally-sanctioned Rhodesia with a colleague from Senator Kennedy's office (Bob Bates), we found that it was possible to buy just about anything in the shops in Salisbury that we could have bought in the US.

19. See Maurice Fitzpatrick, *John Hume in America : From Derry to DC* (South Bend: Notre Dame University Press, 2019).

20. See Jimmy Carter, "Northern Ireland Statement on US Policy," August 30, 1977, *The American Presidency Project*, Curators John Woolley and Gerhard

Peters (Santa Barbara: University of California at Santa Barbara, n.d.). Accessed at: https://www.presidency.ucsb.edu/documents/northern-ireland -statement-us-policy.

21. See "Good Friday Agreement," *Wikipedia.org*. Accessed at: https://en .wikipedia.org/wiki/Good_Friday_Agreement.

22. "In the councils of government, we must guard against the acquisition of unwarranted influence, whether sought or unsought, by the military industrial complex." Dwight D. Eisenhower, quoted from "Military-Industrial Complex Speech, Dwight D. Eisenhower, 1961," 17 January, 1961, in Papers of Dwight D. Eisenhower, *The Avalon Project: Documents in Law, History and Diplomacy*, Lillian Goldman Law Library, Yale Law School, Yale University, New Haven, CT (New Haven: Lillian Goldman Law Library, 2008). In the original text, mostly written by his brother, Milton, president of Johns Hopkins University, Eisenhower was preparing to say "military-industrial-congressional complex," but the word "congressional" was crossed out in the Teleprompter text just before he spoke. Xerox copies of that text were given out by President Eisenhower's granddaughter, Susan Eisenhower, at a fiftieth anniversary commemoration of the speech which I attended. Digital document speech excerpt accessed online at: https://avalon.law.yale.edu/twentieth_century /eisenhower001.asp.

23. The Egypt-Israeli conflict included a military balance that could have encouraged Egypt (that is, also the "Arabs" in general) to attack Israel at some point, as had happened in 1947, 1967, and 1973. Given the Soviet Union's ties to Syria and Egypt (per the latter, until Sadat expelled Soviet troops) and US ties to Israel, the conflict was a major locus of US-Soviet confrontation. With the Egypt-Israeli Peace Treaty, however, it was no longer credible for any combination of Arab states to pose a serious military threat to Israel (in this sense, various terrorist and other attacks are not as strategically "serious" as had been the 1967 and 1973 wars), thus the Cold War dimension of the Arab-Israeli conflict also collapsed, along with the principal strategic basis of US-Israeli relations from the US point of view.

24. https://www.youtube.com/watch?v=wRf1cdw4IAY.

25. Zbigniew Brzezinski, already slated to play a major role in a Carter presidency should Carter be elected, asked me in January 1976 to prepare a study on the history of US human rights policy; this was useful to Brzezinski in this helping to shape the practice of Carter's human rights commitments.

26. See "The Helsinki Final Act," at https://www.osce.org/helsinki-final-act. As I predicted at the time—indeed, had predicted as early as 1969 in a book titled *Security in Europe*what became the Helsinki Final Act had a major impact on bringing the Cold War to an end and also the collapse of the Soviet Union, though I did not foresee the latter. The tradeoff was, in effect, for the United States, finally to accept the Yalta Agreement of 1945—in short, that European

borders could not be changed by force—in exchange for penetration of the Soviet Union and the Eastern bloc states by ideas and information which ultimately were instrumental in "hollowing out" the communist states The Helsinki Final Act also represented the Soviet Union's partial acceptance of some commitments made at Yalta toward Eastern and Central Europe, which it had then soon violated. Notably, everyone in the Soviet Union could read Moscow's commitments in the Final Act on aspects of human rights because it was printed in its entirety beginning on the front page of *Pravda* (none of the US media did more than quote a few passages).

27. At one point, in 1996, fully half of all the time spent by uniformed members of the US Air Force based in Europe was on PFP missions.

28. See "National Endowment for Democracy," at https://www.ned.org/, *passim*. The other institutes were the Free Trade Union Institute, the National US Chamber Foundation; the International Republican Institute, and the National Democratic Institute, on whose board I once sat.

29. See "National Endowment for Democracy," at https://www.ned.org/, *passim*.

30. For a basic primer, derived from my experience on the Carter NSC staff, see my book, *Presidential Control of Foreign Policy: Management or Mishap? Washington Papers*, with a Foreword by Brent Scowcroft (Westport: Praeger, 1982), *passim*. Its principles and practices are basic management and thus relevant to any administration.

31. See, for instance, Nigel Hamilton*, FDR at War*, 3 volumes (New York: Harper-Collins, 2020), *passim*. Worth reading in any event.

32. See "Nassau Agreement," at Nassau Agreement—Wikipedia.

33. In the creation of a US second-strike nuclear deterrent—including competition between the Navy and the Air Force Minuteman—Polaris was the Navy's premier project and attracted many of the government's top civil servants: it was "the place to be." With Polaris safely established and successful, civil servants started moving to the next high-priority government program, NASA, following JFK's "moon shot" speech.

34. I discovered by the time I left the White House in May 1965 that virtually all of the senior officials working for Johnson who were deeply dedicated to the war—with some notable exceptions, such as George Ball, who was essentially isolated—had been appointed by President John Kennedy. Presumably, in order to enhance his own credibility and to have a good transition from an administration that had been cut short, Johnson stayed with the Kennedy foreign policy and national security team, which he sometimes referred to with hardly disguised distain as "my Harvards." Notably, at the time of the French battle at Dien Bien Phu in 1955, when Paris asked for US support, Eisenhower consulted the congressional leadership. A major voice arguing to keep out was, the then-Senate Majority Leader Lyndon Johnson! Of course,

after the 1968 election, Nixon and Kissinger prolonged the war another four years, which led to almost half of all American casualties, plus the bombing of Cambodia, letting loose that nation's instability that produced the slaughter of more than a million Cambodians by the Pol Pot regime. In the late 1970s, I had reason to be convinced that President Kennedy planned to escalate the Vietnam War, had he been reelected in 1964.

35. He, and thus I as well, were also involved in the North Atlantic Assembly, comprised of members of NATO parliaments, and travelled to its meetings and Europe; we also went to the Soviet Union in April 1974 which included a four-hour meeting with Leonid Brezhnev; in addition we met with top leaders in London, Paris, Bonn, Rome, Athens, Jerusalem, Cairo, Riyadh, Baghdad, Amman, Teheran, Geneva, Bucharest, Brussels, Vienna, Tbilisi, Lisbon, and Belgrade.

36. Thus even then I was working on the integration of different instruments of power and influence, in this case the European Economic Community and NATO.

37. Some public-opinion polling has put at the extreme, that fifty percent of the entire US government's budget goes for foreign aid, whereas the actual level is far less than one percent; even so, the US regularly ranks near the bottom among members of the Organization for Economic Cooperation and Development in percentage of GDP provided for foreign aid, and far below the internationally-agreed norm for Official Development Assistance of .7 percent of GDP. In the last complete accounts (2019), while the US is the largest single donor of Official Development Assistance, at $32.62 billion, in terms of Gross Domestic Product, it is placed only twenty-fifth of twenty-nine members of the Development Assistance Committee, at .16 percent. For more details, see "List of Development Aid Country Donors," *Wikipedia.org*. Accessed at: https://en.wikipedia.org/wiki/List_of_development_aid_country_donors#Net_official_development_assistance_by_donor.

38. The US Agency for International Development was narrowly saved from extinction in 1999, at the time that both the Arms Control and Disarmament Agency (ACDA) and the United States Information Agency (USIA) were merged into the State Department. Credit goes to USAID's director Brian Atwood who had close ties to President Clinton, and managed to thwart efforts by the chair of the Senate Foreign Relations Committee, Jesse Helms (R–NC), to put USAID on the chopping block along with USIA and ACDA, to which the secretary of state had unwisely acquiesced.

39. The same need for relative independence is also true for the Voice of America, which, like the BBC, always had a reputation for "telling it like it is," and thus had wide listenership around the world until it was "brought to heel," especially in the Trump administration, thus costing the United States a

significant instrument of influence. VOA can be restored to its former reputation with the right leadership.

40. I once (1971) asked Robert Komer, who had been in charge of the Phoenix
development program in Vietnam, why it had so little success. Komer, who
never minced words, retorted: "Give me as much money as the US military,
and I could pacify the whole country!"

41. During preparations for one of the Pentagon's Quadrennial Defense Reviews
(QDR), in which I was involved as part of an outside research organization
doing the review in collaboration with the Pentagon's Joint Staff, a three-star
admiral complained that State was not pulling its weight. I replied that DoD
might consider "buying the State Department—out of petty cash."

42. One counter remark by allies in Europe over the years is that "we will be
providing the battlefields." The US percentage of GDP spent for military is
by far the highest in the NATO alliance, but that figure counts all US defense
spending worldwide. A strict account of US military monies actually spent
devoted to the European Theater would place the US below the two percent
threshold.

43. When I worked the NSC and again at NATO, I was told by my State Department staff that unless my performance reviews called officers "superior"
or even "superlative," that would damage their careers—the whimsical,
term-of-art needed was "walks on water." Thus objective assessments could
annihilate careers. My NSC colleague Henry Owen, who was in charge of
international economics, simply asked his State Department subordinates
to list all the "buzz words" for performance reviews that would be helpful to
them, and he used them in their reviews. I sought similar advice from my
State Department team at NATO.

44. While I was working on Middle East issues at the NSC, 1979–1981, I found
that this was not true regarding Arab-Israeli issues: but that depended, I
discovered, on the high quality of the particular assistant secretary, Harold
Saunders (and his NSC colleague, William Quandt), and also, to no small
degree, on the fact that Arab-Israeli issues are highly technical and are not
that popular or "career-enhancing" compared to, say, matters about Europe.

45. The problem of training is not just at State or for diplomacy. When I was
at the National Defense University, I discovered that a sizeable fraction of
officers getting a master's degree at the Army War College did far less to earn
it than would have been useful to the Defense Department. It was a "block to
be checked" on the way to promotion.

46. She notoriously supported the Argentine junta, with its mass killings of political opponents, and also favored Argentina over Britain in the Falklands War.

47. On 12 September, 2001, NATO invoked Article 5 of the North Atlantic Treaty
for the first time in its history and, among other things, sent AWACs aircraft to patrol US skies. This course was proposed at NATO, not by the US

ambassador but by the Canadian ambassador, and Washington agreed with it.

48. Thus, as US ambassador to NATO, in my first formal briefing at SHAPE (Supreme Headquarters Allied Powers Europe) in July 1993, the military briefer predicted that by 2000 Russia would have built up an army of at least one-hundred divisions. The SACEUR (Supreme Allied Commander Europe) was embarrassed for his briefer when I expressed a doubt!

49. Anthony J. Blinken, US Secretary of State, "A Foreign Policy for the American People," speech, March 3, 2021, Ben Franklin Room. Digital document, online at *US Department of State*, Office of the Spokesperson, press release, Washington, D.C. (Washington: US Department of State, 2021). Accessed at: https://www.state.gov/a-foreign-policy-for-the-american-people/.

50. *Integrating Instruments of Power and Influence: Lessons Learned and Best Practices*, Report of a Panel of Senior Practitioners, Ser. Conference Proceedings. Co-chairs: Robert E. Hunter (principal author), Edward Gnehm, and George Joulwan. Rapporteur: Christopher Chivvis. (Santa Monica: RAND Corporation, 2008). Free download, accessed online at: https://www.rand.org/pubs/conf_proceedings/CF251.html#download.

51. There is an important point of nomenclature. The National Security Council is a statutory body consisting of a limited number of cabinet-level officers, plus the president and vice president. The term "NSC" is often used to mean the staff, and confusion sometimes arises outside of government contexts.

52. One "iron law," at least in the national security field, is "there ain't no such thing as cabinet government."

53. Even when Henry Kissinger was secretary of state, the National Security Council system remained important, as did the NSC advisor. For a time, Kissinger held both jobs. It did not work: other "players" could not accept it.

54. Henry Owen, one of the better Directors of Policy Planning (1966–1969) and an outside expert with considerable prior government service, argued that the choice at Policy Planning was to have ideas or to be relevant in the bureaucratic give-and-take; the NSC staff (or Council) can't do both, and it often becomes mostly a speech-writing staff for the Secretary. That can be changed if a secretary demands it and appoints the right people.

55. The NSC also always has a committee structure, with the National Security Council itself rarely meeting, except for purposes of media photography. Most of the work gets done at the level of cabinet officers (one name has been Principals Committee), and ideally, without the president in the room, since that necessarily "distorts" discussion in the presence of the "boss," and limits his capacity to keep his own counsel. Below that, at the deputy or undersecretary level (Deputies Committee) and farther below that, Interagency Working Groups. Indeed, one objective is to push the level of decision as far down as possible, so that the issues reaching the president are of

"presidential quality." I did a riff on Harry Truman's desk sign, "The buck stops here," joking that on the back of the sign in small letters is the following: "If it isn't of presidential quality, it had better not get here."

56. At the NSC and NATO, I used to joke that for too many people in the Foreign Service, mostly at entry and even middle levels, "the most 'foreign' country in the world is Capitol Hill."

57. Perhaps the most luckless was Gouverneur Morris, who represented the United States in France during the Terror.

58. See "The Treaty of Guadalupe Hidalgo," digital article, *National Archives and Records Administration* (website), Educator Resources. Accessed online at: https://www.archives.gov/education/lessons/guadalupe-hidalgo#background.

59. See "The Treaty of Ghent," article, *Wikipedia.org.* Accessed online at: https:// en.wikipedia.org/wiki/Treaty_of_Ghent.

60. By the end of the nineteenth century, the Trans-Atlantic cable (and later the Pacific cable) did speed things up. Thus Assistant Secretary of the Navy Theodore Roosevelt was able to instruct (via London to Hong Kong cable) Admiral Dewey, on board the *USS Olympia,* to seize Manila. The Secretary of the Navy, who had taken the weekend off, returned on Monday to discover that the United States was at war with Spain. See Andrew Liptak, "Admiral Dewey and the Battle of Manila Bay, 1898," digital article, *HistoryNet.com*, *Military History*, 18 July, 2017 (Arlington: HistoryNet LLC, 2023). Accessed online at: https://www.historynet.com/admiral-dewey-battle-manila-bay -1898.htm.

61. In September 1964, I needed to place a call back to the London School of Economics from the White House. I picked up the phone for the operator line, which was answered in about a second, "Yes, Sir," and asked to place a call to London. In about two more seconds, a voice said "10 Downing Street," which shocked me, and I went from there. During my first two years at LSE, 1962–1964, I had placed only two phone calls back to the "States." It is of note that the White House operators are probably the best and most resourceful anywhere.

62. See Robert E. Hunter, *The European Security and Defense Policy: NATO's Companion–or Competitor?* Ser. Monograph Reports, digital document (Santa Monica: RAND Corporation, 2002). Accessed and downloadable at: https://www.rand.org/pubs/monograph_reports/MR1463.html. Notably, France never withdrew from the political side of the Alliance, its integrated air defense system, the NATO pipeline, or Article 5 of the North Atlantic Treaty.

63. At NATO, I once went out on a limb, when the United States was trying to get NATO approval for airstrikes in Bosnia and the British were opposing it. My British counterpart woke me up in the middle of the night to say that the US position had been "overtaken by events" because of something

that had been happening in Bosnia. I "smelt fish," and phoned the State Department—six time zones behind us. I went to work, determined that it was, indeed, "fish," and then President Clinton phoned the British Prime Minister in the middle of the night and got matters back on track. So in that morning's meeting of the North Atlantic Council, I set forth a US position for which I had no formal instructions. But then, "just in time," I got cabled instructions to the same effect, before the British ambassador got his, telling him to agree with the US—the position I had just advanced, that is. He was shocked when a member of my staff came into the meeting with my cabled instructions, and he learned that I had been acting without instructions. That, of course, reflected the degree of confidence, created over time, between me and my mission with Washington.

64. When I was the lead official on the NSC staff for the Middle East, one US ambassador to the UN at the time regularly tried to "get off the reservation" on sensitive Middle East issues, because of his own strong, negative feelings about Israel. Thus all of his draft presentations in this area, especially to the UN Security Council, had to cross my desk for approval. In one case, I took one such unacceptable draft that I had marked up to Vice President Mondale, who took it to President Carter, who personally initialed every change I had made.

65. In January 1979, the Big Four heads of state and government met in Guadeloupe, a French Overseas Department, to discuss a wide variety of matters, including the issue of Euromissiles (though that was not made public). See "Guadeloupe Conference," at Guadeloupe Conference—Wikipedia. I was not present but had written the basic briefing paper that Brzezinski sent to Carter. When the team returned, I told Brzezinski that we needed to apprise our ambassadors in the NATO countries who had not been engaged, of what had happened. Brzezinski said he did not have time to write a debrief, so he suggested that I just have State send out the pre-summit briefing paper I had already written for Carter and say that that was what was agreed. So that is what I did.

66. There is far less of a problem for the German government. Given that these are almost always coalitions and the federal chancellor tends to be of a different political party from the foreign minister, the first thing the chancellor does after a summit meeting, even one held just with his opposite number, in the German phrase, *unter vier Augen*—that is, "under four eyes"—is immediately to dictate a memo for his or her foreign minister: *de rigueur* in German politics.

67. The onsite representative of the Chairman of the Joint Chiefs of Staff and US member of the NATO Military Committee.

68. Given that work at NATO as well as the composition of USNATO staff is both civilian and military, early in NATO's life formal arrangements were agreed

which conferred authority for the US ambassador to NATO to deal directly with the Secretary of Defense as well as the Secretary of State. This is unique among all US missions and embassies abroad. The top DOD person on my staff was also the Defense Secretary's representative in Europe but was subject to my authority. This State-Defense "treaty" from 1952 is regularly updated. See: "Defense Representation, United States Mission to the North Atlantic Treaty Organization (USNATO) and Europe," Department of Defense, Directive, no. 5105.20, 27 June, 2017, incorporating Change 1, effective 14 May, 2022. PDF. Accessed at: https://www.esd.whs.mil/Portals/54/Documents/DD /issuances/dodd/510520p.pdf . Many State Department officers naturally dislike this arrangement.

69. A most unfortunate example of the practice was in 1982, when NSC staffer Lt. Col. Oliver North went to Beirut as part of the effort to deal with Iran regarding some US hostages held in Lebanon—the famous "cake in the form of a key." The local US ambassador allowed North to act on his own, but the mission eventually blew up in North's face and also President Reagan's. One institutional change resulted. Every newly-appointed ambassador eventually gets a four-page personal letter from the president, laying out his or her formal responsibilities—they generally arrive many months after the ambassador gets to post, which shows how little functional importance this document has. But after the "Ollie North affair," a line was added to the president's letter to ambassadors: "You will undertake no action without formal direction from me or, acting on my behalf, the Secretary of State." Barn door closed.

70. Just before I left NATO, I saw a reference in a cable to a classified email on which I was a recipient. I asked my secretary what that referred to, since I knew of no such system. She told me that it had existed for about six months. When I logged in, there were several hundred messages to me in backlog. Apparently, however, none of them had really mattered!

71. A significant occasion was an open-line phone call in February 2014, between the assistant secretary of state for Eurasian affairs and the US ambassador to Ukraine—despite the existence of a secure telephone system— in which the assistant secretary discussed who Washington wanted to be president of Ukraine, to replace an elected pro-Russian president who had been chased from the country by protestors. This was, in effect, a coup attempt (it succeeded). The phone call was intercepted and published on the Internet, presumably by the Russians. See "Ukraine Crisis: Transcript of Leaked Nuland-Pyatt Call," *BBC News*–Europe, February 7, 2014. Accessed online at: https://www.bbc.com/news/world-europe-26079957. Two weeks later, Vladimir Putin seized Crimea, and Russian-backed separatists began a conflict in Southeast Ukraine that in 2022 Putin expanded to an assault against all of Ukraine.

SIX

DAVID DUNFORD

Effective Diplomacy is a Team Sport

Introduction

Most close observers of US diplomacy would agree that our diplomatic effectiveness has been in decline over the past several decades. This essay recounts the lessons I learned, the changes I witnessed in how we conduct diplomacy, and the inflection points I recall in our diplomatic decline. I conclude that a) training, mentoring and experience are key to producing effective diplomats, b) a critical mass of experienced diplomats serves as an early warning system for potential crises, c) well led teams of diplomats at home and abroad are those that create positive team chemistry and effective channels of communication with all relevant actors, d) a better balance is needed between security and the necessary work of diplomacy, and e) our diplomats must earn the trust of our political leaders and the people they represent so that critical assessments of proposed policies are weighed constructively.

There were several distinct periods in my diplomatic career. While together they span well more than a generation, each shaped my thinking about how and why our diplomacy has declined. The first extends from entry into the Foreign Service in 1966 until my assignment to Cairo in 1981. The second includes the next six years I spent working either in or on Egypt during the Reagan administration. My time as Deputy Chief of Mission (DCM) in Saudi Arabia 1988–1992 deserves separate coverage. During the Clinton years, I was in Oman as ambassador and then back in Cairo to work on a proposed development bank. The 9/11 attack presented a whole new set of challenges. My experience was either in multilateral economic and political diplomacy or in maintaining important relationships. Each such relationship was with an Arab country led by a monarch or, in the case of Egypt, an autocrat. The challenge was to balance US interests in democracy and human rights with other US interests like nuclear non-proliferation, counterterrorism, oil and other economic issues, and Israel. I did little direct negotiating with adversaries like Russia, China, or Iran, although that is also a critical dimension of diplomacy.

Early Career

I joined the Foreign Service on June 6, 1966, an easy date to remember. The Beatles were at the peak of their popularity, America was wracked with race riots, and the Vietnam war was escalating in intensity. I was one of a large incoming class in the orientation course known as A-100. I counted eighty-seven in our class pictures (we needed two), seventy-six men and eleven women. It was three years after Martin Luther King's "I Have a Dream" speech, Texas Western had won the NCAA basketball tournament with an all-African American starting team, and President Johnson had just appointed the first African American cabinet member.

Our class was all white and few of us, if any, gave that much thought. We were, however, geographically diverse with only a handful of Ivy League graduates. Dean Rusk had been Secretary of State since 1961 and seemed a cold and distant figure. I could walk into the State Department entrance on C Street and visit the upper floors without showing any ID. State Department security officials focused on preventing Soviet and other foreign intelligence agencies from leveraging personal vulnerabilities like sexual orientation, financial difficulties, or drug use. Less attention was given to the physical security of the State Department or our embassies and consulates abroad.

Following eight weeks of orientation and four months of Spanish language training, my first assignment was as a Junior Officer Trainee (JOT), an apprenticeship opportunity that no longer exists, in the US embassy in Quito, Ecuador. I was subject to the military draft, but the State Department requested I be deferred, and my draft board acquiesced. Five members of our class were assigned to Vietnam, most to the embassy in Saigon. Classmate Steven Haukness was assigned to Danang and killed during the 1968 Tet Offensive. Had I entered the following year, I almost certainly would have been sent to Vietnam to staff the CORDS (Civil Operations and Revolutionary Development Support) program. History repeated itself after the 9/11 attack when many incoming Foreign Service officers (FSOs) were sent to Afghanistan and Iraq.

I was fortunate to start in an embassy with professional leadership.

Ambassador Wymberley deRenne Coerr was a seasoned professional but also a poster figure for the image that the Foreign Service is still trying to live down. He was pale, male, a Yale graduate and had a unique patrician-sounding name. About nine months into my tour, Ecuadorean President Arosemena, unhappy with Coerr's public defense of the Alliance for Progress aid program in Ecuador, forced Coerr to depart declaring him *persona non grata*—(PNG'ed in diplomatic lingo). The US government left the position vacant for nearly a year, to signal its displeasure.[1] The embassy continued to run smoothly under the leadership of Jack Crowley who as deputy chief of mission (DCM) became the *chargé d'affaires* or *chargé*. Unlike junior officers recruited in subsequent years, I could accumulate all-around experience in administrative, consular, political, and economic work. In each section, I found a mentor willing to give me as much responsibility as I could handle. Friendships with several of these individuals lasted well beyond my time in Ecuador. Memories of Ecuador include going to the port of Salinas to assist American captains whose tuna boats had been seized for violating Ecuador's self-declared 200-mile territorial limit, keeping an American tourist out of jail who had gone on a drunken and naked romp in a Quito hotel, and being sent to our consulate in Guayaquil to take over visa issuance when malfeasance was uncovered. I was in Quito during the 1967 Six-Day War that transformed the Middle East landscape. I had no inkling then how much of my future would involve the Middle East.

When I went to Quito, I had no "cone." Today called "career paths," cones of that time were labeled administrative, consular, political, and economic/commercial. Today's public diplomacy career path in the State Department was then the responsibility of a separate agency, the United States Information Agency (USIA). I liked working in the economic section, so I asked for an economic assignment in Europe. I was mystified when an August 1968 telegram (in all caps) arrived, directing me to report to the Foreign Service Institute (FSI)[2] in Rosslyn, Virginia the following month to "FINNISH LANGUAGE TRAINING." "Finish what language training?" I asked a colleague. He peered at the telegram and said, "There are two n's in Finnish. You're going to Helsinki." Finnish was an exotic language, but I liked language learning and was too naïve to recognize what a useless skill Finnish would be later on in my career.

As 1968 rolled into 1969, I was studying Finnish during tumultuous times: as the Vietnam war escalated, LBJ announced he would not run for reelection, Martin Luther King and Robert F. Kennedy were assassinated, the Democratic convention took place in Chicago against a violent backdrop, the Woodstock music festival defined my generation, and Richard Nixon was elected president.

Val Peterson, a former Republican governor of Nebraska, was Nixon's choice as ambassador to Finland. This was my first encounter with a political appointee.[3] While he derided the Finnish press for its unbalanced coverage of the US and the USSR, and also obsessed about security in one of the safer places in the world, Peterson was affable and did no real damage to US-Finnish relations. Finns occasionally marched to protest the ongoing Vietnam conflict but never posed a serious threat to the Embassy. Peterson's DCM was a career officer comfortably on a trajectory toward retirement. I enjoyed Finland. Both my children were born there. I became a decent cross-country skier and played goalie for a Finnish amateur soccer team. I invented projects to keep busy and accumulated numerous Finnish contacts and friends but chafed at the lack of energetic Embassy leadership. The SALT I talks between the US and the Soviet Union took place in Helsinki while I was there, but there was little interaction between the delegation and the embassy except on the administrative side.[4] My time in Finland witnessed the end of an era where spouses were also pressed into service and evaluated along with their husbands, although they were not compensated.[5] Citing our two young children, Sandy declined to assist the wives of senior officers during social events.

Helsinki was an important assignment for CIA officers (because the Soviet Union was nearby) and the station was staffed by officers I knew and admired. I thought about quitting and applying to the CIA, but abandoned the idea when I was assigned to the six-month economics course beginning in September 1972 at the Foreign Service Institute.

The economics course was then a relatively new addition to Foreign Service training. Outside economists were brought into FSI to design and run it. State's Bureau of Economic and Business Affairs (EB) looked on the course as a farm team.[6] Frances Wilson, a tall woman with a stutter and fierce determination, was the legendary executive director of the bureau and she took charge of recruiting and developing young officers. She worked closely with FSI to identify the best students and made sure they got challenging jobs, an incentive to study hard given the clear payoff. Assistant secretaries came and went but everyone knew EB was her bureau. It was never good to disappoint Frances Wilson and I did so, twice. One was a questionable personnel decision, and the other was my decision to pass on the opportunity to be staff assistant to incoming assistant secretary

Tom Enders. Physically imposing at six feet, eight inches tall, Enders had a towering intellect and not a lot of charm. I was forever grateful that Frances Wilson continued to support me despite these choices.

I was assigned to the Office of International Trade division which handled trade with developing countries. Trade was a front-burner issue, given the pending legislation that became the Trade Act of 1974 and the looming Tokyo Round of multilateral trade negotiations. The Trade Act created a US version of the generalized system of tariff preferences (GSP). Drawing on basic computer skills acquired during the economics course, I wrote a multiple regression program that predicted how much US imports from developing countries would increase with these preferences applied. The trade legislation and negotiations were the responsibility of the Special Trade Representative's office (STR) in the Executive Office of the President, but the STR staff was focused on trade with Europe, Canada, and Japan. They left GSP to State and I was now the US government expert. A year and a half later the deputy division chief was transferred, the division chief departed unexpectedly, and I was suddenly acting chief of a busy office.

The State Department sent me in 1975 to Stanford University for graduate economics training. When I returned to State, Frances Wilson welcomed me back to EB and watched over me through a year as division chief in the Office of International Trade, two years as director of the Planning and Analysis Staff (staffed mainly by non-career professional economists), and a year as director of the Office of Development Finance.

The State Department emerged from World War II with the lead role for international economic policy, long considered a critical element of overall foreign policy.[7] Responsibility for trade policy was shifted during the Kennedy administration to the newly created Office of the Special Trade Representative (STR) but EB was still continuing to play a major role in all elements of international economic policy when I joined the bureau in 1973.

The Organization of Petroleum Exporting Countries (OPEC) embargo, following the 1973 Arab-Israeli war, shook Americans who wondered throughout the winter of 1973–74 where their next tank of gas would come from. It represented a major challenge to US foreign policy and EB played a leading role in our response. EB, for example, was at the center of the creation in Paris of the International Energy Agency, designed to ensure the security of oil supplies. OPEC's initial success resulted in a massive transfer of wealth to oil-producing countries which in turn gave developing countries more leverage in economic negotiations. Creating a bloc known as the Group of 77,[8] they sought to rewrite the rules on international trade and investment through the UN and its affiliated organizations like the UN Conference on Trade and Development. In the UN General Assembly, the Group of 77 proposed a Charter of Economic Rights and Duties of States which contained many proposals that were problematic for the US and other developed countries. Dubbed the North-South dialogue, these negotiations on multilateral economic issues were treated as a high priority by the Nixon, Ford, and Carter administrations. EB took the lead on energy and North-South issues and also played a strong supporting role in trade issues. The trade preferences contained in the Trade Act of 1974 represented a "carrot" that the US could offer to the developing countries. EB also became a key player in the preparations for Group of Seven (G-7) summits shortly after they began in 1975. EB was clearly a center of excellence during this period.

Although not a fan of political appointees at the deputy assistant secretary level because of their adverse impact on career-service morale, I do understand the case for bringing in talented outsiders. I worked for three in EB, and each was personable and capable. Bill Geimer, a lawyer and highly-respected political insider, oversaw the Office of International Trade. Bob Hormats came from the National Security Council (NSC) in 1977 as senior deputy assistant secretary. He brought with him the portfolio of Sherpa[9] for G-7 summits and he used the Planning and Analysis Staff (then my office) as his staff. Chuck Meissner, my boss in my last EB job, died tragically in a 1996 plane crash on a Croatian mountainside.

EB had to balance the foreign policy concerns of other parts of State with the domestic political concerns of other agencies like Commerce, Agriculture and Labor. Many of State's regional bureaus were unhappy when EB reined in initiatives that attracted strong opposition from the other economic agencies, because those agencies considered State to be insufficiently attentive to business and labor interests. Supporters of reorganization wanted more aggressive promotion of US exports and stronger enforcement of US laws aimed at unfair competition from imports. In June 1979, President Carter signed the Trade Agreements Act of 1979 which transferred overseas commercial programs from State to the Department of Commerce, leading to the creation of the Foreign Commercial Service the following year. This formally moved the lead role on export promotion, especially in the bigger markets, from State to Commerce. Under pressure from Congress, Carter later issued an executive order on trade reorganization which renamed the STR the US Trade Representative (USTR), greatly expanded the office and, within it, centralized the US government policymaking and negotiating functions for international trade.[10] According to Jules Katz, the much-respected EB assistant secretary at the time, the implications for US foreign policy were adverse: "I thought that the reorganization plan was a very bad idea, that it would really gut the State Department role, which was important from a foreign policy point of view, but also it would dissipate a very strong resource in the government. At the time, the Economic Bureau was really at a peak in effectiveness. I had five deputies who were just outstanding, all of whom went on to other important posts."[11]

With a stronger USTR (now a cabinet position), the new Department of Energy created in 1977, and a new Foreign Commercial Service, EB inevitably went into eclipse. Jules Katz left for the private sector. I lost track of Frances Wilson, also a career civil servant and very much an unsung hero. I am told she died in the 1980s, but I never found an obituary. With the trade reorganization, Hormats became deputy USTR, and I followed, putting off an overseas assignment long enough to allow time for my wife Sandy to complete her CPA-practice requirement. Given the impressive title of deputy assistant USTR, I worked on trade issues with Europe and Canada. I came away convinced that a detail to another agency is a key step on the road to becoming a successful Foreign Service leader.

Egypt During the Reagan Years

By 1981, now a senior FSO at age 38, I realized an overseas assignment was a must. With Sandy's strong encouragement, I approached the Bureau of Near East and South Asian Affairs (NEA)[12] and found myself headed to Cairo to run the embassy's economic section. I used my last months in Washington to get the job reclassified from counselor to minister-counselor to give me more influence in Cairo with the US Agency for International Development (USAID) director and the counselors for agriculture, commerce and science. I read a few books about Egypt and the Middle East before I went but I neither spoke Arabic nor had experience in the Arab world. While I was immersed in international economic diplomacy, major changes affecting the Middle East and US politics occurred that would shape my future. The 1977 election in Israel produced the first non-Labor prime minister, Menachem Begin. The American Israel Public Affairs Committee (AIPAC) emerged as a powerful lobby in Washington that could make or break political careers[13] and would fuel the suspicion that Arabists (FSOs fluent in Arabic)[14] in the State Department had too much influence.

I arrived in Cairo in June 1981, less than three years after the Camp David Accords that led to peace between Egypt and Israel and two years after the Iranian revolution, the Soviet invasion of Afghanistan, and the attempted seizure of the Holy Mosque in Mecca by Saudi religious zealots. The eight-year war between Iran and Iraq had begun the year before. Israel would not complete its withdrawal from the Sinai Peninsula (except for 250 acres of Red Sea beachfront called Taba) until the following year. During my first week in Cairo, Israel attacked an Iraqi nuclear reactor near Baghdad, a harbinger of what I could expect in the coming months and years. Four months later, Egyptian president Anwar Sadat was assassinated by Islamic militants.

The Embassy was a large two-story villa located near Tahrir Square, just a block from the Nile River. The USAID mission, with well over a hundred direct-hire Americans, was in the upper floors of a nearby high-rise building. USAID managed a portfolio that received an annual inflow of $815 million. Military assistance, at an annual level of $1.3 billion, was managed by a military assistance group headed by an American flag officer. Embassy access was controlled but security was minimal compared to more recent years. Americans with children tended to live in the southern suburb of Ma'adi which contained an American school called the Cairo American College. Our house was close, allowing our son and daughter to walk to school.

Embassy Cairo, following the Egypt-Israel peace agreement, had become one of our most important posts and was staffed accordingly. Ambassador Roy Atherton was a former NEA assistant secretary of state. Henry Precht, DCM and my immediate boss, had worked in Tehran and also had run the Iran desk in Washington. Nick Veliotes, also a former NEA assistant secretary, replaced Atherton in 1983. All three were highly respected career professionals. At least seven other FSOs who served at Embassy Cairo during my time went on to become ambassadors.

Our presence in Cairo had two major objectives: preserving the peace between Egypt and Israel and propping up an economy badly in need of reform. There was always tension between these objectives. There was widespread consensus both in Washington and in the embassy that both objectives were important but disagreement arose frequently about how hard to push the Egyptian government on economic reform. Many US government agencies were represented on the country team and both the Reagan administration and Congress were keenly interested in our relationship with Egypt. A steady flow of Congressional delegations and administration officials came to Cairo. Atherton and Precht were determined to maintain some coherence in our overall relationship. Henry had a close relationship with then-director of Egyptian affairs Wingate Lloyd in Washington. He was on the phone with him daily (or more often) and they also exchanged daily official-informal telegrams (a form of diplomatic communication known as an o-i).[15] Following three years in Cairo, I was transferred back to Washington to replace Lloyd as director of Egyptian affairs. The office had a staff of five officers and two secretaries, and I adopted the same close relationship (telephone calls and informal cables) with Henry.

NEA was known as the "mother bureau" and considered one of the best in the department, particularly by those who worked in it. Assistant Secretary Richard Murphy's previous assignment had been as ambassador to Saudi Arabia. His deputy, Arnie Raphel, was a rising star. Arnie and I both joined the Foreign Service at the same time and were good friends. Ed Djerejian, who replaced Arnie in 1986, was also a strong leader from the same mold. My immediate boss was Bob Pelletreau, later an NEA assistant secretary. My fellow office directors were all capable officers with great upside potential. Communication up and down in the bureau was excellent. Frequent staff meetings kept us current on what others in the bureau were doing. NEA was clearly another center of excellence. Morale was high and there was an impressive team spirit and a solid sense of shared mission.

The Egypt office continued its frequent contact with Embassy Cairo as Henry Precht stayed on for a fourth year there. Bill Clark, whose expertise was East Asia, replaced Henry and he maintained the close relationship with the office. Frank Wisner was nominated to replace Veliotes, and Jock Covey came over from the NSC to be his DCM. Both were "hands-on" managers who welcomed the daily communication with the Embassy. Wisner's confirmation, like many others, was delayed by opposition from Senator Jesse Helms and Frank became a daily presence in my office for several months. He generated a significant workload, but I was able to develop a close partnership both with him and with Jock which worked well when they got to Cairo.

NEA's excellence did not translate into significant success in our Middle East policy. Sadat, and his successor Hosni Mubarak, wanted the Camp David agreements to result not just in return of the Sinai to Egypt but also to serious negotiations between Israel and the Palestinians. Menachem

Begin had no interest in seeing that happen and the Reagan administration didn't press the matter. Al Haig, Reagan's first secretary of state, enabled Israel's decision to invade Lebanon in 1982 which eventually led to a disastrous intervention by the US. When the dust cleared, our embassy in Beirut had been attacked (April 1983), a truck bomb killed 241 marines (October 1983), other Americans were killed or taken hostage in Lebanon, and the region was rocked by a wave of hijackings orchestrated variously by Palestinians or a Lebanese Shi'a group that became known as Hezbollah. On the plus side, Egypt and Israel remained at peace and Egypt eventually reached agreement with the International Monetary Fund on a modest package of economic reforms.

The attacks in Beirut in 1983 led to the Inman Report on security improvements and the creation within State of the Bureau of Diplomatic Security, a major inflection point for US diplomacy. Today, US diplomats generally operate out of fortress-like embassies. Trained to move around in foreign cultures and establish productive relationships with a wide spectrum of the country's population, diplomats often find themselves at odds with additional security requirements. FSOs are conditioned to accept some risk, and several have been killed on the job over the years. The murder of Ambassador Chris Stevens in Benghazi in 2012 and the political circus that followed even further circumscribed the ability of diplomats to do their jobs.

George Shultz took over from Haig as secretary of state in July 1982. NEA played a major role in three separate crisis task forces in the fall of 1985 dealing with several hijacking events: TWA 847, the Achille Lauro, and an Egyptair flight to Malta.[16] The NSC-inspired Iran/Contra initiative was revealed the following year. Our job in the Office of Egyptian Affairs was to keep the Egyptian-Israeli relationship from going completely sour and Egypt's economy from tanking.

George Shultz was my favorite secretary of state.[17] The NSC was relatively weak under Reagan, and Shultz was clearly the president's chief advisor on foreign policy. When he hosted a luncheon for visiting Egyptian foreign minister Esmat Abdel Meguid, I was invited even though ranking several layers down in the bureaucracy. One night, while I was working the crisis task force on the hijacked Egyptair flight to Malta, he telephoned me for an update. These were small examples of how he trusted the career professionals. He encouraged a "hands-on" approach to foreign policy which dovetailed smoothly with the working relationship between the Office of Egyptian Affairs and Embassy Cairo. Shultz saw the management of US foreign relations as analogous to gardening: you needed to keep a careful eye on all parts of your garden or weeds would take over. Our office, with help and encouragement from Embassy Cairo, kept a close eye on trends and events that could derail our relationship while looking for opportunities to strengthen that relationship.

Reflections on Training and Lessons Learned

In my first decade, the Foreign Service provided me with thirteen months of training in two languages, six months of in-house economics training and an academic year of graduate economics. This was in addition to the A-100 orientation course and a twenty-month apprenticeship in Quito. Later generations of junior officers were not so lucky.

Now it was time for more training. I left the Office of Egyptian Affairs in the summer of 1987 and entered the senior seminar, a nine-month program designed to prepare its members for leadership responsibilities. The course featured monthly trips to different US regions to give participants a better sense of the country we would be representing. I still have vivid memories of time on a family-run dairy farm in Minnesota, riding with the night shift in a Detroit police patrol car and riding around with the Border Patrol in El Paso.

I used a senior seminar assignment to write an essay on leadership. I chose to reflect on why EB in the 1970s and Embassy Cairo and NEA in the 1980s were centers of excellence. I started by describing a visit the seminar class had made to the North Anna nuclear power plant in Virginia. The control room's walls were jammed with dials and meters monitored by the staff to understand what was going on inside the plant and detect any issue which could lead to a reactor meltdown. I concluded that the shared mission of the Office of Egyptian Affairs and Embassy Cairo was early detection of issues that could lead to the meltdown of the US-Egypt relationship. The meltdown could start anywhere: in the host government or in the host society; in the country-team or in one of its diverse elements; in a relationship between the host government and a third country; or within the US itself, in its government, Congress or society. I was proposing a diplomatic service sufficiently staffed to anticipate instead of merely reacting to crises.

Although a Foreign Service leader is not surrounded by gauges and dials, and since alarm bells do not actually go off when a potential crisis is developing, I still saw a clear analogy to diplomacy. Instead of gauges and dials, responsible diplomats need to access all important communication channels directly affecting a relationship. For the Office of Egyptian Affairs, this included communication up, down, and laterally in the US federal bureaucracy, with Congress, key interest groups and all other relevant Washington embassies, in addition to core channels to Embassy Cairo and the consulate general in Alexandria. If these channels do not exist or become blocked, they either need to be created or unblocked. An effective embassy will have contacts with all important elements of the host society. All these channels yield information and information is the power to anticipate problems. However, effective communication is based on trust. If you or one of your team misleads, misinforms, or fails to protect those who are relied upon for information, the needed channels will be cut, and information will dry up or be routed around you.

The other essential element of a successful bureau or office is good team chemistry. I played or coached sports most of my life and I recognize its power. Teams without it, no matter how much talent is on their roster, do not win. The team chemistry during my time in EB, in Embassy Cairo, and in NEA was outstanding. Success or failure in building team chemistry is a function of leadership. It requires a combination of listening, acknowledging contributions, participation in team events, transparency, and accessibility. In EB, Jules Katz provided the leadership, and he was respected within State and throughout the Washington economics community. In Cairo, Roy Atherton and Henry Precht led. It certainly helped that there were so many talented FSOs on the staff and that the channels of communication with the State Department were wide open and utilized constantly. I was privileged to work on the Washington end of those communications and to work with many other talented FSOs. Dick Murphy and Arnie Raphel were our leaders. In the seventies, Jules Katz enjoyed the confidence of Secretary Cyrus Vance, although Vance did acquiesce to the reorganization that reduced EB's influence. The leaders in Cairo and in NEA would not have been successful without the implicit trust and confidence of George Shultz.

The senior seminar was abolished in the early 2000s during the first term of the George W. Bush administration. Secretary of State Colin Powell thought it too costly, given the small number of FSOs who went through it. FSOs assigned to lead or participate in the seminar were regularly pulled out to take "real" jobs. Powell replaced the seminar with leadership training available to all officers who crossed the senior threshold. I hope that senior training today allows participants to get to know their own country better and get the chance, away from the constant pressures of hourly deadlines, to think about leadership and the challenges now facing the Foreign Service. One common criticism of FSOs is that they are out of touch with their own nation. The senior seminar was clearly designed to remedy that. Ambassador Jim Bullington, who ably ran the seminar during my months there, was subsequently pushed out of the service at age forty-eight by "time in class" regulations. He noted in his oral history that "training has long been regarded by the Foreign Service as where you shuffle people off when you've got nothing better for them to do."[18]

Saudi Arabia 1988–1992

Hume Horan, perhaps the most accomplished Arabist in the Foreign Service, was confirmed as US ambassador to Saudi Arabia in 1987. He welcomed my assignment as his DCM which was to begin in summer 1988. The US significantly expanded its economic and security relationship with Saudi Arabia after the OPEC embargo was lifted in 1974. Embassy Riyadh had grown into one of our largest embassies. The US presence included two large military assistance missions and a US Treasury-run technical assistance program designed to teach the Saudis how to operate the bureaucracy of a modern state.[19]

My relaxed year in the senior seminar was cut short by what became known as the Chinese missile crisis. The US government discovered in March of 1988 that Saudi Arabia had purchased and was installing intermediate-range Chinese ballistic missiles south of Riyadh. The Saudi-Iran relationship was at the time quite tense, and the Saudis wanted missiles that could reach Tehran. Because the missiles could also reach Israel, they became a major political and strategic problem for the US government.

Poor coordination between State and the White House left Horan hanging out to dry. Saudi King Fahd had already been uneasy with Horan for several reasons: his Iranian heritage,[20] his flawless Arabic, and his meetings with Saudi Muslim clerics. In Fahd's mind, Horan had Iranian blood and knew too much about Saudi Arabia. Horan, under instructions, delivered a harsh message, drafted in the State Department, calling on Fahd to halt all construction and training related to the missiles. At the same time, the King was getting a softer US message through Prince Bandar, his ambassador in Washington. The King concluded that Horan was responsible for the tough message and made it clear that Horan was no longer welcome in Saudi Arabia. Even though Horan recommended, to signal our displeasure, that Washington let a decent interval pass before nominating a successor, he quickly received instructions to seek agrément[21] for Walt Cutler, who had preceded Horan, to return as ambassador. I would remind readers that when Ecuadorean President Arosemena sent our ambassador home in 1967, we left the post open for a year.

Ned Walker, who had been Horan's DCM, had already departed so my transfer to Riyadh was moved up to April. I had been spoiled by the close relationship between the Office of Egyptian Affairs and Embassy Cairo. The Office of Arabian Peninsula Affairs (ARP) seemed more distant. The reason was simple. The director of ARP had seven countries to cover and was too busy for daily contact by phone and official-informal telegrams. I tried to understand and still regarded NEA as my trusted backstop. Cutler did not arrive until August, giving me over three months of on-the-job training on how to run a large embassy.

George H.W. Bush was elected president that November, and he chose his good friend Jim Baker as secretary of state. Many argue that Baker was the best secretary of state we ever had. He presided over the collapse of the Soviet Union, the reunification of Germany, our muscular response to Saddam's invasion of Kuwait and the reinvigoration of the Middle East peace process. I had an opportunity in Riyadh to personally witness Baker's impressive negotiating skills. As his memoir makes clear, Baker did not come to the job with a favorable impression of the Foreign Service.[22] He was particularly concerned about "clientitis," the tendency to identify more with host country interests than with US interests. Baker showed up in Foggy Bottom "determined to clean house."[23] He consciously chose to manage the State Department much differently than George Shultz had done. He did not want to be captured by "the building." "Unlike George Shultz, who famously showed up without a single aide of his own, Baker brought his own 'plug-in unit' with him to the State Department."[24]

Baker's choice for NEA assistant secretary, John Kelly, surprised many. Although he doesn't discuss his reasoning in his memoir, If you assume that he wanted a totally different NEA from the one Shultz presided over, it makes perfect sense. Kelly's only Middle East experience was as ambassador in Beirut where he incurred the wrath of Shultz for communicating directly with the NSC on the Iran/Contra affair. Kelly, like Baker, wanted a fresh start and he informed all of former NEA Assistant Secretary Murphy's deputies that they would be replaced. The replacements, except for the now-mandatory political appointee, were all career FSOs who I knew and respected: Jock Covey (as Kelly's senior deputy), Skip Gnehm, Dan Kurtzer and Tezi Schaffer. But even from the distance of Riyadh, I could sense that good team chemistry was gone under Kelly's leadership. I heard grumbling about his volcanic temper and Jock's micromanagement.

I saw NEA under Murphy and Raphel as a championship team. Raphel went to Pakistan as US ambassador and was killed in a tragic plane crash there in August 1988. Ed Djerejian was appointed ambassador to Syria, Murphy retired with the change in administrations. Kelly, in what the media dubbed the "Friday night massacre," cleaned out the next level of leadership. I am reminded of what happened to the Chicago Bulls after the Bulls won the NBA Championship for the sixth time in 1998. Bulls General Manager Jerry Krause is widely blamed for the departure of coach Phil Jackson, along with superstar Michael Jordan, Scotty Pippen, Dennis Rodman, and Steve Kerr. The Bulls faded into a generation of mediocrity.

Cutler stayed until April 1989, and I was again left to run the Embassy until Chas Freeman could be confirmed which, thanks in part to Senator Helms, took until November. Chas has a brilliant mind, he radiates innovation and creativity, and he is a genuine strategic thinker. He wanted very much to share his energy and ideas with policymakers in Washington but the reaction to Chas's well-crafted cables was usually silence. One memorable set of cables sent in early 1990, was known within the State Department as the Wooly Mammoth cables. Their basic theme was that, with the end of the discipline of the Cold War, ancient ethnic and sectarian tensions would reemerge like wooly mammoths at the end of the Ice Age.[25] I am reminded that our Cold War strategy evolved from a long telegram from George Kennan, a career Foreign Service officer writing from Moscow.

Embassy Riyadh was staffed with many talented officers who went on to multiple ambassadorships, including Anne Patterson, Dick Jones, and Rick Olsen. Communication within the Embassy and with the consulates-general in Jeddah and Dhahran was excellent. Communication with Washington was another story. Much has been written about our inability to anticipate Saddam's 1990 invasion of Kuwait. I doubt, however, that better communication between Washington and our embassies in the Middle East would have made much difference. Saddam's government made it almost impossible for April Glaspie, our ambassador in Baghdad prior to the invasion, to establish the kind of channels that would have helped us read Saddam's mind. Where better communication with Washington could have made a difference was in the aftermath of the invasion, on issues like the protection of American civilians, impact of the war on Saudi social and financial stability, and options for continued Saudi military cooperation going forward.

One of my main preoccupations in Riyadh after Saddam's invasion of Kuwait was the protection of the thousands of American civilians who were instrumental in keeping Saudi oil flowing and bolstering Saudi defenses. I have written elsewhere at length about our frustrations with Washington on this issue.[26] In the end, with the help of General Schwarzkopf and his Central Command staff, we managed this issue in Riyadh in a way that kept Americans safe without damaging the war effort.

The war ended in early March 1991 but the disconnect between Riyadh and Washington continued. Chas had argued fervently to an unresponsive Washington audience that some thought needed to be given to how the war would end and what we hoped to accomplish in ending it. Chas was not alone. Tom Pickering, the highly-respected career FSO who was then our ambassador to the UN, also argued passionately for a definition of war aims.[27] The fighting ended in March 1991 with a meeting between Schwarzkopf and Iraqi military leaders in Safwan in southern Iraq which had zero political input. The war resumed at a low level for twelve years until March 2003 when we made the disastrous decision to launch a full-scale invasion of Iraq.

With the first Gulf War over, the US government focused on collecting $16.8 billion from the Saudis and a comparable amount from the Kuwaitis. The Saudis had already spent billions of dollars on fuel and other supplies not only for American troops but also for the militaries of several other countries that agreed to join the US-organized coalition against Iraq. The Embassy elected to push back on the decision to charge the Saudis such a high amount based on our own analysis of the Saudi economy. I have few insights on how Washington arrived at the $16.8 billion figure.[28] Conventional wisdom in Washington was that the Saudis were fabulously wealthy. Many members of the Saudi royal family were indeed billionaires. Had King Fahd then adopted the tactics his nephew and current crown prince Mohammed bin Salman (MBS) used years later,[29] he could easily have raised the money. Jim Baker was not happy with Embassy misgivings, charging Chas with "clientitis."[30] After we threatened to withhold military equipment destined for Saudi Arabia, the Saudis managed to pay in full.

The downturn in the world economy following the war led to lower oil prices leaving the Saudi royal family even less money to buy off potential opponents and to employ the many young Saudis coming into the job market. Embassy Riyadh was reporting extensively back to Washington on popular Muslim preachers, Salman al-Ouda and Safar al-Hawali, who challenged the legitimacy of Saudi crown rule. We also drew attention to the battle-tested young Saudis and other Arabs including Osama bin Laden who were returning victorious from Afghanistan to their home countries looking for new battles. We called them Arab Afghans. Bin Laden's adamant opposition to the US presence in Saudi Arabia was a major reason for his growing influence among Saudi Islamists. Looking back, it is not hard to connect the dots between the deployment of troops to Saudi Arabia in 1990 and the way we so poorly managed the aftermath of Desert Storm, to the later 9/11 attacks and our subsequent invasion of Iraq.[31] Our reporting did not attract much interest in Washington. Meanwhile, the 1992 US elections loomed.

While we were pressing the Saudis for payment, the Department of Defense was gearing up to preposition military equipment in Saudi Arabia for use elsewhere in the region. This led to a visit by Secretary of Defense Cheney accompanied by a large military delegation. I do not recall any dialogue we might have had with Washington on the prospects for Saudi agreement or whether we were asked for advice on how to present this proposal. I do remember that the presence of 500,000 US troops in Saudi Arabia had mobilized strong religious opposition to the royal family. The widely publicized demonstration by Saudi women driving around a Riyadh shopping center in November 1990 had a key role in energizing militant Islamists. I attended the Cheney meeting with Saudi Minister of Defense Sultan in Riyadh in April 1991. Since the Cheney delegation was huge, the Saudis included all their service chiefs in the meeting. After initial pleasantries, Cheney turned to a one-star general who began reading from a briefing book. His first sentence included the acronym "POMCUS"[32] which clearly was untranslatable to those Saudis present, including Sultan who did not speak English well. The Saudis began talking to each other in Arabic in what appeared to be consternation. Prepositioning US military equipment in Saudi Arabia was a non-starter. I suspect, no matter how carefully we crafted the presentation to the Saudis, the idea had no chance of acceptance. The Saudis eventually did agree to host a US Air Force unit, well out of sight of any populated area, to enforce the southern Iraqi no-fly zone but even this much US presence was controversial.

The Clinton Years

In 1992, Serbian troops initiated the siege of Sarajevo, Rabin was elected Israel's prime minister, and the US Marines went into Somalia. Both Chas and I departed Saudi Arabia that year. Chas was the last career FSO to be ambassador in Saudi Arabia until 2023.[33] Jock Covey was the administration's initial choice to replace Chas, but the Saudis didn't want a professional—they wanted someone close to the President who would not probe too deeply into Saudi society—and Jock was apparently on the long list of Foreign Service professionals that Jesse Helms didn't like. The post was left empty for the next two years. I was nominated as the next US ambassador to Oman.

While I didn't have the profile to attract the attention of Helms, my confirmation was rocked by an anonymous letter, penned by a young officer in Embassy Riyadh and designed to derail my nomination. The author blamed me for a personnel decision that he believed unfairly disadvantaged his wife. The letter contained several accusations, all of which I was able, with considerable effort and much support from my colleagues in Riyadh, to demonstrate were false. The Senate Foreign Relations Committee insistence that I prove my innocence delayed my confirmation for months. I was lucky. Some fine career FSOs have been less lucky.

The nearly three years I spent in Oman created many pleasant memories. Bill Clinton was elected president during my first week in Muscat, so I had to submit the obligatory letter of resignation required whenever there is a change in administration. I set about opening as many channels of communication as possible and building a positive team chemistry. Not surprisingly, communication with Washington was minimal, but establishing effective relations with Omani decision-makers went quite well. The country team, while certainly smaller than that of Embassy Riyadh, was well staffed. We had a small USAID mission, three military units, a CIA station, and a public affairs officer. I encountered some bumps in the road with respect to team chemistry. I had to curtail the assignments of two military officers and deal with a nasty accusation of sexual harassment against the USAID director. Nevertheless, by my third year in Oman, I sensed that the chemistry was where I wanted it to be.

Bill Clinton came into office pledging to focus on the domestic economy. There was a sense of complacency about foreign policy since we were firmly established as the only remaining superpower. Clinton wanted the government to be less expensive and more efficient so he put Vice President Al Gore in charge of reinventing government. When the Republicans won the November 1994 midterm elections handily, new House Speaker Newt Gingrich was even more eager to cut government funding and Jesse Helms, now Chairman of the Senate Foreign Relations Committee, made sure fiscal belt-tightening was extended to the international affairs budget. The Clinton Administration and the Congress did considerable damage to the Foreign Service, to which I had dedicated a considerable part of my life.[34]

New USAID Director Brian Atwood was under pressure to cut expenses and he produced a plan to eliminate several USAID missions around the world. The modest $15 million program in Oman caught his eye, particularly given Oman's rapid economic advances. On a Friday (the Muslim sabbath), I was notified two hours in advance of an Atwood press conference announcing the closing of many USAID missions, including the one in Oman. The economic assistance was provided as our contribution to an Omani-American Joint Commission on the understanding that Oman would grant us the right to pre-position Air Force equipment on three Omani air bases located in Seeb, Masirah and Thumrait. Put simply, the aid was a quid pro quo for military access. I remain stunned to this day that a) either no thought was given to the linkage or b) that thought was given to it, but nobody thought to inform the US ambassador in Muscat or seek his input. The kind of close cooperation that NEA had with its posts abroad during the Reagan-Shultz period ten years earlier was long gone. The new administration compounded the damage by seeking to claw back money already committed to Oman but not yet spent.[35]

During Clinton's first term, the Middle East peace process, relaunched at the Madrid Conference in late 1991, was showing promise. Clinton kept Dennis Ross, Baker's policy-planning director, and gave him the new title of Special Middle East Coordinator (SMEC). The Madrid meeting launched a two-track process of bilateral and multilateral negotiations. Successes on the bilateral track included the Oslo Accords signed in September 1993 and the peace treaty between Israel and Jordan signed in October 1994. The multilateral track consisted of five separate working groups. These multilateral groups were designed to reinforce the bilateral track by bringing Israelis and Arabs together to deal with concrete issues and, in so doing, allow for the participation of European and other countries outside the region as well as building personal relationships and mutual confidence.

The US chaired the Multilateral Committee on Water Resources which met for the fifth time in Beijing in October 1993. I received an evening call from the State Department asking me to get approval from the Omanis that night to host the sixth meeting in April 1994. I reached Omani Foreign Minister Yusuf bin Alawi to make the request. He called me back an hour later with agreement. This would be the first meeting of any of the five committees, in any of the Arabian Peninsula countries, and the first time an official Israeli delegation would visit any Arabian Peninsula country.

The meeting itself resulted in an agreement to create a Middle East Desalination Research Center (MEDRC) in Muscat. The Israelis sent a delegation headed by Deputy Foreign Minister Yossi Beilin and a large Israeli press delegation also came along. The Israeli press members came to the US embassy for a briefing, and the excitement among them was palpable. The visit led to an exchange of trade offices and a visit to Oman by Israeli Prime Minister Rabin late in 1994. It also allowed us to repair the damage caused by the abrupt termination of our economic assistance program and to get negotiations on the renewal of our military agreement with the Omanis back on track. Vice President Gore visited Oman in March 1995 with a check for $3 million to support the creation of the desalination research center. While most elements of the multilateral track ground to a halt during Clinton's second term, the desalination center in Muscat continues to function to this day.[36]

As my time in Oman wound down, I was subject to mandatory retirement under the rules of the Foreign Service. I had been promoted into the Senior Foreign Service in 1980 and allowed fourteen years to be promoted to Career Minister.[37] Although I had done well in the Foreign Service, I was not, as a reviewer of my recent book indelicately put it, a "superstar".[38] Given the austere budgetary climate in the mid-nineties, there was no incentive to relax the regulations.

Cuts in budget and personnel meant the Foreign Service had no "bench strength" so less than two years later I found myself rehired. I left my teaching position at the University of Arizona and in early June 1997 I returned to Cairo to head the transition team for what was to become the Bank for Economic Cooperation and Development in the Middle East and North Africa (MENABANK). At full strength there were eight of us representing the US, Canada, the Netherlands, Italy, Japan, Egypt, Jordan, and Israel. Agreement to set up the bank, a proposal endorsed by the core parties (Israel, Palestinian Authority, Egypt, and Jordan), was reached at the second Middle East/North African Economic Summit held in Amman,

Jordan, in October 1995. Israeli Prime Minister Yitzhak Rabin addressed the summit with a call for everyone to work for peace and economic cooperation. He was assassinated only days later by an Israeli right-wing zealot.

By the time I arrived in Cairo, work on the bank was moving forward in the face of heavy political headwinds. Benjamin Netanyahu was now Israel's prime minister, and he did not share Rabin's enthusiasm for either moving forward on the Oslo Accords or regional economic cooperation. Israeli actions in Jerusalem (in particular opening an archaeological tunnel near the Temple Mount and building a housing development in East Jerusalem) had angered the Arabs across the region including Egypt. Congressional support for financing the modest amount of capital required to start the bank was lukewarm at best.

My work in Cairo was supported by the two State Department bureaus that were my professional home for nearly two decades, EB and NEA. EB ably provided the administrative support I needed but had little clout on the policy side. In NEA, I found that the Office of Egyptian Affairs had been merged with the office overseeing all the other North African countries. The office director reported to two deputy assistant secretaries, one a political appointee essentially working for Dennis Ross, who continued overseeing the peace process. Career FSO Bob Pelletreau had just retired as assistant secretary, and political appointee Martin Indyk was the incoming assistant secretary. Indyk had worked for AIPAC and then the pro-Israeli think tank, the Washington Institute for Near East Policy. Morale among career professionals throughout the bureau was low due to the significant politicization of the bureau and a fragmented chain of command. When I arrived in Cairo this time, I learned that the political and economic sections had been merged as one of Embassy Cairo's contributions to Gore's initiative of reinventing government. Ironically, the Embassy assigned me to live in the same apartment where the last person to hold the title of minister-counselor for economic affairs[39] had resided. While the Embassy readily provided the administrative support the transition team required, continuing to elicit Egyptian government support for MENABANK was not a high Embassy priority.

Ross was focused on reviving the Oslo process in the face of Netanyahu's foot-dragging and had little interest in the multilateral track. MENABANK needed a champion within the administration and incoming Undersecretary for Economic Affairs Stuart Eizenstat was willing to play that role. I accompanied him to what was the last of the MENA economic summits in Doha in November 1997 where he pledged that the Clinton administration would press Congress to fund the bank. Both Egypt and Saudi Arabia boycotted the Doha event, citing Israeli behavior. We brought most of the transition team to Washington in March 1998 to lobby the key House and Senate committees. House Foreign Affairs Committee chairman Lee Hamilton was a staunch supporter. Senate Foreign Relations Committee chairman Jesse Helms was not. We were told that any US contribution to the bank would have to come out of the annual assistance we provided to Egypt and Israel. Neither Egypt nor Israel loved this idea although Egypt was reportedly prepared to agree if Israel did as well. The team kept working for the balance of 1998, but the handwriting was on the wall. The transition team was the last remnant of the multilateral track, and the administration pulled the plug on us in December 1998.

When Israeli elections resulted in Ehud Barak becoming prime minister, there was new optimism that a final peace deal between Israel and the Palestinians could be achieved. That hope was dashed by the dismal failure of the Camp David negotiations in the fall of 2000 and the subsequent outbreak of violence dubbed the Al Aqsa intifada. I have long believed that, had the Clinton administration put more energy into championing the multilateral track during the first Netanyahu era, enough progress could have been made to outlast the political obstacles. The desalination research center still functions in Muscat and reflects continued cooperation at the technical level between Israel, Oman, and several other countries. A Middle East development bank in Cairo would have created multiple constituencies for peace and continued economic cooperation, and the price tag for the US was only $52.5 million annually for five years.

9/11 and the Militarization of Foreign Policy

I returned to teaching at the University of Arizona in 1998 and was surprised, although not as surprised as many Americans, by the attack on the World Trade Center on September 11, 2001. I knew who Osama bin Laden was and so did my students. We had traced the growing threat of militant Islam since the end of the 1991 Gulf War. The most serious attacks included the 1995 attack on the American military unit assisting the Saudi Arabian National Guard in Riyadh, the 1996 attack on American soldiers housed in the al-Khobar Towers in Saudi Arabia's eastern province, the 1998 attacks on American embassies in Nairobi and Dar es Salaam and the 2000 attack on the USS Cole in Aden harbor. It was no accident that fifteen of the nineteen hijackers were Saudi nationals. We were underprepared for 9/11 and we overreacted after the attack.

I supported the initial decision to go on the offensive in Afghanistan: the 9/11 attack had originated in Afghanistan and the Taliban-controlled government was protecting al-Qa'ida. I watched with disbelief as we shifted the focus to Iraq. Declaring a war on terror, which is after all a tactic not an ideology, and lumping Iraq, Iran, and North Korea into an "axis of evil" made no sense to me. Declaring our adversaries "evil" relieves us of the task of understanding why significant societies around the world support attacks against Americans. We had too few of the diplomats and intelligence operatives needed to do that work. If your adversaries are regarded or perceived as irredeemably evil, then there is no option other than a military solution. Militarization of American foreign policy became inevitable.

Most Americans, shaken by 9/11, were initially willing to support the Bush administration's bizarre shift in focus away from Afghanistan and onto Iraq. The decision to invade Iraq and overthrow Saddam's government inevitably resulted in the kinds of challenges that diplomats and development workers are best equipped to handle. But, thanks to the budget-slashing reinvention of government during the Clinton administration, there weren't enough civilians around to handle even existing priorities much less a surge to rebuild Iraq and Afghanistan. While some might argue that the State Department had become a military organization, with retired general Colin Powell as secretary of state and former assistant secretary of defense Rich Armitage as deputy secretary, many outstanding career FSOs were in positions of leadership. NEA was led by FSO Bill Burns, currently CIA Director, and his talented deputies included FSOs Jim Larocco, Ryan Crocker, and David Satterfield. Given that Liz Cheney occupied the political deputy position in NEA, I can appreciate how awkward it must have been for these career professionals to push back against the White House and the Pentagon on the direction of US policy.

The Iraq policy was driven by Dick Cheney, Don Rumsfeld, and the neoconservatives in senior Pentagon jobs. They insisted on creating a military organization to deal with the aftermath of the invasion. Retired general Jay Garner was chosen to run the Organization for Reconstruction and Humanitarian Assistance (ORHA). Garner, not an ideologue, was looking to State and USAID to recruit the kind of staff he thought he needed. Although I had argued in a speech in Tucson, only days before, that invading

Iraq was a bad idea, I agreed to become one of a second tranche[40] of eight retired FSOs recruited by the State Department to help staff ORHA. We were to be what the media called "shadow ministers." The formal title would be senior ministerial liaison. Rumsfeld opposed any additional recruiting by the State Department, and we eight were caught in the middle. I volunteered to run the graveyard shift of the State Department's Iraq task force while the battle over us was waged between Rumsfeld and Powell. The resulting compromise gave State only four of the eight remaining shadow minister positions. I was initially out in the cold but shifted to the Ministry of Foreign Affairs position when the leading candidate had to drop out because of health concerns.

When I arrived in Baghdad on April 24, after waiting eleven days in Kuwait for the US military to allow us into Iraq, I was part of a small cadre of active and recently retired career FSOs trying to mitigate the damaging effects of what we considered a wrong-headed policy. The administration's initial strategy was to drive Saddam out of power and turn the governance of Iraq over to a group of exiles favored by the Pentagon. When we arrived, most of the ministries had been looted and burned, communication systems had been destroyed and putting Iraq back together was a far greater challenge than anticipated. Garner was soon replaced by Jerry Bremer, a retired FSO with little Middle East experience and ORHA morphed into the Coalition Provisional Authority (CPA). Bremer immediately ordered the exclusion of thousands of senior Iraqi officials who knew how to run the country but belonged to the ruling Ba'ath party. He followed that with a decision to abolish the Iraqi military and intelligence services. Those of us with Middle East experience tried to push back on the de-Ba'athification policy but Bremer was clearly sent to Iraq to implement the Cheney-Rumsfeld playbook. The new policies proved to be the perfect recipe for an insurgency. Al-Qa'ida, which had no presence in Iraq prior to our invasion, happily swarmed in.

My job was to get the Ministry of Foreign Affairs back up and running. Our starting point was a looted and abandoned ministry complex and some fifty or more Iraqi diplomatic posts still run by Saddam appointees. My modest multinational team included an Arabic-speaking retired consular officer, an Army Reserve lieutenant-colonel, a Romanian ambassador, and a British diplomat. We pulled together an Iraqi steering committee of senior-level ministry employees, including a talented woman named Aqila al-Hashemi. We somehow managed to keep it largely intact despite pressure from those administering the de-Ba'athification process and from Iraqi exiles who sought to push out those Ba'athists who had remained in Iraq. Being retired with no career to protect and subject to minimal supervision, I had the autonomy that most FSOs can only dream of. When I departed in mid-June, most Iraqi diplomatic posts were under control and restoration of the physical ministry complex was well underway.

As the insurgency gained momentum after I departed in mid-June, however, three of the six Iraqis from the steering committee running the ministry were assassinated including Aqila al-Hashemi. Some years after I left Iraq, I co-authored a book with Ghassan Muhsin Hussein, the Iraqi who headed the Ministry of Foreign Affairs steering committee, about our collaboration in 2003 to get the ministry up and running.[41] I also devoted a chapter of my most recent book, *From Sadat to Saddam,* to summarize my experiences in Iraq in 2003.[42] Ghassan, a talented artist, went on to be Iraqi ambassador in Bahrain and subsequently retired there until he lost a fight with mesothelioma. Of the two surviving members of the steering committee, one continues to work in the ministry in Baghdad, and the other moved to Jordan where he applied to come to the US as a refugee and is today a US citizen.

We were now engaged in two wars which we had no idea how to win. Once the administration's rationale involving Saddam's alleged nuclear program dissolved, President Bush turned to nation building and democracy promotion in the middle of a homegrown insurgency. The military was in charge, as is appropriate in conflict, but nation-building is really the province of diplomats and development experts. Our military leaders understood and looked to civilian help from agencies still reeling from the budget-cutting during the Clinton years. The Bush administration did attempt to create a civilian surge-capability, which led to what is now the State Department Bureau of Conflict and Stabilization Operations (CSO). Overall, the initiative never advanced to the point of real relevance because of insufficient Congressional funding, interagency rivalries, and lack of forceful Administration leadership. Many of our best career professionals who did go to Iraq and Afghanistan worked effectively with the military. The cooperation between Ryan Crocker and David Petraeus in implementing the 2007 surge in Iraq is a good example.

Having twice gone back to work in the Middle East to plug gaps in our diplomatic readiness, I was now looking for something closer to home. Between 2004 and 2011 I was living in Tucson, juggling teaching at the University of Arizona with consulting for an organization called Leadership Development and Education for Sustained Peace (LDESP) which was run by retired military officers and funded by the Pentagon. LDESP provided short education programs for US Army and Marine units about to be deployed to Iraq and Afghanistan. Subjects included the politics and economics of the country, its culture, Islam, negotiations, ethics, and dealing with the media. After participating in more than fifty such sessions at military bases in Korea, Germany and around the US, I understood better the challenges of trying to prepare military units to advance diplomatic and development goals. The military is a true profession and most who rise through the ranks to the leadership level are impressive. Our political leaders have asked them to undertake tasks that historically we have called upon civilians to do. They salute and do their best with what they have.

In the initial years of our operations in Afghanistan and Iraq, the military focused on killing and capturing as many of the "enemy" as possible. Recognizing that this strategy was creating enemies faster than we could destroy them, General David Petraeus oversaw the rewriting of our counterinsurgency doctrine, in order to shift its emphasis toward protecting the population. I was enthusiastic initially, given our short-lived success during the 2007 Iraq surge. I eventually concluded, as did the Obama administration, that we were not capable of sustaining an effective counterinsurgency strategy.

Some years into my consulting work for the military, I was invited to speak at a conference funded by the Pentagon on the subject of "developing diplomatic skills inside the military/overseas/intercultural environment."[43] I argued that you can turn a soldier into a diplomat in a short time, just not a very good one. Further, I pointed out that many recruits have not been out of the US, have poor communication skills, and have learned from our media that most Arabs are terrorists. You can provide them with a list of cultural tips, but few soldiers come into the military with a mindset open to cultural differences. I explained that I kept my advice simple. My basic message drew from T.E. Lawrence, Major General John Wood (who I met during a short consultancy in Korea with the Second Infantry Division) and common sense:

It is their country, and your time there is short.[44]
Make friends not enemies.
Be part of the solution not part of the problem.
Always be collecting and always be transmitting.[45]

These guidelines for diplomacy must be balanced against the soldier's need to carry out the mission and protect the force. I also argued that you can turn a diplomat or development professional into a soldier, just not a very good one.

The Impact of Technology on Diplomacy

Routine Foreign Service communications moved at glacial speed when I joined the Foreign Service. I arrived in Quito on January 11, 1967. By the end of March, I was not being paid and my wife Sandy and I were burning through our State Department Credit Union loan. Then working in the administrative section, I drafted with my supervisor's help, an Operations Memorandum (OM) documenting the lag in arrival of the "authorization to pay" for me and several other newly arrived employees. We sent it March 30 and received a response, dated May 18, on May 25.[46] I assume both query and response traveled by sea in the diplomatic pouch. During subsequent years, an exchange of telegrams would have resolved the issue, perhaps even the same day.

During my time in Egypt, the State Department invested in Wang computers. They were boxy and clunky, but "state of the art" in 1984. In Cairo, I wrote memos and drafts of telegrams in longhand on a yellow legal pad, or for short items, I would dictate to my secretary. The transition to DC was painful because I had to learn both my new job and word processing on the Wang. The rhythm of work in NEA meant that there were almost always memos and telegrams to complete after secretaries left punctually at 5pm. On multiple occasions, critical paragraphs would disappear into the ether resulting in panic and unseemly cursing as we recreated the language with a deadline looming. When I retired eleven years later, the State Department was still using Wang computers and, by then, they represented seriously outdated technology. State did not get an IT makeover until five years later during Colin Powell's time as secretary. A combination of budgetary pressures and State Department culture appeared to have condemned us to living with inferior technology.

Methods of communication evolved dramatically during my diplomatic career. I began when messages were composed on yellow legal pads and routine messages (airgrams) traveled by sea in diplomatic pouches. Word processing didn't enter my world until 1984. The advent of 24-hour cable news (CNN) in the 1980s quickened the pace of crisis management.

Classified email was available during my last year in Riyadh (1992). I obtained my first personal email account in Oman in 1994 and was then using a personal computer for drafting messages at home (a questionable security practice). I used my first cellphone in Cairo in 1997 (a tremendous aid since I spent so much time in Cairo traffic). We were then using overhead slides for presentations. I used PowerPoint for the first time in 2003 in Iraq and constructed my first PowerPoint presentation in Korea a year later when I began working with the military. Like most military officers, I became addicted. We had satellite telephones in Baghdad in 2003 but they were only useful for calling people outside of Iraq. By 2003, crisis managers could choose among several cable news providers. I was able to surf the Internet and communicate regularly by email both in Washington and in Baghdad. We solved the communications problem in Iraq by creating a Hotmail account for the Iraqi Foreign Ministry and using it to regain control over Iraqi diplomatic posts abroad. Videoconferencing existed when I was in Iraq in 2003 but it was restricted for use by Garner and later Bremer for live communications with the Washington leadership.

Significant advances in communication technology did not change the essence of diplomacy and should facilitate the practice of diplomacy. Today's options make it easier to open and maintain the necessary channels of communication that allow us to anticipate crises. Modern technology does make it challenging for an ambassador to control country-team communications with Washington and to stay abreast of all communications between Washington and the host government. I will long remember Condoleezza Rice's order to the 2003 Iraq task force to collect the fax numbers of foreign ministers and national security advisers of all current and potential coalition members, so that the White House could communicate directly to them without going through our ambassadors.

Conclusions

Much has changed since I entered the Foreign Service in 1966 but there are many constants in what goes into successful diplomacy. The 1960s was a turbulent decade marked by Vietnam and the civil rights struggle, but bipartisan support for a robust diplomacy went hand-in-hand with our military capability. The ongoing Cold War with the Soviets provided incentive for discipline. Every country was important. If we weren't present and effective, we would be ceding ground to the Soviet Union. With the collapse of the Soviets, that discipline deteriorated and, with it, bipartisan support. Now, in this decade, if we aren't present and effective everywhere, we are ceding ground to China and Russia. The September 11 attack united us briefly but our overreaction to the threat of terrorism distorted our diplomacy and made the military our primary foreign policy tool for two decades.

Our diplomacy needs an extreme makeover, although fixing our splintered democracy is necessarily a higher priority. Somewhere, there is a bookshelf crammed with studies of what needs to be done to improve the Foreign Service.[47] As with the Israeli-Palestinian conflict, the destination is obvious but, given the political context the Foreign Service operates in, getting there is hard. A good starting point might be to do what Congress asked us to do in the Foreign Service Act of 1980: "to provide a **Foreign Service** characterized by excellence and professionalism, representative of the American people and operated on the basis of merit principles."[48]

The Foreign Service needs more people and more resources. There are multiple metaphorical dials and gauges to be monitored around the world that require trained and experienced professionals. Even with adequate staffing and resources, it will always be a bargain compared to our defense budget. More resources will allow for more training and more bench strength. Training must also be linked to career advancement.

Those many elements of Foreign Service culture that need to be changed can only be changed by patient and sustained leadership. Individual achievement is celebrated, group achievement not so much. The State Department organizational chart is a nightmare of complexity leading to unnecessary competition and insufficient cooperation between bureaus and offices. The Foreign Service pays lip service to the need for constructive dissent but being right is seldom career-enhancing and there are significant costs to those who press too stridently their concerns about misguided policies. The Foreign Service has many superstars and that is a good thing. I worked for and with several of them. Effective diplomacy is a team sport, however, and no team can be successful without competent role players to complement the superstars.

The Foreign Service lacks a tradition of requiring after-action reports and using case studies in training. Nowadays, we plunge headlong into a crisis, make decisions that either succeed or fail but which often have long-term consequences, and then we move on without looking back. Lessons learned in one bureau or embassy should be documented and made available to all. The Foreign Affairs Oral History Collection of the Association for Diplomatic Studies and Training is a good start, but much more is needed.[49]

I spent a substantial chunk of my career in State Department bureaus that were well-led and in the center of action. I was part of the Bureau of Economic and Business Affairs at a time when international economic diplomacy was a national priority. I was in the Bureau of Near East and South Asian Affairs when maintaining the Egypt-Israel peace was a national priority and when Palestinian and Iranian-inspired terrorism were peaking. Lessons learned from these successful bureaus should have been disseminated throughout our diplomatic service. Unfortunately, something akin to a crab mentality[50] or tall poppy syndrome[51] prevailed in Washington politics and each bureau was reduced from excellent to ordinary. I learned leadership skills from the best—career diplomats who embodied what Bill Burns calls the "crucial trinity: judgment, balance and discipline."[52] I took advantage of the many training opportunities (language, economics, and leadership training) that the State Department offered. I crafted my own leadership style which emphasized creating and maintaining communication channels with all who could affect a bilateral relationship and creating a positive team chemistry. Every entering FSO should get the same opportunities that I received.

Over the last thirty years, politicization has eroded US diplomacy. We are unique in our practice of distributing ambassadorships (generally about thirty percent before the Trump administration) to political supporters and campaign donors. Realistically, this will not change soon. Some political appointees turn out to be inspired choices, but most are not. There has also been a proliferation of special envoys to focus on issues that Congress or the administration believes needs special attention. These special envoys, often also political appointees, bring their own staffs and make the job of balancing various elements of our relationships with individual countries far more difficult.

The collapse of the Soviet Union made us complacent. The Clinton administration bowed to pressure from House Speaker Newt Gingrich and Senator Jesse Helms by substantially cutting the foreign affairs budget. New hires to the Foreign Service practically disappeared for several years. Many diplomatic posts and USAID missions were closed. The US Information Agency was closed, and public diplomacy became a stepchild in the Department of State. Not surprisingly, when the Bush 43 administration decided it needed a more muscular policy after the 9/11 attack, it turned to the military. There was no reserve core of civilians available to plunge into the war zones of Iraq and Afghanistan. For a generation, we organized our diplomacy around supporting the military response to the threat of terrorism. The challenge today for the Biden administration is to build a robust diplomatic capability to take on more compelling threats like climate change, pandemics, and cyber threats. We will need capable diplomats in every country capital (and beyond) and in every international organization in order to adequately protect US interests. We must be staffed to anticipate threats rather than to just react.

The increased focus on physical security, dating back to the April 1983 attack on the US Embassy in Lebanon, has made it harder for diplomats to get out of fortified embassies and build relationships with people in and out of foreign governments. The height of political abuse of security concerns was the shameful exploitation for partisan political purposes of the tragic 2012 murder of Chris Stevens in Benghazi, Libya. Concern for keeping secrets is as old as diplomacy itself but recent massive and deliberate leaks by government employees (Wikileaks and Edward Snowden, among others) have made foreign leaders far more wary of sharing information with US diplomats.

Technological change has significantly increased the range of options for how we conduct diplomacy, but it hasn't reduced the need for experienced and trained diplomats on the spot. Successful diplomacy is about creating relationships of trust, something difficult to do in Zoom meetings alone. On the wall behind Chas Freeman's desk in Riyadh was advice (in Chinese) that Chinese philosopher Zhuangzi gave to diplomats in the third century BC. The essence was that messages must be delivered faithfully, so that truth is not lost, and mutual trust is maintained.[53] To do this successfully requires not just "judgment, balance and discipline" but also a full career of training and experience. A diplomat must understand thoroughly the context in the country capital where the message originated and the context in the place where the message will be delivered. Diplomats absolutely must be trusted by those who employ them. If a trusted diplomat warns that delivering the message will do more harm than good to US interests, the warning should be taken seriously. All this is as true today as it was twenty-three centuries ago.

Notes

1. Coerr remained in the Foreign Service for nine more years but did not get another ambassadorship. The US government waited until populist Jose Maria Velasco Ibarra was elected president, before replacing Coerr. The Ecuadorean government reportedly came to regret the decision to expel Coerr.
2. The Foreign Service Institute (FSI) is the US government's premier foreign affairs training provider. During my career, FSI was in a modest high rise building with very slow elevators in Rosslyn, Virginia. It is today located on the campus of the George P. Shultz National Foreign Affairs Training Center (NFATC) in Arlington, Virginia.
3. Compared to some political appointees, he had diplomatic experience (as US ambassador in Copenhagen) and administrative experience (as director of the Federal Civil Defense Administration in the Eisenhower administration).
4. The delegation did allow Embassy staff to use its dedicated line to Washington for free phone calls.
5. On Jan. 22, 1972, in response to growing protest, the Department of State sent an airgram clarifying that participation by a Foreign Service spouse in the work of a post is a voluntary act and "not a legal obligation which can be imposed by any Foreign Service official or his wife." Use of airgrams ended in 1991.
6. A minor league baseball team that provides players as needed to an affiliated major league team.
7. Robert B. Zoellick, *America in the World: A History of US Diplomacy and Foreign Policy* (New York: Twelve, 2020), 246.
8. Although the members of the G-77 increased to 134 countries, the original name was retained due to its historic significance.
9. A Sherpa represents the president in preparations for a G-7 summit.
10. For more detail on trade reorganization see Thomas R. Graham, "The Reorganization of Trade Policymaking: Prospects and Problems," *Cornell International Law Journal* 13, no. 2 (Summer 1980): article 3. Accessed online at: https://core.ac.uk/download/pdf/80563157.pdf
11. Assistant Secretary Julius L. Katz, Oral History, interviewed by Charles Stuart Kennedy, 12 May, 1995 (initial), PDF, *Foreign Affairs Oral History Collection*, Association for Diplomatic Studies and Training, Arlington, VA, *adst.org* (Arlington: ADST, 1998), 68. Accessed online at: https://adst.org/OH%20TOCs/Katz,%20Julius%20L.toc.pdf
12. A separate Bureau of South Asian Affairs was created in 1992. It became the Bureau of South and Central Asian Affairs in 2006.
13. Congressman Paul Findley and Senator Charles Percy are two prominent examples.
14. Robert Kaplan wrote an entire book about Arabists: Robert D. Kaplan, *The*

Arabists: The Romance of an American Elite (New York: Free Press, 1993) passim.

15. An official-informal telegram or o-i was transmitted in classified channels but, in this case, was not distributed outside the Office of Egyptian Affairs.

16. TWA 847 departed Cairo on 14 June and was hijacked by a Lebanese terrorist group later known as Hezbollah. That led to a seventeen-day crisis which resulted in the murder of a Navy Seal named Robert Stethem. An Italian cruise ship, the Achille Lauro, was hijacked while docked at the Egyptian port of Alexandria on 7 October by members of the Palestinian Liberation Front. The hijackers shot a Jewish American confined to a wheelchair named Leon Klinghoffer and dumped his body overboard. The Egyptians decided to fly the hijackers to PLO headquarters in Tunis. The US Navy intercepted the flight, forcing it to land in Sicily, leading to a crisis in US-Egyptian relations. On 23 November, Palestinians associated with Abu Nidal hijacked Egyptair 648 and forced it to land in Malta. The hijackers shot two Israelis and three Americans (one died). Roughly 50 more passengers died when Egyptian commandos stormed the plane.

17. The only secretaries of state that I interacted with personally were Shultz and Baker. I did meet Colin Powell in Riyadh when he was Chairman of the Joint Chiefs and Madeleine Albright in Oman when she was US ambassador to the United Nations. I liked them both.

18. James R. Bullington, Oral History, interviewed by Charles Stuart Kennedy, 31 July, 2001, PDF, *Foreign Affairs Oral History Collection*, Association for Diplomatic Studies and Training, Arlington, VA, *adst.org* (Arlington: ADST, 2003), 58. Accessed online at: https://adst.org/OH%20TOCs/Bullington, %20James%20R.toc.pdf

19. Known as the Joint Economic Commission Riyadh (JECOR), it resembled a USAID program but was paid for by the Saudi government.

20. Horan's birth father was an Iranian diplomat.

21. Agrément is the agreement by a state to receive an ambassador.

22. James A. Baker III, *The Politics of Diplomacy* (New York: G. P. Putnam's Sons, 1995), 28–31.

23. Peter Baker and Susan Glasser, *The Man Who Ran Washington* (New York: Doubleday, 2020), 326. Foggy Bottom is the name of the neighborhood in Washington, DC where the State Department and the Kennedy Center are located.

24. Ibid., 328.

25. As reported in Christian Alfonsi, *Circle in the Sand* (New York: Doubleday, 2006), 23–24.

26. David J. Dunford, *From Sadat to Saddam: The Decline of US Diplomacy in the Middle East* (Lincoln: Potomac Books, 2019), 81–92.

27. Alfonsi, *Circle in the Sand*, 101–107.

28. Kelly, in his oral history, recounts that he came up with the figure. He didn't explain how. Ambassador John Kelly, Oral History, interviewed by Thomas Stern, 12 December, 1994 (initial), PDF, *Foreign Affairs Oral History Collection*, Association for Diplomatic Studies and Training, Arlington, VA, *adst.org* (Arlington: ADST,1998), 194. Accessed online at: https://adst.org/OH%20TOCs /Kelly-John-H.pdf.
29. He put them under house arrest and wouldn't let them out until they paid up.
30. Baker, *The Politics of Diplomacy*, 373.
31. *Circle in the Sand* does connect the dots.
32. POMCUS is an acronym for prepositioned overseas materiel configured in unit sets.
33. In 2022, President Biden nominated Michael Ratney, a career FSO, to be the next ambassador to Saudi Arabia. He arrived at post in April 2023.
34. See https://www.politico.com/magazine/story/2017/05/04/tillerson-trump -state-department-budget-cut-215101/
35. In USAID jargon the "pipeline" represents funds obligated but not yet disbursed. Rescissions were based on an obscure budgetary provision dating back to 1974, used by the Clinton administration but not subsequently until the Trump administration.
36. See www.medrc.org
37. Roughly equivalent to a three-star (lieutenant) general.
38. The *Foreign Service Journal*, September 2020, 85–86.
39. I was the first in 1981.
40. The first tranche departed for Kuwait on 16 March three days before the war started.
41. Ghassan Muhsin Hussein and David Dunford, *Talking to Strangers* (Winfield: Southwestern College Academic Press 2013).
42. Dunford, *From Sadat to Saddam*, 157–188.
43. The title was given to me; I never would have come up with it myself.
44. Misquotes of T.E. Lawrence abound. His exact words were "Do not try to do too much with your own hands. Better the Arabs do it tolerably than that you do it perfectly. It is their war, and you are to help them, not to win it for them." From T.E. Lawrence, "Twenty-Seven Articles," *The Arab Bulletin*, 20 August, 1917. Digital transcript in: 1917 Documents, World War I Document Archive (digital collection), Harold B. Lee Library, Brigham Young University, Provo, UT. Accessed online at: https://wwi.lib.byu.edu/index.php /The_27_Articles_of_T.E._Lawrence.
45. I worked with the Second Infantry Division in Korea in August 2004 as it was preparing a brigade to deploy to Iraq. The 2nd ID was commanded by Maj. Gen. John Wood. Wood wanted every soldier who met an Iraqi to be "always collecting and always transmitting." "Always collecting" means collecting

intelligence about people and places and getting it to people who need it. "Always transmitting" means having talking points ready about why the brigade is in Iraq and why it is good for the Iraqis.

46. I recall that I got my first check in April.

47. A recent one is "American Diplomacy at Risk," published in 2015 by the American Academy of Diplomacy, retrieved from https://www.academyofdiplomacy .org/publication/american-diplomacy-at-risk/

48. The Foreign Service Act of 1980 Turns 35, *The Foreign Service Journal*, September 2015, accessed online at https://afsa.org/foreign-service-act-1980-turns-35

49. *Foreign Affairs Oral History Collection, Association for Diplomatic Studies and Training,* Arlington, VA, https://adst.org/oral-history/

50. Any crab trying to escape the bucket is pulled down by the others.

51. Any poppy growing taller than the ones around it gets cut back.

52. William J. Burns, *The Back Channel* (New York: Random House, 2019), 408.

53. The entire translation is: "If relations between states are close, they may establish mutual trust through daily interaction; but if relations are distant, mutual confidence can only be established by exchanges of messages. Messages must be conveyed by messengers [diplomats]. Their contents may be either pleasing to both sides or likely to engender anger between them. Faithfully conveying such messages is the most difficult task under the heavens, for if the words are such as to evoke a positive response on both sides, there will be the temptation to exaggerate them with flattery and, if they are unpleasant, there will be a tendency to make them even more biting. In either case, the truth will be lost. If truth is lost, mutual trust will also be lost. If mutual trust is lost, the messenger himself may be imperiled. Therefore, I say to you that it is a wise rule: "always to speak the truth and never to embellish it. In this way, you will avoid much harm to yourselves" https://www.britannica.com/topic/diplomacy/History-of-diplomacy.

SEVEN

EARL ANTHONY WAYNE

Modern American Diplomacy

Core Skills, New Demands, and a Changing Global Stage

Diplomacy has been at the heart of relationships between governments and nations for much of recorded history, and certainly before. The core skills needed to successfully establish and maintain relationships between culturally, politically, linguistically, and otherwise distinct groups remain vital to the heart of successful diplomacy. However, the evolving ways in which governments and societies interact and try to work through problems and opportunities reveal that modern diplomatic practice has become much more complex. There are many more issues to master, greater pressures for rapid results and effective public messaging, and increased to involve wide swaths of the public than even two decades ago. While diplomacy remains at its core the relationships among nations and governments, the numbers and types of non-governmental actors engaged in diplomacy continues to grow significantly in our hyper-connected world. The global stage and power alignments have shifted significantly in this century, along with relative declines in US clout. There is no reason to believe that such changes in the diplomatic arena will not continue.

The basic mechanics of diplomatic practice have also become more complex. With more interactions among nations, US embassies have become larger, with more US government agencies present, more American citizens and companies needing assistance, plus growing sets of issues and tasks to manage, along with new internet-based tech tools and threats in the diplomat's workspace. Many more portions of the population seek to play a role in an expanding list of "global" issues that touch their lives, and do not respect national boundaries. And thus, increasingly, relations among nations are also issues of domestic debate and vice versa, so diplomats need to address domestic policy agendas and domestic audiences, as well.

The growing diplomatic workload is evident in the ever-more compli-cated policy processes within the State Department and the executive branch which must accommodate Congress and other agencies' concerns. Policy making has become more convoluted and difficult as domestic and international issues become more intertwined, and Americans are putting more blame on international factors for challenges they face, as under-scored by the bitter divides over trade and migration.

These changes have been paralleled by evolving relationships among great powers, emerging rivals, allies, and partners, as well as zones of in-stability, all of which continue to evolve and play out in a variety of policy and other substantive arenas in different parts of the globe and in multi-national forums. Challenges posed by cybersecurity, climate change, inter-national crime, global health crises, rapidly evolving transformative tech-nologies, such as AI, and mass movements of people, continually touch every continent.

Since the end of the Cold War, this changing international scene has been very difficult for successive US administrations to manage well. The United States has had great difficulty in crafting and implementing a cred-ible and effective strategic vision within which to produce good results over time. Thus, we have seen significant shifts in Washington's inter-national visions, with the most dramatic shift being the "America First" doctrine under the Trump Administration. Diplomats were key players in shaping the strategies and policies, as well as transforming them into the day-to-day workings of bilateral and multilateral relationships. They must play their roles even when they do not agree with some or all of Washing-ton's decisions and while they are scrambling to understand important emerging issues and dynamics. There have been many American diplo-matic victories along the way, but the trend has sadly been a relative de-cline in US influence and an increasingly complex playing field. The clear challenge for US diplomacy and its diplomats is to find ways to revitalize, reimagine and sustain America's role in the world.

Change as a Constant

For US diplomats, these developments mean that upskilling and reinven-tion has become even more of a constant in a diplomatic career. A funda-mental element of a Foreign Service career is, for example, that a US dip-lomat expects to change jobs and responsibilities every two to four years, often having to learn new cultures and languages and to establish new networks of contacts. This means that reskilling and career-long learning are built into the profession. However, the multiplication of substantive issues needed, from climate change, the environment, health, and international crime, to negotiating norms and rules for the internet economy, handling technological innovations, the introduction of new tools such as digital diplomacy, and the frequently evolving mix of policy priorities, all combine to make upskilling and reinvention a much higher and more frequent priority for successful American diplomacy and for individual success as a diplomat. The American system of diplomatic practice has not kept pace with the changes underway and has for some time been in dire need of modernization and additional resources. Happily, we are seeing more attention to these needs.

This increasing pressure for changes to diplomacy has been evident in the numerous thoughtful studies over the past several years recommending significant transformations and re-imagining for US diplomacy, the Foreign Service, and the Department of State. It is encouraging that the current US administration under President Biden and Secretary of State Blinken has taken up this agenda, and congressional authorization and appropriations legislation has begun to reflect the needed investments for future US diplomatic practice. But to succeed, this must be a sustained, long-term process of investment and implementation of reforms.

The agenda going forward must involve regular review and rethinking of how the United States develops and implements its policies as well as the efficacy of the policies themselves. To succeed, America must more regularly invest in adapting and improving the skills of its diplomats and the ways in which the State Department and the US Embassy teams around the world engage others (including in Washington and across the US) to achieve US objectives.

Similarly, the formation and implementation of US international policy must become more efficient, effective and seamless, to assure good results. The Biden Administration, for example, has come up with excellent conceptual frameworks for talking about a foreign policy that benefits the middle class, that provides worker-centered trade and economic policies, and that restores alliances, builds partnerships, and fortifies democracy. It has also mandated close linkages between the National Security Council, the National Economic Council and the Domestic Policy Council, as well as for related overlapping issues such as homeland security, health, and the environment. The administration successfully worked with Congress during its first two years to approve key legislation that aims to shape and fund changes. However, turning these good steps into a well-functioning policy process and positive results will be challenging, as all were reminded quickly by the US withdrawal from Afghanistan, and subsequently by the ongoing need to deal well with Russia's invasion of Ukraine. The challenges for effective international policy and for successful diplomacy are going to become more difficult to manage with the increasing pace and complexity of change in domestic and global arenas, not the least of which is a progressive weakening of democratic institutions and practices in many countries and continued polarization in US politics and the US congress.

Skilled Diplomatic Gardening

The speed of change, the scope of today's diplomacy, and its more immediate connection to domestic issues, may all be new factors, but the steep, demanding learning curve for diplomats has been quite evident over the forty-plus years that I have worked on diplomacy. The core skills and talents that are essential for a successful diplomat and for successful diplomacy remain constant.

While individuals seek a diplomatic career for a variety of reasons, for me and for many of my most successful colleagues, in addition to seeing the world and learning about different cultures and countries, the essential motivation for joining the US diplomatic ranks was to have the opportunity to build bridges between governments and nations, and to resolve and help avoid conflicts.

At a fundamental level the normal business of US diplomacy continues to be engaging others in ways that assure good communication and mutual understanding, and that maintain a peaceful international environment which allows the US to pursue its interests, and its values to flourish. Avoiding disruptive surprises and conflicts and finding solutions to disputes are also at the heart of US and much of international diplomacy. To do this well, US diplomats need to give deep and regular attention to what other nations are seeking, perceiving, and prioritizing, in order to nurture relationships that allow the US and those nations to find common ground (if possible).

This process is what former Secretary of State George Shultz called diplomatic gardening. This process builds and maintains relationships with enough trust to produce good results, whether one is dealing with "friends" or "rivals." This "gardening" is vital and takes place at all levels in diplomatic relations among countries. Doing it well starts with understanding others. Three of George Shultz's tenets have stayed with me during much of my diplomatic career, even though I worked with him directly for less than one year: 1) successful diplomacy demands regular tending or "gardening" to build and maintain productive relationships; 2) careful observation/listening, patience, endurance, determination, creativity and optimism are essential diplomatic gardening qualities (at home and abroad); and 3) never forgetting that the United States is your country and that its interests and political processes are always at the heart of one's diplomatic mission.

Core Skills

Understanding Others and Drawing Sound Conclusions

At the heart of diplomatic work is the ability to understand and analyze arcuately and adequately the "others" with whom you are working or dealing in another country, as well as comprehend the decision-making within your own country. In public diplomacy parlance, this is called "listening" to key audiences. Understanding the goals and motivations that drive governments, societies, and cultures, and being able to determine accurately any overlapping and conflicting objectives with the national interests of one's own country, is foundational for crafting and implementing international policy. We often use the phrase "to walk in another's shoes," to describe being capable of understanding the pressures, hopes, desires and fears of your interlocutor.

Assessing the Context

The assessment a diplomat provides also needs to accurately consider the relative strengths and weakness of the countries involved, the broader priority of objectives for each government, the limitations on their ability to act, and the decisions and actions that one can anticipate and try to influence. The assessment needs to be regularly revalidated, as it sets up the context for the strategic and policy frameworks within which diplomacy will seek to implement and achieve its goals.

Creating a Network of Contacts

From my first diplomatic jobs through to my last assignment as Ambassador to Mexico (and since), it was vital to create a network of contacts to consult with and rely upon for understanding the goals and political dynamics of your host country or international organization, as well as in one's own capital. One is often dealing with starkly different sets of cultural and historic experiences. It is also beneficial to avail oneself of the trusted views and analysis of close embassy colleagues, especial local-country embassy staff, who can often provide additional perspective. Doing this well enables one to better inform and guide Washington policy makers to devise good strategies and tactics for achieving US objectives. To be most effective, these networks need to go far beyond easy official contacts (e.g., in the foreign ministry or diplomatic corps) to encompass a wider range of people who could allow one to gain a meaningful and practical sense of the real-life dynamics of another society, government or key multilateral organization, such as for example, the European Union. The cultivation of trust and mutual understanding are vital principles of diplomacy, including to whatever degree is possible with rivals or enemies.

Building Relationships of Trust

From the perspective of individual diplomats, developing the skills needed to create broad and reliable networks of contacts can be challenging, especially for those who are not naturally outgoing. It was hard for me to learn how to "work a crowd," or to smoothly initiate social conversation with complete strangers. I worked methodically and persistently at building networks of contacts. Very importantly, for me, was to focus on the good qualities I could see in my interlocutor and on perspectives that we shared, (even if there also were important perspectives that we did not share). This combination was a successful formula for me both overseas and in Washington. Others developed their own strategies. But strong skills and talents in building trusting relationships with others and being able to communicate their views clearly to Washington served as pillars of success for me.

In general, diplomats and diplomatic missions are essential sources of "intelligence," and of analysis and recommendations to their governments for how best to deal with other countries or international entities. Of course, good reporting or analysis can't guarantee good policy decisions, but poor analysis and assessment of other states and societies by governments can certainly help lead to foreign policy disasters, as was starkly observed in the 2003 decision to invade Iraq and then the approach at first taken by the US toward post-invasion governance in Iraq.

In sum, the ability to gather insights, analyze a situation accurately, note potentially important developments in progress and then to communicate a good analysis and its potential ramifications for your country's interests are, in sum, core skills for diplomats.

State Department's Value Added

In this connection, it is important to remember that the greatest advantage which the State Department, US embassies and the Foreign Service bring to Washington policy discussions is the deep, experience-based understanding they can provide about other countries. Diplomats may not be as well informed as Treasury on ways to restore an economy in crisis, or as familiar as Defense with how to mobilize forces for a conflict intervention, but they should have the in-depth understanding of the political, cultural, and historical contexts for managing a problem. This value-added ranges from the analysis and reporting for Washington, to recommending the most effective implementation of US policy decisions. Good diplomats know the best methods to use to deliver key messages to the right people in the countries they serve, in order to build support for US objectives and steps to achieve them.

Effectively Informing and Influencing US Policy

Interestingly, the best diplomats apply their same analytic skills they use to understand other countries' dynamics to understanding how Washington is operating and how best to influence the policy decisions and action plans that are going to be made in the US government. When done well, just like with a host government in another country, the analysis and advocacy skills within the US government to all the key parts of a decision-making structure, including the legislature. However, I will focus on the Executive branch.

Impactful Drafting

It is far from enough to understand another country, culture, or political system, or even to write a good analysis and send in good recommendations. Those all need to be read, heard, and acted upon in one's own national capital. For US diplomats, that means a busy Washington DC. Clear, crisp drafting that tersely presents insights and arguments in a compelling order, linking them to US policy priorities and recommending doable next steps, are vital. This lesson was drilled home to me when I worked in the Secretary of State's office for two years. I read hundreds of messages from embassies each day, which in the State Department we still call "cables," plus many policy memos to the Secretary from various parts of the agency and emails. Embassy cables had a much better chance of being read and considered seriously if their titles caught the readers' attention, and if they had pithy, clear, and insightful summaries up front telling the reader why this cable is important to read. They needed to present well-organized, convincing arguments in the body of the cable, and a good conclusion stating what should be done, with recommendations about how to do it. I used and advocated for these essentials in all my subsequent overseas posts including in giving guidance to the reporting officers in embassies when I was Ambassador.

Similar patterns were true for memoranda sent to the Secretary of State, with adjustments for the required formats. A clear, convincing analysis of the issues and bureaucratic state-of-play which combined realistic sets of options with persuasive pros and cons that gave the Secretary real choices was the ideal we strove to achieve—often sending memos back to drafting bureaus for recrafting. Even so, under the pressure of time, we accepted many memos that fell short. This made subsequent in-house discussion of options very valuable. During my time in the Secretary's office, we also worked toward these goals in what we sent to the White House and other agencies. During those years, for example, on most evenings the Secretary of State sent a one-page "Night Notes" memo to the President. To increase the chances that they would be read, my special assistant colleague and I had to produce crisp versions of the drafts provided by Under and Assistant Secretaries of State for the Secretary to approve. We sought versions that would entice the President and others to read them. I want to add here that I had additional training on drafting from my two mid-career years as the National Security Correspondent at The Christian Science Monitor— my editors gave me daily instruction on how to grab people's attention on complex issues.

From then on, I consistently applied and adapted these lessons when writing or approving memoranda at the State Department from the Counter-Terrorism Office, the European Affairs Bureau, and the Economic and Business Affairs Bureau, as well as from the National Security Council's Europe office where we wrote memos for the President and others at the White House. Busy people, whether at the State Department, in the White House, or elsewhere are often looking for good insights into key issues and potential solutions to challenges, but one needs to bring the insights and ideas to their attention first. Conceptualizing the issues in a well drafted, concise form is a good start.

Finding the Right People at the Right Time to Help Shape Policy

In addition, with either embassies overseas or in the Washington bureaucracy, finding the most effective ways to flag the messages or memos to the "right" people is very important. Over my decades at the State Department, it became clear that the "best" US diplomats, embassies, and State Department bureaus were consistently able to get their good ideas to the right people consistently to propose new policies, strategies, and tactics, and they also were talented at identifying the right timing to do so. A great cable or message that arrives too late has lost its potential impact. The best diplomats regularly adapted to the systems, processes, personnel, and technology in use, to identify the target audience well and the best moments to command their attention. Many times, from my overseas posts, we would carefully time our messages to arrive with just enough time to entice policy makers to read them. We would add specialized addressing by naming the policy makers we hoped would receive the message. And when possible, at times we would send messages from several missions together to amplify their potential impact. The use of formal messaging is often accompanied by using informal networks to offer ideas and help shape the policy process in Washington via phone calls or emails.

Remembering that Washington Process is Important

Beyond identifying the key actors and timing, diplomats need to know how the policy process in a given administration is working or not working. These factors change between Presidential administrations as well as when key officials change within an administration. It really does matter how well the "policy process" is working in Washington, however, as scholars have well documented. Through much of the Reagan administration, for example, the National Security decision-making process did not work well. This resulted in many nasty and unproductive bureaucratic battles that impeded policy making and led to frequent revisiting of issues and very high tensions. Such bureaucratic infighting often made it very hard to craft and implement policy, for example. During the years that I worked for Secretary of State Haig and followed by Shultz, the State and Defense Departments were often feuding and relitigating divisive issues. The internecine infighting and resultant dysfunctional processes certainly had costs for the effectiveness of US foreign policy during the Reagan administration.

The dysfunction was so bad that I (successfully) sought to take a year off to attend Harvard University's Kennedy School and study leadership, decision-making and how to manage bureaucratic conflict. It was a very valuable educational experience that helped me think through some of the issues identified in this chapter and greatly benefited my future work, enabling me to assume higher responsibilities overseas and in Washington with a better set of tools and insights. I came arrived at the firm belief that the State Department was greatly underinvesting in the management and leadership skills of its diplomats. Interestingly, Secretary of State George Schulz also became a champion of further professional education for US diplomats, and it was the topic of the final article he wrote before passing away.

Following the Reagan years, the Administration of President George Herbert Walker Bush set the model for what a National Security decision-making process should be. Many good books describe the outstanding characteristics and processes that defined Brent Scowcroft's skills as National Security Advisor, and James Baker's skills as Secretary of State. I had the opportunity to observe firsthand what a difference a well-run policy process could make, from both the State Department's Counter-Terrorism Office and the staff of the National Security Council. The work was very intense, but good ideas had the opportunity to be heard and seriously debated within a disciplined policy process which was built by a solid, top-level team that did not regularly re-fight policy battles. The "Scowcroft" system was designed to recognize the importance of effective policy implementation. The United States was fortunate to have such a good team and system in place as the US exited the "Cold War" and began the transition to a multi-polar, globalized and more complex international situation, which continues to evolve.

From the perspective of US diplomacy, subsequent administrations, with varying degrees of success, sought to preserve the "Scowcroft" model for National Security decision-making, while adapting it to the new dynamics of big-power relations and the expanding set of issues and challenges on the agenda. For US diplomats during those years, and still today, it remains vital to know how best to inform and influence the State Department and Washington decision-making processes. Among the subsequent administrations, the Trump years reminded everyone that a well-functioning national security process matters, and that disruptions and dysfunction can come from the very top.

Not Neglecting Congress and Other Players in DC

A key item to mention briefly is that the US Congress is often a major player in shaping the diplomatic work to be done and determining how it can be done. Congressional funding and earmarks frequently limit what is possible overseas. Good diplomats invest heavily in getting to know key legislators and their staff, briefing them well, and testifying well before Congress. Many times in my career, Congressional action has determined a core part of my priorities. A good example was the Helms-Burton legislation which mandated sanctions on companies investing in Cuban property that had been taken from US citizens by the government of Cuba. This law set off a major spat with the European Union and its member-states who disagreed that the US had the right to impose sanctions on their companies which had legal leases from the Cuban government. My colleagues and I spent several years "negotiating" a solution to this dispute with the Europeans. These efforts enabled the President to finally create a waiver of the sanctions for the Europeans.

The big lesson for US diplomats, however, is to develop and nurture relations with key members of Congress along with key actors in the Executive branch, in order to have some input and influence for good on their legislation.

Other key influencers around Washington, including the media, have a big impact on policy making. Perhaps the major lesson I gained from my two-year leave of absence from the State Department, while working as the national security correspondent for The Christian Science Monitor, was that much of America's international policy is shaped outside of the State Department: in Congress, as well as by the media, thinktanks, lobbyists and respected experts, and also by the diplomats of other nations serving in Washington. US diplomats ignore them at great risk. A diplomat needs to be comfortable working with all these actors, particularly the media, while also being well educated in respecting the bounds of confidentiality around policy making and implementation.

Effectively Implementing Policies and Forging Agreements

At the heart of good diplomacy exists a cluster of skills that promote US national objectives abroad, that effectively implement agreed US polices and decisions by engaging other governments and elements of their societies, and that help avoid conflicts and seek solutions to disputes with other countries.

These skills include: communicating clear and precise messages from one's government to another; looking for and cultivating overlapping areas of interests between your government and others; negotiating ways forward to resolution where differences arise; devising joint policy frameworks and action plans; building coalitions of like-minded partners; maintaining, creating and building frameworks for long term partnerships and projects; and, effectively communicating with key audiences (among both elites and the broader public) regarding the "diplomacy" and international work underway. As noted earlier, these are all part of the toolbox for a successful diplomatic gardener, as George Shultz would put it.

None of these skills are particular to diplomats or only for use with other diplomats. They are often used by non-diplomat professionals such as lawyers, businessmen and politicians as well as when working with other agencies pr branches of one's own government. However, US diplomats are expected to be effective at these skillsets and to hone them with experience to apply them to wider and more diverse sets of actors and circumstances, as they rise to more senior positions.

Delivering Messages Well

An essential task for diplomats of all ranks is delivering messages from one's government to the host country government (a "demarche"), and in turn, passing back accurately and with explanation the response from the host country. From junior diplomats to the most senior ambassadors and officials in capitals, all are expected to do this. When not done well, the chances for misunderstandings between nations are greater. This is equally important when the initial messages are coming to Washington from another government. Many times, I saw messages in both directions being shaded and interpreted, sometime for good and sometimes with bad results. I remember distinctly, for example, a State Department reporting cable on US leadership communications with Iraq before the invasion of Kuwait that seemed at the time and subsequently to inadequately make clear the threat of what the US would do if Kuwait was invaded by Iraq. However, in other instances US diplomats, including me, did not deliver the messages precisely as written by Washington because the goal was to achieve a desired outcome from the host-government official, and the words crafted in Washington would have been counterproductive. This is where I learned that a diplomat's knowledge of his locale and counterparts can help produce better outcomes than following the exact words as crafted in the Washington bureaucratic clearance processes. Conveying the spirit of the message in ways that are most likely to get the desired outcome is vital. Recognizing this some State Department bureaus would even present key points to be made, and indicate they trust that the diplomats in the field would find the best specific wording to use. Then, of course, it is also vital that the response from the other government be reported clearly and as close as possible to their exact wording, as well. This reporting back to capital should also include appropriate interpretation, as in when a "yes" really means a "no," along with ideas for recommending any further action.

Assuring Clear Communication and Good Coordination

An important additional point and one of the most worrisome developments that I encountered, first in the 1990s, was Washington actors who would visit other countries to engage directly with foreign officials and not keep the Ambassador or the embassy (or at times not even the State Department) in the loop. In principle, there is nothing wrong with direct contact between officials working on a topic but if progress, agreements, or clashes are not shared with others, including with US embassies, it can lead to serious policy disconnects and unforeseen problems.

This links to a much bigger point: it is vital that components of the US government coordinate well in policy implementation and that there is no "stove piping." It is vital that whatever government team you are working with is in good communication with other US policy makers that are working on the same issues, in order to be aware of interactions and negotiations that might be taking place in other channels about those issues. This must be a priority whether one is working at an embassy overseas, in "bureaus" at the State Department or in interagency work across Washington. Good or bad coordination can boost or sink a policy process as well as implementation of policy. I learned to invest a great deal of time and effort into building "teams" within State, with other US agencies in Washington and, as an ambassador, between the embassy and the key players in Washington as well as among agencies and offices in the embassy. Assuring good coordination was an ongoing effort.

My foreign counterparts held similar concerns and made similar efforts as they worked within their own government and with the US government. I distinctly remember comparing notes with contacts in the European Commission in Brussels, with contacts in Brussels representing various EU member-state capitals, and a wide range of contacts from other governments in Kabul and in Mexico City, to avoid problems in what kind of communication was going on between different elements of our own governments. In Washington, working from the Economic and Business Affairs bureau, it was essential that we build effective and trusting coordination not only within the State Department but also with our counterparts at the National Security Council, the Treasury Department, the Commerce Department, the US Trade Representative's office, and many more players. This was often challenging given bureaucratic rivalries and different perspective on issues, but it was required for getting the work done well.

More broadly, although today's easy and rapid international communications bring many benefits to diplomacy, they can also very much complicate successful diplomacy and demand even closer oversight and coordination than the slower-paced and less connected diplomacy of the post-WWII world order did. Farther on, I will mention complications for diplomacy from this highly interconnected world. However, the key point here is that a successful US diplomat will endeavor to maintain fluid communications within his embassy team, with key actors in his capital, and with his local counterparts.

Pushing Back and Influencing Decisions Early

Providing an alternate perspective for a set of instructions from one's own Capital sometimes requires a delicate balancing act from Ambassadors and other senior diplomats. In some cases, Ambassadors will need to find ways to push back on Washington to change the instructions received, often best done via informal messages back to key players. This tactic can work if the arguments for changes are made well, but it can also run into a solid wall of resistance or accusations of "localitis," especially if much negotiation in Washington and very senior-level involvement contributed to the decision. In these instances, Ambassadors have hard decisions to make about the damage that might be done by delivering the message as stated, versus the damage to their own future credibility in Washington by refusing to do so.

If possible, it is much better to be involved in the Washington policy process along the way and beneficially try to influence the instructions long before they are sent to post. This gets back to the importance of having networks of trust and good communication in State, in the White House and with other agencies. The network is a vital means of knowing what is going on, and to shape and influence policy and decisions. A good understanding of your own capital, the administration in which you are serving, and knowing how to help shape outcomes is essential for successful diplomacy.

For example, while serving as Deputy Chief of Mission at the US Mission to the European Union (the number two position in a US diplomatic mission) in Brussels, we found it very important to work with other US embassies in Europe to forge common approaches to key issues on how best to achieve US objectives while addressing Europe-wide and EU member state preferences. We made a point to share policy ideas as well as specific proposals through various formal and informal channels to Washington, before the State Department and the administration had completed its complicated interagency process. At that time, many key players in Washington did not appreciate the emerging importance of the European Union in Europe and the need to adjust US policy to work closely with the EU as well as with NATO and key national capitals. Our interventions were favorably received and had good impact. One of the Ambassadors in the group soon returned to a senior post Washington, assuring that the ideas shared among the group would have practical policy effect.

Similarly, in working on US-Mexico relations as Ambassador from the US embassy in Mexico City, the embassy team needed to work with a wide variety of US government agencies who often had conflicting views on issues and who all played important roles in the Washington policy process. In many of these cases, we found it useful to develop our own embassy-wide strategy and ideas to share with the respective agencies in Washington. We did this in formal proposals but, importantly, ahead of time we prepared the way through individual calls with key agency officials, to introduce and shape our proposals and to build a coalition of support within the US government for the proposals we offered. We often worked to forge new and improved proposals in these informal discussions with Washington.

In Afghanistan, on the other hand, the pressure of daily operations, the many actors involved in DC, Kabul and elsewhere, and the rapid turnover of US personnel in Afghanistan all combined to make this kind of coordination and shaping of policy very difficult. The lack of effective communication and coordination of ideas at times contributed to serious policy differences between military and civilian players in Kabul, as well as in Washington. It also regularly resulted in mixed and poorly coordinated messaging to the Afghans. That did not stop US actors in Kabul from pushing back on US policy and trying to influence outcomes. Nor did it stop various players in Washington from trying to micro-manage many aspects of US diplomacy in Afghanistan. This all made for an intensely complex policy situation during a very complex and dangerous conflict.

Building Coalitions Well

Whether a diplomat is seeking to win support only in one country on one specific issue, or is working to build wider support among a group of countries for an issue or set of issues of broader import, the ability to assemble and build support of partners is vital. In my experience, it was in practical terms always better to have a group of countries supporting a US initiative than to have the US pursuing it alone. Even in cases where the US was trying to bring about a change in a single government's policy or practices, US diplomats often needed to build a local coalition to support the desired change.

Working for Secretary of State Haig and then Shultz during the Cold War era, one of the first questions on any issues raised was "how can we get the allies on board?" That management of allies was often not easy or uniformly successful diplomatic work, whether it was selling our approach to Intermediate Range Ballistic Missiles or on handling leftist governments in Central America. However, efforts to gather support and build coalitions was vital then and continued to remain vital throughout the subsequent decades, even if the Trump administration diverged significantly from giving it the priority it deserved. (Interestingly, even though the GW Bush administration pushed ahead with THE invasion of Iraq, they quickly pivoted to get as much partner support as possible, for example on economic reconstruction in Iraq.) The Biden Administration has made coalition building and alliance strengthening a core principle, recognizing that in a world where US clout is relatively reduced it needs partners even more than before in recent decades. The importance of effective diplomatic efforts to build coalitions and partnerships will remain essential for the foreseeable future, fueled by China's rise and Russia's aggression in Ukraine.

One of my formative experiences showing the value of a well-conceived diplomatic coalition-building campaign was evident during the US effort to combat terrorism in the late 1980s, which in some ways prefigured our post-9/11 global campaign against Al-Qaeda. The US faced a difficult time convincing some of our close allies and partners, as well as some countries that were more non-aligned, of joining together in a unified effort to act against terrorist groups. The State Department, working with the intelligence community, both designed special intelligence briefings and organized traveling delegations of senior officials, to explain the need and value of collective action and to address concerns face-to-face, with personal diplomatic engagement. These briefings and diplomatic engagements produced good results in convincing other governments of the dangers the specific terrorist groups posed and enhanced collective cooperation against these terrorist groups. Then, after Iraq invaded Kuwait in 1990 and threat of terrorist attacks against the US and its embassies increased during subsequent US efforts to liberate Kuwait, the State Department launched a worldwide campaign to obtain unified action against terrorism using the same diplomatic coalition-building approach it had described above. This effort prompted scores of countries to work supportively with the US with practical steps to stop Iraqi terrorism. For many of the participating governments this was the first time they had ever worked directly with the US on counter-terrorism. A decade later, the US deployed an updated version of this type of diplomatic campaign to build a broad coalition for placing new limits on Al-Qaeda and the financing of terrorist activities.

Helping to guide and shape the effort against Iraqi terrorism was my first serious learning experience for what became a series of coalition-building efforts in subsequent assignments including as Principal Deputy Assistant Secretary of State for European Affairs and as Assistant Secretary of State for Economic and Business Affairs. While working on Europe, the coalition-building diplomacy included forging an agreement in 1999 on how to end the fighting in Kosovo, and move forward to build peace and prosperity in Southwest Europe. In the Economic Bureau, this coalition-building work included convincing over 100 countries to join in outlawing the financing of terrorism after 9/11. It required building large coalitions of donors willing to invest many billions of dollars in aid for rebuilding Afghanistan and Iraq after initial fighting had ended in the early 2000s. International coalitions of donors also had to be built to pay for damages caused by a massive tsunami in East Asia and an earthquake in Pakistan.

Each of these partner-building efforts required a well-conceived set of objectives and arguments, often devised in partnership with key non-US government (USG) partners (nations, international organizations, and international and regional financial institutions). Combined with heavy reliance on diplomatic skills and knowledge of US diplomats around the world, these coalition building efforts led to successes that were beyond anything the US government could have achieved on its own. Success demanded heavy investment in working patiently and often laboriously with other partners in regular, at times daily and weekly, conversations. For example, we worked very closely with Japan, the EU, Saudi Arabia, the

World Bank, and the UN Development Program in the case of the first Afghan donors conference, occurring from late 2001 to early 2002. Succeeding also required a willingness to apply good ideas from any of the partners, for building trust and to share the credit, as Secretary of State George Shultz taught.

Within a particular country or grouping (like the EU), building partnerships and coalitions is also vital. It is often very difficult to convince another government to accept a US policy recommendation, no matter how brilliant or well-founded it is, unless there is also a group of stakeholders in that country who are willing to lobby in favor of this collaborative approach. This conclusion became very evident during my years of heading the Economic and Business Affairs Bureau at the State Department as we tried to encourage economic reforms, changes to commercial practices, or regulatory changes in countries around the world. US Embassies, in working with Washington agencies, regularly needed to reach out to members of the local business community or the legislature, or even to leaders of geographic regions, to find those who might have an interest in the reforms or changes the US favored and thus would be willing to promote a reform or change from within the target country.

Public diplomacy messaging, including the use of social media, was also a very useful tool for building support, whether with articles, photos, speeches, or interviews, to explain the benefits of a policy change and to build support for the change in a target country. In countries where there was not a substantial potential domestic coalition in favor of a change or reform, US efforts frequently did not achieve good results, regardless of whatever merits the US policy proposals held for the economic well-being of the country in question. This is also an excellent example of how domestic and international agendas overlap and can collide. Much of the time, unless one can find a way to influence the domestic debate over policy, the international arguments will not carry the day.

I experienced the same basic rule applying to our work with the European Union. For example. I worked with the EU directly and indirectly for about fifteen years. I found that the degree to which we could get various elements of the European Commission and/or enough member states to support the direction that we sought to move, our chances of success were greatly improved. This often took daily hand-to-hand diplomacy in Brussels and EU capitals in order to build like-minded coalitions and then forge solutions in diplomatic exchanges. It often meant supporting "deals" among EU actors and flexibility in our own approaches. But without this skilled and multifaceted diplomacy, stalemate would have been much more likely on a host of transatlantic issues touching billions of dollars in economic activity, and the US could have stood to lose invaluable European support in managing key international economic and foreign policy issues. The overarching objective in much of this effort was to create a working partnership with the EU within which we could together manage a broad agenda and forge solutions to difficult problems and disagreements.

Maintaining and Deepening Relationships with Careful Tending

In this connection and as noted earlier, at the core of good diplomatic practice is maintaining and strengthening long-term relationships with allies, partners, and rivals as well. For diplomats, one key set of responsibilities is arranging visits, summits and regular senior-level meetings, as part of building relationships that endure. This work, like the rest of diplomatic gardening involves patience, persistence and working creatively with your partner-teams, to make visits and meetings successful. This often includes designing a set of "deliverables" or outcomes to make meetings worthwhile. Some of them may be largely symbolic but the best encounters solve problems or at least open the door to solutions and create new possibilities for doing beneficial cooperative work going forward. This was certainly the case for the many US-EU and G-8 summits on which I worked as well as the many dozens of bilateral head-of-government meetings on which I worked.

One of the big lessons I learned early on was that, while it is very important to focus on having a successful visit or summit and it takes a lot of diplomatic work to get good outcomes, the summit or visit is only as good as the follow-up work. The effect of a successfully negotiated communique is brief. Shortly afterwards must begin the vital work of making sure outcomes are implemented well and that progress is made toward achieving its goals, both of which often require continued engagement and detailed follow up. In many cases, US and other diplomacy falls short in this implementation phase. I thus learned that it is very important to monitor implementation and to report back to leaders on progress made (or not made). I spent a great deal of time when working on US-European relations doing just that kind of diplomatic gardening which is crucial for maintaining and deepening relationships among nations.

Constructing for the Longer Term

For diplomats there are at times also opportunities to open new phases of relationships between countries or organizations. The greatest example of that during the last century was the tremendously creative work by leaders, supported by diplomats, to establish the United Nations, the World Bank, the International Monetary Fund, NATO, and other institutions. While relatively few diplomats have the opportunity to help build global institutions as was done in the post-World War II years, there are and will continue to be opportunities to create mechanisms, processes and frameworks that will deepen, expand and extend relationships between countries, beyond run-of-the-mill diplomatic gardening. Many of these involve establishing mechanisms and processes that institutionalize the work of managing key issues, addressing problems and seizing opportunities quickly. These creative opportunities can also come in the forms of negotiation and international agreement that helps change practices and norms among nations. The diplomatic skills valuable to undertaking this work are not different from those discussed above, but at these pivotal moments, it can be key to foster the ability to think "big," and creatively so to develop and maintain deeply trusting partnerships, to build favorable outlooks from capitals, and to do the detail work well are vital. Let me share two examples.

In the mid-1990s, as the European Economic Communities (EEC) were becoming the European Union (EU). and both Europe and NATO were adjusting to the end of the Soviet Union and Warsaw Pact, the US was also looking for additional partners to help deal with problems in Europe and around the world, including newly-emerging global issues such as the environment and international crime. The stage was set for rethinking how the newly consolidating European Union should engage the US beyond purely trade issues, while also preserving the important role that NATO should still play in transatlantic security relations. Several diplomats on both sides of the Atlantic obtained authorization from their superiors to explore how to do this, and over months of negotiations they designed a new outline for cooperation between the EU and the US, called the New Transatlantic Agenda. This new collaborative mechanism for transatlantic cooperation covered the entire gamut of economic issues, foreign policy coordination, foreign aid cooperation, and dialogues on a range of global issues including crime. I had the opportunity to co-lead the US team negotiating with the European Commission. During the months of negotiations, the two sides found massive areas of agreement. The negotiating teams developed a set of shared objectives and together built a large coalition of actors from both sides of the Atlantic centered around a forward-looking vision. The agreement itself, however, basically set the stage for an series of summits, ministerial meetings, "senior level" working groups, and sectoral and agency exchanges among officials from a very wide set of agencies and European EU member states, including private as well as civil society sectors, all dedicated to turning that vision into practical results over the following years. Just to mention in passing, it is of note that the US and the EU have the largest and broadest economic relationship in the world and the EU has become a major diplomatic and development partner with the US in many key regions as well as on key areas like the environment. In subsequent years the form and names of these EU–US meetings and engagements have evolved, but the overall framework has remained and today still functions very closely, to maintain and deepen a very close transatlantic relation alongside NATO. The EU still today considers the New TransAtlantic Agenda as a key marker in developing relations with the US.

Another example from my diplomatic experience of building for the long term involves the US-Mexico relationship. This relationship is unique for both the US and Mexico because it touches the daily lives of so many Americans and Mexicans—more than relations with any other country in the world for each country. This bilateral relationship carries the weight of an often-troubled history, close family and cultural ties, well over million dollars a minute in trade, and a very challenging border to manage as is highlighted by deadly illicit drug trade and massive flows of migrants. My years in Mexico coincided with US and Mexican administrations that both recognized the importance of the relationship and sought to improve that by building stronger mechanisms and processes for solving problems together. With senior officials on both sides willing to consider ways forward, the US Mission Mexico team and I worked "diplomatically" with Mexican and US colleagues, to offer and support new ideas for better cooperation on the border; on handling migration with a series of new agreements and regular consultations; on coordinating against organized crime with a new senior-level, cross-agency coordinating group; and on military-to-military relations with an unprecedented series of regular exchanges. The US and Mexico teams greatly expanded educational exchanges and agreements between universities and other educational institutions that were supported and encouraged by the two governments. We increased business-to-business ties by supporting creation of a new CEO Dialogue (which brought CEOs for their own discussions of how to strengthen bilateral commerce and then to have exchanges with officials) and by establishing programs to support innovation and entrepreneurs. A new High Level Economic Dialogue was also created and chaired by then-US Vice-President Biden, to coordinate the vast array of economic issues not covered by the North American Free Trade Agreement (NAFTA). While a number of these new institutions were put aside during the Trump years, they have since been revived by the Biden Administration. This creative burst of US-Mexico diplomacy is an example of what can be done toward fortifying international relations through serious diplomacy, when partners are committed, innovative and realize the need to invest in longer term relations.

Negotiating to Solve Problems, Build Partnerships,
Contain Rivalries, Avoid Conflicts, and End Wars

Evident throughout most every diplomatic activity is the ability and skill to negotiate understandings well with other governments. It would be impossible to succeed as a diplomat if one can not negotiate well with friends, partners, rivals, and adversaries. The most dramatic negotiations revolve around avoiding or ending fights and wars. Many books have been written about those dramatic and important negotiations, and diplomatic colleagues during my years in service have excelled when thrust into such high-tension and high-stakes situations. Richard Holbrook and James Dobbins stand out in my experience as two successful diplomats with very different styles of negotiating during crises but both with track records of note. Yet many dozens of others, through negotiations, have succeeded in bridging very difficult and broad divisions between the US and other countries with good results. Many diplomats have brokered issues that resulted in significant benefit for the US and others which otherwise could have cost the US dearly. It is important to note in key cases, that the US and others have repeatedly needed to negotiate around conflict or potential conflict situations, with mixed records of success. The experiences surrounding the fighting in the Middle East (e.g., Israel, its neighbors and the Palestinians, the conflict in Syria, the various challenges in Iraq and the long US intervention in Afghanistan) as well as in South Asia, are reminders of the serious challenges to achieving successful negotiations, even with excellent diplomats and skilled negotiators involved.

Negotiations are perhaps the perfect example of diplomacy as a contact sport—and as a sport with a season that will last longer if relationships among involved countries remain important. One needs to understand as clearly as possible your own and your counterpart's available room to maneuver, to determine if there is a possible overlap of interests and objectives, and further, to consider whether you have any leverage to change that situation.

For me, this meant regularly putting myself in my counterpart's shoes and then stepping back mentally to think of ways forward. It also meant creatively thinking through what tools and steps might increase my leverage and/or change my counterpart's room to resist, and in addition, examining what factors seriously limit the flexibility available for me and the others engaged. I also learned the importance of thinking several steps beyond a specific negotiation to consider whether the outcome would allow or promote further future progress and benefits for the parties. In that sense, just as in good diplomatic gardening, I was frequently reminded that negotiations should build trust. Sharp tactics might win a round, which I saw in several cases, but one needs to avoid over-reliance on them, as they are unlikely to win the broader war or help prevent another conflict. In most cases, there need to be positive benefits for both sides for a solution to prosper. I found negotiations to be a series of encounters in which one defines potential common ground and outcomes that can point to a way forward, even if not entirely a win-win. Success also can require letting others play key roles in attaining the outcomes one desires. The ability to step back at certain moments and let others offer solutions can at times be important for success.

Let me briefly recount one set of negotiations at the end of the fighting in Kosovo in 1999. The discussions were focused on getting to agreement on how to bring Kosovo and surrounding countries of southwest Europe to a consolidated path of peace which could build prosperity and integrate the region more effectively into the rest of Europe and the larger transatlantic community. I had the opportunity to help lead the US team in this diplomatic dance during the summer and fall. Our aim was to solidify peace in and around Kosovo, and that required forging agreement among the G 7 countries, the European Union member states, the Central and Southwest European countries, Russia, and several international institutions, including United Nations agencies and international financial institutions. Anger and tensions still ran high, for some. Progress required negotiating bilaterally, negotiating in the G-7 and G-8 groupings in June and in several larger forums, negotiating with some sixty participants around the table. It required that that the US also build agreement with EU leadership (in those months, Germany then Finland, and the European Commission) on the overall vision and plan.

Then, once that key understanding was achieved, US and EU diplomats set out to bring all the others around, including Russia. Moscow was adamant about protecting Serbia's interests regarding its claims to sovereignty over Kosovo. Germany did not want to press Russia too hard to reduce its support for Serbia's positions, even though agreeing with US objectives, and the UK and France shared that perspective. This basically meant that our US team was negotiating simultaneously on multiple fronts while also facing some hesitant support from some of our most prominent allies.

During key negotiating moments on the margins of the June G-8 in Cologne Germany, we stepped back to recalculate our strategy and decided to build on the strong support from Central Europeans for checking Russian influence in the regions. In a series of quickly arranged private meetings, we reached agreements with most of the Central European delegations and several smaller EU/NATO members, for making aligned interventions at key points in the next day's meetings which could keep the "big" Europeans in line if they wanted to yield too much to Russia. In this way, "the US could avoid giving the appearance of trying to impose its will, and instead a group of countries was pursuing a position that happened to align with that of the US. That strategy worked perfectly, and we emerged with an agreed position among all the EU and NATO countries, including those who had previously waivered. Thus, when the Russians were isolated, the Germans and I devised a wording that would allow the Russians something that allowed them to save face. With approval from the US and German foreign ministers, a senior German diplomat privately shared the language with the Russians as their idea, and the Russians accepted.

Following the Cologne summit in June, we had to rapidly negotiate agreement on the specifics of a "Stability Pact" for the region, which was to be blessed at a Summit meeting in Sarajevo on July 30, 1999.

This turned out to require negotiations among some sixty delegations. The Russians sent a lead negotiator with a reputation for being very tough and having a difficult personality. I consulted with several experienced US diplomats and decided to make a specific effort to pull him aside from the session's main proceedings and try to establish some degree of mutual understanding and trust, even if our respective instructions clashed. At the margins of a sixteen-hour negotiation session, the Russian negotiator and I met several times. I told him our aims in frank terms including not leaving Russia out, and eventually we built enough mutual confidence, that he told me what he could not accept. Working with other delegations, we were able to resolve all but one issue. The Russian and I agreed to refer that issue to our foreign ministers who in several hours were going to meet on the other side of the world. The ministers reached agreement on how to handle the remaining issue, thus we attained agreement to proceed with the Sarajevo Summit at the end of July (1999).

One final crunch point in this sequence of diplomatic negotiating came in Sarajevo after the summit speeches had begun. Unexpectedly, Albania decided to demand certain language aimed at protecting Kosovars of Albanian ethnicity that the Russians would not accept, and both threatened to walk out of the Summit. I huddled with the Finnish diplomat who was leading the EU's team for the summit. In coordination with me, he had been shuttling back and forth between the Russians and the Albanians. He and I came up with a formulation that we thought could meet all needs. I got a senior White House official and the Secretary of State to concur, and the Finn then got the Russians and Albanians on board The Summit statement was agreed in time for all the gathered leaders to bless it.

For me this experience underscored the importance of building and using partnerships in negotiations, of creating as much trust and understanding as possible even with rivals, and of being open to creative adjustments along the way to achieving one's objectives. In this case, the outcomes supported processes and interactions that continued to help the region, long after the summit itself.

Meeting Short Term Objectives and Accounting for Long-Term Effects and Fallout for Issues

One important perspective a good diplomat brings to his/her craft is how to succeed in the near-term, and simultaneously, how to achieve good long-term outcomes as well. The diplomat also needs to consider the potential fallout and impact for other issues that are not necessarily connected directly to the one being discussed or negotiated. Can one turn a near-term success into an expanding and enduring path for cooperation, for example? Conversely, how can one limit the negative fallout of one issue or negotiation from encroaching into other important areas or over the longer-term. Good diplomacy will do best to think through the potential connections to other issues, and to think about longer term consequences and opportunities, as well as how one's actions will fit into your home country's broader strategy.

When managing an important issue with the EU, for example, I would ask might our handling of it have an impact on cooperation in other parts of the US-EU partnership, or on NATO-related initiatives, or on cooperation with key EU member-states? Similarly, in dealing with various individual disagreements over a particular border management issue with Mexico, my team and I would regularly talk through whether we could translate this into building a broader gain for bilateral cooperation on public security, or conversely, we would explore how to avoid negative impacts on bilateral anti-crime cooperation or on the public's image of the US government in Mexico. This was also a regular calculation of senior officials, with whom I worked in the early years of the Reagan Administration, regarding rivalry with the Soviet Union. I sat in many meetings where these officials would debate how moves of the US or Soviets in Central America, Southern Africa and other regions could set off reactions elsewhere in the world, e.g., the Middle East or in US-Soviet relations. In today's diplomacy, with so many interconnections between issues and between agendas both domestic and international, this kind of cross-checking for potential effects is more vital than ever.

Conducting Effective "Public Diplomacy"

The ability to influence foreign publics with effective speeches, media interviews, press conferences, articles, etc. has long been a hallmark of a successful senior diplomat and ambassador, but the importance of public diplomacy has grown immensely, as communication has become global and immediate, and as social media, combined with smart phones, has exponentially multiplied the ways in which millions share information, and disinformation as well. Modern diplomacy demands greater skills in knowing how to influence the right audiences with more tools, doing so rapidly and frequently, and countering the disinformation that flows from many sources about issues vital to diplomatic objectives.

Senior officials and diplomats in Washington and overseas need to be much better synced with one another, and ready to use the evolving range of public diplomacy tools so that US policy messages are getting through effectively to a broad spectrum of key target audiences. Indeed, one also needs to listen to, analyze and understand the audience one is trying to influence and find the best ways to engage them, so they absorb and are open to the messages one is seeking to deliver.

Unless one was specialized in the public diplomacy field as a more junior or lower-ranked diplomat, it used to be that one did not have to worry very much about public diplomacy until reaching the more senior level where speeches and media interviews were required. However, with the global communications revolution and widespread use of social media for good and bad, most every diplomatic interaction can have a public diplomacy impact (for good or bad). Major segments of another nation's public today are quickly plugged into what the US is "doing," And the US public has practically immediate access to information generated around the world. In Argentina and Mexico, I frequently reminded all my embassy section heads that the public diplomacy section of the embassy was a vital partner for each of them, with opportunities to improve the US image in those countries and to avoid carefully any steps that could harm the US image. A key part of our daily routine was to identify the public diplomacy issues that needed to be managed and to make sure that the Embassy team and their partners in Washington were working in sync to deliver message in ways that they would be heard by key audiences whether they be elite decision makers, young people, certain geographic or social groups in a country etc.

Beyond just getting the message out, diplomats and public diplomacy teams must evaluate if the outreach is having a positive impact for the advocacy objectives set, and if not, the outreach strategy needs to be adjusted and improved. Integrating public diplomacy into all aspects of US diplomacy, whether emanating from Washington or from individual embassies, is an area for continued investment in tools and training, improved coordination across government, and smarter use of the public diplomacy tools currently available and regularly emerging as technology evolves.

Managing People, Programs and Resources Well

Many successful Secretaries of State have looked to shape, formulate, and implement policy from Washington, as well as to negotiate solutions to problems or forge new opportunities. However, most have not given enough attention to how important it is to invest in the skills and development of US diplomats, or to effectively manage the programs, institutions and other resources needed to carry out with excellence America's diplomatic practice around the world. Some of our very best negotiators, for example, were poor at leading people, teams, and institutions. This similar weakness was evident among ambassadors and assistant secretaries of state, especially those who entered the State Department via political appointment of a given presidential administration.

However, some secretaries of state (and officials at other levels) have understood the importance of investing in the State Department as an institution and in its diplomats, foreign service, and civil service. Secretaries of State George Shultz, and Colin Powell "got this" and supported increases for State Department training, funding, and investment in the "infrastructure" of a successful foreign affairs agency. It is very welcoming that Secretary of State Antony Blinken is of this same tradition and has defined such an ambitious modernization process for the State Department. He successfully sought additional funds, staffing and authorizations needed from Congress during his first two years in office.

The priority of focusing on excellent management and leadership of institutions needs to be instilled and rewarded among US diplomats and made part of the State Department's permanent culture. It is necessary but far from sufficient to just devise good policy and draft good cables. Embassies and state department bureaus need to be capably and creatively led. Policies need to be well implemented by trained staff and funds need to be responsibly used and monitored. Staff need to be mentored and trained/educated consistently throughout a career. US diplomats change jobs every 2–4 years and jobs are being reinvented with new areas of expertise required regularly.

There are much better efforts to instill this learning culture and provide that level of leadership and management training in today's State Department, but through most of my forty-year career, essential leadership and management skills and talents were not systemically encouraged, taught or promoted. It was much more a "learn-as-you-go" system in which individual officers had to seek out on their own much needed additional training and skill-building. I started learning how important these skills were during the 1990s when I was named as a Deputy Chief of Mission at the US Mission to the EU in Brussels, and subsequently when I was giving the responsibility to help manage EUR, the largest and most well-funded geographic bureau in the State Department, as the Principle Deputy Assistant Secretary of State. I was learning on the job and made mistakes along the way, but fortunately in EUR, I had a boss and several colleagues who saw the value of enhancing our management and leadership skills, and together we put a priority on improvements.

Subsequently, when I had the opportunity to lead the Bureau of Economic and Business Affairs in Washington, I learned the importance of clearly defining a mission and yearly action plan, of breaking down stove piping, of encouraging learning and creativity, of proactively supporting the career development of employees and much else. With more "on-the-job" learning as an assistant secretary for the State Department's economic work, I also discovered that there was a serious need to strengthen, support and encourage economic officers in the US foreign service around the world if US economic diplomacy was to produce consistently better results. The need to encourage and train a diverse, talented workforce through difficult circumstances and demanding tasks was further driven home during my service in Argentina, Afghanistan, and Mexico. It became clear to me that there was just not enough support for US diplomats, FSOs, civil servants and staff to promote excellence, to sustain good morale and to encourage development good leaders.

Over the last twenty years of my diplomatic service, it became increasingly clear to me that the United States was not investing enough in the training, capacity-building and support of its diplomats, nor in the ability of senior managers and leaders to effectively carry out their responsibilities. I kept learning through successes and mistakes the importance of career-long efforts to improve how diplomats manage (assure good functioning of the organization) and lead (help the group solve problems it faces). Though those functions may overlap, a good senior diplomat recognizes that both are keys to success for the individual and for broader diplomatic endeavors.

Protecting Your People and Your Citizens

One related point for Ambassadors and Deputy Chiefs of Mission leading overseas posts is the vital importance of providing security for your employees, their families, and for visiting US citizens, in the country where one's post is located. This is a heavy responsibility and in my last two posts. Kabul and Mexico City, I often would awaken at night, worried about the safety of our staff around the country as well as the US-citizen travelers, particularly in Mexico. We devised decision-making systems that carefully weighed safety precautions and had regular reviews of the situation to help assure that the precautions were sufficient. In the case of employees, it was very important that we work to balance our concerns for safety and security of our staff with the need for accomplishing the diplomatic work and national security goals of engaging with host country officials and key figures around the country.

In Afghanistan, for example, despite the often real threat of violence, it was important to visit parts of the country to meet with local officials and our staff serving their as part of the overall effort to counter the Taliban insurgents, to help develop the local economy and services for the population, to fight corruption and to promote the partnership that would be essential for success in the long-term.

In Mexico, where the mission employed some 2700 US and Mexican staff around the country, we also had regular reviews of the security situation in various parts of the country. Additionally, we gave much attention to developing and honing travel warnings for US citizens as millions of our fellow citizens regularly visited the country including some of its most violent states. We worked very hard to provide US citizens with the same guidance that we gave our own employees in ways that the citizens could absorb and understand easily. We also worked with host-government officials so they would understand what information we were sharing and why we were sharing it. We were working closely with the Mexican government to reduce the violence and influence of drug smuggling, criminal organization, and they were often very sensitive if did we talked publicly about the security situation in their country. Thus, US diplomats had to understand the threats at hand, develop plans to address those threats, devise communications plans to inform employees and US citizens and negotiate a workable set of guidelines and mechanism to build good cooperation with host country authorities. The bottom line is that this attention to security of embassies, employees and US citizens is a massively important task for the leadership in US embassies around the world.

The Evolving Global Context: From the Cold War to a Messy, Hyper-Connected, Tech-Infused, Multi-Power World

End of the Cold War

Diplomats apply the skills discussed above within the global alignment of powers, the evolving international setting and overall strategy that their country leadership forges. For the United States, that context has changed radically from the days of the Cold War and will likely continue to change for my US diplomatic successors. Multiple changes are underway: a relative reduction of US power, wealth, and influence; a multiplication of geopolitical and geo-economic actors; the ongoing transformation of "globalization"; the rise of new global threats such as climate change and pandemics; and transformative technologies regularly being developed and deployed. The demand for creative and effective use of the diplomatic skills previously explored will continue to grow in a more complex setting.

While there were certainly many serious crises following World War II, the global context was largely fixed, for the decades during the US-Soviet Cold War. That was the reality, from the time I joined the diplomatic service in 1975, until 1989–91 with the fall of the Berlin Wall and the end of the USSR. Up until those events, the diplomacy that I had practiced, observed, and participated in was largely within the context of the US-USSR rivalry. US relations with China, as important as they were and later would become, when I worked on China issues in the mid-1970s, at that time they were still considered largely through the lens of the US-USSR rivalry and in the context of creating additional worries for Moscow. That rivalry was regularly in-mind during efforts to bring peace between Israel and its neighbors, or when confronting Iraqi and Syrian misbehavior during the 1980s. Indeed, the Reagan administration's ill-conceived policies in Central America flowed from concerns about Soviet-Cuban inroads there, and initial US efforts to mediate a solution to the Falklands/Malvinas War between the UK and Argentina were fueled by considerations in Washington that the Argentine junta had been supportive in our Central America proxy-wars. Of enduring import, our support for the Afghan mujaheddin was fueled by a desire to counter the Soviet invasion. And as we now clearly see in hindsight, that support helped create empowered Islamic radicals who later attacked the US, and it also left Afghanistan to suffer a cruel civil war which brought the Taliban to power in the 1990s. In turn the Taliban's decision to host and support al-Qaeda led to a twenty-year US engagement which left Afghanistan still suffering terribly at present and proved costly to the US, some of its partners, and the region surrounding Afghanistan as well.

US Preeminence

The bottom line is that the end of this East-West rivalry brought with it a new context for US diplomacy. This new and significant shift in global power alignment opened the possibility and need for innovation. The US for a time became the preeminent global power. US policy makers and diplomats set about to reinvent NATO, to redefine relationships across Eurasia and, in my specific work area, to build new partnership with the European Union.

My first experience with the new opportunities for a post-Cold War world was leading teams of counter-terrorism experts to Poland, Hungary, Czechoslovakia, and Bulgaria, to open up opportunities for coordination with countries that had previously provided "safe haven" for terrorist groups behind the "Iron Curtain." In this new geopolitical setting, the Central Europeans were very eager to cooperate against terrorist groups as part of their efforts to join "the West." Beyond Europe, even the Syrians, concerned that their Soviet patron was fading, invited the US to attend the first serious counterterrorism talks in memory as part of a "warming" in US-Syria ties. While not as forthcoming as the Central Europeans on the specifics of CT work, the Syrians went out of their way to be hospitable. They apparently realized that as part of the new geo-strategic context, the Syrian governments might need to change some of its practices regarding terrorism. And the Russians themselves also sat down with a US team of anti-terrorism specialists from the State Department for serious CT talks in 1990–91.

When I went to work at the National Security Council in the summer of 1991, I found very creative work underway to adapt NATO to the new geo-strategic reality, through dialogues and partnerships with the former Warsaw Pact countries. There were efforts to engage Russia constructively, and also, to allow the Europeans to start exploring some coordinated defense initiatives alongside NATO. This process was very difficult within the USG for a variety of reasons, including continuing mistrust of Russia. Some good, creative new partnerships were agreed that allowed expansion of NATO, but at the time, I hoped we could make efforts to embrace an evolving Russia and build cooperation to help assure a more lasting change what had been for many decades a deep rivalry. in retrospect, I concluded that more should have been done to involve the Russian government and to address lingering fears and doubts in Moscow at the time. With such actions, we might have been able to avoid the subsequent return to sharp rivalry in the 2000s.

The portfolio of issues on which I directly worked on throughout the 1990s was to create a new relationship with the European Community, soon the be renamed the European Union (EU). It became clearer to me during these years that the United States needed new partners to deal with a range of challenges that stretched far beyond the traditional issues handled by NATO. Economic and trade issues increasingly became more important for US prosperity in a world no longer dominated by the prior East-West rivalry and now open to the development of expanding and more important global networks of trade, investment, innovation, and production. More global transnational issues like the environment and crime were also taking on more importance.

The European Union seemed to me a preferred partner given the democratic values we shared, relative prosperity and stability, strong economies, massive mutual private investment on both sides of the Atlantic, and the ample resources that the EU could bring to bear on a range of regional and global problems. It was not easy to convince all US-agency players that while we should invest in building this partnership, we could still protect the role of NATO and important bilateral relationships with key European countries, both of which had been very useful for achieving US interests. My EU Commission counterparts faced similar opposition in Europe from EU member states. But with a good deal of hard work and confidence-building, by the end of the decade our diplomatic work had set up a new, stronger, and multifaceted cooperation with the EU in Europe and in other regions of the world where the EU brought new and substantial resources. This collaboration also included wide range of issues on which we had not cooperated in the past from meeting humanitarian crises, development aid, international terrorism and crime, migration, and various environmental projects. The cooperation often was not easy because the EU and its members states were still working out how much power the EU's common institutions should play (vs member state governments), but it allowed for hammering out common transatlantic approaches and increasingly coordinated efforts to use resources and diplomacy for shared ends.

A Globalized World Emerges

The expansion of the internet and cyberspace facilitated a new global setting for commerce and public global engagement, on a wide range of issues from trade to climate. Increased internet-based communication supported rapidly globalized businesses which expanded the spread of global supply chains, bringing new countries into the mix and offering them access to additional source of income and thus moving more of their populations into the middle class, while at the same time that very process began to threaten portions of the US and European workforces with job loses, economic restructuring, and the need to develop new skill sets and work-related knowledge to maintain their standard of living.

For US diplomatic practice, these trends and transformations signaled to me that international trade and economic issues were of growing importance for US well-being and strategic interests. The State Department and US diplomacy, however, remained primarily focused on the political and military security issues that had dominated for decades. In this situation, I worked, first from Brussels, then in the European Affairs Bureau and later, from the Economic and Business Affairs Bureau at the State Department, to give more priority to Economic Diplomacy as well as strengthening the capacity and role of State's economic diplomats both overseas and in inter-agency policymaking in Washington. That meant bringing increased policy focus on economic or trade issues as key pillars of US foreign policy and highlighting their importance for US jobs and US consumers in this "new" international setting.

I also came to believe that US foreign policy needed to give more priority to specifically thinking through economic strategies to complement broader US strategic objectives. This was the case, as mentioned above, when the US and the EU worked together to devise the "Stability Pact" as a way for Southwest Europe to transition away from the fighting in Kosovo (and the other simmering tensions from the bitter breakup of Yugoslavia) and toward a more secure and prosperous future with economic ties to the European Union and the transatlantic community, including closer relations with NATO. Economic diplomacy and economic partnerships needed to take their influential place alongside political-military and geo-political diplomacy in this new geo-strategic setting and the strategies devised should be made to reinforce each other wherever possible.

Also, during the 1990s, it became clearer to me that that more members of the public, in both the US and Europe, wanted to have a say in international policies, particularly regarding trade and the environment. This was part of the birth of a more globally connected civil society which would profoundly change diplomacy, to include embracing, informing, and involving the public in new ways. Diplomacy had to find ways to better embrace and include this more activist public often plaguing roles as active and outspoken non-governmental organizations. This transformation was brought home to me when I attended the November 1999 WTO meeting in Seattle. I had the pleasure of working my way through thousands of American demonstrators protesting globalization. Many of them clearly felt excluded and threatened by what was happening in this globalizing world. This was a new experience for most diplomats and trade negotiators.

In the transatlantic diplomatic space, we tried to deal with this evident disconnect by creating transatlantic dialogues on environmental, consumer, labor, and business issues to bring non-official actors and groups into our "diplomacy." Interestingly, only the consumer advocacy and business groups accepted our openings and began regular dialogues with US and EU teams on relevant issues in the trans-Atlantic context. The environmental groups were more skeptical of joining in a dialogue and were more divided among themselves, and sadly on the labor issues, the US labor union leadership was not very interested.

This was just one example of a trend that would transform diplomacy making it essential for to incorporate stakeholder dialogues with interested public groups and to be better at explaining publicly want diplomats were doing behind closed doors.

Looking back on that era and the deepening of the anti-globalization sentiment in the US and Europe, the irony was that many of us working in American diplomacy were very hopeful that this new era of globalization and US preeminence would help democratic and free market practices spread and flourish. In fact, democracy did spread during this time with many US diplomats and embassies working hard to promote and support this trend toward democracy in countries and regions around the world. A major focus of our work in Europe was trying to help the Central Europeans strengthen their new democracies. Studies also started to show that global poverty was beginning to decline and that the middle class was expanding in less developed countries which were connected/connecting to global production and supply chains.

At the end of the decade, my boss and I in the European Affairs bureau at State proposed a strategy to Secretary of State Albright for the US to frame its international efforts with two major goals: 1) supporting countries to become more democratic, and 2) supporting countries to become integrated into the global economy, with better economic practices and thus becoming more prosperous. We were still hopeful that energetic and creative US diplomacy, including economic and governance assistance, could encourage such results if empowered by strong partnerships with countries that shared similar objectives. We did not get to fully test that strategic framework as the US administration changed, and the 9–11 terrorist attacks refocused US diplomacy to what became the global war on terror.

While the US did not successfully stabilize a new power balance in the 1990s, American statespersons and diplomats successfully forged new partnerships and launched new international groupings like the G20, APEC, the US-EU partnership, the North America Free Trade Agreement, and the Summit of the Americas. The US had begun to invest more attention in a series of issues from trade to the environment to democracy promotion that would assume greater importance for US diplomacy in this "new" world. It was a creative period for US diplomacy.

In retrospect, it is clear the anti-globalization demonstrations in Seattle were an important signal that there was a disconnect growing between the vision of a more democratic and prosperous "globalized" world and pressures being felt among workers and others from those same forces of globalization in the US and other economically developed countries. The US' international and the domestic policy agendas were generating sparks of friction that would only grow. These tensions between domestic and international perspectives reappeared with a vengeance after the 2008 Financial Crisis.

Looking back the end of the twentieth century and the first decade of the twenty-first century, it seems clear that the US political leadership (and leaders elsewhere) had not seriously addressed the hardship at home created by a new major international actor on the global trade scene and by technological transformations in the economy, especially affecting the manufacturing and trading sectors. First, China was emerging as a major economic power, fueled by its 2001 entry into the World Trade Organization and beginning to generate massive changes in international supply chains. This new competitor, China, not only started the impressive growth of Chinese exports to the US but also helped fuel a massive transformation of the US manufacturing economy. Businesses both invested more in China and in the US felt to pressure to become more competitive turning to significant technological innovations. This meant they required fewer US workers to produce the same level of production. Businesses and manufacturing sectors took increasing advantage of cheaper labor markets in other countries as well as the US to do simpler manufacturing tasks and to do them without unions. It is fair to say that the resulting domestic tensions have rocked US diplomacy for the last 15 years or so and lead to serious challenges to relationships with friendly countries and rivals alike. The clashes became particularly sharp during the Trump years, shaking the US' closest partnerships. The Biden administration has made restoring alliances and partnerships a top priority and has made progress, but the economic tensions have not yet been fully addressed as the US is seeking to rebuild its own economic strength and global competitiveness with a focus on reshoring and adding incentives for the domestic market. The tensions between the benefits of trade and the pressure of protecting home economies are far from being resolved.

War on Terror and Transformational Diplomacy

While these economic and trade transformations were underway, the attacks of September 11, 2001, abruptly reminded many of us that globalization had a very dark and dangerous side. Globalization did not just help businesses, some developing economies, and parts of the concerned public to become more engaged. It also allowed terrorists, criminals, radicals, and bigots to become more global in reach and impact.

The 9/11 attacks set off a new focus in US policy circles on fighting terrorism to assure homeland security, redefining priorities for US diplomacy during the next two decades. The attacks indirectly prompted very difficult efforts at nation building with "long wars" in places like Afghanistan and Iraq, for which the US was poorly prepared. They resulted in a shift to heavier reliance on US military tools as distinguished from US diplomatic, development and economic tools. These changes created new priorities and challenges for US diplomats, including the notion of engaging in more "expeditionary diplomacy" aimed at being better at helping countries on the front lines of the "war on terror."

These shifts did not do away with the important basics of diplomacy, and in ways they made clear that diplomatic skills were as important as ever in building and maintaining international coalitions to support the new policy focuses. The "war on terror" did lead to tensions between US diplomacy and US military activities in many countries and regions. Eventually, the need to work together in key conflict countries and regions, brought about closer partnerships between the State and Defense departments and between Ambassadors and Generals/Admirals. But it took a lot of "learning" by both camps.

Whereas throughout history diplomats were often withdrawn from a country where the US was at war, this new approach developed in the early 2000s poured US diplomats and development experts into Iraq and Afghanistan to try to help develop the country and strengthen host government capacities in the midst of a hot war, with bullets, missiles and bombs a daily concern for the diplomats and aid experts, as well as for the US military, host country partners, and developments assistance contractors.

In this new era, many US diplomats were urged by the State Department to serve in war zone countries where they had previously had no intention of working. The new model for diplomacy also forced diplomats to learn more about the economic, development, financial and governance issues that are essential in trying to help (often fragile) governments and nations in conflict situations. Being assigned to live and work together forced civilians and military staff to learn more about how their counterparts did their jobs and organized to achieve objectives. Eventually, in most cases, they were able to forge joint strategies. And, importantly, these situations were often terribly difficult to manage for everyone.

The Obama and Trump administrations each tried in distinct ways to pull back from the post-9/11, expanded US engagement against terror and radicalism, and the temptation to engage in overly ambitious efforts to nation-build. The Trump Administration first tried a militarily successful effort to increase pressure on the Taliban and then shifted to trying to negotiate an exit strategy via an agreement with the Taliban. They made serious negotiating errors along the way and handed a weak had to the incoming Biden Administration. The new Biden team took a bold and very costly step to rapidly withdraw troops and security support from Afghanistan. The human costs for Afghans of the way that was done for Afghanistan continue to be enormous, even if the strategic benefit has some merit.

Still, the Biden Administration remains engaged in counter-terrorism missions around the world in the Middle East and Africa, as was the Trump Administration, and is still trying to find the right mix of managing the on-going needs to counter terrorism threats and violent radical groups, some of which have US connections.

The years since 2001 drove home to many in Washington and in the US diplomatic service the limits of reliance on military tools to solve international problems and the dangers of too much reliance on them to achieve US objectives that involve goals other than winning a direct conflict with other militaries. As many of us increasingly repeated, "if the only tool you have is a hammer, problems tend to look like nails."

It is important to note, however, that many military leaders became convinced that they needed much more diplomatic and development assistance capacity to be applied even when conflict was going to be part of the solution. At the same time, the State Department and USAID came face to face with the sharp limits in their abilities to rebuild other countries' institutions, economies, and societies into well-functioning systems in relatively short period of time (or perhaps even in long periods of time, if the local citizenry was not leading the way). Under the pressure of conflict and enduring divisions in Iraq and Afghanistan, diplomats and development professions ran repeatedly into the hard limits of America's capacity to guide and help achieve such transformations. We also repeatedly encountered the serious costs of trying to take on too much without enough understanding of the special challenges in a country and without enough modesty and wisdom in the policy and implementation efforts to accurately estimate and grasp what was realistically possible to accomplish depending on the timeframe for action and the resources available. Consistently, people underestimated how long transformational projects would take and the cost needed to approach the end state US policy makers desired.

Hopefully going forward, US diplomats and America's leaders will draw good lessons from the many mistakes made during the almost two decades of trying to implement transformational diplomacy. Fortunately, there were also programs and approaches that did produce good results, and which should provide best practices to apply to other conflict and rebuilding situations. We need seriously done studies that get read and use making very clear the best and worst practices in decision-making, policy making and implementation.

While the US was engaged in its "long wars" and war against terrorism, the world kept globalizing and systems for trade, production and manufacturing continued to evolve and connect countries, communities, and workers in new ways, for good and for ill, as noted above. Simultaneously, resentment and concerns about that system deepened inside societies of the wealthiest countries and in many of the poorest countries. Technology accelerated changes in workplaces around the world eliminating and creating millions of jobs. Communications/public diplomacy transformed further with increased use of globally available and instantaneous social media, including widespread disinformation. And a new powerful rival emerged to US economic and political influence in China while the old one, Russia, worked to reassert its role at least in its periphery.

New Priorities for Economic Diplomacy

As Assistant Secretary of State for Economic and Business Affairs from June 2000-June 2006, I was engaging with globalization through an economic lens, dealing with the importance of trade, investment, and financial and other economic ties between the US and the world. I had seen the importance of these issues for America's economic security and prosperity while working on EU-US ties in the 1990s and now I had the opportunity to learn first-hand on the breadth and depth of economic security issues in the 2000s. This work took on the new focuses in fighting terror, in dealing with what became the long wars through reconstruction and development plans and adding new mechanisms to support the development of other countries as part of the US's economic tool chest. This work went beyond what the economic part of the State Department had done previously. During this period, the US added significant new tasks to our priority economic diplomacy agenda and thus to the work of embassies around the world, while continuing to support work on trade agreements, US investment, energy security, debt refinancing, macro-economic reform in countries facing financial crises, the development of international norms on corruption, aviation, international communications, and much more. Let me share examples of this new economic diplomacy which paired diplomats in Washington and embassies working on new priorities with core diplomatic skills.

Stopping Terrorist Financing

On 9/11, I was in Lima Peru with Secretary of State Colin Powell. We were meeting with Peru's president talking about how to help Peru expand exports to the US and better attract US investment, when we learned of the 9/11 attacks. On the flight back to Washington (we could still see the Pentagon still smoldering from our plane when we arrived), I was wondering how the State Department's Economic diplomacy team could help. My previous work on countering terrorist groups and working with our European partners helped spark the idea of passing a UN Security Council which would impose mandatory sanctions on any who finance and otherwise provide material support for terrorists. Our EB team huddled on the first day back to work to put these ideas into proposal which we sent to the top levels the State Department. They and White House staff quickly supported the idea. Then, we worked with the International Organizations bureau and the US Mission to the UN.

The US was able to win UN Security Council (UNSC) approval for resolution 1373 on September 28. UNSCA 1378 set out new objective for cutting off financing and other kinds of support to terrorist groups and organizations, and for many countries this Security Council Resolution had the force of law. For US diplomacy, this UNSC resolution set off a multiyear diplomatic effort to get other countries to implement the new rules to stop terrorist financing. The Economic Bureau of the State Department worked with the NSC, Treasury, law enforcement and the intelligence community as well as the State Department's geographic bureaus and embassies around the world to orchestrate a massive diplomatic campaign. That diplomacy persuaded over 100 countries to actively join the effort and to freeze many terrorist assets.

This took a great deal of good diplomatic work overseas and in the UN to persuade other governments to change their laws and regulations and to implement new controls effectively. The effort also involved very difficult interagency discussions in Washington where the State Department at times had sharp differences with others about how best to persuade other governments to join the effort based on in depth knowledge from US embassies and about who to sanction. The US relied heavily on the "understanding" our diplomats provided to identify the best ways to forward in creating workable international collaboration. US diplomats used their skills to open doors, to persuade foreign officials to take steps that met opposition in their own governments and to build partnerships that made it harder for terrorist groups to function. The December 2005 report by members of the 9/11 Commission reviewing all the steps the US took after 9/11 gave this new anti-terrorist financing work the highest mark of any other post 9/11 US workstream (an A- grade). Interestingly, the second highest mark given in this report (a B+) was for efforts also led by US economic diplomats, working with colleagues from Treasury, USAID and USTR, to provide economic support to countries on the "front line" of the new anti-terror efforts, e.g., Jordan, and Turkey.

Investing in Post-Conflict Economies

As the diplomatic campaigns on terrorist financing were being waged, US economic statecraft also began to weave together international efforts to rebuild after the initial fight in Afghanistan against the Taliban government and Al-Qaida in 2011–02, and again later after the 2003 US invasion of Iraq. It took a tremendous amount of work by American diplomacy to forge a united international approach to initial development and economic frameworks to help both countries recover, as well as to attract sufficient donor and international agency funding to begin providing the assistance needed. In both, Afghanistan, and Iraq the development, governance and related technical assistance continued for years after as did the need for close coordination among international donors and the host governments. Particularly with Afghanistan, the development, governance, humanitarian, and technical support continued until the Taliban's 2021 victory and the humanitarian assistance continues as of this writing.

In each case, key allies, international institutions (UN, World Bank, and International Monetary Fund) and emerging leaders from both countries needed to agree on initial reconstruction/rebuilding/transformation plans, how to solicit funds to donate, and policy priorities. as well as frameworks for ongoing coordination and monitoring. Afghanistan and Iraq were very different cases, of course. There was much more international support for rallying together to help with Afghanistan, for example, than was the case with Iraq where many countries did not support the US decision to invade. Also, the human capital and economic foundations in Afghanistan were much weaker than in Iraq which had a well-educated middle class and substantial oil wealth.

While there are many complex stories to tell of successes and serious mistakes that the US and partners made in both countries, a key point is that diplomats had to use their networks and persuasive, analytic and implementation skills to build agreement to support these countries with funds and sustained involvement in trying to help them rebuild (and transform) their economies and governance/political structures. Many diplomats and development professionals were assigned to work in the countries to help support and implement the rebuilding programs—some had good background in the region, but many did not have deep regional or cultural knowledge, and many had not worked in conflict zones previously. These of tasks around economic and institution building, and transformation was very complicated, especially in a war-zone environment.

The US quickly and repeatedly discovered that it did not have enough diplomats and development experts (or military personnel) with the experience to guide what some called nation building efforts. The State Department and its diplomats were in what seemed like a perpetual effort to keep up with the new demands of this new phase of American global involvement, often without the skills or knowledge they needed, and the work did not get easier as the twenty-first century advanced.

A Costly Strategic Mistake: Invading Iraq

While there were plenty of diplomatic and military missteps, the greatest American strategic blunder during my forty-year career was the decision to invade Iraq. It was initiated with false justifications and with seriously faulty assumptions about America's ability to manage the post-invasion situation. The invasion and the mismanagement of the subsequent situation in Iraq led to tens of thousands of Iraqi deaths, many US casualties, very serious US human rights violations, a tremendous blow to the US image in the world and much more. The emergence of the ISIS terrorist organization was one result which continues to plague several countries today. The US decision to invade also seriously distracted US attention from the effort in Afghanistan, which was already showing signs of problems, ahead and thus contributed mightily to the heavy human and financial costs in that conflict. The United States continues to pay the price of this blunder today.

At the time of the decision to invade Iraq, I dutifully prepared to deal with the expected economic consequences, but it was very upsetting and distressful. I could not sleep at nights for several weeks ahead of the announcement of the invasion because I was so troubled by what I thoughts would be immense costs to the US and others.

A diplomat can decide to resign over a policy decision, or he/she can salute and hope to serve the country better by staying engaged, working to moderate damage. I found that often the best way forward for me was to try to do something constructive and beneficial around the policy or decision with which I disagreed. In the case of the Iraq invasion, I chose to try to help build an international consensus around ways to help Iraq's new government to rebuild Iraq's economy. Once the US went into Iraq, I worked hard to get good advice to the civilian team on the ground (even having to do it through my private email because the Secretary of Defense had ordered the team in Baghdad not to communicate with the State Department).

I then spent many difficult months organizing and managing the international donor reconstruction efforts. This included a very intense preparation for the Madrid Donors Conference in October 2003, which mobilized $33 billion in aid pledges for the four years ahead. We had weekly donor phone calls with 10–15 key governments and institutions in the run up to the Madrid Conference, and then I maintained intense work of donor coordination to implement those pledges and to work with the new Iraqi government on plans to use the funds in the months that followed. We moved to calls every two weeks and organizes a series of follow up conferences in the region to hone plans and encourage countries to follow through on their promises as well as to get the Iraqis to stay focused on reforms and implementation of good policies. During these months, we worked hard to mend relations among donors, especially those in the region. My work on these efforts continued well into 2004 when I was able to hand implementation off to the Near Eastern Affairs bureau of the State Department. I was happy to have been able to contribute something positive to the ramifications of a terrible decision by the US government and a really challenging situation on the ground in Iraq.

I was also very pleased to work on other programs doing much good during the Bush Administration including the creation of the Millennium Challenge Corporation and the deployment of successful assistance programs including the President's Emergency Plan for AIDS Relief (PEPFAR). These were excellent programs that have helped many millions around the world. They could mitigate, but not undo, the damage that was being caused by the war in Iraq. I continued to see the costs of that decision for America's image when I was transferred to serve in Latin America.

Soft Power and Public Diplomacy
Temper Anti-Americanism

In 2006, I had the honor of being nominated and confirmed as US Ambassador to Argentina. There were many enjoyable opportunities in helping to guide US relations with a country that had so many creative and talented citizens. Also, since Argentina was not at the center of US priorities, there was a good deal of freedom to maneuver for an ambassador. It was not that Washington did not care, but rather that the assumption was that the embassy would handle the issues and let Washington know if help was needed. Given the busy Washington agenda, that is the situation for many US embassies in the world.

In the case of Buenos Aires, my embassy team and I had to craft a way to pursue US objectives with a skeptical government that was critical of the US, and the levels of anti-Americanism among the Argentine population were the highest in the Western Hemisphere at that time. There were many causes for this anti-American sentiment. The most recent reasons came from strong opposition to the war in Iraq among the Argentines and the US mistreatment of some Iraqi detainees during interrogation, as well as negative impressions of the way the US was pursuing the broader "war on terror". There was also a strong sense that the US had not done enough to help Argentina emerge from its devasting 2001 economic crisis which more than doubled the percent of Argentines living in poverty to 57% by 2002.

One of my first projects was to work with my embassy team to craft a country strategy. We agreed that a major focus of our work had to now be improving the image of the United States. I encouraged the country team to look at every embassy activity as an opportunity to improve the view of the US working hand in glove with our public diplomacy section. I tried to enlist all the embassy sections in this work from the consular/visa section to our defense attaches. I instructed all sections to work closely with the Public Diplomacy section in identifying ways to send out positive messages to the Argentine public, even if they had not approached their work this way in the past. This shift was very new for many parts of the embassy, and it put additional responsibility on our public diplomacy team to think beyond existing programing. (Some of them had only focused on traditional public diplomacy programs without much innovation.

As the embassy was pursuing this effort to change our standard operating procedures, I realized more clearly than before that the United States has tremendous "soft power" in the world because of the popularity of our music, movies and authors, the reputation of our universities, the richness of US society and the "best" objectives that many Americans pursue whether it be seeking a free press, civil liberties, and respect for human rights. It turns out that many Argentines like those aspects of the United States.

Drawing from my lessons in building international coalitions and partnerships, we set out on a concerted campaign to build visible alliances with Argentine NGOs and to champion popular causes like press freedom, and countering drug abuse, trafficking in persons and domestic violence. With progressive members of the US and Argentine business community, we supported educational exchanges, recognizing Argentine innovators and achievers, and investing in local communities where US companies operated. We positioned ourselves to be spokespersons for the "best" US democratic practices, independent of what was going on in Iraq.

Then, I realized a particular way that we could use US soft power. I observed that Argentines really love US rock music and had developed their own excellent form of Argentine rock. One evening I saw much larger numbers of Argentines flocking to see a rock band concert in a nearby stadium (by Soda Stereo, a super group of the 90s) rather than to attend a government-sponsored stadium rally with Venezuela's President Maduro making anti-American proclamations, even though the government was busing in attendees and promising free food and drink. Going outside of traditional public diplomacy programs, we started reaching out to visiting US music groups with the request asking them if as a charitable outreach would they be willing to meet with young Argentine musicians and poorer Argentines who would not normally be able to attend their very popular concerts. Almost all the artists and groups who we could reach said yes. They often offered the Argentines free tickets and invited them backstage. This outreach was made possible by Embassy volunteers who saw the value of these opportunities. We did not have enough public diplomacy staff to take on these new efforts, but they could work with the volunteers from other embassy sections and then the PD staff would promote our encounters on social media or via radio and TV connections. The PD officers and volunteers were able to work with local schools and NGOs and organize transportation to events and accompany the Argentines. I often did too and held several "workshops" with American musicians at my residence with young Argentines in attendance. I started talking about American rock music on youth-oriented TV programs from concert venues—and when they asked about Iraq, I would talk about the diversity of views in the US and the creativity of American society and how much we had this in common with Argentines. The coverage often started out critical of US international policy, but as we continued to engage and highlight our two countries shared love of much about music and culture in different events and venues (including at the embassy), we started getting increasingly positive reactions from young Argentines and in local media.

Our outreach and public diplomacy work also focused on specific US policy objectives that would enhance the positive image of the US. For example, Argentina did not have a federal law against trafficking in persons, which we wanted to help change. Our deputy public affairs officer was introduced to a courageous Argentine mother looking for her trafficked daughter. We decided that her story was so compelling that our PD section introduced her to an Argentine TV channel which decided to produce a dramatized series about her search for her daughter. We also supported this mother's meeting with Argentine officials and legislators. We worked with leading female politicians, and I privately urged top officials, including the President's spouse, to support the law. Meanwhile the TV series was success and generated more public support to pass a federal law against trafficking in persons. The law was passed, and I then worked with the Public Security minister to implement it. I simultaneously worked with that same minister to deepen cooperation against growing drug trafficking and addiction throughout Argentina—a common objective that both governments could share. We made sure to publicize this

US-Argentine cooperation generating more positive images of what the US and Argentina could do together.

Similarly, when we saw a local press report about a group of mothers fighting addiction in a very poor and crime-ridden neighborhood, we found another opportunity to do good and support a good cause. The public diplomacy section investigated and saw the tremendous efforts that these very poor mothers were making to save their children from addiction without much support from government authorities at any level. I went to visit the mothers despite the concerns of my security detail. We brought more media attention to the mothers' work including with events at my residence, found ways for embassy sections and partners to donate needed supplies, and to better link them to government social services. This generated very good public attention and good will as well as pressuring the federal and state governments to help these mothers. The woman heading the neighborhood effort was later named "woman of the year" by a well-known Argentine magazine. Her neighborhood and the children started receiving more government services to help deal with the addiction problems. It was a big boost for the neighborhood. It was far from what was needed in other poor areas around Buenos Aires but is showed that the US embassy could be a force for good.

As a result of these and other outreach efforts by the embassy team, the embassy was increasingly associated with doing "good" for Argentina and things that Argentines liked about the US. The impact of this hard public diplomacy work showed when the Argentine government was angered with the US administration over a serious law-enforcement case that threatened the President's reputation. She ordered that no federal government officials meet with me or other senior members of the embassy.

Several partners with whom we had worked boldly spoke out in defense of the embassy and helped encourage the government to enter confidential negotiations to forge a solution (which we did). The Embassy also tried to monitor the effectiveness of this work more broadly. We found that polls showed the Embassy's image and that of America was improving, even though the Argentine public remained very critical of US Iraq policies. From the perspective of US diplomatic practice, I learned that a whole of embassy "public diplomacy" effort could significantly improve country to country relations, and that public diplomacy was becoming a much more potent tool for diplomacy.

Obama Corrects Course but Finds Rising Rivals, Domestic Divisions, and Priorities Multiplying

President Obama assumed the US presidency during a devasting financial crisis affecting much of the world and fueling anti-globalization sentiments in many developed countries including the US. His election was greeted very enthusiastically in Argentina (where I was serving), in Latin America more broadly, and elsewhere. Many, including US diplomats, welcomed his intentions to extricate the US from the excesses of the Bush years' version of the war on terror and deep involvements in Iraq and Afghanistan. He guided the US to economic recovery and initiated international initiatives, which bore good fruit. However, President Obama's administration did not successfully move the US to a new international paradigm with a clear mission for the US or set of priorities. In retrospect, the administration also did not give enough attention to the growing alienation felt by many US workers that they were being left behind in large part because of a globalizing trade system, the rise of China's economic prowess, and no effective public policies helping America's workers to cope with the transformations underway in US manufacturing sectors.

As a senior American diplomat, during these years it appeared to me the world became even more complex and that the US had relatively less influence, while still being the strongest global power. The US was not able to successfully support the Arab spring, could not successfully pull out of Iraq, made serious missteps regarding Syria, and undertook a largely unsuccessful surge of the US military and civilian presence in Afghanistan. A US pivot to Asia which initiated to deal with a rising China was a promising move, but it was not brought to fruition as exemplified when negotiations took too long to get agreement on the Transpacific Partnership (TPP) fully approved in the US before the end of Obama's second term.

The TPP was the Obama team's biggest (and a clever) move to check China's growing clout, but it was just finalized too late. That allowed President Trump could pull the US out of that agreement. This was one of the first of many flawed decisions Trump was to take. Also, the new trade agreement with Europe that the Obama team sought to help bring to that vital economic relationship in the modern age never came to fruition, (in part because of rebellions against globalization on both sides of the Atlantic), and elsewhere in Europe. That was another serious lost opportunity.

Also, during these years, Russia moved into Crimea signaling a reassertion of its aggressive nationalism and willingness to challenge and harass

US objectives. The foreboding of letting that action stand was brought home by Russia's 2022 invasion of Ukraine, and the tremendous costs that invasion imposed on Ukraine, the region, and the world, and it became the main priority for US diplomacy and for fortifying the transatlantic partnership.

In the final four years of Obama's presidency, there was a lot of good diplomacy going on and many positive results were achieved. However, from my perspective, it seemed that America's foreign policy was dealing with an increasing number of "priorities" without a clear overarching strategy. There was an emerging toxic mix of domestic and international issues clashing, as signaled in the growing sharp discourse about trade and migration which was only going to become more divisive.

I was among those who thought there were too many special envoys dealing with too many issues often outside of a well-coordinated policy and management structure. In a world with more rapid and immediate information flows and too much information for even the most capable to sort through, the US's vision and key messages were difficult to project clearly. Dangerous trouble was brewing, and it was far from clear that the US had the right overall international strategy for the challenges ahead. Plus, the US leadership in the executive and congressional branches were not dealing well with the reactions at home to the evermore globalized and multipolar world and the impacts on America's economy and society. This was already showing up with more polarized policy discourse and "culture wars."

Afghanistan: Rebuilding the Plane, While Flying the Mission

President Obama and his national security team decided to adjust US policy by reducing involvement in Iraq and focusing on achieving a better outcome in Afghanistan. Given my earlier work on economics and on reconstruction, I was asked to go to Kabul as part of the "civilian surge" to match the surge in military forces which was trying to push back against a more powerful and capable Taliban to strengthen the Afghan government. I was happy to help and wanted to be able support the Afghans who were working to establish a more modern and democratic country. I had a tremendous amount to try to learn very quickly about the situation in Afghanistan, however, and the over $4 billion in ongoing civilian assistance programs that I would oversee and try to make more effective. Plus, there were massive amounts of military funding going into assistance related projects as part of a "hearts and minds" effort by US commanders. These were not well coordinated with the civilian assistance efforts or those of the Afghan government and the rest of the international community.

I became one of four Ambassadorial ranked diplomats serving in Kabul in June 2009, with a fifth added in 2010. Working under one senior US Ambassador, this was an effort to boost US civilian operations and to better since them with the massive US and partner military presence which was over 100,000 strong accompanied by many generals and admirals serving under a senior NATO and US commander. I was initially asked to coordinate US civilian assistance and economic policy working with the Afghans and other international donor partners. During my second year, I was the "Deputy Ambassador," sort of like the COO and second ranked among the five Ambassadors present.

The idea behind adding so many senior diplomats was that with a large military and civilian surge we need more civilians of sufficient rank to get the attention of and partner well with the many three- and four-star generals and admirals involved on the military side in charge of the many US troops in the country. During 2010, there were about 130,000 NATO and partner troops in total, plus a good number of partner embassies, aid programs, a large UN civilian presence and a large contingent of assistance contractors and NGO workers.

There are so many lessons that came from this experience. Many have written compellingly about these lessons in books, and there has been an outpouring of analyses following the collapse of the Kabul government and the US government's poorly managed withdrawal from Afghanistan in August 2021.

During my two years there, we would joke that our job was like flying a complex combat mission in an aircraft that was taking enemy fire, being rebuilt, getting new instructions, and changing crew regularly, all while worrying that we were not getting it right and might crash. We were learning and adapting constantly and making our share of mistakes along the way.

People worked intensively, were dedicated, became exhausted and stressed and kept trying hard to do the work well. It was very hard to assure coordination among civilian agencies and that our aid programs were not well coordinated or monitored/evaluated for results as much as needed. It was very difficult for civilians to oversee development contractors and monitor projects during a hot war where they could often to get to the project sites and where there was significant corruption at all levels of government. There was poor coordination on assistance programs between military units providing aid, international partners with significant aid programs, and the many Afghan government ministries and agencies helping to implement programs and charged with monitoring its integration into the government's own work.

Plus, the US embassy had big challenges in coordinating with policy makers in Washington. It took continual effort, with long hours seven days a week to try to get all this collaboration working well or a least to minimize big disconnects. Only after a year and arrival of a new US/NATO military commander, for example, did we start to get real unity of vision and effort between the Embassy and the US/NATO effort. In the fall of 2009, the Embassy sent cables detailing opposition to the proposals for major increase in US military presence and a strategy to guide the US for the next several years. The US commander's recommendations were largely approved despite embassy objections. Several cables which detailed the embassy's differing perspectives were leaked to the press in Washington. This caused serious problems in the Embassy's relations with the Afghan government as well as in relations with various key actors in Washington DC.

It was clear to me before I went to Kabul that many flaws in the US approach had undermined the opportunities for success, starting with the decision to invade Iraq which put Afghanistan on the backburner of policy attention in Washington. Many of these flaws became very clear to me once I arrived in the country. The US effort, for example, was seriously undermined by the short tours of duty of many civilians (one year) and military which prevented the US from having enough people with a deep understanding of Afghanistan. Many critics argue that the US really fought 20 one-year wars, rather than one 20-year war. I saw that problem clearly during my two years in the country: when the embassy staff turnover took place in the summer of 2010, I needed to help educate very rapidly a new generation of embassy and civilian leaders across the country. It amounted to a severe brain/memory drain.

Similarly, it was quickly evident to me that the Foreign Service, the State Department and USAID did not have enough expertise in managing complex conflict situations where we were trying to help a host-nation government build an economy, improve governance, develop effective government services, and bring its population into the modern world with so many other related tasks accomplish during a real shooting war. We were trying to learn as we went and there were few with past lessons learned to help guide the various teams or with the depth of cultural and lan-guage knowledge that would have been so valuable in dealing with Afghan partners.

The dedicated enemy fighters (Taliban) had a sanctuary (in Pakistan) where they could escape to refresh and retrain in a neighboring country that was simultaneously vital for US supply routes. This was a major flaw in the US plans approved in late 2009. We could never convince Pakistani authorities to stop providing support for our enemies, even as they worked closely with us on a range of issues. So, our military colleagues would pound the Taliban inside Afghanistan, but they could retreat to havens in Pakistan. And in the process of the US attacks, many civilians on both sides of the border became increasingly alienated with the US efforts.

Our Afghan partners were a very mixed bag. Many were dedicated, hard-working, courageous, and ready to sacrifice and die for the future of their country. At the same time, corruption, patron-client relationships, tribal allegiances, family commitments, and other practices undermined their effectiveness and the legitimacy of the Islamic Republic in Kabul in the eyes of their own people. It became clear to me during my first months in Kabul that the US had to find a way to staunch the corruption and abuses of power if our efforts were going to prevail.

However, as my colleagues and I discovered again and again, it is almost impossible to change a society more rapidly than that society is ready to change. Clearly many younger Afghans wanted change and accepted the values and objectives we promoted for a more democratic, educated, and "modern" Afghanistan, but much of Afghan society was still rooted in a world view that was far from what Americans would consider "modern."

It was worth the effort to invest in these younger Afghans and in stron-ger Afghan institutions, I concluded. The younger generations who had progressed through the new educational and training opportunities were very promising. But the US effort needed more modest views of what could be accomplished and an understanding that the long timelines required for progress in Afghan society and in the political model still dominating non-Taliban Afghanistan. I came to believe the polling results in the coun-try that only some 20% of Afghans really agreed with the Taliban's 14th century views of society and religion, but creating a more efficient, honest, and democratic regime in Kabul and other cities would take many years of consistent effort solid Afghan leaders and partners like the US.

Sadly, for understandable domestic US reasons, the US kept setting unrealistic deadlines for the end of our involvement. This had pernicious effects. It signaled to the Taliban and other opponents that they just needed to be patient and the US would leave. Again, this was another major flaw in the policy that President Obama and his team approved in late 2009.

Assuring whole of government and coalition collaboration was an ongoing challenge.

I came away from my intense two years in Kabul convinced of how vital it is to try to remain clear eyed even in the most exhausting and complex conflict situations. This meant working constantly to assure as good a coordination as possible among civilian agencies, with the US and NATO military, with Afghan officials and with decision makers in DC. A "whole of government" and "whole of coalition" approach was vital, as I had learned earlier in very different circumstances in European Affairs and the Economic Bureau. That meant working very hard to keep listening closely to what your team members and partners were saying and processing the messages with good analysis.

Doing what was possible to maintain morale, health, and discipline among so many team members dealing with much stress and exhaustion was extremely difficult but crucial. In all of this, establishing trusting relationships remained vital as was encouraging people to think outside of the box, to identify the strengths and shortcomings of the teams and coalitions, to keep innovating, to try to pass on lessons learned and to assure continuity.

And of course, serious investment had to be put into building understanding and coordination with the Afghan government, while trying to deal with the flaws encountered including serious corruption and lack of capacity. I gradually came to understand areas where the US and Afghans were communicating clearly and areas where cultural, social and history gaps left great room for misunderstanding and diverging practices.

It was also very hard to maintain strategic vision and tactical adaptability under such war-time pressure. And, in addition Washington was offering direction and second guessing decisions regularly. It became clear that it was very hard for Washington to accept/demonstrate the strategic patience that would be needed to produce the changes it sought among our Afghan partners and in Afghan institutions. This was a major challenge to success, and seen in retrospect, these differences in perceived "timelines for success" made it highly likely that we could not succeed.

Trying to Do Too Much with Too Little Understanding

Each US administration made serious mistakes in handling Afghanistan along the way from 2001 to 2021. The largest strategic mistake was diverting attention and effort from Afghanistan to Iraq. Of course, we could not have assured that the USG would have made good choices in Afghanistan even without the invasion of Iraq (and we had already made some poor choices in 2001–03). Overall, however, the US and US diplomacy took on much more that it could handle in trying to reshape Afghanistan in relatively short timeframes. We did not have the tools or the skills to do this well, nor was it clear that such a transformation was possible until enough Afghans were ready and able to lead such a transformation. Our most successful programs were those that strengthened and built human capital (education and public health), but to continue to be successful, these programs would have required many years more of investment. This was also very true with our programs aimed at building institutions for better governance.

I supported the 2009 Embassy cables arguing that military might could have a big impact, but military tactical success was far from enough to achieve a sustainable situation in for US strategic interests. Similarly, after two years in Kabul, I concluded that diplomatic and development tools and programs could help improve performance in the short term, but they would not produce the lasting progress needed until and unless we found a way to successfully address some of the basic weaknesses in Afghan governance, including massive corruption. If our Afghan partners were not building credibility with their population, which they were not, it was hard to foresee good prosect for success, even if were made tactical military gains. Indeed, increasingly we would become seen as part of the problem and the Taliban would make progress in painting us as a dangerous foreign invader. America's Afghan partners needed to be seen as credible and legitimate leaders who could deliver for Afghans.

I left Kabul, however, deeply committed to the principle of helping our Afghan partners who sincerely wanted a more democratic, more effective government to bring their country into the modern world. After retiring from the State Department, an Afghan with who I had worked in Kabul, and I organized an informal study group on Afghanistan in Washington. Talking regularly with other Afghanistan hands from 2016 through the present, it appeared that the United States was still making similar errors in trying to move that country toward peace and was faced with a still strong Taliban.

Though it was never going to be a quick or easy process to get the parties to the negotiating table, to forge a credible and enforceable agreement and to support a process to implement an accord successfully, the US needed a sustained diplomatic, assistance and military effort and a strategy to encourage movement toward peace negotiations. Working with several Washington think tanks and then with a group for distinguished former Ambassadors, we offered advice on the steps that could help foster peace over a multiyear effort. However, we were not effective in getting the Trump administration to adopt and sustain the approaches we suggested, nor to convince the Biden administration to invest in a longer withdrawal process. The results of the US approach in 2019–22 are clear for all to see and have clearly produced horrible outcomes for the Afghan population. The Trump Administration negotiated a poor agreement with the Taliban, under the President's desire to withdraw US troops, and the Biden Administration was not willing to revisit that nor to adjust to the Taliban's clear signals that it was not interested in a serious peace discussion with non-Taliban Afghans. Rather the Biden Administration's moves to draw down led to collapse of morale among Afghan security forces and other non-Taliban leaders.

Military victories, tactically successful campaigns, and the elimination of terrorist leaders can be successfully undertaken in relatively short timeframes but transforming societies of other countries and fostering stable political arrangements are much more difficult and will require sustained investments. Such efforts demand longer commitments using many tools but with diplomacy as a vital pillar.

In the future, US diplomacy should strive to approach such large and complex challenges involving conflict and likely prolonged involvement with wisdom and modesty, assessing clearly what is achievable and in what timeframes. And a note on sustaining domestic support for such long engagements: this is possible, if the messaging is clear and compelling as we have seen with US deployments to South Korea and Europe, but if the messaging from the top is contradictory, the US public like most publics in democracies, will tire of supporting the US involvement. I continue to hope that the US diplomatic and military institutions can learn and absorb the many valuable lessons from the failures of the US efforts in Afghanistan and Iraq.

Mexico: The Quintessential "Inter-Mestic" Relationship

Ambassador to Mexico was my last Foreign Service assignment. Being Chief of Mission of the US embassy in Mexico City and nine consulates is a daunting assignment. This bilateral relationship touches the daily lives of more Americans than any other US bilateral relationship in the world. History weighs heavily on attitudes on both sides of the border and is reflected in the deep family and cultural ties between the two countries, as well as the memory in Mexico of the US invasion and war of 1847. The two countries trade about a million and a half dollars a minute, and that same border supports lethal flows of drugs headed north and guns headed south, plus much illegal migration by Mexicans and other nationalities. All the irregular and illicit flows have become increasingly hard to manage well and very costly on both sides of the border.

When I arrived September 2011, Mexico was working hard to strengthen its democracy, to pull itself into more prosperity, and to struggle through a very violent and corrupting conflict with organized criminal groups that made many billions of dollars each year selling drugs to the US. The US not only had a large embassy but maintains more consulates in Mexico than the US has in any other country in the world. Mexico has an astounding 50 consulates in the US. The US-Mexico relationship involves most every government ministry in Washington and Mexico City and demands very complicated, careful handling of policy and public diplomacy/messaging on both sides of the border. News in the US and Mexico covers developments involving the other country daily. Managing the relationship also demands careful attention to millions of "stakeholders" who are invested in the relationship through trade and commerce, and the many millions of US and Mexican tourists who visit the neighboring country each year. I was asked to serve in Mexico, after Mexico's President requested that my predecessor be removed.

All the best lessons from my previous assignments were needed to handle these four years, and I was stretched regularly to learn more and to operate more effectively. Looking back one major take away was the importance of building coalitions and partnerships in support of problem solving and taking advantage quickly of new opportunities in both countries. This approach required finding champions in both governments, including in the legislatures, and building as many solid partnerships as possible in and outside of government. It meant mounting a vigorous public diplomacy and media effort to bolster the US image and objectives and to deal effectively with problems as they arouse, including with vigorous use of social media.

This work focused on collaboration with colleagues from both governments and civil society to construct processes, mechanisms, and institutions that would foment better management of key issue sets for the long term across this vast relationship. Also very importantly, it meant giving regular attention to the safety of the millions of US citizens visiting or living in Mexico, as well as sustaining morale and security in a diplomatic mission of 2,700 employees representing 29 different government agencies that worked on trade, investment, tourism, migration, law enforcement, border security and much more.

As a new Ambassador, I arrived in Mexico facing a few challenges. First, I was coming from Afghanistan without a real opportunity to decompress. I did not realize until months later that I was still running on adrenalin from Afghanistan, and I was still very stressed from my two years there. Also, some of the Mexican press focused on my Afghanistan experience saying it was an indication that the US now saw Mexico as a failed state. However, my talks with Secretary of State Clinton led me to believe it was my experience in economics and trade as well as experience overseeing development plans in various environments including Afghanistan that contributed to my selection. I understood that my nomination was intended to signal the US intention to work closely with Mexico across the board.

I was not a Mexico specialist which meant I had a lot to learn, and Mexicans had a lot to learn about me, as did the Mexico specialists at the State Department who were skeptical of my ability to manage the relationship.

Secretary of State Clinton, who had gotten to know me in Afghanistan, also gave me one specific task for my first four months. She wanted the USG to have delivered $500 million in assistance to Mexico through the public security and anti-crime cooperation program called Merida by the end of the year (2011). This would be a sign of good will to Mexico's president, Felipe Calderon, who had sought the change of Ambassador and asked for speedier assistance deliveries. He wanted to be more effective in his administration's fight against the drug cartels. The Merida program, which was established in 2007–08 under President Bush, had been slow in getting set up and delivering assistance because of problems encountered by the US and Mexico as they tried to launch this massive new initiative. The US and Mexico had not tried to undertake a cooperative public security effort like this before.

When I arrived in Mexico, I observed that the embassy did not have the sense of urgency that I had been working with for the past two years in Kabul, and I worried about meeting Secretary Clinton's goal. I was also concerned that the public diplomacy section in the embassy was working on a traditional model and not adapted to the new world of social media and rapid outreach to broad swaths of Mexico's social media savvy public. We were too often caught backfooted by critical stories and faced anti-American tone in commentaries. There were also serious bilateral tensions over how to manage the border and migration as well as operationally how to best counter the rise in organized crime and drug smuggling activity. There were serious tensions between some parts of the Mexican public security team and their US counterparts as well as between different Mexican law enforcement, intelligence and justice agencies who suspected each other of being penetrated by various criminal groups.

I worked persistently to address each of the problem areas I encountered and tried to deepen cooperation on the areas with evident opportunity, such as trade and commerce and education exchanges. I immediately set about rapidly building contacts and relationships across multiple Mexican ministries and Washington agencies and making sure that I was seen via the social and traditional media as engaging with elites and common Mexicans. Interestingly, some members of my embassy team and the regional bureau in Washington thought I was moving too quickly given the experience of my predecessor, but I had learned in my previous jobs the value of building relationships and of being seen to be committed to the bilateral relationship.

I gradually developed a network of trusted contacts/partners in both capitals to help solve problems and help create new opportunities. In the US, this network of partners stretched far beyond the State Department. Commerce, the White House Homeland Security Advisor, the CIA director, and the Commander of Northern Command and the Secretary of Homeland Security emerged as key partners beyond various parts of the State Department. Similarly, the Mexican government and I worked hard to build good working relations with key actors willing to work seriously on common problems. This group of partners varied between the two Mexican presidential administrations with whom I worked, but over my four-year stint included a very wide range of agencies such as Foreign Affairs, Public Security, Economy, Justice, the Intelligence center, and the Presidency in the federal government. With one close partner minister, for example, we would regularly meet to talk about how to better build a good coalition across both governments willing to help deepen relations and to deal with tough problems. This exemplary relationship did not produce perfect results (given the many governmental and political actors that had an impact on bilateral relations), but it helped enormously to get through the often-serious lack of interagency trust and coordination on various issues, with better results. This networking also encompassed the business community from both countries, key media figures, active NGO, academic institutions, state, and local government leaders, and much more. These non-federal government actors were often essential in making progress and helping to solve problems.

The progress made could not have been done without excellent embassy teams working hard and in coordination across many important issues. Collaboration among the Country Team is vital for success in every embassy. I worked diligently to foster interagency teams that could generate "whole of mission" approaches to key issues and encourage creative problem solving. We hired new staff in the public diplomacy section to start ramping up our use of social media and to build a range of partnerships that could help extend our impact and outreach across Mexico.

Simultaneously, I told the entire range of agencies and our consulates that they had to work closely with the public diplomacy section and that they each had an important role in the embassy's public outreach in Mexico. The leaders in our PD offices established new and deeper relations with Mexican counterparts and partners in Washington to generate daily collaboration that helped manage press "crises" and develop plans for longer term efforts to strengthen bilateral collaboration involving education, science, entrepreneurship, commerce, investment and much more.

On issues surrounding anti-crime work, we met together at least once a week to go over progress. When we uncovered problems, we called together representatives of agencies who were not cooperating or coordinating well to try to resolve differences. We sadly had to send home a couple of representatives home who were not good team players. At one point, we felt the need to convene a face-to-face meeting at the embassy with US-based and embassy representatives to tell them to stop pursuing uncoordinated actions in activities to crack down on one crime group and to work better together on a key case. They listened and subsequently produced a breakthrough based on very good US interagency coordination and good coordination with Mexican counterparts.

In the economic field, our embassy team conclude that a new step forward was needed as there was no agreement in Washington or with Mexico on a framework for dealing with an important cluster of issues that would help build prosperity for both countries, but which were not being addressed in the framework of the existing trade agreement, NAFTA (the North American Free Trade Agreement). The senior member of the economic section came up with an excellent conceptual proposal for such a framework. We polished and refined the idea and first shared it informally with key senior players in several Washington agencies. Our idea was that they could also then claim credit for the proposal as it was developed and would have "buy-in." The embassy ideas and approach generated a serious interagency discussion. In which the embassy participated. This process successfully builds a coalition of actors who could claim parentage for what became a productive High-Level Economic Dialogue (HLED) overseen by the US Vice President and powered by the leadership of the US Commerce and the Mexican Finance Secretaries.

The HLED and other mechanisms were developed in part to address the very lively in the domestic political debates on both sides of the border about the challenges of managing trade, migration, and illicit trafficking across and around the border. This meant that we were dealing regularly with many members of both countries' congresses and executive branches as well as interested private sector leaders and sub-national politicians. This lively work with so many stakeholders resulted in a series of productive and innovative initiatives beyond the HLED for which many could claim success.

This team working in Mexico City and with Washington actors also helped launch and manage a Mexico-US Entrepreneurship and Innovation Council and new energy and environmental dialogues. We encouraged the creation of a first ever US-Mexico CEO Dialogue. Trade, investment, and tourism all grew significantly during these years.

As noted above, public security issues were also top priorities. We met Secretary Clinton's promised goal for delivering $500 million in Merida assistance by January 1, 2012, and Mission Mexico went on to delivered over $1 billion dollars' worth of capacity building support to Mexico's law enforcement and justice systems initiating over 90 new programs under the $2.3 billion Merida Initiative to support anti-crime reforms. Working with Mexican and Washington counterparts, we improved law enforcement, justice, security, defense, border, and consular cooperation by creating new bilateral coordination mechanisms and protocols. Results included increased arrests of criminal bosses, reduced cross-border violence and unprecedented levels of military-to-military cooperation.

Recognizing that the long-term country to country relationship needed to be reinforce and sustained by stronger people-to-people programs, we fostered close partnerships with two Mexican cabinet agencies and various universities and foundations to build education cooperation grew through a new US-Mexico Bilateral Forum on Higher Education, Innovation and Research. Together, we doubled the number of Mexican students and teachers who studied in the US in 2014 and fostered over 50 university partnerships. The Mexican federal government provided most of the funding for this education surge.

All of these "positive" new cooperative efforts were reinforced by much more vigorous outreach to the Mexican public with speeches, interviews, visits around the country and a much stronger social media program. The embassy, for example, grew Facebook likes from 9,000 in 2011 to 960,000 in mid-2015. We innovated in use of music, youth programs and other means to reach the public.

We still frequently encountered "mini crises" to manage that often touched on the domestic politics and sensitivities on both sides of the border. Using a whole of mission approach to problem solving and using the wide range of partnerships and coalitions built within and without both governments, we were able to diffuse and disentangle controversies.

Managing cross-border crime and migration remained very challenging longer term challenges that clear would demand sustained work overtime to manage well between the two governments. But, importantly, the embassy and partners in Washington and Mexico City put in place a series of institutional arrangements and trusted relationships that made progress easier to achieve. These steps set the groundwork for continued problem solving and for helping to weather the expected crises, big and small, while expanding prosperity and good outcomes on both sides of the border. Many of these good steps lasted even through the trying years ahead following the election of President Donald Trump who took a different approach to US-Mexico relations.

American First (in Reducing Global Influence)

As former Secretary of State George Shultz continued to remind America during these years as he had practiced when in office, diplomatic gardens demand daily tending, and that work is more likely to succeed if you have fellow gardeners committed to keeping the garden alive and flourishing. That is certainly the case with US-Mexico relations flourishing.

The relatively good US-Mexico interactions continued after my 2015 departure through the end of the Obama administration, but they were put under great strain with the arrival of President Donald Trump. Trump did not value institutional relationships or George Shultz' regular "diplomatic gardening." Rather he treated the US-Mexico relationship in large part to strengthen his political base at home on issues of migration, border management and trade. He was quite willing to use bullying and insulting words as well as US economic leverage, including sanctions, to score points with supporters and force Mexican cooperation. He seemed to give much less regard to the longer term importance of bilateral cooperation on these and other issues.

This approach made the US-Mexico relationship much more difficult across the board and mobilized anti-Americanism in Mexico that had been deeply submerged by the work of earlier years. Trump also used similar diplomatic strongarming with the other NAFTA partner, Canada, as well as with allies and partners around the world including rival China. Russia and North Korea were standout exceptions to this more coercive form of diplomacy. Trump also undervalued the State Department and initiated several alarming efforts to slash its budget and staffing, setting of a serious decline in morale and the departure of many senior diplomats, even as China was greatly expanding its diplomatic presence and influence-building efforts around the world.

As a former diplomat who cared about America's diplomatic and foreign policy capacity and strength, I opted to say involved. I began working with the American Foreign Service Association (AFSA) and the American Academy of Diplomacy (AAD) to help build resistance to the Trump team's concerted effort to undermine America's professional diplomats and to weaken our ability to compete effectively with China's economic and commercial diplomacy. Representing many respected former diplomats, we set about influencing congress to resist the Trump administration proposals (which they did) and informing the American public of the dangers of weaking America's diplomatic tools.

Also, I started working several thinktanks in Washington to try to raise public awareness and influence policy thinking with events and writings regarding Mexico and North America (with the Woodrow Wilson Center); on Afghanistan and development issues (with the Center for Strategic and International Studies); and on transatlantic economic relations (with the Atlantic Council). I sought to address the importance of recognizing the interconnection between domestic and international issues and urging the US to act on the pressures and misconceptions that were causing many Americans to be so sympathetic to President Trump's hard line policies on trade-related issues. So, for example, I wrote two long papers with ideas of how the US should be investing much more on developing the skills and capacities of US and North America's workers to have good jobs and "grow" prosperity in the future.

Now, working again outside of government, I found that though there was opportunity to educate, inform and support diplomatic gardening, the impact on Administration policies and actions was hard to measure. Working with many colleagues, we did have impact encouraging Congress to push back on Trump's efforts to slash the State Department's budget, for example, and by keeping constructive dialogue alive with Mexico through the difficult times.

I re-discovered first-hand how many smart, dedicated people in the Washington community are sharing good ideas with the hope of influencing policy. This alternative track for diplomacy is valuable, but it is not a replacement for good first track policy and diplomacy.

Nor, specifically, could the efforts in which I participated stop the drain of good and experienced diplomats from the State Department or the evident decline in US influence and diplomacy capacity. COVID and its poor handling by the Trump Administration added to this sense of disorder and decline. Not surprisingly, morale among my former diplomatic colleagues at the State Department continued to suffer throughout these years. Others on the outside of government produced excellent proposals for reform and revival of the US diplomatic capacity, which I supported, and several which are now being implemented. But there is no question for me, that they US ceded influence and clout to China and Russia and seriously harmed international partnerships and undermined positive images of America built over decades of hard work.

I do have to add that on the more positive side of the ledger, the Trump administration did negotiate a new north America trade arrangement, the US-Mexico-Canada agreement which usefully modernized NAFTA and has so far proven to be a good framework for taking trade forward since it came into force in July 2020. From my perch, in the thinktank world, I weighed in regularly in writing and events to support good outcomes.

Building Back Better Will Be a Long Effort Requiring Superior Diplomatic Skills, Better Capacity, and Less Polarization

President Biden and his team came to office with excellent strategic proposals for spurring domestic investment and job creation, for addressing the lingering effects of the pandemic and for restoring America's partnerships and alliances. He and his team have importantly sought to restore momentum to democracy in the tug of war with authoritarianism in the world.

Having a foreign policy to meet the needs of the middle class and American workers is a good way to describe the Biden teams efforts to create a positive synergy between domestic and international policy and to start building bridges across domestic divides. However, this massive agenda put a tremendous burden on the new administration to coordinate across policy lines effectively, to manage well a very complex and demanding set of priorities, and to build back from COVOD and the serious damage Trump has done to America's institutions and capacities, while trying to lead a still badly divided country.

As of this writing in mid-2023, the Biden administration has made significant progress with important domestic legislation funding important investments in competitiveness and has done a good job in rebuilding US international coalitions, as highlighted by the excellent diplomatic efforts responding to Russia's invasion of Ukraine. The Biden Administration and Secretary of State Blinken have also initiated an excellent and thoughtful effort to modernize the State Department and the tools of US diplomacy including the Foreign Service. The have started adding needed staff, training, recruiting, and funding for the State Department and US overseas presence. This investment and focus need to be sustained. The initial steps bode well for future US international capacities, but the return of deep domestic political polarization does not.

The fiasco of the US withdrawal for Afghanistan in 2021 was a terrible start, however. It was a poor decision, poorly implemented. For me, it was also a serious reminder to me of how hard it is to influence a US administration from the outside. I joined other former US ambassadors and senior officials in offering alternatives to the Trump and Biden administrations for managing out withdrawal from Afghanistan between 2019 and the summer of 2021. All of us working on these op-eds had concluded that US policies (under both presidents) would lead to bad outcomes for the US and Afghans, but, though we believe many still working inside the USG shared our assessments, we could not influence the outcomes with our words, articles, and opinion pieces. Sadly, many Afghans continue to pay a high price for US policies and actions in the last four years or so.

Diplomacy Is More Vital Than Ever

The United States and America diplomacy can rebound from the relative decline in America's global role and the rise of alternative global powers, networks, and models of governance. It will require sustained investment in US personnel, skills and institutions as well as having good policy making processes, which include close consultations with partners and allies, producing wise outcomes. The federal leadership team will need to continue strengthening efforts to build domestic support for a foreign policy and diplomacy suited for the evolving international scene of at least two powerful rivals, a range of global threats, and many countries needing to be persuaded to work closely with the United States. Forging a more peaceful and prosperous world order that reflects America's tradition of democratic values remains a tremendous challenge in a world where democracy has in decline.

But, of course, a vital central factor will be if the US can overcome the polarization that has characterized American domestic politics and move back to a more consensus based approach to US international policy. As of this writing, such an outcome is not clear.

Nevertheless, the core skills and practices of diplomacy discussed earlier will be essential for US success. It will also take diplomats better educated and trained to deal with the expanding agenda of topics from climate change and migration to managing the continued rapid evolution of technology and its effects on so many aspects of daily life and relations between nations. And many of these topics will be sharply debated at home as well as with other governments and international actors.

Diplomacy more than before needs to be a "whole of government" undertaking, drawing on the expertise and participation of a wide range of actors in government as well as partners outside of government. Coordination and collaboration are more important than ever. The "inter-mestic" nature of foreign policy and lack of public understanding about the importance of good diplomacy means the State Department, ambassadors and diplomats need to communicate better about their mission and work to the American public as well as to host country publics. These trends will underscore the value of diversity among new generations of US diplomats.

Diplomacy is also going to be more challenging because the world's communications landscape is faster, more crowded, more competitive, and more filled with misinformation. Technologies have accelerated the speed of the news cycle and thus of diplomacy and national security decision-making. This world of rapid-fire communications is transforming operations of foreign policy machinery in capitals and in embassies. Disinformation and propaganda will continue to be enabled by social media and new technology tools, influencing public opinions and adding complications to diplomatic practice.

As is evident looking back at the many US international missteps in recent decades, the United States must make serious investments in reimagining how the US makes policy and conduct diplomacy, and it must do so with humility and modesty. Building and enhancing partnerships, alliances and problem solving institutions are even more vital for American influence in this world of multiple powers, alliances, and partnerships.

This requires ongoing effort to fund, energize, train, and up-skill US diplomats. The US needs a "top of class" system that recruits diplomatic and international staff better, trains and retrains them better, and better rewards and motivates them. The world in which American diplomacy works is going to keep evolving and demanding more and better performance of its diplomats to produce the best results possible for US interests and values.

The diplomatic garden is getting bigger, with more varieties to tend, more predators to fend off, more competitors to manage, more health risks for which to prepare, and more unpredictable weather to anticipate. We need a diplomacy that can successfully manage the many challenges ahead.

Annex: Some Crucial Career Lessons Along the Way

- As a China analyst in the State Department's Intelligence and Research bureau: It is vital to understand others in the context of their history, politics, and culture as well as possible. Given that knowledge, solid, readable, concise analysis of what events mean is a great contribution for busy policy makers.

- As a political officer in Morocco: it is important to work creatively to build a wide network of contacts and build trust that allows for deeper understanding; that will be valued. You never know when your humblest contacts might turn out to provide the most valuable insight or access.

- A "line officer" in the State Department's Executive Secretariat: One needs to "know" and understand how the policy process works (or not) to influence decisions. Recognize that poor process encourages poor decisions and mistakes by policy makers. Knowing the player's strengths and weaknesses helps greatly.

- As a special assistant to the Secretary of State: Bureaucratic infighting can distract immensely from good policy making and debilitate an administration. Patiently working the "system" and building networks of allies pays off in the longer term; in crises, one may need to press through the decision-making process if it works well or not; endurance and determination are essential for success; "Diplomatic Gardening" takes constant, careful, patient tending; never forget the interests of "your country" and the importance of being able to understand and influence its policy making.

- At the JFK School, Harvard: Leadership is helping the group solve problems and not a function of the position one holds in the hierarchy. Watch out for group pressures to act in certain ways; don't get forced into unwise moves; don't just get caught up in the fight but look for solutions and ways to get to good solutions.

- Embassy Paris political officer: One can build relationships of confidence even with individuals of very different backgrounds and political outlooks if you know and focus on areas of common interest and work with integrity to build trust. Building trust often opens doors for new, mutually beneficial collaboration. Building networks of trust unleashes insight and opens the doors and windows to build creative ways ahead.

- The Christian Science Monitor, national security correspondent: There is much more to the Washington foreign policy process that just State, DoD and the White House. There are many other key actors and channels who influence on policy and outcomes. Know, follow, and influence them if possible. Catch people's attention with you title and lead! Then you can better help educate and influence.

- State's Counter-Terrorism office: Building coalitions is a great way to achieve objectives and extend influence; senior officials are looking for good ideas to solve problems no matter where you might be sitting; creativity well-presented will be rewarded.

- National Security Council staff: Good process, Good teamwork, and Good ideas ready at the right moment can produce great results.

Building inter-agency agreement and trust facilitates breakthroughs. Work at the top is intense. Stamina, discipline, good humor, and a commitment to quality are vital.

- US Mission the European Union: Economic, regulatory, and often technical issues can have very big impacts for a country's security and were more important in the post-Cold War world. Global issues were of increasing importance demanding more attention and expertise. The US needs more partners and different types of partnerships in a more globalized world. it is possible and valuable to create new policy frameworks and institutions to help face a newly emerging global scene. Coordination and collaboration are more important than ever to get to good outcomes and to create new opportunities.

- European Affairs Deputy Assistant Secretary: "Diplomatic Gardening" takes a lot of attention in Washington with a range of domestically facing US agencies as well as US agencies not oriented to collaborate with the State Department, plus with other governments and international organizations, NGOs, and businesses. It is essential to invest in one's staff: in recruitment, training, rewards, and on-ward assignments and promotions. You and your staff need to be very good at working in the US bureaucracy as well as with other countries. In difficult negotiations it is vital to build coalitions and to use partners to achieve successful outcomes whether you are working within the US government or internationally. The public, NGOs and civil society groups are increasingly engaged in and concerned about international issues and the effects of those issues on their lives. You need strategies to involve them, influence them and build partnerships. Diplomacy must become more public facing both at home and in other countries. Public diplomacy would be entering a new era of importance.

- Assistant Secretary of Economic and Business Affairs: Economic work is filled with arcane, technical issues that have massively important impacts on people's lives in most every country. You need to put technical expertise in strategic context to explain its importance to policy makers and the public. One needs to help craft the teamwork needed to bring good policy out of silos of expertise that often do not communicate well. The international agenda is growing more complex and more deeply interconnected with domestic politics and outcomes: there is often no clear dividing line between the domestic agenda and the international agenda—they are interconnected. Big geo-strategic issues have important economic and development aspects that are key to success in handling those challenges going forward, even if policy makers do not initially understand that. They need to be educated on the connections. Increasingly, the US needs to build and maintain coalitions to take on big international projects across a range of issues and countries. The US needs to draw on the spectrum of economic, development, financial and technical tools at its disposal in crafting a strategy to succeed. This work can be done effectively working with multinational teams. It takes serious investment of time and effort in building cohesive teams and partnerships inside the USG and internationally. But one can build excellent outcomes if this is done well. It is important, however, to have solid processes for implementation and coordination. Sanctions can be a very effective tool if used well, for example, in fighting terror, authoritarian governments, criminals, human rights violators and other bad actors, for example, and with hard work, others will join. But there are clear limits to the effectiveness of sanctions and even more so if not done with others. Having coalitions or groups impose sanctions is most always the better way to apply the pressure of sanctions than acting unilaterally. Overuse of sections just to signal undermine their effectiveness, and it is clearly possible to overuse and misuse sanctions. The State Department and the NSC/NEC at the While House need to fully integrate economics into the policy process. The State Department needs invest more in strengthening its economic and commercial diplomacy., this means establishing strong partnerships with agencies and with the private sector. The State Department and Foreign Service also need more resources and better skilled/trained staff to build support for US economic interests and initiatives, for supporting US business trying to open overseas markets and to succeed in the competition with commercial rivals seeking advantage in international markets. Neither trade policy nor international financial policy should be conducted outside of a robust inter-agency policy process in Washington that brings all US capacities to bear in a coordinated way. The same holds true for US development efforts: coordination among the agencies involved needs to be strong with regular evaluation of results. The aid the US offers and the agencies delivering them can make a big difference for good, if coordinated and implemented well.

- Ambassador to Argentina: US soft power and effective public diplomacy are potent tools to persuade other publics of US good will, but they need to be used as an integrated part of diplomacy and as part of a "whole of government" effort especially at US embassies and consulates overseas. Partnerships and strong relations with civil society, business and NGOs supporting democracy, free press, social justice, and related causes can be vital in building and sustaining good relations with other nations. These partnerships show their value during tense periods of relations between governments. A coordinated use of US soft power assets can soften and dissolve anti-Americanism if done well.

- Ambassador-ranked positions in Afghanistan: Overestimating what is doable in a realistic timeframe is a serious, costly problem and hard to escape. Build in processes to understand when one is caught in tasks that are beyond your capacity to manage well and then reassess likely outcomes and timeframes. Deeply absorb how difficult it is to change another government, economy, or society, and keep investing in deeper understanding of local culture, norms, and power structures. Take a humble approach. The US often does not have the best answer at first. Expect mistakes and incorporate ways to learn from those mistakes and implement lessons learned. Build in the regular capacity to reflect seriously on the core issues inhibiting success rather than learning similar lessons repeatedly during a war. Set modest goals with modest investments and be willing to be patient. Change and transformation take time and persistence—and they may not come out where one expected. Try hard to explain this publicly, rather than playing down the challenges. Try to be honest about achieving significant results quickly. Be candid about your capacity to bring about change, the limitations of your partners, and the resistance you will face in the society, political body, and economy you are trying to reform/change. Honestly assess the capacity of your own staff and of the programs you can offer to achieve the desired results. Recognize and address your internal weaknesses, especially when implementing policy. Try to check the temptation to throw money at the problems. Institute strong monitoring of results. Don't underestimate the dangers of corruption, and don't overestimate the overlap of shared goals and values with your local partners. There will be mistakes and diversions of resources. Don't underestimate the importance of coping with micro-managing from Washington and managing bureaucratic infighting among the US team. Don't underestimate the pressure to set unrealistic, short timelines. You likely will not have the time needed to bring about the changes desired.

- Mexico: Domestic politics and foreign policy are inextricably inter-twined for both Mexico and the United States, more so than with any other relationship except with Canada. Successful management of the many "inter-mestic" issues means that one is regularly messaging with, working with, negotiating with, a host of actors on both sides of the border and constantly paying attention to public diplomacy and media messages. The media and the public need to be regularly (daily) addressed with a strategy and tactics. Engaging with other actors from both countries is vital be they legislators, governors, mayors, businesses, NGOs, civil society groups, youth and many more. Having "champions" and committed partners is essential to solving problems and developing opportunities for new gains.

- Getting agreement on a strategic vision about the overall relationship is very helpful and building coalitions of partners to work on key issues and in support of that vision is terribly important. Consider carefully how to reduce resistance and create "win-win" circumstances, if possible.

- Share success—be modest about ownership, share it to get buy in and a sense of progress. Work hard to show that you are contributing to the success of the host country and its citizens as well as in your home country. In big relationships the substantive agenda to be address is likely to keep growing as the global scene, technology, societies, domestic politics continue to evolve. It is vital for you and your team keep learning and innovating.

- One needs to invest heavily in encouraging shared vision, collabora-tion, and coordination on the embassy team. Make sure it is a well-functioning team. Don't forget about your people in the press of events. One's staff need to be cared for and they need to be kept secure—true in Mexico as it was in Afghanistan. Similarly, it is important to figure out ways to bolster resiliency, adaptability and preserve ability to reflect, innovate, recognize creativity, foster optimism in demanding job and posts.

- Never forget the duty to watch out for the safety of US citizens as well as your own staff—this is the responsibility that keeps a leader up at night, especially in locations where the threats are high.

- Post State, Washington: One can influence thinking and policy from outside government, but it is not easy and is hit and miss. There are many good ideas shared regularly in Washington by think tanks and smart thinkers. Busy people in government often do not have time to see, hear or absorb them. However, one advantage of being out of government is that you can take deep dives and offer more serious reflections on important issues that you would otherwise not have time to do. Just as when practicing diplomacy in government one needs persistence, networks, optimism, and "gardening", with the additional channel now of helping to informing the public and, for me as a professor, helping inform the next generation of diplomats. The US needs them to be as wise and skilled as possible. Opportunities to educate and to keep learning are invaluable.

EIGHT

KEN GROSS

On Diplomacy

Prologue

As I tried to sleep and shivered in my sleeping bag in the subfreezing temperatures, I listened to the Tibetans outside my flimsy shack loudly celebrating their new year. I was in Langtang, a Tibetan village in northern Nepal close by the Tibetan (Chinese) border, and the enthusiasm of the Tibetan festivities did little to ease the numbing cold that encased me although I was wearing every piece of clothing I carried with me. One thought kept racing through my head while my body struggled to stay warm and drift off to sleep—so this is the Foreign Service?

My assignment to Kathmandu provided the antithetical experience to my first posting in Germany. In Frankfurt, I enjoyed all the comforts and conveniences you expect in Europe. In Nepal, besides official treks to meet Nepali officials in places like Langtang, I helped cremate American citizens who passed away, used the King's helicopter wing to rescue ill or stranded Americans, witnessed and reported on the revolution that erased the King's status as a god and ushered in multi-party democracy, and began to truly appreciate all the advantages that my country offered its citizens. My first two assignments in Germany and Nepal helped lay the groundwork for the experiences and skills I would need to become a successful diplomat and Ambassador. I witnessed in both of these diplomatic missions the qualities of leaders that are essential to a well-run Embassy and the factors that make its diplomacy effective.

Essential Qualities of a Diplomat and Ambassador

What attributes should an Ambassador have? There are a multitude of characteristics listed by commentators and practitioners that a diplomat—and especially an Ambassador—should possess. I looked closely at what two practitioners who predated the modern era had to say, taking a glimpse back at traditional views of diplomacy and comparing them to today's world. Alexis Saint-Léger Léger, the preeminent French diplomat in the era between the World Wars, listed several of the necessary qualities: imagination, foresight, courage, and patience, while noting that she should be an innovator though limited by the discipline of the civil service.[1] Harold Nicolson, a former British diplomat who wrote a penetrating analysis of the 1919 Versailles peace conference,[2] said that an ideal diplomat or Ambassador should be truthful, precise in her actions, remain calm, possess a good temper, enjoy patience and perseverance, be modest, and always be loyal.[3] Interestingly, other qualities such as intelligence, knowledge, discernment, prudence, hospitality, charm, industry, courage, and tact were not cited; Nicolson said that these qualities were all taken for granted.[4]

These very general characteristics are still needed today for an Ambassador and diplomat. The US Foreign Service is unique in not requiring certain experiences, languages, or background in its candidates for Foreign Service Officers. Instead, budding American diplomats must pass a written exam that covers knowledge in various fields, an oral assessment that provides illustrations of key experiences that could be essential for a career in the Foreign Service, a physical examination, a background check that determines whether a candidate can be granted the needed security clearance, and finally an overall evaluation of the candidate's suitability for a Foreign Service career. Some of the qualities cited by Léger and Nicolson should be evident in the written and oral examinations, but no particular expertise or educational level is required.

Like my colleagues in the US Foreign Service, I brought with me many varied experiences when I joined the Department of State. Our different backgrounds were emblematic of our country, and as representatives of the United States abroad, these differences helped illustrate the heterogeneity of America. My entering class was composed of several professions, including teachers, a retail specialist, a forester, a director from the movie industry, several lawyers, and a Ph.D. in international relations, among others.

Our many different backgrounds were the bedrock upon which we built our diplomatic careers. There is a short introductory course that all new Foreign Service Officers must take, but the real training to become diplomats is experiential from serving in positions mostly in our overseas and domestic assignments. Meeting the Tibetans living in Langtang, making contact with them, learning their culture, and talking about their lives and expectations were part of my diplomatic education.

Assignments in the Foreign Service

Foreign Service assignments, both abroad and domestically, are determined by a potpourri of factors. "Service need" is the overriding and most stated element in determining where a Foreign Service Officer will serve— if the Department of State needs you in a particular job, that is where you will be assigned. That said, it is very rare for a Foreign Service Officer to be assigned to a post against her or his wishes. When the Department was searching for officers to serve in Iraq during the early days after the 2003 invasion, much was made of "service need", but officers were induced to volunteer for service in Iraq by a generous financial package and the lure of extra consideration for promotion. All Foreign Service positions were filled by volunteers.

Foreign Service Officers "bid" on their assignments and compete against their colleagues for them, and an individual's experience and language skills play key roles in determining qualifications for a position. If I had applied for a senior position in China overseeing the management of our Embassy, I would not have met the minimum qualifications of language and experience. Language could be learned—if there were time—but I never served as a Management Officer and would have not had the knowledge necessary to head up the management section of a large Embassy.

The Department prides itself on its promotion system and tries its best to make it as objective as possible and to eliminate any possibility of favoritism. The opposite is true in its assignment system. Though you must be generally qualified for a position, a choice must sometimes be made from among scores of well-qualified candidates, and the person who might be deemed the most qualified is not always chosen. This is where your "corridor reputation" comes into play along with a need for senior mentors to lobby for you. Your corridor reputation is what people throughout the Department think of you—good, bad, or indifferent. From the first days in the Department, the importance of it is drilled into new Foreign Service Officers, and it plays an important role in assignments. Having Foreign Service Officers who know you and will lobby for you for particular jobs is just as important. Though it usually pays to have senior or well-connected officers going to bat for your particular candidacy, your corridor reputation can be advanced by lower-ranked officers too. When I was up for a particular job I wanted in the European Bureau, I was fortunate to have the strong support of my Ambassador, a very senior officer. But as was related to me later, an entry level officer was present when the decision was made on which candidate to choose, and his endorsement sealed my candidacy.

All Foreign Service Officers start their careers with a basic orientation course in the Department called A-100. It is during this short, five-week course (unfortunately reduced from 10 weeks when I took it) that they begin to learn about the Department and the many jobs they could possibly have throughout their careers. Foreign Service Officers also begin their careers in a "career track" (formerly called a "cone," and still commonly referred to as that)—an area of specialty in which they will be expected to spend the majority of their careers. Though Foreign Service Officers are "generalists" and theoretically can serve in any position they are qualified for, the conal system can limit what they actually can bid on and which jobs they can hold. Luckily, the strong strictures of the conal system have lessened in recent years, though I still view it as an anachronism.

My Assignment History

From the start, I would like to emphasize that there is no one "typical" Foreign Service career. Everyone's career path is different, based upon their preferences in assignments, where they served, and how successful they were in their positions. I always advised new Foreign Service Officers that they should try to fill positions that they either liked, thought were important, or hopefully both. There is no one path to become an Ambassador, and to me that is one of the beauties of the Foreign Service. All of my colleagues had "typical" Foreign Service careers, though they differed substantially based on where they served and what positions they held. Persons entering the Foreign Service today should expect to serve in positions and posts they never anticipated and should welcome the variety of opportunities offered.

Once in A-100, an exotic and varied list of posts potentially available to my class for our initial assignments was presented to us a few days into our training. It included many different postings, including London, Karachi, Taipei, Lima, Stuttgart, Seoul, Port-au-Prince, Paramaribo, Cebu, Maputo, and Athens. Having lived in Germany as a child, I hoped to be assigned to one of the four German-speaking posts on our list, and during our class assignment ceremony I was fortunate to be presented with a small flag of Germany indicating my assignment to Frankfurt. This was the last time, except for my Ambassadorial assignment and my final tour in Iraq, that my overseas assignment matched up with my initial wish for a particular post.

My short 18-month tour in Frankfurt was a great introduction to life in the Foreign Service. Our Ambassador to Germany at that time was a political appointee with an extensive military background and was stationed at the Embassy in the then-capital of West Germany, Bonn. I met him only one time when he visited the Frankfurt Consulate and shook hands with me briefly, and my view of him from my perch as a lowly first-tour officer was as an apprentice looking up to an accomplished master, especially since that was my only contact with him. As is true of many of the Ambassadors at large posts, he was not a career diplomat, though he did have substantial foreign policy experience. His deputy, in US diplomatic parlance called the Deputy Chief of Mission, also visited Frankfurt once during my tour. As is true of almost all Deputy Chiefs of Mission, he was a career Foreign Service Officer. During his visit to the Frankfurt Consulate, he met with me and the other new officers in a group and informed us that the quality of incoming officers to the Foreign Service had diminished substantially in recent years. After that pep talk, we were particularly glad we were working in Frankfurt instead of Bonn, and we never heard from him again.

My first tour was followed, as I indicated earlier, by my assignment to Kathmandu, Nepal. Nepal is a breathtakingly beautiful country, though it is one of the poorest in the world. Before I left Germany, a colleague in the Frankfurt Consulate had regaled me with stories of visitors to Nepal who suffered for years from unknown and severe diseases they had caught while visiting Nepal, and when I arrived in Kathmandu and witnessed firsthand the absence of sanitation and disease control, I started to believe his stories. But Nepal was a magical place to live, and Kathmandu was infused with the aura of its many gods and a culture that had developed in seclusion from the rest of the world for many centuries.

In the late 1980s it also was still relatively isolated. Though mountaineers, backpackers, and those seeking an alternative lifestyle had made their way there for several years, outside news and western goods were in short supply, and it was not easy to travel in country or internationally. The Embassy was a relatively small post, though it boasted an excellent recreation facility located in a former palace that sat across from the King's own palace.

My Ambassador was a political appointee, but her deputy was a professional Foreign Service Officer, and my dealings with the front office (the usual term for the office in the Embassy containing the Ambassador and Deputy Chief of Mission) were much more productive than my experience in Germany. Though the Deputy Chief of Mission had initially rebuffed my offer to help with reporting by instructing me to concentrate on my consular duties, my contacts and after work perambulations throughout Kathmandu provided substantial background for reporting during and after the democratic revolution that swept through Nepal in 1990. The Ambassador had a favorable opinion of my consular skills, partly thanks to the faxes she received complimenting my assistance to American citizens. There was one case in particular that provided a boost to my standing in her eyes. I had helped organize a helicopter rescue of an ill American who was trekking far away from Kathmandu, and because of a dearth of means to communicate with the Embassy, the individual's family faxed the Ambassador with details of my deeds and its heartfelt appreciation. Communication, even by faxing, was not reliable at that time, so the family repeated its fax to the Ambassador two additional times in the following weeks. The Ambassador, not realizing that the three faxes referred to only one case, congratulated me on my many exploits rescuing Americans by helicopter. My supervisor, however, understood that the original fax had been sent to the Ambassador two additional times and noted to me that I would receive credit for only one rescue.

Having a political appointee instead of a career Foreign Service Officer as Ambassador does not necessarily mean that the political Ambassador cannot perform her duties with distinction. I have known several political appointee Ambassadors who, because of their close relationship with the President or their previous experiences, were excellent Ambassadors. Professional diplomats have years of experience in living overseas, understand the culture and political situations in which they work, and are focused on serving US Government and not their own interests. I agree with George Kennan that professionalism in foreign affairs requires professional training and experience.[5]

After Nepal, I returned to the Department of State for a short stint on the Intelligence Bureau's 24-hour Watch, followed by a tour in Kuala Lumpur, Malaysia. My Ambassador was a career Foreign Service Officer, and my Deputy Chief of Mission was an exceptional officer who took a personal interest in my career and served as a mentor for me. She encouraged my reporting on political events and helped me with my bidding for my next assignment. Through her lobbying for me, I received word that my number one choice of assignments—a human rights reporting officer in Ankara via Turkish language training—was agreed to and would be supported by the European Bureau. But in one of the many vagaries of the Department's assignment system, the assignment panel rejected my bid and instead assigned the job to a political coned officer. At that time, it was difficult for an out-of-cone officer (I was consular coned) to be assigned overseas to a position that was other than in her or his particular cone. As explained earlier, a "cone" is the functional area that you will be expected to work in for most of your career. I consider it a relic that has outlived its usefulness.

Searching for an overseas assignment tied to language training, I ended up assigned to Port-au-Prince, Haiti, via language training in French, becoming the only mid-level officer that year to receive training in a world language before assignment overseas. My Ambassador in Haiti, Bill Swing, was a superb diplomat who was serving in his fifth consecutive Ambassadorship. I learned more from him on how to treat his officers and staff than from any of my other Ambassadors. He epitomized the best of the US Foreign Service—he possessed a high intellect, exceptional knowledge of the political realities of Haiti and its social fabric, and perhaps most importantly, he knew how to value and treat people, both his American staff and his Haitian interlocutors.

With his help in the bidding process, I moved on to my next assignment working as a desk officer in the Department for the office that coordinated Austrian, German, and Swiss affairs. A desk officer is responsible for an individual or a small number of countries and manages the relationships both within and outside of the Department relating to those countries and interacts closely with both the US Embassies and the foreign Embassies in Washington. Having to work closely with the many different offices in the Department and understand their responsibilities toward the countries in my office served as a primer on how the Department functioned. In managing the many issues for my countries, I had the opportunity to observe and participate in meetings with high-ranking Department and US Government officials, a key ingredient for my diplomatic education.

My next assignment, also in Washington, was in the Economic Bureau where I served as an Aviation Negotiator. In this role, I worked closely with private industry and other Federal agencies to establish or modify bilateral and multilateral agreements on flights between countries. I left this position early to start language training for my next job, Deputy Chief of Mission for our Embassy in Dushanbe, Tajikistan.

Tajikistan, a former Soviet republic neighboring Afghanistan, had undergone a violent five-year civil war after independence in 1992, and was the poorest of the Central Asian countries. It also was severely affected by the fighting in Afghanistan, and the Embassy faced security threats that modified how we worked and lived in country. At that time, our Embassy in Tajikistan was actually "removed" to Almaty, Kazakstan, because of the danger to our diplomats in Dushanbe from terrorists. Our local staff in Dushanbe was sequestered in the former residence of the Ambassador, and US diplomats flew in every few weeks to talk to Tajik officials. The attacks of September 11, 2001, changed this model of working remotely in Tajikistan since we needed to spend almost all of our time in country. Though I was officially assigned to the Embassy to Tajikistan in Almaty and had an apartment there, I spent almost all of my time in Tajikistan on "temporary duty." Nonetheless, it was a great opportunity to work with Franklin "Pancho" Huddle, an outstanding Ambassador, and to gain experience managing an expanding Embassy.

Following two years in Tajikistan, I returned to the United States and spent a year at the National War College. This institution, one of several war colleges for the different branches of the armed services, was attended by officers from all the services, foreign officers from around the world, and civilian employees from executive branch agencies. State Department employees formed the majority of the civilian employees in attendance. The National War College[6] provided an opportunity to study not just war, but more importantly how the US Government works at high levels, an essential tool for senior officers. It allowed us to discuss theories and "look over the horizon," instead of reacting to the immediate challenges always present in our different jobs. I left after a year with a M.S. degree in National Security Strategy.

Many of my military colleagues had fought in Iraq or Afghanistan, and I decided I wanted firsthand experience in the United States' role in Iraq. I volunteered to head our Regional Embassy Office (REO)[7] in Basrah, which was responsible for the four southern provinces of Iraq. This was my first experience serving in a war zone, though because of the very real threats from terrorists we had been required to utilize bodyguards and armored vehicles in Tajikistan. The repeated rocket and mortar attacks of our facility in Basrah, especially during my last three months at post, forced me to reduce our staffing from over 400 people to below 300; of those that remained the vast majority were responsible for our security. As the officer heading up the REO, I worked alongside the few Foreign Service Officers at post and maintained close contact with the Deputy Chief of Mission at Embassy Baghdad.

From my perspective in the south of Iraq, it was obvious that we had entered into the conflict without an understanding of neither the history or culture of Iraq. The analogue used by many of the leaders of our intervention and continuing presence in Iraq was the occupation of German after World War II, a comparison that was as fanciful as it was far-fetched. The lack of understanding of Iraq's culture and history, combined with the efforts to instill democracy and a peaceful society by throwing money into projects that never reached the Iraqi people—electrical sub-stations built without lines connecting them to the grid, modern water treatment plants that were doomed to immediate obsolescence due to a lack of supplies and trained personnel—were just some of the failed projects that accompanied the failure to help institute a viable Iraqi government.

After my 12-month tour was completed, I returned to Washington, but within a few months I was asked to return to Iraq, this time to Baghdad, to help initiate the Embassy's new Office of Provincial Affairs which coordinated the work of the Provincial Reconstruction Teams throughout Iraq. Even though the number and severity of attacks on the Embassy compound in Baghdad were much less than what we endured in Basrah, I much preferred the independence of action I had enjoyed in Basrah and the many fewer bureaucratic in-fights than were part of the atmosphere at the much larger Baghdad Embassy.

Upon returning to Washington I served in a couple of one-year positions (Director of the Middle East Partnership Initiative office and Senior Level Career Development Officer in our Human Resources Bureau) and was chosen to be the next Ambassador to Tajikistan. I looked forward to returning to Dushanbe where I knew the country well, the President, many members of government, and most of the local staff at our Embassy. Because of my time in Tajikistan as Deputy Chief of Mission, I had many friends and acquaintances there, though of course all of my fellow diplomats were new to me. The way the government in Tajikistan is run, the only key contact for me was the President. It was five years after I left Dushanbe as Deputy Chief of Mission that I returned to be Ambassador.

Soon after I arrived at post, I notified my superiors in Washington that I was in Dushanbe and was ready to begin my tenure as Ambassador. I thought that I would receive some cabled guidance on specific strategies or certain initiatives that I should first pursue, but I received no instructions. This was somewhat disconcerting, but I quickly took advantage of the seeming independence from Washington to determine how I should best represent US interests. I decided that I would move ahead on most issues without asking for specific guidance from Washington, hoping that my superiors trusted my judgment. If there were issues that were of prime importance to Washington, I would be sure to keep people there fully informed of developments. And if occasionally there were extremely significant issues for which I believed I first needed Washington's approval before acting on, I would request it, but I thought there would not be many such instances. I believe I only asked one time for Washington's prior approval of my course of action.

I learned that I was not unique in not receiving much specific guidance from Washington. While stationed in Dushanbe I drove to neighboring Uzbekistan and Turkmenistan for vacation, and while in the latter's capital city of Ashgabat I visited the US Embassy to meet the newly arrived Ambassador. After a pleasant introductory conversation, he took me aside to lament that he had not received any particular directions or instructions from Washington. I told him not to worry and explained to him my system for managing issues and initiatives in Dushanbe. Evidently I was not alone in being able to enjoy a certain independence of action. Non-career Ambassadors would have to rely on the guidance provided by their Deputy Chiefs of Mission, and there is much care taken by the Department to ensure that people with the appropriate experience are chosen to be their deputies.

Following three years as Ambassador in Tajikistan, I returned to the State Department and worked in a series of jobs in the Human Resources bureau. After these positions, I thought about pushing my candidacy for another Ambassadorship. Foreign Service Officers are limited, by law, to serving until they reach the age of 65, and I had only two years left before I had to retire because I would "age out." There were not many chief of mission positions available at that time for which my background and experience qualified me, and I decided to request that I be assigned to the Consulate General in Erbil, Iraq, as the Consul General. After serving in Basrah and spending a short tour in Baghdad, I looked forward to completing my service with the State Department by achieving the trifecta of US posts in Iraq (Basrah, Baghdad, and Erbil) and working with the Kurds in the Kurdistan Region of Iraq for my last tour in the Department of State.

Security at all three posts in Iraq was very strict, and when I arrived ISIS was still ensconced in Mosul, just over 80 kilometers distance from Erbil. Because of the continuing fight against ISIS, the massive displaced person and refugee issues, and the virulent animosity between the central Iraqi government and the Kurds, who strongly believed they should be independent, the Kurdistan Region received a surfeit of attention from many different power centers in Washington and from our own Embassy in Baghdad. Luckily, the United States had one of its premier diplomats as Ambassador to Iraq, Doug Silliman. But even he was subject to the demands of numerous visitors from Washington, some of whom had extensive experience in the area and some of whom did not, who visited the Kurdistan Region and offered or demanded their own courses of action or solutions to the many problems bedeviling the region. Unlike in Tajikistan, where I had a fairly free hand to implement initiatives, many different individuals or groups in Washington determined policies at a granular level in Iraq, often without possessing the firsthand knowledge of the actual up-to-date situation on the ground. This was my last assignment in the Department of State.

Lessons Learned

Like any profession, the accretion of experiences of diplomats and professional Ambassadors inform their actions. I served in the Foreign Service for over 31 years, and like everyone who remains in a career for that length of time, I witnessed many changes. Some were natural, such as the increase in the use of technological tools in diplomacy. Others were evolutionary and could be expected to occur over time. And some were unnecessary and harmful to the conduct of US foreign relations.

The following seven lessons are my "takeaways" from my Foreign Service career. Like almost all of my colleagues in the State Department, there are many things that I would have done differently if I had had the authority. And there are several institutional changes I still would make in the Department. But I will concentrate on the more general aspects of serving as an American Ambassador or diplomat that I believe should be followed, changed, or avoided—here are the lessons I learned from my Foreign Service career at the Department of State.

1. No One Is Indispensable

The United States has had several extremely talented career Foreign Service Officers who have held the rank of Ambassador and performed exceptional services. However, as you might expect, Ambassadors tend to have large egos that need regular feeding and some believe they are irreplaceable. Actually, though there are some extremely well-informed officers who are recognized experts in discrete areas, the nature of the US diplomatic profession ensures that one rarely remains at a posting or holds a position at the Department of State for a period longer than three years. The normal tour of duty abroad for US diplomats ranges from twelve months to three years, depending upon the danger and hardships present at each particular post. Though they serve at the pleasure of the President, Ambassadors usually serve for a maximum of three years. Thus, the Department's rules tacitly acknowledge the fact that no one Ambassador or Foreign Service Officer is indispensable.

The education of Foreign Service Officers is dependent on gaining a wealth and variety of assignments and experiences. Formal training, at all levels, is woefully inadequate, and the present service relies on officers learning their craft from their Foreign Service experiences. Secretary Colin Powell, in my opinion the best of the Secretaries of State I served under, was well-known for empowering his troops. He asked to be briefed on certain issues by mid-level officers rather than the senior-level office director and generally looked to the functional experts rather then the senior officers heading up offices.

Though an Ambassador may be *the* expert for her country, there is a recognition that there are no sinecures, and other officers should have the opportunity to lead the US Embassy in that country and gain needed experience. The limitation on length of assignments furthers the goal of ensuring that experience and responsibility is spread among many officers who will have the opportunity to lead an office, a section, or an Embassy. However, as you might expect, the constant reassignment of officers means that officers are continually having to "learn" new jobs. There is a canard among mid-level Foreign Service Officers that for a three-year tour, you spend the first two years learning your job and your last year trying to obtain your next one, but the overall assignment system works well.

2. The Ambassador Must Lead the Embassy

You will notice that in Léger and Nicolson's definitions of an ideal diplomat, there was no mention of leadership skills. Perhaps that is a difference in how American diplomacy is now conducted in the twenty-first century as opposed to over a century ago. An American Ambassador in the early twentieth century in most cases had a fairly small staff and personally conducted the majority of the Embassy's diplomatic work. The welfare and professional development of less experienced Foreign Service Officers was not necessarily a priority for the Ambassador. Today an Ambassador heads up a large, diverse team that conducts diplomacy in numerous areas and at several levels. It is impossible for an American Ambassador to be the "point person" for all of the many policies and facets of modern diplomatic relationships. She needs a strong team, but the Ambassador must also know how to lead it.

Besides managing the large number of diverse issues pursued by the average American Embassy, the Ambassador must embody leadership traits that induce her staff to support her initiatives and policies. It is no longer sufficient for an Ambassador to simply state a policy to be followed; the Ambassador must ensure that her team understands the reasoning behind it and how the policy will achieve a particular objective. An Embassy should be a team, united in its pursuit of its foreign policy goals. Additionally, an American Ambassador today, in tandem with the Deputy Chief of Mission, should evince concern for the careers of the officers in the Embassy and provide them opportunities to develop their skills. My Deputy Chief of Mission in Malaysia was exceptional in this regard; she not only provided me with valuable career advice, but she lobbied extensively for me to obtain my next assignment.

Embassy employees expect and deserve a transparent set of achievable goals and a sense of support from the top management. Though the Ambassador may lead the Embassy pursuit of certain goals, the contributions of many officers go into formulating and pursuing these goals. A fractured Embassy, because of the discordant pursuit of policies or the lack of support from the Ambassador, will not be an Embassy that achieves its objectives or attracts Foreign Service Officers to bid on assignments there.

3. The Embassy Should Be the Entity That Conducts Foreign Relations Abroad.

The art of diplomacy abroad, at least at some levels and in some instances and countries, morphed from the semi-autonomous conduct of diplomatic relations to minutely Washington-directed interactions with host country officials. As I mentioned earlier, when I was Ambassador to Tajikistan, I and my officers were responsible for forming relations with representatives of the Government of Tajikistan, establishing relationships with other countries' diplomats, and implementing US Government policies. Though we had several official visits from senior US Government representatives from all branches of government and from many departments, the visitors were not there to push or promulgate separate policies. On a particular issue, the US Government policy was clear, and whether the visitor was the Commander of Central Command, the Secretary of State, or a Congressperson, the policy was understood and there was no divergence of opinion evident to Tajik Government representatives.

Conversely, when I was in Erbil, the plethora of visitors we hosted frequently had their own interests or agendas which sometimes competed with the Department of State's stated policies. The experts on the ground in the Kurdistan Region, our Ambassador and me and my officers, frequently were reduced to providing transportation and security for the visitors. Soon after my arrival in Erbil, my Ambassador tasked me with developing and evaluating contacts with leaders from Mosul and its surrounding area. It was under control of ISIS at that time, but by talking to important members of the Mosul community, many of whom had fled to Erbil and other parts of Kurdistan, we could determine who might be responsible future leaders and what their plans would be. My team and I devoted three weeks to doing this and reported our findings to our Embassy in Baghdad and Washington. Soon after this intensive three-week period, a team from a semi-independent office in the State Department arrived and immediately ordered us to set up meetings over the next few weeks with the same potential leaders for post-ISIS Mosul. My political section had to arrange and attend meetings with the exact same individuals we had just spoken with so that our visitors could ask the same questions. Perhaps our Iraqi contacts believed we were just being thorough, but it was a poor and unnecessary use of my overworked political officers' time that taxed our security resources and offered nothing new.

Instead of the Department of State being the premier agency responsible for implementing the foreign policy of the United States, in both Washington and Iraq we often had to follow the directives of political elements in the National Security Council, other federal agencies, or members of Congress. Unfortunately, the State Department at this time either could not or would not fight for its preeminence in the implementation of foreign policy. This maelstrom of divergent interests and programs severely reduced the effectiveness of United States Government policies in Iraq and the Kurdistan Region, and the incoherence it induced mystified our Kurdish counterparts. And, needless to say, the occasional overreach by Washington offices ignored the competence of my officers in the Erbil Consulate and adversely affected our morale.

4. Conduct of Foreign Affairs Within the
US Government Should Not Be Too Diffuse.

The advantages of having one department or agency coordinating foreign affairs policies in a country appear self-evident. Just as different Washington agencies offering competing policies within a country is a recipe for ineffectiveness, different sections or offices within an Embassy promulgating divergent courses of action lead to an uncoordinated and unproductive Embassy. A strong Embassy front office, composed of the Ambassador and Deputy Chief of Mission, must ensure that all Embassy offices understand and have bought into the policies the Embassy is seeking to achieve. Today's Embassies are an amalgam of offices working for and representing many different federal departments and agencies. Besides the many sections staffed by Department of State officers, a typical Embassy could be composed of representatives of the Department of Defense, Army, Navy, and Air Force, Department of Commerce, Department of Agriculture, Drug Enforcement Agency, Federal Bureau of Investigation, Central Intelligence Agency, Customs and Border Protection, Internal Revenue Service, US Marine Corps Security Guards, and Secret Service, to name just some of the component offices.

These separate offices report to and follow the instructions of their home offices in Washington while at the same time they must abide by the direction of the Ambassador. When inconsistencies arise between the two lines of authority, problems can ensue. The Embassy front office must work closely with agencies at post and in Washington to head off any divisions of purpose. In one of my tours in Tajikistan, the Office of the Defense Attaché, which broadly represented the Department of Defense, in one instance edged into the territory of the political section, which was responsible for the conduct of our political relations with the Tajik Government. I had to gently pull back the Defense Attaché from his "competition" with the political section chief since the matter fell within the latter's authority.

The blurring of lines of authority or activities within an Embassy can also occur among the sections of the Embassy made up of Foreign Service Officers and lead to animosity. I have seen this discord between Embassy sections composed of State officers most often when valuable contacts of the political section are unsuccessful applicants for visitor visas. Political officers frequently want their contacts to be issued visas, but Consular officers have the primary authority in determining who qualifies for visas.

On occasions, the denial of visitor visas for contacts of the political section led to disruptive behavior between the political and consular sections.

The Ambassador and Deputy Chief of Mission must carefully manage the relations between different agencies and the State Department and among the various State and other offices within the Embassy. A successful front office will work with all the offices and sections of the Embassy to refine the policies it will pursue and set internal policies that define how potentially troublesome situations can be avoided or quickly resolved. The Ambassador must invest substantial amounts of time at the State Department and with other federal entities in Washington and at post to make certain she has the contacts and the understanding of policies to keep her Embassy productive and working at an even keel.

5. The Ambassador and Staff Must Practice Personal Diplomacy

This sounds obvious: Foreign Service Officers stationed abroad are in their countries to understand the political and economic situation, learn the culture so that they can interact effectively with host nationals, and establish relationships with the decision-makers and the average citizens in their country of assignment. But there are a wealth of competing duties or distractions that limit the time or diminish the inclination to interact with others outside of the Embassy community. A US Embassy can be a self-contained little bubble in which officers and staff spend a majority of their work and free time. Much of this is necessary—handling the bureaucratic demands of the State Department, getting to know your fellow officers, ensuring your family feels at home in a country far away from the United States. But there can be a tendency to have this little bubble turn into a comfortable world separate and detached from the country they are living in.

It is the responsibility of the Ambassador to model the proper behavior and create opportunities for officers to develop contacts outside of the Embassy and more broadly in the host country. The Ambassador can easily do this by having officers join in her travel throughout the country, participate in events hosted by the Ambassador and the host country, and take advantage of speaking opportunities with local groups, to name just a few possibilities. But the Ambassador must encourage officers, especially those newer to the Foreign Service, to make this outreach a normal and necessary part of their jobs. And to do this, the officers must have the opportunity and time to make these interactions. Foreign Service Officers have a formal work plan, called a Work Requirements Statement, that is revised every year and lays out the activities the officer must complete during that rating period. Making outreach to host country nationals and gaining understanding of the local situation should be an important part of each individual's work requirements, and the person's supervisor must provide the work time needed to do so.

When I was stationed in Kathmandu, the Deputy Chief of Mission initially turned down my offer to help with reporting efforts and told me to concentrate on my consular work. But consular work gave me unique insights into the political unrest that led to the revolution against the monarchy, and by necessity he allowed me to report on activities since my contacts had increased my understanding of the situation. He should have encouraged me in my interest in learning more about Nepali society and reporting on events even if that was not my main responsibility as a consular officer. While stationed in Kuala Lumpur, I made several trips throughout the country because of consular issues, but I always met and talked to local officials about important political and economic developments and reported on them, thus increasing the Embassy's understanding of issues outside of the capital and extending the reach of our Embassy. My Deputy Chief of Mission encouraged and valued my reporting.

One essential quality for an Ambassador, not mentioned by Léger or Nicolson, is to be proficient in the language of the host country. The best way to communicate with your host nation, whether you are speaking to the president or to a shop keeper, is in the native language. On the day I presented my credentials to the President of Tajikistan and began making public appearances, I spoke at the graduation of a medical school class in Dushanbe. A Tajik Minister spoke before me and like many of his generation he was more comfortable in Russian and gave his remarks in that language. After I had spoken in Tajiki, the students immediately peppered the Minister with questions and complaints about why he had spoken in Russian rather than in the national language. Tajikistan at that time did not have many diplomats who could speak Tajiki, and early in my tenure as Ambassador I recall speeches being interrupted by applause after just a few sentences solely because I was speaking in their native language. Even the President of Tajikistan, while speaking in Tajiki, made a comment at a diplomatic gathering that I was the only Ambassador present who could understand what he was saying. The ability to speak the local language benefits the Ambassador in so many ways—to understanding the complaints of the taxi driver on issues relevant to the national course of events, to speaking to politicians disaffected with the governments, and to establishing bonds with local officials, to name just a few.

Given the funding shortfalls the Department of State has suffered through, it is not surprising that the requirement of language proficiency is sometimes waived because there is a need to get personnel to post. Secretary Powell tried to implement an increase in hiring to provide a "training float" so that we would have enough officers to staff our positions while other officers were in language or other training. Unfortunately, unlike the military, we have never had the funding necessary to allow for the training needed by the Foreign Service. This shows up most markedly in the staffing of our Embassies in non-world language countries.

Finally, an Ambassador must interact closely with and form personal relationships not only with the local officials, but also with her foreign diplomatic counterparts. In Dushanbe I worked closely, in public and privately, with the Ambassador from the United Kingdom, the Russian Ambassador, the chief UN representatives, and the Ambassadors from other countries resident in Tajikistan. The UK Ambassador and I traveled together throughout Tajikistan, eliminating the need for local officials to schedule two different meetings and reinforcing our common policies. The Russian Ambassador and I met on a regular basis at lunches and dinners to discuss important bilateral issues and the conduct of relations with the Tajik Government; we hosted him and his chief Embassy staffers at our Embassy, and he in turn hosted us at his dacha. We appeared together at the Russian-Slavonic University in Dushanbe to answer questions by the students, illustrating to the students and the media that the United States and Russia can work together.

In many countries national diplomacy is not conducted in a vacuum, and it is very helpful for a group of countries to combine their diplomatic efforts to achieve a desired outcome with the host nation. Respect and friendship among the Ambassadors can make such coordinated action must easier and viable. During my first tour in Tajikistan, I led a group of countries in protesting the Tajik Government's failure to properly care for Afghan refugees, and in Erbil I led a group of my colleagues to urge the Kurdish Regional Government to resolve some of its difficulties with the government in Baghdad. Foreign governments sometime listen more acutely to Ambassadors that unite in their démarches to a host government.

Many of the Ambassadors and diplomats also socialized together, and I hosted dinners with other missions so that my officers and theirs could get to know each other better and understand our common goals. The UK

Ambassador and I wagered a friendly bet on a United States—England World Cup match and together hosted a dinner for our compatriots to watch the game. The terms of the wager were that the losing Ambassador would jump into the UK Ambassador's pool fully clothed; the game ended in a tie, so at a dinner at his residence we both jumped in the pool.

6. Technology Should Assist Diplomacy Not Subsume It

In my career with the Department of State, I witnessed the many ways that technology amplified and improved our capacity to conduct foreign affairs, particularly in the area of communications. The ability to reach so many more people in country quickly with our messages via the Internet, chat rooms, Zoom meetings, or just simple emails is radically different from when I first started with the State Department in 1987. The Embassy's almost instantaneous communication with the Department of State permit Washington to participate in conversations the Embassy is conducting, and vice versa.

The unrelenting advance of technology is the most important development in the conduct of diplomacy. Just over 100 years ago, the victorious countries in World War I sent their representatives to Paris and Versailles to hammer out a peace treaty. President Wilson headed the US delegation and remained in Paris for six months conferring with his French and British counterparts and representatives from several other countries. Besides being an amazing example of "personal diplomacy" that kept the President outside of the United States for half a year, the length of the peace conference and the plethora of issues it reviewed while in session are difficult to imagine today. Having one individual responsible for the bulk of the decisions seems ludicrous today. If a similar conference took place now, almost all of the work would be done by experts remotely with perhaps a few key negotiators engaging in direct talks on occasion. President Wilson viewed himself as the chief negotiator or arbiter for the United States; thanks to today's technology, if a future President felt the same responsibility (hopefully, this would not be the case), instantaneous and encrypted messages could keep the President fully informed while she remained in the White House.

Technology has allowed the average Embassy to engage in the full ambit of issues present on the diplomatic plate of a country and to keep Washington informed and up-to-date of the progress on issues. My only quibble with technology is that we should use it as a diplomatic tool, not as a substitute for diplomacy itself.

As a tool and a means of communication for the individual Ambassador or diplomat, technology is unsurpassed. But if the global reach and instantaneity of technology diverts the Ambassador or diplomat from investing in much-needed personal work or transfers all of the decision-making from the post to Washington, this creates problems. Keeping Washington informed and the diplomats at post advised of Washington's guidelines are two of the most important benefits of technology. Transforming Ambassadors into mere information conduits impinges on the normal responsibilities of an Ambassador and could limit the input of the experts on the ground who deal with the country's leaders on a regular basis. The Department of State provides instructions and guidance to the Ambassador, and she—the chief interlocutor with the country's leaders—must execute them in the manner known best to her. Otherwise, you risk proving the quip uttered by Peter Ustinov in one of his plays that "[a] diplomat these days is nothing but a head waiter who's allowed to sit down occasionally."[8] This is an obviously humorous overstatement, but it contains a solid germ of truth.

Diplomacy directed by too heavy a hand from the capital, made more possible by technology, is directly linked to my my first five issues. I have seen too many senior American diplomats visiting at post who are so tied to their Washington contacts by texts and emails that they ignore the opportunities they have to forge better relations with host country officials and to interact or mentor Foreign Service Officers at post because they cannot stop reading messages on their iPhones and responding to their texts. Obviously, senior officials need to stay in touch with others in Washington and elsewhere, but to continue to conduct your Washington work when you have left someone in charge at the Department and to forego the opportunity to connect with staff at an Embassy, mentor the newer officers, and interact with citizens and officials of the host country is not good diplomacy.

When I was stationed in Dushanbe, a senior official visited and did not bother to meet with staff in the Embassy. I and a few others joined him on a long flight for a meeting in a neighboring country, and his attention never left his iPhone even though there was no pressing urgency in Washington. Attempts at conversation were futile. For him, staying in constant touch with Washington was much more important than talking to us. Conversely, another senior visitor who visited frequently made sure to meet and spend time with new officers, and with his permission I formed a rotation of first-tour officers who took turns acting as his control officer for each visit, thus giving them the opportunity to spend time with him and to practice their craft. He graciously agreed to this arrangement to help educate our young diplomats.

7. Moral Authority in Foreign Policy Counts

No country's domestic and foreign policies are universally admired. In this diverse multipolar world there are too many issues that divide us and affect how other countries view the United States. But countries, rightly or wrongly, have an overall good or bad "general reputation" among foreign citizens, and their moral example is important. I recall during my first few overseas assignments that the United States enjoyed a fairly good overall reputation even though certain issues could be problematical. I witnessed demonstrations in Germany against some of our policies, but I also attended post-revolution public gatherings in Nepal that celebrated the United States as an exemplar of democracy. Many of our policies that were disfavored were viewed by citizens of foreign countries as wrongheaded but conducted without animus. It was rare to have our policies, with discrete exceptions, viewed as being inherently bad and designed for male fide reasons.

This started to change after the United States invaded Iraq. I was serving as Deputy Chief of Mission in Tajikistan then and conducted a press conference that explained and had to defend our invasion of Iraq. At that time the general population of this former Soviet Republic viewed the United States positively, a symbol of democracy, human rights, and hope that many Tajik citizens wished to emulate. The US invasion of Iraq, particularly its long aftermath, confused them and caused many to question US Government motives in Iraq. Our moral suasion lessened.

When I was in Basrah and later in Baghdad, I viewed firsthand the extent of the destruction wreaked on Iraqi society and the ill feeling toward the United States that formed over time. No longer was the United States the liberator of Iraq from Saddam Hussein, but instead many Iraqis considered it to be a foreign occupying power that continued to ravage the country long after Saddam was gone.

As I witnessed in Tajikistan and Iraq, the dimming of public perceptions of the United States and its policies was evident. This does not necessarily equate to a lessening of America's overall power, but there is no question that the United States' authority—across the policy spectrum—and image diminished. In Tajikistan, our chief competitors for influence were Russia, which dominated the countries of the former Soviet Union and maintained a military base in country, and China, the new hegemonist whose investments, loans, trade, and infrastructure improvements were quickly overwhelming the country. The United States was immersed in Afghanistan, and its focus in Central Asia was the ongoing fight against the Taliban and the withdrawal of troops. Russia and China played up US missteps in Afghanistan in Tajik media and to the public in an attempt to portray the United States as a malevolent influence. We at the US Embassy countered these characterizations, but any civilian casualties or inadvertent destruction of homes in Afghanistan was fodder for negative stories about the United States. Over time, public appraisals of United States' actions and policies became less laudatory.

That said, a number of US programs continued to reinforce positive interpretations of the United States. US exchange programs, at all levels, are a bargain for the United States Government whose benefits continue to pay off for years. Cultural programs, person-to-person encounters, and public outreach could and should all be increased to combat misperceptions fostered by other countries and encourage better country-to-country relationships. These simple and cost-effective measures help illustrate to foreign citizens the continued moral relevancy of the United States.

Conclusion

The seven "lessons learned" listed above are not extraordinary revelations or proposals, but I believe they are common sense prescriptions that would improve the general conduct of foreign affairs by the United States. The implementation of them would, in some cases, require a change in mindset but not necessarily a large increase in funding for the State Department. A good friend of mine in Basrah, a British officer, remarked that every conflict boils down to one thing—personal relationships. These are best pursued and fostered by the Ambassadors and diplomats stationed in a foreign country. Similarly, a high-ranking Kurdish official, soon after I arrived in Erbil, spent a considerable amount of time with me over several cups of coffee explaining how all the rivalries and struggles among Kurdish officials harkened back to some personal slight or misunderstanding. Time spent in developing relationships and understanding in a country pays off for the United States.

It is not always just what we do as a nation, but also how we do it that matters to other countries. In my experience, diplomacy is not a zero-sum game that one side wins or loses. Diplomacy is not defined by wins and losses, but rather by working toward acceptable solutions for two or more entities. And to be a successful Ambassador and diplomat, you must relate to and understand the individuals sitting across from you at a negotiation table or standing behind a produce stand. My chief takeaway from my career as a Foreign Service Officer is that personal development, interactions, and friendships are the most critical elements in developing a professional cadre of diplomats who can work with others to promote effectively the policies of the United States.

Notes

1. Elizabeth R. Cameron, "Alexis Saint-Léger-Léger," in *The Diplomats 1919–1939,* ed. Gordon A. Craig and Felix Gilbert (Princeton, New Jersey: Princeton University Press 1953), 378.
2. Harold Nicolson, *Peace Making 1919* (New York: Grosset & Dunlap, 1965).
3. Harold Nicolson, *Diplomacy* (New York: Harcourt, Brace and Company, 1930), 110–125.
4. Ibid., 126.
5. "Conversations with Eric Sevareid" (Washington, D.C. Public Affairs Press, 1976), reprinted by permission in *Interviews with George F. Kennan*, ed. T. Christopher Jesperson (Jackson: University Press of Mississippi, 2002), 153.
6. The National War College is one of many colleges established for military officers of a certain grade and experience level. There are individual war colleges for the individual military services, but the National War Colleges is the oldest and to me the premier war college of all of them. The State Department had approximately 30 officers attending the NWC; besides the US military officers in attendance, civilian employees from several executive branch agencies and foreign military officers were in my class.
7. REOs were established throughout Iraq after the coalition invaded and functioned as undeclared consulates. During my time in Basrah there was no government established in Iraq to replace Saddam Hussein, and I was not accredited to Iraq and was not subject to any visa requirements or border controls by the Iraqi Government.
8. Ustinov, Peter, *Romanoff and Juliet,* (New York: Random House, 1957), 13–14.

NINE

MARC GROSSMAN

This chapter was completed January 27, 2023.

What is the Purpose of American Diplomacy?

I n a world overflowing with new and old challenges and fresh opportunities, what purpose will American diplomacy serve in the twenty-first century? Like other contributors to this volume, I was proud to be an American diplomat. I believe diplomacy has a role to play in solving many of the problems that confront individual citizens and the nations in which they live. Diplomacy can also identify paths to a more prosperous and peaceful future.

These outcomes are not assured. To make them possible, Americans must bridge the divisions that consume our public institutions. Simultaneously, the purposes, processes, culture, and supporting institutions of US diplomacy must change if today's diplomats have any chance of carrying out their vital work effectively.[1]

There have been vivid, fanciful, disparaging, and sometimes even useful descriptions of diplomacy. I appreciate this contribution from former Secretary of State Henry Kissinger who wrote that diplomats must work to achieve their nation's objectives with an understanding of the other side's "history, culture, and goals."[2]

This chapter begins with three observations from my diplomatic experiences:

Successful diplomacy is based on strong national institutions and capabilities. A nation's economic growth, health care, education, and technological development determine a diplomat's capacity to influence allies, friends, competitors, and adversaries.

Diplomacy is not a synonym for engagement. Connecting and negotiating are important tools of statecraft, but when we talk about

     diplomacy, we should focus on the comprehensive strategies that
     promote and protect national interests.

Diplomacy is not the answer to every question; effective diplomacy
     is often backed by the threat, and sometimes the use, of force.

American diplomacy will be tested by what *Washington Post* columnist
Josh Rogin describes as "three 'tectonic' trends" at work in the world: "The
rise of nationalism and populism due to the unequal distribution of benefits from globalization; the rise of emerging and foundational technologies that have altered daily life and the way governments, companies,
and people interact; and the fraying of a world order which was built for
an era when the United States was the only superpower and the spread of
democracy everywhere seemed inevitable."[3]

As we consider the future of American diplomacy, it is essential to recognize the core challenge underlying these trends: the profound misalign-
ment between citizens and elites in how they understand, define, and describe the national interest.[4]

The COVID pandemic starkly exposed this gap. Millions in the US and
other nations discovered that their countries did not produce critical medical equipment. Hospitals were overwhelmed. Key pharmaceuticals had
to be imported. Global supply chains were disrupted, economies around
the world shrank, and millions lost their jobs. Many leaders failed to anticipate these risks or made decisions that perpetuated them. The attack
on the US Capitol on January 6, 2021, further exposed the political and
cultural chasm that some elected leaders in the US have chosen to exploit.

Americans must make it a priority to realign citizen and national interests. To succeed in today's world, Americans need to embrace a national
strategy in which both domestic and foreign policies are designed to preclude the worst outcomes while creating opportunities to produce optimal
results. To achieve these goals, Americans must strengthen the country's
diplomatic institutions.

Preclude

A high-functioning American diplomacy can support the realignment
of citizen and national interests by creating and executing national policies that can make operational the concept of "preclusion" introduced by

Philip Bobbitt in his book *Terror and Consent: The Wars for the Twenty-first Century.* Bobbitt argues that nations today find it more and more difficult to assure their publics of "increasing equality, security, and community."[5] In the future, he says, nations will need to pursue policies designed "to preclude a certain state of affairs from coming into being."[6]

This is not a pessimistic notion, as Bobbitt writes: "Making the world safer than it would otherwise have been might strike some commentators as a pathetically modest, even commonplace goal, but it is hardly that. The most remarkable feature of preclusive victory is precisely this anticipatory, precautionary attention to possible futures."[7]

Diplomats have of course practiced preclusion without explicitly using the name.[8] Over the course of my career, I participated in creating and executing what I now think of as preclusive policies, including:

The strengthening of NATO's conventional weapons capabilities in the early 1980s to make nuclear war less likely.

During that same period, the deployment and then withdrawal of intermediate-range missiles (INF), which foiled the USSR's plan to deploy its destabilizing SS-20 missile system in Europe.

The effort to save and return home 500,000 Kurds who had been forced by Saddam Hussein into the mountains between Iraq and Turkey after the first Gulf War. Their entry into Turkey would have further inflamed Turkey's unstable southeast.

The creation of the Baku-Tbilisi-Ceyhan pipeline, which reduced Russian energy influence in the Caucasus and brought economic benefit to southeastern Turkey.[9]

Two rounds of NATO expansion in 1999 and 2004, which avoided leaving vulnerable "border lands" subject to Russian domination. (It is impossible to imagine an effective Western diplomatic or military response to President Putin's February 24, 2022, invasion of Ukraine without Poland and the Baltic states as members of the Alliance.)

Other examples of preclusive policies during my career included strategies to choke off terrorist financing and to promote international anti-corruption efforts. Both Plan Colombia, the US "whole of government" effort to support Colombians in their fight for their democracy, and the pursuit of US interests in Afghanistan 2011–2012,[10] were designed to prevent the worst and produce as close to the best outcomes as possible.

A good test of the utility of preclusive policies is to measure them against issues that today preoccupy citizens and policymakers: the war in Ukraine and its consequences, including the war's disruption of global energy supplies and impact on climate change; the rise of China; and the future of global trade and investment.

Putin's invasion of Ukraine is a costly example of the failure to produce a policy that might have deterred Russian aggression. Western leaders did not understand the full meaning of Putin's defaulting on the agreement he signed at the 2002 NATO-Russia Summit in Rome guaranteeing the right of nations—including Ukraine—"to choose the means to ensure their own security, and the inviolability of borders."[11] Other factors were the ineffective responses to Putin's annexation of Crimea in 2014 and his extensive efforts to subvert and control Eastern Ukraine. NATO's leaders made a promise they could not keep by offering NATO membership to Ukraine and Georgia at the 2008 Bucharest Summit. The failure of many NATO allies to meet their promise to spend at least 2 percent of GDP on defense led to Russian miscalculation about NATO's capacity to defend its interests and values.

Are there policies that can be fashioned and carried out today to create a relatively positive outcome in Ukraine? Elements would include maintaining the so far remarkable military support from allied and friendly nations for Ukraine's courageous resistance to Russian aggression and connecting this effort to planning for a negotiated end to the conflict. Preclusion would focus on mitigating the plight of Ukrainian refugees and those who are internally displaced. A post-war strategy will need to mobilize human and financial resources, including creating incentives for private sector involvement, to support Ukrainians as they rebuild their nation in ways that are sustainable, support Ukraine's EU aspirations, and encourage good governance.

Russia's invasion of Ukraine is a reminder of the need for a preclusive strategy to maintain peace and prosperity in Europe. This will require a focus on further strengthening NATO, not just by expanding membership to Finland and Sweden, but also by committing to increased defense spending on interoperable, rapidly deployable systems, and by engaging in ever-closer political consultations. NATO must also now consider how to deter or win wars, which the fighting in Ukraine has shown will include cyber-attacks, drones, and advanced, data-enabled command-and-control systems.[12]

The US-Europe transatlantic relationship has been reinvigorated by Putin's attack on Ukraine. In tandem with strengthening NATO, US and

European governments can find ways to shape a common agenda that promotes the freedom and dignity of individuals, the rule of law, and an economically sustainable, rules-based international order. The Transatlantic Trade and Technology Council and the US-EU Trade and Labor Dialogue can be examples of ways to create and pursue policies designed to produce better outcomes.

The war in Ukraine disrupted global energy markets. The price of oil rose from ~$63 per barrel in March 2021 to ~$120 per barrel in March 2022, accelerating global inflation and a scramble for energy resources.[13] The fact that Europe's energy security had been mortgaged to Russia is another example of how Putin's invasion exposed the failure to pursue preclusive policies. Prior to the invasion, Europe was importing 155 billion cubic meters of natural gas annually from Russia. Europe's total energy commodity imports from Russia were approximately €400 billion in 2021.[14]

Faced with their vulnerability, Europeans are now pursuing an alternative path, with a plan to slash Russian gas imports by 70 percent, setting a price cap on Russian natural gas deliveries at ~$191 per megawatt-hour, and moving rapidly to import LNG from the US and other producers.[15] Combined with the remarkable effort across the continent to install or expand more than 20 LNG regasification facilities, these policies limit Russia's ability to recoup the costs of war in Ukraine through natural gas exports and will ultimately reduce Europe's dependence on Russian energy.[16]

The early analyses of the impact of the war in Ukraine on the global effort to meet the climate change challenge was a depressing litany of reversals of the very modest progress that had been achieved. China, for example, has plans to construct 258 new coal-fired power plants.[17]

But a more preclusive view has begun to emerge. Nations are recognizing that sustainable alternatives such as wind and solar can play a role in decreasing dependence on foreign sources of fossil fuels. The $225 billion European RePowerEU plan, for example, is expected to shift 45 percent of Europe's energy use toward renewables by 2030.[18]

In the United States, both the Inflation Reduction Act and the Bipartisan Infrastructure Package contain significant provisions, totaling more than $400 billion, devoted to green energy investment and environmental remediation.[19] As part of the administration's goal to connect foreign policy objectives more explicitly to citizen interests, US leaders argue that domestic job creation is directly connected to international climate diplomacy. In his first State of the Union speech, President Biden said, "For too long, we have failed to use the most important word when it comes to meeting the climate crisis: jobs. . . . For me, when I think of climate change, I think jobs."[20]

Meeting and managing the rise of China is another area where the pursuit of preclusive policies can meet the challenge without succumbing to the belief that violent conflict between the US and China is inevitable.

To promote and protect US interests and values in the Indo-Pacific, America must strengthen its national capacities and work actively with our allies and friends. As China expert Jude Blanchette observed in *Foreign Affairs*: "The United States can disprove Beijing's contention that its democracy has atrophied, and that Washington's star is dimming by strengthening the resilience of American society and improving the competence of the US government. If the United States and its allies invest in innovation and human capital, they can forestall [President] Xi's efforts to gain first-mover advantage in emerging and critical technologies. Likewise, a more active and forward-looking US role in shaping the global order would limit Beijing's ability to spread illiberal ideas beyond China's borders."[21]

A strong military component is of course required for any strategy of deterrence in the Pacific. Increasing Taiwan's capacity to defend itself is a lesson already learned from the war in Ukraine. A policy to compete successfully with China in the Indo-Pacific must also have effective diplomatic, economic, technology, and commercial components. India, Japan, Australia, and the US have, for example, substantially strengthened a forum called the "Quad" to coordinate their policies in the Indo-Pacific on issues including pandemic response and vaccination availability, the defense of democratic values, climate change (including exploring hydrogen energy alternatives), deterring cyberattacks, supply chain security, and infrastructure.

How effectively Quad nations work together to ensure that China does not dominate the technology future in critical areas like 5G, semiconductors, advanced battery technology, and artificial intelligence will be a key measure of the group's success. The American administration, with the strong support of Congress, has taken steps to curb China's semiconductor industry. Most recently, the Department of Commerce announced that it would prohibit American citizens from exporting high-performance chips and manufacturing equipment to China without a license.[22] US allies have cooperated with these efforts for the most part, with Dutch semiconductor lithography equipment manufacturer ASML unable to export its most advanced equipment to China under current export rules.[23]

The US has also taken steps to build up its own semiconductor capabilities, with the Chips and Science Act appropriating $52.7 billion toward domestic semiconductor research and manufacturing investments.[24] While not a Quad member, the European Union proposed its own €43 billion chips legislation in February 2022, which includes policy initiatives to develop "partnerships with like-minded countries."[25] It remains to be seen whether these are sufficient to counter China's own activities in the semiconductor space—the party is currently drafting a ~$143 spending package to strengthen chip manufacturing capabilities in the wake of western export restrictions.[26]

Finally, there is the need to shape a future in which trade and foreign investment bolster US international strategic objectives. These include support for multilateral approaches when that is the best path forward, and transparent, fair global competition that encourages new ideas and commercial innovation while simultaneously promoting other important citizen interests, including creating American jobs.

Globalization has been a positive force for many citizens around the world, especially the almost 1.2 billion people lifted out of poverty before the pandemic. But globalization's benefits were unequally shared. Communities were undermined as jobs were exported and automated; a sense of purpose in daily life evaporated. As political scientist Zaki Laïdi argued in his prescient book *A World Without Meaning*, "globalization is a state and not a meaning."[27]

Observations from different perspectives highlight many attitudes today. President Trump's US Trade Representative, Ambassador Robert Lighthizer, wrote in *Foreign Affairs*: "What should the objective of trade policy be? Some view trade through the objective of foreign policy, arguing that tariffs should be lowered or raised to achieve geopolitical goals. Others view trade strictly through the lens of economic efficiency, contending that the sole objective of trade policy should be to maximize overall output. But what most Americans want is something else: a trade policy that supports the kind of society they want to live in. To that end, the right policy is one that makes it possible for most citizens, including those without college educations, to access the middle class through stable, well-paying jobs."[28]

In remarks in December 2022, President Biden's US Trade Representative, Ambassador Katherine Tai, said, "trade must become a force for good for ordinary Americans and people around the world. . . . And that is why we are placing workers and everyday people at the center of our trade policy, to craft a durable and fair tomorrow by pursuing resilience, sustainability, and inclusive prosperity."[29]

Is it possible, as journalist Sebastian Mallaby suggests, to "reframe the nation's attitude toward globalization?"[30]

A part of any attempt to achieve this "reframing" will require active diplomacy to create a domestic and international consensus around answers to the questions economist Dani Rodrik poses in his book *Straight Talk on Trade:* "How much globalization should we seek in trade and finance? Is there still a case for nation-states in an age where transportation and communications revolutions have apparently spelled the death of geographic distance? How much sovereignty do states need to cede to international institutions? When does globalization undermine democracy? What do we owe, as citizens and states, to others across the border? How best do we carry out these responsibilities?"[31]

Rodrik lays out a framework for thinking about these issues: "We need a pluralistic world economy where nation states retain sufficient autonomy to fashion their own social contracts and develop their own economic strategies. . . . Global governance does remain crucial in those areas such as climate change where the provision of global public goods is essential."[32]

Some of America's efforts to meet the challenges posed by China, especially in the competition in semiconductors and US efforts to build and buy in America, have angered US allies and friends. American diplomats will be called on to find a way to create jobs in America while working with others to recognize their legitimate needs.[33]

Other opportunities to preclude as part of the effort to realign citizen and national interests include:

Prepare for the next pandemic by domestically manufacturing and stockpiling personal protective equipment and pharmaceuticals;

Recognize that technologies such as artificial intelligence and machine learning already have, and will have even more in the future, crucial national security implications;

Continue to fight terrorism in a world of great power competition;

Actively support global human rights, the sanctity of the individual, the rule of law, and the promotion of the role of women in societies;

Reform immigration policies, highlighting the right and responsibility of nations to protect their borders, to admit immigrants who can contribute to economic growth and innovation, and to offer safety to those who flee political persecution; and

A preclusive diplomatic approach would resuscitate arms control negotiations among the nuclear powers while keeping Iran from acquiring nuclear weapons.

Strengthen

Just as it accelerated economic, technological, and social changes and trends, the COVID pandemic demanded new thinking and new ways of practicing a more competitive diplomacy. Philip Seib, a farsighted writer on the impacts of new media on diplomacy, maintained in 2016 that: "Traditionalists who believe that fast diplomacy is almost always bad diplomacy face a disconcerting reality. They must adapt to a strange and inhospitable new world in which the interests of diverse publics must be addressed quickly and deciding what to say may take precedence over what to do."[34]

The pandemic also exposed the need to change the ways diplomacy is executed, who is chosen to do this crucial work, and how they are made professionally ready to do the jobs they are assigned. Today's international challenges must be met by focused and vigorous American diplomacy. US diplomacy and US diplomats have, for example, played a critical role in forging the strong Western response to Putin's invasion of Ukraine.

The Biden administration came into office having received several studies recommending important changes in how America carries out its diplomacy. The recommendations of these studies were varied but reinforcing. All called for bipartisan support for a substantially larger, better funded, more diverse, inclusive, and professionally trained diplomatic workforce—a workforce more actively connected to and focused on the needs of the American people.

The reports shared the premise that US diplomacy, with its long and proud history, staffed today by a remarkable group of patriotic, committed, and effective employees, confronts a crisis both from external attacks on its core functions and an internal culture that creates roadblocks to change and needs a brutally honest self-assessment of how best to meet its vital responsibilities.[35]

These and other important observations are the foundation for the November 2020 report, *A US Diplomatic Service for the twenty-first Century,* published by the Harvard Kennedy School's Belfer Center for Science and

International Affairs. I was a co-author of the Belfer report along with Ambassador Marcie Ries and Ambassador Nick Burns, who is now the US Ambassador to China.[36]

Forty years after the passage of the Foreign Service Act of 1980, which provides the structure of the current Foreign Service, the time had come to identify what about the Foreign Service needed to be upgraded, modernized, or changed to meet contemporary challenges. During his tenure, Secretary of State Mike Pompeo recognized the need to rebuild, restarting the hiring of new Foreign Service Officers, for example, and supporting the effort of the then Director General of the Foreign Service to promote a conversation in the department about diversity and inclusion. In a speech in October 2021, Secretary of State Antony Blinken outlined his thinking on diplomatic reform.[37]

Some of the reforms mentioned in the Belfer report have been adopted, including the appointment of a State Department coordinator for diversity and inclusion, a down payment on a training "float" or complement, paid internships that will broaden the socio-economic base of future applicants, the opening of more leadership positions to career officers, new parameters for risk management, and plans for career-long professional education for both the Foreign Service and Civil Service.

After the positive response to the Belfer report, Ambassador Ries and I pursued a Phase II effort focused on four achievable, affordable, urgently needed, high-impact recommendations.[38]

Blueprints for a More Modern US Diplomatic Service, released in September 2022, is a detailed plan ready to be implemented.[39] The Blueprints cover four areas:

A revised mission and mandate for the Foreign Service and a new framework for communicating with the American public.

Expanded professional education and training to deepen our diplomats' expertise as leaders and preeminent experts and a plan to create sufficient positions to make it possible.

Modernization of the personnel system to build in more diversity, accountability, flexibility, and accommodation of the needs of accompanying families and partners at home and overseas.

A plan for a diplomatic reserve corps to provide surge capacity in geopolitical crises and natural disasters.

The administration and Congress need now to work together to produce for the American people the high-functioning diplomatic service they should demand and that they deserve.

In his biography of John Adams, David McCullough recounts that Adams was criticized during his assignment as America's first minister to England after the American Revolution by a Loyalist who had fled to London: "He is not qualified by nature or education to shine in courts. His abilities are undoubtedly equal to the mechanical parts of his business as Ambassador; but this is not enough. He cannot dance, drink, game, flatter, promise, dress, swear with the gentlemen, and small talk and flirt with the ladies; in short, he has none of the essential arts or ornaments which constitute a courtier."[40]

That was never my job description. It is not the job description of the people who represent America today around the world.

When young people ask me if they should become diplomats and represent their nations, and especially those who wish to represent the United States, my answer is, "absolutely." America needs professional, creative, and courageous diplomats who represent the values, diversity, and strength of the United States to promote and protect America's interests, values, and citizens around the globe.

Those who answer the call to service today will do this honorable work in a rapidly changing and increasingly dangerous world. They will succeed only if they strengthen and adapt their practices and procedures, culture, and institutions. They can help fashion and pursue policies designed not only to preclude the worst but also to create a more promising future by aligning the interests of their fellow citizens with the definitions and objectives of US national interests.

Acknowledgments

The author thanks Dominic Pacoe and Emma Timken for their fantastic research and production support. Teddy Weiss and Terrill McCombs provided greatly appreciated substantive and technical advice. Kathy Gest offered expert and astute editing. Ambassador Tony Wayne, Jill O'Donnell, and Mildred Patterson read drafts of the chapter and made many suggestions to greatly improve it. All errors are the author's responsibility.

Notes

1. This chapter will focus on American diplomacy, but many other nations confront similar issues, especially in seeking ways to reform their diplomatic capacities.

2. Winston Lord, *Kissinger on Kissinger* (St. Martin's Press, 2019), x.

3. Josh Rogin, *Chaos Under Heaven* (New York: Houghton Mifflin Harcourt, 2021), xxii.

4. A key report in shaping this conversation is the Carnegie Endowment for International Peace/University of Nebraska, *US Foreign Policy for the Middle Class: Perspectives from Nebraska*, Salman Ahmed, Editor, 2020. See also: John Walcott, Gregory F. Treverton and Pari Esfandiari. "Foreign Policy on the Home Front," *Global TechnoPolitics Forum*.

5. Philip Bobbitt, *Terror and Consent: The Wars for the Twenty-First Century* (New York: Alfred A. Knopf, 2008), 87.

6. Ibid, 198.

7. Ibid, 207.

8. For example, William J. Burns, *The Back Channel* (New York: Random House, 2019). Robert Hutchings and Jeremi Suri (eds), *Foreign Policy Breakthroughs* (New York: Oxford University Press, 2015). Robert Zoellick, *America In the World* (New York: Hachette, 2020).

9. Steve LeVine, *The Oil and the Glory* (New York: Random House, 2007).

10. "Seven Cities and Two Years: The Diplomatic Campaign in Afghanistan and Pakistan," Yale Journal of International Affairs 8, no.2 (2013).

11. Lord George Robertson, "What's Driving Putin's Invasion of Ukraine? A Former NATO Chief Who Met Him Explains.," Atlantic Council, February 28, 2022, https://www.atlanticcouncil.org/blogs/new-atlanticist/whats-driving -putins-invasion-of-ukraine-a-former-nato-chief-who-met-him-explains/.

12. David Ignatius, "How the Algorithm Tipped the Balance in Ukraine," *Washington Post*, December 19, 2022, sec. Global Opinions, https://www .washingtonpost.com/opinions/2022/12/19/palantir-algorithm-data-ukraine -war/.

13. "Crude Oil Prices 1983–2022 Historical Data," Financial Data Aggregator, *Trading Economics*, January 16, 2023, https://tradingeconomics.com /commodity/crude-oil.

14. Jonah Fisher, "EU Reveals Its Plans to Stop Using Russian Gas," BBC News, May 18, 2022, sec. Science & Environment, https://www.bbc.com/news /science-environment-61497315; "*A 10-Point Plan to Reduce the European Union's Reliance on Russian Natural Gas—Analysis*," International Energy Agency, March 2022, https://www.iea.org/reports/a-10-point-plan-to-reduce -the-european-unions-reliance-on-russian-natural-gas.

15. "Can American Liquefied Natural Gas Rescue Europe?," *The Economist*,

November 10, 2022, https://www.economist.com/business/2022/11/10/can
-american-liquefied-natural-gas-rescue-europe; Kate Abnett, "EU Countries
Agree Gas Price Cap to Contain Energy Crisis," *Reuters*, December 19,
2022, sec. Energy, https://www.reuters.com/business/energy/eu-countries
-make-final-push-gas-price-cap-deal-this-year-2022–12–19/.

16. *LNG Database*, "Gas Infrastructure Europe," accessed January 16, 2023,
https://www.gie.eu/transparency/databases/lng-database/.

17. "Global Coal Plant Tracker," *Global Energy Monitor*, July 2022, https://
globalenergymonitor.org/projects/global-coal-plant-tracker/summary-tables/.

18. "REPowerEU: Affordable, Secure and Sustainable Energy for Europe," European Commission, May 2022, https://commission.europa.eu/strategy
-and-policy/priorities-2019–2024/european-green-deal/repowereu-affordable
-secure-and-sustainable-energy-europe_en.

19. For specific figures, see "Inflation Reduction Act Guidebook," The White
House, January 2023, https://www.whitehouse.gov/cleanenergy/inflation
-reduction-act-guidebook/ and "FACT SHEET: The Bipartisan Infrastructure
Deal," The White House, November 8, 2021, https://www.whitehouse.gov
/briefing-room/statements-releases/2021/11/08/fact-sheet-the-bipartisan
-infrastructure-deal-boosts-clean-energy-jobs-strengthens-resilience-and
-advances-environmental-justice/.

20. President Joe Biden, State of the Union Address, April 28, 2021.

21. Jude Blanchette, "Xi's Gamble" *Foreign Affairs* 100, no. (4):19.

22. Mario Mancuso et al., "Restricting Exports of Sensitive Technology to China,"
Reuters, October 17, 2022, sec. Legal Industry, https://www.reuters.com/legal
/legalindustry/restricting-exports-sensitive-technology-china-2022–10–17/.

23. Jillian Deutsch et al., "US Wants Dutch Supplier to Stop Selling Chipmaking
Gear to China," *Bloomberg*, July 5, 2022, https://www.bloomberg.com/news
/articles/2022–07–05/us-pushing-for-asml-to-stop-selling-key-chipmaking
-gear-to-china.

24. "FACT SHEET: CHIPS and Science Act," The White House, August 9, 2022,
https://www.whitehouse.gov/briefing-room/statements-releases/2022/08/09
/fact-sheet-chips-and-science-act-will-lower-costs-create-jobs-strengthen
-supply-chains-and-counter-china/.

25. "Digital Sovereignty: Commission Proposes Chips Act," European Commission, February 8, 2022, https://ec.europa.eu/commission/presscorner/detail
/en/ip_22_729.

26. Julie Zhu, "Exclusive: China Readying $143 Billion Package for Its Chip Firms
in Face of US Curbs," *Reuters*, December 14, 2022, sec. Technology, https://
www.reuters.com/technology/china-plans-over-143-bln-push-boost-domestic
-chips-compete-with-us-sources-2022–12–13/. See also: Chris Miller, *Chip
War: The Fight for The World's Most Critical Technology* (New York; Scribner,
2022).

27. Zaki Laïdi, *A World Without Meaning: The Crisis of Meaning in International Politics* (New York: Routledge, 1998), 1–14.

28. Robert Lighthizer, "How to Make Trade Work for Workers," *Foreign Affairs*, 99, no. (4): 78.

29. "C. Peter McColough Series on International Economics With Katherine Tai," Council on Foreign Relations, December 19, 2022, https://www.cfr.org /event/c-peter-mccolough-series-international-economics-katherine-tai.

30. Sebastian Mallaby, "Biden Needs Allies to Keep China and Russia in Check. Here's How to Do It.," *The Washington Post*, January 8, 2023, sec. Editorial-Opinion.

31. Dani Rodrik. *Straight Talk on Trade: Ideas for a Sane World Economy.* (Princeton, NJ: Princeton University Press, 2018), 13.

32. Ibid, 14.

33. "What America's protectionist turn means for the world," *The Economist*, January 14, 2023, https://www.economist. com/finance-and-economics /2023/01/09/what-americas-protectionist-turn-means-for-the-world.

34. Philip Seib, *The Future of #Diplomacy* (Cambridge UK: Policy Press, 2016), 3. See also Philip Seib, Real-Time Diplomacy (New York: Palgrave Macmillan, 2012).

35. Ambassador Nicholas Burns, Ambassador Marc Grossman, Ambassador Marcie Ries, *"A US Diplomatic Service for the twenty-first Century,"* The Harvard Kennedy School Belfer Center for Science and International Affairs, November 2020; CAP National Security and International Policy Team. *The First 100 Days: Toward a More Sustainable and Values-Based National Security Approach.* Center for American Progress, October 19, 2020; Gina Abercrombie-Winstanley, Joaquin Castro, and Chris Murphy. *TRANSFORMING STATE Pathways to a More Just, Equitable, and Innovative Institution*, March 2021; Council on Foreign Relations, John Finer, and Uzra S. Zeya, *Revitalizing the State Department and American Diplomacy* § (2020).

36. Ambassador Nicholas Burns, Ambassador Marc Grossman, Ambassador Marcie Ries, *"A US Diplomatic Service for the twenty-first Century,"* The Harvard Kennedy School Belfer Center for Science and International Affairs, November 2020, 45.

37. Antony Blinken, 2021. "A Foreign Policy for the American People." (Speech delivered at the State Department, Washington, D.C., March 3, 2021.)

38. Ambassador Marc Grossman and Ambassador Marcie Ries, *Foreign Service Journal*, March/April 2023.

39. Ambassador Marc Grossman and Ambassador Marcie Ries, "Blueprints for a More Modern Diplomatic Service," The American Diplomacy Project (Arizona State University, September 2022).

40. David McCullough, *John Adams* (New York: Simon and Schuster, 2001), 349.

TEN

RONALD E. NEUMANN

Reflections on Half a Century of Diplomacy

The discussion of what has changed in diplomacy and what should be done to increase American diplomatic effectiveness has been continuing over the more than half a century that I have been involved, first as a diplomat for 37 years and since my retirement as president of the American Academy of Diplomacy. As a diplomat, my direct experience was primarily with postings in the Middle East, Iran, Yemen, the United Arab Emirates, Iraq after the US occupation and three ambassadorships, in Algeria, Bahrain and, finally, in Afghanistan. In terms of experience, this means that mine is mostly with the Middle East and entirely in the so called "regional bureaus" and not in the "functional", that is, those dealing with cross cutting issues like drug trafficking or climate change. Those interested in details of my life, including as an infantry officer in Vietnam, can refer to my book, *Three Embassies, Four Wars: A Personal Memoir*.

Fourteen years as president of the American Academy of Diplomacy (the Academy), a non-governmental and non-partisan organization dedicated to strengthening American diplomacy, has given me an opportunity to take a more holistic look at our diplomatic institutions, strengths, and weaknesses. It has also led me to study the history of State Department reform efforts. What stands out from articles over 50 years is how many of the problems have remained constant. The lack of professional education, the discussion of need for on the ground presence of diplomats, the difficulty of managing separate personnel systems are only a few of these perennial, seemingly never resolved issues.

Over this time, I have come to believe, as the great diplomat George Kennan wrote, that diplomacy is "outstandingly an intellectual task. It is just as much an intellectual task as teaching or scientific research or medicine. It will absorb all that anyone can give it in the way of reflectiveness. It yields to no other profession in the demands it places on the capacity for scientific analysis and creative thought. It is, in fact, a species of scholarship."[1] Yet while this is true, diplomacy has had difficulty establishing itself, and being accepted, as a profession. Partly this stems from a lack of standards and a clear definition. As the Academy noted in 2015 "diplomacy today is virtually unique among professions in the US in its lack of stringent pre-entry requirements relating to its field, formal accreditation and the absolute requirement for continuing education, and/or re-certification during the career, according to a comparison of nine other professions."[2] Improvement in all these areas is possible as shown by the regular practices of other major powers.[3]

To this might be added the impressionistic conclusion that Americans may well not see diplomacy as a profession worthy of particular respect. Few would brush their teeth with a toothpaste not certified safe by chemists or drive across a bridge not designed by engineers but pretty much everyone seems to conclude that they can have a valid opinion on diplomacy. That may well be an exaggeration. And no profession, certainly not diplomacy, has been free from error over time. Still, I have the impression that the plumber's opinion is often accorded more immediate acceptance than that of the diplomat.

Of course, despite this continuity, much has changed over this time. But watching the recurring discussions of many similar ideas over the years has prompted me to ask why so many ideas with broad consensus have not led to change. This has generated some reflections on larger impediments to change and what might lead to more effective action.

As this is written there is a renewed discussion of fundamental change taking place. Papers written by the Belfer Center at Harvard,[4] the Council on Foreign Relations[5], and several others call[6] for fundamental reform and a new law to renew the Foreign Service Act of 1980.[7] A new study, *Blueprints for a More Modern US Diplomatic Service*[8] goes beyond previous studies in laying out new concepts and legislative details and the 2023 State Department Authorization bill demands that the State Department study the idea of establishing a Foreign Service Reserve and establishes a two year Congressional study of reform for State. Perhaps this time will be different. Improvement in the diversity of our diplomatic representation are overdue and the most likely to show progress given the attention being devoted to the issue by Secretary of State Anthony Blinken. But in a sharply divided Congress reform efforts may fall short. My own experience has led me to two basic conclusions. One is that more progress may be made by incremental change than by efforts to enact sweeping reform. The other, which may sound contradictory at first, is that some big reforms are possible but must couple a long-term vision or plan with incremental progress over time. Perhaps these conclusions may be clearer if one begins with a discussion of some basic obstacles to reform.

One might be summarized as a lack of understanding of the problem of implementation. Large bureaucracies are hard to change. Some of the problem is that institutions become set in their ways. Laws and regulations undergird continuity and cannot easily be ordered away. And some of the resistance may lie in human nature and be better explained by a sociologist or a psychologist than a diplomat. I leave the analysis of causes to others. The fact that change is slow needs to be accepted because it has consequences for what is more and less likely to succeed.

If bureaucracies are slow to change then it follows that decisions for change will need substantial time to be put into effect, for change to be accepted, for habits to change; in short for the change to become the new pattern. But this logic is rarely followed by a new administration.

Whatever ideas for fundamental reform a new administration brings with it, few are ready for instant implementation. Time is needed for the selection and confirmation of senior officials. This process itself is becoming longer as partisan divisions have sharpened. The old idea that some deference should be extended to a new president in selecting his cabinet and senior officials has largely faded. Confirmation of cabinet officers now takes roughly twice as long as it did in the Reagan administration.[9] Hence, an administration lacks its own team to begin the work. And when its people are in place, and in between crises that demand the attention of senior policy makers, it begins to focus on reforms beyond the cosmetic, there tends to be a long period of study. Committees are formed. Studies are done, either internally or by outside consultants (who rarely start with any understand of the organization they are studying).

Consultations with employees are started; a good thing to develop support for later change, but also time consuming. The result is that decisions about reform tend to arrive late in the administration without the two or three years that are likely to be required for successful implementation. It is as though policy makers had the implicit assumption that if their decisions are sufficiently brilliant others will just automatically follow and implementation can be left to the bureaucracy; the very group whose resistance needs to be overcome in the first place. The result is that a great many reforms are essentially still born; administrations change, new leaders come in and the process starts over again. And this is often a best case, because if the Secretary of State changes part way into the administration the whole process may be aborted. Perhaps the worst example of a reform effort occurred during the brief tenure of Secretary Rex Tillerson.

Tillerson was determined to shrink the State Department. To do so, he implemented a hiring freeze for the Civil Service.[10] Foreign Service hires were reduced and various bureaucratic tools employed to shrink the senior ranks of the Foreign Service.[11] However, there was no plan for the future shape of the State Department. When senior leadership was asked for guidance on the structural vision to be achieved by reduction they could get no answer.[12] It was just "cut" without plan or defined purpose. So the removals were chaotic and the chaos lasted, and lasted. It was as though one decided to halt running trains while the schedule was reconsidered and a year later the trains were still sitting on the sidings.

The institutional damage was extreme. Embassies went years without ambassadors. Assistant Secretaries were not appointed. One bureau two years later was massively short of its Civil Service employees.[13] Several working groups were formed to consider new ideas. From corridor gossip and oral reports of those on the working groups, they actually did come up with some important ideas for reform. But with Tillerson's departure all his efforts were halted and the results of the working groups were locked away as being anathema, somehow poisoned by the leader who had called them into being.

Secretary Mike Pompeo took a different direction. He realized that being well into the administration he lacked time for any major reform so he decided to work on repairs at the margin.[14] Some of the worst abuses were ended. The hiring freeze was ended. Recruitment and promotions increased, partly by the Secretary's direction and partly by Congressional order. Hiring of family members overseas was expanded. Some new reforms were considered, from an ethos statement prominently displayed at the main entrance to the Department to an effort to fill ambassadorships (although problems stemming from the White House persisted). Whether these new reforms were good or bad they had no time to show results. The pandemic and tumult in the streets overshadowed everything and when the Trump administration left office most changes were shoveled out the door. The much-ballyhooed ethos statement disappeared.

Many of the changes of the Trump period were badly conceived from my perspective but that is not the point of this account. Rather, two lessons stand out from this history. One is that without time for implementation reform efforts die with the executing administration. The second is that without a guiding vision large scale change may produce more chaos than progress. This is why I often favor more incremental reform that can be executed without the time lost in long studies. The numerous efforts now underway to increase diversity in the State Department may yet validate this point.

All this is magnified by the fact that in my experience only three secretaries of State really paid attention to the well being of the institution. One was George Shultz, the second was Colin Powell, and the third was Hillary Clinton. In the last fifty years they are the only ones who actually fought for the Department's budget or paid attention to issues of the well being of the staff. Shultz is remembered decades later for having threatened to resign rather than let his employees be subject to lie detector test. Powell and his deputy Richard Armitage were explicit in telling ambassadors that they had a duty to care for the welfare of their staff. And Clinton strove particularly to expand the role of women.

The State Department may again be blessed with such leaders but that will be a matter of chance. Secretary Anthony Blinken has made reform a significant priority. Some changes have taken place, but implementation lagged for most of the first two years of the Biden Administration. Thus the jury is still out on whether Blinken will go down as the fourth Secretary to really work on institutional change.

In the military, the service heads, the Chiefs of Staff, Commandant of the Marines, and Chief of Naval Operations come from the career and are appointed to look after the well being of their services. The State Department does not have this. The Director General of the Foreign Service is the closest equivalent, but that position lacks the stature or authority of a service chief and in recent years has often gone to an ambassador who has presided over a fairly small embassy.[15] Whatever the personal qualifications of such an appointee, and generally they have been high, they lack the position and stature of the service chiefs. Hence leadership care for the institution will be episodic. This again suggests that reform is unlikely to be successful if too much is attempted too late in the administration.

No such generalization is immutable. One major reform of the Department occurred because Secretary George Shultz had a vision and stayed in office long enough to bring it about. This was his decision to move State's training facilities from a depressing collection of rented building to a permanent campus and create a real professional training center. Because he drove the vision and held to it over several budget cycles it came into being. The National Foreign Affairs Training Center, generally referred to as FSI for the Foreign Service Institute that is its predecessor and core, still has a long way to go to fully achieve Shultz's vision of professional education. But it's creation was a major reform in diplomatic training and would not have happened without his leadership.

Shultz's success in creating FSI was particularly noteworthy because of the structure of the State Department budget. Funding is generally provided by the Congress on a yearly basis. Funds not obligated by the end of the fiscal year must be returned to the Treasury. And each year's budget is subject to fights, compromises and periodic swings. Big projects may be rebuffed as too costly and incremental funding over time can be derailed by the yearly budget battle. There are ways to avoid this, including provisions allowing for money to be expended over multiple years or building in automatic replenishment. This simply illustrates how vital it is that an administration build a substantial supporting body in Congress to maintain a project over time.

Despite this success, the problems of FSI reflect many of the larger points about reform made earlier. Study after study, including several by my own organization, have pointed to the need for expanded professional education for diplomats.[16] This recommendation has been fundamental to every study for decades. But little has happened despite substantial efforts by often talented officers. The military war colleges have become accredited degree granting institutions. The military regularly sends officers to civilian universities to acquire advanced degrees. FSI remains basically an institution for excellent profession training, particularly in languages, but lacks the resources to provide long term, professional education. It does not have the funding to even prepare a cost analysis of what would be required to become an accredited degree granting institution such as the military war colleges, nor the resources or staff to undertake such an effort. Nor, fundamentally, does State have the personnel to be able to free them for long term professional education. The military is able to send personnel to long term training and education because it is staffed at approximately 15 percent over the numbers needed to fill all operating positions. State has no such excess to allow it to take people out of line positions and send them for long term education. Secretary Powell did create such a "float" but it was sucked up into the expanded requirements of the Afghan and Iraq wars.[17]

Yet the need remains. It is unrealistic to believe that this can be fixed quickly by the efforts of a single administration, particularly given the likely budgetary and personnel requirements that will certainly exceed a single year's budget. This brings back the need for vision and time. The Department would have to convince congress of the value of professional diplomatic education. The Congress would need to provide direction, supervision, and a commitment to multiyear funding to undertake such an effort. Mounting a legislative effort of this scope is possible. But it is not quick. An administration would need to begin the effort early in its tenure, lead it at the top, and push it for the entirety of its term.

Many discussions of reform in diplomacy focus on what is new in the world. This is important, and even wise. But it needs to be coupled with an understanding of what is not new, what is unchanging so that one avoids assuming that resources for new functions can come easily from giving up what is outdated. In saying this I do not suggest that reallocation is not possible or necessary. It is. But figuring out what to give up is harder than many suppose.

I have often challenged audiences to name a single major responsibility of a nineteenth century diplomat which is not also a responsibility of today's diplomat. I've not had a response. This is because the basic functions of earlier diplomats remain. Diplomats are still responsible for taking care of Americans overseas, as diplomats at US embassies and in the State Department did magnificently during pandemic evacuations from multiple countries. Support for American commerce has been a core task since the beginning of the Republic (although it was once entrusted to a separate consular service rather than main line diplomats). Persuading foreign governments to do things our way remains one of the most basic diplomatic tasks.

Of course, we have given up our quill pens and electronic communications have been vastly speeded up. But these are tools, not basic responsibilities. They come with their own demands for additional personnel for IT work, and vast numbers of security personnel for an increasingly dangerous world. And some of the tools have added their own forms of stress and workload.

For many years I was supported by office management specialists (OMS) who, as the name implies, were far more than secretaries. I learned over the years how to most effectively use these incredibly qualified people to increase my efficiency. Now they are largely gone. So each officer has to deal with everything in his or her electronic inbox. All of the administrative load which able OMS's handled, from travel planning to vouchers to reimbursement for petty expenses, is now handled by the officer concerned. For the system as a whole there may be a gain in saved personnel costs. But ask any officer who has to deal with making out a travel voucher or arranging a household transfer, and who has dealt with the balky electronic systems, encumbered by masses of regulation about what is and is not allowable, if the system has made them more efficient. The only question is whether the reply will be in polite language.

One particular two-edged sword of technology is the handheld device, still represented by the Blackberry for official business. There is a world of efficiency in being connected. We would not give it up if we could. But there are also strains and vulnerabilities. Officers are now reachable at all hours of the day or night and replies are expected by senior officials. One is never "off duty" and the strains tell on families and relationships when the officer deals with frequent crises and high-profile matters; dealing with these matters are the basis for the best jobs to have, but workloads that were always intense have grown worse. When I served in Baghdad shortly after the invasion, a period that now looks very early in the development of technology, I kept a log long enough to discover that we were regularly working 90 to 100 hours a week. I gave up the record keeping as too discouraging, especially since diplomacy knows no overtime pay. Conditions have gotten worse in this regard.

Another problem of our electronic communications is that approved encryption technology has not kept up with speed. The pressure to report quickly is nearly overwhelming. The result is problems. Reports that should be classified are not so alert adversaries have easy access to our communications. And sometimes reports that really are classified are stuck into unclassified emails or texts because there is no equivalently speedy way of conveying something important to a senior official in a timely manner. This was certainly a factor in some of the troubles into which Secretary Hillary Clinton fell with her emails, or actually, mostly emails sent to her by others. It is perfectly correct to say that some of the material sent to her should have been classified (or was). It is just as perfectly unreasonable to suggest that every such message should have been separately driven to her residence or that the Secretary of State should routinely be called into the office late at night. The Wikileaks that resulted in the removal of several ambassadors from their posts illustrates the danger on one side of the problem. Being caught by surprise, either diplomatically or in the tough politics of Washington, lies on the other side.

This is a modern problem that did not exist when we had only landline telephones once we left the office. It is the flip side of progress, and a problem not yet solved. Equipping our diplomats with mobile and hand-held encrypted capabilities that meet government security standards needs urgent attention.

Still another problem of modern communications that is harder to quantify is the ability of every agency and office in Washington to reach out to officers at all levels in an embassy and ask for information or give instructions. One problem is that such "instructions" are often neither well thought out nor coordinated to insure that they do not conflict with some other policy. When embassies have become platforms for the entire US government, with more than twenty agencies and cabinet departments now represented overseas and the actual diplomats a minority of the staff, the problems of coordination and carrying out a coherent policy are extreme.

A separate part of the same problem is that officers find themselves spending too much time at their desks answering email from Washington and not enough time doing the basic contact work and relationship building that is essential to the craft of diplomacy. In a recent discussion with a group of mid-level officers I found that this problem has only grown worse since I left the service. There is no technological fix for this. It takes a strong ambassador to insist that demands from individual offices in Washington go unanswered in the name of more important tasks. But if such judgment is not exercised our best diplomats will spend all their time regurgitating old information rather than collecting new insights and influencing foreigners.

These issues of leaked secrets, inefficiencies of the technology that was to have freed us, and individual stress and burnout are probably not the matters of high policy the editors of this volume had in mind when they asked for reflections on changes in diplomacy. But they do affect the quality and achievements of our diplomacy and, as such, are worthy of mention.

To raise the focus of this essay, I turn to three problems of the modern scene. One is the imbalance between institutions and emerging problems. The second is change in America's position in the world brought on by the combination of the end of the cold war and our own changes in direction. A third is the gross mismatch between America's ambitions and its patience, exacerbated by an unchanging intellectual arrogance. Each of these areas is essentially an aspect of policy. But each has consequences for how diplomacy must adapt.

For over seventy years the post WWII institutions have undergirded stability and prosperity in the world. But even as these institutions, such as the World Bank and the IMF, are challenged by Russia and the raising power of China, the world is also grappling with major new challenges of climate change, pandemics, and transnational crime. Yet while international cooperation is needed more than ever to address transnational challenges, action still lie mainly with states. States are jealous of their authority and will not easily surrender sovereignty to international bodies. One need only look to the US refusal to join the International Criminal Court[18] or the Landmine treaty[19] or the refusal of the Senate to ratify the Law of the Sea treaty[20] for over 30 years. Many other states are at least as reluctant to surrender sovereignty. The United Nations is not in a position to do much about this because it is a collection of states, unable to act beyond measures on which states can agree. Even if a majority of countries pass resolutions in the General Assembly, any enforceable decisions require action in the Security Council where five states hold veto power.

The mismatch between the demands posed by the challenges and the monopoly of power by states is one of the gravest challenges today for policy and diplomacy. Yet even if states still hold the majority of power, that power is itself challenged by a growing array of other actors and the fast-moving developments in the breakdown of alliances, the rise of nongovernmental organizations, and the multipolar nature of the post cold war world.

The divisions of the cold war were dangerous and not conditions that one would wish to see back, even if that were possible. But they did provide a basic intellectual framework around which much diplomacy could be organized. Now, many of these alliances are gone or under stress. The Organization for Security and Cooperation in Europe's (OSCE) Minsk Group has lost out to Russian efforts to be the primary deal maker in the war between Armenia and Azerbaijan.[21] Other institutions like the European Union are under strain with the departure of Great Britain and the strains of the covid-19 pandemic.

Efforts to organize new relations are difficult. The Trans Pacific Partnership treaty was one approach during the Obama administration to bring into being a new alliance with Asian states founded on an economic basis, not only to improve trade but to confront China. American participation in this effort died under the assaults of domestic politics and the refusal of President Trump to continue the effort. The result was that the other powers went ahead anyway, but suspended from the new agreement some 22 provisions carefully negotiated and fought for by the United States.[22] Among the items lost were provisions for protection of intellectual property and investors' ability to litigate disputes under investment agreements and investment authorizations.[23] The bilateral agreements that were proposed to replace the TPT have not come into being.

Other organizations have come into being without US participation. One example is the Asian Infrastructure Investment Bank.[24] Proposed by China it now has over one hundred members, including many US allies such as Australia and South Korea. US efforts from the time of the Obama administration on to block participation have all failed to keep our friends and allies from joining this organization which is, to some extent, a competitor to the US dominated Asian Development Bank.

One exception to the disintegration of alliances is NATO, the North Atlantic Treaty Organization. While some questioned its long-term utility in the post cold war world, NATO found new purpose in so called "out of area" missions like Afghanistan where 20 years into the war NATO found common purpose until President Biden decided to lead us all out. The more recent challenges of Russia, particularly in Ukraine, have also solidified NATO.

This solidarity was weakened by the transactional approach of President Trump. That has now passed and President Biden has declared a return to alliances. But European states are left to wonder whether the populist forces Trump led in America will return to power and resume his directions. Thus NATO states may question whether the basic bargain of the alliance will be maintained in the future. American diplomats attempting to find partners for future actions will have to wrestle with the fallout from such doubt.

America is not alone in dealing with populist forces that push against alliances. Within NATO, Turkey is bent on policies that increasingly challenge alliance solidarity. Authoritarian policies in Poland and Hungary challenge the framework of European unity even as Britain's departure from the EU has weakened the cohesion of the alliance and sparked new challenges and strains, particularly in Ireland.

"Coalitions of the willing," as the George W. Bush administration named them, can sometimes be put together. But as the Iraq situation worsened it became increasingly evident that under strain the "willing" become unwilling and the grouping fell apart. There were many reasons for this in Iraq but the contrast with NATO in Afghanistan does say something about the value of alliances.

As many commentators have noted, the change to a multipolar world has led to a more transactional style of diplomacy in which today's partners may be tomorrow's adversaries. President Trump's approach to foreign policy strengthened this tendency but it was an approach with broad support among the American electorate and may yet return.

The fraying of alliances, challenges to institutions, development of a more multipolar world, and shifts to transactional arrangements all pose immense challenges to American policy and to the organization of effective diplomacy to successfully execute policy even as it seeks to deal with new transnational challenges. American diplomacy is not well organized to be effective in meeting these expanding challenges. Throughout my career the better jobs were seen as being in the so-called regional bureaus, those handling bilateral relations with states. The "functional" bureaus, those handling cross cutting issues like economics, oceans, technology, and narcotics, were often avoided by Foreign Service Officers as being less likely to lead to promotion. The combination of Foreign Service avoidance and the need to build up deep technical expertise led the functional bureaus to become staffed predominately by the civil service. This division was not maximized for effectiveness, although it did result in the growth of experts in the civil service who have been outstanding in both the formulation of policies and the international negotiations to support them.

The downsides, however, have become more obvious in recent years. Foreign Service officers have not received the experience and training in the functional bureaus to be optimally effective with their foreign contacts in pressing US viewpoints. The civil servants often found themselves stuck in jobs that, while reasonably senior, provided no avenues for professional growth or promotion. Additionally, the functional bureaus often lacked the bureaucratic weight to get needed attention for policy changes and actions. Foreign governments, particularly among our major allies but also competitors like the Chinese, often outplayed us in international organizations. Increasingly, studies of American diplomacy from the American Academy of Diplomacy and, more recently those new studies previously mentioned, have recommended a blending of civil service and Foreign Service assignments in the functional bureaus.

The uniformity of these recommendations have not, thus far, led to significant change. In 2015 a project led by the Academy in cooperation with the Partnership for Public Service,[25] recommended major changes for the civil service to allow more flexibility of assignment; a plan we saw as having gains for all three stakeholders, the civil service, the Foreign Service, and the flexibility of State's personnel management. We believe this plan is worth trying, particularly the initial pilot program we recommended.

However, this study did not go far enough in addressing the manifold challenges of multilateral diplomacy in the twenty-first century. For that reason, with generous support from the Una Chapman Cox Foundation (which also funded the previous study), the Academy produce a new study of multilateral diplomacy that examines the need, what other major powers are doing to make their diplomacy more effective and recommends changes.[26]

In addition to multilateral diplomacy, a catalogue of what makes diplomacy different today must add the return to confrontation with Russia and the challenges of a rising China. The latter development has altered a basic approach to China that had guided American policy for more than 30 years.

The confrontations with Russia and China have each brought new diplomatic challenges. It is not my purpose here to analyze either the causes or the policies involved in these two areas but, rather, to note how they have brought about diplomatic challenges different from those of the cold war. Russia seems more interested in domination of its immediate neighbors and a general weakening of the west than in any ideological challenge. One result has been that diplomatic allies in some areas are on different paths in other areas. NATO has held together well in its main response to Russian actions in Ukraine and potential threats to the Baltic states but some members, particularly Germany, long disagreed with the United States on the need to block a major gas project to Germany, the Nordstream 2 pipe line.

Similarly, Russia's forays into Libya and Syria have confronted the United States with policy challenges that, to date, have no clear policy response. Libya is a particular example of the problems of the current era. The refugee flows, not only from Libya itself, but from Africa and even Iraq and Afghanistan that flow through Libya are a significant human rights problem and a challenge particularly for Europe, the destination for most of the refugees. The swirling conflict in Libya drew in outside powers: Russia, the United Arab Emirates and Egypt joining the side of those seeking to seize Tripoli; and Turkey intervening in defense of the weak but internationally recognized government. The UAE and Egypt have been motivated particularly by fears of the expansion of radical Islamic forces. Russia has seized the opportunity for a low-cost strategic foothold on NATO's southern flank.

Europe and the United States have backed strenuous efforts by the United Nations to broker a peace arrangement, resulting in a ceasefire that has held since last October and the selection of an interim unity government in March. But all sides have continued to ignore the UN arms embargo. US policy under the Trump Administration was particularly confused. On the one hand the formal policy supported the UN. Yet at the same time, President Trump was widely perceived to have given a "green light" in April 2019 to self-styled Field Marshal Khalifa Haftar's offensive on Tripoli. That offensive failed, but observers were left puzzled as to what the real US policy was. Meantime, refugees continue to flow, instability and the proliferation of armed groups has spilled over into neighboring countries such as Chad, the Islamic State and Al Qaeda could potentially resurge in ungoverned space in Libya's south, and external actors like Russia continue to challenge Libya's sovereignty.

It remains to be seen whether the UN-facilitated political process will produce elections the type of policy challenge the US may increasingly confront. US interests and resources are too limited and domestic opposition to major foreign interventions are too large to justify a large engagement. Europe is more directly threatened, as are Libya's neighbors, but key states such as France and Italy have differed in the past over how to handle refugees and it remains to be seen if the current alignment is just superficial. Above all, the fractious nature of the Libyan body politic make it difficult even to design an effective role for outsiders. But all see—or claim to see—US influence as being decisive in moving events in a positive direction.

Unlike the Cold War, where regional conflicts were often perceived (sometimes wrongly) as part of a larger conflict, Syria and Libya are seen more as regional problems than as any broader form of Russian aggression. Our interests are limited. Russia's actions do not fit within any pre-existing intellectual or policy framework. Without going further into the cases, my point is simply that with Russia we have a hybrid challenge, from military in the Ukraine to semi-covert in Libya, to election interference and propaganda inside the United States. We have individual decisions but are still grappling with the need for an integrated policy response. The diplomat cannot explain a policy until it exists.

With China the challenge is much broader. Over Taiwan and in the South China Sea the military issues are evolving but fit within familiar concepts even if there are arguments over which policy to choose. But there are whole new realms of diplomatic challenges in the realm of technology. In 2020 I was on a selection committee for awards for economic performance of Foreign Service Officers at various levels of seniority. Many of the award citations documented the work of individual officers and teams in persuading host governments to resist Chinese technology in 5G networks. From Panama to Asia officers were engaged in these efforts, finding and explaining to their host governments not only the problem but demonstrating alternative choices.

The United States has also begun a broad effort to question and, in some cases, argue against China's belt and road initiative. These efforts are limited by the old adage, you can't beat something with nothing. Chinese diplomatic staffing in Africa seriously outnumbers American diplomats on the ground. US credit and commercial programs have difficulty matching Chinese largess. The challenge is multifaceted, involving economic and commercial tools as much as access to host governments. Our diplomatic tools seem inadequate to the task.

The world is full of new challenges. Not all policy issues require new diplomatic tools. However, I cite the Russian and Chinese examples because they are conceptually new. In the Russian case it is the alteration from the Soviet Union, where numerous different problems could still be fitted within the containment and coexistence mental boxes. In the Chinese case, what is new is that the challenge has fundamentally reoriented a policy of cooperation that began in 1972 with President Richard Nixon's opening to China. The issue now requires us to develop technological and economic tools to deal with a China which is now an equal or near equal peer competitor. In the Chinese case in particular there is the additional problem that we are operating without fixed alliances with common goals. We do have particularly strong friends in Japan, with whom we have a treaty relationship, South Korea, which has political strains with Japan, and Australia. But as the Chinese challenge has been seen as growing the transactional approach of the Trump years worked against developing a broad framework of friends with common goals. Finding ways to harmonize actions with others on such key issues as economic rules of the road or the challenges of the South China Sea is clearly a new diplomatic problem of major proportions.[27]

In many ways, the Chinese challenge is particularly acute with regards to other east Asian states, such as Malaysia, Singapore, Vietnam, India, and Bangladesh. In each case we have multiple interests involving not only trade but democracy promotion. The newly proclaimed "values policy" of the Biden administration has still to take shape. However, as a recent article pointed out, we may face considerable tension between strengthening our common purposes with these states and our conflicting push for democratization.[28]

But all is not new in the world of diplomatic challenges. There are at least three perennials conditions that continue to hamper the development of effective diplomatic approaches to major problems. One is the tension between morality and realpolitik, with each having a tendency to over reach while the tension between them causes policy swings that undercut credibility. The second is the problem of impatience and the third that of an intellectual arrogance that leads to "Made in Washington solutions" that repeatedly fail because they fail to take into account local circumstances or the mentality of foreign leaders. Each of these elements seems to me somehow inherent in the American character and therefore each needs some consideration if one wants to design more effective diplomatic approaches.

For example, balancing between interests and values is likely to be required between our shared interest with Asian states in dealing with China, noted earlier, and our proclivities to press for more democracy and human rights. Balancing between the two will disappoint those who wish clear priorities would be uniformly applied to all situations. Unfortunately, American's national interest will not always accommodate such purity of purpose. The diplomat will be left to explain the fall from virtue.

This problem, of the tension between morality and realism seems to be a permanent characteristic of American foreign policy. When President John Quincy Adams in 1821 said that America "goes not abroad, in search of monsters to destroy" he was speaking directly against trying to put our morality into our foreign policy. In Adam's view of America, "She is the well-wisher to the freedom and independence of all. She is the champion and vindicator only of her own."

In 1920 the British newspaper *The Spectator* summed up this tension in the American character, "The American nation has a dual personality Americans are at once the most idealist and most practical people in the world. They vibrate between Emerson and Edison."[29]

Two centuries on, the pendulum continues to swing back and forth between these views. President Nixon's realism, and his almost wholly realpolitik deputy Henry Kissinger, were clearly of the realist school of foreign policy. But Nixon was followed by Jimmy Carter who introduced the idea of human rights reports and thought and thought that America should address the wrongs it documented.

The pulling and tugging between these policies continues. During 20 years of war in Afghanistan we have preached on the values of and spent millions to bolster women's rights, a free press and freedom of expression. But when President Biden explained his decision to pull US troops out of Afghanistan, the only goal cited was that of destroying al Qaeda, a goal the president said had been achieved. Women and freedom were left to Afghan forces to defend from the Taliban.[30] This is not to argue with the decision to withdraw. It is only an illustration from my own experience of the inconsistency that develops out of the tension between morality and realpolitik.

The desire to achieve moral ends frequently leads leaders to overstate goals without reflection on whether we have the means to achieve them. Often our words lead others to expect more than we can or will deliver. Hungarians expected help when they rose against their communist dictatorship. When Soviet tanks rolled in, no help was forthcoming. When Iraqis rose up against Saddam Hussein at the end of the first Gulf War they thought that the words of President George H. W. Bush promised support—they didn't. Our planes bombed Libyan soldiers to help topple Qaddafi but we took no responsibility for the aftermath. These examples are not to argue for or against any of these decisions. They are cited only to underscore the tension between our words, frequently based on high principles, and the limited action in support of our words that reality seems to impose.

The problem for diplomats is that our leaders rarely like to speak in limited terms, to suggest that we will not help some people or some cause (although President Trump seemed not to have this problem). Diplomats who must explain our policies and persuade foreigners to support us have a difficult task as a result.

Another perennial is what I would call an intellectual arrogance that leads policy makers in Washington repeatedly to design policies without regard for the situation on the ground or the personality of local leaders. Three examples may illustrate the point. The first is Vietnam, where one US policy decision after another failed because of the inability to understand the local conditions. Speaking of one set of recommendations to Vietnamese President Diem, William Colby, a CIA official who spent 15 years involved with Vietnam, wrote, "we defined the necessary 'psychological shock' in terms totally counter to Diem's personality and the realities of the Vietnamese power structure and society."[31] As Colby ruefully noted, "the conviction [was] widespread among the Americans that the failures of the various American formulas for success in Vietnam could be due only to the unwillingness or inability of the Vietnamese to perceive their validity—indeed, their brilliance—and then apply them as indicated."[32]

That this example is not from an outdated past may be seen in two more recent instances, one from the Obama period and one unfolding in the Biden administration. In 2009, President Obama began an extensive reconsideration of US policy in Afghanistan, following a shorter review at the beginning of that year. The review took many months. In the end, Obama somewhat reluctantly accepted military recommendations for a major surge of US forces into Afghanistan. The policy was to be time limited and, also, limited in purpose with the goal being to focus on the destruction of al-Qaeda and pushing back the Taliban while, explicitly, avoiding nation building.

However, while this policy appeared coherent in Washington it contained several contradictions when applied to the field. One was implicit in the effort to build a greatly enlarged Afghan military to which we could turn over the fight. An army is a reflection of the society it represents. Therefore, to build the army we wanted the Afghan state had to be strengthened. And to have a functioning state one must have an economy. This logic, which actually translates into state building, was applied to a massive increase in economic assistance even as we denied that nation building, better called state building, was actually a goal.

In the policy review these was extensive discussion of whether the military goals were achievable in the time frame stipulated.[33] I once asked a senior participant in that review whether the associated civilian goals had received equivalent attention as to the reality and probability of achieving them in the time frame stipulated. The answer was no.[34]

When the review was translated into action on the ground the US military faced an impossible task. To achieve the stability they thought necessary they identified some 80 districts in Afghanistan as requiring not only military stabilization but the building of state structures of governance and administration to keep them safe. The goal was set as achieving this in two years with the districts divided in half for achievement n each of the two years. Civilian governance and AID officers constantly warned that there was no way the Afghan state could achieve this institutional development in two years.

In 2010 this division of views led to considerable friction on the ground with the military alleging that the civilians were too slow to make the necessary progress and the civilians arguing that the military was "rushing to failure." On a visit to Afghanistan that year I witnessed this friction playing out at high levels of command. Military and embassy officers of very senior ranks were bad mouthing and criticizing the other in meetings where both were represented. The ill will was palatable and certainly hindered effective cooperation.

But the problem was neither that the US military was stupid nor that the civilians were lethargic. The problem was that the military had been handed a time-bound, made in Washington mission that simply could not be achieved in the time given. In its herculean efforts to accomplish this mission the military instituted all sorts of programs and fielded district level teams in virtually all the critical districts. But since the Afghan state had no capacity to generate an effective civilian presence in the required time, almost all the progress vanished after the military withdrew. The civil-military ill feeling certainly impeded discussion of any possible strategies to bridge the time needed for the Afghan state to meet the challenge. But the basic problem was that the strategy adopted in Washington simply ignored the realities of Afghanistan.

One particular aspect of that Washington combination of arrogance and ignorance jumped out at me from the strategy memo approved by President Obama himself. In it, he wrote that the first of four elements for working with the government of Afghan President Hamid Karzai would require: "Working with Karzai where we can, working around him when we must" to enhance sub-national governance and strengthen counter corruption.[35] This approach was absurdly unrealistic but it was often followed in the field. Visiting military teams scattered about Afghanistan in 2010 I frequently found Americans depicting the Kabul government as irrelevant to their operations. They had the money and the power in the field and they would establish the policies they thought best.

In many conversations I tried to point out that this would not work because President Karzai had the ultimate power to hire and fire provincial officials. He would use that power when he felt the foreigners were going too far in undermining him. Further, Karzai was engaged in a complicated game of political maneuver to keep various competing Afghan political leaders and tribes under his control and to prevent others from becoming too strong. A local governor might be incredibly corrupt, inefficient, or both, but if he was in place for a political purpose Karzai deemed essential he would retain the official.

In 2010 I tried to make my point by noting what had happened to the British in Helmand province, the region for which Britain was responsible within the NATO division of responsibility. In Helmand, a reasonably effective governor named Mohammed Daoud was lauded by the British. Praise of him was loud in the British press and British officials in Helmand were impressed by Daoud's efforts at reform. Unfortunately, Karzai was dealing with multiple tribal and political issues in Helmand. Finally, Karzai removed Daoud. The British were outraged. But for several days Karzai refused to even take a protest call from the British Prime Minister or to explain to the British the reasons for his actions (although he explained them to me, or at least what he said were his reasons). It was a not very subtle signal from Karzai that Afghanistan was his country and was not going to be run by a foreign government. If even the British Prime Minister could not prevail against this, how much less likely was it that a US battalion, brigade, or even division commander would be able to organize things in the provinces in opposition to Kabul's wishes. I failed completely to make any headway with this argument.

Also, while the US military with its vast funds could build clinics and schools quickly, it was only the Afghan ministries in Kabul that could keep them supplied with drugs, books and personnel over time. Even when the Afghan government recognized the worth of a project, they lacked the resources to simply add them to an already overextended budget. So good projects that were quickly built often deteriorated after our departure. The unfolding effort, waste and sacrifice of this period was an almost perfect example of the ignorance and arrogance against which Colby warned four decades earlier.

To carry the story to the current day, one can look at the Biden administration's rapid and short-lived effort to stimulate a peace agreement with the Taliban in Afghanistan. The signing of a US troop withdrawal agreement with the Taliban during the Trump administration was supposed to have opened the door to a substantive negotiating effort between them and the Afghan government. In the year following that signature there was some motion on process and none on substance; that is, meetings were held but the Taliban refused to discuss any actual arrangements for reaching a peace agreement.

In the brief period between President Biden's inauguration and his decision to withdraw the remaining US troops, the US embarked on a rapid-fire effort to generate progress in the peace talks. The administration called for a regional states peace conference in Turkey, pressed the Afghan government in harsh terms to present new peace proposals, invited the United Nations to play an enhanced role and launched an intensive round of consultations with allies; all to occur within a three months. Yet all this came in the context of clear signals from the Taliban that they were not interested in the kind of peace we were proposing, based on maintaining the Afghan constitution, women's rights and modern freedoms.

Nothing whatsoever in the Taliban's operations during the preceding year or its intensified military operations suggested that they would suddenly swing behind the sort of peace being proposed. Still less would they do so if all American troops were about to leave and thus remove a major obstacle to the chances of a Taliban victory. Furthermore, nothing in the twenty years of the American involvement in Afghanistan suggested that political developments of the magnitude discussed could be moved at the pace suggested. More broadly, even the briefest comparative examination of other long running internal conflicts solved by negotiations would suggest that resolution takes years.

The issue is not the whether or not the decision to withdraw troops was correct. Rather the point is that if the Biden administration thought that its rapid-fire peace proposals had any chance of success then it, like successors over many administrations, was indulging in a "made in Washington" intellectual fantasy divorced from any understanding of the realities of Afghanistan or its surrounding region. Of course, it is possible that the administration did not believe in its own proposals but was going through the effort to show it had tried before making the final withdrawal definitive. In that case the effort, to create an illusion of having tried something they had no intention of sticking with, would have been less foolish but scarcely more honorable.

In discussing matters such as Washington's habit of making foreign policy without regard to foreigners or the tensions between realism and values it is important to remember that these issues are actually matters of policy and that policy and diplomacy are not the same thing. Editorial and popular discussions frequently confuse the two matters as they also confuse the distinction between strategy and policy. Thus an editorial may ask what is our strategy in, say, Syria, when what is needed is to understand what are we attempting to accomplish. The latter, the statement of goals, is a policy. The strategy has little to do with the value of the goal and everything to do with how to accomplish it.

Fundamentally, policy, setting the goals, belongs to elected officials; the president and the congress. It is in the design of strategy, how one is to achieve the goals that diplomacy begins to play its part. This is a simplistic and somewhat theoretical distinction. Much policy toward countries or issues that are not of top interest to policy makers is actually made in the middle ranks of the State Department, other cabinet agencies and posts in field. And the top-level leadership may be deeply involved in the design of strategy; too deeply as the Obama example illustrated. Yet even if oversimplified the distinction is important because so often I have seen us seek to fix a problem through changes to policy when the problems actually lie in implementation. There is a significant cost to our diplomatic effectiveness when we fail to understand the difference.

Over the years that I have been involved in our policies in Afghanistan I have watched administration after administration confuse these points and grapple with the resulting problems. By my count, we have had ten different policies in Afghanistan in 20 years.[36] The constant reassessment and re-conceptualization of our goals has badly undermined confidence in our purpose, weakened support from our partners, and made long term coherent plan execution nearly impossible. Yet rarely if ever did we ask whether what was needed was adjustment in how the policy was being implemented. Rather administration after administration chose to look for a new policy.

One rather small example of this problem was special envoy Richard Holbrooke's decision to redo the justice program in Afghanistan. The program had undoubted problems. Holbrooke's answer was to stop the program cold so that it could be redesigned. The executing contractor demobilized, letting go of staff, getting rid of equipment and giving up office space. It took about a year until USAID, after several efforts, got Holbrooke to approve a new concept and was able to re-bid new contracts, one of which was won by the same contractor who had previously demobilized. During the year nothing was accomplished. I believe that focusing on and fixing specific problems would have been far more effective than the stop and start process we followed. But this is simply a micro example of the cost of not understanding that the hard work is in policy execution.

Similar examples could be pulled from our Iraq experience as well as from each of the policy shifts in Afghanistan. Suffice it to say, the problem of coherent execution or implementation of policy is a major headache for diplomacy. Whether senior American officials jump to this defective default approach because of deficiencies in academic education or some other cause I do not know. Certainly, the propensity to focus on policy is replicated in most popular writing about foreign policy. Perhaps it is just that it is easier to deal with high policy than to truly understand the problems of trying to execute policy in complex foreign societies. In any event, we show little inclination to learn.

But if the disinclination to understand foreigners is a long-term issue, the change in how we view security is a significant change in how we conduct diplomacy and one with serious costs. Risk is not new to diplomacy. How we respond to it is, and it is weakening our effectiveness.

There are 320 names inscribed on the walls in the entrance to the State Department of American diplomats who have died in the line of duty. In the early years of the Republic these were sometimes from things like storms at sea and yellow fever. A distant predecessor of mine who headed our first mission to Algiers died of pneumonia while trying to deliver a demarche to Napoleon during the winter retreat from Moscow. In the twentieth century violence became a significant factor with deaths recorded from assassination, the blowing up of embassies, and terrorist attacks. Over 20 died during the Vietnam war. My own father once carried a pistol to a Christmas eve mass when under threat of assassination in Afghanistan, where he was then the ambassador. But diplomacy carried on as I saw in my tours in Algeria when there was a blanket death threat against all foreigners and in my later tours in Iraq and Afghanistan. Diplomacy was a risky profession, but we carried on.

This began to change in the early years of this century as political pressures in Washington and fears of casualties began to restrict movement. This tendency moved into high gear after the massive politicization of the attack in Benghazi. The legislation governing the accountability review board process (ARB)[37] came to be seen more and more as a process interpreted as an overriding requirement to find fault if there is a serious security incident. As former assistant secretary for diplomatic security Greg Starr and I wrote "when security is defined as the first priority, the basic purpose of stationing diplomats abroad is undermined if they cannot perform their jobs. Diplomatic functions—to influence host governments and other foreigners; to explain, defend and advance US policies and objectives; and to gain information and access needed to conduct analyses—require making personal contact. Diplomacy is an incremental business in which numerous contacts and observations contribute over time to generate larger results. Secure telephone technology and video can supplement traditional meetings, but they cannot substitute for building personal relations and trust with foreign contacts."[38]

The time has now come to alter this state of affairs. The Academy's report on *Changing the Risk Paradigm*[39] recommended rewriting the legislation to bring the State Department into conformity with the practices governing the military and intelligence community. Our discussion with the Congress are showed understanding of the need for change. Getting legislation passed was a difficult task despite the support we have from the American Foreign Service Association, and former senior diplomats, generals, and USAID mission directors but the legislation was changed at the end of 2022. However, legislation is a necessary but not sufficient condition. Changes are necessary in diplomatic training and culture. But change is essential and the time for change is now.

Much has changed in the practice of diplomacy over the years I have been involved in the profession even as much has remained the same. Diplomacy is fundamentally about getting foreigners to want to accept our views and to do so in ways that allow one to continue working harmoniously with foreign partners.

The world is full of challenges to American foreign policy. Diplomacy is basically about executing policy so there are limits to what can be done by improving the tools of diplomacy if the policies that direct the tools are deficient. But some of the changes continually mentioned over the years are overdue. One that I have not mentioned is the selection of ambassadors and senior leaders in the State Department. The United States is the only major power that appoints large numbers of non-career (political) appointees to ambassadorships and turns over so many senior positions at home with the changes of administrations.

The problem of non-career ambassadors has generated a great deal of writing. The issue of who staffs State's senior positions at home is actually more serious but has received less attention. The first problem of ambassadorships is an old one.

I do not wish to recapitulate the extensive writing of others on the issue. Those interested in the details can turn to Academy reports, academic studies, and the recent writings of Ambassador Dennis Jett.[40] Every administration since that of George Washington has used at least some diplomatic postings to reward political supporters. Some have been excellent, some total duds. In modern times the number of such appointments has been around 30 percent of ambassadorial postings with higher percentages during the administrations of presidents Kennedy, Regan, and Trump. The law states that "Contributions to political campaigns should not be a factor in the appointment of an individual as a chief of mission."[41] However, that provision is regularly ignored. Suffice it to say that since both political parties find the practice convenient, it is unlikely to change. The issue which deserves attention is that of competence.

The Senate has the constitutional responsibility to confirm ambassadors. It could exercise some control over quality but has rarely done so.

It is unlikely that more legislation will succeed when existing law is regularly ignored. Talking with colleagues who have been involved in presidential appointments and in projects to improve practice has clarified some points. One is that on the rare occasions when an appointee is shown to be really substandard, the practice of the Senate Foreign Relations Committee (SFRC) is more often to leave the nomination lingering until the administration withdraws it than to actually reject the appointee. Another conclusion is that the SFRC has exercised this power most frequently when a leading senator was particularly committed to the issue. This seems to have been true to some extend during the periods of Senators Paul Sarbanes and of John McCain. Because it takes a particular type of character with a secure political base to push back against prevailing political practice one cannot count on this being a normal occurrence. Thus, the problem is likely to continue.

That being the case, more attention needs to be paid to training the non-career ambassadors, most of whom are serious people who want to do a good job. This is more difficult than it sounds. Until a non-career ambassador is confirmed by the Senate the State Department can neither hire the individual not give direction. Attendance in the three-week long course for new ambassadors has to be voluntary for the non-career appointee, usually done on their own time while they continue to hold their civilian job. Although it is widely recognized that the course is too short for the appointee with no previous State Department background, it is almost too long for the patience of those not yet appointed. Further, because the appointee has not been confirmed they, whether career or non-career, are prohibited from any US government consultations outside the State Department lest they appear to be taking the Senate's consent for granted. With many issues involving other cabinet departments, this limitation clearly hampers the appointee from developing a full understanding of issues for which he or she is about to become responsible.

Of course, more training and consultations are possible after confirmation. Yet the reality is that after waiting for months for the lengthy appointment process to finish most ambassadors are in a hurry to get to post. And in many cases the Department is in a rush to get them out the door. When I returned home after almost a year and a half in Iraq where danger precluded my wife from joining me the pressure to leave immediately for my new post as ambassador to Afghanistan was intense. I had to reduce my consultations for Afghanistan to eight days in order to hold to the one month off I had promised my wife before we were again separated.

Of course, I could have reduced my vacation but I reasoned that some personal "recharging" was essential between postings to two critical threat posts. In any event, the incident illustrates the pressures not to linger at the door on the way to a new post.

If the issues of qualifications for non-career appointees and adequate training time are longstanding, the problem of having fewer and fewer career appointees in senior positions in the Department of State is a newer one. The Academy calculated that from the 1970s to 2014 the number of senior positions filled by career employees had declined from about 60 percent to about 30 percent.[42] This decline was massively accelerated during the Trump years. Of more than 50 positions at the assistant secretary level and above, only two career officers confirmed by the Senate were in place when President Biden took office.

This is not to argue that all such positions should be filled from the career ranks. Presidents are entitled to appoint officials who they believe share their policy preferences. The problem occurs when the balance between career and non-career appointees gets too far out of balance. The career officers can draw from their experience of foreign cultures and leaders to suggest how to make policies more effective, to identify potential problems in policies suggested, and to guide the complex Washington process of guiding implementation. Final decisions rest with elected leaders but to remove the career service from the discussion leading to policy decisions is simply to magnify the potential for error.

Additionally, if the opportunities for promotion to leadership positions is cut down too far then the result is to chop the top off the professional career pyramid. Over time, that makes the profession as a whole less desirable and weakens the development of a professional service. At the present time, the balance seems to be shifting back toward more career assignments. It is unlikely that the potential problem can be fixed by legislation given the power the Constitution grants to the president in matters of appointment. However, it might help if the press would balance its fascination with the ambassadorial appointments with an understanding of the problem of senior appointments at home. This too seems unlikely. Time after time I have pointed out to journalists that because policy is ultimately made in Washington the issue of appointments there is more serious than that of the ambassadorial appointments. This argument has almost never had an effect or been reflected in the stories they publish. Perhaps I am not sufficiently persuasive. Perhaps the issue just isn't as easy to make interesting. And perhaps it is a small part of the larger problem of getting American interest focused on the need for a strong professional diplomacy.

George Kennan understood this when he wrote that, "diplomacy is always going to consist to some extent of serving people who do not know that they are being served, who do not know that they need to be served, who misunderstand and occasionally abuse the very effort to serve them. This, . . . adds to the strains of the Service; it does not detract from its dignity.[43]

In the same speech, Kennan said to his colleagues, "Let us take special pride in the fact that we of this profession serve, not because of, but in spite of many of the popular attitudes by which our work is surrounded. It takes a special love of country to pursue, with love, and faith, and cheerfulness, work for which no parades will ever march, no crowds will cheer, no bands will play."

In any event, it is the issues of having the best possible professional diplomacy for America that deserve continuing attention. Selecting the best people from diversified backgrounds, giving them the best possible mentoring and professional education throughout their careers, and accepting the importance of professional and physical risk in the service of the nation will continue to be major challenges of the twenty-first century. I am sure the discussion will be continuing long after I have left the field.

Notes

1. George Kennan, *Diplomacy as a profession*, Foreign Service Journal, July-August 2015, https://www.afsa.org/george-kennan-diplomacy-profession.

2. Academy, *American Diplomacy at Risk*, April 2015, pg. 34 https://www.academyofdiplomacy.org/wp-content/uploads/2016/01/ADAR_Full_Report_4.1.15.pdf.

3. For a comparative examination of other nations' diplomacy see Robert Hutchings, *Modern Diplomacy in Practice*, Palgrave McMillan, 2020.

4. Nicholas Burns, Marc Grossman, and Marcie Ries *A US Diplomatic Service for the twenty-first Century*, Harvard Kennedy School, 2020, https://www.belfercenter.org/sites/default/files/2020-11/DiplomaticService.pdf.

5. Uzra S. Zeya and Jon Finer, *Revitalizing the State Department and American Diplomacy*, Council on Foreign Relations, November, 2020, https://cdn.cfr.org/sites/default/files/report_pdf/csr89_final.pdf.

6. William J. Burns and Linda Thomas-Greenfield, *The Transformation of*

Diplomacy. The Transformation of Diplomacy, Carnegie Endowment for International Peace, September 23, 2020, https://carnegieendowment.org /2020/09/23/transformation-of-diplomacy-pub-82766, Task Force, *Transforming State: Pathways to a More Just, Equitable, and Innovative Institution*, Truman Center, March 2021, http://trumancenter.org/wp-content/uploads /2021/03/Truman-Center-Task-Force-Transforming-State-Final.pdfSSHOMAS.

7. Foreign Service Act of 1980, PUBLIC LAW 96–465—OCT. 17, 1980, https://www .govinfo.gov/content/pkg/STATUTE-94/pdf/STATUTE-94-Pg2071.pdf.

8. Marc Grossman and Marcie Ries, *Blueprints for a More Modern US Diplomatic Service*, Arizona State University, 2022, https://www.academyofdiplomacy .org/wp-content/uploads/2022/09/American-Diplomacy-Project-2-pdf.

9. Ian Smith, *Confirmation Process of Political Appointees Now Takes Longer Than Ever*, FedSmith, January 22, 2020, https://www.fedsmith.com/2020/01/22 /confirmation-process-political-appointees-takes-longer-than-ever/

10. State has three personnel system; the Foreign Service, about 13,000, which comprises most of the diplomatic personnel who serve abroad, the Civil Service, about the same who serve mostly domestically, and foreign nationals employed overseas, about 50,000.

11. For example, Federal law requires that after the appointment of a career officer in a presidential appointment, such as an ambassadorship, the officer must either have another assignment in 90 days or retire. As the Trump Administration appointed almost no career officers to senior level jobs in Washington a great many had to retire as they were replaced or their appointments ended. As a result, the Foreign Service lost approximately twenty five percent of its equivalent to three and four star generals.

12. Private conversation with a senior officer in Personnel.

13. Department of State Office of the Inspector General, *Inspection of the Bureau of South and Central Asian Affairs*, February 2018, https://www.stateoig.gov /system/files/isp-i-18–11.pdf.

14. Private conversation with senior State official, 2021.

15. The Academy has recommended strengthening the DG's position. See American Academy of Diplomacy, *American Diplomacy at Risk*, April 2015 https://www.academyofdiplomacy.org/wp-content/uploads/2016/01/ADAR _Full_Report_4.1.15.pdf.

16. American Academy of Diplomacy, *Strengthening the Department of State*, May, 2019 https://www.academyofdiplomacy.org/wp-content/uploads/2021/01 /AADStrengtheningState.pdf; *American Diplomacy at Risk*, April, 2015, https://www.academyofdiplomacy.org/wp-content/uploads/2021/01/AAD StrengtheningState.pdf; -content/uploads/2015/12/Diplomacy_in_a_Time _of_Scarcity.pdf, with the Stimson Center, *Diplomacy in a Time of Scarcity*, October, 2012, https://www.academyofdiplomacy.org/wp, Academy with the

Stimson Center, *Forging a twenty-first-Century Diplomatic Service for the United States through Professional Education and Training*, February, 2011, https://www.academyofdiplomacy.org/wp-content/uploads/2016/01/*Forging -a-twenty-first-Century-Diplomatic-Service*; *A Foreign Affairs Budget for the Future Fixing the Crisis in Diplomatic Readiness*, October 2008, https://www .academyofdiplomacy.org/wp-content/uploads/2015/12/Long_Final_10_22_08 .pdf, David C. Miller Jr., Thomas R. Pickering, and Rand Beers, *Revitalizing State: Closing the Education Gap*, Foreign Service Journal, May, 2021.

17. See Blueprints (note 8) for detailed proposals to expand the training complement and protect it from misuse in the future.

18. Rome Statute of the International Criminal Court, 2002, https://www.icc-cpi .int/resource-library/documents/rs-eng.pdf.

19. The Convention on the Prohibition of the Use, Stockpiling, Production and Transfer of Anti-Personnel Mines and on their Destruction, September 18, 1997. https://treaties.un.org/Pages/ViewDetails.aspx?src=IND&mtdsg_no =XXVI-5&chapter=26&clang=_en.

20. United Nations Convention on the Law of the Sea, 1982, https://www.un.org /depts/los/convention_agreements/texts/unclos/unclos_e.pdf.

21. Vladimir Socor, *The Minsk Group: Karabakh War's Diplomatic Casualty*, Eurasia Daily Monitor, November 25, 2020, https://jamestown.org/program /the-minsk-group-karabakh-wars-diplomatic-casualty-part-one/

22. Colin Dwyer, *The TPP Is Dead. Long Live The Trans-Pacific Trade Deal*, NPR Nov. 8, 2018, https://www.npr.org/sections/thetwo-way/2018/03/08/591549744 /the-tpp-is-dead-long-live-the-trans-pacific-trade-deal.

23. Mathew P Goodman, *From TPP to CPTPP*, Center for Strategic and International Studies, March 8, 2018, https://www.csis.org/analysis/tpp-cptpp.

24. See David Dollar, The AIIB and the 'One Belt, One Road', Brookings, Summer 2015, https://www.brookings.edu/opinions/the-aiib-and-the-one-belt-one -road/

25. Op cit, *Strengthening American Diplomacy*, chapter II.

26. Jo Ellen Powell, *Bringing America's Multilateral Diplomacy into the twenty-first Century,* The American Academy of Diplomacy, February 2022, https:// www.academyofdiplomacy.org/wp-content/uploads/2022/03/Bringing -Americas-Multilateral-Diplomacy-into-the-twenty-first-Century-FINAL.pdf.

27. On example of new efforts at strengthening our Pacific alliances is the launch of on informal grouping of the United States, Australia, Japan, New Zealand and the United Kingdom aimed at boosting economic and diplomatic ties with Pacific island nations. See Jarrett Renshaw, US, Japan, Australia, New Zealand and United Kingdom form Pacific group, Reuters, June 24, 2022, https://www.reuters.com/world/us-japan-australia-new-zealand-united -kingdom-form-pacific-group-2022–06–25/

28. Elbridge Colby, Allied Interests, *The National Interest*, May/June 2021.

29. Quoted in Robert B. Zoellick, *America in the World, A History of US Diplomacy ad Foreign Policy*, page 182, Twelve, Hachette Book Group, 2020.

30. Remarks by President Biden on the Way Forward in Afghanistan, April 14, 2021 https://www.whitehouse.gov/briefing-room/speeches-remarks/2021/04/14 /remarks-by-president-biden-on-the-way-forward-in-afghanistan/.

31. William Colby with James McCargar, Lost Victory, A Firsthand Account of America's Sixteen-Year involvement in Vietnam, Contemporary Books, 1989, pg. 75.

32. Colby, op cit, pg. 13.

33. The review is described extensively in Bob Woodward, *Obama's Wars*, Simon & Schuster, 2010.

34. Private conversation of the author, reflected *in Failed Relations between Hamid Karzai and the United States: What Can We Learn?*, USIP, May, 2015, https://www.usip.org/publications/2015/05/failed-relations-between-hamid -karzai-and-united-states-what-can-we-learn.

35. President Obama's Memorandum for the Principals, transmitted from the National Security Adviser but generally considered to be penned largely by Obama himself. It is reproduced in Woodward, op cit, page 385.

36. Ten policies in 20 years; my analysis. 1. Invasion, light footprint. 2. Later Bush years, a substantial effort at state establishment. 3. Obama early 2009, troop reinforcement of 17,000 and start withdrawal by 2011. 4. Obama policy of fall 2009 to further increase troops, major expansion of Afghan security forces (ASF), and economic aid. 5. Obama decision to turn all fighting over to the Afghanis by 2013 which had not been a factor in any of the decisions about how to expand the ASF. 6. Obama decision in 2014 to cease air support for the ASF, saying "we are not at war with the Taliban" (quoted to me directly by a senior NSC official)) and withdraw all but 1,000 troops by the end of 2016. 7. Facing failure in 2016 Obama halted the troop withdrawal and resumed air support for ASF. 8. Trump policy review of only conditions-based withdrawal and pressure on Pakistan. 9. Trump withdrawal deal with the Taliban and gives up on conditions-based approach, accelerating withdrawal ahead of conditions. 10. Biden decision to withdraw all troops by 9/11/2021 but continue diplomatic and other support.

37. H.R.4418—Omnibus Diplomatic Security and Antiterrorism Act of 1986, https://www.congress.gov/bill/99th-congress/house-bill/4418.

38. Greg Starr and Ronald E. Neumann, Diplomacy Requires Taking Some Risks to Fulfill the Mission, *The Hill*, January 17, 2021, https://thehill.com/opinion /national-security/534399-diplomacy-requires-taking-some-risks-to-fulfill -the-mission.

39. Academy, Changing the Risk Paradigm for US /Diplomats, January 2021

https://www.academyofdiplomacy.org/publication/changing-risk-paradigm
-for-diplomats/

40. Op cit, American Diplomacy at Risk, Ryan M. Scoville. *Unqualified Ambassadors*, Duke Law Journal, 2019 https://scholarship.law.duke.edu/cgi/view
content.cgi?article=3991&context=dlj, Dennis C Jett, *American Ambassadors The Past, Present, and Future of America's Diplomats*, 2014, Palgrave
Macmillan.

41. Foreign Service Act of 1980, 22 USC Ch. 52: FOREIGN SERVICE, https://uscode
.house.gov/view.xhtml?path=/prelim@title22/chapter52&edition=prelim.

42. Op cit, Diplomacy at Risk, page 15.

43. Kennan, op cit.

ELEVEN

THOMAS PICKERING

A Prescription to Heal US Diplomacy in the Twenty-First Century

An ancient and arcane subject, still more of an art than a craft, diplomacy has become increasingly dominant in international and national thinking and activity. This is in part due to the failure to solve world problems through military action, especially by the United States. Military efforts to influence events in Iraq and Afghanistan as a substitute for diplomacy failed, It would be better to try diplomacy first, backed up as possible by military actions for leverage.

This chapter looks at this challenging subject from three perspectives or through three lenses:

The first section is those overarching issues which color and in part determine state attitudes toward policy. They set for some states an ideological construct of how to look at preserving interests in foreign affairs. They include such topics as global or world order, the militarization of diplomacy, the tension between domestic and foreign affairs, concepts of sovereignty and war-making in self-defense and the pursuit of wars of choice.

The second section is devoted to current high-profile foreign policy challenges—a description of the controversies and some thoughts on ways forward in diplomacy to deal with them. The topics include arms control and disarmament, particularly regarding nuclear weapons; non-proliferation; the Covid pandemic; global economic developments; dealing with China and Russia' and conflicts in the developing world.

The third section examines to the structure, organization and staffing of US diplomacy and what might be improved and reformed. The discussion touches on the foreign service and civil service, structure and effectiveness of the State Department and relations with the White House, the skills of diplomacy, the emerging role of technology and science and new fields of foreign affairs, multilateralism and the need to treat diversity more considerately and carefully.

State Views on Foreign Policy

Academic study and principled research have developed both theories of international relations and a set of ideas and parameters which are believed to influence or even pre-determine the outcomes of the application of force and persuasion in their resolution. In this regard, the definition of diplomacy as the art of solving international problems through the cooperation of states and international organizations leaves a broad area open for careful consideration. While war and the use of force describe processes, much of their application is devoted to inter-state and now increasingly intra-state differences over everything from boundary and territorial disputes to ideological, economic and political differences. Similar differences exist in the economic and social areas. They are the daily grist for the grinding of diplomatic mills around the globe. They constitute a mega-challenge to all diplomacy.

Above and behind them are transcendental and philosophical approaches which in one way or another impact thinking about these issues, often subliminally and politically. In many cases these are not considered to be central to the work of diplomacy, but which ineluctably influence considerations of policy approaches and choices and as a result, success or failure. Often large scale and all encompassing, sometimes value-connected, and at times considered to be at the heart of political thinking about approaches to solutions as well as paths to be followed in seeking outcomes—they occupy a kind of stratosphere over and above the process of problem resolution itself.

World Order

The most salient current example is the issue of which systematic and ideological approaches to state organization and action are best equipped to serve the interests of the state and for some states the strength and prosperity of the international community within which those states operate. The stark choice now competing is what has been termed on one side as the "liberal progressive" order or approach, and on the other "dictatorship or authoritarianism". Much is being written about these approaches and comments are legion. The purpose of this section is not to resolve those differences, but to examine their role and purpose both politically and philosophically. Some commentators divide the liberal progressive order into subdivisions reflecting past and current practices in its pursuit.

The US and China are seen as the respective champions of the two, with US friends and allies and many of the nations of the globe gathered around the former, while China, a few of its near neighbors like North Korea and Russia, and perhaps Iran are closer to the latter vision. Arguments on each side have been developed and ran the gamut between what is efficient and most effective to what is fair and equitable. Short term and long-term considerations also play a role with many seeing the more dictatorial approach better equipped to serve meeting short term targets and goals and the liberal order better suited to dealing with states which have democratic objectives and a variety of ideas about solutions, a set of objectives and longer-term preoccupations.

Resolution of this ideological and institutional conflict will not be easy. The fact that public preferences generally align with freedom, equality and justice in the liberal order in, and the alignment of more states with what was called the "free world" during the Cold War, provides added opportunities for the creation of a more solid, self-correcting and self-perpetuating alternative to autocratically-dominated relations. The latter is characterized by leadership differences, authoritarianism and a willingness to make submission to such an order the basis for organizing the international community. But it does mean that the liberal order needs open and participatory leadership not dominance and diktat if it is to survive and prosper.

Militarization of Foreign Policy

The international community, largely led by the US, has been through a multi-decade period of attempting to resolve diplomatic differences through military intervention. It began with the Korean War launched by the Democratic People's Republic of Korea's (DPRK), commonly known as North Korea, blessed by the Soviet Union and aided and abetted by the Peoples Republic of China when fighting grew close to their Yalu border with the DPRK. The Vietnam, Iraq and Afghanistan wars, with the US taking the initiative, followed as major defining points of this period. The search is now on for an alternative with little promise that harmony between the US and China or with Russia will emerge. Seemingly the larger the states involved and the larger the conflicts become, the more intractable the solution. Smaller, less important countries like Grenada and Panama seem easier to deal with and more likely to produce the political arrangements necessary to resolve battlefield victories. Diplomacy is the major alternative to wars of choice and the use of force to impose a solution. This is not by any means a new conundrum, but the famous question asked of the then Chairman of the Joint Chiefs of Staff, Colin Powell, by Secretary of State Madeleine Albright: "What do you have this magnificent military force for?" epitomizes the rationale for engaging in such a use of force. The failure after 20 years of military engagement to achieve a political solution after every military conflict and to do so to US satisfaction is part of the answer to the disutility of this approach.

These differences extend further. The United Nations Charter prescribes only two approaches legally to go to war. The first approach, self-defense, is the simplest and seen in the past as obvious and self-evident when it occurs. It is allowed practically without any test of why and how it is being used by the state claiming the right to do use force in response to an attack on it. Recently however, claims for pre-emptive rights to conflict on such grounds, or preventative rights to do so, have muddied the waters and left open room for debate about the definition of self-defense. Both pre-emptive steps to conflict and preventative justifications for the same, cloud the differences between self-defense, on the one hand, and wars of choice, on the other. These make for both legal and political confusion and turmoil in the international community and as a result have helped to promote both intra-state and inter-state conflict and inhibited the task of the international community to attempt diplomatic resolution of those disputes.

The second approach contained in Article 42 of Chapter VII of the UN Charter deals with a UN Security Council authorization of the use of force and has been applied in a very few circumstances. The US (Iraq, 2003) among others which include Russia (Ukraine and Georgia) and China (Vietnam) have ignored the mandatory language of the Charter or otherwise claimed self-defense to use force in such circumstances.

Legally, under international law there is a dispute about wars of choice with a number of states ignoring the need for UN Security Council action. But clouded areas, even with a strict interpretation of the UN Charter, remain. The UN Charter authorizes the use of force in self-defense. It is entirely up to the state concerned to decide it has and can use that authority in Article 52 of the Charter. Traditionally, before 9/11, the US had a tight definition of when to use force in self-defense—solid evidence that an attack had taken place against the country being defended. Since then, discussion of preventive and pre-emptive bases for self-defense have raised uncertainties in making choices about self-defense.

In 1990 at the United Nations, the US used a series of a dozen resolutions leading up to authorization for use of force to counter the Iraqi invasion of Kuwait on August 1, 1990. This served two purposes: exhausting the use of sanctions and other remedies before turning to a war of choice and secondly, preparing the members of the Council for their responsibility to use force only when other methods under the UN Charter had failed. The dozen resolutions included a demand for Iraq to withdraw, the imposition of wide-ranging sanctions against its failure to do so and individual steps designed to thwart any international cooperation with on-going Iraqi activities to absorb Kuwait as its nineteenth province.

The three western permanent members of the UN Security Council—Britain, France and the US—took the lead.[1] Daily US and UK consultations in the early morning set the plans for the day. The strategy led by the US was not to let a day pass when the Council in one form or another was not dealing with the Iraqi invasion. Once a resolution had moved to the vote, or even before, the three coordinated on a text for the next step. Saddam Hussein never failed to provide a reason for a follow-on resolution. Once the three had agreed on a text, it was taken to a meeting of the permanent five members of the Council. That process had been set up for other purposes at UK initiative a year before the Iraqi invasion but readily served the new purpose. There was a monthly rotating presidency of the group among the five and Russia and China cooperated in holding meetings and ironing out differences over text which were, more often than not, small and easy to do. The UK and France worked both their own capitals and through them in Washington to provide support for early US agreement.

The next step, a resolution assembly line process, was for the P-5 to take the text to the non-aligned members of the Council -usually 7 members, which was sufficient if they stayed together to block passage of a text—a potential sixth veto. The meeting was held at the UN in a room devoted to informal Council meetings and provided with very limited UN staff and interpreters. Of the P-5, we always had four members in addition to the Western three, that was always Russia. The non-aligned grew used to the idea that if Russia came to the meeting, then China had agreed to support the resolution. China preferred in its low-key posture not to push the non-aligned. Usually, agreement was quick and the four permanent members accepted on the spot all changes. Where the non-aligned wanted to refer the text to their capitals, it was usually accomplished overnight or in a few days. The text was then officially distributed and printed in "blue" ink which meant it would be voted on within roughly one-day.

On one occasion, China objected to a text it claimed authorized the use of force. To resolve the problem, I was able to arrange that China would speak during the explanation of its vote after everyone else and explain, without objection from others, it did not consider its abstention vote on the resolution as allowing for the authorization of the use of force. The President of the Security Council arranged the speaker's list so no one spoke after China and its interpretation went unchallenged. In other words, the use of diplomacy in this case meant allowing China to offer an interpretation of the text of a resolution that was not challenged by the other powers.

Another use of force, nuclear deterrence, occupies a special place in thinking about conflict. Deterrence has been used to justify the possession of nuclear weapons frequently linked to defining their sole purpose as preventing the use of such weapons by another state. Coupled with two other significant conclusions, the issue remains unresolved and perhaps even more dangerous today than it has been in the past—Presidents Biden and Putin recently re-agreed to what Presidents Gorbachev and Reagan jointly articulated years ago—"Nuclear war cannot be won and must never be fought". We too should keep in mind that despite many intensive efforts, there is no convincing argument that once a nuclear exchange has begun that we have a clear way of stopping it. The inability to stop nuclear war once begun makes imperative both the continued efforts through prevention, reduction and other steps to make more stable and unlikely any nuclear use and to seek to define what might be feasible conditions for the elimination of such weapons globally.

Nuclear war is the most tragic and destructive use of war and cannot be separated from conventional conflict. It is important to note that any war can begin conventionally, but end with nuclear exchanges, war.

So far, our experience with unfinished long wars has raised again the need to use diplomacy to stop the use of force by choice, support predictable and effective deterrence to the degree possible and end as soon as possible any conflicts which breakout to save human life, spare us from humanitarian disasters and prevent escalation.

Military force alone as a solution has failed. Instead, there is always, as noted above, at the end of conflict a political solution. In the case of Afghanistan, many of us sought an early effort at a negotiated outcome prior to the use of military force knowing that this is the most advantageous period for such a dialogue. The US military resisted our efforts and wanted further to improve the military balance in their favor before opening negotiations. They ignored however that to engage to resolve a conflict you need a long effort to begin; that to be successful in negotiations you have to be able to improve your military position as negotiations proceed not just create a favorable status quo; and that the absence of diplomatic communications means you have yielded much situational dominance to your opponents in a key area—determining a favorable political outcome. Pure force used to bring pressure to collapse the will of the opposing side may be theoretically possible but in the world of asymmetrical and popular war loses salience. We have rarely been able to achieve resounding success in crushing the will of an opposing side through military dominance alone. While diplomacy never guarantees success, its continuation always presents an alternative to either having to expand the use of force or back away from the process entirely. Late comers to negotiation, as in Vietnam and Afghanistan, pay more and risk more. Failure to harmonize military thinking with diplomatic experience has served to lose more for the United States than perhaps any state in history. We have consistently forgotten the lessons of previous conflicts; ignored the post- World War II maxim—"No land Wars in Asia"; and failed to heed the lessons that wars of choice have complex, very often negotiated, exit strategies.

Discord Between Domestic and International Issues

A third set of related issues which provide a framework for considering solutions to diplomatic problems while not prescribing distinct answers are differences over internal issues. There is a view in the US that there is pre-eminence in deciding elections of domestic questions over international considerations. Dictatorships almost by definition are structured to resolve such issues through a decision-making process based on authoritarian principles and most often guided and decided by a single leader at the top of that hierarchy often based on an ideology. In some cases, China perhaps, and less likely Russia, such ideological considerations are relied upon in the decision-making process to provide authoritative "evidence" of the correctness of the decision rendered despite at least some arbitrariness in the confection of and selection of those "principles" from the ideological structure behind the decisions. Such a propensity toward war, or the fear of others of that propensity, plays a malign role in the effort of bringing states together.

Liberal and progressive supporters flatter themselves, and in a number of cases with good reason, that they depend on open and wide-scale debate about such decisions, applying the scientific method and relying on judicial and legal precedents in deciding and acting in an attempt to marry the most effective decision with the fairest and most equitable outcome. Compromise is seen in many of these cases as a responsible approach and wise in finding the best policy or answer to an international challenge. (There is in the United States however a burden attached to the idea of compromise—if you are always right, a view of the US public—why should you be required to recognize the opposing views of the other side as having validity and therefore allowing them to be accommodated in a solution.) This approach builds into negotiations an additional burden to be overcome and an automatic domestic consideration to every foreign policy difference which is resolved by compromise—seemingly almost all of them. Much the same consideration is present in US public thinking about how to deal with the "other side" over such differences. Since they are by US public opinion definition wrong or largely so, any compromise is a mistake and often the mere question of speaking to them is seen as offering too much, too early in the process of seeking resolution.

Both systems thus seem to mix domestic and international issues with clear evidence they understand that a mixture of both is often present. The "inter-mestic" characterization given to such, while it has not erased considerations of domestic and international issue differences, has added a sense of inter-relatedness to them. It has heightened the reality that surgical separation of the two is not easily achieved and the dominance of domestic issues, in the US at least, widely accepted by commentators, is less likely to be true, while a blending of the two exists and is real.

Sovereignty—Snare and Delusion?

Another problem is that encompassed in the Westphalian principle of the absolute equality of sovereign states and the obvious differences of size and strength actually present among them. Even the United Nations, widely influenced by equal sovereignty considerations, recognizes the differences with permanent membership of the 5 victors of the second World War in the Security Council and the awarding of veto rights to them. Behind the scenes the reality is even more stark. Large states with significant economic and military power can mobilize those strengths to do better in both bilateral and multilateral negotiations. The US and Russia, in possession of over 90 percent of the world's nuclear weapons, are seen by others as needing to be treated with care and respect compared to other states, which do not possess such power capabilities.[2]

Sovereignty itself has some of the facets of a snare and delusion. While absolute equality is presented as a basis for international relations, particularly conservatives in the United States do not see things that way/ They have had strong influence in reducing US participation in treaty ratification by stalling or blocking Senatorial advice and consent to that process. They often argue that the US could have and should have negotiated a "better deal" and in any case should be free to exit any international obligation any time it wishes, despite the attention paid to observing international law in the US constitution.

Keeping Treaties

Sovereignty is a word the extended meanings of which go so far as to incorporate the idea that the state and its actions cannot be questioned and as a result those with the power to do so can act as they choose. Reconciling that approach with international law and the creation of treaties raises problems for some whose views support an extreme interpretation of sovereignty. That include actions such as the US unilateral withdrawal from the Joint Comprehensive Program of Action (JCPOA) negotiated between Iran and seven other parties in 2015 and from which the Trump Administration took the action of nullifying US participation in May of 2018. The agreement, an executive agreement in US terms, limited Iran's nuclear program in ways to prevent development of a nuclear weapon in less than a year and provided for extensive inspection and monitoring in return for relaxation of economic and other sanctions against Iran. There were a number of arguments deployed by Trump to justify this, including some connected to treaty ratification in the United States. The Obama Administration treated the arrangement as an Executive Agreement and those in favor of US unilateral withdrawal claimed it had relevance only for the administration which concluded it as a "political" agreement. International law makes and accepts no such distinctions in the binding character of an international arrangement which is permanent and complete unless the agreement itself contains a mutually agreed limitations such as a withdrawal clause. The latter, usual in many agreements, allows for the withdrawal of a state party often under defined conditions including when notice must be given and then how much time must elapse before withdrawal becomes effective. Since the JCPOA agreement contained no clause permitting withdrawal, the step of withdrawing was seen by other parties, particularly Iran, as a violation of the arrangement and freed them to act as no longer bound by the agreement. Differences over sovereignty and its precise definition and application have fueled international disagreements, allow uncertainties to be exploited for narrow advantage, and often buttressed the idea that 'might makes right'. Both the claim that treaties can be nullified unilaterally and that states have the power to do so are advanced. This adds to uncertainties and disputes in international diplomacy which do little to enhance peace and break a major maxim of international law—*pacta sunt servanda*—that treaties must be kept.

The Conflict Between Interference in Internal Affairs and The Right of Self- Determination

The UN Charter's prohibition against interference in the internal affairs of states (UN Charter, Article 2.7) and the support of the organization for self-determination also presents controversy. The issue is further complicated by the need to deal with states which are unable or unwilling to protect their own population from pressure or use of force against them bordering on genocide and the concern of the world community about the need in such cases to act in concert against such actions.

As in the case of the break-up of former Yugoslavia, the differences turned on the fact that direct, forceful intervention violates sovereignty and the UN Charter and the failure to do so permits steps which are morally and internationally offensive and illegal.

R2P: A Bridge Too Far or Not Far Enough?

This led to adoption a decade or more ago of the view that outside states could so act—the "Responsibility to Protect" (R2P)—as long as it was a situation of genocide or other crimes against humanity. Subsequently, as consideration of the issue advanced, some states became concerned that R2P might open an opportunity to use force against them to re-establish colonial domination or intervene in their internal affairs instead of merely protecting vulnerable populations. The current resolution of the problem is to fall back on the UN Security Council and provide that R2P can become operative authorizing the use of force only when the Council decides to invoke the use of force under Chapter VII of the UN Charter. This latter has been rarely done under any circumstances and given the deep differences over the application by the Council of the use of force among the permanent members holding the veto—principally China and Russia on one side and Britain, France and the United States on the other—this is unlikely to produce widespread use of R2P to protect the public from state-sponsored abuse—leaving as yet unsettled another important issue for the world community.

The issues discussed in this chapter are not meant to be an exhaustive list, but rather an example of such issues that run the gamut from the serious and hard to resolve to the slightly less serious but equally hard to reconcile. States engage in them, often picking and choosing a position which seems most likely to support an important position they might care to take to deal with a current, emergent and important problem. Some, such as the future form of world order between the liberal and authoritarian approach, will be with us for some considerable time, even though we might have come close to a clearer answer in the period of the early 1990s following the collapse of communism in the then Soviet Union. Others relate to questions which could and should be discussed in any future reform of the United Nations. That is now not likely to take place with any alacrity given the increasing polarization of views in the organization, particularly among the principal UNSC veto-wielders—China, Russia and the United States. Failure to resolve them does little to enhance the future of diplomacy or indeed the ambition to make progress in a post post-Cold War era. They provide a clouded and unresolved coterie of background issues with which to contend even as current demands and requirements for solutions increase.

Diplomacy: A Current Menu of Challenges

The massive destructive power of nuclear weapons provides a paramount challenge to diplomacy. Specifically, what to do about and with nuclear weapons is an existential issue and threat and needs major attention. While there are many such questions—nuclear proliferation in Iran and North Korea and efforts to reduce and stabilize the nuclear equation, particularly between the United States and Russia, with a growing interest in including China, are pre-eminent.

Nuclear Weapons: The Threat That Keeps on Giving

The early agreement between the Biden Administration and Putin's Russia to extend the New Start agreement in 2021, as provided for in its terms for an additional five years, marked a shift away from the Trump Administration policy of successively abandoning previous arms control arrangements.[3] The June 16, 2021 bilateral Summit meeting between the two leaders in Geneva marked the agreement of both sides to begin a further series of strategic stability conversations within which it is assumed the questions of additional steps to improve nuclear stability could and ought to play an important role.

While exact steps have not been agreed or even outlined by the two sides, past proposals have included an Obama administration suggestion that a further reduction of deliverable nuclear weapons numbers from 1550 on a side to 1000, or perhaps even 900, should be considered. Some have suggested as well that the 5000 to 6000 total nuclear weapons holdings by both sides, which include both weapons already subject to reductions and so-called reserve weapons might also be included in the reductions. While New Start verification and monitoring is sufficient for the inspections under the extension, additional work will be needed to assure that further steps also are given the high standard of verification assurance provided under New Start.

New technology for delivery vehicles now presents a new challenge. Both the US and Russia, in addition to proposing to spend large sums on nuclear weapons modernization, have also announced continuing work on hyper sonic glide vehicles, space conflict, nuclear propelled delivery vehicles, anti-satellite weapons and new Anti-Ballistic Missile (ABM) interceptors among others. The disparity between reduction and build up has probably never been as great or as pervasive since the Kennedy administration which can only be dealt with using special efforts and innovative thinking. Coupled with the disappearance of the INF treaty, the earlier cancellation of the ABM treaty, the withdrawal from Open Skies, the nuclear weapons and associated arms control challenges are as large and dangerous as we have seen for a number of decades. The INF Treaty (Dec 1987) blocked the deployment by Russia and the US of ground-based missiles in Europe (with a range of 500 to 1000 kilometers). The US withdrew in August 2019. The ABM Treaty (May 1972) provided for ballistic missile defense by the US and Russia of no more than 100 interceptors at a single defended site; the US withdrew in June 2002) The Open Skies Treaty (June

2002) provided for the parties to engage in aerial surveillance over the territory of other parties to provide for great nuclear stability and predictability from which the US withdrew in Nov 2020.

The Biden administration, facing perhaps the largest assembly of significant problems at home and abroad as any new American administration, has worked hard and intelligently to sort out its priorities and organize its efforts. But entering into complex talks with Russia and the slow confirmation of newly appointed officials by the Senate Foreign Relations Committee is not moving a demanding process forward.

The Trump administration made a major effort to include China in the nuclear disarmament effort even as it sought to dismantle and junk that effort widely. China has resisted the notion it might join and the Biden administration, while appearing to recognize the long term need to include China and perhaps others in the nuclear disarmament efforts, particularly regarding land based intermediate range missiles in the East Asian region, has proceeded slowly and carefully.

An early effort on the part of the US and Russia, separately and confidentially, to keep China briefed on their strategic stability discussions would be a useful way of beginning to inform China and of building a case for later inclusion. In the meantime, China is, according to press reports, thought to be building toward about 300 deliverable nuclear weapons, something well short of the 1000 or 900 in the next stage of US Russia consideration, but not so inconsequential as totally to exclude China. Recent reports based on commercially available satellite photography show China constructing over 100 missile silos in each of two remote desert areas of Gansu and Xinkiang provinces.

Similarly, tactical nuclear weapons have not been included in US and Russia discussions. Russia clearly depends on them for defense of its long border with China. The US commitment to extended deterrence for its allies in Europe and Asia also comprehends depending on dealing with such weapons. One suggestion is to encompass in a global maximum figure all holdings of deliverable weapons, both tactical and strategic, and let the parties individually describe the mix they prefer. That could be a step forward with the flexibility to meet the varying needs of the parties. Further down the road, separation of warheads from delivery vehicles might increase stability. Others have suggested wider acceptance of "no first use" of nuclear weapons as an additional basis for stability, as well as establishment of missile limitations and a WMD free zone in the Middle East or the Gulf, both issues that have key problems based around the limitations to be imposed and the necessary parties to participate to give assurance of balance and stability.

The pre-eminence of this topic in the listing above is based in part on the capacity of nuclear weapons for mass destruction and the current state of only partial or minimal control over their use. The end of the Cold War marked a period of new optimism about controlling nuclear conflict— the threat it seemed had disappeared—which tended to put it on the back burner from which it has not re-emerged. This threat must be addressed. The tendency to see the nuclear danger has passed, at the same time to treat those weapons as if there were just somewhat larger versions of conventional arms. To spend in the future large sums on "modernizing" them also creates dangers. At the same time, to renew threats of use as an ostensible way to enhance deterrence while pulling down the admittedly inadequate structure we had built for nuclear stability during the Cold War, have all presented additional challenges and require new concentrated diplomatic action and thinking.

Non-Proliferation: Nukes for Kooks

The sub-title above may be doing a severe injustice to Iran, if not to North Korea (DPRK). However, it is meant not to characterize the states involved, but to emphasize the thinking behind non-proliferation. That is fairly simple. The more states that possess nuclear weapons, the greater the statistical chances are for the use of nuclear weapons in war. The greater the chances are for use, the greater the chances are that such use becomes widespread and the harder it is to end such use. The obvious conclusion is that no further states should have such weapons. We should seek by determined diplomatic action to reduce and eliminate such weapons, blocking the acquisition by more states and reducing and eliminating those previously acquired.

Two immediate problems pre-occupy us now. Iran, which has a significant nuclear program and has declared itself against acquiring nuclear weapons but has sought to expand its nuclear program in response to the unwise Trump violation of the arrangement—Joint Comprehensive Program of Action (JCPOA). Iran agreed to restrict its nuclear program. It now seeks to respond to pressure from the Trump administration and the continuation of it by Biden, by expanding its nuclear program while also re-establishing the JCPOA. Negotiations are proceeding indirectly between Iran and the US, the two of the seven parties who are no longer abiding by the terms of the agreement, facilitated by the European and other partners. Progress has been made but there appear to be at least four important issues to be resolved: For Iran—US "guarantees" that it will not withdraw from the JCPOA again; a request that all nearly 1600 Trump era sanctions passed after US withdrawal be removed; For the US—requests for the destruction of new model Iranian centrifuges; and a requirement that Iran agree now to follow-on talks for further nuclear steps and associated other limitations on missiles and related vehicles. Whether and when the return to the JCPOA on an intended compliance-for-compliance basis will take place is both unknown but hopefully close.

The US and the other parties intend to follow return to the JCPOA with further negotiations aimed in the first instance at closing loopholes in it on the timing of "sunset" provisions and access by the International Atomic Energy Agency (IAEA) for UN inspection purposes to certain Iranian sites where it is now restricted by Iran. Such further negotiations are also considered likely to involve missile delivery and other such vehicles on a regional basis; Iranian and other support for non-state-actor militias such as Hizbollah; Iranian civil and human rights treatment of its own citizens; and the important issue of providing a regional security balance and stability in the Gulf and Middle East.

Secondly, less likely of success and more challenging is dealing with North Korea which has tested nuclear weapons and acquired an estimated 20 to 40 of them. The previous US administration made an effort at holding three summit meetings between Trump and Kim Jong Un in Singapore, Hanoi and Panmunjom to achieve a denuclearized DPRK or at least some real progress toward that goal. Grand bargains are hard to put together, particularly when each side seeks from the others full concessions while retaining some of its own, and the efforts of the Trump administration were unsuccessful in achieving a denuclearized DPRK.

China, which borders the DPRK along the Yalu River plays an important role. China is influenced in its approach of supporting Kim jong Un by seeing the DPRK as a helpful border barrier keeping both Republic of Korea and US forces at bay below the 38th parallel while at the same time supporting Kim to avoid any incursion of Korean refugees into Northeast China and losing a major role in the management of the issue in its own interests. The US, South Korea (RoK) and Japan are necessary for a positive conclusion but not sufficient. The DPRK seeks elimination of all sanctions against it, a peace treaty for the Korean War, energy support and reassurance of its continuation in control for which it is unlikely to agree to complete denuclearization of the peninsula to say nothing of uniting the two Koreas on terms which do not preserve the DPRK in full.

President Biden has appointed an experienced and capable negotiator, started a re-examination of the issue and more than likely will move toward a process of step-by-step progress, perhaps with an early freeze of some or all of Pyongyang's nuclear activities at Yongbyon, a center for plutonium production and uranium enrichment. The more likely outcome is a long and drawn-out negotiating effort with little promise of success. A change in Chinese and Russian views would be a help, but the state of distrust between these two and the US is such that it is unlikely to be part of any mix. Both China and Russia appear prepared to live next to a nuclear armed DPRK perhaps counting on their own capacities to prevent thoughtless or radical nuclear decisions there as a better bet than seeing change which might lead to the DPRK's disappearance and a united peninsula dominated as they fear by Seoul and Washington.

The Pandemic from Hell

The world was ill-prepared for an unexpected onslaught of a deadly pandemic the origins of which are unclear and still disputed. Close ties to a zoonotic event and focused work on producing vaccines offset international unpreparedness and weak organization at the World Health Organization and similar circumstances in most states with a few rare exceptions. The US had disbanded all previous preparations in terms of strategy and institutional preparation for dealing with a pandemic; the Trump administration denied its potency and spread—and failed to organize successful efforts in health practices—masking and separation—in hospital care and preparation; inadequate therapy, coming late to the use of monoclonal antibodies; and was hindered by the complexity of devising, developing and distributing vaccines.

While vaccines were rapidly developed, early efforts by wealthy states which could produce them, to monopolize supply in their own country and denial by other producers of exports to the developing world, left small and poor states without a supply. International cooperation in vaccine development to poor states under the GAVI organization was quickly extended to Covid vaccine under a Covax initiative. GAVI is an international organization founded in part by the Gates Foundation to provide vaccines to states with per capita income levels according to World Bank statistics below $US 1550 per anum. Covax is an offshoot of GAVI dedicated to insuring the low-income countries receive a useful and fair share of covid-19 vaccine. Initially it provided up to 20 percent of poor state needs. Vaccine shortages complicated the effort and the US and others both released limitations on technology patents for vaccine production and made large contributions—collectively over a billion doses—which met only immediate needs out of the 11 billion estimated requirement for worldwide immunization and the achievement of herd immunity on a widespread basis. Further vaccine use has been stymied by anti-vaxers—spreaders of vaccine hesitancy—using misleading and untrue information, often from the United States where vaccine acceptance has become subject to a high degree of political polarization.

Meanwhile, the virus has not been quiescent. Its capacities to develop new and more infectious and perhaps more rapidly spread variants has been aided and abetted by the time taken both to develop, certify and distribute vaccines to the billions needing them and over time without vaccines likely to be infected and become hosts for the evolution of new variants. The so-called India variant, Variant Delta, has played a large role in spreading the disease and began to raise questions about the adequacy of vaccines. However, most experts conclude the vaccines are capable of preventing serous infection, hospitalizations and death as a result of Variant Delta's and other variant's spread as long as the patients have been vaccinated. Interest has been peaked, in part by big Pharma, in booster shots, obviously further money spinners for them. Current contention around boosters turn on the point that most experts agree administration of boosters now, particularly while large segments of the world's population do not have access to the initial stages of vaccination and based on possibly limited data from a narrow source, is to distort priorities and deny fair and equitable administration which is in the best interest of the world population. The Biden administration is now moving toward providing boosters especially to medically disadvantaged people after 6 to 8 months following a second dose. Study of booster effectiveness should obviously take place as a necessary step before certifying for emergency or regular use and should be done transparently and at the highest standards of certification.

While careless and non-scientific based talk and rumor has convinced temporarily at least a significant percentage of some populations to eschew vaccination, the damage is not limited merely to the vaccine deniers. The fact that they can become hosts to the development of new more lethal variants is ever present and a danger to the world at large. Experts tell us, the longer we refuse vaccination and the larger the group that does so, the higher the chances are of evolving a variant which may well require complete development of a new vaccine rather than the administration of booster shots. This would be another serious setback in the battle to save lives and the return of people, economies and social structures to the kind of normal to which we had become used and now hope to re-establish.

The US and World Economy: Debilitation and Recovery

Much has been and will be written on this important subject. There are few simple answers. It is clear that the pandemic had a very large negative impact on economic activity including growth; on employment; investment; trade and state incomes—all of which were linked to steps taken to practice good health measures to stop the spread of the Covid-19 virus and its emerging variants—masking, social distancing, lock downs, and self-isolation. The early emergence of effective vaccines has helped the turnaround, as well as in some states like the United States able to afford it, of infusions of funds to areas hardest hit and less able rapidly to rebuild. Time will tell whether the lessons learned in the recovery are relevant and repeatable or misguided and misconceived. The current betting is on the former conclusions and this is a bright spot, but there is still a long distance to go in the US and elsewhere. Less fortunate countries will suffer economic impacts and declines longer and require more assistance from donors, international organizations and humanitarian agencies.

One test will be whether recovery is differential favoring the wealthy states and classes over the poor and disadvantaged and the effect that will have on global recovery as a whole. Under constraints of stress, the globe seems destined to turn to 'me first' and 'local self-interest' strategies, forgetting that we are increasingly bound together—economically and socially in particular—and what happens in one country or region will impact others on supply and demand. This effects trade as a whole and the centrality of supply chains which in a competitive world economy should favor lowest costs of production of competitive products rather become than artifacts protected by high costs and unable without distorting subsidies to survive in an open trading globe. That battle will go on for a long time. So far, with some exceptions, the new US administration seems tilted toward a more open global trading relationship rather than a narrow, protected economy subventioned by subsidies and sourced often to those least able to pay the taxes required to keep it going. But US labor is not fully reconciled to the need to compete, and to retrain and re-equip unemployed workers for the new, not the old challenges. The US share of world manufacturing is down, but its continued dominance of the information economy and its future development is healthy and strong. Can we use the willingness to bring funding to the answer to the pandemic problem to build a changing and new economy fit for the next decades of the twenty-first century? Can we afford not to do so? And can we find a fair sharing of the tax burden built on our progressive traditions about taxation, rather than free rides for some where capacity to pay and a fair balance to permit continued investment in economic expansion can be considered and be equitably adopted.

This is at first glance often seen as a primarily domestic issue. But once the globe is concerned, particularly around trade, competition, efficiency and opportunity, it becomes international. Trade negotiations are a special realm of diplomacy and require expertise, a careful assessment of what matters to the US economy and growth and innovative answers. I worked for The Boeing Company for 5 and a half years principally in organizing and overseeing its emergence as a global enterprise.

In the production and development of commercial aircraft our principal competitor was and is Airbus. A European government-supported entity, Boeing had deep concerns about subsidization at Airbus where if a new aircraft was developed and failed, the loans from government to help it do so were forgiven. Boeing had to go to the financial market for its money and pay principal and interest as required by the loan agreements whether its new airplane investment succeeded or failed. Boeing took Airbus to the WTO dispute mechanism over the issue. Airbus responded with its own suit on areas where it saw subsidies going to Boeing. Boeing won its suit but lost to Airbus on the latter's initiative. Seventeen years of consideration and appeals failed to end the controversy. Boeing and Airbus have now asked the EU and US government to renegotiate the subsidy issue to assure fair treatment, something I and my colleagues recommended to Boeing after conversations with Airbus some 17 years back.

A relative bright spot on the world horizon, economic recovery in its largest economies shows promise. While China's statistics remain suspect, predictions for the US are optimistic even as there is a resurgence in new Covid cases, especially in red states where vaccination is politicized. The Biden Administration has overall done a better job than Trump. Nevertheless, inability or failure to influence positive attitudes toward vaccination and to meet 70 percent vaccination targets is likely to have its own negative drag on economic recovery despite anticipated recovery figures hinged around 7 percent growth rates. Such figures are unusually high for a large economy like the US and one where there are local-level failures to meet essential vaccination needs. World recovery is likely to be slower, particularly in the developing areas where assistance is necessary and unlikely to be fully forthcoming from the US and China. The linkage with the pandemic and the fight against it remains obvious despite assessments and conclusions which seek further to separate the two in hope that the health crisis can somehow be defeated by larger efforts at economic recovery leaving the health battle to proceed separately and on its own.

China

US assessments of China have gone over two decades from a relationship characterized by differences but within which there was considerable overlap of common interests and cooperation to one where US views on the right have begun anticipating both a continuing cold war and a potential hot one. Military judgments to increase their budgets are part of increasingly shrill warnings. Those who look for a more balanced way forward are perplexed and confused. President Xi has taken on the mantel of an incorrigible autocrat and many of his policies have come to justify conclusions of a catastrophic ilk. China has accepted that widescale US decline is in progress, inevitable and perhaps a permanent condition. It has sewn and is wearing publicly the clothes of historical national greatness which it saw stolen from it during the pre-Communist, war-lord period of the first half of the twentieth century. It has assumed with both endless wars in the Middle East and the semi-naivety of Trumpism, that US decline was general, un-stoppable and likely to be complete—a risky but not unwarranted set of conclusions, with which Biden and his administration will have to work hard to dispel.

US China watchers look at a continuum that runs between acceptance of Middle Kingdom hegemony at one end and US military opposition almost inevitably shaped to enforce a general conflict on the other. These unappetizing and dangerous conclusions have pushed hard for an approach somewhere along the central section of the continuum which can foresee push backs coupled with selective cooperation as being successful short of conflict. The obvious answer is there but defining it and using it is not easy. This is especially true when there is an added requirement to overcome what is seemingly a Chinese misinterpretation of decline in the US and too much of an allocation of success to China in the decades ahead. One approach is to look among the possibilities for some cooperation where we inevitably share a significant sense of common interest and where the importance of the issue is existentially focused for both parties. That occurred with the Soviet Union on the nuclear issue, particularly over time following the Cuban missile crisis.

With China, there have been long standing hopes that state capitalism under communist party direction would and could lead to a political approach where China would fit into the world community as fashioned in large part by the US after the end of the Cold War. Xi, a leader whose abandonment of the 10-year term limit and his seeking after presidency for life, has determined a harder line more nationalist course for his country. However, climate change and China's relative isolation in the international community where the belt and road and related policies seem based on buying not building influence may be two areas of potential common interest worth following up on more closely. Certainly, former Secretary Kerry in his lead on climate change is well aware of the possibilities and China has sown willingness to invest in renewable energy—wind and solar—but is doing much less of the same in rapidly moving away from coal.

The US, to develop a more settled relationship with China, will have to combine in creative and innovative ways progress on the win-win issues such as climate change. This will require a determined firmness on areas where we believe China is over-reaching and seeking to revise a world order where it wishes to protect, control against or fend off US presence and contention in areas such as Taiwan, Hong Kong, the South China Sea and the East Sea islands with Japan.

With Taiwan the current apparent China-US agreement that there will be no use of force to settle differences between Beijing and Taipei and no support for independence on Taiwan unless agreed by both parties is under growing pressure on both sides.

At sea, it has always seemed that the major test should be does China really intend to convert the Law of the Sea Treaty (LOS) to make freedom of navigation a part of an outcome rather than merely a defense of rights. It appears they wish to turn the LOS which insures wide access to high seas of the world into a nine-dashed line national preserve off its east coast. Here too there should be room for communication and discussion based on assuring full and open access by all users to all international air and sea routes in the South China Sea, while contending territorial claims are resolved through diplomacy. US reconnaissance activities on the China coast should be no more nor anything less than we are prepared to see China and Russia exercise on our coasts. We further need to revive and improve the Incidents at Sea arrangements now more observed in the breach.

A few years ago a Republican expert with deep knowledge of China and Mandarin answered my question about what was the most important step we could take to deal with China over the South China Sea by saying "Ratify the Law of the Sea Treaty!". Certainly, we have a common interest in keeping open these sea and air lanes to the traffic of all states as guaranteed in that agreement. China's claims to high sea sovereignty in the nine-dashed line failed in court and within the community of nations to become acceptable international law. The LOS would protect all settled Chinese territorial and economic zone interests and form a basis for a negotiated set of solutions to the territorial disputes in the region. They certainly cannot be settled by adverse occupation and island enlargement. If China were willing to stop temporarily expansion of these rocks and reefs, we should be willing to accept any internationally supported bilateral basis for settlement as recognized in the UN Charter or conventional international law—from bilateral negotiations between contending parties to judicial decision at the International Court of Justice (ICJ) and any method in between. ASEAN members states would have a large role to play in making such a solution possible and the US should be fully behind them in doing so. In the meantime, it would be useful also to have a fisheries agreement for the region to prevent full destruction of the valuable catch which would include all distant water participants in the fishery. That too should be followed by an arrangement that covered hydrocarbon extraction including the adopting for disputed areas of full and equal sharing of the oil and gas offtake among all valid claimants until a final settlement could be negotiated.

Trade as a separate issue with pressures designed to force China to accept US objectives seems to lose sight of several factors of importance. Our negative balance of trade in goods with China is not the only statistical measure of significance. Services play an increasing role in US and world prosperity. China's large but declining holdings of dollar instruments is a countervailing asset to US pressure and not a trivial one. China's poaching on western technology can be best fought by staying ahead of the R and D game in this and other regions as much as seeking weakly policed legal methods of restricting Chinese illegal use. Restricting and protecting trade—in a curious effort to free it and expand it in our favor—seems to belie an understanding of reality.

There is much more required to reach a fair arrangement with China. Indeed, one fundamental question to be resolved is whether both states can agree on that course of action- at least for a series of questions which if not resolved raise questions of an existential nature for both of them. In this regard it would seem best to combine the elements of a cessation of contentious activities with work together on developing a settlement or a modus vivendi with which we could live even if preferred outcomes were not available. That will require careful exercise of diplomacy and effective communication as well as a full understanding of interests and red lines and a testing of what could be achieved through a process which was not ideal but did serve to reduce the risks of use of force in conflict. A solid but sensible defense posture, the ability to push back on areas of disagreement and an exploitation of common interests in assuring mutual survival and prosperity would seem to be a solid basis for such an approach. Resolution of existential issues should help address secondary problems and build currently absent trust as we go forward.

Russia

Putin's Russia is not the Soviet Union and the US is not the unilateral leader of a Cold War coalition against it. These are both conclusions widely forgotten or never clearly learned in Washington and Moscow respectively. They inform a growing sense of contention and opposition which, as in the case of China, has its dangers and potential disasters. (More also on Russia and China below).

Russia's strength lies in its nuclear weapons and delivery systems not in its economy or Russia's political attractiveness to the rest of the world community. Putin's power is widely assured by a system and institutions which serve to promote and prosper that power, but which are heavily based on a nationalist policy lodged in a belief that the US and its allies continue to be arrayed against it in an aggressive attempt to nullify Russian influence in the world, if not fully control it. Putin stands as the bulwark against that fear and his strength grows as he convinces Russians of his success and wanes with failure to do that.

Recent contacts at the Summit in Geneva and an effort to re-establish relations in the diplomatic sphere have begun a process of communication, contact and potentially constructive talk. As president Biden wisely pointed out in his post-Summit press conference, it will be six months before we know whether this combination of seeking areas for cooperation and change and of containing areas of difference can make a shift in relations possible. It will not come as a result of re-labeling; "reset"—is not an attractive option because of past failure. But a selection of strategic stability, cyber and possibly expanding areas of existing interest and cooperation against terrorism and in Central Asia drug trafficking and use to list a few, can be a better basis for the future. Washington and Moscow need to seek to advance a future less fraught with nuclear danger or stymied by a failure to communicate and even more significantly by a failure to understand each other's red lines and objectives.

Putin's international isolation is in part a reaction of the international community to his promotion of Russian nationalism and attempt to intrude, particularly in the area of the former Soviet Union, his political and strategic influence. Overtime, Putin has not paid the same kind of attention to economic prosperity that he has to politics. He has ignored underpinning his interest in being a recognized world player by economic success relying almost solely on strategic and political outreach. That has meant that efforts to split off Western European from American influence have failed; they have raised fear and suspicion in that region rather than a search for harmony and cooperation with Russia—with Germany at times perhaps being an exception.

The Trump Administration was unusual in regard to Russia. Trump's apparent admiration for Putin's *mensch* status hid a willingness to ignore differences over aggression in Crimea and Ukraine, and a sense, not yet proven by fact, that Trump for reasons of Russian *kompromat* and large loans may have had a "special" influence with Trump. All of that was clouded by a relationship which was otherwise dominated by traditional Republican conservative suspicion of and indeed enmity toward Putin and Moscow. At times Trump himself in his public statements adopted a suspicious and negative view toward Russia, if not Putin, but never in Putin's presence or even within his direct hearing. (Trump analysis is a special preserve and could well dominate a book and will occupy only a small portion of this chapter.)

There are solid reasons noted above why the US should seek a balanced relationship with Russia—pushing back hard where differences predominate to seek to assure they do not worsen as a result of inattention or lassitude, and seeking cooperation, especially where we have common existential concerns such as around nuclear weapons and delivery vehicles, thereby hoping to broaden the basis for cooperation. In doing so we have a chance at the same time to make contention of less significance. Opening the door through important cooperation either to trying in areas of contention to reduce mutual harm, or if not, contain and compartment those concerns so they stay within a box which can be watched carefully and be part of an effort to keep them from intruding on areas of potential positive mutual involvement makes sense. Much as I have outlined with China, but based on entirely different existential factors and scale, these similarities and differences are of a scope and purpose that takes into account the distinguishing characteristics between the two relationships. Consistent and regular communication is also important for effective diplomacy.

Many observers are concerned that with the apparent growth over the last two decades of China-Russia cooperation we are headed into a triangular relationship where that cooperation will dominate confrontation with the US and lead to an irreversible loss of US leadership. This is not a trivial concern. But it is worth understanding and analyzing with some care. Central to US leadership is its ability to bring together coalitions and alliances of key players around the globe. Both the two 'endless wars' in the broader Middle East and the role of the George W Bush administration and much more importantly Trump, have undermined an acceptance of the US as the major world player. While some of us never accepted the 'unilateral' moment or period in the 1990s—when the US could operate as it wished with no help from friends—US power and influence predominated around the globe, but declined after 9/11 and the invasion of Iraq, to be won back with major effort and perhaps only in part under President Obama. President Biden faces an even higher hill to climb in that regard.

On the other side of the ledger, Chinese and Russian efforts to gather around them coalitions and allies have not prospered. Their isolation is in part offset by China with the Belt and Road Initiative (BRI) but the terms and conditions of those economic relationships have brought in hardships for the players not easily offset. Russia, at the center of the old Soviet unity has not yet succeeded in rebuilding it, especially around a Moscow centric control. Russian dominance of military technology has opened the door to defense trade with China, but almost always limited to one technical innovation below current Russian superiority. China's manpower along the border has caused Russia to rely on tactical nuclear weapons in addition to its strategic nuclear superiority to offset any weakness in numbers of conventional forces. Neither Russia nor China is ready to cede to the other political leadership of the bilateral partnership and thus in any showdown they are likely to end up more apart than together. None of these is a permanent condition, but none of them is easily overcome. Much of the balance in the relationship depends on how the Biden administration orients and conditions its strategy toward both of them. Giving pre-eminence to China in these concerns is justified by the realities but at the same time losing sight of Russian nuclear strength and capacity is an oversight neither history not reality will forgive lightly. Diplomacy has become even more necessary as military pre-eminence neither assures pre-dominance nor provides ready at hand the political answers to the bedeviling problems which characterize the present complex world relationship around multipolar challenges.

Regular diplomatic exchanges through well-staffed and led Embassies in Beijing and Moscow are a must. Frequent contacts at the highest level through carefully scripted and strategically planned and motivated Summit-level calls and, when valuable, Summit meetings, are a central part of the right process. Building on areas that can reduce conflict and structure common interest in cooperation should be a long-term part of strategy. How one set of bilateral relations is managed against the other is central. The value of good relationships with both sides makes it imperative to keep them open as an objective. Hard reality mitigates against full success. But what must be carefully avoided is the risks of allowing either of the bilateral relationships to descend to the point of open conflict or even an unnecessary break in diplomatic communications, especially at the highest levels.

The relationships, beginning with China, should have a real claim on some of the valuable time of the Head of State. But that too should be balanced in a way that assures that better relationships with one of the two do not inhibit or detract from similar possibilities with the other. Alliances of two against one ought to be avoided but economic, political and social cooperation on key issues such as nuclear weapons and climate change should be seen as a central part of the arena for collective work. Agility, innovation and a serious, continuing effort to repair rents in the fabric of these relationships should be part of the strategy and seen by others to be so. US lead is critical—by example, by mutual respect for allies and friends, by firmness and by exercise of strategic care—no problem allowed to overwhelm, no concern allowed to disappear. It goes without saying that there is a need for well trained, experienced, language and history familiar and competent diplomats to work on a daily basis in Washington and Beijing and Moscow as sources of solid analysis and information to guide and advise on policy. Carefully chosen senior leaders from among them are even more necessary. Both State and the NSC should be the locales for debate, understanding and counsel to the Secretary of State, the National Security Adviser and the President.

The Middle East: Won't Come Along, Won't Go Away

Despite solid efforts to reduce US preoccupation with the Middle East, it has not responded cooperatively. Two decades ago it was dominated by the three "I" word countries—Iran, Iraq and Israel and its neighbors. Now, the list has grown almost exponentially to include Syria, Lebanon, Yemen, Libya, Algeria and Sudan along with others. Gulf state differences between Iran and Saudi Arabia in the lead of the GCC States have overtaken an effort on the part of the United States to look at the strategic threats of China (and perhaps Russia) as pre-eminent, and Asia as the new center of world political and security focus.

President Obama favored a shift of intensity of focus from the Middle East which was eating up US resources and assets toward Asia which he saw as more challenging and requiring more attention. Some of that is taking place under Biden. But there is not a free choice given US allies and friends in the Middle East, their preoccupation and ours with a series of important issues including access to energy. No administration has all the resources it needs to meet a wide panoply of foreign affairs issues and downsizing has its own "rewards" as we have just seen in Afghanistan and are likely to see with regard to Iraq if that endless war is to be eliminated.

Hydrocarbons have declined as a center of the world energy challenge and climate change and renewable energy have grown to push out coal and even oil and gas, with US fracking a new major source for energy. With the post-pandemic period has seen a surge in higher prices and an unwillingness by OPEC to increase production to ease cost increases the energy situation has changed. The Middle East still plays an important if different role than it did in energy three decades ago. Still a necessary source, but less sufficient than it has always been and less needed by the US, although that has been offset by increased dependence by our allies and friends. Strategically those players have become more significant in maintaining both a global balance in favor of a liberal world order and in support of US leadership and aspirations for its own and shared interests.

While dependence has shifted but not decreased, unpredictability and uncertainty have gown. There are no ready-to-hand solutions to the problems in the states listed above. Outside player participation has grown with Russia, to a lesser degree with Europe, and regional leaders such as Iran and Saudi Arabia increasing their roles. The US, in part paying the price for the "unending wars" in Iraq and Afghanistan now is seen as less significant but not indispensable.

We and others have learned some bitter lessons. Military force on its own does not, even with battlefield predominance, lead to a political solution of essentially diplomatic problems. Asymmetrical and hybrid warfare have added to complications. Diplomacy, long neglected and dismissed as too complex and demanding, has returned but with players whose leverage has diminished, understanding drained and patience reduced.

Israel-Palestine has fallen on hard times with right wing resistance to compromise in Israel and fractured and weakened Palestinian leadership divided between al Fateh and Hamas.

Syria badly needs a strategic approach which can treat with the humanitarian crisis, develop future governance acceptable to a majority of Syrians and reflect the interest of the outside players in a solution they can live with. The complexities have defeated the possibilities. The red lines are established too high to see acceptance. Too many related side issues are present—Syrian president Assad's newly found dominance of Syrian affairs on the ground with Russian help; the center of his opposition in the area of Idlib's holding out for a central change in government, Turkey's effort to assure a non-Kurdish control of its border regions; Iran's use of Hizbollah especially to challenge Israel are but a few of the major such complications. US interest has declined at a time when the US has concluded that its chances of effecting change are very low—as indeed are those of others. The unlikelihood of the Sunni Shia and Arab Persian contests leading to a solution on their own or even with US leadership is real.

Yemen has many of the same challenges and an even more disastrous humanitarian situation. Iran and Saudi Arabia should be able to find an answer but have not. The UN which has just changed negotiators struggles for answers and the central and side players appear paralyzed in providing enough essential help to break through the barriers the conflict has thrown up to crossing red lines and providing humanitarian aid.

Libya has two main protagonists and other outliers contesting the future of the small (8.0m population), oil wealthy state. Outside players from Egypt, Turkey, Russia and the US and Europe all have interests but none has a predominant influence. So far, no single coalition of inside and outside players has emerged and none seems likely on the horizon. In the meantime, Libyans continue to pay the price both for foreign interest in their wealth and their own incapacity to bend and blend enough in a solution to get it to hold.

Iran and the US are seeking to return to the Joint Comprehensive Program of Action (discussed briefly above) while so far non-productive but initial talks have begun between Iran and Saudi Arabia which could prove of value in beginning to work toward some balanced agreement on security of the region.

Without a significant change, the region looks condemned to stumble forward with conflicts dominating the outcome and diplomacy relegated to a secondary and not very influential function. The US could change that but bearing the heavy burdens of other preoccupations as already outlined that seems unlikely. Russia could be a major partner but that is unlikely given the zero-sum nature of recent US-Russia relationships and Mr. Putin's apparent tilt toward staying in power by playing a strong Russian nationalist card wherever he can even at the risk of not winning overall but keeping his public supportive with tactical gains and some strategic dominance of an unsettled and potentially unsettling situations .China seems, perhaps very wisely, to have opted out of a central role while building carefully its tactical influence. Turkey, Iran, Saudi Arabia and others, including Europe, have relegated their leverage and influence to a secondary status which in the absence of the US being willing to gather it and Russia unable to do so, seems dispersed and ineffectual. The Middle East has a reputation and capacity for producing conflicts. Conflicts at times have helped the region along to change and stability. The opposite is even more true. It is not too early to be truly worried about such developments, even as the region looks now more stuck in stasis than it is in malign change.

Latin America: Democracy in Distress

We have learned to live with uncertainty, conflict and contention in Latin America and Africa (next). Small wars, coups, and instability have

multiplied even as it looked like the end of the Cold War would bring stability and democracy. Democracy miles wide and a millimeter deep served
to bring only more fragility. Bi-polar political contention, a radicalization
on the fringe from Cuba and Venezuela to Bolivia and for a time Ecuador
added to the uncertainty and disruption. Struggles in Colombia with civil
war and implementing a challenging peace agreement between right and
left mean disruption. Chile has perhaps the best record but even Santiago
went through a period of political dispute. Brazil, long seen as the colos-
sus of the south has not been well served by its swerve to the right under
President Jair Bolsonaro whose Trumpian outlook and tactics left him and
his people badly vulnerable to the virus.

This multiplying uncertainty came at a time when any help under Trump
from the United States to build back better was unavailable, uncertain,
and unknown. While the US long had special interests in the Hemisphere,
its governance and cooperation in the grand days of Franklin Roosevelt
and John Kennedy have not yet reappeared on the Biden platform. Part of
that may be the necessary requirement to prioritize the Western Hemisphere below other needs. But that neither helps to sustain good neighbor-
liness on the one hand or a new-found capacity within the Hemisphere to
sail successfully alone. US leadership decline has handed Latin America
an opportunity and a challenge. The first is to develop its own particular
answers to its problems without depending overly on the 'gringos'. The
second is to operate to meet its needs in growth and maturity with its own
not imported Anglo-Saxon solutions.

A continent of great promise, Latin America is wealthy in minerals and
agriculture, well established in business and academia, strongly proud
of its linguistic heritage and developing new ways of thinking and acting from dealing with gang problems to evangelical religious observance,
from strong capitalism infused in many places with corruption, to more
careful attention to its unique indigenous heritage long suppressed by the
dominant 'white' ruling classes in many if not all of its states.

Caribbean culture, long monopolized by colonial heritage, more English, French and Dutch speaking than Spanish, is now in a multilingual
struggle for a place in the Hemispheric sun as a whole. The large, Latin-
dominant players—*hispano-parlantes*—who yield to no one in their aspirations for Hemispheric dominance and leadership, leave the islander 'also
rans' with little or no chance of a gold medal or blue ribbon.

Were the Latin American institutions stronger, we might see more
creativity and innovation. Nevertheless, standouts in literature, poetry,

cinema, music and theater remind us constantly that we are the minority on this side of the ocean. Afro-Caribbean heritage is strong and abiding. We should adopt the respect for dignity and mutual appreciation we so badly lack and which was so widely abandoned in the nineteenth century age of Yanqui Filibuster.

Africa: Last but Not Least

American analysts, at least those not familiar with Africa and even some who are, inadvertently I am sure, tend to push it way down the list of US priorities, to treat the continent as a whole with little distinction between countries, ethnicities, languages and historical traditions; and thereby to assign it widely and much too often to African-Americans for dominance of informed comment and criticism. We forget if we even tried to remember the innate racism adopted in that approach. It is still with us and makes putting Africa into a realistic perspective as hard as untying the Gordian Knot. I am doing it here at the end of a section, but with full assurance there are many other areas which I would like to have included in this section of the chapter that time and lower priority forced me to drop -Southeast and South Asia, the Pacific Island states and a host of functional issues such as terrorism to name a few.

Africa includes 55 states. Its emergence in post colonialism has been a significant phenomenon of the late twentieth century. Success in Africa gets widely ignored in the press, failure monopolizes attention, bad news drives out good news, and generalities cover over pertinent facts and details.

Success stories are not so easy to find, but include in the north, Morocco and Tunisia; in West Africa, Benin and Senegal; in East Africa, Kenya, Tanzania; in Central Africa, Malawi and Zambia; in Southern Africa, South Africa, Namibia, and Botswana. None of these states is perfect and each has committed errors but what modern country has not?

No region as a whole faced more problems at independence than this continent; no peoples were more poorly educated, had lower levels of health care, more primitive agriculture and less capacity in mining and manufacturing beginning in the early 1960s. External support has been helpful, in some cases generous and in others restricted, made major positive inroads in dealing with HIV/AIDS and threatens now to collapse in the face of the onslaught by the Delta Variant of Covid-19.

Africa has worked hard to build African Unity (AU), peacekeeping in the west through the Economic Community of West African States (ECOWAS) (with its regional cooperation in peacekeeping in Liberia and Sierra Leone led by Nigeria) and seeking to improve East African cooperation after an initial try at tearing it up. China seeks cooperation and influence, access to minerals and agricultural land and has maintained a program of assistance and building that has failed widely to incorporate Africans for leadership and labor and relied heavily on Chinese direction and debt traps to assure returns in the short term for Beijing. The US has participated widely, with success in Pepfar (a heavily funded George W Bush initiative to combat HIV/Aids), peacekeeping and development programs in all parts of Africa. France and Britain have maintained contacts with and support for their former colonial territories with France most predominant in providing military aid to those facing terrorism and internal disruption.

Africa is not without problems. In the north differences between Morocco and Algeria over the Western Sahara and beyond, Libya split in two parts and more through internal conflicts: West Africa from Cote d'Ivoire to Nigeria which has disputes both internal and over Islamic extremism and terrorism; in central Africa the DRC a classic failed state struggles to stay together, block further corruption, deal with electoral malfeasance and respond to the UN's largest and perhaps least successful peacekeeping effort; in the south, Angola is finding its way past the excesses of the Dos Santos period, South Africa is dealing with the riots of Zuma supporters over his arrest and a reasonably new administration is seeking clean and democratic government under Cyril Ramaphosa and Mozambique with domestic splits and Islamic armed intervention in the new northern oil and gas province—to name just a few. Africa has no monopoly on failed and failing states but is far from devoid of their presence, with outside intervenors less than certain to be able alone or in concert to help pick up the pieces.

Our tendency to lump all Africans together, to treat it as a basket case in general, to ignore its challenges and benefits and to see it often as a contested area both in the past Cold War and now with China, distort and deceive our efforts at a coherent and constructive strategy. The Biden Administration has a new opportunity to rethink Africa. It should not be done under the pressure of unrealistic and thus too tight deadlines, but not so stretched out that no conclusions are reached, no risks evaluated and taken, and no changes adopted where it is necessary to do so. Greater respect for African leadership, more serious attention to corruption and maladministration, more listening to local and regional leaders and more careful preparation of US specialists and experts should be part of a new formula. Fifteen percent of Americans had their past in the continent, many in totally unacceptable conditions of servitude both there and here. Hopefully they will play a constructive role in dealing with Africa, but the continent should be of interest to us all and its role and influence in the US widely appreciated, admired and treated with dignity and humane respect.

How Diplomacy Works

Exchanges of envoys goes back 2000 years. It was the beginning of how to influence friends, enemies and neighbors in the interests of a country short of war, annihilation and occupation. A careful choice of good people as diplomats often made a positive difference. Before American independence, both diplomacy and its importance were understood and luminaries like Benjamin Franklin were sent to Europe to help assure that our diplomacy complemented our defense in the successful outcome of breaking with Britain. Two hundred and forty-seven years later it is even more important that we get the people, processes and purposes right to assure our interests and survival.

People: The Centerpiece

American diplomacy in particular is people centered. No other aspect of working with other states is more important. Until 1924, our diplomats were politically chosen and appointed. Professionalism was then only beginning and the Rogers Act of 1924 helped put us in the forefront of building a coterie of career diplomats to support us.

The objective was to use rigorous, 3-day examinations to pick meritorious people who could succeed. Out of 15,000 to 30,000 applicants around 400 each year are chosen. The State Department then must train them, put them into positions of growing responsibility, assign them worldwide, use merit and success as the basis for advancement, rely on near peers to assure that quality and merit is recognized and rewarded and to provide for those not measuring up to leave the career. The US Navy promotion system was used as a model. The Foreign Service thus established served through both wars and peace, underwent modifications and reforms in additional legislation, opened up to women, sought wider diversity but too timidly so for many and brought into senior positions experienced and thoughtful leaders. Mistakes were made—and recognized and corrected—and they in turn brought about further change. A service early clustered around graduates of Ivy League institutions gradually expanded and strengthened intake to cover much of the country even though for some in the press the myth of Ivy League attachment continues. Women competed but not without a long and contentious legal struggle and controversy. Minorities entered but in too small numbers and through a process that at first rewarded those able to afford a solid education—until three decades ago when programs to provide scholarships to needy entrants, particularly minorities, began to function. These ROTC-like programs need expansion.

Reflecting all of America is not just an obligation it is a better way to make policy, friends, and understand the world. Trump failed and pared down diversity from intake to retention. Biden seeks to change that with the appointment of a Chief Diversity officer and staff to assure that more minorities from all groups enter the service and those that do have a voice and a champion next to the Secretary of State.

With worldwide service and rotation of jobs every two or three years, the Foreign Service has expanded from a few hundred in the 1920s to over ten thousand officers today. They work alongside civil service officers and employees and Foreign Service specialists who fill a myriad of jobs requiring specialized, highly trained competence. The civil service in the State Department operates under rules set for it as a whole in the US government. Job rotation depends on promotion and advancement which in turn depends upon vacancies in the system out ahead of the candidates. Once in a job, civil service officers, in the absence of removal for cause, enjoy permanent occupancy. This brings conflict over jobs with the Foreign Service which ought through two and three-year rotations to spend a balanced amount of time overseas and at home and where selected civil servants should be given the chance of overseas service. Ideas have recently been propounded for solving this issue including a limited Excepted Service for a small percentage of State Department civil servants which would permit rotations overseas and other flexibilities.

The Foreign Service is looked to provide for staffing of overseas missions—embassies, consulates and others—from junior officer and specialists to Ambassadors. Traditional targets on Ambassadorial selection have looked at 30 percent from the outside public, often political donors and others brought in by the White House and the president, and 70 percent from the career service. These ratios are far from fully settled and under Trump moved strongly in favor of more political appointments.

Over past decades, many have favored a ratio closer to 90 to 10 percent in favor of career officers, including former Vice President Gore while he was a serving Senator from Tennessee. The argument has been that such offices should not be for sale through political contributions and the fact that our military after the Civil War professionalized and—while apocryphal—the first job to be made professional was probably brain surgery!

With the advent of the Biden Administration and in the aftermath of Trump, studies have shown reform and change is needed and likely. Many creative ideas have emerged. Some have focused on better training and education.

For many years the Foreign Service relied on preparation by America's universities although there was no requirement to hold a university degree to enter. The Foreign Service Institute (FSI), established before World War II, undertook training and exceled in language learning among other subjects. Recent studies have pointed out a growing need for more advanced courses in politics and related issues, improved entry-level training, more time allocated to Ambassadorial preparation and a one-year mid-level course for officers on their way up. Traditional reliance on "On the Job Training" and mentoring seems to have failed in meeting the growing needs for officers with a wide diversity of knowledge, the ability to absorb new subject matter rapidly, and a solid background including in subjects such as science and technology which play an increasing role in US diplomacy. A small group of us have begun raising money to improve the offerings of the FSI in new areas, supporting pilot projects which if successful will be regularly budgeted, as well as the use of gaming techniques and wider university offerings from around the country.

The Foreign Service has been organized around concentration of its' officers in five 'cones'—political, economic, consular, administrative and management and public diplomacy. Recent recommendations have questioned this approach and suggested other approaches including more time spent on multilateral relations and managing and participating more widely in that field. While the US holds its own internationally, there is much we can learn from others. Longer more thorough entry courses is one, another is greater professionalization of Ambassadors.

The National Security Council (NSC) plays a major role in preparing the president for decisions in foreign and security policy. The legendary Brent Scowcroft, seen as one the best NSC leaders, taught us that making sure the president has all the views and considers them in policy decisions is a principal purpose of the NSC staff. Carrying out those decisions is the work of the mission departments and agencies and the NSC has a role in assuring the president gets that support. For the State Department, Foreign and Civil Service officers are seconded to the NSC and serve the NSC advisor and president from the White House.

Ambassadors are often called upon to act without referring to Washington and even more to provide Washington with foreign policy advice as conditions and circumstances change. In the mid-1970s in Jordan, we committed to provide 12 Hawk anti-aircraft rocket batteries to the country. It followed the 1973 Yom Kippur/Ramadan War and King Hussein was acutely conscious of Jordan's vulnerability to air attack. A week after we had completed the sales contract which provided for certain restrictions on the use and deployment of the missiles, I received a highly restricted cable from Washington telling me we had just provided the US Senate with a letter containing even greater restrictions at the behest of a neighboring state. I knew this letter if followed would end the sale and leave our relations with Jordan in tatters. I spoke to the Prime Minister and he agreed with my assessment as did King Hussein who was out of town after the PM briefed him. It was a Friday night and I asked the two to make no decision until the PM and I talked again on Saturday morning. I spent a long sleepless night thinking about ways forward. What I came up with was that Jordan would insist that it was fully bound by the sales contract, but nothing more, and would for a few days say so to the press who had by then begun to get word of the letter. I wrote back to Washington that morning about what I had done after talking with the PM and he and King Hussein had both agreed. Washington never replied. The Jordanians had a public relations field day on us and after two weeks I asked the Jordanians to stop the press play since the US had not pushed back on them. This was the first and only time I actually advised a foreign government to come out against a US proposal—and at least then it worked in our interest!

Process: Who Acts Where and When to Form Policy

Foreign policy is the sum total of decisions and statements by a country defining how it will view existing and future issues. Policy changes often as a result of changing situations. Diplomats must keep up with those situations and recommend to their capitals when and how to change.

The able, accomplished diplomat understands very quickly that one of the principal tasks is to learn and listen to others as a valuable technique. Listening in my experience has several facets. The first is to understand what is being said—and to use dialogue to assure that the understanding is as complete and thorough as questions and answers can make it. The other side of that dialogue is almost always designed to promote the interests of a foreign power. That does not mean the dialogue is not of value or untrue, but it invariably involves a selection of statements and issues which provide the truth in ways that support the other state's national interests.

Carried to a longer conclusion, listening has other uses as well. One is to capture not just what is being said, but more deeply what may be the meaning or intentions in saying it. This is often harder. Governments prepare their statements with great care to avoid saying what they intend or propose to do until they are ready to do so. Often the maker of the statement and those repeating it fail themselves to understand the full meaning. It is only with an extended dialogue that others can begin to determine what is being set forth and what it might mean for a bottom line in problem solving. These are some of the most interesting challenges for a diplomat in listening and learning.

The third "L" word in the triumvirate here is 'lead'. Learning and listening contribute to a new look at policy often based on a revised understanding of the other sides' red lines. Many techniques can be employed. Finding a past precedent for a new effort at change and compromise is one. Noting how the change provided benefits can help. Being aware of the political forces at work in another state and understanding and then using that to fashion a compromise solution also helps.

Much of the information gathered that informs the need for a policy or a change in policy comes from our intelligence community as well as from our diplomats reporting from abroad. Some of it is carefully guarded while much of it is in the public domain. Foreign Service officers must build trust with their contacts at home and abroad. That trust often results in identifying approaches to problems and issues that can be to our benefit.

Sound strategy is a pillar of successful diplomacy. The US has multiple competing strategy makers—in State, Defense and the NSC. If would do well to combine or coordinate them. Strategy is a sensitive subject. Secrecy is important and having your opponents knowing what you think about strategy is a weakness not easy to overcome. In the end, in the US, the ultimate strategy is in the head and heart of the senior elected official— the president. Strategic advice can assist but cannot replace dealing with decisions about objectives and process at the time and place required and appropriate. This is especially true regarding vital, or existential issues—as Harry Truman defined them 'survival and prosperity' and perhaps that of our allies.

Closely aligned with strategy is the growing imperative of addressing foreign and security policy on a 'whole of government basis. This means that the Scowcroft approach to the NSC is even more important—the president needs to know what each of his cabinet advisors thinks about a policy decision, not just the view of the NSC adviser.

American diplomats are called upon to undertake negotiations on a regular basis, both formally for agreements and informally for greater understanding. Such does not happen overnight and requires long hours. Knowledge of a foreign language can help develop agreement, particularly where the subject is complex and the choice of explanations of what is being sought allows for some latitude. A final resort to ambiguity may be necessary but it should not be the first choice of an outcome. Ambiguities left around the landscape often result in creating even greater difficulties in the future and certainly help to undermine trust. And trust is one of the exemplary tools you can deploy to build confidence and cohesion in diplomacy. Trust and truth go together. Nothing undermines trust as rapidly as untrue or misleading statements.

Our system does not make diplomacy very easy. Some US diplomats have noted that in a tough negotiation often up to 40% of their problems are with Washington. The Congress has its own role. The failure to approve important treaties over the last decade has raised mistrust and uncertainty for our potential partners. The current effort at returning to the JCPOA with Iran is in part held up by an Iranian insistence that the United States commit not to withdraw again as Trump did in 2018—a difficult problem to cure or address in a democratic state where political change by elections frequently takes place.

The policy process in the United States often involves other departments and agencies. The NSC has the task of bringing together policies which need White House commitment. Within the purview of the State Department there are areas for agreement open to its policy making. Similarly, as other department's activities impact overall relationships with foreign states, there is a State Department interest in coordinating that often presents interagency differences.

Starting new talks with opponents has its own psychological ambiance. Generally, the costs of speaking with an 'enemy' are high, often in an electoral democracy where demonization of the 'other' is frequently present and politically costly to deal with. But there is no alternative to doing so even if you start indirectly and work through others to do that.

Respect and dignity describe behavior designed to bring about trust and understanding. Lies do not support trust, neither does anger. You do not have to tell all of the truth but all of what you do say should be true. Similarly, you should not allow emotion to control your words. If judged necessary and you have reached the point where other approaches have clearly failed, controlled anger may be the only way forward. If so, be sure you do not let the emotion override your purpose.

Much of today's foreign and security policy is informed by science and technology. Mastery of the subject matter no matter what its origin is central to achieving a diplomatic purpose. Innovative thinking is a genuine asset. It can take many forms—new ideas to bring around an agreement. Be careful of too much dependence on explaining why an approach is in the interest of the other side. It tends to breed suspicion and distrust and a belief that your own arguments are weak. But making concessions to facilitate the concerns of the other side in terms you can accept may help.

Purpose: US Interests

Diplomacy has a significant importance. Diplomacy without result can leave negative impacts which harden mistrust and build animosity. Results that are positive can go on to build a relationship of confidence, purpose, and value.

Win-win answers are not always easy to find. And parties generally begin their approach to a negotiation on the basis of hope for a zero-sum outcome in their favor. This is often engendered by the press treatment of the issue which in turn, because of domestic politics, brings from the parties what they believe the public should hear to support their own political popularity. Even autocracies without elections have politics and in time politics must be separated from interests if there is to be a valid answer. Not all marriages are made in heaven. Not all international disputes are ready or even close to settlement. Negotiation as a process can often bring them closer together and the negotiators themselves over time while engaged in an agreement process often begin to put aside the unworkable and think about how to make the difficult less problematic for the other side as their resolve to solve the problem takes hold. It also means that if the overriding interest is to find an answer you can live with, then the pain of getting there and the risks of making such moves may be worth the cost to achieve an acceptable if not necessarily ideal outcome.

Diplomacy seeks to avoid conflict. Although at times conflict intrudes in diplomacy. Sometimes there are advantages to conflict which make clear early and on a timely basis to both parties that a military solution is not a realistic, likely outcome for either side. And indeed military solutions without the capacity to use them to shape an acceptable political outcome are often not solutions at all but merely another stage of unproductive conflict whose costs are rarely if ever offset by the losses suffered in the fighting.

Several thoughts in conclusion are worth noting:

- Wars of choice should not be fought.

- Shaping the diplomacy before during and after a conflict is most helpfully done sooner rather than later; best done before a conflict breaks out.

- Diplomacy requires time and patience, innovation and good sense, political leadership and careful preparation, friends and allies, and an ability to speak with enemies despite the costs of doing so.

- Diplomacy is a first resort and the costs are not monetarily high but politically and economically they may be more expensive than we first suspect.

- Professional competence almost always beats committed amateurism.

- Diplomacy is almost always a careful balance between short term gains and long-term consequences—both should be considered carefully.

- Military leverage without diplomacy in place most often leads no-where even with political demands on the other side; military leverage with diplomacy in place can be applied to an on-going outcome of shaping a benefit.

- Wars of choice by large powers against small states may work in the short term but leave reputational wreckage for the victor; wars of large powers against larger states produce, with hybrid and asymmetrical conflict, lengthy, costly commitments usually ended only after unpro-ductive withdrawals.

And from Secretary of State George Shultz:

1. Trust is the coin of the realm.
2. Diplomacy like gardening requires daily tending.
3. When you are in a deep hole, stop digging.

Notes

1. Under the Charter, Britain, China, France, the Soviet Union (now Russia) and the United States are Permanent Members of the UN Security Council alongside ten rotating, elected, non-permanent members. They have the right individually to veto (block the passage) of any proposed resolutions of the Council.
2. The October 1648 Peace of Westphalia resolved in Europe most of the issues of the thirty-years war. Its most important contribution was to accept "sovereignty" and "equality as a universal attributes of states, empowering them at home to do as they wished and often to pursue the concept abroad, raising issues.
3. New Start provided for limits on the number of deliverable nuclear warheads by the US and Russia under an advanced and improved verification system.

TWELVE

P. MICHAEL McKINLEY

This chapter was completed in March 2023.

From Morning in America to January 6
Perspectives on Diplomacy, 1982–2022

Introduction

I was 28 and had lived less than six years in the United States when I joined the State Department in September 1982 to represent a country I knew as a concept as much as a reality. If there is a common thread running through my experiences in government across thirty-seven years, it is the friction between America's idealism and self-image, and the cruder realities of world politics and our national interests.

There were parallels then with the uncertainties of today's world. I began my diplomatic career almost two years into President Ronald Reagan's first term in office, when the dip in our international standing and self-confidence was still part of the country's fabric in the aftermath of the Vietnam War and the economic and political crises of the 1970s. The term "Morning in America" was only introduced in the 1984 presidential campaign, but it reflected a mindset for the entire decade. The national recovery in the 1980s was as much psychological as economic and political, and it helped lead to the literal and ideological collapse of the Soviet Union and the end of the Cold War in 1989. The Iran-Contra scandal of the period, which hobbled the Reagan presidency for a time did not change that reality.

It was to be followed by a period of American dominance and influence on the international stage—political, military, economic, and cultural—until the terrorist attacks of November 11 gradually sent the United States on a more troubled path again. The last twenty years of my career were witness to how the triumph of American ideals of democracy and free markets was accompanied by a relative decline of influence as the United States was drawn into the costly conflicts in Afghanistan and Iraq which undermined its broader focus on global developments.

In the same timeframe the rest of the world was transforming at one of the fastest rates in human history. Other countries and ideologies emerged to challenge the post-Cold War status quo, and we seriously under-invested in our own society. The United States downplayed the alliances and political and economic relationships which had provided the foundations of our national security for the better part of a century. The fall of Kabul to the Taliban in August 2021, where I had once been ambassador, embodied the mistaken priorities of two decades of policymaking.

As 2023 begins, therefore, and as Russia's invasion of Ukraine dominates the headlines, we are at another of those inflection points, much like 1945, 1989, and 2001, but with considerably less leverage globally. As the United States responds to the moment, there are underlying realities that have held over time, and which determine how we interact with the world: the state of the global economy; the threat and realities of conflict; the dangers of nuclear proliferation; the importance of alliances and multilateralism; evolving transnational challenges; and the principles that govern interaction between states. It is tempting to conceptually define our way forward on foreign policy within this framework, adapting and updating approaches which have served American interests over the past 70 years. The National Security Strategy (NSS) released by the Biden administration in October 2022 does that, while reaffirming values that the United States considers universal and enduring.[1]

There is a strong caveat, however. Today's global challenges defy the neat categories we grew comfortable with and will write their own rules of engagement with the future. They include the rise of China; the wider implications of Russia's invasion of Ukraine; populism and the rise of authoritarianism; the role of technology; the changing nature of globalization; an increasingly multi-polar world; the renewed challenge to values the US sees as central to international relations; and the impact of new transnational issues from pandemics to climate change.

In addition, while the world was changing over the last twenty years, we did too. The current polarization of American politics, the failure to address societal inequalities and to modernize our economy, and the undermining of our own system of governance were a long time in the making and impact foreign policy. The debate over whether the United States can still lead effectively internationally is symptomatic of the wider challenges we face as a nation. There is the need for new concepts and strategies that can accompany the underlying continuities and strengths of our foreign policy and the relaunch of our own democratic credentials.

Most of all, we need to break the pattern of defining foreign policy in terms of ideological confrontation and of American supremacy and exceptionalism. These characterized our approach to the Cold War (1945–1989) and post-Cold War periods. They are not appropriate now. Casting relations with adversaries or competitors as an existential struggle between systems that will determine the future of the world, or to reassert American global leadership on everything from climate change to the future of democracy when the world has fundamentally changed, is to revert to our historical comfort zone. We cannot do so any longer and succeed.

About My Career

All of us are informed by our personal experiences. I grew up and was educated mostly overseas, in Latin America and Europe, the son of expatriate parents. Once in the State Department, I did not specialize in one region. I spent almost a dozen years working sub-Saharan African issues in the field and in Washington; I spent eight years in Europe; another ten in Latin America where I was ambassador to Peru, Colombia, and Brazil; and I was ambassador to Afghanistan. I spent six years working multilaterally with the UN system, NGOs, and the EU—and almost three years for senior leadership on the Department's Seventh Floor.

This essay is also informed by the kind of work I did throughout my career before resigning in response to the Ukraine scandal in 2019. I was the Angola-Namibia desk officer when we had missions in neither country and as negotiations for Namibia's independence and the withdrawal of 50,000 Cuban troops from Africa were concluded with Castro's Cuba, the Soviet Union, communist Angola, apartheid South Africa, and the UN. I was an intelligence analyst for El Salvador and (at times) Nicaragua when the Iran-Contra scandal broke in Washington. As a Deputy Assistant Secretary, I was charged with restarting the refugee resettlement program which was shut down after 9/11 (something President Trump aspired to but never achieved). In the same position, I worked on Guantanamo and Abu Ghraib as the latter became by-words for America's violations of its own principles. I was Deputy Chief of Mission at the US Mission to the European Union when the reset with Europe took place after the invasion of Iraq.

Across my career I worked on conflicts and peace negotiations in Central America, Angola, the Congo, Darfur, Liberia, Ethiopia, Colombia, and Afghanistan—and on our counter-narcotics policy in the latter two countries. For ten plus years across the 2000s, in Brussels, Lima, and Bogota I worked on free trade negotiations, with successes in Peru and Colombia. I was senior advisor to former Secretary Pompeo in 2018–2019 as the Trump administration made decisions on the withdrawal from Afghanistan, on Indo-Pacific strategy, on migration, on negotiations with North Korea, and as State Department capabilities were undermined.

In short, I was a generalist. As I seek to answer some of the questions posed by the authors of this anthology, I am fully aware that there are many other ways to look at our nation's diplomacy. There can be only one conclusion, however: that the United States needs to engage the outside world as much as we think it needs us if our nation is to prosper and be secure.

The Starting Point: The Importance of Ideals in America's Foreign Policy

There is no other country that quite defines its purpose as "the shining city on a hill", as a beacon to the world's dispossessed, as the torchbearer for global democracy, as the "indispensable nation," and as leader of "the free world." Our engagement with other countries strongly draws on our perceptions of American exceptionalism, America as the indispensable nation, America as the global leader. As President Biden set off in June 2021 for his first G-7, NATO, and US-EU summits, he reaffirmed the widespread sentiment in our country that "the United States must lead the world from a position of strength . . . flanked by nations that share our values and our vision for the future."

America's self-definition on the world stage drove a highly ideological and successful foreign policy after World War II in response to the earlier fight against fascism and the rise of communism. We never really adapted it to a changing international landscape after the collapse of the Soviet Union in 1989. This was partly because it did not seem like we had to, at least initially. Much of the rest of the world adopted representative democracy and market economies in the 1990s, including eastern Europe and Russia, parts of East Asia, and most of Latin America. These could differ in form from the American model, but it is hard to argue that this transformation would have occurred absent our influence and example—and the umbrella of American security commitments. The virtues of American exceptionalism and leadership seemed self-evident. By the 2000s, however, the US was struggling to apply the same approach to profoundly shifting global and strategic realities. By the late 2010s, the limitations were more apparent as a domestic debate intensified over what role we should have internationally.

American foreign policy over the past seven decades, therefore, was not just the product of a traditional defense of national interest or responding to international developments and threats—it was inextricably linked to how the United States saw itself on the world stage. Our self-belief was often transformative for the better at home and abroad. Our certainty, however, also approached dogmatism, with more negative consequences, as the world became more complex, and especially when we sought to define challenges in black and white.

The 1980s: Restoration

In hindsight, the 1980s represented the successful culmination of the combination of American military power, economic dominance, and idealism to advance national security for the United States and for our allies against existential threats over a period of decades. The hope that we could, was very much a part of the work environment when I first joined the State Department in 1982, and an inspiration and sense of purpose for many of us in the foreign service. It is hard to overstate, even at that late stage of the Cold War, how stark the divide seemed between the world represented by the United States and its allies, and that of the Soviet Union and other communist nations like Cuba, Vietnam, and China, and the countries of eastern Europe. Much of "the West" was only beginning to emerge from the economic downturn of the 1970s, and the United States did not seem on the verge of winning the ideological war against communism. The Soviet military and nuclear threat to Europe remained a serious concern.

There was a simplicity to the way President Reagan's administration presented the issues, but the reframing of American global leadership, the economic recovery of the United States, and the robust response to efforts by the Soviet Union to extend its global influence helped give renewed substance to American idealism by the time the Berlin Wall came down on December 9, 1989. While there are many reasons the Soviet Union and its eastern European allies collapsed, not least their internal weaknesses, our example, our international alliances, and our tactical and strategic military and political responses helped define and speed the moment.

My personal experiences with the strategic issues of that period date from 1985 to 1990, when I worked on the "regional conflicts" or proxy wars with the Soviet Union and its allies, first in Central America and then Africa. There is a tendency to gloss over those conflicts, with primacy rightly given to more signal achievements of the era to include facing down the Soviet Union in Europe. Our engagements in regional conflicts, however, also helped prevent the communist takeovers of Central American nations; helped lead to the withdrawal of Soviet troops from Afghanistan; resulted in Namibian independence and the departure of Cuban troops from Africa; contained an expansionist Libya allied with the Soviet Union in northern Africa; and provided security for freedom of navigation in the Persian Gulf which, at that time, was the source of most world energy supplies and was being threatened by an Iran hostile to the United States.

There was another understated aspect of American diplomacy in these and subsequent years. American participation, and often leadership, led to negotiated breakthroughs on conflicts—across borders, and internal to countries. The list of successes across the last thirty years is long: the Contadora process for Central America; the quadripartite negotiations securing Namibia's independence and the withdrawal of Cuban troops from Africa; the Sant Egidio negotiations which led to an end to Mozambique's civil war; the peaceful dissolution of Ethiopia and Eritrea; the Dayton accords in the Balkans; the Good Friday agreements for Northern Ireland; the Camp David Accords on Israel and Palestine; the agreement reached by the FARC insurgency and the Colombian government; the talks leading to the independence of South Sudan; and the border settlement between Ecuador and Peru.

We had significant interests in some of these wars, much less so in others. American idealism to make the world a better place drove much of what we did. There were also failures which I experienced first-hand: in Darfur, the Liberian civil war, and the diplomatic efforts to end the war in the Democratic Republic of Congo. The underbelly of American engagement on conflict was our belief that there was always a difference to be split, underestimating enmity and differences between warring parties, and over-estimating our influence. That lack of awareness was to become a formidable obstacle in our responses to the post 9/11 period.

The United States appeared to strike the right balance between ideology and substance in its international policies towards the end of the Cold War. There were wrong calls: the effort by some to slow German reunification in late 1989, for example, which I witnessed as a special assistant on the Seventh Floor, but they had little lasting impact. I did, however, see another side to the equation as I worked on El Salvador and Nicaragua as an intelligence analyst. Our government minimized the killing of civilians by Central American security forces we supported; we undertook a proxy war against Nicaragua's Sandinista government, funding and arming a resistance, the "contras", which had little support inside the country; and we engaged in a hostages-for-arms and money operation which, as the "Iran-Contra" scandal, rocked the Reagan presidency, and violated the "no negotiations" with terrorism maxim. The almost parodic invasions of Grenada and Panama led to chest-beating about our military prowess oblivious to what the Latin American region saw as the neighborhood bully in action.

The United States had exhibited this kind of willful blindness and hubris before, on a much larger scale in Vietnam, but the successes at the end of the Cold War seemed to bury undue concern about mistakes we made in the regional conflicts, and our selective approach to human rights and democracy as we embraced friendly authoritarian governments too closely in our drive to win the Cold War. What I saw then, in retrospect, presaged part of our approach to the "global war on terror" and the invasions of Iraq and Afghanistan in the 2000s.

The 1990s: America Triumphant

The 1990s were a golden age of American influence and ideological self-confidence. Frank Fukuyama was prescient: ideological confrontation receded to vanishing point.[2] The US embodied the new paradigm of liberal capitalism and was thriving. Far from being eclipsed by Japan and Germany as seemed possible only a few years earlier, the US economy continued to grow and, critically, began to emerge as the innovation center for the coming information technology revolution in the world. The US promoted free trade agreements within the Western Hemisphere; multilateralism in world trade; and embraced globalization. Our traditional military alliances with Europe through NATO, and with Japan and South Korea were expanded, even as we cut spending on our own armed forces. China was invited to apply to the World Trade Organization, with Americans confident capitalist economic growth would lead to that country's political liberalization.

The dissolution of the Soviet Union and emergence of fifteen new countries during the Bush and Clinton presidencies, saw Russia democratize, reduce nuclear stockpiles in tandem with the United States, and join the G-7 (to become G-8) grouping of the world's leading democratically led economies. The Oslo and Camp David accords promised the possibility of resolving Israeli-Palestinian tensions. The successful reversal of Iraq's invasion of Kuwait seemed to posit a new benchmark for principled interventionism on behalf of international law—and a successful new military doctrine of "overwhelming force" as the shadow of failures in Vietnam faded. Late, but critical, US military and diplomatic interventions led to peace in the Balkans. US support for democratization in Latin America, East Asia, the former Soviet Union states, and in Africa saw the emergence of dozens of new more representative and liberal governments.

The United States also led the world in developing a more robust response to humanitarian crises caused by famine, natural disasters, and war. This included building UN agency and NGO capacity, but it was also a time when the doctrine of humanitarian intervention took shape, galvanized in no small part by the failure to act early during the Rwanda genocide of 1994. Early manifestations (the creation of the "exclusion zone" for Kurdish populations in northern Iraq after the Gulf War, the intervention to help end the 1992 famine in Somalia) were followed by multilateral efforts to both create security for and assist affected populations in Bosnia, the Democratic Republic of Congo, Haiti, Liberia, and Sierra Leone.

Humanitarian intervention as a concept has come under heavy criticism in recent years, and the policy was necessarily selective in its approach, but, having worked on Somalia and the Congo in the 1990s, and lived in Mozambique as it transitioned from twenty years of war to democratic elections under UN auspices, it still seems to me today that doing something is considerably better than watching humanitarian catastrophes unfold unchecked. Nothing is absolute; but acting, where it is possible to act, still seems a moral imperative and a value worth preserving.

By the end of the decade, the US was the undisputed global power with the collapse of the Soviet Union, with no challenger in sight. The American share of the world's GDP had grown, as challengers to the economic throne seemed to recede. The US had led successful responses to the Mexican and Russian financial crises of 1994 and 1998 respectively. American political values were reinforced by the emergence of new democracies.

Perhaps unsurprisingly, the signs of emerging ideological hubris became more evident as the decade progressed. There was a marked contrast in tone in speeches given six years apart by President H W Bush in his 1991 address to the United Nations General Assembly, and after the victories over Saddam Hussein's Iraq and the fall of the Soviet Union, and one by President Clinton in 1997 at the swearing-in of Secretary of State Albright:[3]

"Let me assure you, the United States has no intention of striving for a

Pax Americana. However, we will remain engaged. We will not retreat and pull back into isolationism. We will offer friendship and leadership. And in short, we seek a *Pax Universalis* built upon shared responsibilities and aspirations." (President Bush)

"America must continue to be the world's greatest force for peace and freedom and prosperity (and remain) the indispensable nation . . . (an America that) "leads the fight for a world that is safer from weapons of terror and mass destruction; where America leads the fight for a world that is safer from organized crime and drug trafficking and all terrorist activity; and where expanded trade brings growth and opportunity; where peace and freedom know no frontiers." (President Clinton)

The ambition may have been admirable, but it also reflected an ideological conviction that the United States had found the way forward for a prosperous and peaceful global future, that what we did benefited the world, that our principles were clearly the right ones, and that others should follow our example. It was a view articulated in other official speeches of the time, and by the succeeding George W Bush administration as it dealt with a vastly changed geopolitical landscape after 9/11, and a world less inclined to follow Washington's lead.

By 2000, there were already indications of discomfort internationally, and new political realities began to intrude: Yeltsin's Russia was evolving into Putin's Russia, resentful of the expansion of NATO and of what Russians increasingly saw as a deliberate effort to diminish the country. Allies in Europe had their own reservations, born of dealing with a Washington that seemed to consider the continent yesterday's news. I saw that attitude as a political officer in London, and again as Deputy Chief of Mission in Brussels in 2000. Washington officials were particularly dismissive of the growing influence and power of the European Union, with demarches asking for support for US positions worded almost as demands. The irony that Europe writ large was our first port of call for responding to any pressing global concern seemed entirely lost.

French foreign minister Vedrine spoke for others in warning against the "hyper-puissance" of the United States. In a 1998 interview, when asked how to counter US influence, he responded: "Through steady and persevering work in favor of real multilateralism against unilateralism, for balanced multipolarism against unipolarism, for cultural diversity against uniformity."[4] The implicit criticism of the United States should have been a wake-up call. There were echoes in the United States, with Richard Haas pointing to underlying trends which were beginning to change the foreign policy landscape.[5] Vedrine, in any case, was only slightly ahead of his time: the "unipolar world" apparently first coined by an American commentator, Charles Krauthammer, in 1990, was about to end abruptly.[6]

9/11 and the Aftermath

It is a truism that the attack on September 11, 2001, changed the United States and, to a lesser extent, the world. Our national response, and the swift success of the military operation in Afghanistan, suggested that the tragedy could soon be placed in a broader context of the largely still positive developments on the global stage.

That did not happen. The United States, as it had done during the Cold War, found a new existential confrontation—"the global war on terror." We defined what we did—our alliances, our relations with troubled regions of the world—in terms of how others responded to our definition of what was at stake. We used moral terminology unrelentingly. In the process, we also sought to remake the map of the Middle East, strengthen Israel's security, and topple Saddam Hussein in Iraq. And we sought to "nation-build" and transform Iraq and Afghanistan into modern democracies ignoring historical, political, and cultural realities of those countries which made the task extraordinarily difficult.

As the hubris of early military victories in both Afghanistan and Iraq carried us forward, we stumbled into the "forever wars'; we violated our own values by engaging in torture and other human rights violations; we spent three trillion dollars which could have gone to urgent domestic needs; and we sent more than two million young Americans to fight and sometimes die in these conflicts. We sidelined global diplomacy and sought to remake the State Department fit for "expeditionary and transformational diplomacy" which was conveniently focused on those wars. Doing so provided a scapegoat for the failure of other security agencies and departments to achieve desired objectives. We alienated allies, contributed to the destabilization of the broader Middle East, and overlooked or belittled emerging new challenges from Russia and China, countries we had deemed "former adversaries" in the 1990s. If this assessment seems harsh, it is no more so than the retrospective commentaries on former Secretary of Defense Rumsfeld in June 2021, the architect of so much that went wrong—or those of an increasing number of analyses of what went wrong in Afghanistan (7).

It would be easy to suggest that the United States made mistakes during the Cold War too, and certainly the intervention in Vietnam had a dramatic and negative impact inside our country and on global opinion. That war, however, took place in the broader context of an agreed sense of purpose (containing communism) which had critical support from allies. Our approach to the global war on terror clearly did not generate the same international consensus.

How to explain the decision to stay the course on the war on terror for as long as we did? Part of the reason is that no country willingly accepts defeat on the battlefield, and we kept moving the goalposts on what defined success. Those opposed to President Biden's decision in 2021 to withdraw fighting forces from Afghanistan, did the same, as the decision lay bare the failures to achieve our objectives in that country. Another part of the rationale for the military interventions in the Middle East, combatting the emergence of ISIS in 2013–2014, even as the latter also begged the question of whether the Caliphate would have come to power without the destabilizing impact of the international occupation of Iraq.

Part of the explanation for staying on a war footing, however, was a national worldview which saw us as right: we characterized the global war on terrorism in much the same terms as we had the Cold War. President Bush, in a defining speech in 2001, spoke of the coming conflict in stark moralistic terms: "Every nation, in every region, now has a decision to make. Either you are with us, or you are with the terrorists."[8] President Obama's May 2010 National Security Strategy, while openly acknowledging the rapid change taking place in the world, focused heavily on the "forever wars" highlighting that the US would continue to "underwrite global security" by committing to allies and partners and to preventing nuclear proliferation but also through "our focus on defeating Al Qaeda and its affiliates in Afghanistan, Pakistan, and around the globe."[9] A neutral reading the document could still conclude our country was consumed by war but also by our self-imposed obligation as leader of "the free world."

The document also begged the question of what the rest of the world saw as their security challenges. Most countries did not see things in quite the same terms. It is striking the extent to which Americans did not focus on the nuances at the time of global public opinion on the 9/11 attacks. According to Pew Research, approximately 40 percent of the population in Western Europe thought that US policies in the Middle East were to blame.[10] The percentage moved into the 60s and 70s in other parts of the world. Countries sympathized with the suffering of Americans, but worldwide, a striking 70 percent of elites believed that the populations of their region thought it was good for the United States to feel vulnerable.

It is also the case, as already suggested, that other countries and regions had other priorities—growing and modernizing their economies and societies. As the decade progressed, East Asia, Latin America, and the Middle East—emerging economies in general—underwent an extraordinary transformation. In 2001 the term BRICs was first formulated to describe Brazil, Russia, India, and China's emergence. That year they represented about 10 percent of world GDP; by 2020 the figure for BRICS, now including South Africa, was closer to 25%.[11] Their political saliency increased. The European Union's (EU) soft-power influence on the world stage, and emergence as an economic competitor to the United States also became more evident notwithstanding detractors with Cold War mentalities in Washington, embodied by the dismissive attitudes inside the State Department of the role of the EU during the 2014 Ukraine crisis.

All of us who were in government at the time remember where we were on 9/11. I began work on September 7 at the State Department as a Deputy Assistant Secretary in the Bureau of Population, Refugees, and Migration (PRM). I walked out of the building on the morning of September 11 with almost everyone else. I turned back after some time had passed, re-entered, walked the empty, halls and visited the front office of Diplomatic Security. No one could think about how to react in that moment.

React we did. The early success of the war in Afghanistan led to a decision to remove Saddam Hussein in Iraq in March 2003, a move which received bipartisan support in the US Congress but very little internationally and opposition from key European NATO allies. The downside of sidelining our ongoing unfinished mission in Afghanistan was ignored. The failure to find weapons of mass destruction, the stated rationale for intervention, was dismissed as almost an afterthought by a triumphalist official Washington. The rapid success of the invasion of Iraq led to an occupation meant to remake Iraq as a democracy and to transform the region "by advancing freedom in the Middle East."[12] The hubris of victorious American military interventions—from Grenada and Panama through the liberation of Kuwait, the Kosovo intervention, and Afghanistan—colored expectations for a quick drawdown in Iraq and transition to peace and democracy. By 2006, however, the country was now being described as "the central front" in "the war on terror."[13]

That was not the way the build-up to the war in Iraq began. I attended a meeting in the White House in late January 2003 where it seemed to me that war aims did not appear to include nation-building and US security and foreign affairs agencies agreed that there was no need for a radical purging of Iraqi officials or of the country's military hierarchy. By March, however, the hawks in the administration had decided on an approach which led to a series of rapid-fire missteps which took us in another direction.

The over-confidence was astounding to me at the time: I was alarmed at how quickly we moved to declare victory and acclaim the support of the Iraqi people—which was not in evidence. American television replayed endlessly the image of a few hundred persons who gathered to watch American soldiers pull down a statute of Saddam Hussein in Baghdad—with hardly a qualifying observation on what this might mean about Iraqi ambivalence about "liberation" in a city of five million persons. The ransacking of government ministries, including the country's register of land holdings, was dismissed by then Secretary of Defense Rumsfeld as "stuff happens." Our failure to protect the basic infrastructure of governance in the country was to cost us dearly in the years to come, as was recognized at the time by State Department officials I worked with and who would later be expected to pick up the pieces of an occupation largely led by political appointees and security personnel with little understanding of the Iraqi environment.

As our engagement in Afghanistan and Iraq deepened, our ties with allies in Europe worsened, as we sought to measure the relationships largely through the prisms of the broader Middle East conflicts and the primacy of NATO "out-of-area", and as we were caught out on human rights abuses and torture.

As Deputy Assistant Secretary in PRM, I met with International Committee of the Red Cross (ICRC) officials regularly as they quietly raised the mistreatment of prisoners in Guantanamo, in Iraq, and Afghanistan. Their reports were more than disturbing: they were, for me, conclusive proof that torture was taking place. With a close colleague in Legal Affairs, Edward Cummings, a widely respected expert on human rights and war crimes, we raised our own deep concerns with our superiors and the Seventh Floor—well before the Abu Ghraib photographs emerged in May 2004.[14] While it was clear that the Department at its senior levels opposed the use of "enhanced interrogation techniques," it was also clear that other agencies and the White House at the leadership level did not. And they carried the day.

Our government never really seemed to realize the damage torture did to the international image of the United States as champion of democracy and human rights. We expected others to accept our rationalizations. Even after the widespread condemnations of Abu Ghraib by our political leaders and the US Congress, I remember having to accompany senior USG officials to meetings with the European Union where we sought to explain what constituted torture and what did not; where we asserted the primacy of American interpretations of the Geneva Conventions; and where we defended renditions of terrorism suspects to countries where there were no guarantees of due legal process. More widely, we resolutely defended the advances of democracy in Iraq as that country descended into civil war, as tens of thousands died, as we pressured European allies to participate in a conflict of our own making, and as we sidestepped the actions of problematic allies in the region.

Our international standing was also impacted by the military ups and downs of the "forever wars." As we "surged" first in Iraq in the mid-2000s to defeat an extremist insurgency, and then in Afghanistan to confront a resurgent Taliban, the United States found new justifications for extending our military engagements in the broader region. Our combat in the so-called Sunni triangle in 2004–2005 was presented as a victory, which it was, but which also led to the death of hundreds of young Americans and the further fragmentation of Iraq and sowed the seeds for the rise of Islamic State (ISIS). President Obama's draw-down of US military forces in Iraq had to be reversed by 2014 once ISIS began to control territory and populations in the north.

In the meantime, we ignored strategic concerns closer to home. The United States sought to reduce its "Plan Colombia" assistance to that country, arguably our most successful post-Cold War intervention in a conflict overseas. As ambassador in Bogota from 2010–2013, I found the policy short-sighted, and could not understand how we found tens of billions of dollars for Iraq and Afghanistan but held back meaningful assistance to Latin America more generally. It is certainly clear in 2022 that a more systematic and sustained engagement in the region could have helped us address issues like migration, narcotics, climate change, and economic growth which are of concern today. Instead, the prostitution scandal involving the Secret Service and Southern Command during the Summit of the Americas in Cartagena, which I had to contend with as ambassador, came to symbolize for me Washington's dismissive approach to the region.[15]

By 2013, I was in Afghanistan. It was striking the extent to which, year after year, the Pentagon and State Department submitted reports to Congress about advances being made in the conflict against the Taliban, and in developing the country's democracy and economy.[16] Our internal need to justify our actions in terms of broader policy objectives and principles, led to contortions which masked deteriorating realities on the ground. We extemporized on the prevalence of rampant corruption; on human rights abuses; on the failures of the Afghan military in the field. I made my concerns known to Washington to include my belief the government would not survive without US support. I was convinced as I left Kabul in December 2016 that the "eroding stalemate" designation used to describe events on the ground was accurate and that it was only a matter of time before the Taliban made significant gains.[17]

There was continuous debate in Washington on the long-term implications of our support for Afghanistan, and there were successive withdrawals of our military forces, but there was no conclusion to that debate until President Trump made the decision in 2018, against the recommendation of his national security advisers and the Department of Defense, to withdraw US troops from the country as quickly as possible. The result was the agreement between the Taliban and the US concluded in February 2020.

The fall of Kabul in August 2021, in the aftermath of President Biden's decision to complete the withdrawal of our forces from Afghanistan negotiated by his predecessor, was not a surprise to me. I agreed with the decision, if not with its execution. As I wrote in Foreign Affairs on August 16, one day after the Taliban entered the capital, "the situation on the ground is the result of two decades of miscalculations and failed policies pursued by three prior US administrations and of the failure of Afghanistan's leaders to govern for the good of their people. Many of the critics speaking out now were architects of those policies."[18]

There were other elements to US foreign policy after 2001, but, in hindsight, they did little to address the challenges that were emerging beyond our focus on the broader Middle Eastern wars and terrorism. Evaluated on their own merits, however, they were significant.

The Bush administration made historic commitments to fighting HIV/AIDS and malaria in Africa through the PEPFAR program—a lasting success benefitting tens of millions of people and perhaps a blueprint for assistance in the post-COVID pandemic world. Global economic issues were also a growing concern for the second Bush administration after 2004. Debt forgiveness for some of the world's poorest and most indebted countries charted a more strategic response to the challenge of unequal growth in the age of globalization. Again, the approach would appear to be an early model for how the developed world can help emerging economies address post-pandemic recovery, climate change and the economic impact of the war in Ukraine. US free trade agreements expanded from three to seventeen and seemed then to be the right strategic response to the opportunities of globalization.

At the US Mission to the European Union in Brussels from 2004–2007, I supported a myriad of visits of US cabinet and sub-cabinet officials who sought common ground with the EU on agriculture, banking regulations, and approaches to WTO negotiations. Washington, however, was more focused on reaching agreement on issues related to security—the sharing of passenger name records on transatlantic travel, the governance of international financial transfers through SWIFT, and discouraging the development of a separate security pillar among EU countries which could detract from NATO.

The focus was short-sighted. The 2000s were a period when the EU greatly expanded its global economic ties, and established conformity regulations and standards for everything from banking and accounting oversight to consumer products and the use of GMOs—all of which increasingly gained acceptance in global markets. European multinationals and financial institutions were challenging American rivals in more international markets. There was little strategic recognition inside the US government of how fundamentally transforming these trendlines were.

President Obama saw the dangers of a focus on the "forever wars" and a need to recast US engagement with the rest of the world. His 2008 campaign speech spoke about how the wars in Iraq and Afghanistan had robbed the United States of the opportunity to face twenty-first century challenges domestically and internationally.[19] It is nonetheless striking the extent to which the wars dominated that first speech—and his administration. It is also striking how reluctant successive administrations have been to acknowledge a central fact: by any number of definitions of success, including military, we lost the "forever wars." Our country has yet to come to terms with that hard reality.

Obama did restore a more collaborative approach to international diplomacy in contrast to the Bush administration. International public opinion became more favorable towards the United States again, and towards our government. The United States was instrumental in helping achieve the landmark Paris Climate Accord in 2015, still the reference point on climate change worldwide. Diplomatic relations with Cuba were restored—

a welcome, if short-lived, break from almost sixty years of failed sanctions policies which had done nothing to change the political system in that country, and which had complicated our relationship with Latin America as a whole. The JCPOA nuclear agreement with Iran promised a more strategic approach to the threat of proliferation in the Middle East—with the benefit of acting in concert with Russia and China as well as European partners.

The administration resisted the pressures to intervene in the Syrian conflict, tragic as the humanitarian consequences were. Doing so would have greatly expanded American military exposure in Middle Eastern conflicts and risked more direct confrontation with Russia. Obama in his final State of the Union in 2016 laid out the stakes starkly: "We also can't try to take over and rebuild every country that falls into crisis. It is the lesson of Vietnam and Iraq—and we should have learned it by now."[20] The Libyan civil war after "the Arab spring" and the triumph and subsequent overthrow of the Muslim Brotherhood in Egypt made clear the limits of US influence in the wider region. The reset with a resurgent Russia also abruptly stopped with the invasion of Crimea and the Donbass in Ukraine in 2014, but Moscow's belligerence did lead to a strengthening of US commitments to NATO's eastern European allies.

There was one other belated effort on trade and globalization. The pivot to Asia after 2012, and major initiatives like the Trans-Pacific Partnership (TPP) and the Transatlantic Trade and Investment Partnership (TTIP), were recognition of the rise of China and the importance of restructuring and modernizing our political and economic priorities. In retrospect, however, these initiatives came late as more negative global currents made themselves felt to include anti-free trade sentiment in the US Congress. These were not new. Throughout the negotiations in the 2000s to conclude the Peru and Colombia free trade agreements with the US, when I was ambassador in both countries, I was struck by the opposition from representatives and senators to accords which promoted markets and jobs for Americans as well as strategic economic alliances which would become more critical as China became more of a global economic heavyweight.

It appeared, as 2016 ended, that the United States was restoring its credibility as a global leader in the multilateral, economic, and transnational arenas, and beginning to take a tougher stand on the emerging challenges from Russia and China. That said, it is striking how little attention the afore-mentioned State of the Union address or Obama's farewell speech gave to foreign policy achievements or issues beyond terrorism and conflict even while extolling "the wealthiest, most powerful, and most respected nation on Earth." A reference to the challenge of "autocrats in foreign capitals who see free markets and open democracies and civil society itself as a threat to their power" was, however, a preview of things to come—inside democracies, including ours, as well as emerging authoritarian states and dictatorships.

The Trump Years 2017–2020:
The Internal Challenges to America in the World

It is facile and misleading to personalize what President Trump did—to the country, and to the foreign policy of the United States. The US had already spent much of the previous fifteen years consumed by the "forever wars": it was also undergoing significant political and social polarization domestically; and economically, a wrenching transformation laid bare by the 2008 Great Recession exposed inequalities and structural weaknesses that had been ignored over decades. We, like many other countries, turned inward after the financial crisis, becoming increasingly nationalistic, skeptical, and fearful.

As I have written elsewhere, Trump's approach in part reflected a broader consensus inside the United States about what should be our revised priorities going forward.[21] These included: ending the "never-ending" wars; confronting China; modernizing our security capabilities and greater burden-sharing within our alliances; levelling the playing field in international commerce where the United States was seen as losing ground to unfair competition from China and others; and retreating from globalization and international engagement.

Trump also reflected the breakdown in bipartisanship in US Congressional support for common foreign policy objectives. Bipartisanship beyond our shores may have been a myth at times, but an almost exaggerated sense of respect between the parties was always on display for outsiders. As I supported what seemed like dozens of congressional visits to Brussels, Lima, Bogota, and Kabul from 2001–2016, however, even the appearance of civility all but vanished. I remember Republicans telling me how they were going to block President Obama's priorities; Democrats spoke dismissively of Republican concerns.

By the time I reached Afghanistan in 2013, the hostility was open. On one occasion, I welcomed the late Senator McCain to my residence, only for him within a minute to tear into President Obama for the failures in Afghanistan—to include repeatedly referring to him as "your president." I told McCain he had been part and parcel of the policy decisions since 9/11 and the failures were his as well.

More broadly, the Trump Administration, which I served first as ambassador to Brazil and then as senior adviser to secretary of state Pompeo, was very much part of the global challenge underway to the post-1945/1989 world order. It was far broader than autocrats in China and Russia. The political and even ideological challenge questioned the relevance of an international model defined by the emergence of liberal democracies, open markets, globalization, security alliances, and a codification of universal human rights. In other words, the challenge internationally and in the United States was to the very ideals which had driven much of American foreign policy for almost seven decades.

Political populism as a governing model became increasingly manifest in Europe, in Latin America, in Asia—and flourished in the United States under Trump. He was reinforced by the pantheon of nationalist, authoritarian, and populist leaders which included longer-standing ones in Russia, China, and Turkey, now joined through the democratic process, by populist leaders in the Philippines, Italy, India, Hungary, Poland, Mexico, Brazil, the United Kingdom, and Japan. Many had in common an approach to foreign policy which defined national interest in narrow and unilateralist terms that tended to subsume multilateralism.

The Trump Policies

The Trump administration policies certainly had an impact, and some reflected new world realities.

Trump made economic prosperity the key feature of national security policy but with a profoundly different take. Globalization was rejected. Nationalistic and inward-looking economic objectives drove and dominated our ties with major trading partners—often to the exclusion of other longstanding rationales for the relationships. His administration did, however, renegotiate agreements with South Korea (KORUS) and Mexico and Canada (USMCA) which could be presented domestically as levelling access to foreign markets for goods produced by American firms and workers. He also forged a sanctions-based approach to China with domestic support, and which reflected a growing concern elsewhere about China's growing security, economic, and political challenge. He helped crystalize the urgency of the new challenge to cybersecurity from our adversaries.

His administration's actions on security reflected a widely shared view in Congress and his cabinet that the United States was over-extended and that our allies did not do enough for themselves. Burden-sharing did improve somewhat; and our involvement in the conflicts of the broader Middle East was reduced. The 2020 agreement between the United States and the Taliban appeared to allow for a defined exit strategy from Afghanistan. The diplomatic breakthrough of the Abraham Accords, between Israel and Arab states lowered tensions in the broader Middle East. The nuclear negotiations with North Korea were an important initiative to revive a moribund process as Kim Jong Un became ever more threatening to Seoul.

The efforts to reduce US military involvement in conflicts overseas were the product of a view that these wars had little strategic importance for the United States and of a growing reluctance to be "the policeman of the world." While successive administrations had shared these goals, there was a singularity of purpose to the strategic repositioning of US military resources and priorities around the globe under President Trump.

Diplomatically, and in a profound challenge to American engagement internationally since 1945, the Trump administration rejected multilateralism at almost every level, driven by a worldview that prioritized the primacy of bilateral ties and national self-interest as the bedrock of national security. The natural corollary was to reduce the emphasis on collective action to address human rights or global threats like climate change or health pandemics. It also resulted in the unilateral abrogation of international security agreements on nuclear weapons with Russia and Iran. Bilateral relations with countries became ever more transactional, with an emphasis on what they could do for US interests—abroad and domestically.

Again, Trump had elements of domestic or international support depending on the issue. The withdrawals from the JCPOA nuclear agreement with Iran and the Paris Climate Accord were warmly welcomed by those in the United States who had opposed them in the first place. The muted response internationally to the abrogation of the security and nuclear treaties with Russia reflected US and NATO concerns that Russia was violating its own commitments.

The negative fallout, however, of Trump's policies was glaring, throwing into question the direction of US foreign policy and values.

On the economic front, the decision to drop the Trans-Pacific Partner-ship (TPP) agreement, which was the strategic counterweight to China's expansion in the Asia-Pacific region, shook the confidence of our East Asian allies and led to alternative groupings that exclude the United States and include China. European and Asian leaders grew increasingly concerned about the intensifying rhetorical, economic, diplomatic, and security confrontation between China and the United States. Separately, trade frictions with some of our closest partners in Europe, Asia, and Latin America arose over the arbitrary imposition of tariffs on products like alu-minum and steel. Meanwhile, our own large trade and investment rela-tionship with China barely shifted despite sanctions and efforts to curb imports. I was also struck by the extent to which Secretaries of State and Commerce focused on re-shoring production facilities in the United States and seemed to ignore the economic and strategic benefit to the United States of the operations of American companies overseas. "America First" as a policy to rebuild the United States failed to factor in how firmly our economy was tied into the world's.

On the security front, Trump administration policies undermined our strategic rationale for working inside broader collectives. This helped weaken commitments to the alliances that had kept the United States se-cure for decades to include NATO and with our key East Asian partners. Trump's confrontational approach to burden-sharing with NATO, Japan, and South Korea, and threats to withdraw American troops from these theaters damaged our reputation as a reliable defense partner on defense. I was witness to ministerial meetings with allies including Britain, France, Germany, and South Korea in which the body language and the careful words chosen by interlocutors suggested that they were engaged in man-aging a difficult relationship.

Abandoning the JCPOA agreement was meant to weaken Iran; instead, Iran proceeded to enrich uranium at accelerated rates and to meddle with greater intensity in Lebanon, Iraq, and Yemen, and to threaten our Gulf allies. The Abraham Accords ignored the plight of Palestinians, strength-ening the hand of hardliners in Israel inclined to abandon the two-state solution which had been the bedrock of American diplomacy for decades. The growing tensions with China lessened the inclination of Beijing to cooperate on the North Korean nuclear negotiations, one of President Trump's most important diplomatic initiatives.

Diplomatically, key allies in Europe and East Asia began to re-think whether close ties with the United States could be sustained. African and

Latin American nations, whatever their political make-up, increasingly realized they factored even less in American foreign policy calculations than they had in prior administrations. The range of withdrawals from multilateral institutions diminished US influence on climate change, human rights, nuclear proliferation, trade rules, and in mobilizing a global response to COVID-19.

The mercurial nature of some of the decision-making disrupted policy and international perceptions of where the United States stood on issues. I was in Singapore when, on the eve of the first meeting with North Korea's leader, Trump threatened to pull-out of the summit flummoxing his advisers; in Washington, when the president's invitation to the Taliban to visit Camp David led to a rearguard action by the cabinet to have it withdrawn; and again in Washington, as the threats were made to close the Mexico-US border within hours if an immigration agreement was not reached. Allies noticed.

On a related front, the credibility of the United States as a "values" leader for the world had been fraying since 9/11. It now took a battering as Trump became a willing partner of a constellation of global authoritarians and populists intent on undermining the principles as well as the institutions and alliances of the liberal international order. As leaders from President Putin, President Xi, and President Kim Jong Un were embraced by Trump, allied leaders like President Trudeau of Canada, President Macron of France, and President Merkel of Germany were belittled.

American values were diminished on so many levels. As I and others worked on the migration accords with Mexico, for example, it was hard to escape the impression that the motivation included keeping persons of a different ethnic background out of the United States. I argued for sustaining even a symbolic commitment to an intake of refugees as the White House pushed for a complete stop to any resettlement program for people fleeing persecution. Senior cabinet officials were indifferent or hostile to what they saw as elite universities making the case for keeping the door open to international students. I heard comments that universities should focus instead on educating Americans to a higher standard rather than worry about ties to the outside world. It all seemed to me a return to the ideology of nativism from an earlier part of our national history.

Secretary of State Pompeo's creation of a Commission on Unalienable Rights in 2019 placed a primacy on religious freedom and sought to reinterpret American civil rights.[22] It was widely seen internationally and domestically as an effort to limit broader interpretations of human rights dating back to the UN Universal Declaration of Human Rights of 1948 which had served as the basis for expanding rights for women, for the LGBT community, and for fighting racial discrimination.

Domestic political developments also had a negative impact on foreign policy. As I wrote in the Financial Times on January 20, 2021, the assault on governance in Washington during the Trump years, to include the State Department and national security agencies, was significant.[23] It is hard to convey to outsiders what happens to bureaucracies when their most senior career leadership is sidelined or pushed out; when political loyalists subvert rules and regulations built up over generations to ensure the integrity of government departments; or what happens when simple facts and truth are turned into Orwellian-like speech.

It happened across the federal government, at State, at the Environmental Protection Agency, at the Department of Justice, at the Department of Education, at the Department of Defense, and inside the National Security Council itself. Most egregiously, the lessons on how to bull-doze your own experts were not lost on COVID-deniers overseas. The Trump administration appeared to systematically undermine the work and recommendations of the Center for Disease Control (CDC) and the National Institute of Health (NIH), which in turn seemed incapable of pushing back on the president. There was also the sustained effort by the Trump administration to use the national COVID response as a battleground between red and blue states. The independence of American media was assailed. At State, I found myself arguing against efforts to curtail access for media critics of our foreign policy.

At the State Department, and under both Secretaries of State Tillerson and Pompeo, the assault was on resources, process, people, and values. Tillerson sought to slash budgets and personnel, and to sideline the foreign service from decision-making. Well over 100 senior foreign service officers left or were forced to leave the building during his one year at State. Pompeo restored process, personnel systems, and promoted career officials to ambassadorships. Increasingly, however, and especially after the Ukraine scandal, the building became more politicized.

Even before I resigned in October 2019, I witnessed a significant change in the working environment. The denigration of the loyalty of civil servants by some political appointees was persistent. The development of a "Professional Ethos" for State Department employees, to which I voiced my opposition early on, resulted in an intimidating "loyalty oath" banner hung at the "C" Street diplomatic entrance. It was not intentional, but there were echoes with what authoritarian governments might seek to impose. One senior career person told me, only partly in jest, that a Seventh Floor-chaired meeting we both had attended was more like a session of the North Korean politburo. The shock of the early Tillerson months passed; among foreign service colleagues what I sensed was a greater degree of resignation to the status quo.

I have written elsewhere in some detail about just how much the building was undermined across the four years and will not belabor the points further here.[24] I do want to note that the decline in diversity inside the State Department was noticeable. There appeared to be antipathy to the advocacy of LGBT rights internationally. The absence of African Americans from positions of authority in the State Department and the steady decline in the number of senior female leaders was pronounced—despite efforts by a few career officials to change that reality. The relative silence of senior State Department officials, as the murder of George Floyd and the Black Lives Matter movement impacted the building, was striking. At the time, I wrote in the Foreign Service Journal about the racism at Foggy Bottom that urgently needed to be addressed by department leadership and included accounts of the prejudice my own family of mixed race and heritage had faced.

Finally, there was the scandal over the political extortion of Ukraine in 2019 which resulted in the first impeachment of President Trump. Enough has been written about this episode that it does not require elaboration here. As I wrote in my statement to the investigating congressional committee in October of that year, my resignation from the department was driven both by the failure of State to support Ambassador Masha Yovanovitch and other colleagues drawn into the controversy, and by the effort to extort Ukraine for domestic political gain.[25] I had already had political appointees all but label me as "deep state" earlier in my time on the Seventh Floor, but there was an additional chill to hear that there was the possibility of the White House targeting me as well. I also knew that civil servants in other departments had faced their own moments of difficult reckoning over different issues. The whole atmosphere had echoes of the drift to authoritarian rule I had seen in other governments. It did not surprise me to see reports after President Trump left office that General Milley, among other senior former administration officials, are reported to have used terminology from the 1930s to describe what they had experienced.[26]

The spectacle internationally of a United States president using development and security assistance to pressure another country for political dirt on an opponent sent a clear message to American friends and allies everywhere. There were no more rules of the game, let alone "values," in play. For these countries, foreign policy was becoming a question of managing a wayward United States the way they might other powerful countries that could hurt as much as help their interests. Without a change in administration in January 2021, it is hard to see how our long-term US alliances and relationships could have been sustained in a second Trump presidency, certainly not as we had come to know them over the previous seventy years.

Looking Forward

The United States remained the most powerful economy in the world, and still had the strongest military, but by 2021 found itself less influential than just a few years earlier. The incoming Biden administration clearly had thought through the implications. In its first two years, it has carried out a broad range of initiatives to reengage multilaterally, meet transnational challenges, rebuild alliances, and tackle simmering and full-blown crises around the globe. Critically, the change in approach and tonality from the Trump years has also been significant, with an important emphasis on listening to and working with allies and friends.

The breadth of ambition internationally is sometimes lost given how much of the Biden administration's focus has been on our domestic recovery from the pandemic and transforming the American economy. As the following list suggests, the administration's foreign policy has addressed the strategic landscape. The United States rejoined the Paris Climate Accord and the World Health Organization and broadened our multilateral engagement with US-sponsored initiatives like the Leaders' Summit on Climate Change and the Democracy Summit. Washington highlighted the importance of international economic cooperation through the G-7 and G-20 and launched a US EU Trade and Technology council to address the challenges of the digital age. It reinforced security alliances from East Asia to NATO and strengthened regional dialogues in South Asia and the Pacific.

The administration also toughened US policy towards China as well as Russia, even before the invasion of Ukraine on February 24, 2022. Washington helped expand the Abraham Accords between Israel and Middle Eastern nations, supported peace negotiations in Yemen and Ethiopia, and deepened economic ties and assistance in the Indo-Pacific. There has been outreach to Africa and Latin America with leaders' summits hosted by President Biden. Efforts are underway to intensify cooperation in the western hemisphere to address the surge in migration, the environment, and near-shoring. The US response to Russia's invasion of Ukraine has galvanized NATO and Europe into displaying a unity of purpose not seen for a generation.

That said, the damage in recent years to our foreign policy and standing in the world has been significant, and the challenge we face is not simply about reversing individual decisions by the Trump administration—or about successfully mobilizing a response to an inflection point in international relations, which is what Ukraine represents. It is also about adapting for a vastly changed global landscape, where, once again, most of the world is not defining foreign policy in unequivocal terms or looking for American leadership to help determine the path forward. The war in Ukraine has not fundamentally changed that reality.

In this context, it seems fair to ask whether the United States would have quite the same profile internationally as it does now without Russia's invasion of Ukraine. Even a cursory look at other issues suggests that our influence or primacy is not so easily restored. The Summit of the Americas in June 2022 laid bare Washington's divide with Latin American countries on a host of issues. The presidential visit to Saudi Arabia later that month only served to highlight the weakened state of US ties with Gulf states. The withdrawal from Afghanistan was seen in South and Central Asia as reflecting a decline in American interest in the wider region. Washington's message at the US-Africa Leaders' Summit in December 2022 was heavily focused on the challenge from China and appeared to fall flat with an audience of the continent's presidents and prime ministers. The new Indo-Pacific Economic Framework (IPEF), also launched in 2022, is seen as thin on substance by South and East Asian allies. Before Russia's invasion of Ukraine on February 24, 2022, western European governments were openly skeptical about the staying power of the administration's reset of the transatlantic relationship. President Macron argued openly for Europe's "strategic autonomy" from the United States.

Additionally, the initiatives in Washington to rebuild capacity, resiliency, and innovation inside our nation seem to other countries a variation on the "America First" policies of the Trump administration that caused global trade frictions earlier. The administration's by-line for international engagement "a foreign policy for the middle class" and criticism of free trade agreements suggest as much. Although American initiatives like the Inflation Reduction Act and Chips and Science Act are driven in part by concerns about the "systemic" rivalry with an emerging China, there has been little outreach by the United States to trading partners and allies on how to work together to meet the challenge. European governments are dismayed by what they see as growing American subsidies and protectionism in the economic sphere, which they believe will harm their economies.

In East Asia, the IPEF initiative offers no concessions on access to the American market and is driven more by US concerns with China than anything else. The corollary is the growing concern of regional countries with the deteriorating relations between the two superpowers. The United States has not rejoined the Trans-Pacific Partnership, now known by the acronym CPTPP, the single most important step it could have taken to address both its concerns about China and promote trade and investment with East Asia. As for near-shoring or friend-shoring supply chains of critical products, there has been no sustained effort by the United States to define what that might entail in practice in Latin America or elsewhere.

More generally, the many countries governed by authoritarian or populist leaders are unlikely in the near term to change policies or leadership that are problematic for the United States. They include American partners or allies in every region of the world at a moment of growing international tension and conflict. That reality alone would suggest the need for greater nuance in American foreign policy.

Domestically, our reckoning with the fallout of the January 6 insurrection is far from complete and highlights our continuing democratic vulnerabilities and affects foreign policy. Our political fault lines are again being exposed by efforts to restrict individual freedoms at state level and as candidates line up to contest the 2024 presidential elections. The opposition to multilateralism inside the Republican party remains strong, and there are broader questions about how extensively the United States should commit to conflicts abroad.

In response, however, and just as we did during the Cold War and the global war on terror, we are reverting to a Manichean vision of good and evil. The National Security Strategy and other statements by American political leaders may speak analytically about broader international concerns and the strategic competition with China, Russia, and autocracy, but the tonality is of an existential confrontation where, again, it is the United States that will be at the forefront of the battle for what is right: "Around the world, the need for American leadership is as great as it has ever been . . . the need for a strong and purposeful American role in the world has never been greater." We are in "the contest for the future of the world," and "we will not leave (that) future vulnerable to the whims of those who do not share our vision for a world that is free, open, prosperous, and secure."[27] The competing visions entail "whether the world should be safer for democracy or authoritarianism . . . (and) whether the strong can bully the weak." In the coming years, "the terms for geopolitical competition between the major powers will be set."[28]

These are strong words and beg the question of what the rest of the world thinks is at stake and what the role of the United States should be. As articulated, our vision does not lend itself to the complexity of dealing with wary allies and partners, sophisticated adversaries, audiences skeptical of our political authority, and the dozens if not majority of countries who are not interested in taking sides. Their view of global challenges is not necessarily ours; our view of our role is not necessarily theirs.

I began this chapter suggesting that there are significant continuities in the foreign policy context. There is common ground internationally on the nature of some of the key challenges the world now faces. The new National Security Strategy does address many of the issues I have raised. The United States can be expected to play a key role internationally whatever happens.

The NSS, however, also acknowledges that "the post-Cold War era is definitely over." If that is the case, then it is also time to abandon our default position of defining foreign policy challenges in terms of American exceptionalism, leadership, and, as I said earlier, in black and white. A more pragmatic approach to foreign policy would seem to be in order, one that still finds a way to uphold our values but recognizes the multi-layered complexity of today's world.

It may yet arrive, but not without additional effort. President Biden and

Secretary of State Blinken have made clear on many occasions, that the United States must heal itself. "Shoring up our democracy is a foreign policy imperative," but much will depend on whether a next administration shares that belief. Partnership is again part of foreign policy; but without clearer indications that the US is prepared to work on a global stage with many players and interests, rather than simply seek to reimpose a modified status quo of American leadership and objectives, the efforts will be for naught. There does appear to be greater pragmatism in working our security alliances and multilateral institutions, as opposed to focusing on their limitations. Again, however, there will be a need to strengthen and modernize them to face down those who want to see the international order weakened. Our own resource commitment to foreign affairs and security agencies must increase in a more troubled world but may be difficult to achieve in a divided Washington. As we continue to promote values we believe to be universal, we are in danger of over-estimating our influence.

Institutionally, there is also a requirement to rebuild the State Department to reverse the damage done by Secretaries Tillerson and Pompeo. Serious initiatives are underway to reform and modernize the foreign service, to add resources, and to carry out a much-needed makeover on race, on gender, and generationally. It will also be important to formalize safeguards for process and personnel. To date there appears to be an assumption that the page can simply be turned by not being the previous administration. History suggests that is not how things work. In the meantime, old habits die hard to include the high level of political donors appointed to ambassadorships. This is the spoils system by any other name and undermines the integrity of the department. There is also an insidious perception that State has lost primacy to other government agencies since 9/11 because of intrinsic institutional weakness. State's centrality, however, is heavily determined by the influence of its political leadership and the priorities determined by the White House. If those policies are directed to engaging the world, instead of shutting it out, the State Department will continue to be the at the center of foreign policy.

Finally, the United States should avoid finding new crusades to mobilize its international engagement. That means rethinking China and Russia. This is not the place to debate policy towards both countries, but it should be possible to suggest that the proliferation of conflict-laden rhetoric does not contribute to a strategic approach to the most consequential challenges of our time—and may lead to unintended military conflict. We also risk losing sight of the many other concerns we should address around the globe—and inside our own country. Ideals can continue to be at the center of America's self-image and motivation; they do not need to lock us into the past as we confront the future.

Notes

1. https://www.whitehouse.gov/wp-content/uploads/2022/10/Biden-Harris -Administrations-National-Security-Strategy-10.2022.pdf

2. https://www.jstor.org/stable/24027184

3. https://2009–2017.state.gov/p/io/potusunga/207269.htm, and https://1997 –2001.state.gov/statements/970123.html

4. https://www.nytimes.com/1999/02/05/news/to-paris-us-looks-like-a -hyperpower.html

5. https://www.foreignaffairs.com/united-states/what-do-american-primacy

6. https://www.foreignaffairs.com/articles/1990–01–01/unipolar-moment

7. https://www.theatlantic.com/ideas/archive/2021/06/how-donald-rumsfeld -deserves-be-remembered/619334/ and https://www.sigar.mil/pdf/evaluations /SIGAR-23–05-IP.pdf

8. https://georgewbush-whitehouse.archives.gov/news/releases/2001/09/20010920 –8.html

9. https://obamawhitehouse.archives.gov/sites/default/files/rss_viewer /national_security_strategy.pdf

10. https://www.pewresearch.org/global/2001/12/19/americas-image-post-911/

11. https://www.goldmansachs.com/insights/archive/archive-pdfs/brics-book /brics-full-book.pdf and https://journals.sagepub.com/doi/full/10.1177 /09749101211067096#:~:text=The%20role%20and%20contribution%20of,(US %24%204%20trillion).

12. https://georgewbush-whitehouse.archives.gov/news/releases/2005/12 /20051214–1.html

13. https://georgewbush-whitehouse.archives.gov/news/releases/2006/04 /20060406–3.html and https://www.cnn.com/2007/POLITICS/09/11/iraq .senate/index.html

14. http://www.washingtonpost.com/archive/local/2006/03/17/edward-cummings -lawyer/421231f4–4412–4638-bf0b-f6d299fc772f/?tid=ss_mail

15. https://www.washingtonian.com/2013/03/25/secret-service-prostitution -scandal-one-year-later/

16. https://dod.defense.gov/Portals/1/Documents/pubs/October_1230_Report _Master_Nov7.pdf, and for subsequent years, passim

17. https://www.washingtonpost.com/news/checkpoint/wp/2016/10/14/an -eroding-stalemate-in-afghanistan-as-taliban-widens-its-offensive/

18. https://www.foreignaffairs.com/articles/united-states/2021–08–16/we-all-lost
-afghanistan-taliban

19. https://www.nytimes.com/2008/07/15/us/politics/15text-obama.html

20. https://obamawhitehouse.archives.gov/the-press-office/2016/01/12/remarks
-president-barack-obama-%E2%80%93-prepared-delivery-state-union
-address

21. https://jia.sipa.columbia.edu/online-articles/nationalist-and-populist
-challenge-foreign-policy

22. https://www.nytimes.com/2019/07/08/us/politics/state-human-rights.html

23. https://www.ft.com/content/31ddc0e5–4f95–4f1f-a188-a906ebec9296

24. https://www.theatlantic.com/ideas/archive/2020/10/state-departments
-politicization-almost-complete/616795/

25. https://www.politico.com/news/2019/11/04/michael-mckinley-impeachment
-deposition-read-full-text-pdf-065495

26. https://www.theguardian.com/books/2021/jul/16/i-alone-can-fix-it-review
-donald-trump-fuhrer-mark-milley-leonnig-rucker and https://www.cnn.com
/2021/07/07/politics/donald-trump-adolf-hitler-book-claims/index.html

27. https://www.whitehouse.gov/wp-content/uploads/2022/10/Biden-Harris
-Administrations-National-Security-Strategy-10.2022.pdf

28. https://www.politico.com/news/2022/05/26/blinken-biden-china-policy
-speech-00035385

THIRTEEN

J. STAPLETON ROY

Superpower Diplomacy

Understanding how the United States can and should use its power responsibly in a world where we have, until recently, had uncontested military supremacy is the number one foreign policy and national security challenge facing our country. Anyone who reads the morning newspapers knows that we are facing many difficult trials, both domestically and abroad. Our position in Afghanistan has collapsed, twenty years after terrorists based in that country dealt the United States the most damaging blow on our soil since Pearl Harbor. We responded by committing our power to transforming the situations in Afghanistan and Iraq.

We are still living with the consequences of those decisions. In North Korea and Iran we are facing dangerous nuclear challenges. Many of our traditional allies are skeptical of our motives and reluctant to assist us to deal with a threat that many think we brought on ourselves. Public opinion in countries that have been close US allies for over fifty years is now prone to view unilateral use of American power as a bigger threat than their traditional enemies.

Of particular concern, anti-Americanism is strong enough to deserve more attention than we are giving it, and it is not being artificially fanned by a Cold War opponent. Such sentiments are not simply found in traditional bastions of anti-Americanism as the Middle East and the Muslim world. They are now strong in Europe and Russia, where they extend far beyond the irredeemable leftist intellectual circles that still cling to outmoded Marxist concepts. They have been important factors in elections in Germany, South Korea, and Spain, where the winners in each case were those who used anti-Americanism to their advantage.

Americans quite rightly are troubled by this phenomenon. As the hands-down winner in the Cold War showdown between the side favoring freedom and democracy and the side mired in the repressive misconceptions of communism, we should, by rights, be acclaimed by a grateful world. And yet this is not the case. Some attribute this to the petty envy of less successful nations. According to this school of thought, it is natural for people to resent the wealth and power of others. They dismiss such envy as an inevitable consequence of leadership. Others do not care and argue that the opinions of other countries are irrelevant.

In a sense these attitudes beg the question. Is it the fact of leadership or the style of leadership that is feeding anti-American sentiments in the world? Our society has many wealthy and powerful individuals. Some are arrogant, demanding, and abusive. Others do not flaunt their wealth and are modest, generous, and considerate. Most people respond differently to these two extremes. So, it is risky to blame our unpopularity on our power and leadership alone. What we need, I would argue is a different conceptual framework for thinking about many of these issues.

It may be helpful first to take a broader look at our current foreign policy environment. It is an indisputable fact that we are still the preeminent nation in the world. Most if not all Americans want and expect us to be a force for good. Our problem is that we have been cast into this role without a consensus, either nationally or within the administration, on how we should use this power. In that sense, we have not yet adapted our foreign policy to our new role in the world.

This is important, because a foreign policy, to be effective, must be based on a strategy that integrates our goals with a realistic understanding of the constraints on what we can accomplish. It is also important to achieve the proper balance between our ideals and our interests. We now have fewer constraints on use of our power because of the absence of a superpower competitor, although China is on the path to becoming one. This has created two related problems: how to use our power wisely in the absence of constraints on use of our power; and how to handle the balance between domestic and international drivers of our foreign policy. We are not handling either of these problems well.

In a sense, the end of the Cold War did not represent the end of history, as some have argued, but rather the end of geo-politics in the United States. What I mean is that with the removal of the Soviet threat, domestic considerations became the principal drivers of our foreign policy. Obviously, domestic factors are always relevant to foreign policy in a democracy. Policies cannot be pursued effectively if they lack the necessary domestic base of support. We have seen numerous instances of this in recent decades. However, domestic factors should not be the drivers of foreign policy. Domestically driven foreign policies are usually ineffective, misguided, and particularly vulnerable to the law of unintended consequences.

To be effective, foreign policies need to be grounded in a sound understanding of the real world with which we have to deal. A prime function of our diplomatic missions around the globe is to provide the US government with the information necessary for such an understanding. As you would expect, Americans do not pay sufficient attention to our international interests to provide sound guidance. This is what governments are for. It is the responsibility of government to ensure that properly conceived policies retain the domestic base of support necessary for their effective implementation.

This requires that our interests be pursued with due regard for our values. When we face severe threats, Americans are prepared to set aside our values as necessary to deal with the threat. When threats recede, the values reassert themselves. The most effective policies result when our interests and values are in congruence. Most of the time this is not the case, confronting us with the same challenge that we have confronted throughout our history, which is reconciling the discrepancies between our ideals and the actions we take in pursuit of our interests.

Values and Interests

Two decades ago, Henry Kissinger wrote a book entitled *Does America Need a Foreign Policy?* In it he noted: "In the face of perhaps the most profound and widespread upheavals the world has ever seen, has failed to develop concepts relevant to the emerging realities." This is not an indictment of us, since he also notes that "The United States finds itself in a world for which little in its historical experience has prepared it."

Three decades into the post-Cold War period, we have still not developed a coherent vision of how we should use our power to promote our ideals and advance our interests. We reject the concept of empire as applying to us, but in much of the world we are perceived as peremptory and domineering—imperial, in fact.

The United States as an Accidental Sole Superpower

At the core of my argument is the proposition that we, the people of the United States, are essentially unprepared for the role we have been thrust into in the world? This is not due to any deficiency in our capabilities as a people but because of two intertwined considerations.

- Our historical experience has not prepared us for the situation we now face. At times in our past, we have been isolationist in our thinking. At other times, we have played an active role in bipolar situations where the contest, in our view, has been between good and evil, between the free world and the evil empire. This was the case during our brief intervention in World War I, following which we rejected participation in the League of Nations. This was also the case during World War II and the Cold War that followed it. In both these cases, our interests and our ideals were mutually reinforcing.

- There is another and arguably more important strand in our history, which is the role we have played in the Western Hemisphere, the only region of the world that has been subject to domination by a regional superpower, the United States. In the Western Hemisphere, we have been neither isolationist nor engaged in a battle between good and evil. On the contrary, with no significant checks on our power, we have been both interventionist and high minded, often acting without due regard for the contradictions between the principles which we espouse and the interests that we intervene to protect.

Now we find ourselves thrust into a leadership role in a globalized world that is not bipolar. The threats come not only from specific countries, but also from issues such as terrorism, the danger of proliferation of nuclear weapons, and global warming. In dealing with these issues, we find we need to cooperate with countries such as China and Russia, whose domestic structures do not fit the model of mature western democracies.

The second reason for our mental unpreparedness is that we were thrust into the role of the world's sole superpower not by conquest but because of the unraveling of our principal opponent, the Soviet Union. This did not happen at a time of confrontation between the two superpowers. On the contrary, it occurred during a period of détente when Gorbachev was pursuing policies of *glasnost* and *perestroika* that were opening up the Soviet Union to outside influences as never before.

In looking back through history, I have been unable to identify a single comparable case in which the dominant country achieved its position of preeminence by the domestically driven collapse of its principal rival. The net result is that we are still struggling to define how we should use the sudden increase in our relative power position in the world. This confronts us with a number of conceptual challenges.

First Challenge:
Applying American Political Principles to Foreign Policy

The first challenge lies in how to apply American political principles to foreign policy. A good place to begin is with the debate that accompanied the establishment of our nation. The genius of our founding fathers, as expressed in The Federalist Papers, lay in their understanding that power is dangerous and corrupting and that unchecked power in the hands of government will inevitably lead to improper use of that power.

This concept found expression in President Washington's farewell address, where our first president offered this sage comment after eight years in office: "A just estimate of that love of power, and proneness to abuse it, which predominates in the human heart, is sufficient to satisfy us of the truth of this position. The necessity of reciprocal checks in the exercise of political power, by dividing and distributing it into different depositaries, and constituting each the guardian of the public weal against invasions by the others, has been evinced by experiments ancient and modern; some of them in our country and under our own eyes."

Our founding fathers applied this concept to the formulation of our system of government, and their insight forms the basis for every modern system of government in the world. In theory, that concept is just as relevant in international as in national affairs.

Yet, curiously, our thinking about our global role seems to attach no importance to this concept. On the contrary, many Americans are proud of our role today as the sole superpower. We glory in our ability to stamp out evil regimes with only token support from friends and allies. Our defense budget exceeds the collective defense budgets of all of our principal allies and adversaries. What is missing is recognition that American political theory suggests that being a "sole superpower" will lead inevitably to abuse of that power in the absence of appropriate checks and balances, as our behavior in the post-Cold War period has demonstrated.

We are giving too little attention to this issue. Perhaps we should be asking ourselves: What is the nature of the global system that can, in the no-longer-bipolar post-Cold War era, ensure that extended US preponderance will not lead to improper use of US power? This is in our own interest. If we are seen as using our power wisely, other nations will be comfortable with our leadership and will not attach high priority to challenging us. Conversely, if we are seen as abusing our power, this will inevitably hasten the emergence of countervailing checks on our power. I address this issue later in this essay.

Second Challenge:
Finding the Right Style of Leadership

The second challenge, perhaps even more difficult than the first, will be finding the right style of leadership for current world conditions. Some time ago, an Asia Foundation Task Force report on Asian views of the American Role in Asia is replete with references to a flawed US style of leadership, which Asians characterized as heavy-handed, lacking consistency and sensitivity, and prone to unilateralism. The problem is not restricted to Asia, since we find such attitudes in Europe as well. Most countries in Europe and Asia still want and expect the United States to provide leadership. But as the Asian report makes clear, they want more consultation and sensitivity. Three decades into the post-Cold War era, the United States has not yet adjusted its leadership style to the type of leadership required by the different threat perceptions we now face.

Third Challenge:
Defining the US Role in the World

The third challenge is defining the type of world that we would like to see emerge, and the role that the United States should play, both in helping to create that world and in using our power within it. Our efforts to reconcile these contradictions are complicated by the divergent views within the US policy establishment on this question.

Elements of a variety of contending schools of foreign policy thinking are all present in recent administrations. In the George W. Bush administration, the principal struggle, a highly ideological one, was between the neo-conservative (hegemony) view of how to use US power and the more traditional view. Since then, anti-globalization views have strengthened, and the Biden administration has yet to clarify whether it will maintain our traditional free trade position or retain the protectionist elements that gained strength in the Trump administration.

A case can be made that the United States and Iran are the two most ideologically-driven countries in the world today. In essence the United States has become a revolutionary power, prone to intervene in other countries to impose our concepts of governance but without the knowledge of the world necessary to use our power wisely. In successive administrations, a public consensus has not emerged on the question of how to use US power. This lack of consensus undermines our ability to convey a coherent message, whether to friendly ears or to those skeptical of our intentions.

Role of Diplomacy

Diplomacy is the art of influencing others through persuasion to act in ways that are compatible with your own interests. It is shaped by the power relationships among the parties, by the degree of commonality, or lack thereof, among the respective interests, and by the vagaries of human nature as reflected in the individual personalities of those involved. It normally requires compromises of greater or lesser significance to reach agreement. When diplomacy fails, this can result in conflict or in disgruntled acquiescence to the wishes of the dominant party or parties.

In the international sphere, agreements reached through diplomacy help to stabilize bilateral and multilateral relationships as long as the common interests that underpin the agreements remain intact. If the common interests diverge, compliance with agreements suffers. The American record of compliance with commitments that we consider outmoded is poor. This is one of the weaker aspects of our diplomatic traditions. This is true of other countries as well, but we tend to be more vociferous in extolling the virtues of upholding the rule of law, while willfully breaking the rules when we see this as serving our interests at the moment.

Personality factors are important in diplomacy for a variety of reasons. You need to be able to understand the motivations of the other side without being captured by them. You need to gain the confidence of the other side while not losing the confidence of your own government. Of the two, the most important consideration is to keep the confidence of your own government.

Diplomacy is a competitive profession. You must never forget that the government you are dealing with abroad has its own ambassador in Washington. If officials of your own government prefer to convey messages through the ambassador of the country to which you are accredited, your influence in Washington will shrivel, as will your knowledge of the current state of affairs. This was a major problem for American diplomats during the Nixon administration, when Soviet ambassador Dobrynin had access to the White House that American diplomats lacked in Moscow. For those of us serving in Moscow, this meant that we often knew less about the bilateral relationship than our Soviet counterparts and well-informed American journalists.

Diplomatic skills in dealing with your own government are just as important as in dealing with the foreign government. It can even be harder, especially when a change in administration has shifted the cast of senior policy-making officials in Washington. Ideological factors are often strongest when a new administration takes office. The Chinese have a saying that new officials arrive brandishing three torches, meaning they are eager to put their own stamp on affairs. This was the case in both the Reagan first term and the Clinton first term.

I arrived in Bangkok, Thailand as Deputy Chief of Mission in the American embassy during the first year of the Reagan administration. One of the final actions of my predecessor, who was acting ambassador (in diplomatese this is expressed as Chargé d'Affaires ad interim, or Chargé for short) following the departure of the previous Chief of Mission, was to send a telegram to Washington strongly recommending against publicly charging the communist regimes in Indochina with a form of biological warfare called "yellow rain." This quaint moniker was adopted because various hill tribes had reported seeing puffs of yellow smoke being emitted from communist jet aircraft, following which people on the ground reported various illnesses. The toxic substance was identified by government analysts as a mycotoxin, a toxic substance produced by certain fungi.

The evidence for this charge was skimpy at best, but the Reagan administration was eager to put communist regimes on the defensive. As a result, they ignored the US embassy's advice and launched at the United Nations a high-profile propaganda war against the communist regimes in Indochina, accusing them of engaging in biological warfare. The American embassy in Bangkok was tasked with collecting samples of these mycotoxins on assorted plant twigs, which were shipped to Washington for analysis. Unfortunately, the analytical process took up to nine months, which seemed excessively long when dealing with a deadly pathogen.

We in the embassy concluded that the weight of the evidence pointed against the validity of the claim that the communist countries were engaged in "yellow rain" warfare. However, the ideological fervor in Washington was such that openly disputing the claims would have resulted in discrediting the embassy's reporting. Instead, we persuaded Washington that given the gravity of the charge, we needed professional biological warfare specialists on our staff to validate the claims. Washington acquiesced and sent us two highly qualified US army biological warfare specialists whose sole function was quickly to investigate any instances of alleged yellow rain. Their reports were uniformly negative. Washington never repudiated the claim, but as the weight of the negative evidence accumulated, the administration quietly dropped the campaign. An eminent American scientist concluded that the droplets of alleged yellow rain were actually bee droppings colored by pollen from yellow flowers.

Another example of how ideological fervor can impact on foreign policy was provided by the Bo Gritz affair, which also occurred early in the Reagan administration's first term. In the wake of the Vietnam War, we attached high priority to tracking down evidence of American military personnel reported as missing-in-action in the war. A special unit of the American embassy in Bangkok, staffed by US military personnel, was devoted to this task. We investigated every claim, however scant the evidence. They became skilled in identifying fraudsters who tried to sell the American embassy chicken bones, claiming they were the remains of American military personnel.

Enter Bo Gritz. He was a decorated special forces veteran of the Vietnam War, who became convinced that substantial numbers of American missing-in-action were being held in prison camps in southern Laos. We had gotten wind, through the informal grapevine in Washington, that with his impressive military credentials, Bo Gritz had gained informal backing from the White House to undertake a secret mission to Thailand, behind the backs of the alleged skeptics in the US embassy, to locate and liberate these unfortunate US personnel.

Bo Gritz arrived in Bangkok, avoided any contact with the US embassy, and immediately fell into the hands of the chicken-bone sellers. Together with him, they organized a foray into Laos. Starting from eastern Thailand, the intrepid group swam across the Mekong River to Laos and trekked into the jungle, whereupon the chicken-bone sellers took him prisoner and held him for ransom. Bo Gritz, with his impeccable military skills, managed to escape and swim back across the Mekong to Thailand, where he was promptly arrested by Thai border forces for illegal entry. As soon as the US embassy learned of these developments, we dispatched consular officers to the border, who succeeded in getting Bo Gritz released and repatriated to the United States.

This is indicative of another feature of American diplomacy: we provide prompt and unbiased assistance to any American citizen who runs into difficulties with the law in foreign countries, without regard to the background of the individual. If American citizens break the law in foreign countries, of course, they are subject to local jurisdiction. But our embassies and consulates monitor their treatment, witness their trials, visit them regularly, provide reading material, and help to repatriate them once they are released.

When I served in the American embassy in Taiwan in the early 1960s (when we still recognized the Republic of China on Taiwan as the government of China), one of my duties was to witness the marriages of Americans to Chinese so that I could provide an English language certificate to supplement the Chinese language marriage license, which had little utility in the United States. Most of the Americans were young military personnel who had fallen in love with local girls.

Impact of Experience on Understanding

When I retired from the Foreign Service in January 2001, I was entering my 45th year in the US Department of State and had served as an American diplomat for over 20 percent of our history under our present constitutional system. The United States was at the height of its power, and I always felt extraordinarily fortunate to have the opportunity to represent my country abroad in both Asia and Europe. Nearly half of that time was focused on dealing with China and the Soviet Union, the two communist countries that constituted our most formidable international challenges.

By joining the Foreign Service at the tender age of 21, my state of mind was of having an endless time horizon ahead during which I could master the art of dealing with foreign countries of differing sizes and inclinations. I loved my work and was more focused on having interesting assignments than on rapid advancement. I could afford the luxury of spending three years in full time language training assignments before I reached the average entry age for new foreign service officers.

This slowed my promotions. At one point, one of my supervisors cautioned me, after I had agreed to spend a year studying Mongolian, that I needed to pay more attention to getting promoted since the most interesting and challenging jobs were at higher levels of the Foreign Service and would be out of reach if I was not competitive with my colleagues. This was good advice, which I largely ignored for another ten years, while reaching professional level fluency in Chinese and Russian, in addition to Mongolian. Newly-minted officers who entered the Foreign Service in their thirties could not afford this luxury.

Speaking the language of your post of assignment is an enormous asset, even if you can get by speaking English or a widely known language such as French or Spanish. Aside from improving your understanding of local history and culture, your range of contacts is greatly expanded by being able to converse in the local language, especially if you are able to achieve a high level of fluency. My practice was to be guided by the language preference of whomever I was talking to. Often, foreigners want to practice their English and resent it if you persist in switching to their own local language.

Through observation, however, I learned one of the advantages of speaking the local language well. In Taiwan, I noted that many senior government officials spoke English fluently, making easy conversation possible. Visiting American officials, however, would make the mistake of assuming that if the foreign official spoke fluent English, that meant the official thought the way that Americans do, which was not the case. This gave the other side a subtle advantage.

I saw the same situation in reverse in Beijing. In one case a well-connected university professor I had met agreed to assemble a group of young vice-minister level officials from various ministries for a dinner party at my residence. The conversation was entirely in Chinese, and as the dinner progressed the officials relaxed and began to swap stories and gossip. One of them observed, for example, that 84 percent of the high-octane Maotai liquor sold in Beijing was counterfeit. The water for the liquor was supposed to come from a particular spring in a southern province, but neighboring towns were producing counterfeit versions from their own local springs.

This resulted in a lively discussion of what the government should do. The counterfeit liquor was of a quality making it nearly indistinguishable from the authentic liquor, and the livelihoods of thirty thousand workers depended on the counterfeit trade. Should the government destroy the jobs of these workers over a minor difference of quality in the end product? Sharply differing views were expressed in a convivial atmosphere. No state secrets were revealed, but it was unusual for a foreign diplomat to be exposed to this type of interplay among Chinese officials. The conversation would have been impossible in English, or through interpreters.

During my years in the Foreign Service, the US government devoted substantial resources to language training. In every embassy and consulate that I served in, we usually had the highest percentage of language officers among our personnel and were considered to be among the best-informed diplomatic establishments.

In retrospect, I can see how fortunate I was to have landed in a profession that perfectly suited my interests. For four and a half decades I was privileged to work alongside colleagues of uniformly high integrity and of an intellectual caliber that made judgments of relative "smartness" completely irrelevant. Nobody referred to a colleague as being brilliant or less than brilliant. We all had the qualities to do our jobs. Moreover, from my earliest assignments in the Foreign Service, I always had the sense that my supervisors were more experienced and better qualified than I was. They knew how to teach me the ropes, and I profited greatly from their advice and guidance.

As Foreign Service Officers, we served under both Republican and Democratic administrations. Never once, in my long years of service, did I encounter the slightest bias on the part of my colleagues for one political party over another. As Americans, we wanted the administration in office to do the best job possible in advancing US interests, and we devoted our efforts to that end. In my experience, the tendency of political appointees to mistrust the "bureaucracy" is misguided. When I reached more senior policy levels as an ambassador, I encountered the anomalous situation of trying to prove myself wrong by seeking successful implementation of policy decisions with which I disagreed. I never once doubted that my colleagues would do the same. It is a luxury to work in such an environment.

Another source of pride was in discovering that in well-led American diplomatic missions abroad, all the components of the US government could work together as a team to advance the interests of the United States, without the petty rivalries that mar cooperation among government departments in Washington. It was heartening to see State Department economic officers willing to go all out to support the visit of a Commerce Secretary alongside their commercial officer colleagues, and vice versa. In Beijing the political section worked hand in hand with the Defense Attaché Office on a political-military assessment that was so good that portions of it were incorporated word for word into a National Intelligence Estimate. During the Tiananmen disturbances in Beijing in 1989, Ambassador James Lilley maintained high morale among all components of the mission at a time when the embassy was under severe strain.

My three ambassadorial assignments were in Singapore from 1984–86, the People's Republic of China from 1991–95, and in Indonesia from

1996–98. All three countries are in East Asia, but they are radically different in terms of their characteristics. Two of them, China and Indonesia, are among the largest in terms of both population and geographic space. China has the largest population in the world, while Indonesia ranks number four, after China, India, and the United States. China has a land mass roughly comparable to that of the United States, while Indonesia is the world's largest maritime country, consisting of over 17,000 islands spanning an area from east to west equivalent to the distance from Boston to Los Angeles.

Singapore is one of the smallest countries in the world, both in size and population. It is a tiny, island state covering an area of less than 300 square miles, with a population now numbering under six million people. In the CIA World Factbook, its global ranking is 190th in terms of size and 114th in terms of population. Do not be misled by these statistics. Singapore is an economic dynamo, with a per capita GDP that ranks 5th in the world, as opposed to 15th for the United States. Its long-serving Prime Minister when I was there, Lee Kuan Yew, was a world-renowned statesman who had graduated from Cambridge University in Great Britain with a Double First, an honor indicating an unusually high level of academic achievement.

This emphasis on academic achievement was reflected throughout the Singapore bureaucracy, with the best and brightest graduates being recruited into the civil service and the military in large numbers. Singapore is probably the closest equivalent of a meritocracy in the world.

Not surprisingly, size matters and is often reflected both in how the citizens of a country view themselves and in national behavior at the leadership level. With over thirty provincial units, China's three largest provinces together have a population equivalent to that of the United States. Five of China's provinces have populations larger than Germany, the most populous country in Europe except for Russia. California, our most populous state, would rank about 14th in China.

Indonesia now has a population of about 270 million. Some 87 percent of the population is Muslim, making it the country with the largest Muslim population in the world. Roughly ten percent of the population is Christian, two-thirds protestant and one-third Catholic. However, given Indonesia's massive population, that means that there are more Christians in Indonesia than there are people in Australia.

Top Communist Party leaders in China have normally served one or more times as party secretaries or governors in country-sized provinces in making their way to senior positions. While normally too polite to show awareness of such disparities, under stress Chinese leaders can reveal their inner feelings, showing distain for foreign leaders they encounter who in their view would qualify for county level positions in China.

Status consciousness can affect negotiating behavior, as can time pressures, egos, and other personal considerations. In my experience, negotiating with big countries such as China and the Soviet Union, logical arguments carried more weight than with smaller countries.

When I was the Deputy Chief of Mission in the US embassy in Beijing in 1980, one of my responsibilities was to handle the final stages of the negotiations for our Consular Treaty with China, during which the most difficult issues had to be resolved. We had made conclusion of a Consular Treaty a requirement for opening additional consulates in each country. China at the time, had not yet adhered to the Vienna Conventions on Diplomatic and Consular Affairs, which establish the privileges and immunities enjoyed by diplomatic and consular representatives.

In all such treaties, the United States attaches particular importance to being promptly notified by the host country when an American citizen is arrested or detained, and to have prompt access to the detained citizen. Having served in Moscow, I was familiar with the terms of our Consular Treaty with the Soviet Union, which provided for notification within 48 hours and access within three days. Given the relatively backward state of transportation and telecommunications in China at the time, we were prepared to agree to notification within three days and access within four days. The Chinese only had a limited number of consular treaties at that time, and none of them provided for such prompt notification and access. The Chinese offered notification within thirty days, which was completely unacceptable.

To complicate matters, the French were also engaged in negotiations with China for a consular treaty, and they reached agreement on a text that provided for notification within fifteen days. The Chinese adopted this as their new bottom line. They were adamant that they could not offer more than their agreement with France. We were at an impasse.

Fortunately, I was aware that we had consular treaties with all of the East European countries of the Soviet Bloc that had provisions for notification and access comparable to the US-Soviet consular treaty. We broke the impasse by providing the Chinese with copies of these treaties and explaining that given these precedents, it would be a waste of time to seek Senate confirmation of a US-China consular treaty that did not have comparable provisions. The Chinese were eager to open new consulates in the United States, so reaching agreement was important for them. Presented with persuasive evidence, they agreed to provide comparable terms in our treaty. Not surprisingly, the French were furious that we had achieved better terms, complaining bitterly that they would now have to renegotiate their recently concluded consular treaty with the Chinese.

As it happened, a year earlier I had also negotiated our first Science and Technology Agreement with China under heavy time pressure. Both sides wanted the agreement concluded before Chinese Vice Premier Deng Xiaoping's visit to the United States at the end of January 1979, shortly following our establishment of US-PRC diplomatic relations on January 1st that year. The negotiations moved quickly because both sides were prepared to compromise on thorny issues.

A few years later, I was also the US negotiator for a science and technology agreement with a Southeast Asian country. In contrast to my experience in China, the negotiations were long and tedious. Determined to demonstrate their toughness, the other side insisted on conceding nothing without getting a comparable benefit. It reached the point of absurdity when they refused to correct a typographical error in the draft text unless we made a concession on some other point.

This is not uncharacteristic of smaller countries in dealing with larger ones. In some cases, they adopt a chip-on-the-shoulder attitude to underline their unwillingness to be bullied or pushed around by a larger country. Diplomats need to be alert to, and make allowances for, such behavior patterns, which may appear irrational on the surface but are reflective of demeaning treatment in the past.

Technology and Diplomacy

Technology has radically transformed diplomacy since my early days in the Foreign Service, but it cannot replace it. Communication links between Washington and our vast array of overseas posts have become much speedier and more reliable. Cell phones, email, Zoom, Skype, and jet aircraft, to cite a few examples, have all greatly facilitated travel and messaging. Washington-based officials can get to foreign capitals in a few hours, whereas before it took days. They can pick up the telephone and talk to overseas posts or foreign officials in the twinkling of an eye.

Nevertheless, technology cannot provide the personal touch, the empathy that two human beings can develop with each other, the "feel" one can develop through frequent meetings, both official and social. Such factors can be important.

In negotiating an aviation agreement with a Southeast Asian country, we kept getting closer and closer but could not bridge the final relatively minor differences. In consultations among ourselves on the problem, we realized that the chief aviation official had an ego invested in taking credit for successful conclusion of the agreement. If we concluded the agreement in his country, credit would be shared with others. So we invited him to go to Washington for the final round of negotiations, and he returned triumphantly having signed the agreement.

In every foreign capital, you find there are officials who like to solve problems, and others who delight in being as difficult as possible. Knowing your counterparts, and dealing with the right people, when possible, can facilitate resolving difficult issues.

At times, diplomacy requires utmost secrecy. In negotiating diplomatic relations with Beijing, when a leak could have aborted the process, secrecy was maintained by giving Ambassador Woodcock a key role in the negotiations, which could be conducted in Beijing without drawing attention. If senior US officials had traveled to Beijing for the negotiations, it would have greatly increased the danger of leaks.

The human factor is always present in personal contacts. While many considerations contribute to resolving problems, you gain an edge if the other side respects your negotiator. In the normalization negotiations with China, when we could not resolve a thorny issue, Deng Xiaoping turned to Ambassador Woodcock and asked his opinion on what we should do. He responded that the issue would be easier to handle within a diplomatic relationship than without one. Deng agreed, and the negotiations came to a successful conclusion. Conversely, I have seen situations where the other side held our negotiators in such contempt that they were reluctant to reach agreement and give our envoys credit for a successful agreement.

If is far easier to judge the mood of your counterpart in face-to-face meetings than in telephonic or video conversations. This can be important in determining when a touch of humor may help overcome an obstacle and when you need to be deadly serious.

Technology is a tool for diplomacy, not a substitute.

My entry into the Foreign Service occurred in December 1956, six months after graduating from college. My class of thirteen new recruits was the smallest in recent memory and came from diverse backgrounds. I was the youngest at 21, while the oldest member was a 31-year-old lawyer.

In the fall of 1956, the Foreign Service had just completed an organizational reform that expanded the number of Foreign Service grades from six to eight. If we had entered the Foreign Service two months earlier, we would have entered at the FSO-6 level and then been downgraded to the new FSO-7 level. We just missed that window and entered as FSO-8s, the new entry level for FSOs. This was our first exposure to the peculiarities of the Foreign Service personnel system.

The State Department was in the process of implementing reforms recommended by the Wriston Commission, which had concluded that the Foreign Service was not representative of the country as a whole since recruiting had excessively focused on graduates of eastern colleges and especially the Ivy League. This process was known as Wristonization, which had the goal of expanding recruitment from non-eastern educational institutions.

Needless to say, this approach had generated some controversy among more traditional members of the Foreign Service, who feared that this new emphasis would lower the quality of new recruits. One of my earliest memories in the Foreign Service was reading an article in the Foreign Service Journal bemoaning this new trend. Taking issue with Horace Greeley's famous exhortation to "Go West, young man," which gave voice to the spirit that drove our nation's rapid western expansion, the article's author reminded the reader that "the road to the West leads to the setting sun."

In reality, the Foreign Service was in need of modernization, both of its personnel structure and of its communications. At that time, the US State Department relied on two means of communication: the airgram and the telegram. Airgrams were used for the bulk of routine communications. They were written in normal English and were transmitted to the State Department in diplomatic pouches that were escorted to Washington by diplomatic couriers, who traveled by the fastest means of transportation available, which in those days included ships, trains, and propellor-driven aircraft. This meant the pouches took one to three weeks to reach eager readers in Foggy Bottom, where the State Department is located. In line with this archaic means of communication, until the early 1950s, airgrams began with the set phrase: "I have the honor to report. . . ." Fortunately, this quaint practice had been dropped by the mid-1950s, although State Department files were filled with examples of this courtly form of address.

For more urgent communications, telegrams were used. These reached Washington in a much timelier fashion but were costly, with the amount dependent on the number of words. Accordingly, in our training courses for fledgling diplomats, we were instructed on how to compose telegrams in a new form of English that ignored the strictures of grammar and omitted all unnecessary words. This made sense from a fiscal standpoint, but incautious officers periodically discovered that they inadvertently strayed into "cablese" in their unofficial communications with bemused correspondents, who were struck by the grammatical inadequacies of US government employees.

By today's standards, these means of communication were primitive indeed. The problem persisted for several decades, making only gradual progress with the introduction of electric typewriters. The breakthrough occurred with the emergence of computers and early forms of word processing in the 1970s. The State Department adapted slowly to these technological innovations. In the more gentlemanly traditions of the old Foreign Service (there were very few female foreign service officers in those days), officers dictated their reports to secretaries, who then transcribed them for approval. Typing skills were not a common characteristic among officers. Junior officers who could not type, and more senior officers who lacked access to a dedicated secretary, were reduced to drafting their reports in long hand.

An article in the Economist magazine several decades ago made a strong impression on me. It cited evidence that the introduction of new technologies requires a forty-year-long process before they are used properly. It cited evidence from the introduction of electric-powered machines in the late nineteenth century. Water-powered machines were lined up in long rows. With the introduction of electric-powered machines, the work place could be organized more efficiently. But it took years for managers to recognize this obvious reality. Twenty years after the introduction of electric power, only five percent of machines were driven by electricity.

My reaction to the article was skepticism. Surely, new-age managers, driven by the quest for efficiency, would leap at the opportunity to introduce productivity-enhancing equipment. The process of introducing computers into the State Department proved that I was wrong. As it happened, I had spent two years in college as an engineering student before I realized that my interests really lay in history. But I had taken enough advanced mathematics courses so that I was comfortable with binary numbers and hexadecimals. For me, computer-based word processing equipment offered a giant leap forward in productivity. No more correcting multiple carbon paper copies. No more taking a day and a half to correct typos in a memorandum sent to executive suite principal officers. No more waiting endless hours while an unskilled secretary labored to produce an error-free product.

The communications revolution in the State Department was more like a crawling snail. Too many officers could not type and preferred to dictate or draft in long hand. The word processing machines were given to the secretaries rather than to the drafting officers, thus requiring a two-stage process of writing drafts and then having the secretary reenter them into the word processing machine. Embassies turned up their noses at computer equipment because they disliked seeing unsightly wiring running down hallways.

Gradually it became clear to me why new technologies may require forty years for proper utilization. The power over acquisitions and budgets in organizations lies at the top, which is the level least likely to understand the new technologies. For proper utilization the generation that grows up with the technology, and is comfortable using it, needs to rise to the level that controls acquisitions and budgets before sensible decisions are made.

A second problem lay in the differentiated functions between the producing officers and the supporting highly-skilled technicians. The technicians kept the computers running, but they did not use them to write reports. Often lines of communication in such situations are less than perfect. The technicians would order word-processing software but omit the spell-checkers to save money.

I discovered in Singapore that Foreign Service administrative officers did not know how to use spreadsheets. They supervised local employees who did the spreadsheet work. When Washington instructed embassies to submit proposals for five percent, ten percent, and fifteen percent reductions in total embassy budgets, as ambassador I wanted a spreadsheet that could examine the various options. The traditional way to deal with budget cuts in embassies was to postpone acquisition and maintenance, thus passing on equipment shortfalls to successors. My philosophy was to pass on a fully functional embassy to a successor.

Rather than postponing needed acquisitions and maintenance, I wanted to be able to consider reductions in American and local personnel as part of the process of meeting the budget targets. But we could not ask local personnel to prepare options involving cuts in their own jobs, and the US administrative and personnel officers did not know how to use spreadsheets. Since I had fallen in love with spreadsheets when I discovered they could assist me in preparing my income tax, I sat down one Sunday and produced the needed spreadsheet, which we used to select the best mix of budget and personnel reductions.

Another problem involved late-night reporting to Washington. There is a 12-hour time difference between Beijing and Washington in summer (with daylight saving time in the United States but not in China) and a 13 hour difference in winter. Washington is no respecter of time differences and does not scruple to telephone or cable an ambassador in the middle of the night to make an urgent demarche and report back.

When we opened our embassy in Beijing in 1979, telecommunications in China were very backward. International calls were not only prohibitively expensive, but it could take many hours to get an international connection. I recall an incident in Beijing at that time, when I was awaked by a call from Washington in the middle of the night regarding a member of a Chinese dance troupe that was visiting Houston. The dancer had tried to defect, but had been seized by Chinese consular personnel and was being held in the consulate. I was instructed to contact the Chinese Foreign Ministry and demand her immediate release. I carried out the instruction but then spent the rest of the night trying to get an international line to report back to Washington. This was a frustrating experience.

By the time I became ambassador to China ten years later, the telecommunications situation in China had much improved, to the point where you could direct-dial an international number. This greatly facilitated unclassified communications with Washington. Dealing with classified cables was another matter. If an urgent action was required in the middle of the night, you had to take the duty car to the embassy, carry out the action, prepare a report, and summon the duty secretary to prepare the classified cable. These steps could consume hours of time when you were yearning for sleep. I wanted a more efficient procedure, especially one that bypassed the need for a secretary.

The problem was that cables had to be in a precise format for successful transmission. Secretaries had mastered the process, whereas most drafting officers had not. Moreover, the State Department software for sending cables was clunky and slow. For example, most diplomatic cables go to multiple addressees. We have over 200 diplomatic posts around the world. The official software required you to select each addressee by scrolling through a list of over 200 posts.

At the time, we were using Word Perfect software to draft our messages. Fortunately, I had mastered the WordPerfect macro language, which I used to streamline my own personal communications. With a little experimentation, I was able to write a program that made it possible to format a cable with multiple addresses in 20 seconds rather than 20 minutes. All that was necessary after that was to write the report and hit a key that sent the cable. This removed the need to bring in the duty secretary for late night communications with Washington.

When I moved from Beijing to Jakarta as ambassador, I was dismayed to discover that the State Department had switched from WordPerfect to Microsoft Word. Software programs were written in Basic rather than in the WordPerfect macro language. The State Department's software had still not been improved, so formatting cables was once again a lengthy process. I was not familiar with Basic, but computer languages are all based on the same Boolean logic. With some trepidation I ordered a couple of books on Basic to see if I could rewrite the WordPerfect program in Basic.

Fortunately, this proved possible after several months of experimentation. We switched to using the new software program that greatly speeded the process of transmitting cables. Unexpectedly, this proved very handy in 1998, when the turmoil in Jakarta that forced President Suharto from office required us to evacuate the American community and reduce the embassy staff to a skeletal level.

The turmoil gave us another useful lesson. All embassies have emergency plans in place for dealing with evacuations and terrorist threats. We had reviewed our emergency plan well in advance of the turmoil and thought we were well prepared. Our plan included provisions for renting the busses necessary to transport Americans to the airport if an evacuation was needed. When the rioting began to encroach on the residential areas of the American community, and the government was unable to provide the police and military forces necessary to secure those areas, we made the decision to evacuate Americans.

To our dismay, we discovered that the bus companies considered the roads unsafe and were unwilling to provide the promised busses unless we could secure military escorts for the vehicles, which naturally the military could not supply. Fortunately, the embassy's Defense Attaché had attended the Indonesian Command and Staff school many years earlier and was personally acquainted with the Indonesian senior military commanders. Through his intervention, we were able to secure military escorts for the busses during the period from midnight to 4:00 am, when the rioting crowds had dissipated.

This proved the wisdom of a saying attributed to President Eisenhower that "plans are worthless but planning is essential." Our evacuation plan had proved faulty because of unforeseen circumstances, but because we had earlier thought through the problems, we were able to adapt quickly to alternative approaches.

Adaptability is important in diplomacy. In the fall of 1997, the Asian financial crisis erupted. Indonesia had a strong economic and financial team, many of them trained in US universities, and this had enabled Indonesia to weather earlier and less severe financial crises. This time it was different. Indonesia's currency had been stable for many years. Since loans in dollars for repayment in Indonesian rupiahs carried much lower interest rates than loans in rupiahs, and since the Indonesian currency had been stable for a long time, the country had accumulated tens of billions of dollar-denominated debts.

Unexpectedly, in the face of the Asian financial crisis, the Indonesian rupiah collapsed in value, making the country technically bankrupt. For the first time, it turned to the World Bank and the International Monetary Fund for financial support. This was a matter for the US Department of the Treasury to handle, not the Department of State. However, the State Department had been slow to establish linkages with other government departments for the transmission of official cable traffic. Treasury cables for transmission through State Department communications facilities had to be hand-carried to the State Department. Unsurprisingly, Treasury balked at this procedure.

We resolved the problem through two ad hoc procedures. First, on an emergency basis, we arranged for a Treasury officer to be assigned to the American embassy in Jakarta. This greatly smoothed telephone communications with Treasury. Second, since most communications did not need to be classified, we switched to the use of email for two-way communications with Treasury. As a result, we were able seamlessly to coordinate with Treasury on fast-breaking events, avoiding bureaucratic battles. Once again, it was heartening to see different US agencies working together for a common purpose.

Post–Cold War Diplomacy

The first thirty-five years of my diplomatic career covered the final three and a half decades of the Cold War. The United States was at the height of its power, but our freedom of action in the world was constrained by the military capabilities of our principal adversaries, the Soviet Union and the People's Republic of China. In the conflicts in Korea and Vietnam, we had to settle for less than victory, in large measure because of the success of Moscow and Beijing in lending material support to the forces we were fighting.

In retrospect, we can, perhaps, recognize that the principal motivating factor for both Pyongyang and Hanoi in their respective conflicts was the desire to reunite divided countries, not to expand the scope of communist rule in the world. At the time, this was far from clear. The Soviet Union had an expansionist ideology that provided the theoretical basis for fomenting communist revolutions throughout the world. The United States was traumatized by the unexpectedly rapid collapse of the Nationalist forces in the Chinese civil war, which added China's vast territory and population to the communist camp. This coincided with the clamping down of the iron curtain in Europe, which brought most of the East European countries into Moscow's communist empire. Against this background, we would have needed extraordinary foresight to conclude that nationalism was a more important factor than communism in the Korean and Vietnam conflicts.

During the Cold War, because of the tenuous balance of power between East and West, we needed our friends and allies in Europe and Asia in order to hold the line against further territorial losses to the communists. Unlike the Soviet Union, we relied on diplomacy rather than military force to keep our allies and friends part of our united front of countries determined to block further communist expansionism.

All of this changed with the unraveling of the Soviet Union in 1991. George Kennan, in his Long Telegram in 1946, had predicted that this might happen eventually, but he had not pointed toward a particular time frame. Gorbachev had unsettled western analysts of the Soviet Union by his unforeseen success in consolidating his position in the Soviet Union, in launching bold measures (such as his *glasnost* and *perestroika* policies), and in his massive reductions of Soviet troop strength on the Chinese border.

The collapse of the Soviet Union in 1991 produced an unprecedented situation. The United States suddenly found its power greatly enhanced not by victory in a military conflict but by the unanticipated collapse of our principal adversary. We were mentally unprepared for this outcome. We did not have a strategy in place for what we should do if we achieved victory in the Cold War, other than dance in the streets and pat ourselves on the back.

The problem was exacerbated by the fact that then President Bush, George H.W. Bush, lost his bid for reelection in 1992. Before becoming president, he had served as a US Navy pilot in World War II, been the chief US representative at the United Nations, served as Chief of the US Liaison Office in Beijing, headed the Central Intelligence Agency, and spent eight years as Vice President of the United States under President Reagan. In terms of foreign affairs and national security strategy, he was the best prepared US president since President Nixon and President Eisenhower. He had skillfully handled the coming down of the Berlin Wall, the unraveling of the Soviet empire in Eastern Europe, and the early stages of the collapse of the Soviet Union.

It is interesting to speculate on what might have happened if the first President Bush had been reelected in 1992 and served as President of the United States during the first four years of the post-Cold War period. Instead, we elected four consecutive presidents—Clinton, Bush Two, Obama, and Trump—who had never served in the US military (Bush Two served in the Texas Air National Guard), evaded being drafted during the Vietnam War, and had no background in national security affairs and foreign policy. Two had been state governors, one had served for two years in the US Senate, and one was the only president in United States history to take office with no prior political or military experience.

At the pinnacle of our power, we spent twenty-four years under presidents who lacked the experience to guide us through the fast-evolving world that emerged from the end of the Cold War. Presidents are not one-person shows, of course. They can draw on the wisdom and advice of experienced officials on their staff to compensate for inadequacies in their own backgrounds. Three of our four post-Cold War presidents did exactly that. However, the opportunities and pitfalls confronting us at the end of the Cold War cried out for skilled and experienced executive leadership, which our electoral process was unable to supply.

As noted earlier, with the collapse of the Soviet Union we needed a check on our power other than through the emergence of another hostile power. What we should have done was to seize the opportunity to reform and strengthen the international system, which still reflected the outcome of World War Two and had not been adapted to the emergence of new power centers such as Japan, India, the European Union and Brazil. This would not have been easy, but it was worth the effort, even if it failed. Our goal should have been to strengthen global rules that we were prepared to honor, and to put ourselves under the discipline of those rules. Instead, we did the opposite. We became less supportive of international institutions, fearing that they would constrain the free exercise of US power, a thoroughly "un-American" attitude.

If we had accepted the constraint of global rules, we would still have been able to intervene in Afghanistan to oust the supporters of the terrorists responsible for the September 11, 2001 attacks in the United States. However, to the extent that nation-building was required in Afghanistan, that should have been an international responsibility, not one unilaterally assumed by the United States and its allies. Nor would we have launched the war of choice in Iraq.

It still baffles me why there is such unwillingness on the part of the United States to recognize the applicability in the international sphere of the concept that power must be checked and balanced. To my chagrin, with the collapse of our principal opponent, my own country became more arrogant and demanding, less inclined to listen to advice from others, and more prone to lecture other countries on their failings.

When I was the Assistant Secretary of State for Intelligence and Research toward the end of the Clinton administration, our bureau was in charge of international public opinion polling for the United States government. We did not do the polling ourselves but commissioned competent polling organizations to do the legwork, while we supplied the questions. The polls revealed that throughout the world the United States as a country was generally viewed favorably, but our style of dealing with other countries was uniformly viewed negatively. We regularly shared these results with senior officials of the US government, with no discernable effect.

As the United States ambassador in China, I kept track of the number of times that my instructions from Washington used phraseology in messages for the Chinese government such as "you must" or "you should." That is not a style that is productive in dealing with other people on a personal level, or with foreign governments. I periodically sent informal messages to the East Asia Bureau in the State Department conveying these statistics and politely noting that messages phrased in this peremptory manner were less likely to have the desire effect than language designed to persuade rather than to irritate. Naturally, as the United States ambassador, I always faithfully carried out my instructions, but wherever possible, I sought to persuade rather than to anger.

It would be useful for ambassadors to keep on their desks the following passage from the Federalist Papers:

An attention to the judgment of other nations is important to every government for two reasons: the one is, that, independently of the merits of any particular plan or measure, it is desirable, on various accounts, that it should appear to other nations as the offspring of a wise and honorable policy; the second is, that in doubtful cases, particularly where the national councils may be warped by some strong passion or momentary interest, the presumed or known opinion of the impartial world may be the best guide that can be followed. What has not America lost by her want of character with foreign nations; and how many errors and follies would she not have avoided, if the justice and propriety of her measures had, in every instance, been previously tried by the light in which they would probably appear to the unbiased part of mankind?

A similar type of problem emerged in Indonesia during my tour there as ambassador. Indonesia has the largest Muslim population in the world, but Islam is not enshrined in the constitution as the official religion, in part because over ten percent of the population practices other religions. Indonesia has a tradition of tolerance towards other faiths, and this is reflected in Indonesia's practice of Islam. For example, the head of Indonesia's largest Muslim organization in the 1990s sent his daughter to study in Israel and served on the board of the Shimon Perez Institute.

Given the Muslim character of Indonesia's population, it should not be surprising that many Indonesians are predisposed to view the United States as biased against Islam because of our strong support for Israel. While they were not well-disposed towards Saddam Hussein's style of rule in Iraq, they nevertheless viewed him as the leader of an important Muslim country. In the second half of the 1990s, when I was the American ambassador in Jakarta, we were still flying air patrols over Iraq as a legacy of the Gulf War. These air patrols periodically resulted in incidents when the Iraqis fired missiles at our military aircraft and we responded in kind by attacking the missile batteries.

Under these circumstances, Washington periodically instructed me to convey to the Indonesian government our justification for these actions. As American ambassador, I believed our actions in Iraq were defensible, but the instructions were worded in language that took no account of the Muslim nature of Indonesia's population.

I did not expect US government officials as a group to be familiar enough with Indonesia to be alert to such nuances. However, the State Department has many superb Arabic-speaking Middle Eastern experts who know well the Islamic world and are aware that many Muslims do not share our attitudes and assumptions about regional issues. If there was one US government agency that should know how to draft messages for Muslim audiences, it should be the State Department. And yet this was not apparent from the instructions I received in Jakarta.

Lessons from Government Service

My years in government service gave me a better understanding of the interplay between domestic and foreign factors in the formulation and implementation of foreign policy. Both are important, but the proper balance must be maintained for maximum effectiveness.

Democratic forms of governance often encounter difficulties in balancing external realities against domestic pressures. Representative systems rest on the support of the governed, who may have strong views about how to deal with foreign policy issues, while lacking well-informed or current awareness of complicated circumstances abroad. If these pressures are strong enough, this can result in foreign policies that primarily reflect domestic attitudes without adequately taking into account the feasibility of their implementation. This can have two deleterious consequences: the president may be unable to gain support for his/her policies; or the president may adopt domestically-driven foreign policies that have no realistic possibility of success in the light of external conditions.

When presidents feel it necessary to cater to domestic attitudes in their negative comments on particular foreign countries, this can undercut their ability to gain support for their own policies toward those countries, thus tying their own hands. This is a recurrent problem in American foreign policy, reflecting improper management of the contradictions inherent in reconciling Americans interests with those of foreign countries.

Americans are conditioned by our educations to think in terms of principles rather than contradictions. We uphold freedom and equality for all, while giving less attention to the inherent contradiction between the two principles: freedom leads to inequality because of the disparities in human capabilities. Proper management of the contradiction can maximize both. Ignoring the contradiction produces less desirable results.

Such contradictions often find expression in our approach to human rights. Too often we fail to recognize that democracies, by their nature, cannot be even handed on human rights issues. Why, for example, did we give acute attention to the fate of political dissidents in China in the 1990s while largely ignoring the genocide in Rwanda during which hundreds of thousands were slaughtered, while we turned a blind eye? The answer is there was no domestic constituency for Rwanda in the United States, while politicians were able to gain media attention by lambasting China's human rights practices.

If we pause to reflect, it should be obvious that democracies inescapably reflect the passions, prejudices, and priorities of their people. This point was understood by our founding leaders. In the debate over our Bill of Rights, James Madison pointed out that "in our Government the real power lies in the majority of the Community, and the invasion of private rights is chiefly to be apprehended, not from the acts of Government contrary to the sense of its constituents, but from acts in which the Government is the mere instrument of the major number of the Constituents. . . ."

This does not mean we have a double standard. Rather, it means that in practice we apply a different standard to every country we deal with, depending on the mix between popular attitudes, including those in Congress, and government policies. It is, I would argue, properly the role of responsible governments to even out these discrepancies and to strive for evenhandedness and consistency in our approach. But in practice, this is accomplished imperfectly, and the imperfections are the more striking when we fail to understand the problem.

Promoting human rights is one of the most exciting and difficult tasks that we face as diplomats. It is exciting because it is directly linked to what should be one of the core values of public service, which is a commitment to providing prompt, courteous, and efficient service to the public, or, to put it another way, a commitment to helping people. It is difficult because our efforts to promote human rights can expose us to charges of hypocrisy, can give rise to serious misunderstandings of our motives, and can be counterproductive if pursued with an excess of zeal over wisdom. These problems arise all the more readily if we are inadequately informed about ourselves, our history, and the nature of our society. In promoting human rights, as in fighting wars, we need to know both ourselves and the other side in order to find the best approach.

Even then, the task is not easy. Countries at different levels of economic development and with social, cultural, and religious backgrounds that differ from our own may have attitudes and priorities on human rights that differ from our own. Moreover, in countries where the governments are major contributors to human rights abuses, those governments will be unsympathetic to and uncooperative with efforts to address those abuses. And, more often than not, there are trade-offs between short term and longer-term objectives that can easily lead to differing views on the best approach.

The inescapable conclusion must be that the importance of promoting human rights should be matched by the seriousness of the thinking that we devote to the topic.

Why Do We Behave the Way We Do?

Given the fact that promotion of human rights is not only part of our foreign policy but can also create problems in our relations with other countries, it is worth reflecting on why we behave the way we do. There are dozens of democracies around the world, many of whom share our commitment to human rights but are less high-profile in their approach. Would a less assertive approach be more effective and make us less subject to charges of insincerity, inconsistency, and interference in internal affairs? The answer is: perhaps. But the other side of the coin, from my subjective viewpoint, is that oppressed people and victims of mistreatment throughout the world look to the United States for sympathy and support precisely because they know that we attach importance to the issue. So, we need not be ashamed of our high posture, even though we need to behave wherever possible so that this is not equated with arrogance, high-handedness, and hypocrisy.

In reality, our behavior is largely a product of our own history, where our high ideals have often contrasted with our actual practices. In a sense, our activism reflects the struggle we have had to wage, and need to continue to wage, to address our own shortcomings. From our earliest days as a republic, thoughtful Americans were aware of the fact that despite the stirring declaration of our founding leaders that "all men are created equal," we accepted the continuation of slavery for over seven decades as the price of achieving union among our original thirteen colonies. This inconsistency between our ideals and our practices was glaringly obvious from the beginning, and it required decades of intense domestic activism before we were able to abolish slavery, just as it took nearly a half century of suffragette agitation before we were able to let women exercise the right to vote. More recently, it required the activism of the civil rights movement in the 1950s and 1960s to overcome our own resistance to providing meaningful equality to all our citizens. That struggle is still far from over.

I have found that many foreigners have difficulty understanding the intensity with which we pursue human rights issues because they are not aware of our own history of domestic struggle that has, in a sense, spilled over into our international style. This was driven home to me when we sent a group of Chinese academic specialists on human rights to the United States in the early 1990s. When I met with them on their return, I was struck by their surprise at finding that most US attention to human rights is focused on our own domestic situation. No wonder, then, that they had the impression that we spent all our time poking into the domestic affairs of other countries.

Interests, Values, and National Myths

Just as our domestic behavior may not always be consistent with the values we uphold, the same, unfortunately, can be said about our foreign policy. For us, as for most if not all countries, interests (such as trade and national security) and values (such as promoting democracy and human rights) are both important. Conceptual problems arise, however, when we fail to appreciate the distinction between interests and values or fall into the trap of treating them rhetorically as being on the same level and as occupying an equal place in our priorities.

If we review our own history, several things become evident. Our policies are most reliable and consistent when our interests and values are congruent, such as when we fight to defend a democratic ally. When our interests and values are not in harmony, our behavior (as opposed to our rhetoric) more often than not is driven by our interests, not to the exclusion of other factors, but to a significant degree.

A few examples will underline this point. As I have already noted, we tolerated slavery during the formative years of our republic, knowing it was wrong, in the interests of national unity. Our record of adhering to treaties and agreements with Native Americans during our period of national expansion was less than perfect. During World War II, we worked with Joe Stalin to defeat Adolph Hitler. And during the Cold War, we supported dictatorial regimes in various parts of the world because of the perceived—and, in my view, very real—threat of communist expansion.

A review of our history will also show, however, that such accommodations, which are inherently in contradiction with our principles, are unstable and cannot outlast the circumstances that gave rise to them. In other words, there is a constant and healthy thrust in our national policies to resolve contradictions between our interests and values by bringing them into congruence with each other.

What conclusions can we draw from this? If we are aware of these contradictions in our behavior, we can seek to manage the contradictions more effectively and at less cost to our values. If we are blind to the contradictions, or deny their existence, we may fool ourselves, but to others we will appear as arrogant, domineering, and hypocritical, a perception that makes it more difficult for us to achieve our foreign policy objectives.

Successes and Missteps in American Foreign Policy

Without question, one of the great successes of American foreign policy was the normalization of relations with the People's Republic of China in 1979. Since that time, Taiwan has prospered within the framework negotiated by the United States. Taiwan's per capita GDP is now equivalent to that of Canada. Cross-strait tensions have been low when the government on Taiwan has respected the concept of one China. There are domestic political pressures in Taiwan for the government to seek an international status inconsistent with one China. It is not in the interest of the United States or Taiwan for such efforts to succeed.

Beijing has made it clear that it will use military force to prevent Taiwan from formally separating itself from China. Nevertheless, on July 1, 2021 PRC President Xi Jinping reiterated that Beijing's policy is to "advance peaceful national reunification." For the moment the threat lies in separation, not in unification.

China's rapid rise poses a massive challenge to American interests and values. Skillful diplomacy, backed by credible military capabilities, provides the best answer. Actions that increase the danger of military confrontations will not serve our interests nor our fervent desire to see democracy continue to thrive on Taiwan.

The two biggest mistakes made by the United States during my service in the US government were the Vietnam War and the handling of relations with Russia in the post-Cold War world, including the beginning of the reckless expansion of NATO, which reached its predictably tragic climax after I had retired.

The Vietnam War demonstrably failed to achieve its goal of preventing communist North Vietnam from swallowing up the non-communist southern portion of the country. The cost of this failure was nearly 60,000 American dead and over 210,000 total casualties, a price nearly sixty percent higher than our successful effort to stem communist aggression in Korea. Whether our effort in Vietnam was worth the cost is still debated in the United States, with most concluding it was not. However, Prime Minister Lee Kuan Yew of Singapore always argued that the US war effort in Vietnam bought nearly ten years of time for the newly independent countries of Southeast Asia to consolidate themselves, without which the dominoes might indeed have fallen. Such concerns should not be lightly dismissed.

When I served in Thailand from 1959 to 1961, there were communist guerrilla forces in the jungles between Thailand and Malaya that made the roads unsafe to travel without an armed escort. Local authorities showed me Chinese language propaganda materials bearing recent dates that had been seized from guerrillas they had apprehended. During that same period, the roads from Thailand to South Vietnam became subject to guerrilla attacks. I also encountered mistaken beliefs on the part of well-educated Thai that Moscow's success in launching the first sputnik in October 1957 demonstrated, in their view, that the Soviet Union had surged ahead of the United States in scientific achievements. Moreover, communist influence in Indonesia at that time was significant and growing, and there was concern in Washington that it might tilt further toward the communist bloc.

Nevertheless, in my observation, the most destructive long-term consequence of the Vietnam War was its impact on the moral fiber of the American people. Opposition to the war became so strong that even our institutions of higher learning, which in my youth had been bastions of resistance to the false claims of McCarthyism, became complicit in a nation-wide draft-evasion campaign that corrupted the grading systems in our colleges and universities, denied US government speakers access to college campuses, stigmatized Americans who dutifully accepted military service in Vietnam, and sanctified the view that lies and evasion are justified in opposing an immoral war. This produced a generation of young Americans who rose to leadership positions in our society embracing the slippery proposition that the end justifies the means.

Another consequence was that our first four post-Cold War presidents became commanders-in-chief of our arms forces having evaded in one form or another honorable service in Vietnam. In the 1950s, college classmates of mine who looked forward to political careers volunteered for the draft, if necessary, so that they could include military service on their resumes because failure to serve was a black mark on a political resume. Now, in contrast to then, most of our top civilian leaders have never served in the military, including most members of the US Congress.

The impact on integrity in government is discernable. When I moved to Washington to join the Foreign Service in the mid-1950s, the White House was expected to uphold the appearance of high standards of integrity. Being caught in a lie, had consequences, real or reputational. When President Eisenhower was implicated in a false cover story for the U-2 flight over the USSR in 1960 that was downed by a Soviet missile, there were troublesome repercussions for the president, who even briefly considered resigning. Later, the publication of the Pentagon Papers demonstrated the degree to which the US government was covering up information about our military activities in Vietnam.

In recent years, lying by the White House, whether the President, senior officials, or White House spokespersons has become commonplace. Distorting the truth has always been part of politics, but the scale of such behavior directly correlates to the degree of confidence that citizens have in our governing institutions. Accountability in government is degraded if lying becomes an acceptable practice. In my career in the Foreign Service this was never the case at working levels of the civil service.

The second adverse consequence of the Vietnam War was its negative impact on the constitutional war powers that the president shares with congress. Following the war, Congress eliminated the draft in favor of an all-volunteer military force. This has limited the impact of military conflicts on the general population, reinforced by greater reliance on high-tech weapons to limit casualties.

However, our success in fencing off the consequences of combat from the general population has given our presidents more leeway to engage in discretionary combat operations, or wars of choice, while increasing incentives to conceal from the public the true state of affairs regarding the financial and human costs of such conflicts. The overall impact on government integrity has been negative, and the human costs have been disproportionately placed on a small percentage of American citizens. In my view, when we undertake discretionary military interventions abroad there should be immediate consequences for every American citizen. This could take the form, for example, of tax increases or other measures designed both as a check on the power of the president to risk American lives in foreign operations, and as an acknowledgement that it is a national effort when our armed forces fight to defend our country. Certainly, this issue deserves more attention in our public discourse.

The other most serious mistake was the tragic mishandling of the new situation in Europe that followed the collapse of the Soviet Union and our emergence as the sole superpower in the world. We made the collective error, together with our European allies, of failing to transform NATO from a defense alliance into a collective security organization for Europe, including Russia, with the aim not of dealing with an existing threat (now greatly reduced) but of preventing new threats from emerging.

Instead, success administrations, with European support, pursued a deeply flawed policy towards Russia that brushed aside historic Russian interests that are the driving elements in Russian behavior. If we do not acknowledge the existence of these interests, we cannot understand the motives for Russian actions. Putin is driven by far more than the desire to upend the current international order, where the United States is the dominant player and Russia assigned a subordinate role. For a country obsessed by historical memories of the invasions by Napoleon and Hitler, we must assign some importance to Russia's historic fear of Germany and its desire to ensure the security of its western frontiers.

Successive US administrations have refused to acknowledge that NATO's eastward expansion has been a major factor influencing Russian behavior. If you remove this factor, which you can learn about by talking to any Russian, then Russian behavior can only be explained by the malignant intentions of Russia's rulers. Putin did not jump overnight to the conclusion that the international system was inimical to Russian interests. He was driven to that conclusion by the persistent refusal of the United States, the other NATO countries, and the EU to acknowledge that Russians felt threatened by the two-step expansion eastward of EU and NATO membership. Russian red lines were cavalierly ignored.

Warned that western support for Kosovar independence would have consequences in the Caucasus, NATO responded at its Bucharest summit in 2008 by confirming that the door was open to Ukraine and Georgia for EU and NATO membership. In short, the counter-strategy to Putin's warning was to wave a red flag at the bull. The Georgia crisis, predictably, followed soon after. Significantly, Putin enjoys overwhelming support from Russians on this question, indicating that these feelings are not simply a reflection of Putin's personal whims.

The unpleasant reality is that NATO now has less credibility as a defense organization because of its reckless expansion that could only be justified by the perceived absence of a credible threat, not by the vital importance to US interests of the new members. This is very different from the Cold War NATO, where each side recognized that the dividing line between NATO and the Warsaw Pact reflected national interests too important to be violated. If Putin's domestic repression depends on the existence of external threats, we have been more than generous in meeting this need in Russian minds.

With respect to Ukraine, US policy has been portrayed as seeking to help Ukrainian leaders build a successful political system that Russia seeks to subvert. The reality is that three decades after Ukrainian independence no Ukrainian government has sought to build such a political system. Ukraine is constituted from eastern and western parts with different histories and attitudes regarding relations with Russia and the west. The number one requirement for the new country was leadership that gave top priority to forging national unity, if this was possible. The only way to accomplish this was by not letting the country be pulled apart by a tug of war between Russia and the west over the fragile new country's orientation.

Far from recognizing this problem, US and EU policy grabbed the rope and blithely sought to pull the country into the western embrace. Russia seized the other end of the rope. Ukrainian leaders were too busy looting the country to pay much attention to the issue of forging national unity. A country that had a military numbering some 600,000 personnel at independence ended up in a few short years with a military incapable of defending the country's borders.

Americans are properly outraged over Russian efforts to subvert the Ukrainian political system, along with that of the United States, where we have seen President Putin's aggressive election meddling. This is indeed deplorable behavior, but in the Ukraine the United States does not have clean hands. Credible press stories have laid bare a deep degree of US involvement in Ukraine affairs that Washington officially says are for the Ukrainians to resolve.

The larger question is whether there are correctives to the policy errors we have made in dealing with Russia. An important first step would be to get rid of the ideological blinders that have distorted our vision of the road ahead, and to stop blaming Putin for all the ills in the bilateral relationship. We do not have to assume Russian good intentions towards us.

On the contrary, we can assume the existence of important differences in national interest between Russia and the United States. But as a minimum any sensible approach must be based on recognizing that Russia has historic national security interests that deeply influence how Russians view the outside world. Brushing these interests aside with bland assertions that pushing EU/NATO membership to the borders of Russia should not be of concern to the Kremlin is one of the principal ways in which we have fooled ourselves. Much will depend on whether we have the wisdom to build a more stable relationship based on realities rather than illusions.

The irony is that one of the great successes of American foreign policy was the skillful manner in which the George H.W. Bush administration, in partnership with our NATO allies, managed the final three years of the Cold War. The unexpectedly rapid unraveling of the Soviet empire, followed by the reunification of Germany and the disintegration of the Soviet Union itself, was a process fraught with dangers that were largely avoided. There were solid grounds for hope that a better future lay ahead. Instead, we find thirty years later that Russia has been alienated from Europe and driven into the arms of China. Europe proved incapable of handling on its own the problems in the Balkans spawned by the unraveling of Yugoslavia, and the danger of conflict between major powers in Europe has reemerged.

Weaknesses in America's Approach to the World and Possible Improvements

An embedded element in America's diplomatic tradition is the belief that skillful diplomacy backed by credible military power is the best posture to be in. This is true much of the time, but not always. In fact, a case can be made that our diplomacy is weakened by the knowledge that if negotiations cannot produce a successful outcome, we can turn to our military power to resolve the impasse. Most countries do not have that option. In negotiations with equal or stronger countries, they must rely on the skill of their diplomats to protect national interests. Too often, the United States has relied on military power rather than diplomacy to impose our will on other countries.

In diplomacy, it is always important to understand the interests of the other side. When we were negotiating with Thailand for permission to locate an international broadcasting tower in their country, the Thai were reluctant to agree. Washington kept sending our Bangkok embassy stronger and stronger instructions to tell the Thai how important the issue was for us. My experienced ambassador sent back a message to Washington, noting that the Thai were fully aware that this was an important issue for us. They did not understand why it was an important issue for them. Washington responded positively to this reminder and sent revised instructions offering the Thai part-time use of the broadcasting tower and a $5 million training program for Thai telecommunications personnel. The agreement was promptly signed.

For the first time since the Civil War, the United States political system is in crisis. Two-fifths of American voters and over two-thirds of the members of one of our two major political parties, including a shockingly large number of the representatives of that party in both houses of Congress, refuse to acknowledge the legitimacy of the 2020 presidential elections. Now, more than ever, is a good time to reflect on how we can improve and modernize our governing institutions.

We should begin by sharply modifying or eliminating the 18th century spoils system we use to fill the top-most positions in our government, positions that carry heavy responsibilities for policy formulation and execution. Far too many of these positions now entail Senate ratification, a requirement that can leave many of these positions unfilled for much of the first year of a new administration, and in some cases for several years. No other major country is so irresponsible in staffing its government.

This outmoded and unnecessary practice eliminates any corporate memory at the policy level with each change to a new administration. The problem is particularly bad in the case of ambassadors. Administrations from both parties, and the nation's foreign policy elite, including our leading newspapers, continue to regard ambassadorial posts primarily as political plums rather than as positions that can play important roles in the formulation and conduct of foreign policy. This applies, in many cases, even when the ambassadorial positions are located in countries and regions facing complex and even dangerous problems where the United States needs the best possible advice and envoys whose views carry weight both with their own governments and with the governments to which they are accredited.

This does not automatically require a career diplomat. For example, I was privileged to work with Ambassador Leonard Woodcock, a seasoned negotiator who earned the respect of China's top leaders and whose views carried weight in Washington. Having served as a Deputy Chief of Mission in two major posts (Beijing and Bangkok), I am also personally aware of the gulf between being the deputy and the chief of mission. Highly competent staff, which is almost always the case in our major diplomatic establishments, can head off disasters but cannot substitute for a chief of mission whose understanding of the host country and whose policy instincts are flawed.

The problem is compounded by the fact that the US Government, including the State Department, lacks figures in high positions with the experience, continuity, and institutional influence to give promising candidates the pattern of assignments that will best prepare them for the most demanding positions. The result is that we often do not have in place career diplomats with gravitas sufficient to override the political considerations that play such a major role in ambassadorial assignments.

We would not tolerate such a situation in our military, which is the only fully professional service from top to bottom. The US military illustrates the point that even senior career people can, on occasion, screw up, misjudge situations, and fail to rises to the demands of the job. But, in the case of the military we recognize that accumulated experience is an invaluable commodity that often makes the key difference between brilliance and wisdom. By having our top military positions filled 100 percent by professionals with decades of experience under their belts we maximize the odds that our senior military can handle the most demanding assignments.

In other areas of the government, including the Foreign Service, it is hit and miss. Top career diplomats, such as Tom Pickering, Frank Wisner, or Bill Burns, have shown their competence in a series of demanding positions. All gained their reputations not in minor out of the way posts but by skillfully handling assignments in major countries. And each of those examples continued to use their accumulated experience for years inside the US government instead of taking it back to the private sector.

This is the fundamental problem when the spoils system is applied to vitally important ambassadorial positions: regardless of whether the incumbents perform well or badly, their experience goes back to the private sector rather than providing the US government with the cadre of senior, experienced foreign policy experts that we need to maximize our effectiveness in dealing with the challenges we face.

One would hope that the challenge China is posing to our position in East Asia and the world would be sufficient to shock us into correcting some of the lax patterns of behavior that we could indulge when we were protected by two oceans from major threats. One wonders what it will take to cause us to mend our ways.

The problems of the spoils system can be seen in comparing the first and second terms of two-term presidents. During my career in the Foreign Service, I found, with few exceptions, that the personnel appointments in the second term were improvements over the first term, in large measure because presidents discovered the negative consequences of filling important positions with people who lacked the knowledge and management skills for effective performance.

Diplomacy cannot function without resources. The harsh reality is that for years, we have been devoting the bulk of our discretionary spending to the military and neglecting the funding of all the other elements of our comprehensive national power. The contrast with China is striking. Beijing is putting tens of billions of dollars into funding the non-military components of its comprehensive national power, such as the Belt and Road Initiative and the Asia Infrastructure Investment Bank. We need to do better in this area.

Administrations I Have Known

Curiously, the Carter administration is frequently viewed as a failed presidency, in large measure because of the collapse of the US relationship with Iran, the hostage-taking of the US embassy personnel in Tehran, and the failed rescue attempt, which prompted the resignation of Secretary of State Cyrus Vance. In addition, his difficulties with Congress, and his inability to curb the raging inflation created the impression of a weak president.

And yet in the first two years of his administration, President Carter accomplished three stunning foreign policy achievements: conclusion of the Panama Canal Treaties in 1977, the Camp David Accords in 1978, and completion of the normalization of relations with Beijing in 1979. He also signed the SALT II Treaty with the Soviet Union in 1979, which was observed by both sides for six and a half years, although it was never ratified by the United States. These were more significant foreign policy accomplishments than most two-term presidencies accomplish in eight years.

Dr. Henry A. Kissinger was perhaps the most cerebral of our post-World War Two secretaries of state. He was notorious as National Security Advisor under President Nixon for his exclusion of the State Department from key foreign policy issues, in part because this was the preference of the President. This was dispiriting for those of us working on Soviet and Chinese affairs because we often lacked inside knowledge of what was occurring at high levels in these critically important bilateral relationships. I recall the frustration of our ambassador in Moscow when Dr. Kissinger, in his role at the National Security Council, made a secret visit to Moscow without the knowledge of the ambassador, who only learned of the visit as Dr. Kissinger was departing Moscow.

However, when Dr. Kissinger moved to the State Department as Secretary of State in the final year of the Nixon administration, and throughout the Ford administration, he relied heavily on Foreign Service and State Department personnel for policy ideas and implementation and leaned on them just as heavily for top quality inputs. It was exciting to feel challenged to engage in serious foreign policy thinking, despite the heavy demands.

Secretary of State George Shultz was outstanding in his ability to motivate the bureaucracy to take responsibility for foreign policy issues. He was particularly effective at empowering his Assistant Secretaries in the geographic bureaus to share the burden of dealing with foreign governments.

In one instance, when Secretary Shultz was visiting East Asia, there was an incident in US relations with Japan that required immediate attention. To handle the matter, he instructed the Assistant Secretary for East Asia and the Pacific, who had a special relationship with the Prime Minister of Japan, to break off from his delegation to visit Tokyo and resolve the matter with the Prime Minister.

As Deputy Assistant Secretary of State for China, I accompanied Secretary Shultz on a visit to Beijing, after which he sent me to Australia and New Zealand to brief the governments on his conversations in the Chinese capital. In both cases, I met with the respective Prime Ministers of the two countries. Those of us who worked in the East Asia Bureau, under Secretary Shultz, had a sense that it was our responsibility to come up with creative foreign policy initiatives for top level approval rather than waiting to be instructed what to do. Foreign Service Officers were eager for such challenges. I held monthly lunches with counterparts at the National Security Council and the Defense Department to discuss the situation in Asia and consider possible policy initiatives. If we agreed that a particular policy action was desirable, we then coordinated our efforts to gain approval for the action in our respective agencies.

The George H. W. Bush administration was a special case in terms of the smoothness of relationships between the State Department and the White House, the National Security Council, and the Department of Defense. I have mentioned earlier the President's skill in managing the end of the Cold War, assisted by a superb national security team. Secretary of State James Baker regularly spoke with the president by telephone several times a day, National Security Advisor Brent Scowcroft had a long-standing friendship with Deputy Secretary of State Eagleburger, and the Secretaries of State and Defense took hunting trips together.

Early in the first Bush administration, a coup occurred in Panama during a visit by a foreign leader to Washington, which tied up senior officials. This crippled coordination procedures that had not yet been fully tested. We ended up with three separate streams of information from our mission in Panama: the embassy, the US military, and our intelligence resources, each with a different version of events. Fortunately, the coup collapsed, but the Washington response had been wanting. Corrective measures were instituted.

Four months later a coup attempt by disgruntled military officers took place in Manila, while the US president was enroute to Europe. The Philippine government requested US military intervention to suppress the coup. An urgent decision was necessary. Within minutes, the State Department was able to set up secure video links with the Vice President, the National Security Council, the Defense Department and the Philippine Defense Minister to review the options. The decision was made, and approved by the President over a secure telephone line, to send a flight of US jet fighters over Manila at roof top level. The coup collapsed. In contrast to Panama, coordination had been superb and timely.

The first Bush administration's decision to expel Iraqi forces from Kuwait following Saddam Hussein's occupation of that country provides a model of effective national security policy, once the President made the decision that Saddam's aggression could not go unanswered. Within a few months an international coalition was formed (including Arab countries) with the goal of liberating Kuwait, troops and equipment were deployed, Saddam Hussein was dealt a crushing defeat, and the costs were largely borne by Saudi Arabia and Japan, the two principal beneficiaries of securing Saudi oil fields. Coalition casualties were minimal. With the goal accomplished, the war ended, even though the road to Baghdad lay open. The coalition would have fractured if the goal had shifted to regime change in Iraq. The impressive display of American military power had a global impact.

Final Challenge: How to Play Our Role Effectively

Our greatest challenge as a major power whose actions affects lives and fortunes throughout the world is to prepare ourselves to play this role effectively. To put it bluntly, as a nation we are insufficiently informed of the world around us. Our media do not provide adequate coverage of foreign policy issues. Our knowledge of foreign languages is inadequate. Our schools of higher learning are second to none, but they do not teach Americans enough about the rest of the world in terms of geography, history, and culture. This is an intolerable situation for a country that bears the responsibility of being the world's sole superpower and that has the ability, as President George W. Bush put it some years ago, "to strike at a moment's notice in any dark corner of the world."

As many of us have learned from personal experience, it is dangerous to delve into dark corners unless we know what we are doing. Alexander Pope, several centuries ago, captured this thought in his poetry, when he noted that: "A little learning is a dangerous thing" because "shallow draughts intoxicate the brain And drinking largely sobers us again." The United States cannot afford to have a brain intoxicated by inadequate knowledge of the world in which we are now playing such a dominant role.

Why does this matter? Because how the United States defines its own objectives is of critical importance to the future of our relations with other countries, especially China. If the United States defines its national security goals in terms of preserving unchallengeable supremacy for the indefinite future, as we are now doing, there will be several inevitable consequences:

First, none of the world's other power centers will support the central objective of US national security strategy. Successful foreign policies are based on finding common interests with other countries. Defining our goals from the narrow standpoint of US interests alone places a heavy burden on our foreign policy.

Second, if our goal is perpetual hegemony, China's rise, or the rise of any other country, will inevitably become threatening at some point. Sooner or later, regardless of Chinese behavior, the United States would have to adopt a policy of containment toward China.

If, on the other hand, the US goal is defined as ensuring the prosperity and security of the American people, then we are likely to see a different set of consequences. Most importantly, this would signal US acceptance of the concept of a world in which other countries have an equal right to pursue the well-being and security of their people through means other than force and conquest. In this case, the United States need not feel threatened by a stronger and more prosperous China that behaves responsibly. The goal of US China policy, then, would be to maximize prospects for a good US-China relationship and responsible Chinese behavior.

These are two very different foreign policy goals. The first presupposes an eventual confrontation with China, not because of its behavior but because of the increase in its wealth and power. The second assumes that a strong and self-confident United States can coexist with a stronger China that is a responsible stake-holder in the international system.

This underlines why the number one challenge facing each new administration will be determining how the United States can and should use its power responsibly in a world where we wield more military and financial power than other first-rank countries. To do so they must, in Dr. Kissinger's words, "develop concepts relevant to the emerging realities." Defining such concepts is long overdue. To prolong our leadership, we must be seen by other countries as a responsible steward of the unprecedented relative power that we now hold. This is both consistent with our interests and with our most fundamental political principles.

FOURTEEN

MICHAEL McFAUL

Twitter Diplomacy

Lessons from an American Experiment in Russia

n my last meeting with Secretary of State Hillary Clinton before leaving Washington for Moscow to take up my new post as the US Ambassador to the Russian Federation, she gave me some last instructions. As she recounted in her book, *Hard Choices*, "When Mike McFaul . . . was preparing to move to Moscow as our new Ambassador, I told him that he'd have to find creative ways to get around government obstacles and communicate directly with the Russian people. 'Mike, remember three things,' I said, 'be strong, engaged beyond the elites and don't be afraid to use every technology you can to reach more people.'"[1]

After three years of working directly for President Barack Obama at the National Security Council, Secretary Clinton was my new boss. (Of course, we both still worked for President Obama.) I took her guidance seriously. Before arriving in Moscow, I worked with the State Department's communications team to produce on introductory video of myself on You-Tube.[2] On one of my first weeks at the American embassy in Moscow, I opened my first Twitter accounts, @McFaul. A few weeks later, on January 29th, I opened @Макфол, with this message: Добро пожаловать! Здесь я хочу общаться с вами напрямую исключительно на русском языке. До встречи! [Hello! Here I want to interact with you exclusively in Russia. Until we meet!] However, after a few months of experimentation with the two accounts—one in English and one in Russian—I shut down the second account and just used @McFaul to tweet in both languages. I used other social media platforms to carry Clinton's instructions to me. But Twitter soon emerged as the most important platform for me. Overnight, I became a pioneer in Twitter Diplomacy.[3]

Secretary Clinton made "twenty-first Century Statecraft", which included using new technologies to citizens around the world, a central component of her work at the State Department.[4] In her memoir, she devoted a whole chapter to "twenty-first Century Statecraft: Digital Diplomacy in a Networked World."[5] Well before most, Clinton understood that social media had to be harnessed as an additional tool of public diplomacy. In January 2012, however, very few ambassadors—American or otherwise—were active on Twitter. A few American ambassadors had started to experiment with this new modality for communicating to citizens where they served, but most stuck to safe topics, like food, music, and culture. A small handful of non-American diplomats were already using various social media platforms by then. For instance, while serving as Sweden's Minister for Foreign Affairs, the Swedish politician and diplomat Carl Bildt was a successful first-mover in virtual diplomacy. But in 2012, most diplomats shied away from this new method of communication. Many still do.

Eager to implement the instructions from my Secretary of State, I went all in. Headed by Joseph Kruzick, my press office in Moscow also embraced this new mission with great enthusiasm. Others at the embassy were skeptical. Who would clear our tweets? Did they even need to be approved by Washington? Given Twitter's informality, was tweeting appropriate for a US Ambassador? How would we separate personal communications from official messaging? Was this assignment for me personally or my entire public affairs staff? What if we made a mistake?

These were all legitimate questions. I'm sure they were also asked by diplomats when radio and television first were invented. But in my mind, answers were available, even if we would have to learn from experimentation and not a handbook of best practices on Twitter Diplomacy, but such a manual did not exist. We were going to make mistakes; of that, I was sure. But that was acceptable for me. You cannot be a pioneer if you are afraid to make mistakes or too worried about conservative conventional wisdom. I did not want just "to be" a US Ambassador. I wanted "to do" things as US Ambassador. In 2012, with the return of Vladimir Putin to the Kremlin for his third term, the opportunities to achieve win-win outcomes with the Russian government were rapidly diminishing. The Reset in US-Russia relations, which I had helped to launch in 2009, was over in 2012.[6] So the chance to do something creative regarding public diplomacy appealed to me. Soon after my arrival at post, I began tweeting.

Tweeting, however, was only a very small part of my job, and even only one component of our public diplomacy efforts. In fact, I put in place some ground rules for my use of Twitter and other social media platform, including Facebook and Livejournal. (We decided not to use VKontakte, a successful Russian copycat of Facebook, because the company at the time was violating the intellectual property rights of several American video and music companies.)

First, I never let virtual diplomacy get in the way of physical diplomacy. I rarely tweeted during the workday. We used social media to supplement and amplify, not substitute, our physical diplomacy and other media work. Second, and most obviously, there were many dimensions of my diplomatic work with the Russian government that were best left behind closed doors. I tried to be transparent about my meetings with Russian officials and civil society leaders, but not always as transparent regarding the substance of these meetings. Even the fact of some meetings had to be left private; some senior Russian government officials enjoyed meeting with me, but did not want publicity, because Putin and his propogandists were blaming me personally for fomenting a revolution against his government. Third, we tried to engage with everyone on Twitter, not just elites or those with massive followings. Of course, as my account grew in popularity, it became impossible to respond to everyone. But I tried, sometimes with the help of my staff. Fourth, over time, I tried to tweet more and more in Russian. Fifth, our press and public affairs team did not privilege Twitter over other more traditional media and public diplomacy activities. I tried to do it all—television, radio, print interviews, op-eds, my own blog on Livejournal, public talks, and even formal lectures at universities that included slides in Russian. (I've been told that I was the first US Ambassador in Russia to use PowerPoint, but don't know if that's true.) But with Russia's internet penetration in 2012 already at 63.8%, we had to be engaged in social media, not just traditional media.[7]

In parallel, my team and I also engaged in some traditional public diplomacy, including hosting jazz concerts, NBA players, Silicon Valley CEOs, and Governors at Spaso House, as well as sponsoring cultural performances in Moscow and around the country. My wife Donna Norton and I especially leaned into the public diplomacy, hosting over 20,000 guests at Spaso House in two years. And at almost every one of those events, there was a tweet about it!

Achieving Scale

Before taking up my new assingment in Moscow, I met in Washington with Alec Ross, who was then serving as Secretary Clinton's Senior Advisor for Innovation and leading an effort within the State Department to modernize our strategic communications. Alec knew Twitter and gave me a few pointers. He also had someone from his team, Jason Flippen, at our embassy in Moscow who assisted me. Like with any other medium, using social media effectively is a skill. In December 2011, I had a rather inactive Facebook account which I used mostly to track social movements in other countries, including Russia. I did not have a Twitter account. I did not know how to these platforms for anything useful, let alone diplomacy—a skill which I also was just beginning to learn. I was grateful for the early coaching.

The most important lesson Alec taught me was that I could not use my Twitter account just to circulate State Department press releases. No one would follow me to read that. Instead, I had to blend formal and informal content and begin revealing some personal information about myself. That's what most followers really wanted. I had to mix the spinach with the chocolates. In other words, I had to become a public figure. That was new and scary to me. I had been giving interviews on television and radio, as well as giving public talks, since the early 1990s. But before arriving in Moscow, almost all of my previous media appearances had been as an "expert." The subject matter of these interviews was usually Russia and US-Russia relations. On Twitter, I at times was going to be the subject matter as well.

I modeled my behavior on social media (and other forms of media) after President Obama. He and his terrific press team used a variety of plat-forms and tackled a multitude of subjects—some personal, some not—to communicate to the American people and the world. President Obama, of course, delivered many serious addresses and gave hundreds of inter-views focused on policy. But he also did some more playful things, like ride around in a car with comedian Jerry Seinfeld, play basketball with NBA stars, or walk around the White House with a selfie stick. His critics called these actions "unpresidential" or much worse. TV commentator Lou Dobbs called Obama's use of the selfie stick the work of a "self-absorbed ass clown"![8] With clear boundaries, Obama also allowed the public to see him as a husband, father, basketball fan, a Chicagoan, and Hawaiian. He even let the public know what books he was buying and what music he was circulating on his iPod. I tried to do some, not all, of the same. Gen-erally, Russians loved it. For instance, I tweeted about coaching my son's grade school basketball team—that shocked my social media audience! They were accustomed to seeing their own diplomats and American am-bassadors in suits and ties, not sweatshirts and sneakers. As a former (and future) professor, I tweeted often about Stanford University. Because many Russians, especially those on Twitter, value higher education, Stanford themes were always popular. To relate to Russian not living in Moscow or St. Petersburg, I also tweeted about growing up in Montana, or what Russians would call, "the regions." And sometimes, I tweeted about family life, especially when my family traveled together within Russia. I rarely posted photos of my young sons—that seemed too personal—but whenever I did, they were extremely popular. One of the most popular photos I ever tweeted was on Red Square of my parents and siblings visiting from Montana and the state of Washington.

Even little details of my private life generated audience interest. One our first Valentine's Day in Moscow, I took my wife to an Uzbek restaurant to celebrate. The following year, Twitter followers asked if we were going to have Uzbek food again; others made recommendations for other kinds of cuisines. They were paying attention. One night playing basketball at the embassy, someone broke my finger in several places, which required surgery to repair. I tweeted about my surgery and photographed the very elaborate cast. A few weeks later, during a Boeing event at Skolkovo, I ran into Prime Minister Dmitry Medvedev and started to explain my cast, but he interrupted me and said that he already knew all about it because of the internet. More routinely, I tweeted about my daily schedule. My followers loved the behind-the-scenes details and were surprised by how much of my day was consumed by meetings with Russians outside of the government, be it rabbis at synagogues, Bolshoi opera singers, or NBA basketball players. A tweet of my meeting at the embassy with NHL hockey star Alexey Ovechkin generated tons of interest. The photo of him meeting with me at a time when the Putin-controlled media was berating me as a revolutionary created dissonance. So too did the many meetings that I had and tweeted about with government officials, members of parliament in Putin's party, and senior religious figures such as Patriarch Kirill—the leader of the Russian Orthodox Church, who is considered close to the Kremlin. Twitter helped me dispel the myth that I was only engaging with opposition leaders.

To expand our reach in the early, we learned from social media experts the importance of engaging figures with large followings on the platform. Thankfully, some senior Russian officials active on Twitter did engage with me from time to time, such as President Medvedev's closest economic advisor, Arkady Dvorkovich, and Deputy Prime Minister Dmitry Rogozin. These interactions helped to boost our numbers, since Russians naturally were shocked to see the US Ambassador to Russia chatting, and occasionally sparring, with high-level government officials. To generate buzz, I also engaged with some semi-celebrities such as Ksenia Sobchak and Tina Kandelaki, since they had huge followings at the time. Every now and then, I interacted with Russian opposition leaders, including most noticeably with Alexei Navalny. In fact, after responding on twitter to a hit job done on me by a famous television show, Odnako, broadcast on Russia's largest state-controlled television channel.[9] Navalny responded by tweeting "@Mcfaul it is already fun." So I responded for the first time to anyone on Twitter on January 17, 2012, "@navalny Odnaka had no word about the 3 years of reset. Yesterday my mtgs with WH/Kremlin officials could not have been warmer." That was the beginning of a two-year campaign by the Kremlin to cast Navalny was an American puppet. For those who watched only official Russian media, they would have believed Navalny and I were best friends, drinking beers every night, and plotting our next revolutionary move. In reality, we never once met for a formal meeting during my entire tenure as US Ambassador. (We had a one chance meeting at a dinner celebrating the twentieth anniversary of the Moscow Times; although we talked for sixty seconds, dozens of people photographed us, and the photos went viral on Twitter.) However, we did banter on Twitter occasionally, in conversations that boosted my numbers.

Humor was another method for expanding reach. Of course, I shared official State Department or White House statements. I also used social media to communicate my respect for certain Russian holidays. Cosmonaut Day was one of my favorites, and for occasions such as the 70th anniversary of the Battle of Stalingrad, my feed was appropriately solemn. But I also was playful on Twitter and often used self-deprecating humor. I deliberately cultivated an informal voice on the platform that some within our embassy thought was inappropriate for a an ambassador. I cautiously disagreed, instead arguing an accurate and honest portrayal of myself on Twitter would help us communicate tougher and more formal messages later.

At the same time, I drew limits. I refused to play guitar in a Russian band, which would have produced fabulous social media content, but seemed too contrived. Most controversially, I did an interview and photo shoot for a Russian magazine, *GQ Russia*, which I was told was very popular with Russian government officials. But then we pulled the plug on the publication upon discovering that the Russian version of the magazine at the time published risqué photos of women with whom I did not feel comfortable appearing in print together. I wanted to scale, but not at any price.

Bumps and Hard Calls Along the Road

In using Twitter and other social media for diplomacy, I was a pioneer and pioneers make mistakes. Most certainly, I made my share. My biggest challenge was writing properly in Russian. In 2012, I could read and speak Russian pretty well; I felt comfortable doing television and radio interviews in Russian and did many, sometimes hour-long shows on complex topics. But when you are speaking Russian, you can make grammatical mistakes, especially regarding the endings of words and verb tenses, that are less noticeable. The difference between "ogo" and "omu" as the last, unaccented syllable in word when speaking is relatively minor. The difference between "I" and "Y" when speaking is also trivial. But when writing, these mistakes jump out more starkly. The last time I had been in a class learning how to write Russian was 1985! It showed. I was constantly making mistakes, for which some followed berated me. We tried a system in which a Russian member of our public affairs team would read and correct my tweets before sending, but that proved cumbersome, especially as tweets were most popular if published in real time at an event. Moreover, I mostly tweeted at night from home, without staff around.

To compensate for my poor writing skills, I sometimes would cut and paste tiny snippets of text from the tweets of the others into my own. That way, I got the prepositions and endings right. One night, however, this crutch of mine got me into serious trouble. I was tweeting to generate attention for my upcoming trip to Ekaterinburg. For the public event, I wanted to make sure that we invited Russians in a more democratic way than was usually the case for such events, so I was using twitter to find some new participants for our planned events. I also was seeking advice from Ekaterinburg residents about where to eat and what to see. It was typical Twitter banter, but in response to one of my interlocutors that night, I cut and pasted a word from another Tweet that I assumed was an informal reference to the city. It was—but way too informal for a US Ambassador. I Tweeted the word "Yoburg" which I found out minutes later meant "F**kberg." Extremely embarrassed, I quickly apologized.[10] Since Twitter does not allow you to edit Tweets, I had to delete the post—but not before thousands of Russians had seen my mistake. Most of course saw the innocence of my mistake. When

I got to Ekaterinburg a few days later, many young people explained to me that it was no big deal, and they used the word among themselves all the time. But it was a highly embarrassing mistake that those already critical of my social media activity pounced upon.

In 2012, tweets had to be twice as shorter as they are today, and there were also no threads. That meant I had to be creative in my use of words to communicate. In one exchange with the Editor-and-Chief of Russia Today, Margarita Simonyan, I wanted to say that their reporting that day was inaccurate. The word "inaccurate" would have been a properly diplomatic word to describe their reporting. But I ran out of room in that Tweet and instead used a shorter word in Russian—"lie." In retrospect, I regret that Tweet. I used it only because the platform limited the number of words that I could publish. In diplomacy, one often has to use many words to hide or obfuscate the direct meaning. On Twitter, one has to do the opposite: write bluntly and succinctly.

However, the hardest challenge as a diplomat using Twitter was deciding when to express my opinion about a policy issue before getting official permission—or as we called it at the State Department, "clearance"—to do so. Almost always, these hard calls occurred when I believed the Obama administration should speak up in defense of human rights, given that it was our policy to do so. During my three years at the National Security Council at the White House, from 2009 to 2011, I wrote many statements on behalf of the administration criticizing human rights violations or democratic setbacks in Russia. That remained our policy in 2012. The question was always about tone and speed, since Moscow is eight hours ahead of Washington. On handful og occasions, we knew that if we waited for Washington to wake up and give us guidance for a response to a specific arrest or injustice, we would have missed the news cycle in Russia. Moreover, press guidance from Washington went through an internal clearance process within the State Department, and sometimes required as many as a dozen people to clear the language. That process almost always produced a more watered-down statement than what I thought was appropriate.

Two instances, in particular, were difficult calls. The first was when I decided to tweet about what I believe was the wrongful arrest of the band members of Pussy Riot. They had performed their punk rock protest music in one of Russia's most sacred cathedrals, Cathedral of Christ the Savior, without a permit. Some punishment was in order—suspended sentence or fine. However, two years in a penal colony for the group's leaders,

Nadezhda Tolokonnikova and Maria Alyokhina, seemed completely out-rageous. As the news broke of their sentence, I was standing in a security line at the Istanbul airport. I knew if we did not respond immediately, we would miss the moment to be a part of the news cycle. I also knew that if I said nothing before bordering my plane, the back and forth between Mos-cow and Washington, and the clearance process more generally, would delay our response and diminish our impacy. So I jumped in on my own and criticized the sentence. I know some in Washington were displeased, but I decided that the negative consequences for our policy of not acting were greater than the negative consequences for me personally of acting.

In the summer of 2013, I faced another similar dilemma when tweet-ing about the conviction of opposition leader Alexei Navalny. At the time, Navalny was (and remains) Russia's most popular opposition leader. That summer, he was arrested for allegedly embezzling money from a timber company in the provincial town of Kirov, while serving as an unpaid ad-visor to the governor. Most analysts, as well as, our best foreign service officers in the embassy concluded that Navalny was innocent. Through their loyal agents in law enforcement and the courts, Kremlin officials were using a false accusation to silence Putin's greatest critic. On July 18, 2013, I watched online as a judge in Kirov spent hours reading Navalny's conviction. I should have stayed silent during the reading of the convic-tion, but I could not help myself, given how it felt like witnessing live a show trial from the Stalin era. I could not stand by idly and pretend that what was happening to Navalny did not impact everyone who believed in freedom. I recalled Martin Luther King Jr. famous line in his letter from a Birmingham jail: "Injustice anywhere is a threat to justice everywhere." So when Navalny tweeted, "hello everyone,"[11] I tweeted back, "privet, smo-triu," meaning "hello, I'm watching." My two-word Tweet went viral and later became a bit of a meme. Navalny supporters loved it; the Russian gov-ernment hated it. Some even accused me of meddling in the internal legal affairs of the Russian state. Eventually, the judge finally read the shocking verdict—five years of prison time and a 500,000-ruble fine. I felt like we had to react, and immediately. We could not wait for Washington to wake up and plod through their clearance process. For this tweet, I did consult with my most senior colleagues at the embassy. We chose every word of the 140 characters very closely: "We are deeply disappointed in the conviction of @Navalny and the apparent political motivations in this trial." Notice the use of the word, we. I was convinced that this statement was consis-tent with our administration's policy of speaking out about human rights abuses. Even if some within the State Department might not have agreed with the content or speed of our reaction, I was confident that Obama and Clinton would be supportive.

My message produced a massive reaction on social media and bled into conventional media, both locally and abroad. As Andrew Cooper and Jeremie Cornut have written, "Minutes after the tweet was live, it had started generating buzz on the Russian social media landscape, reaching nearly 1,000 retweets, as well as dozens of likes and comments. As a Russian journalist explained: 'Everyone was checking McFaul's Twitter account and quoting what he said.'"[12] Other diplomats conveyed to us later that my Tweet made it easier for them to say something as well. The message also echoed a view held by millions of Russians; a public opinion poll conducted by Levada Center showed that 57% of Muscovites and 44% of all Russians considered the charges against Navalny to be unjust and politically motivated. Later that day, a massive demonstration erupted spontaneously in downtown Moscow.[13] Shockingly, the outcry seemed to compel to the Kremlin to reverse its decision. To the surprise of most, the prosecution asked the court to change the verdict to house arrest, and the court acquiesced. At this moment in Russia's history, popular mobilization appeared to have reversed an unjust conviction. Who knows if our tweet produced any effect on this protest, but that day it felt good to be on the right side of history, if only in a small way. Subsequently, many Russians—not just opposition supporters—thanked me for speaking out. Without Twitter, the American reaction that day would not have been as impactful. Of course, Putin's propogandists accused me of orchestrating the whole thing and even circulated on social media a photo-shopped picture of me sitting in front of a window at a downtown hotel and watching "my work" as the demonstration gathered steam.

The Pussy Riot and Navalny convictions underscored a dilemma. Who should be the voice of criticism within the US government? Some at the State Department, including some at the embassy and others back in Washington, believed that diplomats stationed inside the country should not issue critical statements. Rather, we should leave that assignment to State Department officials in Washington, so that we in Moscow could maintain access with our counterparts in the Russian government. (It's a dilemma journalists covering the US government face all the time— write something too critical and lose you access.) I understood the argument, but ultimately disagreed. I believed that the Obama administration should have one policy, which everyone working for the administration should embrace and express. I also thought it was naive to believe that Russian government officials gave us access or met with us because we did not criticize them. My assumption is that they met with us because they thought it was in the interest of their government to do so, not because I or anyone else working the US embassy in Moscow were nice people. Ironically and perhaps surprisingly, I was outspoken on Twitter and other platforms regarding autocratic policies and human rights abuses of the Russian government, but at the same time, maintained access to senior officials. They met with me because we had business to do. Even during one dark phase, when Foreign Minister Lavrov circulated a communication directing all ministers not to meet with me, some still did, because we had work to do. (Because I had served in the White House during the cooperative era between President Obama and President Medvedev, I had the opportunity to work closely with many senior Russian government officials well before I arrived in Moscow as US Ambassador. Those contacts, plus my close personal relationship to President Obama, gave me an advantage regarding access that not all previous or future ambassadors have enjoyed.)

In retrospect, I also wonder about the division of labor within the US government regarding the issuing of critical statements about a foreign government. I most certainly endured public criticism from Kremlin-controlled media outlets because of my public statements about democracy and human rights. But is that such a bad thing? After all, President Obama asked me to serve as US Ambassador to Russia in order to represent American policies and American values. He did not send me to Moscow to make friends with Putin. While joining up with President Obama in Seoul, South Korea in the spring of 2012 to attend Obama's last bilateral meeting Medvedev on the sidelines or a multilateral meeting, Obama even told me that he loved it that Putin didn't like me; it meant that I must be doing something.

Some to this day still blame me and my critical tweets for the deterioration of relations between the United States and Russia. But that kind of analysis grossly inflates the impact of an individual ambassador on bilateral relations between powerful countries such as the United States and Russia. The downward spiral in US-Russian relations that began in 2011 and accelerated in 2012 was much bigger than me and would have occurred with or without my appointment as US Ambassador to Russia, let alone my Twitter. (The same is true during good times; Ambassador Matlock played a role in improving US-Soviet ties in the 1980s, but Reagan and Gorbachev played the central role, from which Matlock's popularity inside the USSR benefited.) Furthermore, relations worsened considerably after I left. Following the end of my service, Putin annexed Crimea and supported separatists in eastern Ukraine. Those actions were far more consequential to damaging US-Russian relations then all of my critical tweets combined.

The Pluses and Minuses of Becoming a Public Figure as a Political Appointee

There is no doubt that Twitter, as well social media more generally and my active engagement with other media platforms, helped to make me a more public figure in Russia than was usually the case for American ambassadors serving there. By the end of my term, Russians would approach me at public events or restaurants and say hello. At the end of any speaking engagement, I signed many autographs. During the 2014 Winter Olympics in Sochi, I took dozens of selfies with Russians. I was especially popular with students, so much so that the Russian government eventually banned me from speaking at universities. The day I announced on Twitter my plan for going home, thousands of messages filled my feed in praise of my work.

My public profile produced advantages for our diplomatic work. Most obviously, we could communicate with hundreds of thousands—and at times, even millions—of Russian instantaneously. We could explain US actions in Syria, our reaction to Edward Snowden's arrival in Moscow, or President Obama's decision to cancel a summit in Moscow in September 2013 directly to Russian society without mediation by the Russian press. We also could use my personality as a vehicle to get our messaging out.

The greatest downside of developing my personal public profile was that critics—both in Washington and Moscow—could claim that I was just representing myself while tweeting or appearing on television, instead of the administration's policies. Of course, that was not true. When Obama visited Moscow in July 2009, he also practiced dual-track diplomacy, meeting with students, business executives, civil society leaders, and members of the opposition. So too did Vice President Joseph Biden, Secretary Clinton, and Undersecretary of State William Burns. When I allegedly committed a diplomatic foul by meeting with the Russian opposition during my first week as ambassador, I was actually accompanying Undersecretary Burns for *his* meetings with them. But because I had a high public profile, the Russian media focused on me, not him. Moreover, I never said anything on Twitter or elsewhere that was not 100% consistent with our policy. After all, for better or ill, I was one of—if not the—leading architect of our policy towards Russia—the Reset. How could I be out of step with a policy that I helped to craft and implement while working for three years at the White House before arriving in Moscow? More generally, many complained that I was not playing the role of a typical ambassador in certain aspects of my behavior. On that point, my critics might be right. But I was comfortable not being a "typical" ambassador. Those times in Putin's Russia were not typical; so maybe not acting as a typical ambassador was a benefit?

Learning from Social Media

Cultivating an active social media presence produced one unexpected additional benefit—knowledge about Russia. Once I opened a Twitter account, I discovered news personalities and publications that I had never known previously. Twitter was especially useful in tracking events and debates within the Russian opposition. As we all now know, Twitter was an essential platform for following breaking news. But I did not understand its value as a news source until I opened my own account. Because I kept my direct messages open, people from all around the country sent me articles and video clips that I never would have seen from just reading my cables or newspapers. Twitter proved especially invaluable in learning about regional politics. It is impossible for me to imagine serving as a diplomat today and not at least "creeping" on Twitter to keep up with events.

Measuring Impact

Similar to assessing the casual impact of any social media activity or election campaign, measuring the precise influence of Twitter diplomacy is difficult, if not impossible. Embassy Moscow did not take the necessary steps at the beginning of our social media efforts to trace this impact scientifically. (We had no control group and did not run a randomized controlled trial!) Trying to track attitudinal changes with Russian society generated from our modest efforts on social media platforms is a fool's errand. After all, I was a small producer of content in a vast sea of radio, television, print, and social media messaging produced by the Russian government and its allies. Isolating the independent causal effect of our public diplomacy on social media is beyond even the most sophisticated social science methods. Similar problems exist in other fields. For instance, regarding elections, candidates spend enormous resources to generate and disseminate content on both traditional and social media, yet the impact on voter behavior remains not well understood.[14]

These challenges have compelled some to dismiss Twitter diplomacy as a waste of time, a distraction from the "real" business of diplomacy, or an endeavor unworthy of and undignified for an ambassador to pursue. I disagree. Twitter diplomacy should never crowd out other parts of a diplomat's portfolio, and Twitter is only one platform of many that diplomats must use to communicate to citizens where they serve. But social media must be used as one of many tools in the arsenal of public diplomacy. If deployed properly and strategically, it can produce positive effects. Even our short experiment in Twitter diplomacy in Russia from 2012–2014 generated some visible achievements from which future diplomats can learn.

Our first achievement was the scale of our audience. From my first Tweet in January 2012 to my last in February 2014, my followers on Twitter grew to nearly 80,000 with another 13,000 on Facebook. Today, that seems like a small number (my current follower count is approaching 600,000). In 2014, however, this following size was huge. Combined with other accounts on Facebook, Instagram, and Livejournal, I was ranked as one of the top ten micro-bloggers in Russia, alongside President Medvedev and opposition leader Alexei Navalny. *Foreign Policy* ranked me among the top-10 diplomats and politicians in its "Twitterati 100" list, an "honor" I shared with the pope and Hillary and Bill Clinton. [15]

When we conducted hour-long "ask me anything" sessions on Twitter, or I commented on controversial issues, I could generate a half million impressions in a day. At the time, only a small percentage of Russian citizens were on Twitter. But of those who were, we could reach a significant number over the course of a month. Given that government-owned or government-loyal media gradually limited my appearances, Twitter offered us a valuable way to communicate directly to Russian citizens. We essentially had our own newspaper with a circulation much bigger many Russian publications at the time. That reach proved indispensable in a country the size of Russia; in one day, I could reach a number of Russians that would have taken me literally weeks on the road to connect with through physical public diplomacy events. Moreover, during our more traditional public diplomacy events—be it a talk at an American Corners in Volgograd or a jazz concert at Spaso House—we could use social media to connect with many thousands more virtually than we reached in the physical world. Twitter amplified everything we did.

Second, Twitter allowed us to communicate immediately. I did not have to wait for a television network or a radio station invitation to conduct public diplomacy. I could "broadcast" anytime, and at times, this immediacy proved essential for shaping public debates. As disccused above regarding our reaction to Navalny's wrongful conviction, n a world of 24/7 news cycles, speed matters. Twitter provided our embassy with an instant capacity to response to events and shape media stories.

Third, different from television, radio, or print, Twitter is a two-way channel of communication. I was not only "broadcasting," but also "listening" and reacting. Russians loved it when I responded to their Tweets, especially when writing in Russian. Furthermore, Embassy Moscow learned considerably from reading these responsive tweets, such as which messages worked more effectively and when to deploy humor or stay serious. We also discovered when to communicate facts and when to express opinions.

Fourth, in an observation based more on anecdotal evidence, Twitter seemed to serve as a great channel for discussing not only policy issues, but the United States more generally. At a time when the Russian state-controlled media portrayed the United States in sinister terms—a country seeking to "weaken" Russia and overthrow Putin's regime—my tweets about less political matters related to American life was a useful, subtle rebuttal. How could the United States be so evil when all we seemed to care about was who won the Super Bowl? Tweets about everyday life in Montana were especially effective in suggesting that not all Americans were obsessed with Putin, regime change, or Russia. My playful spirit and openness to discuss apolitical topics—from my jump shot to my family tradition of baking chocolate caterpillar cakes for birthdays—helped to undermine the Kremlin's image of me as a sinister usurper or revolutionary fomenter. My willingness to engage everyone and anyone—from deputy prime ministers in Moscow to high-school students in Vladivostok—also surprised many. On many occasions, Russians assumed someone on my staff was posting on my behalf. Ironically, my grammatical and spelling mistakes that so embarrassed me helped people believe that it was actually me on social media.

Fifth, Twitter allowed me to constantly underscore my love of Russian culture, my respect for Russian history, and my admiration for the Russian people. Not everyone in our embassy or back in Washington agreed with the wisdom of expressing these sentiments, but I thought it was important, both to distinguish between our criticism of the Russian government from the Russian people, and because it had the virtue of being true. Well before serving as US Ambassador, I had lived many years in the Soviet Union and Russia. Russophobes don't do that. Over years of consistently emphasizing my admiration for Russia on social media, I think we did achieve a real breakthrough in messaging, in which we could criticize Putin's policies without appearing to criticize Russians themselves. One Putin loyalist told me as much when suggesting that it would have been far easier to attack me in the press if I were a genuine Russophobe.

Sixth, our open engagement on Twitter was in and of itself an indirect promotion of democratic values. By the end of my service, Russians knew much more about me, my family, and my personal life than they knew about Putin, his family, and his personal life. Near the end of my tenure, one colleague familiar with the Kremlin explained that Putin actually was right to believe that my actions undermined his legitimacy. But instead of my tweets criticizing his policies, working as a US Ambassador in a transparent, engaging manner had a more significant impact on his legitimacy.

On a personal level, the volume of praise I received on social media for our public efforts seemed to vastly outweigh the negative reaction. Of course, this impression is not a scientific study, and even if I could verify this observation, it would not imply that we nurtured a decisively positive image for the United States, President Obama, or me among all Russians. After all, only a percentage of Russians used the platform. The anecdotal evidence as measured by me and my team, however, did suggest we were breaking through to some, if not most, of my followers. Just a few months into my service, one Russian [although we do not know for sure it was a Russian], tweeted, "Michael, u're an outstanding ambassador Russia have never seen [*sic*]. Thanks for all your incredible effort&hard work. Reset works." The following year, in February 2013, another wrote, "To my mind you're the greatest US ambassador we ever had." When I announced my departure from Moscow in February 2014, my feed was flooded with messages of sorrow and praise. Among Echo of Moscow radio listeners—a segment of the population more liberal and Western than the average Russian—the vast majority responded in a poll very favorably to my work as US Ambassador. Most had gotten to know me through Twitter.

The Future of (Public) Diplomacy

When John Quincy Adams reported for duty in St. Petersburg as the first US Ambassador to Russia in 1809, he became the most senior American with whom Russian government officials would ever meet. Ambassador Adams would correspond with the Madison Administration, occasionally receive instructions from his government, and deliver demarches to the Tsar's team in person. In those meetings, Ambassador Adams conducted diplomacy. Since connectivity with the State Department was slow, he had to make his own judgement calls about US policy, while meeting in person with his Russian counterparts. He did not have the luxury of having the "inter agency" deliberate on most foreign policy matters and send him instructions. Adams and his team also provided critical information about developments inside Russia, since their cables to the United States were some of the only reporting that American government officials ever read about events in Russia.

Today, both of those critical missions for the US Ambassador to Russia—conducting diplomacy with the government and reporting on the country—have serious challengers. Because of airplanes, the President, the Vice President, the US Secretary of State, the National Security Advisor, the Secretary of Defense, and even the CIA Director can board Air Force One or MilAir and meet their counterparts in Moscow or around the world. Likewise, Deputy Secretaries and Assistant Secretaries from the State Department and several other agencies travel to Moscow, meet their Russian government counterparts in Washington, or interact at multilateral gatherings around the world. When I served as the US Ambassador to Russia, we hosted a visiting US government delegation from Washington nearly every week. Yet unlike Adams' time in St. Petersburg, multiple US government officials—including the president—now conduct diplomacy with the Russian government. Compared to the 18th century, or even several decades ago, the role of the US Ambassador in Russia, as well as all other diplomats based at the embassy, in implementing policy has been greatly diminished. When American visitors came to Russia, be it the President, the Secretary of State, the National Security Advisor, the heads of the FBI and CIA, or lower level officials, I typically accompanied them during their meetings without directly participating in the discussions. They were doing the diplomacy, not me. In addition, Washington-based policymakers in the Obama administration did not always use the US embassy in Moscow to communicate with their Russian counterparts via the demarche modality. They could just call their counterparts directly, and vice versa. As officials across the world have grown accustomed to conducting business on other virtual platforms during the COVID-19 pandemic, the role of the embassies as the intermediaries for communications between capitals has and will continue to diminish further.

In parallel, the US Ambassador and other diplomats serving in Russia (and around the world) have new competition regarding reporting on Russia. Diplomatic cables on Russian elections, environmental issues, or economic developments now compete with dozens of other conventional and social media sources that can be accessed quickly by US officials. Oftentimes, those reporting or tweeting from Russia are greater experts about the topics that they cover than American diplomats on their first tour in Russia. Moreover, thirty years ago, American diplomats interacted with think tank specialists and academics in Moscow as critical sources for their cables. Today, those kinds of sources are producing their own content online (and often in English) for the whole world to read. In addition, more people in the US government are now gathering information about Russia than in previous decades. When senior US officials speak regularly with their Russian counterparts, they rely less on embassy reporting cables for information. For instance, when I was the US ambassador to Russia, Secretary of State John Kerry did not need to read our cables to determine what Foreign Minister Lavrov was thinking; he just called him directly on his cell phone.

These new conditions regarding the conduct of government-to-government diplomacy and State Department reporting require a fundamental rethinking of the role of the American diplomat in the twenty-first century. Of course, ambassadors and other diplomats must continue to deliver demarches, meet with the foreign ministry counterparts, and write reporting cables. But they also must reweight their portfolios of activities to devote greater time and energy to public diplomacy, including on social media. Explaining US foreign policy to local citizens is a task that diplomats remain uniquely qualified to perform. Furthermore, social media must be used as a critical instrument for reaching foreign publics. If the State Department does not embrace this mission as a more central component of diplomatic work, the rationale for maintaining a large staff in embassies around the world will weaken. We should redefine the role of ambassadors and other diplomats in the twenty-first century as agents of public diplomacy first and foremost, beyond other assignments such as issuing visas.

This transformation requires a major cultural shift and a reordering of incentives within the State Department. Most critically, every foreign service officer—not just public affairs officers—should have to embrace public diplomacy as part of their assignment. That should be also true for nearly every American serving in US embassies. As US Ambassador to

Russia, I once walked into my Country Team meeting—that is, the weekly gathering of two dozen section heads and agency leaders—and declared that everyone in the room was hereby deputized to serve part time on the public affairs team. (I gave an exemption to the chief of station of the CIA.) Yes, they had to continue writing reporting cables to Washington—but now, they also had to embrace writing "reporting cables" about the work of their section or agency to the Russian people. I would then circulate this information on social media platforms. In February 2013, we even ran a social media campaign featuring 28 days of good news about US-Russia relations, which required every major section or agency at the embassy to share content about bilateral cooperation with which most people were unfamiliar. It was a fabulous success.

To get more diplomats involved in public diplomacy would also entail a democratization and decentralization of content production and circulation. Big embassies like the US Mission in Russia should have dozens of Twitter accounts, not just one. Lower level diplomats must be allowed to generate and circulate social media content, especially regarding non-political issues. When I served as the US Ambassador to Russia, the head of my political section, Howard Solomon, would post photos of beautiful churches around the country. Dozens of diplomats could be doing that every day, because photos and videos are most popular on social media than wordy official statements.

Third, the criteria for State Department promotion should better reward public diplomacy.[16] An hour speaking to high school students in Pskov, Russia should be valued just as much as a classified cable read by a handful of American officials back at home.

Fourth, more social media experts must be brought onto embassy teams. Budgets show priorities. The size of the public affairs budgets for the US embassy in Moscow during my tenure underscored that we cared insufficiently. Using social media effectively requires hiring trained professionals in photography, videography, and graphic design. When I worked in Moscow, we were amateurs and experimenters, but nearly a decade later, that is not good enough anymore. Furthermore, the proliferation of social media platforms means that US Ambassadors and their senior teams must have experts not only on Twitter, but also YouTube, Instagram, TikTok, Telegram, and Clubhouse.

Fifth, the entire US government—not just the State Department—must restructure to conduct public diplomacy more effectively. In today's ideological competition between authoritarianism and liberal democracy, Xi

Jinping's China[17] and Vladimir Putin's Russia[18] have made major invest-ments in tools for propagating their worldviews and explaining their pol-icies. Given that the United States has not progressed similarly, it is time to catch up. The executive branch and congressional leaders must start by radically restructuring the US Agency for Global Media (USAGM).[19] The Trump administration errored in its politicization of government-supported media organizations.[20] USAGM should make all of its entities that are dedicated to providing news—Radio Free Europe/Radio Lib-erty, Radio Free Asia, the Middle East broadcasting networks, and Radio Marti—completely independent of the executive branch, with funding pro-vided from the US Congress and nonpartisan boards. The highly effective Open Technology Fund, which funds Internet freedom technologies at every stage of the development cycle, should also become an independent organization.[21] The US government should promote independent efforts to provide more resources for public media, including new resources to the Independent Fund for Public Interest Media.[22] Voice of America (VOA) also has to change.[23] One entity cannot serve as a consistently authori-tative source of news, provide a comprehensive projection of significant American thought and institutions, and represent US policies clearly and effectively. In 2021, that is an impossible mission. The parts of VOA that provide news should be incorporated into their counterpart regional media organizations, such as Radio Free Europe/Radio Liberty or Radio Free Asia. VOA Latin America and VOA Africa should be reconstituted as independent entities. The rest of VOA should be reconfigured and mod-ernized (with more TikTok, less TV) to more effectively explain US foreign policy abroad—an assignment that should be more tightly intertwined with the executive branch.

US presidents need a better communications infrastructure to explain their decisions to communities—not just governments—around the world. The United States Information Agency, which served US interests well during the Cold War, could offer a starting point, although the twenty-first century version requires greater nimbleness and flexibility.[24] The ad-ministration and US Congress should expand funding for all educational and cultural exchange programs. Nothing changes the minds of foreign-ers faster about the United States than extended time spent in the United States. (Similarly, we need greater expertise about the world; sending more Americans to study abroad helps to provide that knowledge.)

Of course, the United States should not get back into the Cold War pro-paganda business, nor do we want to mimic the disinformation elements of Russia's RT or China's CGTN today. But if we want to compete in the battle of ideas against populist demagogues[25] and aggressive authoritarians,[26] we must do a better job of explaining ourselves. More effective support for independent media and journalism is another indirect method for supporting liberal democracy.

Notes

1. Hillary Rodham Clinton, *Hard Choices* (New York: Simon & Shuster, 2015), p. 460.
2. Https://www.youtube.com/watch?v=TpeWJ3zNgqE.
3. "Twitter Diplomacy" became a concept. Scholars have begun to study the effects of Twitter and social media more generally on diplomacy. See for instance, Meghan Sobel, Daniel Riffe, and Joe Bob Hester, Twitter Diplomacy? A Content Analysis of Eight US Embassies' Twitter Feeds," *The Journal of Social Media in Society*, Vol. 5, No. 2 (2016), pp. 75–107; Bjola, C., & Jiang, L. (2015). Social media and public diplomacy: a comparative analysis of the digital diplomatic strategies of the EU, US, and Japan in China. In Digital Diplomacy: Theory and Practice, ed. Corneliu Bkola, and Marcus Holmes, 71–88. New York: Routledge; Zhang, J., & Fahmy, S. (2015). The use of social media in public diplomacy. In International Public Relations and Public Diplomacy, ed. Guy Golan, Sung-Un Yang, and Dennis Kinsey, 315–31. New York, NY: Lang Publishing; Radhika Chhabra, 'Twitter Diplomacy: A Brief Analysis', ORF Issue Brief No. 335, January 2020, Observer Research Foundation; Collins, S.D., DeWitt, J.R. & LeFebvre, R.K. Hashtag diplomacy: twitter as a tool for engaging in public diplomacy and promotig US foreign policy. *Place Brand Public Dipl* 15, 78–96 (2019). https://doi.org/10.1057/s41254-019-00119-5.
4. U. S. Department of State. (2009, May 28). twenty-first Century Statecraft. Retrieved from https://www.youtube.com/watch?v=x6PFPCTEr3c.
5. Clinton, *Hard Choices*, chapter 24, pp. 454–464.
6. I chronicle the events leading to the end of the Reset in McFaul, *From Cold War to Hot Peace: An American Ambassador in Putin's Russia* (New York: Houghton, Mifflin, Harcourt, 2018).
7. http://www.internetlivestats.com/internet-users/russia/
8. https://www.youtube.com/watch?v=8YFej3mjsis.
9. https://www.rferl.org/a/mcfaul_gets_frosty_reception_in_moscow/24456070 .html.
10. "Макфол В Твиттере Извинился За Свой «Ёбург»—Информационное Агентство «Европейско-Азиатские Новости»." 4 Июля, 2012. http://eanews.ru/news/scandals_sensations/makfol_v_tvittere_izvinilsya_za _svoy_burg/

11. Account, Alexey Navalny Verified. "'Организовал'. Значит Красивой Сцены С Оправданием Не Будет. Всем Привет, Кстати." Microblog. *@navalny*, July 18, 2013. https://twitter.com/navalny/status/35772835997 6943617.

12. Andrew Cooper and Jeremie Cornut, "The changing practices of frontline diplomacy," *Review of International Studies*, Vol. 45, No. 2 (2019), p. 315.

13. "Протесты После Приговора Навальному." Accessed February 12, 2015. http://rusplt.ru/policy/prigovor_protest.html.

14. Add cites.

15. https://foreignpolicy.com/2013/08/13/the-fp-twitterati-100/; and https://afsa.org/using-social-diplomacy-reach-russians.

16. https://www.atlanticcouncil.org/in-depth-research-reports/issue-brief/upgrading-us-public-diplomacy/

17. https://www.theatlantic.com/politics/archive/2020/05/china-disinformation-propaganda-united-states-xi-jinping/612085/

18. https://www.rferl.org/a/russia-rt-america-funding/31427870.html.

19. https://www.usagm.gov/

20. https://www.lawfareblog.com/trumps-war-us-agency-global-media.

21. https://www.opentech.fund/

22. https://luminategroup.com/ifpim.

23. https://www.voanews.com/

24. https://www.americansecurityproject.org/ASP%20Reports/Ref%200097%20-%twentiethe%20United%20States%20Information%20Agency.pdf.

25. https://www.newyorker.com/magazine/2019/01/14/viktor-orbans-far-right-vision-for-europe.

26. https://www.washingtonpost.com/world/europe/russia-election-putin-navalny-parliament/2021/09/16/d000e6e2-1012-11ec-baca-86b144fc8a2d_story.html.

FIFTEEN

MICHAEL O. SLOBODCHIKOFF

AND G. DOUG DAVIS

Morning or Twilight

American Diplomacy in the Twenty-First Century

T he end of the Cold War saw policymakers in the United States euphoric and develop the attitude that the United States had won the Cold War. What that meant was that the United States was in the unique position of being the most powerful country in the world, with a military that was second to none. In fact, there was no country that could beat the United States military in terms of weaponry, and military capabilities.

This unbridled power led the United States to making several critical mistakes in diplomacy. Instead of ensuring that we maintained good relationships with our allies and focused on negotiating desired outcomes, the United States relied more on its military might to achieve desired goals. No other country could afford to do so. This meant that the United States relied less on season diplomats, and began to lose sight of a grand strategy in foreign policy. The victory of the ideology of the United States led to complacency and efforts to manage conflicts without an overarching ideology and plans for foreign policy.

From the perspective of the military, the military was often called upon to deal with issues without having a diplomatic plan that worked in tandem with military might. As General Clark has argued in his chapter, it is extremely important for diplomacy to work in tandem with the military to achieve our goals. Over relying on military might without ensuring a diplomatic plan or diplomatic support meant that the United States could not maintain its diplomatic might. The wars in Afghanistan and Iraq and the subsequent failure to build democracy in those countries and maintain the peace have challenged US credibility as a moral power in the twenty-first-century.

The rise of China as a power that is challenging the United States and a resurgent Russia in Europe and the Middle East has provided a distinct challenge to the United States and its ability to lead and maintain its power in the twenty-first-century. The challenge to the United States global order is real, and highlights the importance of diplomacy in the twenty-first-century. The dedicated diplomats who have written chapters in this volume have dedicated their lives to improving and serving the United States of America. In these chapters, they have outlined and discussed the realities of diplomacy in the United States, the difficulties facing diplomats, foreign policymakers, and military leaders in the twenty-first-century. We should all be very thankful for the fact that despite the difficulties that they have faced throughout their careers that we have such a dedicated and capable people ensuring the future of diplomatic relations in the United States. It is thanks to these hard-working individuals that the United States has been able to achieve such power and moral authority as it has at the end of the twentieth century. The challenges that the United States faces moving forward or unprecedented and should really worry policymakers moving forward. Will the United States be able to keep its moral authority and maintain its power on the global stage or will it be forced to eventually cede its power to countries like China and Russia?

Ultimately, diplomacy is a vital part of statecraft and must be maintained. The United States is at a crossroads. It can either revitalize its efforts in diplomacy or it can wither away its power in the future. Diplomacy and the art of diplomacy is even more important in the twenty-first-century than it has been in the twentieth century. While the United States still has one of the most effective militaries in the world, the efficacy of that military to bring about changes in behavior or resolve many crises is limited. The military is very effective at waging war and defeating enemies, but less so at nation-building and creating permanent change. The wars in Iraq and in Afghanistan have resulted in sectarian violence, and limited gains in governance.

In addition to the difficulty with achieving long-term goals through the use of military force, the economy of the United States, which had been one of its greatest strengths, has slowed. The crisis in 2008 highlighted how interconnected many economies were and how difficult economic pressure can be used to achieve long-term change. While in the past the United States has been able to use economic pressure and sanctions to achieve changes in behavior such as with the apartheid regime in South

Africa, sanctions and economic pressure have not been as effective in the twenty-first-century. Further, the growth in the economy of China and India are challenging the economic situation in the United States. While almost all trade and economic interactions helped the United States at the end of the twentieth century, countries now have more choices and the ability to achieve economic gains without involving the United States and the twenty-first-century.

Another huge challenge to US superiority in the global system is one of demography. The US population is shrinking. The population and much of Western Europe, our traditional allies, is also shrinking. The population in many African states and India is increasing. The relevance of the United States as a global superpower is slowly deteriorating. What this means is that the US can no longer afford to use its might and strength to force other states to comply with its wishes. Instead, the US must rely on what most countries have long relied upon, which is effective negotiation and compromise with other countries. Most other countries have a professional cadre of diplomats who devote their lives to negotiation and achieving the goals of the countries that they represent. They do not rely upon diplomats who are not professional diplomats to negotiate outcomes. The United States also has a professional cadre of diplomats who are extremely well trained and very professional at their task. However, increasingly the posts of diplomats and ambassadorial positions are given to political supporters of the president, and there is increasing this trust of professional diplomats because politicians worry that their loyalty is not to the politician but rather to the country itself or even more troubling their loyalty to the country can deteriorate the longer they are stationed in another country.

The importance of diplomacy and the twenty-first-century cannot be understated. However, our current system in the United States needs to be revised greatly. It has been argued by some in this volume that more training needs to occur, that there needs to be more reliance upon professional diplomats, and the politics needs to be less present in the State Department. One very interesting recommendation comes from former ambassador Marc Grossman, who recommends developing a cadre of reserve diplomats who are well-trained and can be called upon in moments of crises. They can be sent to countries to help resolve political conflicts and to help in negotiations. This is a very interesting proposal and one that we believe deserves a lot of discussion from policymakers.

While we won't reiterate the points made by all the contributors in this volume, we will state that all of the recommendations made by these professional diplomats and people who have devoted their lives in the service of the United States should be taken very seriously in policy circles. There are decades of service mean that the issues that they present that need to be resolved are truly important issues that keep the United States from being extremely successful in its diplomatic efforts.

We have dedicated this volume in the memory of former Secretary of State George Schultz. In discussions with many ambassadors, it became apparent how important the former secretary was to ending the Cold War. While the former secretary was extremely familiar with the political battles occurring in Washington, he nevertheless truly focused on the professionalism and abilities of those who worked within the Department of State. He relied upon their counsel, he took the time to listen to their arguments, and in an era where technology was making it difficult to take the time to be fully briefed on all events, he would often take several days to become acquainted and fully briefed on issues before entering into negotiations. In discussions with former ambassador Jack Matlock, the last US ambassador to the Soviet Union, former ambassador Matlock described how Mr. Schultz would fly into Finland before summit meetings with the Soviet Union, and would bring Mr. Matlock and other officials from the Soviet embassy to Helsinki to begin face-to-face briefings of what the major issues were that might arise during negotiations, possible pitfalls, and ensuring that everyone was on the same page and clear about their various roles in the negotiation processes. This approach was vital to creating a negotiated settlement to the end of the Cold War, to negotiating treaties on de-escalating the arms race, and setting the groundwork for a more peaceful world order. Former Secretary of State George Schultz's contributions to US foreign policy and to diplomacy in general cannot be understated. It is wholly fitting that this volume is dedicated in his honor.

This volume begins with a touching preface written by former Secretary of State James Baker III. Former Secretary of State James Baker was very involved in the State Department and had an amazing way of navigating the political pitfalls in Washington. He succeeded former Secretary of State George Schultz and had a lot of respect for his predecessor. We are very thankful for his contributions to US foreign policy and for his touching tribute to his friend and mentor.

The volume is organized in such a way that gives an introduction to the functions of career diplomats. The chapter written by former ambassador Richard "Dick" Miles discusses his career at the end of the twentieth and beginning of the twenty-first century. While his career was truly extraordinary in many ways, his career also illustrates a "typical" professional career.

Chapter 3 is written by the former supreme Allied Cmdr. Europe, General Wesley Clark. Typical studies of diplomacy do not examine the military aspect of diplomacy. General Clark's chapter is unique in that it examines how military policy and military force can be used as a very effective diplomatic tool. He also points out the problems of using force in the wrong way which actually hurts diplomatic efforts. In other words, the use of military force can be an effective tool in promoting diplomacy providing it is used in an effective manner and not only on its own. It must be used in tandem with other diplomatic efforts.

The next section of the book identifies problems and challenges facing US foreign policy. For example, former ambassador Robert Hunter discusses a myriad of challenges facing policymakers and diplomats regarding US foreign policy. Former ambassador David Dunford discusses how many different entities are involved in the foreign policy process and often are not coordinated in their efforts to achieve US foreign policy goals.

Several diplomats provide lessons and necessary skills that diplomats should possess. For example, former ambassador Ken Gross discusses the necessary skills that diplomats must possess in the twenty-first-century. Similarly, former ambassador Earl Anthony Wayne discusses not only the core skills that must be possessed by diplomats but also identifies the specific challenges faced by diplomats in service to the United States.

Former ambassador Marc Grossman discusses the fact that US foreign policy is not geared towards the middle class, but rather serves the interests of the policy elites. The middle class has largely been forgotten in the pursuit of US foreign policy goals. Mr. Grossman's proposal of having a reserve cadre of diplomats available in times of crisis is very interesting and one which we believe should be pursued.

Former ambassador Ronald Neumann discusses the global order established by the United States following World War II. He identifies the fact that the global order is currently under attack by the Chinese and the Russians. Further he laments the fact that the credibility of the United States is at a low point. He argues that alliances are necessary to maintain the current global order. The US needs to prioritize its alliances and attempt to improve its relations with its current allies. He also argues that US diplomacy must be revitalized if the United States is to fend off challenges from other states globally.

Former ambassador Thomas Pickering deeply analyzes US diplomacy. First, he looks at what motivates countries. Second, he examines current global crises and discusses the relevance of diplomacy in resolving these crises. Specifically he shows how diplomacy can resolve these crises if it is used effectively. Finally, he analyzes the current structure of US diplomacy and makes recommendations on how to improve that structure so that the United States and become more effective at dealing with global challenges.

Former ambassador P. Michael McKinley looks at a historical view of US efforts in diplomacy from the Reagan administration through the Biden administration. He has a unique experience within the leadership of the US Department of State, and therefore has a very unique perspective of US diplomacy efforts from an administrative perspective as well as the perspective of a former ambassador. He is able to effectively show how diplomacy has evolved from being driven by ideology during the Cold War era to being in serious jeopardy and not being able to meet the challenges of the present era.

Former ambassador Stapleton Roy highlights the fact that superpower diplomacy is different from diplomacy and the rest of the world. While the rest of the world has to use diplomacy to convince other countries to cooperate, the United States is too often relied on its military to threaten other countries and resolve disputes through force as opposed to negotiation. He argues that this approach has to change for diplomacy in the twenty-first-century to be successful. It is very interesting to contrast the views of ambassador Roy with those of general Clark. They highlight the same problem from very different perspectives.

This volume is extremely unique in that it brings together specialists with many decades of experience in US foreign policy. Their expertise is unmatched and vital for policymakers to consult during this transitional era of US foreign policy. It is very difficult to determine whether or not the United States can overcome the challenges that it is currently facing in its foreign policy. However if it is to be successful in doing so, it must truly reform its diplomatic institutions, its approaches to foreign policy, and relying more upon the knowledgeable and professional Americans working to further American interests.

The roots of American power have always lied within the wealth of its country citizens. The United States is truly a unique melting pot of world cultures, languages, and diversity. The United States is a natural leader in the world, and should not relinquish this role. The authors in this volume represent just some of the wealth working to advance US foreign policies and interests. In the future, the United States needs to rely on their expertise in order to weather the current storm. In other words, it is as yet unclear if it is morning or twilight to American diplomatic efforts in the twenty-first-century. The future remains hazy. However, with people such as these experts working to represent the United States, then it is more likely that US diplomacy will adapt and become more and more successful in the twenty-first-century and beyond.

CONTRIBUTORS

James A. Baker III has served in senior government positions under three United States presidents. He served as the nation's 61st secretary of state from January 1989 through August 1992 under President George H. W. Bush. During his tenure at the State Department, Baker traveled to 90 foreign countries as the United States confronted the unprecedented challenges and opportunities of the post–Cold War era. Baker's reflections on those years of revolution, war and peace—"The Politics of Diplomacy"— was published in 1995.

Baker served as the 67th secretary of the treasury from 1985 to 1988 under President Ronald Reagan. As treasury secretary, he was also chairman of the President's Economic Policy Council. From 1981 to 1985, he served as White House chief of staff to President Reagan. Baker's record of public service began in 1975 as undersecretary of commerce to President Gerald Ford. It concluded with his service as White House chief of staff and senior counselor to President Bush from August 1992 to January 1993.

Long active in American presidential politics, Baker led presidential campaigns for Presidents Ford, Reagan, and Bush over the course of five consecutive presidential elections from 1976 to 1992.

A native Houstonian, Baker graduated from Princeton University in 1952. After two years of active duty as a lieutenant in the United States Marine Corps, he entered The University of Texas School of Law at Austin. He received his J.D. with honors in 1957 and practiced law with the Houston firm of Andrews and Kurth from 1957 to 1975.

Baker's memoir—"Work Hard, Study . . . and Keep Out of Politics! Adventures and Lessons from an Unexpected Public Life"—was published in October 2006.

Baker received the Presidential Medal of Freedom in 1991 and has been the recipient of many other awards for distinguished public service, including Princeton University's Woodrow Wilson Award, the American Institute for Public Service's Jefferson Award, Harvard University's John F. Kennedy School of Government Award, The Hans J. Morgenthau Award, The George F. Kennan Award, the Department of the Treasury's Alexander Hamilton Award, the Department of State's Distinguished Service Award and numerous honorary academic degrees.

Baker is presently a senior partner in the law firm of Baker Botts. He is the honorary chairman of the James A. Baker III Institute for Public Policy at Rice University and serves on the board of the Howard Hughes Medical Institute. From 1997 to 2004, Baker served as the personal envoy of United Nations Secretary-General Kofi Annan to seek a political solution to the conflict over Western Sahara. In 2003, Baker was appointed special presidential envoy for President George W. Bush on the issue of Iraqi debt. In 2005, he was co-chair, with former President Jimmy Carter, of the Federal Commission on Election Reform. Since March 2006, Baker and former U.S. Congressman Lee H. Hamilton have served as the co-chairs of the Iraq Study Group, a bipartisan blue-ribbon panel examining a forward-looking approach to Iraq.

Baker was born in Houston, Texas, in 1930. He and his wife, the former Susan Garrett, currently reside in Houston and have eight children and 17 grandchildren.

General Wesley K. Clark is a businessman, educator, writer and commentator. General Clark serves as Chairman and CEO of Wesley K. Clark & Associates, a strategic consulting firm; Chairman and Founder of Enverra, Inc. a licensed investment bank; Chairman of Energy Security Partners, LLC; as well as numerous corporate boards including BNK Petroleum and Leagold Mining. He is active in energy, including oil and gas, biofuels, electric power and batteries, finance, and security. During his business career he has served as an advisory, consultant or board member of over ninety private and publicly traded companies. In the not-for- profit space, he is a Senior Fellow at UCLA's Burkle Center for International Relations, Director of the Atlantic Council; Founding Chair of City Year Little Rock/ North Little Rock, and Founder of Renew America Together. A best-selling author, General Clark has written four books and is a frequent contributor on TV and to newspapers.

Clark retired as a four star general after 38 years in the United States Army, having served in his last assignments as Commander of US Southern Command and then as Commander of US European Command/ Supreme Allied Commander, Europe. He graduated first in his class at West Point and completed degrees in Philosophy, Politics and Economics at Oxford University (B.A. and M.A.) as a Rhodes scholar. While serving in Vietnam, he commanded an infantry company in combat, where he was severely wounded and evacuated home on a stretcher. He later commanded at the battalion, brigade and division level, and served in a number of significant staff positions, including service as the Director, Strategic Plans and Policy (J-5). He was the principal author of both the US National Military Strategy and Joint Vision 2010, prescribing US warfighting for full-spectrum dominance. He also worked with Ambassador Richard Holbrooke in the Dayton Peace Process, where he helped write and negotiate significant portions of the 1995 Dayton Peace Agreement. In his final assignment as Supreme Allied Commander Europe he led NATO forces to victory in Operation Allied Force, a 78-day air campaign, backed by ground invasion planning and a diplomatic process, saving 1.5 million Albanians from ethnic cleansing.

His awards include the Presidential Medal of Freedom, Defense Distinguished Service Medal (five awards), Silver star, bronze star, purple heart, honorary knighthoods from the British and Dutch governments, and numerous other awards from other governments, including award of Commander of the Legion of Honor (France). He has also been awarded the Department of State Distinguished Service Award and numerous honorary doctorates and civilian honors.

G. Doug Davis, PhD is the director of the Master's of Science in International Relations program at Troy University where he is a European Security and Middle East regional expert. In addition to a doctorate in political science from the University of Arizona, he has a graduate degree from the Pontificia Università Lateranense. He has published academic papers and is the coauthor, with Dr Michael Slobodchikoff, of *Cultural Imperialism and the Decline of the Liberal Order: Russian and Western Soft Power in Eastern Europe*. Most recently he is the coeditor of *The Challenge to NATO: Global Security and the Atlantic* Alliance (Potomac Books), which is co-edited with Michael O. Slobodchikoff and Brandon Stewart. His academic work has been translated and published in nine languages. He has international development experience in the Middle East where he has worked on projects funded by the European Union, Italian government, and the World Bank. He has international banking experience and has worked to open financial institutions internationally.

David J. Dunford served three years as U.S. Ambassador to Oman and four years, including the 1990-91 Gulf War, as Deputy Chief of Mission in Saudi Arabia. He worked for General Garner and Ambassador Bremer in Iraq in 2003 as the senior official in charge of rebuilding Iraq's Ministry of Foreign Affairs. His other assignments included Economic Minister-Counselor in Cairo, Director of Egyptian Affairs in Washington, Deputy Assistant U.S.

Trade Representative in the Executive Office of the President, and Coordinator of the multinational team tasked with setting up MENABANK, a proposed regional multilateral development bank in Cairo.

Ambassador Dunford is co-author of *Talking to Strangers: The Struggle to Rebuild Iraq's Foreign Ministry* (2013) and author of *From Sadat to Saddam: The Decline of American Diplomacy in the Middle East (2019)*. He is a member of the Governing Board of the University of Arizona's Center for Middle East Studies. He taught courses on the Arab-Israeli Conflict and the Middle East Business Environment at the University of Arizona for 20 years and consulted for both the government and the private sector on Middle East issues.

Ambassador Ken Gross served as an Ambassador and Senior Foreign Service Officer in the U.S. Department of State for over 31 years in a number of positions that highlighted his foreign policy expertise, crisis management abilities, and negotiating skills. An important part of his skillset was the ability to manage important issues at large posts while mentoring his staff.

His last assignment for the Department of State was as the Principal Officer at the U.S. Consulate General in Erbil, Iraq, where he deepened the U.S. Government's relationship with the Kurdistan Regional Government (KRG). In this role, he helped ensure cooperation between the Iraqi Government in Baghdad and the KRG, convincing the KRG to remain an integral part of a democratic, federal Iraq.

Ken served in Iraq on two other occasions, first as Principal Officer in Basrah and later as Director of the Office of Provincial Affairs at the U.S. Embassy in Baghdad. In Basrah he oversaw U.S. operations in the four southern provinces of Iraq and assisted in the transfer of security control from U.S. forces back to the Iraqi Government. In Baghdad, Ken set up the embassy office coordinated the Provincial Construction Teams, which were important in regaining local Iraqi support.

As Ambassador to Tajikistan, Ken managing the embassy and advanced U.S. policy goals in the poorest country in the region that was embroiled in clashed of influence by its large neighbors, Russia and China. Ken strengthened U.S. security by coordinating a host of issues related to Tajikistan's proximity to Afghanistan, including cross-border issues, Coalition resupply and drawdown, counter-narcotics and border security, and anti-terrorism cooperation.

Ken's service at the Department of State in Washington included directing the office responsible for the assignment and counseling of all Foreign Service Officers and the office that directed
U.S. assistance for good governance and participatory democracy in the Middle East and North Africa.

With a deep interest in mentoring and teaching others, Ken plans to use his Foreign Service experience to train practitioners and students of foreign affairs.

Ambassador Marc Grossman served as the Under Secretary of State for Political Affairs, the State Department's third ranking official, until his retirement in 2005, after 29 years in the US Foreign Service. As Under Secretary, he helped marshal diplomatic support for the international response to the terror attacks of September 11, 2001. He also managed US policies in the Balkans and Colombia and promoted a key expansion of the NATO alliance. As Assistant Secretary for European Affairs, he helped direct NATO's military campaign in Kosovo and an earlier round of NATO expansion. In Turkey, Ambassador Grossman encouraged vibrant US-Turkish political, military, and economic relations.

Ambassador Grossman was a Vice Chairman of The Cohen Group from July 2005 to February 2011.

In February 2011, President Obama and Secretary of State Clinton called Ambassador Grossman back to service as the US Special Representative for Afghanistan and Pakistan. Ambassador Grossman promoted the international effort to support Afghanistan by shaping major international meetings in Istanbul, Bonn, Chicago and Tokyo. He provided US backing for an Afghan peace process designed to end thirty years of conflict and played an important part in managing US relations with Pakistan. Ambassador Grossman returned to The Cohen Group in February 2013.

Ambassador Grossman is the Chairman of the Board of the Senior Living Foundation of the Foreign Service. He also serves as the Vice Chair of the Board of Trustees of the German Marshall Fund of the United States and as a Trustee of the University of California Santa Barbara Foundation. He is a member of the Board of the C&O Canal Trust.

Raised in Los Angeles, California, Ambassador Grossman has a BA in Political Science from the University of California, Santa Barbara, and an M.Sc in International Relations from the London School of Economics and Political Science.

Mary N. Hampton is a political science professor Emerita whose teaching and research fields include national and international security, US and German foreign policy, European security issues, and identity in international politics. She is the author of *The Wilsonian Impulse* and *A Thorn in Transatlantic Relations: American and Europeans Perceptions of Threat and Security* (Palgrave, 2013) and has co-edited two other books, including (with M. Donald Hancock), *The Baltic Security Puzzle: Regionals Patterns of Democratization, Integration, and Authoritarianism* (Rowman-Littlefield, 2015).

Ambassador Robert E. Hunter was the former U.S. Ambassador to NATO under President Clinton ('93–'98), and represented the U.S. to the Western European Union. He was the principal architect of the "New NATO", leading the North Atlantic Council in implementing decisions of the 1994 and 1997 NATO Summits. Ambassador Hunter led the Council in obtaining major air- strike decisions for Bosnia, securing approval for Implementation Force and Stabilization Force. He served on Secretary Cohen's Defense Policy Board and was Vice Chairman of the Atlantic Treaty Association ('98–'01).

During his extensive career in the public sector, he served as Special Advisor on Lebanon to the Speaker of the House of Representatives and Lead Consultant to the National Bipartisan Commission on Central America (the Kissinger Commission. During the Carter Administration, Ambassador Hunter served on the National Security Council staff as Director of West European Affairs ('77–'79), and later as Director of Middle East Affairs ('79–'81). He was a member of the U.S. negotiating team for talks on the West Bank and Gaza, directed the 1978 NATO Summit, and was the principal author of the Carter Doctrine for the Persian Gulf. He also served as Foreign Policy Advisor to Senator Edward M. Kennedy ('73–'77) and foreign and domestic policy advisor to Vice President Hubert Humphrey. He served on White House staff (health, education, welfare, labor) in the Johnson Administration ('64–'65) and in the Navy Department on the Polaris Project. Has written, lectured, and broadcast extensively on foreign affairs and national security issues.

Ambassador Hunter was a Senior Fellow at the Overseas Development Council ('70–'73), Research Associate at the International Institute for Strategic Studies in London ('67–'69), and Director of European Studies at the Center for Strategic and International Studies. Twice recipient of

Department of Defense Medal for Distinguished Public Service, decorated by Hungarian, Lithuanian and Polish governments, and received Leadership Award of the European Institute.

Ambassador Hunter recently published a book called *Building Security in the Persian Gulf* that makes recommendations for a new security structure in the Persian Gulf region in order to promote long-term security and stability, while also reducing burdens on the United States.

Ambassador Michael McFaul is Director at the Freeman Spogli Institute for International Studies, the Ken Olivier and Angela Nomellini Professor of International Studies in the Department of Political Science, and the Peter and Helen Bing Senior Fellow at the Hoover Institution. He joined the Stanford faculty in 1995.

Dr. McFaul also is as an International Affairs Analyst for NBC News and a columnist for The Washington Post. He served for five years in the Obama administration, first as Special Assistant to the President and Senior Director for Russian and Eurasian Affairs at the National Security Council at the White House (2009-2012), and then as U.S. Ambassador to the Russian Federation (2012-2014).

He has authored several books, most recently the New York Times bestseller *From Cold War to Hot Peace: An American Ambassador in Putin's Russia*. Earlier books include *Advancing Democracy Abroad: Why We Should, How We Can; Transitions To Democracy: A Comparative Perspective* (eds. with Kathryn Stoner); *Power and Purpose: American Policy toward Russia after the Cold War* (with James Goldgeier); and *Russia's Unfinished Revolution: Political Change from Gorbachev to Putin*.

His current research interests include American foreign policy, great power relations, and the relationship between democracy and development. Dr. McFaul was born and raised in Montana. He received his B.A. in International Relations and Slavic Languages and his M.A. in Soviet and East European Studies from Stanford University in 1986. As a Rhodes Scholar, he completed his D. Phil. in International Relations at Oxford University in 1991. He is currently writing a book on great power relations in the 21st century.

Ambassador P. Michael McKinley (Ret.) served as a foreign service officer at the U.S. Department of State for 37 years. Over the course of his career, he held senior leadership positions in missions in Latin America, Europe,

Africa, and Afghanistan. His last assignment was as Senior Advisor to the Secretary of State, from which he resigned in October 2019 over the lack of support for career diplomats caught up in the Ukraine scandal.

McKinley led some of the largest US embassies in the world as ambassador successively to Peru (2007–2010), Colombia (2010–2013), Afghanistan (2014–2016), and Brazil (2017–2018). He helped conclude free trade agreements with Peru and Colombia and key security and economic accords with Brazil. His experience with regional conflicts and peace negotiations across three decades on three continents was central to his work as ambassador in Colombia and Afghanistan.

McKinley joined the US Foreign Service in 1982. Earlier assignments included Bolivia, the United Kingdom, Mozambique, Uganda, and Belgium in addition to Washington. Across these postings, he worked on societies in conflict in Central America, Southern Africa, and East Africa. As Deputy Chief of Mission and Chargé d'Affaires at the US Mission to the European Union from 2004–2007, McKinley helped advance the reset with Europe and transatlantic cooperation on security, economic and regulatory issues. As Deputy Assistant Secretary in the Bureau of Population, Migration, and Refugees from 2001–2004 in the aftermath of 9/11, he oversaw policy and almost $700 million in annual USG assistance to the refugee resettlement program in the United States and to refugee populations in Africa, Europe, and Latin America.

Ambassador McKinley is a senior counselor at The Cohen Group in Washington, DC, and a non-resident senior adviser at the Center for International Strategic Studies. He is the author of numerous articles on US foreign and domestic policy which have appeared in the Financial Times, Foreign Affairs, The Atlantic, Just Security, and Politico, among other publications. His book on colonial Venezuelan history published by Cambridge University Press is an acclaimed study of the period. McKinley is a graduate of the University of Southampton, and he earned a PhD from Oxford University in 1982. Raised in Venezuela, Brazil, Mexico, Spain, and the United States, McKinley speaks Spanish, Portuguese, and French. He is married to the former Fatima Salces, and they have three children.

Ambassador Richard "Dick" Miles entered the Foreign Service in 1967 and served abroad in Oslo, Belgrade, Moscow, and as Consul General in Leningrad (now Saint Petersburg), and as Principal Officer of the U.S. Embassy Office in Berlin. "Dick" Miles served as Ambassador to Azerbaijan from 1992 to 1993, as Chief of Mission to Serbia-Montenegro from 1996 to 1999, as

Ambassador to Bulgaria from 1999 to 2002 and as Ambassador to Georgia from 2002 to 2005. In the State Department, he also worked in the Office for Soviet Affairs and the Office for East European and Yugoslav Affairs and in the Bureau of Political-Military Affairs.

Ambassador Miles worked for Senator Ernest F. Hollings (D-SC) on an American Political Science Fellowship in 1983–1984, and in 1987–1988 he was a fellow at Harvard University's Center for International Affairs.

He retired from the State Department in August 2005. From April until December 2006, he served as Executive Director of the Open World Leadership Center headquartered in the Library of Congress. In November 2008, Ambassador Miles was recalled to active duty to serve as Charge of the American Embassy in Ashgabat, Turkmenistan. He returned to Washington, DC and retirement in September 2009. In February 2015, he was asked to go to Bishkek, Kyrgyzstan to serve as Charge of the American Embassy there. He returned to Washington and retirement in September 2015.

Ambassador Miles has been awarded the State Department's Meritorious Honor Award and Group Superior Honor Award (twice). In 1992 he was awarded a Presidential Meritorious Service Award and a national award for reporting. In 2004 he was the recipient of the State Department's Robert C. Frasure Award for peaceful conflict resolution.

Ambassador Miles married the former Sharon Alice O'Brien in 1960. The couple have two children: Richard Lee Miles was a Police Officer in Richmond, Virginia for many years. Elizabeth Anne Miles-Masci is a freelance editor and lives in Alexandria, Virginia.

Ambassador Ronald Neumann, now President of the American Academy of Diplomacy, served previously as a Deputy Assistant Secretary and three times as Ambassador; to Algeria (1994–1997), Bahrain (2001–2004) and finally to the Islamic Republic of Afghanistan from July 2005 to April 2007. Before Afghanistan, Mr. Neumann, a career member of the Senior Foreign Service, served in Baghdad from February 2004 with the Coalition Provisional Authority and then as Embassy Baghdad's principal liaison with the Multinational Command.

In Manama, Bahrain Ambassador Neumann worked on maintaining the balance between urging progress on democratic reform and expanding solid relations with a friendly monarchy. As a Deputy Assistant Secretary in the Bureau of Near East Affairs (1997–2000) he directed the organization of the first separately-funded NEA democracy programs and also was responsible for the bureau's work in developing the North African

Economic Initiative for Morocco, Tunisia, and Algeria. Other assignments included Director of the Office of Northern Gulf Affairs (Iran and Iraq; 1991 to 1994, Deputy Chief of Mission in Abu Dhabi, United Arab Emirates, and in Sanaa in Yemen, Principal Officer in Tabriz, Iran and Jordan Desk officer.

Ambassador Neumann served as DACOR (Diplomatic and Consular Officer Retired) distinguished visiting professor at the Command and General Staff College, Ft. Leavenworth 2008. He is on the board of the American Bahrain Friendship Society and the Nancy Hatch Dupree Foundation, the Middle East Policy Council and the advisory council for School of Leadership Afghanistan. He is the author of *The Other War, Winning and Losing in Afghanistan* and *Three Embassies, Four Wars; a personal memoir.*

Ambassador Neumann served as an Army infantry officer in Viet Nam and holds a Bronze Star, Army Commendation Medal and Combat Infantry Badge. In Baghdad, he was awarded the Army Outstanding Civilian Service Medal. He earned a B.A. in history and an M.A. in political science from the University of California at Riverside.

Ambassador Thomas R. Pickering is currently vice chair of Hills & Company. Ambassador Pickering served as under secretary of state for political affairs (1997–2000) and as U.S. ambassador to the Russian Federation, India, Israel, El Salvador, Nigeria, and Jordan. He was also U.S. ambassador and representative to the United Nations in New York, where he led the U.S. effort to build a coalition in the UN Security Council during and after the first Gulf War. He has held additional positions in Tanzania, Geneva, and Washington, including as assistant secretary of state for the Bureau of Oceans, Environmental, and Scientific Affairs and as special assistant to Secretaries of State William P. Rogers and Henry A. Kissinger. After retiring from the State Department in 2000, Ambassador Pickering joined the Boeing Company, where he served for five and a half years as senior vice president for international relations. He holds degrees from Bowdoin College, the Fletcher School of Law and Diplomacy, and the University of Melbourne.

Ambassador J. Stapleton (Stape) Roy is a Distinguished Scholar and Founding Director Emeritus of the Kissinger Institute on China and the United States at the Woodrow Wilson International Center for Scholars in Washington, DC. Stape Roy was born in China and spent much of his youth there during the upheavals of World War II and the communist revolution, where he watched the battle for Shanghai from the roof of the Shanghai American School. He joined the US Foreign Service immediately after graduating from Princeton in 1956, retiring 45 years later with the rank of Career Ambassador, the highest in the service. In 1978 he participated in the secret negotiations that led to the establishment of US-PRC diplomatic relations. During a career focused on East Asia and the Soviet Union, Stape's ambassadorial assignments included Singapore, China, and Indonesia. His final post with the State Department was as Assistant Secretary for Intelligence and Research. On retirement he joined Kissinger Associates, Inc., a strategic consulting firm, before joining the Woodrow Wilson International Center for Scholars in September 2008 to head the newly created Kissinger Institute. In 2001 he received Princeton University's Woodrow Wilson Award for Distinguished Public Service.

Dr. Michael O. Slobodchikoff is the author of several peer-reviewed publications and of three books. He is the author of *Strategic Cooperation: Overcoming the Barriers of Global Anarchy* (Lexington Books), *Building Hegemonic Order Russia's Way: Rules, Stability and predictability in the Post-Soviet Space* (Lexington Books), *Cultural Imperialism and the Decline of the Liberal Order: Russian and Western Soft Power in Eastern Europe* (Lexington Books), which is coauthored with G. Doug Davis. He has also published an edited volume entitled *The Challenge to NATO: Global Security and the Atlantic Alliance* (Potomac Books) with G. Doug Davis. His most recent book project is currently in press with the University of Michigan Press. Dr. Slobodchikoff is the leading expert on treaty networks and the use of network analysis on treaties in explaining the creation of global and regional order. He specializes in Russian security, international organizations, international conflict and peace, international security, and comparative politics. He is a regular contributor to Russia Direct and has often served as an analyst on Russian relations with Ukraine and the West for BBC World News as well as Voice of Russia Radio.

Ambassador Earl Anthony Wayne is the Hurst Senior Professional Lecturer at American University and a Public Policy Fellow at the Woodrow Wilson International Center for Scholars and Co-Chair of its Mexico Institute Advisory Board. He is a Senior Non-Resident Adviser at the Atlantic Council and at the Center for Security and International Studies. Ambassador Wayne served as a US diplomat from 1975 to 2015, including as Ambassador to Argentina (2006–2009), Coordinating Director for Development and

Economic Affairs and Deputy Ambassador in Kabul, Afghanistan (2009–2011), and Ambassador to Mexico (2011–2015). He was Assistant Secretary of State for Economic and Business Affairs (EB) under three Secretaries of State (2000–2006) and Principal Deputy Assistant Secretary of State for Europe (1997–2000). The US Senate confirmed him as a Career Ambassador, the highest rank in the US Foreign Service, in 2010. He received multiple honors during his government service, including the 2017 Director General's Cup for the Foreign Service and the 2015 Cobb Award for Initiative and Success in Trade Development.

INDEX

10th Mountain Division, 55

18th Airborne Corps, 54

2008 Great Recession, 360

82nd Airborne Division, 55

9/11 Terrorist Attack, 75–78, 86, 100–101, 123–24, 139, 144–45, 153, 174–75, 195–96, 198–99, 304, 325, 345, 348, 351–54, 361, 364, 371, 456

Abashidze, Aslan, 37, 42

Abkhazia, 37

Abraham Accords, 362–63

Abu Ghraib, 345

Adams, John, 265

Adams, John Quincy, 284

Adjara, Province of, 37, 42

AES (Electric Company), 38–40

Afghanistan War, 285

Afghanistan, Islamic Emirate of, 3, 6–7, 18, 20, 38, 44, 47, 65, 72, 77, 86–87, 91–92, 100, 124, 130, 139, 145, 147–48, 162, 173, 175, 180, 187–89, 195–97, 199–201, 206–10, 212–13, 215, 220, 222, 228–29, 238, 252, 257, 269, 279, 281, 285–91, 293, 301, 303, 307, 327–28, 343, 345–46, 348–49, 352–58, 360, 362, 368, 375, 399, 441–42, 452–53, 456–58

Africa, 3, 13, 53, 196, 281, 283, 329, 331–33, 345, 348, 350, 357, 368, 443, 456

Africa, Central, 331

Africa, Sub-Saharan, 345

African Unity (AU), 331

Ahtisaari, Marti, 69–70

AID officers, 286

AIDs, 331–32

Air Force, 63, 71, 139, 141, 245, 435

Airbus, 319

Albania, 32, 183

Albright, Madeline, 35, 53–54, 65, 69, 193, 304, 350

Algeria, 269, 291, 327, 332, 457–58

Algiers, 290

al-Hashemi, Aqila, 146–47

Aliyev, Heydar, 29

alliance, xiv, 2, 6, 10, 21, 50, 79–80, 91, 100, 106, 125, 161, 174, 194, 203, 222, 224, 278–80, 283, 325–6, 344, 347,349, 352, 360–61, 363–64, 367, 371, 408, 445, 451, 453, 459

alliance economic, 359

Al-Qaeda, 145–46, 174–75, 189, 199, 287

Alyokhina, Maria, 427

America First Doctrine, 160, 363, 369

American Academy of Diplomacy, 220, 269, 280, 457

American Corners in Volgograd, 432

American Foreign Service Association, 220, 292

American Revolution, 265

Among Echo, 434

Andropov, Yuri, 14, 16, 18

Angola, 95, 332, 345

Annan, Kofi, 54, 450

anti-Americanism, 375

Anti-Ballistic Missile treaty (ABM), 312

Arab Spring, 359

Arabic Language, 129–30, 135, 139, 146, 401

Arab-Israeli War, 127

Argentina, 185, 187, 189, 202, 204–6, 227

Aristide, Bertrand, 54–55

Armenia, 29, 278
Armitage, Richard, 36, 145, 273
Arms Race, 9, 13, 15, 17–18, 22, 444
Army, 38, 41–42, 47, 65, 83, 146, 148, 245, 286, 383, 450, 458
Army Confederate, 50
Army German, 50
Army Kosovo, 32
Army North Korean, 51
Army Northe Vietnamese, 52
Army Soviet, 2, 3
Artificial intelligence, 260
ASEAN, 322
Ashgabat, 44, 240, 457
Asia Foundation Task Force, 380
Asia Infrastructure Investment Bank, 413
Asian Development Bank, 279
Asian financial crisis, 396
Asian Infrastructure Investment Bank, 279
Asia-Pacific region, 363
Askarov, Azimjon, 45
Assistant Secretary of State for Intelligence and Research, 399
Atambayev, Almazbek, 45
Athens, 84, 234
Atlantic Council, 80, 121, 220, 450, 454
attaché, defense, 32, 38, 58, 203, 245, 308, 386, 388, 395
Australia, 279
Austro-Hungarian Empire, 34
Azerbaijan, 28–30, 278, 457

Baghdad, 130, 137, 146–47, 150, 201, 239–41, 244, 248, 251, 276, 355, 415, 452, 457–58
Bahrain, 147, 269, 457–8
Baker, James, X, 9, 17, 28, 40–41, 136, 138, 141, 168, 415, 444, 449–50

Bakersfield College, 26
Baku, 28, 257
Baku-Tbilisi-Ceyhan pipeline, 257
Balkans, 58, 63, 348, 350, 410, 453
Baltic states, 26–27, 257, 281, 454
Bangkok, 382–83, 410–11
Bangladesh, 283
Banja Luka, 58, 64
Bank for Economic Cooperation and Development in the Middle East and North Africa (MENABANK), 142–43, 452
Barak, Ehud, 144
Basic computer language, 395
Basrah, 238–40, 251–52, 452
Batista, Fulgencio, 87
Battle of Stalingrad, 424
Batumi, 37, 42
Begin, Menachem, 88–89, 129, 131–32
Beijing, 4, 82, 142, 260, 321, 326–27, 332, 363, 385–86, 388, 390, 394–95, 397–98, 405, 411, 413–14
Beirut, 132, 136
Belgrade, 31–35, 48, 60–61, 66–69, 456
Belt and Road Initiative (BRI), 325
Benghazi, 132, 153, 291
Benin, 331
Berger, Sandy, 61, 66
Berlin, x, 28, 74, 457
Berlin Wall, xi, 28, 100, 189, 347, 398
Berlin, East, 25, 28
Biden, Joseph, 10, 85–89, 153, 161, 174, 180, 194, 196, 213, 221–22, 259, 261, 263, 273, 279, 283, 285–86, 288–89, 294, 306, 312–14, 316–17, 319–20, 324–27, 330, 332, 334–35, 344, 346, 353, 357, 367–68, 370, 380, 430, 446
Bildt, Carl, 420
Bill of Rights, 402
bin Alawi, Yusuf, 142
biological warfare, 382–83

Bipartisan Infrastructure Package, 259

Birmingham, Alabama, 427

Bishkek, 44–47, 457

Black Lives Matter, 366

Blackberry, 278

Blair, Tony, 70

Blanchette, Jude, 260

Blinken, Anthony, 161, 186, 222, 264, 270, 273, 371

Bo Gritz affair, 383

Bobbitt, Philip, 257

Boeing Company, 319

Bogota, 360

Bolizia, 330

Bolshoi opera, 423

Bolsonaro, Jair President, 330

Bonn, 28, 59, 107, 235, 453

Boolean logic, 395

Bosnia-Herzegovina, 31, 57

Boston, Massachusetts, 387

Botswana, 331

Brademas, John, 84

Bragg, Fort, 55

Bremer, Jerry, 146, 150, 451

Brezhnev Doctrine, 20–21

Brezhnev, Leonid, 14

BRICS, 354

British press, 288

Brussels, 60, 69, 80, 110, 171, 173, 176, 186, 192, 346, 351, 358, 360

Brzezinski, Zbigniew, 82–83

Bucharest Summit, 258, 408

Budapest, 34, 82–83

Buenos Aires, 202, 205

Bulgaria, 35–37, 69, 190, 457

Bullington, Jim, 135

Bureau of Population, Refugees, and Migration (PRM), 354

Burjanadze, Nino, 41–42

Burns, Bill, 412

Burns, Nick Ambassador, 264

Burns, William, 430

Bush, George H.W., x, 13, 17, 65, 75, 79, 108, 136, 285, 398, 410, 414, 449

Bush, George W., 49, 134, 279, 325, 332, 351, 380, 416, 450

"C" Street diplomatic entrance, 366

Cairo, 123, 129–34, 136, 142–44, 149–50, 451–52

Calderon, Felipe, 215

Cambridge University, 387

Camp David Accords, 130–31, 144, 348–49, 413

Capitalism, 321, 330, 349

Carey, Hugh, 85

Carter, Jimmy, 15, 18, 55–56, 59, 79, 83, 85, 90–91, 98, 102–103, 105, 108, 111, 128, 284, 413, 450, 454

Castro, Fidel, 3, 87, 95, 345

Cathedral of Christ the Savior, 426

Caucasus region, 408

Cebu, 234

Center for Disease Control (CDC), 365

Center for Strategic and International Studies, 92, 220, 454

Central Command, 52, 138, 244

Central Intelligence Agency (CIA), 16, 47, 126, 140, 145, 216, 245, 285, 387, 398, 435, 437

centrifuges, Iranian, 315

Chairman of the Joint Chiefs of Staff, 304

Chatham House, 94

Chechnya, 38

checks and balances, 77, 379

Cheney, Dick, 139, 145–46

Chennault, Claire, 81

Chernenko, Konstantin, 15

Chernomyrdin, Viktor, 69–70

Chief Diversity officer, 334

Chief of Naval Operations, 273

Chiefs of Staff, 273

Chile, 330

China CGTN television, 439

China, People's Republic of, x-xi, 4-7, 10, 19, 21, 35, 44, 51, 72-73, 77-78, 81-82, 85-86, 95, 100-101, 124, 151, 174, 189, 194, 197, 206, 220-21, 224, 233, 252, 258-64, 278-79, 281-84, 301, 303-7, 311, 313, 315-16, 319-23, 325-27, 329, 332, 344, 347, 352, 354, 359-61, 363, 368-71, 376, 378, 384, 386-90, 394, 397, 399, 402, 405, 410-14, 416-18, 438-39, 442-43, 452, 458-59

Chinese language, 406

Chips and Science Act, 261, 369

Chiraq, Jacques, 59, 68

Christian Science Monitor, The, 166, 169, 225

Chubais, Anatoly, 40

Churchill, Winston, 2, 17, 70

CIA Director, 435

CIA World Factbook, 387

Civil Service, 272

Civil War, 335

Clark, Wesley, 6, 9, 11, 33, 441, 445-46, 450

Clarke, Richard, 54

Clinton, Hillary, 216, 218, 273, 276, 419, 421, 430

Clinton, William, 53-55, 57, 59-60, 63, 70, 72, 79, 83, 107-8, 117, 121, 123, 140-45, 147, 152, 349-51, 382, 398-99, 432, 454

Clubhouse, 437

Cohen, William, 66, 453-55

Colby, William CIA, 285

Cold War, ix-xi, xiii-xiv, 1-2, 4-6, 8-9, 11, 13-14, 18-22, 49, 73-78, 81, 83-84, 86-88, 92-94, 96, 99-100, 102, 112, 137, 150, 160, 168, 174, 188-90, 226, 282, 303, 311, 314, 321, 323, 330, 332, 343-45, 347-49, 352-54, 356, 369-70, 375-80,

396-98, 404-6, 409-10, 415, 438, 441, 444, 446, 449, 455

Collins, Jim, 30

Colombia, 257, 330, 345-6, 348, 356, 359, 453, 456

Commandant of the Marines, 273

Commonwealth of Independent States, 19

Communism, 2-3, 5, 74

communist, ix, 2-3, 15, 18, 20, 27-9, 30, 36, 39, 51, 81-84, 87, 90, 92, 96, 99, 285, 320-21, 345, 347-48, 382-44, 387, 397, 404-6, 459

Comprehensive and Progressive Agreement for Trans-Pacific Partnership (**CPTPP**) , See Trans-Pacific Partnership

Congo, the, 345

Congress, 21, 28, 42, 52-53, 79-80, 84-86, 89, 97, 103, 112, 128, 131, 133-34, 141, 144, 151-52, 160-62, 168-69, 186, 220-21, 244, 260, 265, 274-75, 289, 291, 338, 354, 356, 359-60, 362, 402, 407, 411, 413, 438, 450, 457

Congressional Committee, 366

Congressional Delegation, 4, 80, 131

Congressional Funding, 147, 169

Consular Treaty with China, 388

Contadora process, 348

Cooper, Andrew, 428

Cooperation Council for the Arab States of the Gulf (GCC), 327

Cornut, Jeremie, 428

corruption, 42, 188, 198, 209-12, 228, 257, 287, 330, 332, 357

Cosmonaut Day, 424

Cote d'Ivoire, 332

Council of Foreign Relations, 270

Covax initiative, 316

Covey, Jock, 131, 137, 140

COVID Pandemic, 73, 221, 256, 263, 278, 301, 318, 319, 331, 357, 364, 365, 435

COVID vaccine, 316–7
Covid, Delta Variant, 317
COVID-19, 73, 221, 256, 263, 357, 364–65, 435
Crimea, 206, 258, 324, 359, 430
Crimea invasion, 359
Crowley, Jack, 125
Crown of St. Stephen, 82–83
Cuba, 3, 87–88, 95, 99, 169, 189, 330, 345, 347–48, 358
Cuban Missile Crisis, 4, 321
Cummings, Edward, 354
Customs and Border Protection, 245
cyber-attacks, 258
Cyprus, 84
Czech Republic, 83
Czechoslovakia, 20, 190

Darfur, 345
Dayton Accords, 31–33, 63, 65, 68, 348, 351, 451
De Gaulle, Charles, 106
demarche, 170, 248, 291, 351, 394, 435–36
Democracy Summit, 367
Democratic People's Republic of Korea's (DPRK), 303
Democratic Republic of Congo, 348
Department of Commerce, 245
Department of Defense (DOD), 6, 47, 139, 245, 357, 365, 414, 455
Department of Education, 365
Department of Justice, 365
deputy chief of mission, 30, 34, 48, 123, 125, 172, 186, 235–9, 243, 245–7, 251, 345, 351, 382, 388, 411, 451, 456, 458
deRenne Coerr, Wymberly, 125
détente, 378
Diem, Vietnamese President, 285
Digital Diplomacy, 420
Director General of the Foreign Service, 273

Dobbins, James, 180
Dobbs, Lou, 422
Dobrynin, Ambassador Anatoly, 382
Donbass conflict, 359
Drew, Nelson, 60
Drug Enforcement Agency, 245
drug trafficking, 204, 269, 324, 351
Dunford, David, 10, 445, 451–52
Dushanbe, 247
Dvorkovich, Arkady, 423

Eagleburger, Lawrence Sidney, 415
East Asia Bureau, 399
Economic and Business Affairs Bureau (Department of State), 126, 152, 166, 171, 175–76, 187, 192, 197, 226
Economic Community of West African States (ECOWAS), 331
Economist, The magazine, 392
Ecuador, 124–25, 136, 330, 348
Edison, 284
Egypt, 88–89, 123, 129–34, 136, 142–44, 149, 152, 281, 329, 359, 451
Egypt-Israel Peace Deal, 88, 130, 152
Eisenhower, Dwight, xiv, 2, 6, 8, 70. 87–88, 395, 398, 407
Ekaterinburg, 425
El Salvador, 345, 348
Elchibey, Abulfaz, 29
Emerson, 284
Enders, Tom, 127
Energy market, 259
Erbil, 248
Estonia, 13, 26–27
Ethiopia, 345, 348, 368
European Commission, 171, 176, 178, 182
European RePower EU plan, 259
European Union (EU), 75, 94, 106, 164, 169, 173, 176, 178, 181, 190–92, 226, 261, 278, 345, 351, 354, 356, 358, 398, 451, 454, 456

Executive Agreement, 309
extremism, 332

Facebook, 111, 219, 420–22, 432
Fahd, King, 135, 138
FARC insurgency, 348
Fateh, 328
Federal Bureau of Investigation (FBI), 245
Federalist Papers, 379, 399
Financial Times, 365
Finland, 9, 126, 182, 258, 444
Finn, Robert, 28
Finnish Language, 125
Flippen, Jason, 422
Florida, 3, 87
Floyd, George, 366
Ford, Gerald, 128, 414, 449
Foreign Affairs, 82, 260–61
Foreign Assistance Act, 95
Foreign Policy, 432
Foreign Service Act of 1980, 270
Foreign Service Institute, 98, 125–26, 274, 335
Foreign Service Journal, 366
France, 33–34, 50, 57–58, 60, 106–7, 182, 282, 305, 311, 332, 363–64, 388, 451
Frankfurt, 231
Franklin, Benjamin, 333
Frazier, Robert, 60
Freeman, Chas, 137, 153
Fried, Dan, 43
Fukuyama, Francis, 19, 349

G-7, 349
G-8, 349
Gallucci, Robert, 56
Gansu province, 313
Garner, Jay, 145–46, 150, 451
Gates Foundation, 316
Gates, Robert, 97

GAVI international vaccine organization, 316
Geimer, Bill, 128
Genetically modified organism (GMO), 358
Geneva Convention, 356
Geneva Summit, 323
Georgia (US state), 36
Georgia Train and Equip Program (GTEP), 36
Georgia, Republic of, 21, 36–44, 96, 258, 304, 408, 457
Germany, ix, 1–2, 33, 43, 49, 60, 83, 91, 96, 107, 136, 148, 182, 231, 234–36, 251, 281, 324, 349, 363–64, 375, 387, 408, 410
Gest, Kathy, 265
Ghali, Boutros Boutros, 54
Ghent, Treaty of, 104
Glasnost, 17, 378, 397
Global War on Terrorism (GWOT), 76, 86, 100
Global Warming, 22, 378
globalization, 189, 192–5, 206, 256, 261–62, 344, 349, 358–61
globalization (anti), 193–94, 206
Gnehm, Edward, 101, 137
Good Friday, 348
Good Friday Agreement, 86, 348
Gorbachev, Mikhail, 4–5, 14–18, 21, 306, 378, 397, 430, 455
Gore, Al, 141–43, 335
GQ Russia, 424
Grant, James, 95
Great Britain, 2, 278, 387
Great Recession of 2008, 360
Greece, 84
Greeley, Horace, 391
Grenada intervention, 354
Gross, Ken, 10, 445, 452
Grossman, Marc, 8, 10, 443, 445, 453
Group of 77, 128

Guadalupe-Hidalgo, Treaty of, 104
Guantanamo Prison, 345

Haas, Richard, 351
Haftar, Field Marshal Khalifa, 282
Haig, Alexander M., 50, 132, 167, 174
Haiti, 54–55, 237, 350
Hamas, 328
Hamilton, Lee, 144, 450
Hampton, Mary, 454
Hanoi, 397
Harvard Kennedy School's Belfer Center, 263
Harvard University, Kennedy School, 167, 263, 449
hegemony, 74, 320, 380, 416
Helmand province, 287–8
Helms, Jesse, 131, 137, 140–41, 144, 152
Helms-Burton Act, 169
Helsinki Final Act, 83, 90
Helsinki Summit (2018), 108
Hezbollah, 132
Hill, Chris, 33, 60, 62, 65–66, 68
Hitler, Adolf, 404
HIV, 331–32
Hizbollah, 315, 328
Ho Chi Minh Trail, 51
Holbrooke, Richard, 32–34, 59–63, 65–67, 290, 451
Horan, Hume, 135–36
Hormats, Bob, 128–29
Hugary, Invasion of 1956, 20
human rights, 15-6, 45, 90–92, 123, 201, 203, 227, 237, 251–52, 281, 284, 315, 349, 352, 355, 357, 361–62, 364–65, 401–4, 426–29
Hume, John, 85
Hungary, 83, 190, 279, 361
Hunter, Robert E., 10, 445, 454–55
Hussein, King of Jordan, 336

Hussein, Saddam, 68, 251, 257, 285, 305, 350, 352, 354–55, 400, 415
Hutu, 53

Ideology, 2–3, 11, 145, 307, 348, 364, 397, 441, 446
Independent Fund for Public Interest Media, 438
India, x, 5, 7, 260, 283, 317, 354, 361, 387, 398, 443, 458
Indiana University, 26, 30
Indochina, 382
Indonesia, 386-7
Indonesian Command and Staff school, 395
Indo-Pacific, 260, 346, 368
Indo-Pacific Economic Framework (IPEF), 368
Indo-Pacific Economic Framework (IPEF), 368
Inflation Reduction Act, 259, 369
Instagram, 432, 437
Intermediate Range Ballistic Missiles, 174
Intermediate-Range Nuclear Forces Treaty (INF Treaty), 257, 312
Internal Revenue Service, 245
International Atomic Energy Agency (IAEA), 56, 94, 315
International Committee of the Red Cross (ICRC), 354
International Court of Justice (ICJ), 322
International Criminal Court, 278
International Criminal Tribunal, 57, 70, 278
International Monetary Fund (IMF), ix, 93, 132, 178, 200, 278, 396
International Republican Institute (IRI), 40
Internet, 44, 150, 159, 161, 191, 249, 421, 423, 438

Iran, 21, 29, 44, 69, 72–73, 78, 84–5, 89–90, 124, 130, 132, 135–36, 145, 263, 269, 303, 309–11, 314–15, 327–29, 338, 343, 345, 348–49, 359, 362–63, 375, 380, 413, 458

Iran-Contra scandal, 343

Iraq, 6–7, 47, 52, 65, 67, 69, 72, 92, 96, 124, 130, 138, 145–48, 150, 153, 164, 170, 14–75, 180, 189, 195, 197, 199–207, 212–13, 233, 235, 238–41, 244, 251, 257, 269, 279, 281, 285, 290–91, 293, 301, 303–5, 327–28, 343, 349–50, 352–56, 358–59, 363, 375, 399–400, 415, 450–52, 458

Iraq War (US Invasion of), 77, 89, 93, 138–39, 174, 199–207, 274, 303, 325, 345, 441–42

Iraqi invasion of Kuwait, 305

Ireland, 85, 279

Irish Republican Army (IRA), 85

Iron Curtain, 2, 15, 17, 190

ISIS, 201, 240, 244, 353, 356

Islam, 130, 139, 144

Islamic State, see ISIS,

Israel, 43, 63, 85, 88–89, 124, 127, 129–32, 135, 140–44, 151–52, 180, 189, 327–28, 348, 350, 352, 362–63, 368, 400, 452, 458

Ivanov, Igor, 41–42

Ivy League, 334

Izetbegovic, Alijaha, 60, 62–63

Jackson, Mike, 71

Jackson-Vanik Amendment, 82

Jakarta, 395

January 6, 2021, 256, 343–72

Japan, 1, 7, 49, 56–57, 91, 127, 142, 175, 260, 283, 315, 321, 341, 349, 361, 363, 398, 414–15

JCPOA, See Joint Comprehensive Plan of Action,

Jerusalem, 88, 143

Jett, Dennis Ambassador, 292

Johnson, Lyndon, 51, 105, 124, 454

Joint Chiefs of Staff, 51, 53, 61, 304

Joint Comprehensive Plan of Action (JCPOA), 89, 309–10, 314–15, 329, 338, 359, 362–63

Joint Comprehensive Program of Action (JCPOA), 309–10, 314, 329

Jones, Beth, 36–37

Jordan, 336

Joulwan, George, 101

Kabul, 87, 171, 173, 187, 207–12, 216, 287–88, 344, 357, 360

Kandelaki, Tina, 424

Karachi, 234

Karzai, Hamid Afghan President, 287

Kathmandu, 235

Katz, Jules, 129, 134

Kelche, Jean Paul, 71

Kelly, John, 136

Kennan, George, 137, 236, 269, 295, 397, 449

Kennedy, Edward, 79, 82, 84–85, 94–95, 454

Kennedy, John F., 3, 51, 127, 292, 312, 330

Kennedy, Robert F., 125

Kenya, 331

Kerrick, Don, 60–62

Khrushchev, Nikita, 3

Kigali, 53–54

King, Martin Luther, 124–25, 427

Kinzer, Joseph, 55

Kirkpatrick, Jeanne, 99

Kirov, 427

Kissinger Commission, 80, 98–99, 454

Kissinger, Henry, 4, 90, 94, 255, 284, 377, 413–14, 417, 458–59

Kists, 38

Kohl, Helmut, 75

Korean War, 3, 51, 303, 315

KORUS, see United States-Korea Free Trade Agreement, 361

Kosovo, 31–36, 65–70, 72, 175, 181–82, 192, 354, 453
Kosovo Diplomatic Observer Mission (KDOM), 33
Kosovo Liberation Army, 32
Kosovo Verification Mission (KVM), 33
Krauthammer, Charles, 352
Kremlin, 105, 410, 420, 423–24, 428–29, 433, 434
Krol, George, 27
Kruzel, Joseph, 60
Kruzick, Joseph, 420
Kurdish people, 257
Kurdistan, 241, 244, 452
Kuwait, 136–38, 146, 170, 175, 305, 350, 354, 415
Kyrgyzstan, 44–46, 457

Laïdi, Zaki, 261
Lake, Anthony, 53, 59
Landmine treaty, 278
Langtang, 231
Laos, 51, 382–83
Latin America, 3, 6, 99, 202, 206, 329–31, 345–6, 349, 350, 354, 356, 359, 361, 363–64, 368, 438, 456,
Latvia, 13, 26–27
Lavrov, Sergey, 429, 435
Law of the Sea treaty, 278
Leaders' Summit on Climate Change, 367
leadership, ix–x, 28, 50–52, 59, 63, 65, 67, 85, 98–100, 124–6, 133–7, 145, 147–52, 167–8, 170, 182, 186–8, 193–94, 207, 218, 223, 225, 242–43, 264, 272–74, 290, 294, 303, 325–32, 340, 345–8, 351, 355, 365–6, 368–71, 376–80, 387, 398, 406, 409, 417, 446, 455–58
Lebanon, 47, 80, 122, 132, 153, 327, 363, 454
Legal Affairs, 354
Leningrad, 26–28, 30, 40, 456

Levada Center, 428
Levant, 88
Liberia, 332, 345
Liberian civil war, 348
Libya, 72, 153, 281–82, 285, 327, 329, 332, 348, 359
Libyan civil war, 359
Lilley, Ambassador James, 386
Lillis, Michael, 85
Lima, 198, 234, 346, 360
liquid natural gas (LNG), 259
Lithuania, 13, 26–27
LiveJournal, 420, 432
Lloyd, Wingate, 131
London, 59, 71, 79, 95, 107, 110, 234, 265, 351, 454
London School of Economics, 80, 94, 453
Los Angeles, California, 387
Luce, Henry, ix

MacArthur, Douglas, 51, 81
Macron, Emmanuel, 364, 368
Madison, James, 402
Maertens, Tom, 27
Makarios III (Archbishop), 84
Malawi, 331
Malaya, 406
Malaysia, 236, 243, 283
Mallaby, Sebastian journalist, 262
Mandarin, 322
Manichean ethos, 370
Manila, 415
Maotai liquor, 385
Maputo, 234
Marine Corps, xiv, 25, 42, 245, 449
Marshall Plan, 75, 93
Marshall, Andrew, 89
Martin Luther King Jr., 427
Marxism, 375
Matlock, Jack F., 3, 9, 429–30, 444
McCain, John Senator, 293

McCarthy, Joseph, 81, 406
McCarthyism, 406
McCombs, Terrill, 265
McCullough, David, 265
McFaul, Michael, 419, 424, 428, 455
McKinley, P. Michael, 10, 446, 455–56
McNair, Fort, 54
Mecca, Holy Mosque of, 130
Medvedev, Dmitry, 423, 429
Meguid, Esmat Abdel, 132
Mekong, 385
Menendez, Bob, 88
Merkel, Angela, 364
Mexico, 50, 104, 163, 173, 179–80, 184–85,
    187–88, 214–21, 229, 361, 364, 456
Mexico City, 171, 173, 187, 214, 218–19
Middle East, 6, 77, 79, 88–9, 93, 101–2,
    125, 129, 131, 136–37, 141–42, 144,
    146–47, 180, 184, 196, 239, 269, 313,
    315, 320, 327, 329, 352–5, 357, 359, 362,
    368, 375, 401, 438, 442, 451, 452, 453,
    454, 458
MilAir, 435
Miles, Richard "Dick", 9, 46, 444,
    456–57
Miles, Sharon, 26, 28–29, 35–37, 44, 46,
    48, 457
Military-Industrial Complex, 87
Milley, General Mark, 366
Milosevich, Slobodan, 32–34, 58, 60–62,
    64–70
Minsk Group, 278
Mitchell, George, 86
Mladic, Ratko, 58, 61
Moller, Pat, 48
Montana, 433
Morocco, 331
Moscow, 1–5, 13–15, 17, 22, 26–27, 29–31,
    42, 62, 82, 137, 182, 189–90, 291, 323–
    27, 359, 382, 388, 397, 406, 414, 419–24,
    426–31, 433–37, 456
Mosul, 240, 244

Moynihan, Daniel Patrick, 85
Mozambique, 332
Mozambique's civil war, 348
Mubarak, Hosni, 131
Mujahedeen, 3
Muscat, 140–42, 144
Muslim, 57–9, 135, 139, 141, 359, 375, 387,
    400–401
Muslim Brotherhood, 359
Mutually Assured Destruction (MAD),
    78

Nagorno Karabakh, 28
Nakhichevan, 29
Namibia, 331
National Democratic Institute (NDI),
    40
National Endowment for Diplomacy,
    92
National Foreign Affairs Training
    Center, 273
National Guard, 36, 398
National Institute of Health (NIH), 365
National Intelligence Estimate, 386
National Security Adviser, 327
National Security Council, 14, 27, 43,
    54, 60, 82, 88, 102, 107, 112, 128, 161,
    166, 168, 172, 190, 225, 244, 335, 365,
    414–15, 419, 426, 454–55
National Security Strategy (NSS), 344
Native Americans, 404
NATO-Russia Summit in Rome (2002),
    258
Navalny, Aleksei, 424, 427–28, 432–33
Navy, 34, 79, 93–94, 245, 333, 398, 454
NBA, 421, 423
neo-conservative, 380
Nepal, 231, 235–6, 247, 251
Netanyahu, Benjamin, 89, 143–44
Neumann, Ronald, 10, 445, 457–58
New Start verification, 312
New Transatlantic Agenda, 178

NHL, 423

Nicaragua, 345, 348

Nicolson, Harold, 232, 242, 247

Nigeria, 332

Night Notes Memo, 166

Nixon, Richard, 4, 14, 52, 82, 108, 126, 128, 283–84, 382, 398, 413–14

Nord-stream 2 pipe line, 281

North American Free Trade Agreement (NAFTA), 180, 218

North Atlantic Treaty Organization (NATO), ix, 2, 93, 121–22, 279, 454

North Korea, 51, 56–57, 145, 220, 303, 311, 314–15, 346, 362–64, 366, 375

North Vietnam, 405

Northern Ireland, 348

Northern Ireland, Republic of, 85, 348

Norton, Donna, 421

nuclear weapons, 1, 5, 15, 20, 49–50, 55, 76, 89, 263, 301, 306, 309, 311–15, 323, 325–26, 362, 378

Nunn, Sam, 55

Obama, Barack, 21, 87, 89, 103, 148, 196, 206–7, 211, 219, 278–79, 286–87, 290, 309, 312, 325, 327, 353, 356, 358–60, 398, 419, 422, 426, 428–30, 434–35, 453, 455

Odnako, 424

O'Donnell, Jill, 265

O'Donnell, Kirk, 99

Office management specialists (OMS), 275

Okar, Mary Rose, 82

Oman, 123, 140–42, 144, 150, 451

O'Neil, Tip, 85, 99

OPEC, 127, 135, 327

Open Skies Treaty, 312

Open Technology Fund, 438

Organization for Security and Co-operation in Europe (OSCE), 33–34, 38, 278

Organization of Petroleum Exporting Countries (OPEC), 127, 135, 327

Orwellian speech, 365

Oslo Accords, 141, 143, 349

Ovechkin, Alexey, 423

Pacific Islands, 331

Pacific Ocean, 260, 367, 414

Pacoe, Dominic, 265

Palestinians, 131–32, 144, 180, 363

Panama, 52, 55, 283, 304, 349, 354, 413, 415

Panama Canal Treaty, 413

Panama invasion/intervention, 354

pandemic, 316

Pankisi Gorge, 37–38

Pardew, James, 60–62

Paris, 59–60, 68, 107–8, 127, 225, 249, 358, 362, 367

Paris Climate Accord, 358, 362, 367

Paris Peace Conference, 59, 108

Partnership for Peace (NATO), 63, 75, 83, 91

Partnership for Public Service, 280

Patriot Act, 77

Patterson Mildred, 265

Patterson, Bob, 27

Pax Americana, 351

Peace Corps, 36, 46

Pearl Harbor, 375

Pentagon, 21, 47, 56, 65–66, 71, 89, 95, 110, 145–46, 148, 198, 356

Pentagon Papers, 407

Pepfar program, 332

Perdue, George "Sunny", 36–37

Perestroika, 17, 378, 397

Perisic, Momsilo, 32, 61

Permanent members of UN Security Council (P5), 305

Pershing, John, 50–51

Persian Gulf, 348

Persian Gulf War, 80

Peru, 198, 345–46, 348, 359, 456
Peterson, Val, 126
Petraeus, David, 147–48
Pew Research Center, 353
Philippines, 96, 361
Pickering, Thomas, 4, 10, 30–31, 138, 412, 446, 458
Plan Colombia, 257, 356
Plavsic, Biljana, 64
plutonium, 316
Poland, 83, 190, 257, 279, 361
Polaris Project, 79, 94, 454
Politburo, 16, 29
Pompeo, Michael, 264, 272, 346, 361, 364–65, 371
Pope, Alexander, 416
Port Au Prince, Haiti, 55, 234
Powell, Colin, 41–42, 48, 53, 55, 134, 145–46, 149, 186, 198, 242, 248, 273–74, 304
Poythress, David, 36
Precht, Henry, 130–31, 134
president, ix–x, xvii, 3–4, 8, 15–21, 34, 34, 37–40, 42–45,47, 49–52, 54–65, 68–70, 75, 80, 83–84, 86–87, 89–91, 93–98, 102–12, 124–28, 130, 132, 136, 140–42, 147, 161, 166–9, 180, 186, 198, 202–8, 208, 211, 213–6, 218–22, 236, 239, 242, 247, 249, 257, 259–61, 269, 271, 278–80, 282–89, 292–94, 306, 316, 320, 324–5, 327–8, 330, 334–8, 343, 345–7, 350–51, 353, 356–8, 360, 362, 363–70, 379, 395, 398, 401, 405–7, 409, 411, 413–16, 419, 422–23, 429–32, 434, 438, 443, 449-
President, UN Security Council, 306
President's Emergency Plan for AIDS Relief (PEPFAR), 357
Price, Linda, 27, 48
Pristina, 35
Pskov, Russia, 437
Purnell, John, 27

Putin, Vladimir, x, 21, 28, 40, 72, 99–100, 108, 257–59, 263, 306, 312, 323–24, 329, 351, 364, 408–9, 420–21, 423, 427–31, 433–34, 438, 455
Pyongyang, North Korea, 56, 316, 397

Qaddafi, Muammar, 285
Quito, Ecuador, 124–25, 133, 149

Rabin, Yitzhak, 140, 142–43
Radio Free Asia, 438
Radio Free Europe, 438
Radio Liberty, 438
Radio Marti, 438
Ramaphosa, Cyril, 332
Rambouillet, Agreement, 34, 68
Rambouillet, Chateau de, 34, 68, 70
RAND Corporation, 101
Reagan Administration, 271
Reagan, Ronald, xiii, 4–5, 10, 14–19, 21, 123, 129, 131–32, 141, 167–68, 184, 189, 271, 306, 343, 347, 349, 382–83, 398, 429, 446, 449
realpolitik, 284
red Square, 423
Redmond, Charles, 57–58
Regional Embassy Office (REO), 238
Responsibility to Protect (R2P), 310
Rice, Condaleeza, 150
Ries, Marie Ambassador, 264
Rodrik, Dani, 262
Rogers Act of 1924, 333
Rogin, Josh, 256
Rogozin, Dmitry, 423
Ross, Alec, 421–22
Ross, Dennis, 141, 143
ROTC, 334
Roy, J. Stapleton, 2, 4, 11, 446, 458
ruble, Russian currency, 427
Rumsfeld, Donald Secretary of Defense, 352
rupiah, Indonesian currency, 396

Rusk, Dean, 124

Russia, x-xi, 4–7, 10, 19, 21–22, 26–23, 30–31, 33–34, 38–41, 43–44, 46, 59, 70–75, 77–78, 83, 85, 86, 99–100, 108, 124, 151, 162, 174, 181–83, 190, 197, 206–7, 220–22, 247–48, 251–52, 257–59, 278–79, 281–83, 301, 303–5, 307, 309, 311–13, 316, 322–29, 344, 346, 349–52, 354, 359, 361–62, 368, 370–71, 375, 378, 385, 387, 405, 408–10, 419–38, 442, 445, 452, 455, 458–59

Russia Today, 426

Russia Today (RT), 439

Russian Orthodox Church, 423

Russian-Slavonic University, 248

Russophobes, 434

Rwanda, 53–54, 350, 402

Rwanda genocide, 350

Saakashvili, Mikheil, 41–44

Sadat, Anwar, 130–31, 147, 452

Saint-Léger Léger, Alexis, 232

SALT I Treaty, 126

SALT II Treaty, 413

sanctions, 7, 21–22, 84–8, 90, 169, 198, 220, 227, 305, 309, 315, 359, 361, 363, 442, 443

Sandista, 349

Sant Egidio negotiations, 348

Santiago, 330

Sarajevo, 57–58, 60–61, 63, 140, 182

Sarajevo Summit, 183

Sarbanes, Paul Senator, 293

Saudi Arabia, 85, 90, 123, 131, 135, 138–40, 144, 175, 327–29, 368, 415, 451

Schneider, Mark, 94

Schwarzkopf, Norman, 52, 138

Science and Technology Agreement with China, 389

Scowcroft, Brent, 168, 335, 338, 415

Secret Service, 356

Secretary of Commerce, 364

Seib, Philip, 263

Senate Foreign Relations Committee (SFRC), 293

Senegal, 331

Seoul, 234, 316, 362, 429

Sept. 11, 2001, 144, 151, 195, 238, 352, 354, 399, 453

Serbia, 34, 36, 61, 63, 65–68, 70, 140, 182, 457

Seven Point proposal, 59

Shalikashvili, John, 53, 58–59

Shek, Chiang Kai, 81

Shevarnadze, Eduard, 17, 41–43

Shimon Perez Institute, 400

Shultz, George Pratt, v, xi, xiii-xiv, 17, 132, 134, 136, 141, 162–63, 167, 170, 174, 176, 186, 219–20, 273–74, 341, 414

Sierra Leone, 332

Sierra Leone, 350

Silicon Valley, 421

Silliman, Doug, 241

Simonyan, Margarita, 426

Sinai, 88, 130–31

Singapore, 283

Six-Day War, 125

Slocombe, Walt, 55

Snowden, Edward, 430

Sobchak, Anatoly, 28

Sobchak, Ksenia, 424

Sochi, Russia, 430

soft power, 354

Solana, Javier, 66–67, 69–70

Solomon, Howard, 436

Somalia, 53, 140, 350

South Africa, 7, 63, 84, 331–32, 345, 354

South Asia, 129, 152, 180, 331, 367

South China Sea, 282–83, 321–22

South Korea, 7, 56–57, 213, 279, 283, 315, 349, 361, 363, 375, 420

South Ossetia, 37, 43–44

South Vietnam, 406

Sovereignty, 182, 262, 278, 282, 301, 308–10, 322

Soviet Union, ix, 1–5, 9, 13–15, 18–21, 26–28, 30, 36, 72, 74, 76, 78, 81–84, 86, 91, 94–95, 99, 101, 126, 136, 150, 152, 178, 184, 251, 283, 303, 311, 321, 323–24, 343, 345–50, 378, 384, 388, 396–98, 406, 408, 410, 413, 434, 444, 459

Spaso House, 421

Special Trade Representative (USTR), 127

Sperling, Gil, 34

sputnik, 406

Srebrenica, 59

SS-20 Missile system, 257

St. Petersburg, 30, 423, 434–35

Stalin, Joseph, 404

Stanford University, 423

Starr, Greg, 291

State Department, xi, 3–4, 6–9, 16, 25–26, 34–35, 37–38, 45, 47–48, 71, 81, 83, 93, 96, 97–98, 103–5, 107–8, 110, 112, 124, 127, 129–30, 134–37, 142–43, 145–52, 160–61, 165–76, 186–87, 192, 196, 198–202, 209, 212, 215–16, 220–38, 240–41, 244, 246, 249, 252, 264, 269–75, 290–93, 302, 333–38, 343, 345–47, 352, 354–56, 365–66, 371, 386, 391–95, 399, 401, 412–14, 419–22, 424, 426, 428, 435–37, 443–44

Stevens, Chris, 132, 153

Sudan, 327

Suez, Invasion of, 88

Suharto, President, 395

Sung, Kim il, 56

Sunni triangle, 356

Super Bowl, 433

Susak, Gojko, 61–62

SWIFT (Society for the Worldwide Interbank Financial telecommunication), 358

Swing, Bill, 237

Syria, 22, 72, 137, 180, 189–90, 206, 281–82, 289, 327–28, 359, 430

Tai, Ambassador Katerine, 261

Taipei, 234, 321

Taiwan, 260, 282, 321, 384–85, 405

Tajikistan, 44, 237–41, 243, 245, 247–48, 251–52, 452

Talbot, Strobe, 30, 61–62

Taliban, 87, 145, 188–89, 196, 199, 200, 207, 210–13, 252, 285–86, 288–89, 344, 356–57, 362, 364

Tanzania, 331

Tbilisi, 37, 40–43, 48, 257

technology, xiii-xiv, 9, 29, 72, 105, 111, 149–50, 167, 185, 197, 223–24, 229, 249–50, 259–60, 276–77, 280, 282–83, 291, 302, 312, 317, 322, 325, 335, 339, 344, 349, 367, 389–90, 393, 419, 438, 444

Tefft, John, 31

Telegram, 437

Tennessee, 36, 335

terrorism, 76, 86–7, 100, 151–53, 166, 168, 174–75, 190–91, 195–7, 225, 262, 324, 331–32, 349, 353, 356–7, 359, 378, 452

Texas Air National Guard, 398

Thai language, 406

Thailand, 382–83, 406, 410–11

The Spectator, 284

Tiananmen Square disturbances, 386

Tibet, 231–32

TickTok, 437

Tillerson, Rex, 272, 365–6, 371

Timken, Emma, 265

Tito, Josip, 21, 47

Tolokonnikova, Nadezhda, 427

Trade Act 1974, 127–28

Transatlantic Trade and Investment Partnership (TTIP), 359

Transatlantic Trade and Technology Council, 259

Trans-Pacific Partnership, 278, 359, 363, 369
Tripoli, 281–82
Trist, Nicholas, 104
Trudeau, Justin, 364
Trudeau, Justin, 108, 364
Trudeau, Pierre, 108
Truman, Harry, 82, 338
Trump, Donald, 6, 8, 85–87, 89, 97, 102–3, 108, 152, 160, 168, 174, 180, 194, 196, 206, 213, 219–22, 261, 272, 278–80, 282–83, 285, 288, 292, 294, 309, 312–16, 319–20, 324–25, 330, 334–35, 338, 345–46, 357, 360–69, 380, 398, 438
Tudman, Franjo, 60
Tunisia, 331
Turkey, 21, 29, 59, 72, 84, 199, 257, 279, 281, 288, 328–29, 361, 453
Turkmenistan, 44, 240, 457
Twitter, 419; diplomacy, 419

U.S. Marine Corps Security Guards, xiv, 25, 34, 42, 132, 140, 148, 245, 273, 449
U-2, 407
UK (United Kingdom), 85, 248, 361, 456
Ukraine, xi, 18, 21–22, 43, 73–75, 77, 86, 97, 99–100, 162, 174, 207, 222, 257–60, 263, 279, 281–82, 304, 324, 344–45, 354, 358–59, 365–66, 368, 408–9, 430, 459
Un, Kim Jong, 315
Una Chapman Cox Foundation, 281
Unipolar, 20, 74, 351–52
United Arab Emirates, 269, 281, 458
United Nations, ix, 15, 18, 35, 53–54, 88, 107, 178, 181, 278, 281, 288, 304–5, 308, 311, 350, 382, 398, 450, 458
United States-Korea Free Trade Agreement (KORUS), 361
Universal Declaration of Human Rights of 1948, 365
University of California, Berkeley, 26
uranium enrichment, 316

US Agency for Global Media (USAGM), 438
US Central Command, See Central Command
US Information Agency, 438
US Information Service (USIS), 95
US Mission to the European Union in Brussels, 358
US Trade Representative, 261
US-Africa Leaders' Summit, 368
USAID, 36, 39, 42, 45, 129–30, 140–41, 145, 152, 196, 199, 209, 290, 292
US-EU Trade and Labor Dialogue, 259
US-EU Trade and Technology council, 367
USS Lexington, 25
US-UK Nassau Agreement, 94
Uzbekistan, 44–45, 240

Valentine's Day, 423
Vance, Cyrus, 88–89, 134, 413
Védrine, Hubert French Foreign Minister, 351
Versailles, 249
Vienna, 33–34, 109, 388
Vienna Conventions on Diplomatic and Consular Affairs, 388
Vietnam War, 3, 94, 99, 343, 383, 398, 405–7
Visegrad states, 83
VKontakte, 420
VOA Africa, 438
VOA Latin America, 438
Voice of America (VOA), 438

Wake, Doug, 27
Walker, William, 34, 68
Warsaw Pact, 409
Washington Post, 256, 455
Washington, DC, 457, 459
Washington, George, 50, 292
Wayne, Earl Anthony, 10, 265, 445

weapon of mass destruction (WMD), 313

Weinberger Doctrine, 66

Weinstein, Allen, 92

Weiss, Teddy, 265

West Africa, 331

West Germany, 9, 235

Western Hemisphere, 330

White House, xiii, 37, 51, 53, 55, 62, 67, 79, 93, 94, 98, 102–3, 105, 108, 110–11, 135, 145, 150, 166, 172, 183, 198, 216, 225, 249, 272, 302, 334, 336, 338, 354–55, 364, 366, 371, 382–83, 407, 414, 422, 424, 426, 429, 431, 449, 454–55

Wilson, Frances, 126–27, 129

Wilson, Woodrow, ix, 449

Winter Olympics, 430

Wisner, Frank, 412

Woodcock, Ambassador Leonard, 390, 411

Woodrow Wilson Center, 220, 458–59

Wooly Mammoth Cables, 137

WordPerfect, 394

World Bank, 316

World Bank Group, ix, 176, 178, 200, 278, 316, 396, 451

World Cup, 249

World Health Organization (WHO), 316

World Order, 2, 5, 9, 172, 223, 256, 301–3, 311, 321, 328, 361, 444

world order, liberal, 20–21

World Trade Organization (WTO), 319

World War II, 1, 10, 49, 70, 75, 83, 90–91, 93, 108, 127, 178, 189, 239, 307, 335, 346, 378, 398, 404, 445, 459

Wright Patterson, Air Force Base, 63

Wriston Commission, 391

Wristonization, 391

Xi Jinping, President, 260, 320, 405, 437–8

Xiaoping, Deng, 390

Xiaoping, Deng, see Deng Xiaoping,

Xinkiang province, 313

Yalowitz, Kenneth, 39

Yalta Conference, 108

Yanqui Filibuster, 331

yellow rain, 382

Yeltsin, Boris, 13, 18, 351

Yemen, 269, 327–8, 363, 368, 458

Yew, Lee Kuan, 387, 406

Yom Kippur/Ramadan War, 336

Yongbyon, 316

YouTube, 419, 437

Yovanovitch, Ambassador Masha, 366

Yugoslavia, 21, 31–32, 47, 57, 70, 192, 310, 410

Zagreb, 60–62

Zambia, 331

Zedong, Mao, 21

Zepa, 58

Zhvania, Zurab, 41–42